Understanding Human
═══ *Motivation* ═══

Understanding Human

Motivation

A COGNITIVE APPROACH

John Jung

CALIFORNIA STATE UNIVERSITY, LONG BEACH

MACMILLAN PUBLISHING CO., INC.
New York
COLLIER MACMILLAN PUBLISHERS
London

Macmillan Publishing Co., Inc.
866 Third Avenue, New York, New York 10022

Collier Macmillan Canada, Ltd.

Library of Congress Cataloging in Publication Data
Jung, John.
    Understanding human motivation.

    Includes bibliographies and index.
    1. Motivation (Psychology)   2.   Cognition.
I.   Title.
BF683.J86   153.8   76–52913
ISBN 0-02-361550-8 (Hardbound)
ISBN 0-02-979270-3 (International Edition)

Printing: 1 2 3 4 5 6 7 8   Year: 8 9 0 1 2 3 4

To Phyllis, without whom this book would have been written much sooner, but with much less fun.

Preface

Among the most fascinating questions in psychology are those concerned with the underlying motivations of behavior. Academic psychology traditionally has tended to prefer the mechanistic and objective approach to these questions and rejected subjective and introspective accounts as unscientific. Objective accounts of the causes of human behavior are usually unsatisfying in that they rarely deal with any complex human social behavior and are restricted to biological accounts of primary drives such as hunger or thirst. These behavioristic models assume that once the laws of simpler behaviors are determined, one can build on this foundation to encompass more complex aspects of motivation. Unfortunately, this promise is as yet unfulfilled and increasingly shows less potential.

Perhaps it is more appropriate to try a different approach, one that places more emphasis on the perceptions or subjective views of the individual regarding the causes of his or her own behavior. This approach directs more attention to the role of the choices or decisions that the individual often must make prior to engaging in a specific course of action and is in keeping with the current cognitive revolution in the field of psychology.

Part One develops the basic perspective of this book, demonstrating the need for increased attention to the role of cognitive and subjective factors and pointing to the importance of the consideration of individual differences in motivation. Part Two presents arguments and evidence about the importance of viewing humans as decision makers who choose their actions from among numerous possibilities. When such choice and control are absent, the individual experiences powerlessness or helplessness—a pervasive aspect of many motivational problems. A chapter dealing with biological constraints on behavior is included to acknowledge the recent interest in, and renewed attention to, the possible genetic determinants of motivation.

Part Three deals with three selected motivational topics: achievement, aggression, and affiliation or attraction. These phenomena, based on social and individual needs of a nonbiological nature, are emphasized as examples of important human motives. Part Four examines affective determinants and correlates of behavior such as emotions, moods, and need for varied stimulation. Processes such as hunger, thirst, pain, and sex—traditionally the central topics of behavioristic accounts of motivation—are presented in Part Five. The treatment of these topics focuses on the social and cultural factors rather than on the physiological bases of these behaviors. Another chapter deals with motivational analyses of two very important behaviors that are not discussed in most motivation texts—tobacco smoking and alcohol drinking.

Part Six is a speculative section dealing with real life situations that involve the control and change of human motivation in such areas as pornography and the law, littering control, and family size. Finally, there is a brief look at deviancy, a class of behaviors that usually defies rational analyses. Students and laymen often are puzzled by the irrationality underlying such forms of behavior without realizing the active role played by those who are considered "normals" in creating the nonmotivated behaviors known as deviant behavior.

It is a pleasure, as well as an obligation, to express my deep appreciation to Barry E. Collins, University of California, Los Angeles, and Roderick Wong, University of British Columbia, for their generous and constructive prompt critical evaluations of large sections of the material. Their suggestions have greatly improved the quality of both content and organization.

Numerous other colleagues read and commented helpfully on smaller portions of the manuscript, and I gratefully acknowledge the help of Vic Benassi, Ralph Hupka, Ken Green, and Bob Thayer of California State University at Long Beach. Troy Duster, University of California, Berkeley, was especially helpful in providing a sociological perspective for the chapter on deviancy.

The warm hospitality afforded me by Don Cahalan in the stimulating environment of the Social Research Group, University of California, Berkeley, where I spent a sabbatical in 1974–5, is gratefully acknowledged. It provided a welcome change of pace from the lonely isolation most authors inflict upon themselves and helped me maintain a sense of reality during the major period spent on this project.

The encouragement of Baxter Venable during the early stages of this undertaking was indispensible to keeping my morale sufficiently high to continue through many drafts. The confidence and assistance provided by Pat McConahay and the staff of Macmillan are greatly appreciated.To the classes that suffered through earlier drafts of often illegible pages, many thanks for their enthusiastic encouragement, constructive suggestions, and patience.

Finally, I would like to invite you, the unseen audience of students for whom this book was written, to send me any suggestions, comments, and criticisms. In this way, a small step can be made to reduce the lack of contact between author and audience.

J. J.

Contents

Gier-self-esteem? see
             eval

PART FOUR

Some Affective Factors

PART FIVE

Some Biological Factors

PART SIX

Changing Motives and Individual Differences

PART ONE

INTRODUCTION

CHAPTER 1

A Question of Motives

Imagine that someone built a robot that not only looked human but also behaved in ways that were indistinguishable from the patterns of real humans. This mechanical marvel, fashioned out of metal and electronics, would be energized by solar batteries so that it would be more active during the daylight hours. At night, it would gradually wind down into a sleeplike state. While awake, our robot would behave in programmed sequences wired in from "birth." As the years went by, our nuts-and-bolts wonder would acquire or learn new behavioral patterns as a consequence of a programmed ability to receive new stimuli, compare them with previously stored information, retain new information, and modify its behavior to fit the demands of changing situations. Our robot would be able to walk and talk as well.

If we watched this robot in action, we might be tempted to impute human qualities to it. We would speak of its intelligence, its personality, its motives, and its emotions, for example. We might even give it a human name and a gender. In short, even though we knew that our robot was not alive, we would be unable to refrain from generalizing from our own inner experiences and we would attribute to this mechanical device similar inner thoughts, feelings, and motives. This tendency is an ancient one, as humans have always speculated about the force, spirit, or life of inanimate as well as living objects.

An objective and scientific approach to the analysis of our robot's behavior, however, would avoid reference to anthropomorphic and animistic explanations. We would agree, for example, that it would be incorrect and unnecessary to conclude that the robot felt tired or was fatigued if its efficiency decreased. We would search for an objective explanation based on the design of the robot machinery.

In contrast, such parsimony in explaining human behavior is not only unwarranted but foolhardy. Humans do experience a variety of inner states, which must be considered, in our view, if we are to achieve an adequate understanding of human behavior. Motives and emotions, the main topics of this book, are among the inner states that influence human behavior.

In our discussion of motives and emotions throughout this book, frequent emphasis will be given to the role of *cognitive processes*. These processes, usually referred to as thinking, problem solving, and information processing, are inner events, which are not directly observable. Cognition plays an essential role in the analysis of motivation and emotion. The interpretation of the meaning of a situation, the appraisal of alternative responses, and judgments about the possible consequences of responses are all cognitive operations that influence our actions, our feelings before, during, and after our response, and our judgment of and reaction to the behavior of other persons.

However, as we shall see in Chapter 2, the scientific approach to psychology has traditionally tried to restrict itself to the study of overt behavior. Mentalistic and subjective concepts and processes have been regarded at best as superfluous and at worst as misleading. In essence, scientific psychology attempts to view humans *as if* they were machines not unlike the robot described previously.

Defining Motives and Emotions

A simple but accurate definition of motivation is not easy. It must be able to include terms that refer to such diverse states as *desires, wishes, plans, goals, intents, impulses,* and *purposes.* Some of these states imply a deliberate and calculated process involving reason, whereas others convey a flavor of spontaneity.

Emotion is also an elusive category of feeling states, which include *fear, hate,* and *anger* as well as *pleasure, humor, joy, excitement,* and *boredom.* Emotional states are generally viewed as being less rational than motivational ones but they do involve cognitive processes as well. Cognitive appraisal can determine the nature of an emotional experience. In addition, emotions can be seen as factors that alter or disrupt ongoing cognitive processes.

A clearcut distinction between motives and emotions is not always possible, because emotions sometimes operate as motives in generating responses. Thus, anger in one situation may cause an individual to pursue a certain course of action. In this book motives and emotions will often be referred to simply as motives.

In general, when we speak of motives we are referring to the causes or reasons that underlie a given behavior. One can think of few important aspects of our behavior that would not involve motives. Leaving aside accidents and other behavior with unintended consequences, one might expect to find a very large number of motives, because so many different categories of behavior exist. One hope, of course, is that there are only so many basic motives and that all other motives are derivatives of them. In other words, a need to achieve or gain mastery may manifest itself in different forms, such as in academic, athletic, or artistic accomplishments, such that it would be unnecessary to assume that each activity requires a fundamentally different type of motive.

Instead of attempting to define or identify the different motives that exist, one might specify the common features of all motivated activity. This strategy avoids the problem of distinguishing between highly similar or overlapping motives.

What are the essential features of motivated behavior? First, such activity is assumed to be intentional and voluntary behavior that is purposive or goal-directed. The individual holds expectancies, formed probably through past learning experiences, that specific behaviors will lead to the attainment of certain desired incentives. The concept of motivation also implies that energy is involved to activate the individual to a level that enables the performance of the appropriate behavior. Furthermore, motivation is assumed to be selective or directional. The same amount of motivation does not activate all response tendencies equally, but rather it energizes the behaviors relevant to the situation the individual is in at the moment.

Motivation also involves the persistence of behavior over time so that sustained effort can occur even if obstacles or setbacks occur. In the case of satisfying biological needs such as food, the restoration of deficits will terminate the motivated behavior at least temporarily. In the case of more socially based motives such as attaining social approval or recognition, the behavior may be persistent and apparently insatiable. As each goal is achieved, the individual may reset his or her target higher so that absolute fulfillment is never achieved and persistent attempts may be made over many years against often difficult obstacles.

Approaches to the Study of Motivation

COGNITIVE APPROACH

Humans are continually interpreting the complex pattern of behavior they observe in others as well as in themselves. We try to explain our actions in terms of motives that are regarded as causes of behavior. Similarly we try to infer the underlying motivational causes of the behavior of others.

The process by which we make these interpretations or attributions of causal motivation was first emphasized by Fritz Heider (1958). He noted that we often account for events in terms of personal forces such as effort or in terms of environmental factors. Heider argued that the tendency to attribute causality reflected a motivation to understand and organize the influx of behavioral events we observe. His conception of attributions focused on immediate or spontaneous interpretations rather than painstaking and deliberate analysis.

About a decade later, Harold Kelley (1967) directed renewed attention to the process of attribution. His conception of attribution differed from Heider's in that it emphasized the processing of information about behavior as a more rational procedure. Kelley noted that although there was no single attribution theory, as such, the general approaches of a number of independent investigators working on different phenomena were similar in that they dealt with the assumed attributional inferences of actors.

We will refer frequently to attributions about motives throughout this book. Sometimes we will use synonyms of *attribute* such as *infer, impute, ascribe,* and *interpret,* but it should always be clear that we are talking about a rational process by means of which observers try to explain the causes of behavior.

An emphasis on attribution should not be taken to mean that we think observers *always* or automatically make attributions. We often do not explain behavior that is uninteresting or irrelevant to us, for example. Research on attribution, of necessity, overestimates the degree to which attributions are ordinarily made in everyday life. In experiments designed to study the nature of attribution, subjects must be explicitly instructed to make such causal inferences.

RADICAL BEHAVIORISTIC APPROACH

The concept of motive is considered superfluous by extreme behaviorists, such as B. F. Skinner (1971), who feel that if we know the external stimulus conditions that exist when responses are learned, we can predict behavior as well, if not better, without recourse to the inference of internal states such as motives, cognitions, and feelings. Because these inner forces or causes are hypothetical and cannot be observed directly, these behaviorists feel we should not postulate them when we can identify the objective conditions associated with behavior.

In fact, in a lecture at the New York Poetry Center, Skinner (1972) went so far as to question whether a poet should be given credit for writing a poem when he observed, "Having a poem, like having a baby, is in large part a matter of exploration and discovery, and both poet and mother are often surprised by what they produce."

But what about the individual's own feelings about the causes of his or her behavior? Are these of no value? Even if we do not invoke inner causes to explain the behavior of others, can we use them to explain our own actions? How does the radical behaviorist view the role of a person's own inner states?

An example of an extreme behavioristic view (Bem, 1967) depicts the individual as one who first acts, and *then* as an afterthought identifies his or her motive. In essence, Bem suggested that the actor examines his or her own behavior, just as an observer would, in attempting to infer inner feelings, as diagrammed in Figure 1–1.

A person wanting to know, for example, if he liked football, might note the fact that he was attending a football game at that very moment and on that basis draw the conclusion that he liked it. According to this argument, it is

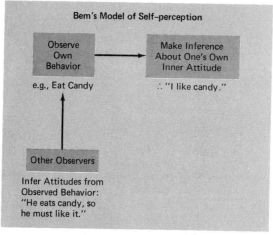

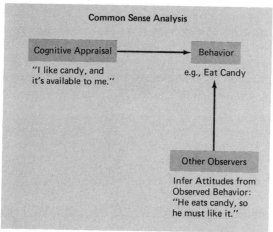

FIGURE 1–1. A comparison of a radical behaviorist's model for identifying one's own attitudes with a commonsense view.

unnecessary even to consider inner feelings that are difficult to measure because one can infer them accurately by observing overt behavior.

This drastically oversimplified attempt to leave out cognitive factors of motivation and thus be objective in the sense that physical science is objective ignores the fact that the actor does in fact have access to private events and feelings ordinarily unavailable to external observers. Even though the actor in this example might be attending the game, i.e., his behavior is consonant with a positive attitude toward the game, his reaction or feeling might actually be quite different. Perhaps he attended to be sociable but actually finds the game rather boring. Observers frequently misinterpret the true intentions and feelings of others. Bem's analysis imposed artificial limitations on the input an individual ordinarily has available for making inferences about his or her own inner motives and feelings.

PSYCHOANALYTIC APPROACH

Are we conscious or aware of the causes of all our behavior? Or is it possible, as psychoanalytic theorists such as Freud and Jung maintained, that much behavior occurs for reasons that are not apparent to the individual. By conscious, one does not require that full awareness of the motives exist when the behavior is performed, but that at least retrospectively the individual be able to identify his or her reasons. On the other hand, the concept of unconscious motives suggests that even with careful reflection and interrogation the person is unable to identify motives. It should be clear that even unconscious motives are goal-directed, usually in some defensive or protective sense, according to Freud. Psychoanalysts assume that with skillful therapy they can help identify these unconscious motives.

The issue of unconscious motives is intriguing but one that is virtually impossible to test scientifically. This is not to say that such motives do not exist or that they are unimportant. On the contrary, they appear to be of great clinical significance. But because the validity of psychoanalytic interpretations is so difficult to determine, there will be no extended discussion of unconscious motives in this book. An example of such an analysis will serve to illustrate this technique and some of its problems.

Freud had just completed the laborious task of proofreading his great book, *The Interpretation of Dreams,* and in writing about this chore to his friend, Fliess, proclaimed that he would make no further changes, "even if it contained 2,467 mistakes." Most people would assume that this specific number was arbitrarily pulled out of thin air, but Freud, attuned as he was to the unconscious meanings of events, attempted to determine why he had picked that very number.

His reconstruction of events led him to the following interpretation. Just before writing Fliess, he had read in the paper about the retirement of a man with whom he had been acquainted many years earlier. To be precise, Freud was twenty-four years old at that earlier time; he thus concluded that this must be the reason for the twenty four in the number 2,467. When he wrote to Fliess, Freud was forty three. Adding forty three and twenty four gives sixty seven, so Freud figured that this must account for the sixty seven in his choice of the number 2,467. Freud elected to add the number twenty four because on discussing his acquaintance's retirement with his wife, she suggested that he should be retiring after a period equal to the interval since his last encounter with the man. In reply, Freud exclaimed that he wished to work yet another twenty-four years before retiring.

Rieff's (1961) analysis of this anecdote argues that it is extremely complicated and contrived and seems to assume that Freud was hiding something from himself. In Rieff's opinion, this example is typical of the Freudian method. He concludes, "What Freud's thoughts were when he set down at random the number 2,467, interpretation cannot disclose—not only because of the ever-present hazard of plural meanings but, more fundamentally, because interpretation always follows, often at great distance, the event." More-over, "When he presumes that he has disinterred the determinant thoughts of the past, actually his method fundamentally alters the sense of the past and its reality." (Rieff, 1961, p. 126)

Freud's study of the unconscious attempted to show the role of past factors in so-called irrational or illogical behavior. Other approaches might be employed to explain what appears to be irrational behavior, especially when one does not have access to, or accept, the verbal report of the person.

Sometimes seemingly irrational behavior is totally rational, but is misclassified because we do not have access to full information about prior conditions. For example, suppose we watch a man steal a loaf of bread in full view of a policeman. He is arrested and sent to jail. We would consider the potential penalty to far outweigh the potential gain so we would judge this behavior to be irrational. Yet, on learning that the man was penniless and had not eaten for a week, we see the behavior as, if not rational, at least comprehensible.

In this example we were able to explain the behavior in terms that did not require the examination of unconscious processes. However, suppose we could not identify any extenuating situational factors, such as starvation and poverty, as possible causes. Assume also that the thief could not report any reasons for his action. It might then be tempting to invoke unconscious motives, motives that are not readily measured by direct means such as a verbal self-report. Verification of such postulated motives, however, is difficult. Unconscious motives are usually formulated only after the observer has learned other information about the background of the person whose behavior is to be explained. Sometimes alternative explanations are possible and there is no clearcut means for choosing among them or testing their validity.

We cited only one specific example, the case in which Freud analyzed his own motives, to illustrate the complexity of psychoanalytic explanations. This example may be atypical of explanations involving the unconscious, but it does show how speculative such accounts can be.

Scope of This Book

This book is concerned with the study of human motivation and emotion. Inasmuch as virtually all behavior involves at least one or the other or both processes a wide range of activities fall within the scope of this book. It should be obvious that the choice of topics must be selective.

Unlike the study of animal behavior in which we cannot identify the nature of inner subjective experiences and must rely on observable behavior, it is possible to achieve some understanding of the thoughts and feelings of humans, which can not only help us better understand subsequent behavior but is of interest in its own right. Granted, introspective verbal reports have limitations, but we believe that such data in combination with the observation of overt behavior is more useful than total reliance on the latter.

Conscious human experience, as noted earlier, varies in the extent to which it is rational and logical. The hedonic tone or degree of pleasantness-unpleasantness of such feelings is another dimension. At times, we will emphasize the rational nature of human cognition as a key factor affecting human motivation, such as in a situation in which a person chooses among several responses and evaluates their costs, payoffs, and likelihoods of occurrence.

In other contexts, such as in a discussion of stress, we will focus on the strong unpleasant feelings that activate the individual to seek means of escape or coping. And, in some cases it will be necessary to consider the joint influence of the cognitive and affective aspects of inner experience, such as in considering the behaviors of gamblers who feel lucky even though they know that the chances of winning are miniscule.

Human behavior and experience are very much socially determined and influenced and this fact will be reflected in the considerable attention we give to social and cultural factors not only in our treatment of affiliation and liking but also in our discussions of more biologically based topics such as hunger, thirst, or pain.

In this book, we will emphasize the attributions that people make about the causes of behavior. It is important to identify the type of attributions made by a person, because these cognitions will be a major determinant of his or her behavior. For example, a person who thinks that he or she is unable to achieve a certain task may not try it, but if the person can somehow be persuaded of a good chance of success, he or she may attempt it. One who perceives the behavior of another as hostile, will react quite differently from one who attributes friendly intentions to the other person.

The Nature of Evidence Obtained by the Experimental Method

Most of the evidence about human motivation discussed in this book is based on research obtained by the experimental method usually with humans in laboratory settings. This method enables one to draw causal inferences that are not logically possible when the evidence is produced by other methods, such as naturalistic observation. The latter method yields uncontrolled observations, which may serve as a fertile source of hypotheses or guesses about causal relationships but do not enable one to rule out alternative explanations. In contrast, the experimental method, which involves controlled observation of events created by the experimenter, is valued precisely because it enables us to arrive at causal inferences. An example, which the advanced student may bypass, will serve to illustrate the difference between uncontrolled and controlled observations.

Consider the question of how anxiety affects learning. Careful naturalistic observation in a classroom setting might disclose a tendency for more anxious students to learn poorly. This correlation or covariation of two variables, anxiety level and learning scores, suggests several possible causal relationships. The differences in anxiety might be the cause of the differences in learning. Or perhaps the opposite situation is the case, namely that poor learning performance generates higher levels of anxiety in students. It is also possible that neither variable is the direct cause of the other; perhaps a third factor such as intelligence or learning ability is the major cause of differences in learning scores.

If such were the case, we can see that anxiety level should not be regarded as a major cause of the differences in learning. What about the hypothesis that anxiety differences are an effect, rather than a cause, of learning differences? Although this idea is plausible, other explanations are conceivable. Perhaps the parents of poor learners are very punitive to their children so that the anxiety levels of such students are elevated. In this instance, the anxiety of the children would not stem so much from their poor learning scores as it would from concern about their parents' reactions.

In this fictitious example, it should be clear that the existence of a correlation may suggest causal relationships, but it is not possible to rule out alternative explanations. A study using the experimental method, however, can reach causal inferences, because it is possible to vary systematically variables hypothesized to affect behavior while equating comparison groups on all other variables.

In an experiment, at least two different conditions are created and observations of behavior under these controlled circumstances are made. One condition, referred to as the experimental condition, involves the presence of some factor assumed to have an effect on behavior, such as anxiety, a drug, or level of room illumination, whereas the other so-called control condition does not. Usually research participants (called subjects) are randomly assigned to the different conditions. This method is assumed to rule out any bias in the assignment of individuals to the different conditions. Therefore, except for chance, the characteristics of the subjects assigned to each condition should be equal, *on the average*. If this is the case, any differences in behavior that occurs during different test conditions should be due to the influence of the factor or variable assumed to have an effect. Other research designs exist such as one in which the same subjects serve under all test conditions but with subgroups receiving them in different sequences. We need not discuss the advantages and disadvantages of different experimental research designs here. For our purposes, it is sufficient to understand the basic logic of the experimental method in arriving at causal inferences.

How would we conduct an experiment on the question of the relationship between anxiety and learning? A simple study might involve the formation of two groups of subjects by random assignment to make them equivalent. Then we could use instructions that heightened anxiety for one group such as telling them it was important to do well while giving neutral instructions to the other group. Thus, we have induced or manipulated the level of anxiety, which would be called the *independent variable.* The group assumed to have high anxiety would be called the *experimental group,* whereas the group assumed to have no or little anxiety would be the *control group.* Comparisons would then be made of the two groups in their learning performance on some achievement task. Learning scores, or the *dependent variable,* will vary within each group, but the main concern would be whether the average scores of the two groups differed by an amount exceeding that expected by chance, as defined by established statistical tests, which we will not describe here. If differences do exist between the experimental and control group scores on the learning task, we can conclude that they are caused by the differences in anxiety levels in the two groups, because they did not differ, on the average, in any other dimension.

This conclusion assumes that the experiment was conducted carefully so that no contaminating source of differential treatment of the two groups was added. For example, suppose after all our efforts to equate the characteristics of the two groups by random assignment of subjects and to induce different levels of anxiety in the two groups, we had inadvertently tested one group before and the other group after lunch. This factor, rather than differences in

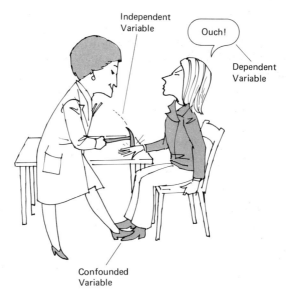

FIGURE 1–2. Relationship of independent, dependent, and confounded variables. The experimenter deliberately manipulates the independent variable and indirectly produces a change in the subject's behavior. If a confounded variable is inadvertently introduced, there is no way to tell whether the independent variable or the confounded variable produced the behavioral change. [From *Fundamentals of Experimental Psychology* by C. Sheridan, Second Edition. New York: Holt, Rinehart, and Winston, 1975. Copyright 1975 by Holt, Rinehart, and Winston. Reprinted by permission.]

anxiety, may have been the major cause of the obtained differences in learning scores. An extraneous and unintended factor that prevents a sound inference about the effects of our independent variable is called a *confounded variable*. Another example of confounding is illustrated in Figure 1–2.

If we can avoid errors such as confounded experiments, this method affords us an advantage over the uncontrolled natural observation of causal inference about the determinants of behavior. It should not be surprising, then, that it has been highly regarded by scientific psychologists.

Some Limitations of the Experimental Method

Although the experiment has distinct advantages and analytical precision, it is not without limitations. First, consider the artificial nature of the experimental situation. This feature is not in itself a flaw, but it may limit the generalizability of findings beyond the laboratory—it may not help us to analyze real phenomena. Experiments in the physical and biological sciences have led to the highest achievements, but experiments in psychology involve humans who may respond differently in the test situation from the way they behave in natural situations. Knowing that it is only an experiment, a human may not act as he or she would normally. He or she may respond to what Orne (1962) termed the demand characteristics of the test situation by reacting in ways that he or she thinks are expected or, conversely, in a lackadaisical, uncooperative, or even subversive manner. Consider studies of induced stress in which some contrived danger is involved. Because most assume (perhaps erroneously sometimes) that the investigator is ethically responsible, a human subject is unlikely to believe that he or she is in any real danger. Such disbelief is not restricted to laboratory studies but may also occur in the real world. Dramatic presentations aimed at producing affective responses such as fear, joy, or grief often fall short, because the viewer keeps in mind that it is only a play or a movie.

Most experiments conducted by university psychologists are based on participants who are college students. Given that the demographic factors such as age, social class, and ethnic background as well as the psychological characteristics such as intelligence, attitudes, and values of college students are unrepresentative of the general population, it is to be expected that many conclusions obtained from such experiments may be limited in generalizability. This criticism may be less valid for studies of phenomena in the field of perception or psychophysics, but it is a serious problem for studies investigating the phenomena of motivation.

Furthermore, generalizability of experimental findings is weakened by the fact that not all individuals will react to a given situation in a similar manner. One person may be stoical when experiencing pain, whereas another may faint. One person may retaliate when insulted, whereas another may turn the other cheek. Precisely what factors account for these individual differences is an important question of a motivational nature.

The experimental method, by focusing on the effects of the factor under the control of the experimenter and disregarding individual differences in reaction, will generate some *average* laws of behavior. Yet, such laws may be inapplicable to the understanding of the behavior of many individuals, even though they provided the original data.

If, as we assume, each individual's behavior depends heavily on his or her interpretation of a given situation, it is necessary to assess this cognitive factor on an individual basis rather than rely on a fictional average. An analysis of the origins of these individual differences in cognition is highly relevant in order to understand many aspects of human motivation.

Contemporary behavioristic psychology places too much emphasis on the use of the experimental method, especially in the study of complex phenomena such as those dealing with motivation and emotion. Experimental situations suitable in studies of perception may be totally useless in the study of momentary or fragile states that occur in motivational and emotional phenomena. It is not suggested that experimental methods be abandoned totally, but that greater use of naturalistic observation, introspective report, and the like be made. Frequently the conclusions provided by different methods will not agree. And why should they? Thus, an observer of aggression, the aggressor, and the victim should have different emotional and cognitive experiences of the same episode. No one account is the true account, because all accounts are valid and necessary components of the total event.

Experiments generally are designed to simplify a situation for more precise analysis. Thus, the study of motivation would call for the examination of a given motive in isolation or possibly in combination with one other motive. In reality, of course, our behavior is the resultant of a number of simultaneous and often fluctuating motives.

Furthermore, motives not only operate in conjunction or competition with other motives but also in the presence of various affective states such as emotional conditions or moods, as suggested in Figure 1–3. A person who is hungry but also depressed due to poor grades will probably differ in eating behavior from an equally food-deprived person who is elated due to receiving high grades. The sexual behavior of a person who is anxious and fearful will probably differ from that of someone who is relaxed and content. Interactions of affective and motivational factors greatly complicate the study of human behavior. The simple assumption that a student need only have high ability and good motivation to obtain excellent academic achievement is often disconfirmed in the classroom.

The point of directing attention to the complex nature of real-life situations that involve numerous interacting concurrent influences on behavior is not to argue that the motivational factors cannot be studied experimentally. However, studies of isolated factors in highly controlled and often highly contrived

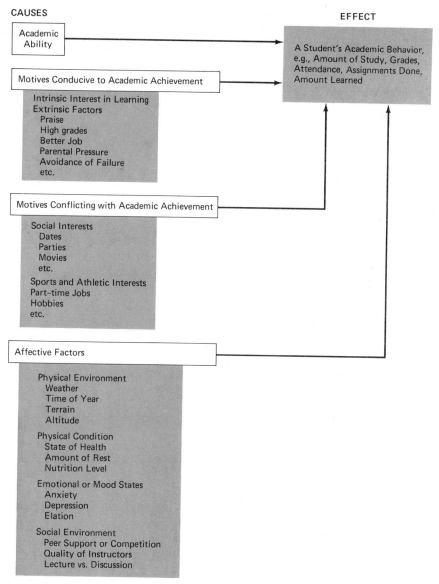

CAUSES

EFFECT

Academic Ability

A Student's Academic Behavior, e.g., Amount of Study, Grades, Attendance, Assignments Done, Amount Learned

Motives Conducive to Academic Achievement

Intrinsic Interest in Learning
Extrinsic Factors
  Praise
  High grades
  Better Job
  Parental Pressure
  Avoidance of Failure
  etc.

Motives Conflicting with Academic Achievement

Social Interests
  Dates
  Parties
  Movies
  etc.
Sports and Athletic Interests
Part-time Jobs
Hobbies
etc.

Affective Factors

Physical Environment
  Weather
  Time of Year
  Terrain
  Altitude
Physical Condition
  State of Health
  Amount of Rest
  Nutrition Level
Emotional or Mood States
  Anxiety
  Depression
  Elation
Social Environment
  Peer Support or Competition
  Quality of Instructors
  Lecture vs. Discussion

FIGURE 1–3.   A given behavior such as academic performance of a student is affected by more factors than the level of motivation for academic achievement and his or her level of academic ability.

settings are often overgeneralized. The laboratory findings should at best be regarded as first approximations rather than as definitive laws of human behavior. We feel this warning is in order, because we will cite so much evidence from experiments throughout this book. We think these findings are important, because they avoid some of the biases and limitations of the views of the layperson.

On the other hand, we are not as optimistic as some experimental psychologists who believe that laboratory research will produce highly generalizable laws of motivations. For as we proceed, we will argue that humans are highly individualistic or idiosyncratic with respect to the causes or motives for many of their most meaningful behaviors. The experimental method is not well suited for this type of emphasis since, as noted earlier, it focuses on average group differences.

Conceptual Problems of Motivation as a Construct

Undoubtedly all of us experience the inner states commonly known as motives and emotions. It is also reasonable to assume that such states could affect our subsequent behavior. Yet, as will be shown in detail in Chapter 2, there has been a traditional reluctance among many American experimentally-oriented psychologists to rely on subjective verbal reports of such factors in trying to analyze the causes of human behavior. In the past ten to fifteen years, there has been a growing reacceptance of the use of subjective evidence.

CIRCULARITY

Constructs such as motives were originally in disfavor because of the tendency for them to be used in a circular manner. A behavior such as singing, dancing, or fighting, for example, would be attributed by an observer to the operation of a motive to sing, dance, or fight, etc. Such explanations do not enable us to identify any of the conditions that instigated the activity. They merely represent descriptive terms of the behavior made *after* the behavior has occurred. Yet, if the construct of motives is to aid in explaining the causes of behavior, they must enable us to predict future occurrences by identifying important antecedent conditions of such behavior.

A similar problem exists with respect to inferences about emotional states when explaining behavior. A student might be said to learn poorly *because* of anxiety or the crying of a child in the presence of a dog might be attributed to a fear of dogs. But why was the student anxious in the first place, and why was the child afraid? This is not to say that emotional responses did not occur in these examples, but the question whether one may safely conclude what causal relationships, if any, existed between the emotions and the behavior is raised. Because the emotions were postulated after the occurrence of the observed behavior presumably caused by these emotions, we have a circular definition.

The example shown in Table 1–1 may illustrate the problem. A baby is seen (and heard) crying. What was the motive? Suppose one postulates the operation of an instinct or motive for crying. Such a statement would tell us

TABLE 1–1. Some Alternative Explanations of the Same Type of Behavior.

What Was the Motive?		
Antecedent Conditions	Motive Inferred	Behavior Observed
Food deprivation	Hunger	Crying
Water deprivation	Thirst	Crying
Falls down, bangs head	Pain	Crying
No afternoon nap	Tiredness, Fatigue	Crying
Playmate will not share toy	Envy, Jealousy	Crying
Toy will not function easily	Frustration	Crying
Mother just left room	Separation Anxiety	Crying
Stranger entered room	Stranger Anxiety	Crying
Loud startling noises	Fear	Crying

nothing other than what we already know, namely that the child is crying. One plausible hypothesis, from our previous experiences with babies, is that the child might be crying from hunger. We could test this hypothesis by offering the baby a bottle to see if the crying will stop. Suppose, however, we had seen the mother feed the baby only a few minutes ago. We would eliminate the hunger motive as a probable cause of the crying and consider some of the alternatives shown in Table 1–1.

Our choice among these alternative explanations in Table 1–1 is not arbitrary or random but is influenced by any information we have about the situation prior to the onset of the crying. If we knew the mother had just left the room, we would hypothesize a different causal factor or motive than if the mother were still present. On the other hand, if we enter the room without knowing that the mother had just departed and found that the baby was already crying, we would be less likely to conclude that separation anxiety was the cause.

The point of our example is that the same general type of behavior, such as crying, can occur as a response to a variety of causes. Knowledge of preceding factors helps us to explain the observed behavior and to predict its future occurrence. In contrast, the postulation of motives to account for behavior after it is observed does little to explain the causes of that behavior.

VALIDITY OF SUBJECTIVE REPORT

Another reason to avoid using subjective experiences in the study of human motivation has been the difficulty in measuring them. Individuals vary in the extent to which they are aware of inner feelings and in the extent to which they are willing to report them accurately. Subjective evidence is biased and therefore not the type of data one would want for a science of psychology modeled after the physical sciences. It is ironic that much of the current readmittance of subjective evidence is due to the growing recognition that subjective factors such as an individual's bias and interpretation of a situation are important determinants of behavior. Psychology cannot fully understand behavior by ignoring subjective experience.

THE SITUATIONAL NATURE OF MOTIVATION

An entirely different type of justification for dropping the use of constructs such as motives and personality traits that refer to stable dispositions of individuals was offered by Mischel (1968). He presented arguments challenging the usefulness of dispositional constructs *by psychologists* in referring to causes of behavior. If motives are indeed stable properties of individuals, he reasoned, then the behavior observed in one situation should be correlated with behavior in similar situations, for example, an honest person should be able to resist temptation in a variety of situations. Citing the work of other investigators, Mischel noted that such predictability of behavior based on assessments of motive traits in one situation with those in another was poor. Honesty, for example, would appear to be not so much a property or trait of a person as a response to a particular situation. Constructs referring to inner processes such as motives, then, could be argued to exist more in the minds of the observers than in the individuals being studied.

ATTRIBUTIONAL DIFFERENCES BETWEEN SELF AND OBSERVERS. It is important, however, to distinguish between the motives attributed to an individual by himself or herself and those attributed by observers. Although there may often be agreement, especially when the observers are close acquaintances of the person, there frequently can be large discrepancies. It is possible for an individual to behave in a manner that is highly consistent with his or her own definitions of his or her motives. But if these personal constructs do not coincide with the formulations or categories of observers, observers will not reach the same interpretation.

A good example of this situation is provided by Bem and Allen (1974) who asked subjects to rate themselves in several dimensions such as honesty and conscientiousness by indicating how variable they were on each trait over a variety of situations, Bem and Allen assumed that those dimensions judged relevant to an individual would be the ones in which their behavior would be of low variability.

Several independent measures were then obtained from each subject in the traits of honesty and conscientiousness to determine the degree of agreement or correlation among the different indices. These measures included self-report, mother's report, father's report, and peer's report for both traits. In addition, group discussion and spontaneous behavior were rated for friendliness. Additional indices for conscientiousness were based on the extent to which requested course evaluations were returned, the extent to which course reading assignments were completed, and neatness of appearance on several occasions during the term.

The intercorrelations among the various measures on a given trait were consistently higher for those subjects who had indicated that their behavior was generally consistent. In other words, people can judge which aspects of their behavior are more important to them. Because individual differences about relevant dimensions exist, the typical procedure of measuring everyone on the same criteria without regard for whether each one considers all these criteria important is unwise, and this approach has contributed to the low predictability.

Proponents of the view that situational factors are the major determinant of behavior must also account for the obvious fact that wide individual differences in behavior often occur in the same given situation. Not all persons, for example, are equally likely to contribute to a charity appeal such as the March of Dimes. Some dispositional factors such as motives or traits would seem to be needed to handle this type of outcome.

Bowers (1973), in criticizing Mischel (1968), pointed out that all individuals do not perceive a given situation in the same way. His view insisted that *"situations are as much a function of the person as the person's behavior is a function of the situation"* (p. 327). The cognitive appraisal of a given situation depends on the individual; thus, it is not meaningful to argue in behalf of either the situation or the person since the two factors cannot be readily separated.

Bowers also made the important point that ordinarily the individual is involved in determining the kinds of situations in which he or she will participate, whereas the typical approach of an experiment requires that all subjects be exposed to the same situation. Although the latter type of control may be necessary for some purposes, it prevents us from noting that situations are a function of the individual when he or she is free to select or influence them.

AN INTERACTIONIST VIEW. The importance of *interactions* between situations and traits in determining behavior was emphasized by Bowers. A given person does not react the same way across a variety of situations as might be implied by the notion that a trait is a invariant aspect of the person. Clearly, behavior is also a function of the situation. However, one should not expect a given situation to elicit the same type of response in everyone even if one believes that situations are more critical in determining behavior than are traits. Individual differences within the same situation suggest that some contribution of traitlike qualities also affects behavior.

In these examples in which the effect of one factor depends on the level of a second factor, we speak of the *interaction* of the two factors. Thus, suppose persons with high honesty did not shoplift, whereas low honesty persons did when store surveillance was low. When store surveillance was high, neither type of person shoplifted. Thus, neither the trait nor the situation alone can predict behavior as well as a consideration of the interaction of both factors.

Endler and Hunt (1966) demonstrated the importance of interactions of variables such as situation, trait, and response mode in their analysis of responses to a questionnaire about reactions involving anxiousness. Using situations such as "You are crawling along a ledge high on a mountain side," or "You are going into an interview for a very important job," they asked college students to rate the intensity of fourteen different reactions including "heart beats faster," "want to avoid situation," "enjoy the challenge," and "experience nausea."

They analyzed the results to determine the relative importance of each factor considered alone, the situation, the type of response, and the individual. None of them predicted behavior as successfully as the interactions among variables did. In other words, the response to a given situation was not the same for everyone, the response that typically occurred for one situation was not the same for another situation, and finally, individuals who reacted with one type of response in one situation gave other responses in other situations. These results support the position that it is necessary to examine interactions among variables in order to predict behavior successfully.

Mischel (1973), it must be noted, changed his views (Mischel, 1968) in which he focused attention on the ignored role of situational determinants. In his later view he clearly acknowledged the interactive relationship between situations and traits or dispositions in the determination of behavior. Both factors must be considered; the question of which one is more important is a useless and misleading issue for which there is no meaningful answer.

WEAKNESS OF ALL-OR-NONE CONCEPTS. There is a tendency to view both situational and dispositional factors in an all-or-none manner, which is perhaps too simplistic. It may be more fruitful to recognize that both factors can vary in degree. Situations in which one person seeks the assistance of another can be either very forceful or subtle; a verbal threat can be used to gain help as well as can a subtle look of helplessness by someone carrying an armful of packages. Similarly, a disposition or trait of altruism is not an all-or-none dimension but rather a continuum. A person may feel kindly and helpful toward friends but not toward strangers.

If either the situational or the dispositional factor is high in strength, one should expect the other factor to have relatively less influence. An emergency situation should produce helping behavior from most persons regardless of their individual levels of altruism. In this case it would appear that the situation is the more important factor. However, if the situation is a relatively minor one, willingness to help will be most strongly affected by dispositional factors such as the level of altruism of the person.

CONCLUSIONS

The fact that psychologists may not have been able to measure motives in a useful manner in the past can not be used to deny the fact that in everyday life people do think in terms of motivational factors when attempting to explain their own behavior as well as that of others.

Despite the fact that attributions of motivational dispositions are often inaccurate, the important point is that everyone uses them. Everyday explanations of the causes of behavior invariably are a question of motives. Furthermore such faulty inferences still influence our attitude and our behavior toward others. Rightly or wrongly, if we judge someone to be motivated by dishonest motives, our reactions toward them will be quite different from those experienced if we perceive that they are motivated by honest motives. In view of these effects, it is essential that we consider the nature of motivational explanations, flawed or otherwise, if we are to improve our understanding of human behavior.

In cases of trivial or habitual behavior such an extended deliberation would not be necessary. Furthermore, we sometimes act in haste on important matters, not really aware of why we acted in the manner we did and sometimes regretting it. But when we do make a cognitive appraisal of our actions, it should be noted that such evaluation occurs *before* the behavior is initiated. This is not to deny that we may periodically reappraise our behavior during its course or later as in the case of second guessing.

These appraisals, being subjective, may sometimes appear illogical or irrational to observers, especially those who might hold different values or goals. The individual who made the decision may also subsequently question the wisdom of his or her own actions, but the point still remains that motivated behavior frequently involves the weighing of risks and benefits of possible alternatives prior to the selection of the eventual course of action. Responses are not, as suggested by many theories, mechanically and automatically triggered by stimuli except in cases of the most highly overtrained habits and reflexes.

Identifying One's Own Inner States

How do we come to label or recognize our own motives and emotions as we experience them? This process is undoubtedly complex. When we are born we do not have many of the motives and emotions we will eventually acquire or develop. As our experience grows, we begin to have the feelings we will eventually learn to label with words such as *hunger, fear, anger, disgust,* or *greed* in various situations. The sight of the milk bottle itself may come to elicit in an infant feelings associated with the hunger state. Similarly, the infant will experience feelings of fear in response to the barking sounds of a dog if he or she had been frightened by a dog previously.

In his famous experiments Pavlov presented a tone just prior to giving dogs food. As a result, a neutral stimulus, a tone in this example, acquired the ability to act as a signal that food was about to appear. Due to this process, known as *classical conditioning,* a response such as salivation, which would occur at the appearance of food, comes even when the tone occurs alone. In a similar manner, we come to recognize situations or stimuli, which hold certain meanings or associations learned sometime in our past. For many of these states we will also acquire verbal labels that we will often use in referring to the actual bodily feelings. A child who is crying because he cannot operate a toy for lack of motor coordination may be told he is feeling *anger* but if he is crying because his parents would not buy him a desired toy, he might be told that he is feeling *disappointed.*

How does a person identify the particular motive or emotion being experienced in a given situation? We argued earlier that cognitive appraisal of the situation occurs in which the individual interprets the meaning of the situation, i.e., what is appropriate behavior here for me? What are the set of alternative responses? What are the consequences of each response? How do my present needs or goals fit in? These are some aspects of an appraisal which a person might make prior to or after embarking on a course of motivated activity.

Inferring Inner States of Others

If we now turn to the question of how observers arrive at conclusions about the motives of others, we would seem to use a different process. If we are limited to observations of overt behavior of another person, as is often the case especially on meeting someone for the first time, we tend to introspect about our own feelings in comparable circumstances. We ask ourselves what we would do or feel if we were in the other person's position and then generalize from our own feelings to conclusions about those of the other person.

However, it should be obvious that observers do not usually have access to important information about the other person, data such as internal feelings, attitudes, and past experiences of the individual, which play an important role in that person's appraisal of his or her own potential conduct. This discrepancy in the process of identification of motives by an individual and someone who observes that person must necessarily often lead to conflicting inferences about the latter's motives.

Consider again the example of honesty. Suppose a student who considered himself or herself to be an honest person was taking an exam where almost everyone else was cheating. He or she might decide to also cheat in self-defense. Is this behavior inconsistent with a self-image of honesty? To the extent that a person can rationalize or interpret this single action as defensible, the individual will probably still view himself or herself as basically honest. Because one knows also that in the past one has generally acted honestly, he or she could attribute cheating to the extenuating circumstances imposed on him or her rather than to any character defect.

In contrast, an observer who witnessed this isolated incident might draw the conclusion that the individual not only cheated on this occasion but did so as a general practice. Not having access to information about the person's past behavior, the observer would tend to attribute the errant deed to a trait or motive of dishonesty.

Jones and Nisbett (1971) have hypothesized that actors and observers generally differ in their causal attributions in precisely the manner described above. Their analysis was speculative in the sense that it was not based on empirical evidence and they suggested that some exceptions to their generalization undoubtedly exist. For example, the tendency of actors to attribute their actions to situational determinants may be limited to cases in which their present behavior is discrepant from past actions in similar situations. If high consistency of past and present behavior in similar situations exists, it is likely that even actors will see their behavior as stemming from internal dispositions. In contrast, observers who saw only the present behavior would be unable to compare it with the actor's past actions and would be less likely to make situational attributions.

Another basis exists for conflicting inferences not only between actor and observer but also among different observers. The concept of personal constructs proposed by George Kelley (1955) refers to categories for structuring the psychological world that vary among individuals. For example, some people judge others in terms of dimensions such as good-bad, other people might employ an alternative or supplementary basis such as smart-dumb, friendly-hostile, or strong-weak. Individuals differ not only with respect to the type but also the number of classificatory dimensions used in assessing others.

To the extent that one person's construct system differs from that of another, it is likely that inferences about the motives underlying a given behavior will disagree. This point is quite obvious when one considers the high frequency of misunderstandings between those who come from markedly different cultures.

In the above example of the honest student who cheated on the test, an observer who valued honesty would judge the student to be dishonest, but an observer for whom this dimension was less salient might judge the student practical or realistic.

Bias in Interpretations

In addition to the possibility that different cognitive bases exist for interpreting behavior, it is also conceivable that the individual will perceive the bases of behavior differently from observers simply because he or she will be "ego-involved." That is, the individual may be motivated, perhaps often without being aware, to interpret motives in a manner that will be most favorable to himself or herself.

SOURCES OF ATTRIBUTIONAL BIAS

Maselli and Altrocchi (1969) suggested that some attributions about one's behavior may be defense mechanisms. Thus, one might make excuses for one's shortcomings by attributing these failures to the evil intentions of others. In addition to placing the blame on others for one's own failures, one might overestimate the credit due to themselves when good fortune happens to them. A classroom example of a student who receives an F grade will illustrate this point. The instructor might attribute the grade to laziness or stupidity on the part of the student but not to the instructor's poor teaching ability. The student is likely to adopt the opposite interpretation. In the case of students who receive A's, the instructor may attribute great teaching ability to such outcomes, whereas the students might emphasize their own ability and effort as being causal factors.

Even though an individual might be biased in perception of behavior in his or her own favor, it is important to note that these self-perceptions are crucial determinants of subsequent behavior. The true causes of behavior, which objective observers may be more likely to identify, may be quite different from those identified by the actor. However, as long as the individual is unaware, his or her biases and (inaccurate) perceptions continue to influence his or her behavior. Accordingly, attribution theorists (Heider, 1958; Kelley, 1967, 1973) attach significance to the subjective and phenomenological perceptions held by the individual about the determinants of his or her performance.

Weiner and Kukla (1970), for example, examined attributions for the performance of subjects on achievement tasks in which success or failure was possible. They wanted to determine the extent to which factors such as ability, task difficulty, amount of effort, and luck or chance might be invoked by subjects to account for their performance. Weiner and Kukla used fake feedback to rig the outcomes so that they would be identical for all subjects. One finding was that individual differences in achievement motivation affected the types of attributions made. A fuller explanation of achievement motivation theory will be provided in a later chapter, but it will suffice here to say that persons with higher levels of achievement motivation perceived their outcomes as caused by internal factors. Thus, they saw their successes as stemming from their ability and regarded their failures as the results of inadequate effort. Low achievement motivation individuals were more prone to attribute their performance to external factors such as luck or the difficulty of the task.

Although such results are consistent generally with the view that self-serving attributional biases exist, Miller and Ross (1975) raised the possibility that explanations of a nonmotivational nature are also tenable. For example, Feather (1969) suggested that the expectations of the subject must also be considered. Outcomes consistent with expectation will be attributed to internal factors such as ability, whereas inconsistent outcomes will be perceived as due to external factors such as chance.

If we make the further assumption that persons with high achievement motivation have greater expectancies for success, we see that this factor may account for their attributing their successes to internal factors. By the same token, the assumption that low achievement motivation individuals have lower expectancies of success can explain why they assign their successes to external factors such as chance or luck.

Miller and Ross (1975) also considered alternative explanations for evidence of self-serving attributional biases. They concluded that the possibility that individuals may interpret their motives in either ego-enhancing or ego-defensive ways may receive better support in future studies.

To the extent that such ego defenses or self-serving biases operate, the inferences that an individual makes about his or her own behavior will differ from those made by a neutral observer. This conclusion does not imply that observers are completely accurate in their attributions about the actor, but that their biases will be somewhat different. It is conceivable, for example, that observers may bias their attributions in favor of those whom they like and against those whom they dislike. Thus, a behavior with a positive outcome might be attributed to ability or effort if a friend is involved, but to luck if an enemy is involved. Conversely, behavior leading to negative consequences might be regarded as due to bad luck when someone we like is responsible, but due to the lack of ability or evil intentions when someone we dislike is involved.

Attributing Intentions to Others

When we interpret the actions of others we cannot assume that the actors always have intentions. Judgements of intentionality are closely intertwined with the identification of the motives of others.

Observers may mistakenly assume that certain behavior is motivated when in fact the behavior is accidental or coincidental. For example, if someone bumped into you and knocked you down, you might assume the actor had motives. However, if the behavior was not intentional and was perceived as an accident, your reaction would be quite different. Intentions, then, are of the utmost importance in assessing motives. Nevertheless, they are generally ignored by the behavioristic theories of motivation. Most of us cannot deny that our introspection can lead to faulty inferences about intentions. For that matter, we are sometimes unsure of the intentions underlying some of our own behavior. Our own experience, then, makes it clear that our interpretations of the intentions of others as well as those of ourselves are important determinants of our behavior.

The problem of how one ascribes intentions to the behavior of others
has generally been referred to as the study of person perception (Tagiuri and
Petrullo, 1958). Persons, like physical objects, are stimuli, but are also perceived in social and psychological dimensions. Fritz Heider, a pioneer in the
study of social perception (1944, 1958), divided person perception into two
phases. First, there is the attribution of causality. Thus, when Person A receives a gift or hears someone call his or her name, Person A wants to know
who (or what) caused the event. His or her causal inference may or may not
be correct. Suppose A correctly identifies friend B as the causal agent. Then
A's task is to determine whether or not B (the actor) *intended* to produce
that event or consequence for A (the observer). In summary, an observer
must (1) determine the location of the causal agent, and then (2) determine
whether the consequence is best explained by the actor's intent or by chance
or some other explanation that does not assume the actor meant or intended
to cause the consequence.

The notion of responsibility assumes that behaviors are often intentional
and that such intentions can be correctly attributed. Thus, in legal matters, it
is important not only to know who committed a crime, but also to determine
whether or not the agent had intent; whether the agent knew the consequences
of the action in advance. If the action is judged to be accidental, Heider
suggests that the actor is less likely to assign responsibility or blame to the
agent for this action.

Pepitone (1958) identified another factor used in evaluating behavior,
which he termed *justifiability;* this concept refers to the degree to which an
act conforms to or meets ethical standards. Even well-intentioned behavior
such as robbing a bank to buy a present for a friend can be found lacking in
justification. Of course, the judgment of intention need not take justifiability
into account, but the total judgment of the action does depend on this factor.

Most theoretical accounts of the process of attribution of intent assume
that observers make inferences, using their knowledge about their own intentions as bases for making inferences about the behavior of other people
(Heider, 1958; Jones and Davis, 1965; Ossorio and Davis, 1968). But why
do observers make such attributions in the first place? Heider suggested that
such interpretations help us find meaning and order in an otherwise chaotic
influx of information. Forming impressions about people and their motives
assists in permitting predictions about subsequent behavior. Although there
is no doubt that attributions of intent, assuming they are accurate, can have
these integrative functions, it is a moot point to maintain that this goal is a
primary purpose for such inferences.

What factors influence how observers attribute intent? One factor is the
degree to which the outcome of an act is perceived as desirable for the
assumed agent. Assuming that the actor appears to know about the act and
has the ability to perform it, he or she is generally assumed to have intended
it if he or she will benefit by it.

It should be emphasized that such attributions are not always accurate. Unintended behavior may erroneously be judged intentional and vice versa. This qualification is not meant as a criticism of the theoretical formulations, because these errors occur frequently in everyday situations. Just as there are illusions in the perception of physical stimuli, so are there biases and errors in the judgment of social behavior and the assumed intentions. Social psychologists are now actively looking for differences in the accuracy of attributions of intent as functions of numerous variables such as judges, actors, or acts.

So far, we have looked at attribution of intent as a process without looking at the consequences for behavior. It is important, also, to examine the influence of these judgments on subsequent behavior. The degree to which we are attracted or repulsed by others may be influencd by our judgments of their intents and motives. Pepitone (1958) has shown that we are apt to like a person perceived as having good intentions toward us, even if that person is seen displaying objectionable behavior. For example, a person who tells you that you have bad breath may be rude, but he or she is less disliked if the apparent intention is to shock you into self-improvement rather than to be hostile.

Observers rely on a variety of cues when they draw conclusions about the intentions of others: prior information, context, consequences of the behavior, and nonverbal cues are examples. Unlike some psychologists, laypeople also rely on verbal reports to some extent. These cues may be used by observers even though the actor is unaware that he or she is being observed. Moreover, these cues are not always interpreted correctly and better cues are sometimes ignored by observers.

Sometimes, however, the observed person is aware of being assessed and may deliberately create cues that he or she hopes will be detected and interpreted in a given manner. Moreover, false signals are sometimes given in an attempt to disguise the behaver's true intentions.

Strategies used in the game of poker are a good example. If you are to win, you must be able to bluff occasionally. A person who either never or always bluffs will eventually be found out. Successful players must even allow themselves to be caught bluffing occasionally so that on future occasions opponents are uncertain about the value of their cards.

Intentions, then, are subjective states that are important to ascertain because they influence our interpretation of many aspects of behavior. Assumptions about the nature of intentions or the presence or absence of them have a decided effect on our responses to the actions of others.

Summary

The constructs, motives and emotions, include a variety of important inner experiences associated with our daily behavior. When an individual is energized and actively involved in the pursuit of a valued incentive or goal, some motive is assumed to be operative. Emotions are feelings that may occur in reaction to motivated behavior, such as when aggression may be accompanied by fear or anger. At other times emotions may serve as motivating factors in themselves, such as when we try to escape from the unpleasant feelings associated with dangerous situations.

After providing a definition of motivation, we gave a brief description of the scope of this book indicating our concern primarily with human behavior and experience. Emphasis on the social, cognitive, and subjective aspects of human motivation and emotion was described.

A review of some of the main reasons motivational constructs have traditionally fared poorly among many psychologists was given. The tendency to use motives in a circular manner, their subjective nature, and their inability to predict behavior well across similar situations were cited.

Despite these problems, motivational constructs are here to stay, so to speak, as everyone uses them in their analyses of the causes of behavior. A discussion of the process by which individuals identify their own motives pointed out why a different process is plausible when we are identifying motives of other persons whose behavior we observe. In analyzing one's own behavior, one has the additional input of knowledge of one's own past feelings, experiences, and background against which comparisons and interpretations can be made. Little or none of this information is available to the observer who tries to make motivational inferences about an individual solely on the basis of observed behavior.

Another important consideration in analyzing behavior is the question of intentionality. All behavior that leads to specific effects does not involve intention. Accidents or examples in which the intent of a behavior was quite different from its actual effect occur frequently. Our reactions to the behavior of others often depend on whether or not we perceive the behavior as intentional.

Inferences about motives and intentions, then, involve cognitive processes such that the individual interprets a given behavior in the light of information such as the context, previous knowledge, and expected consequences. Such cognition, however, is possibly subject to distortion from various types of biases, which may be ego-enhancing or -defensive. Because motivational interpretations, biased or not, strongly influence our behavior, we must consider them in arriving at a more complete understanding of human behavior.

References

Bem, D. J. Self-perception: An alternative interpretation of cognitive dissonance phenomena. *Psychological Review,* 1967, *74*, 183–200.
———, and Allen, A. On predicting some of the people some of the time:

The search for cross-sectional consistencies in behavior. *Psychological Review*, 1974, *81*, 506–520.

BOWERS, K. S. Situationalism in psychology: An analysis and a critique. *Psychological Review*, 1973, *80*, 307–336.

ENDLER, N. S., and HUNT, J. McV. Sources of behavioral variance as measured by the S-R inventory of anxiousness. *Psychological Bulletin*, 1966, *65*, 336–346.

FEATHER, N. E. Attribution of responsibility and valence of success and failure in relation to initial confidence and task performance. *Journal of Personality and Social Psychology*, 1969, *13*, 129–144.

HEIDER, F. Social perception and phenomenal causality. *Psychological Review*, 1944, *51*, 358–373.

————. *The psychology of interpersonal relations*. New York: Wiley, 1958.

JONES, E. E., and DAVIS, K. E. From acts to dispositions: The attribution process in person perception. In L. Berkowitz (Ed.), *Advances in Experimental Social Psychology*. (Vol. 2). New York: Academic, 1965.

————, and NISBETT, R. E. *The actor and the observer: Divergent perceptions of the causes of behavior*. Morristown, N.J.: General Learning Press, 1971.

KELLEY, G. A. *The psychology of personal constructs*. (Vols. 1 and 2). New York: Norton, 1955.

KELLEY, H. H. Attribution theory in social psychology. In D. Levine (Ed.), *Nebraska Symposium on Motivation*. (Vol. 15). Lincoln: University of Nebraska Press, 1967.

————. The processes of causal attribution. *American Psychologist*, 1973, *28*, 107–128.

MASELLI, M. D., and ALTROCCHI, J. Attribution of intent. *Psychological Bulletin*, 1969, *71*, 445–454.

MILLER, D. T., and ROSS, R. Self-serving biases in the attribution of causality: Fact or fiction? *Psychological Bulletin*, 1975, *82*, 213–225.

MISCHEL, W. *Personality and assessment*. New York: Wiley, 1968.

————. Toward a cognitive social learning reconceptualization of personality. *Psychological Review*, 1973, *80*, 252–283.

ORNE, M. T. On the social psychology of the psychological experiment: With particular emphasis to demand characteristics and their implications. *American Psychologist*, 1962, *17*, 776–783.

OSSORIO, P. G., and DAVIS, K. E. The self, intentionality, and reactions to evaluations. In C. Gordon and K. Gergen (Eds.), *Self in society*. New York: Wiley, 1968

PEPITONE, A. Attributions of causality, social attitudes, and cognitive matching processes. In R. Tagiuri and L. Petrullo (Eds.), *Person perception and interpersonal behavior*. Stanford, Calif.: Stanford University Press, 1958.

RIEFF, P. *Freud: The mind of the moralist*. Garden City, N.Y.: Anchor, 1961.

SKINNER, B. F. *Beyond freedom and dignity*. New York: Knopf, 1971.

————. On "having" a poem. *Saturday Review*, July 15, 1972, 32–35.

TAGUIRI, R., and PETRULLO, L. (Eds.), *Person perception and interpersonal behavior*. Stanford, Calif.: Stanford University Press, 1958.

WEINER, B., and KUKLA, A. An attributional analysis of achievement motivation. *Journal of Personality and Social Psychology*, 1970, *15*, 1–20.

CHAPTER 2

Two Sides of the Same Coin: Subjective and Objective Approaches

Our behavior is usually accompanied by inner feelings of awareness and consciousness of such actions. Affective states and emotional feelings are also frequently associated with our behavioral responses. Despite the existence of two aspects of psychological reality, overt behavior and inner experience, American psychology has tended to ignore the latter and focus on the study of observable behavior.

Behavioristic Approaches

The behaviorist or stimulus-response orientation to psychology, inspired by John B. Watson in the early years of this century, excluded the consideration of subjective experiences, because they were regarded as unreliable, superfluous, mentalistic, as well as sometimes misleading. Verbal report, the primary means of gaining insights into the private world of feelings, was considered imprecise and difficult to validate. The scientific approach to the study of human psychology therefore limited its observations to overt behavior for the most part.

Most behaviorists have emphasized the role of the environmental determinants of behavior and have assigned little influence to hereditary factors. The process of learning has been assumed to play a significant part in determining human motivations and emotions. Responses that lead to certain consequences called reinforcers are learned or associated in connection with the stimuli in those situations. Reinforcers were generally defined as primary needs such as food or water. Consequently, knowledge of the external stimuli associated with a given behavior should be sufficient to predict and understand that behavior. There should be no need to analyze the subjective feelings that accompanied the behavior. Admittedly, such states exist, but the staunch behaviorist would regard them as superfluous in predicting behavior.

In the last decade some important changes have occurred and increasing numbers of behavioristic psychologists have abandoned the extreme behaviorism of the past. Recognition of the need to study subjective and cognitive factors is evident in the studies of a wide variety of topics ranging from physiological psychology (Sperry, 1969), to meditation (Ornstein, 1972), to cognition (Holt, 1964), to motivation (DeCharms, 1968), and to emotion (Leeper, 1965). A shift is also evident in the role attributed to biological and genetic determinants of behavior (e.g., Lenneberg, 1969; Seligman, 1970).

In this chapter we will examine the case for both the behavioral and the subjective perspectives. We feel that each aspect is important and that it is necessary to study both. First, we will describe the history and nature of the traditional behavioristic approach. Not all behaviorists are alike, however, and we will distinguish between strict empiricists such as B. F. Skinner and more theoretically oriented behaviorists such as Hull (1943) or Tolman (1932) who were willing to include hypothetical or inferred constructs in their models.

EARLY BEHAVIORISTIC VIEWS

From the early part of this century until about 1950, the traditional emphasis of behaviorists was on biological or so-called *primary drives* such as hunger or thirst. This choice was due to several factors such as the ease of control and measurement of such drives. By recording the number of hours of food or water deprivation, it is possible to achieve an objective and quantifiable index of the stimulus preconditions in existence when some behavior is observed in some test situation. This approach tended to favor the use of laboratory animals, especially the white rat, so that the more complex motives commonly found among humans were ignored. Nonetheless, it was assumed that the principles derived from the study of simpler organisms could be applied toward the understanding of complex human motives. Given this assumption, it is not surprising that research should concentrate on simpler, readily available laboratory animals.

The principles of reinforcement discovered to control maze performance by rats were applied to human behavior. In the case of human social motives such as affiliation, aggression, or altruism, which did not seem tied to reinforcers such as food reward, it was thought that a process of secondary or higher level reinforcement was involved. Thus, stimuli that were originally of neutral value could acquire reinforcing properties by frequent association with a primary reinforcer. A mother who provides food for her infant becomes a source of secondary reinforcement accordingly, because food is always paired with her presence. Eventually, her values and motives become incorporated by the child who wants her approval and affection.

Compared with its predecessor, *instinct,* the concept of drive was a vast improvement as a scientific construct. Whereas drives were inferred from information about the environmental stimulus conditions, instincts were usually postulated in an ad hoc or circular manner. Behavior X was due to an instinct for X, and behavior Y was due to an instinct for Y. Although instincts were popular motivational concepts around the turn of the century, the rise of behaviorism supplanted them with the more precise and objective drive formulation. As Beach and Jaynes (1954) pointed out, the use of instincts often obscured more than it explained. Only with careful empirical observation was it discovered that many so-called instinctive behaviors did not actually occur automatically if certain critical early experiences were prevented or otherwise failed to occur. It should be added in conclusion that contemporary concepts related to instinctive or unlearned behaviors are more rigorous and do not deserve the condemnation received by instincts at the turn of the century. The work of ethologists, such as Tinbergen (1951), on instinctive behavior, which will be described in Chapter 3, involves careful observation and specification of stimulus conditions related to these patterns of behavior. There has been a renewed interest in unlearned or innate determinants of behavior in recent years as a consequence.

Returning to the concept of primary drives, we should note the impact of physiological processes such as homeostasis on such models. Homeostasis refers to the equilibrium or balance of physiological processes. By analogy, behavior should be activated toward some goal such as food only to the extent that there is a deficit; when the balance is restored, the motive for food-seeking behavior should disappear.

The laboratory study of primary drives favored by the behaviorists allowed the investigator to control the environment and thus study the variables of interest. History indicates, however, that such control was not always easy. Pavlov (1927), in his classic studies of conditioned salivation, found, much to his dismay, that his dogs often fell asleep while strapped in their experimental harnesses, that distracting hall noises interrupted their attention and their salivation, and that they struggled to escape when first placed in the test apparatus. Consequently, Pavlov found it useful to postulate the existence of a freedom reflex, an investigatory reflex, and an orienting reflex. These extraneous phenomena interfered with the main topic of interest, the salivary responses, and so were ignored at that time. As we shall see shortly, these phenomena have assumed great theoretical interest a generation later.

The conditioned reflex served as a model for early behaviorists such as John B. Watson who attempted to view the sum total of behavior as a collection of associations formed through conditioning. This interest in the growth and development of a behavioral repertoire as a result of environmental experiences rather than the operation of innate factors led behaviorists to emphasize the study of learning. Learning referred to relatively permanent changes in behavioral tendencies. It was necessary, however, to examine motivational factors that served to energize the organism to perform such acquired tendencies. Observed behavioral performance may involve learned responses but without the appropriate motivational states, they should not take place.

LATER BEHAVIORAL VIEWS

Different learning theorists varied in their precise formulations of the nature of both learning and motivation. We will briefly describe and contrast two major behavior theories. Clark Hull and Edward Chace Tolman, both behaviorists, developed important theories in the 1930s and 1940s. Both of them rejected introspection, a method used by earlier psychologists to study consciousness. But whereas Hull (1943) dealt with a mechanistic and molecular approach, Tolman (1932) operated within a cognitive and molar framework. In either case, formulations about internal processes were treated as intervening variables, abstractions that could not be measured directly but were operationally defined in terms of specifiable antecedent and consequent conditions. For example, concepts such as Hull's *habit* or Tolman's *expectancy* dealt with their views of what was learned by an organism; both referred to unobservable internal constructs. Yet, each intervening variable could be defined only by linking it with variables on the antecedent side, e.g., the number of learning trials and variables on the consequent side, e.g., speed of running a maze or percentage of correct choices.

Behavior can be viewed as a sequence of learned associations or habits as Hull saw it or as a set of cognitions and expectancies according to Tolman. Even so, it is necessary to refer to some motivational constructs in order to translate these hypothetical states into observable performance. Hull formulated the construct *drive,* which referred essentially to the level of deprivation of some primary biological need. Drive was equated with the sum total of all the sources of energy that activate an organism at a given moment. When the responses of the organism lead to *drive reduction,* such as the attainment of water by a thirsty rat, Hull viewed the situation as one in which an association had been formed between a stimulus and a response due to reinforcement. Later versions of his theory changed details of this process but still emphasized the importance of reinforcement as a factor in learning. Since reinforcement is based on the reduction of some motivational factor (e.g., drive), it is clear that a close tie exists between learning and motivation in Hull's theory.

Tolman, on the other hand, did not regard reinforcement as necessary for the learning process per se, although he did acknowledge that the role of motivation was necessary for performance. Tolman placed more emphasis on "confirmation" of *expectancies* than on reinforcement due to drive reduction. In a sense, one may say that knowing that, "I was right," is the nature of the reinforcement process for the successful performance of a learned expectancy. This cognitive view of the consequences of performing learned behaviors, however, does not tell us why the behavior should have occurred at all. As one critic argued, Tolman's theory leaves his rats "buried in thought" with their expectancies and hypotheses.

Both of these behavioristic theories of learning talked about the nature and role of motivation. Their views of motivation, like their constructs of learning, varied in detail but shared some important features. *Operational definitions,* rather than circular ones, were required so that one could identify the variables, such as the number of hours of deprivation, that were linked with the amount of motivation and the variables, such as activity level, that reflected the influence of differences in motivational level. These views of motivation were objective but still lacking in the ability to incorporate many aspects of behavior, especially human behavior.

CRITICISMS OF BEHAVIORISTIC VIEWS

A drive conception of motivation based on biological deficits would suggest that once all deficits were removed, the organism would be quiescent. It would also suggest that an organism could be motivated only by depriving it of some biological need such as food, water, or physical safety. How could one account for the higher order needs of humans that seem unrelated to biological drives? Why are some persons driven to obtain social status, popularity, fame, or fortune? The general solution offered by behaviorists for such seeming exceptions was to argue in terms of *secondary reinforcement.* Some drive theorists might argue that abstract values and goals must have been associated at some time with the satisfaction of primary drives. Thus, a mother who provides food to a child becomes a secondary reinforcer whose beliefs, values, and attitudes are also valued by the child.

This speculative formulation was never held too enthusiastically, but it was the best account that could be offered by the primary drive advocates.

Despite these limitations, it was not until the 1950s that the inadequacy of drive as a motivational construct became generally accepted. The types of phenomena, such as curiosity to novel stimuli, noted by Pavlov in his classic studies of conditioning were rediscovered both here and in Russia (Berlyne, 1960) and assumed importance in emphasizing the weaknesses of the simple drive theories. These phenomena were difficult to accommodate by drive formulations of motivation and could not readily be dismissed. It became necessary to revise theories in order to explain curiosity and exploratory behavior.

A number of empirical studies were undertaken to determine precisely what conditions were necessary for the occurrence of such behaviors. It became clear that even when all primary drives were apparently satisfied, organisms were highly active, curious, and attentive especially in novel, unusual, or complex environments. Such findings were embarrassing to those promoting a model of motivation based on the idea that homeostasis of primary drives was the main factor in controlling behavior.

Harlow and his colleagues (Butler and Harlow, 1954; Harlow, 1953; Harlow and McClearn, 1954) noted that monkeys would learn to bar press merely to be able to observe the environment (electric train set running) or to manipulate mechanical puzzles. Montgomery (1953; 1954) demonstrated in a series of studies that rats preferred the arm of a T maze that led to a complex rather than a simple path. Berlyne (1951) reviewed much of the Russian research on the orienting reflex and the conditions under which it occurs. In addition, Berlyne (1960) summarized his own research, as well as that of others, on curiosity. As a result of these and other studies, concepts such as curiosity drive, exploratory drive, and manipulatory drive were developed; furthermore, it was maintained that these drives were analogous to hunger or thirst drives.

By the late 1950s, however, it became clear that drive theorists were making the same mistake as instinct proponents. Merely naming a behavior did not explain its origins or the conditions for its maintenance. To say an animal explores because it has high exploratory drive is the same as saying it is due to an exploratory instinct—it adds nothing. Of course, the phenomenon of exploration still exists, but the task is to identify the causes of its occurrence. The recognition of these phenomena, nevertheless, served to point out many of the inadequacies of the behavioristic model, because it could not readily account for these behaviors, which apparently were not dependent on tissue needs.

Toward a Subjective Behaviorism

Recent behavioristic views (e.g., Bandura, 1974; Lazarus, 1974; Mischel, 1973) have argued in favor of greater consideration of internal processes of a cognitive and subjective nature in analyzing human behavior. All of them concur in stressing the role of self-regulatory and control processes as determinants of human motivation and emotion. These proposals centering around a concept like the self are significant changes from earlier behaviorism, which eschewed mentalistic and phenomenological constructs.

SOCIAL LEARNING APPROACHES: THE STANFORD SCHOOL

Although in his 1973 statement Mischel's primary thrust seems to be the importance of situational factors as opposed to trait explanations in determining behavior, he also provides an extended discussion of the role of subjective and cognitive factors. Briefly, Mischel proposed that there are personality or individual differences in competences, basic ability, and intelligence that limit behavioral capacity. In addition, there are wide individual differences in how persons process information from the environment. Each person develops his or her own construction of social reality, although it may overlap with that of others to some extent. These cognitive categories are acquired by direct learning as well as by social or observational learning experiences. They seem to be similar to the personal constructs proposed by George Kelley (1955), which were discussed briefly in Chapter 1.

In addition, the individual acquires expectancies about the effects of various matters such as the consequences of specific behaviors or the relationship among different stimuli in the world he or she encounters. Depending on his or her value system, some of these outcomes and contingencies are more desirable than others. The actions an individual chooses to take will therefore be different from those made by someone with a different set of values.

Not only is the individual depicted as an active agent who categorizes and encodes information, assesses contingencies, and makes decisions based on personal values, but as one who regulates his or her own behavior in many ways that are not so immediately tied to environmental input. Mischel notes that people evaluate their own performances against some internal standard of quality and engage in self-praise or self-criticism of their performance. Self-control in the form of discipline, patience, or delay of gratification also occurs, often working in opposition to the impact of stimuli in the environment.

In his presidential address to the American Psychological Association, Albert Bandura (1974) also drew attention to the importance of self-produced consequences as determinants of behavior. Criticizing theories that attribute all behavior to the effects of external factors, Bandura cited illustrations of the role of internal symbolic processes that enable humans to anticipate or foresee consequences and to act accordingly, often in ways unpredicted by theories that emphasize immediate stimulus factors as the determinants of behavior. The whole area of moral evaluation of one's own actions reveals not only the operation of self-control but also how internal processes may take precedence over external reinforcers. In situations in which one might receive immediate positive reinforcement but will suffer self-criticism, loss of self-respect, and impaired self-esteem, for example, the tempting behavior is often inhibited or partially blocked. The opposite situation exists where external consequences are aversive and punishing but actions are undertaken by the individual because they are in some way self-reinforcing as in the case of idealists, martyrs, or the religiously devout.

The powerful influence of self-produced consequences can also be seen in the fact that we sometimes resort to self-deceptive rationalizations in order to justify behaviors that would otherwise be reprehensible. As Bandura (1974, p. 861) observed, "People do not act in ways they ordinarily consider evil or destructive until such activities are construed as serving moral purposes. Over the years, much cruelty has been perpetuated in the name of religious principles, righteous ideologies, and regulatory sanctions." Without our ability to devise rationalizations for self-exoneration, we would be less likely to act in ways that conflict with our self-concepts.

Social learning theorists such as Mischel and Bandura place great emphasis on the role of concepts with a subjective ring, such as self-control, self-evaluation, and self-gratification. It should be noted, however, that their approach is still firmly rooted in the behavioristic tradition. Although they have moved further toward the study of more complex human phenomena than their predecessors such as Hull, Tolman, and Skinner, their method still deals with the identification of antecedent conditions associated with or producing different types of behavioral consequences. The phenomena on which they concentrate, such as observational learning through the imitation of modeled behavior, is assumed to obey laws of learning similar to those found for the behavior of Hull's rats. When Mischel and Bandura refer to processes such as self-control or self-evaluation by the individual, they assume that these internal processes are controlled or created by identifiable external conditions just as the tendency of the laboratory rat to press a bar for food is shaped by the principles of learning.

A COGNITIVE APPROACH

A similar cognitive model dealing with the alteration of emotional states through the influence of self-control processes has been proposed by Lazarus (1974). Building on his earlier studies of coping in stress situations (Lazarus, 1968), he shows how emotions can be controlled by the individual in examples such as managing grief or being a good loser. Various techniques including rationalization, detachment, and denial serve as means of self-regulation of experienced emotion. He emphasized the fact that these coping strategies actually precede the emotion and serve to modify it. This is not to say that additional forms of coping responses might not also occur after the emotional experience, as assumed by the common-sense interpretation.

Lazarus maintained that the organism is not a passive recipient of external stimuli, which then determine emotional arousal. Instead, the individual through self-regulatory actions determines which aspects of the environmental stimuli to attend to or how these stimuli are to be interpreted or appraised.

These new theoretical models are promising and represent substantial improvements in behavioristic formulations, because they incorporate the more complex cognitive and subjective internal determinants. Despite these improvements in conceptual models, one of the limitations of the research generated by these approaches is that of the dominant methodology employed. Although the experimental method is the favorite paradigm in most behavioristic research, it may not be the best approach for assessing subjective processes. This criticism is particularly true of laboratory experimentation, because the participants are aware that they are being studied; it is less valid for naturalistic field experiments in which the subjects are not aware of their participation in a study.

A PHENOMENOLOGICAL PERSPECTIVE

Of central importance in understanding the causes of behavior is the consideration of the individual's phenomenological view of his or her own motives and feelings, as well as his or her perception of similar states in other persons. The way things appear to the actor, accurate or not, represents the essence of a phenomenological perspective. The importance of the conditions of objective reality as determinants of behavior is not denied, but we feel that greater focus needs to be placed on the self-perceptions of the individual whose behavior we wish to comprehend. Furthermore, we believe that a variety of methods, experimental and nonexperimental, can be used to study these processes. Our own experiences make it clear these variables are important, and formal academic psychology only hides its collective head in the sand if subjective variables are ignored in an effort to imitate the physical sciences.

But radical behaviorists such as B. F. Skinner would argue that it is unnecessary to refer to inner feelings, because it is sufficient to identify the reinforcement contingencies associated with these subjective states. In one passage in *Beyond Freedom and Dignity,* Skinner (1971) describes the layperson's description of a young man's behavior and then provides a behavioristic translation, in parentheses, as follows:

. . . he lacks assurance or feels insecure (*his behavior is weak and inappropriate*); he is discouraged (*he is seldom reinforced, and as a result his behavior undergoes extinction*); he is frustrated (*extinction is accompanied by emotional responses*); he feels anxious (*his behavior frequently has unavoidable aversive consequences that have emotional effects*); . . . and he experiences an identity crisis (*he does not recognize the person he once called "I"*).

Skinner suggested that statements about the young man's feelings may allow us "to make some informed guesses about what is wrong with the contingencies, but we must go directly to the contingencies if we want to be sure, *and it is the contingencies we must change if we are to change his behavior.*"

SELF-CONCEPT AS A PHENOMENOLOGICAL CONCEPT

One goal of a phenomenological approach to the study of human motivation is the study of how feelings about one's own self or self-concept can influence other aspects of an individual's motives and emotions. The *self* is a difficult concept to define, although all of us are reasonably clear what the term refers to. The person or individual each of us considers to be *me* is what most of us understand to be the *self*. The self-concept refers to our overall evaluation of the goodness or badness of the self.

As we shall show shortly, physical factors such as physical attractiveness can dramatically affect the nature of one's self-concept. We think it is likely that the attitudes one holds about oneself can affect behavior more strongly than past or immediate external sources of reinforcement for specific behaviors in many cases.

Skinner may be correct *in principle* that some past pattern of reinforcement has been involved in the creation of these subjective states called self-concepts, yet it is not so clear that such concepts are not beneficial for our understanding of behavior. Factors other than reinforcements for behavior such as one's sex, age, race, social class, as well as less obvious factors such as physical features, are crucial determinants of one's self-concept. Knowledge of an individual's attitudes about himself or herself may help explain behavior that might be difficult to comprehend in terms of reinforcement history alone. We will now describe several studies showing how physical attractiveness first affects one's self-concept, which then appears to influence performance on various tasks.

Physical Factors and Self-concept.   Psychologists have given little recognition, at least in their theories, to the importance of physical attractiveness to either the self-concept or reactions by other persons. This omission is surprising, because in everyday life physical appearance is a major factor influencing interpersonal interaction. Whether it be total body shape, facial features, height, or trimness, physical dimensions play a key role in how a person is treated in many situations. Perhaps nowhere is this fact more evident than in the attraction and distraction ability of a beautiful woman, at least from the perspective of most men. The popular saying, attributed to Dorothy Parker, "Men don't make passes at girls who wear glasses," is not without some validity. However, it does not appear that the physical attractiveness of men is such a primary consideration for women.

In theorizing about personality, psychologists focus on traits such as honesty, loyalty, hostility, or warmth. It is conceivable that some relationship exists between physical traits and psychological attributes. Short men might differ from tall men in personality; fat women might differ from thin women in personality. How are such differences explained? Are they determined primarily by physiological or constitutional factors as suggested by Sheldon (1942)? A fat person might be less energetic, because he or she would find it more physically fatiguing. Or do social stereotypes determine the way in which others react to an individual? Thus, the belief that fat people are jovial might be somewhat self-fulfilling in that other people will reinforce fat people for joviality. Or it could be that fat people develop this trait in reaction to the negative affect which most people seem to have towards them (Maddox, Back, and Leiderman, 1968).

Whereas physical factors considered by society to be ugly seem to connote negative attributes, physical beauty is perceived as related to positive qualities. Dion, Bersheid, and Walster (1972) had college students rate photographs of three persons: one attractive, one neutral, and one unattractive. The sex of the persons in the photographs matched that of each subject. Ratings were made of a number of psychological traits as well as of future success in several aspects of life. Male and female subjects alike tended to predict greater success and to attribute more socially desirable traits to the more attractive faces, as Table 2–1 indicates. Of course, whether these expectations are in fact true is a separate question. These expectations might be inferences based on the subject's impressions of what is already true in our society, or they may be totally unfounded. However, if enough people think the same way, it is possible that these predictions could become self-fulfilling.

On the other hand, it could be argued that if most people think well of the physically attractive, this expectancy may be self-defeating. That is, if we place some people on pedestals and worship them, these gods and goddesses could become vain, arrogant, and unbearable. The admiration stems not from any moral character or virtue or from any outstanding artistic or intellectual accomplishment, but is merely a consequence of physical attributes.

The extent to which our concern about our physical features and the reaction of others affects our feelings can be seen in a study by MacGregor (1968), who analyzed eighty-nine patients who sought modification of their noses by plastic surgery in order to alter their appearance and their self-concepts. About half the patients were motivated by a desire to disguise their ethnic background and hoped that the nose change would protect them from

TABLE 2–1.   Traits Attributed to Various Stimulus Others.

Trait Ascription*	Unattractive Stimulus Person	Average Stimulus Person	Attractive Stimulus Person
Social desirability of the stimulus person's personality	56.31	62.42	65.39
Occupational status of the stimulus person	1.70	2.02	2.25
Marital competence of the stimulus person	.37	.71	1.70
Parental competence of the stimulus person	3.91	4.55	3.54
Social and professional happiness of the stimulus person	5.28	6.34	6.37
Total happiness of the stimulus person	8.83	11.60	11.60
Likelihood of marriage	1.52	1.82	2.17

*The higher the number, the more socially desirable, the more prestigious an occupation, etc., the stimulus person is expected to possess.
Source. From "What Is Beautiful Is Good" by K. Dion, E. Bersheid, and E. Walster, *Journal of Personality and Social Psychology,* 1972, *24,* 285–290. Copyright 1972 by the American Psychological Association. Reprinted by permission.

racial prejudice and discrimination. The other half of the sample seemed to be concerned more with aesthetic factors related to their individual personality and wanted their noses "fixed" rather than "changed." They were frequently persons with deformed or unusually shaped noses, which led to staring, teasing, and embarrassing nicknames such as *Banana Nose, Cyrano, Tweedlebeak,* and *Pinocchio.*

A similar negative evaluation of one's own physical features occurred prior to the civil rights and black pride movements of the 1960s in the tendency among blacks to modify their features with skin whiteners and hair straighteners. The classic study of Clark and Clark (1947) indicated that black children realized the advantages of being white and rejected identification with blackness. Although these trends have disappeared (Hraba and Grant, 1970) in the face of growing black identity and pride, this example illustrates further how physical appearance plays a major role in self-concept.

SUCCESS AND FAILURE AS FACTORS.   As a specific example, consider the subjective feelings that stem from success and failure. We assume that these consequences will create different self-perceptions of personal competency as well as differences in affective states such as moods and emotions. Furthermore, these subjective states can serve as causes or modifiers of subsequent events in a behavioral chain. For example, whether a person has just passed or failed an exam creates internal states, which in turn should affect the likelihood that the person will respond positively to, say, an appeal for a charitable donation. In fact this momentary state may be more critical in determining the present behavior than years of previous reinforcement for charitable behavior.

Evidence (Berkowitz and Conner, 1966; Isen, 1970) that bears on this example shows that subjects were more altruistic after they had experienced the warm glow of success in a task that was not associated with the appeal for help. The opposite effect, in which negative feelings created by failure affect behavior, is illustrated by the finding that aggression frequently follows the negative experience of frustration (Dollard, Doob, Miller, Mowrer, and Sears, 1939).

Aronson and Mettee (1968) provide another example of how self-esteem affects behavior. They induced low self-esteem in subjects by providing fake feedback indicating poor performance on a task. The task was arranged then so that the subjects had an opportunity to cheat with detection seemingly unlikely. Compared to those who did not receive such esteem-lowering scores, these subjects cheated more after this negative experience.

Not only can success or failure create affective states that influence reactions toward others, but these feelings can seemingly then determine one's reactions to one's self, which in turn can influence aspects of one's behavior. In one study by Mischel, Ebbesen, and Zeiss (1973), fake feedback of results on a concept learning test of intelligence was used to induce feelings of success or failure. For the next ten minutes, subjects had a chance to study the results of personality tests they had taken a week earlier. Two sets of

IBM cards, one containing what were presumably the subject's twelve best assets and one with his or her twelve worst liabilities, were available, as well as paragraph summaries. Two notebooks with "Actuarial Norms" for positive and negative qualities were also provided. In reality, all subjects received identical materials in this part of the study, although each was told that he or she received his or her own scores.

Observation of the amount of time each subject spent studying the positive and negative information about his or her self was the main goal of the study. The results, shown in Table 2–2, indicated that success led to the subjects' paying more attention to the positive assets, whereas failure led the subjects to focus more on the negative liabilities. Although some personality differences were found, the overall evidence led Mischel et al. to conclude that success causes us to react more favorably toward ourselves, whereas failure has the opposite effect.

TABLE 2–2. Mean Time Spent on Assets and Liabilities in Each Success–Failure and Expectancy Condition.

	Assets		Liabilities	
Condition	Expectancy	No Expectancy	Expectancy	No Expectancy
Success	188	329	330	239
Failure	209	91	221	367
Control	103	125	273	327

Source. From "Selective Attention to the Self: Situational and Dispositional Determinants" by W. Mischel, E. Ebbesen, and A. Zeiss, *Journal of Personality and Social Psychology*, 1973, *27*, 129–142. Copyright 1973 by the American Psychological Association. Reprinted by permission.

Recognition of broad subjective states such as self-concepts as evidence helps us understand paradoxical situations such as those that occur in cases of persons whose behavior seems totally at odds with past reinforcement histories. Dramatic examples such as the child who comes from the best home with loving parents, the finest education, and all material needs but becomes a petty thief, or the child who comes from the wrong side of the tracks, poverty, and a broken home but goes on to become a brilliant scientist or successful in business illustrate this point.

These examples defy logical explanation in terms of objective facts, but when subjective states such as rebellion, resentment, persistence, or determination, are considered, the paradoxes often disappear. Everyone knows of someone who had everything going for them but who never realized their potential due to self-doubt or lack of confidence. Similarly, we all know people who have average ability but whose self-determination and ambition lead them to achieve great success. These paradoxes are difficult to comprehend without considering subjective factors such as the self-concepts each person holds.

One of the objections to the use of self-concepts is the fact that the self must at the same time be both the subject and the object. Epstein (1973) has proposed a view of the self-concept that he feels can satisfy both the behaviorists and the phenomenologists. Specifically, Epstein maintained that the self-concept is a *theory* that an individual holds about himself or herself. This theory serves to guide the individual in optimizing pleasure and minimizing pain, thus making life more livable and emotionally satisfying. In many respects, this approach is similar to that suggested by Kelley (1955), except that it emphasizes emotional factors whereas Kelley stressed cognitive aspects such as personal constructs. In any event, by viewing the self as a theory rather than as an entity, Epstein felt that the self can "no longer be dismissed as unscientific, or as a reincarnation of the soul. . . ."

Choosing Strategy—Objective versus Subjective Approaches?

One criticism of the invocation of internal constructs such as self, self-esteem, self-concept, and the like in explaining behavior is the assumption that characteristics of the self must also have antecedent conditions or past reinforcement histories. Otherwise the conception of self becomes a mysterious inner force pulled out of thin air when all other efforts at explanation have failed. Variations in self-concepts, like differences in overt behavior, must also reflect certain differences in reinforcement patterns.

On strictly logical grounds, the behaviorist view is warranted. The subjective experiences of an individual are but one side of a coin, the other being the set of corresponding stimuli that created these inner states as well as modified behavioral tendencies. The differences in self-esteem that affected helping behavior in studies (Berkowitz and Conner, 1966; Isen, 1970) reported earlier in this chapter, for example, can be traced to differences in prior reinforcements administered by the experimenter in the first phase of those experiments. Subjects who had encountered success were more likely to help others than were those who had experienced initial failure.

One might well wonder, then, if it makes much difference whether we attack from the subjective or the objective side. In favor of the emphasis on objective behavioral analysis is the possibility of interobserver agreement and greater control compared with the less reliable evidence of subjective evidence.

Why not then emphasize the study of behavior and the external conditions related to it? One reason is that one type of behavior is affected not only by the past reinforcement received for it but also by other experiences quite unrelated to it. Consider a simple example, as diagramed in Table 2–3. Suppose we take three groups of rats whose past history is either known or assumed to be equal. All of them are then given identical food reinforcement during twenty trials in running a maze, *A*. On the average, we would

TABLE 2–3.   Differences in Past Experiences Unknown to Observer
May Lead to Unexpected Variations in Behavior to a Given Situation.

Past Experience in Maze B (Unknown to Observer)	Present Experience in Maze A (Known by Observer)	Type of Behavior in Maze A
Group 1 Satiation due to large number of food-reinforced trials	20 trials with food reinforcement available for correct responding	Low or No Activity
Group 2 Numerous electric shocks of painful intensity	Same as Group 1	Agitated high activity
Group 3 Placed in maze for same amount of time as Gps 1 and 2 but received neither food nor shock	Same as Group 1	Moderate Activity, Exploration

predict the average performance of each group to be about the same, based on our knowledge of their identical treatment in *this* maze.

Suppose, however, that the three groups of rats also received other experiences in a different maze, *B,* shortly before receiving the second maze situation. Suppose one group received enough food-reinforced trials there to approach satiation, another group received a number of electric shocks, and the final group was merely placed in the apparatus and received neither food nor shock.

In the light of this additional information, we would not be surprised if the identical treatment of the three groups in the *second* maze did not yield similar behavior. One group would probably be calm and inactive, another group would probably be agitated and fearful, and another group would probably explore the maze actively depending on the nature of the subjective and inner states created by experiences in the first maze. We would expect the different affective states created in the three groups by their experiences in the first maze to lead to variations in response even though the groups receive identical treatment in the second maze.

One might quickly object that even the different affective states created in the first maze involved identifiable external causes. This observation is valid, but the possibility of actually knowing such conditions is usually much lower in real life than in laboratory experiments in which the investigator controls such factors deliberately. How do we empirically assess the external conditions that led to differences in self-esteem, values, and other factors that might lead to differences in reactions among otherwise equivalent students who fail an exam? We cannot be sure that we can identify the critical factors that will interact with the experience of failure in this example, let alone identify the past reinforcement histories of each of these factors.

In other words, even if one allows that every internal state must involve a past history of external reinforcements, one finds it extremely difficult to proceed from this information alone to infer which internal states will interact with the external stimuli in a given situation. One student facing failure will take it calmly, because his or her self-esteem (created by its own reinforcement history, to be sure) is adequate. Another student with similar self-esteem might take the failure as quite a defeat, because that student places a high value (also created by past reinforcement) on academic achievement.

The implication of this analysis is that it is not so easy after all to take the objective approach to what causes human behavior unless there is very little influence of past experience in a given situation, a tenuous assumption at best. The more we suspect that some aspects of the psychological past of an individual will become activated in a situation, whether they be called memories, fantasies, emotions, self-esteem, personal constructs, values, and so on, the more essential it is that we try to assess the nature of the cognitive, subjective, and phenomenological reactions the situation creates in the individual. Our preceding discussion, however, argues that it is unlikely that we can identify the nature of these inner processes and the manner in which they operate by analyzing merely the external stimulus conditions.

Verbal Report Revisited

The best solution in the long run for discovering the nature of many of these inner determinants of human behavior may involve the old but simple procedure of asking the individual to describe his or her subjective impressions of his or her conscious awareness of self, personal values, personal constructs, feelings, moods, emotions, and experiences. This procedure is not suggested as one that will always be highly effective because such a direct and simple technique will encounter many obstacles. People have a multitude of reasons, many of them very valid, for not wishing to divulge all their inner feelings, thoughts, and attitudes to others, especially psychologists. Fear of offending others, fear of retaliation from others, fear of embarrassment or appearing foolish might also be involved. The wish to maintain privacy, personal freedom and control, and dignity are other considerations. Moreover, in many situations an individual may be unable to recognize, identify, or describe accurately the nature of inner processes. Rationalization, defensiveness, and the desire to put oneself in the most favorable light will also occur.

Obviously, the use of a subjective verbal report is a dangerous and risky procedure. Yet, total reliance on observable behavior and the conditions under which it occurs may be even worse, because this strategy prevents the consideration of the contribution of subjective states to behavior. Unless we have reason to suspect the individual of outright lying and deception (an ironic suspicion for psychologists to hold against others), a verbal report from the individual can provide some clues about previous factors that might be interacting with the present situation to determine behavior. Because we cannot empirically determine the nature of the past reinforcement for most of these interacting inner processes, we should at least try to know which ones are operating in a given situation, based on a verbal report from the individual under observation.

How do we know if an individual really believes or feels what he or she claims? Can we trust the truthfulness of our respondents? Will individuals not tend to be defensive, especially in dealing with psychologists? Some psychologists (Jourard, 1968) are optimistic and feel that the problems of openness and cooperativeness could be solved if psychologists would demonstrate their trustworthiness to participants and also show how involvement in research could benefit the participants as well as the investigators.

In contrast, it has been quite common for behaviorists to use deception as a technique for uncovering the individual's true feelings. It is assumed that the individual will hide his or her true feelings and thus it is mandatory for the experimenter to outsmart the participant and trick him or her into revealing these feelings. An extreme example of this strategy has been dubbed the "bogus pipeline" (Jones and Sigall, 1971). In the first phase of the experiment, the subject is hooked up to what acts essentially as a lie detector. A complex set of manipulations is employed to convince the subject that the apparatus has uncanny abilities to detect true feelings and attitudes. Then the subject is tested on the machine about issues such as racial attitudes. It was assumed and shown that subjects who had been intimidated by the awesome accuracy of the machine probably gave truer feelings than control subjects who did not receive this deception. The deceived subjects apparently made no attempt to report socially desirable responses, because their ratings of *Negroes* for example, were less favorable than those of the control group. The implication is that the bogus pipeline identifies truer and more honest attitudes.

CONCLUSIONS. This emphasis on an assessment of how a situation is perceived by the individual, what meaning or significance the situation holds, and the expected consequences of the various alternative responses the individual perceives as viable is needed, in our view, for a more accurate understanding of the determinants of human behavior. Verbal report, as we have seen, has its limitations and should not be used alone or always accepted at face value but should be compared with behavioral measures to check for consistency. This phenomenological perspective of the perceptions of the individual about the causes and effects of his or her own behavior and experience deserves greater attention from psychologists than it has received in the past.

At the same time one must use great caution to avoid allowing speculations about inner factors to serve as excuses or rationalizations for behaviors stemming from other causes. A student who fails an exam and claims afterward that the performance was due to an indifferent attitude and a lack of effort rather than a shortage of ability may or may not be reporting his or her true feelings. If we had independent evidence about the student's prior attitude or amount of study expended, we would be in a better position to evaluate his or her claims.

Similarly, one must avoid circular reasoning when using explanations involving inner processes. A person who donates generously to charity might retrospectively claim that a good mood was responsible. Perhaps, but we would be on safer ground if we had independent verification of this claim, preferably measured prior to the occurrence of the behavior that this mood allegedly influenced.

In summary, by carefully combining information from the person whose behavior we wish to understand with information from independent sources about the same events, we can formulate a more comprehensive and valid explanation.

Greater use of subjective evidence such as verbal report may be of great value in our understanding of motivation, because the perception of a situation, an important factor underlying behavior, varies in individuals. Therefore, general laws based on the *nomothetic* approach (Allport, 1937) of group averages may well be of limited value in accounting for the motivation of different individuals. These fictional averages, although mathematically sound, are often psychologically meaningless. The alternative approach, termed *idiographic* by Allport, has not met with much success despite his articulate advocacy. Perhaps one obstacle, to quote Bem and Allen (1974, p. 511), is that "the problem with concluding that an idiographic approach represents the path to the truth, however, has always been that one is never sure what to do next." The idiographic approach implies that no general laws exist and that each person is more or less unique, hardly an appealing prospect for those who want to develop a science of psychology.

Bem and Allen, however, argue that the impasse can be resolved if investigators do not attempt to compare everyone by the *same* categories. Since the relevant personal constructs or traits do vary in individuals, it is more appropriate to compare persons only according to those dimensions that they themselves consider significant to their lives. Instead of trying to predict all of the people all of the time, a more realistic goal according to Bem and Allen is to predict some of the people some of the time.

A similar dissatisfaction with the limitations of the nomothetic approach has arisen recently in such diverse areas as educational psychology (Cronbach, 1975), the psychology of aging (Jarvik, 1975), and human memory (Underwood, 1975). The interactive effects of person variables such as ability, values, motives, and personality on the operation of experimental treatment variables can no longer be dismissed without creating oversimplified conclusions.

Approach of This Book

We will attempt to present evidence from both the objective behavioral approach and the phenomenological or experiential view, recognizing that behavior and experience are two sides of the same coin and that both need to be examined in order to achieve a more complete analysis. Laboratory experiments will be the major source of evidence, reflecting the state of current research, but naturalistic observations will also be provided wherever possible. As noted earlier, controlled laboratory experiments may be suitable for analyzing behavior, but nonexperimental and nonreactive procedures may be better in assessing subjective states as they occur in real life.

Our conceptual framework will emphasize the role of cognitive processes similar to those suggested by Mischel (1973) and described earlier. The personal constructs used by each individual to categorize his or her world of experiences, the subjective expectancies formed about his or her personal values, and his or her strategies for self-regulation and self-control are among the internal determinants of the individual's motivation and emotion.

We take a somewhat hedonistic approach in assuming that humans approach pleasurable situations and avoid those involving pain. It is important to recognize, however, that the specific sources of pleasure and pain will not be the same for everyone and that these goals will be determined by each individual's way of viewing the world and his or her system of values. Here again, we see the necessity of considering subjective and phenomenological definitions, rather than objective ones, of pleasure and pain, right and wrong, good or bad. The very set of dimensions or personal constructs that exist will also be idiosyncratic rather than universal and objectively definable. As George Kelley (1958) concluded on the basis of his experiences as a therapist, "Over and over again, it appeared that our clients were making their choices, not in terms of the alternatives we saw open to them, but in terms of the alternatives they saw open to them. It was their network of constructions that made up the daily mazes that they ran, not the pure realities that appeared to us to surround them."

None of the arguments presented for the necessity of the inclusion of subjective phenomena is proof that Skinner is wrong and that external stimuli and reinforcements are insignificant. He may be correct, in principle, that all behavior obeys reinforcement principles, but it is virtually impossible to identify all these factors in complex situations in order to test his assumption. Furthermore, we assume that all other things being equal, the individual's perception of situational factors at the present moment are more crucial in affecting behavior than the entire past history of reinforcements in that situation. Sudden and dramatic decisions to take a course of action sometimes seem contrary to predictions based on knowledge of past reinforcement patterns. Human behavior may involve more self-determination and free will than Skinner allows. Feelings about oneself can quickly be altered by the present context, such as when a sudden reorganization of one's perception of a situation can move one from feelings of self-worth to self-pity or vice versa. Understanding behavior may be impossible without taking these phenomenological experiences into account.

Summary

American psychology has been strongly influenced by behaviorism, which historically has emphasized the study of observable behavior. Subjective processes were ignored as mentalistic and unnecessary in the analysis of behavior. Recent years have seen the acceptance among behaviorists of the inclusion of subjective and cognitive processes, especially as strict behaviorism has failed to account for various phenomena such as curiosity or exploratory behavior in which a biological tissue deficit does not appear.

One notable and influential exception to this trend is represented by the views of B. F. Skinner whose radical variety of behaviorism still focuses only on environmental stimuli as possible causes of behavior. His position rejects the use of mentalistic labels such as motivation or emotion in the explanation of behavior. Other behaviorists, however, are proposing models of behavior that suggest it is necessary to include internal processes such as self-regulatory mechanisms for a better understanding of human motives and emotions as well as other phenomena.

An overview of a phenomenological approach to the analysis of motivation emphasized the importance of considering the interpretation of a situation by the individual as a function of values, personal constructs, expectancies, and self-regulatory abilities.

It was recognized that explanations involving subjective states and concepts such as the self can be traced, in principle at least, to past histories of objectively definable reinforcements. However, it was argued that in practice it is difficult to measure these factors. Furthermore, in a given situation, it is also difficult to know which internal processes will be activated and influence motivation.

Although the limitations of verbal report were acknowledged, it was suggested that a return to its use, supplemented where possible by independent evidence, might provide us with some understanding of the subjective and cognitive processes that affect a person's behavior and feelings in a given situation. Such processes may be highly idiosyncratic in individuals so that general laws of behavior derived from group averages may be seriously inadequate and misleading when used to predict or interpret individual behavior.

References

ALLPORT, G. *Personality: A psychological interpretation.* New York: Holt, 1937.

ARONSON, E., and METTEE, D. R. Dishonest behavior as a function of differential levels of induced self-esteem. *Journal of Personality and Social Psychology,* 1968, *9,* 121–127.

BANDURA, A. Behavior theory and the models of man. *American Psychologist,* 1974, *29,* 859–869.

BEACH, F. A., and JAYNES, J. Effects of early experience upon the behavior of animals. *Psychological Bulletin,* 1954, *51,* 240–263.

BEM, D. J., and ALLEN, A. On predicting some of the people some of the time: The search for cross-sectional consistencies in behavior. *Psychological Review,* 1974, *81,* 506–520.

BERKOWITZ, L., and CONNER, W. H. Success, failure, and social responsibility. *Journal of Personality and Social Psychology,* 1966, *4,* 664–669.

BERLYNE, D. E. Attention to change. *British Journal of Psychology,* 1951, *42,* 269–278.

———. *Conflict, curiosity, and arousal.* New York: McGraw-Hill, 1960.

BUTLER, R. A., and HARLOW, H. F. Persistence of visual exploration in monkeys. *Journal of Comparative and Physiological Psychology,* 1954, *47,* 258–263.

CLARK, K. B., and CLARK, M. K. Racial identification and preference in Negro children. In T. Newcomb and E. Hartley (Eds.), *Readings in Social Psychology.* New York: Holt, 1947.

CRONBACH, L. J. Beyond the two disciplines of scientific psychology. *American Psychologist,* 1975, *30,* 116–127.

DeCHARMS, R. *Personal causation: The internal affective determinants of behavior.* New York: Academic Press, 1968.

DION, K. L., BERSHEID, E., and WALSTER, E. What is beautiful is good. *Journal of Personality and Social Psychology,* 1972, *24,* 285–290.

DOLLARD, J., DOOB, L. W., MILLER, N. E., MOWRER, O. H., and SEARS, R. R. *Frustration and aggression.* New Haven, Conn.: Yale University Press, 1939.

EPSTEIN, S. The self-concept revisited: Or a theory of a theory. *American Psychologist,* 1973, *28,* 404–416.

HARLOW, H. F. Mice, monkeys, men, and motives. *Psychological Review,* 1953, *60,* 23–32.

———, and McCLEARN, G. E. Object discrimination learning by monkeys on the basis of manipulated motives. *Journal of Comparative and Physiological Psychology,* 1954, *47,* 73–76.

HOLT, R. R. Imagery: The return of the ostracized. *American Psychologist,* 1964, *19,* 254–264.

HRABA, J., and GRANT, G. Black is beautiful: A reexamination of racial preference and identification. *Journal of Personality and Social Psychology,* 1970, *16,* 398–402.

HULL, C. L. *Principles of behavior.* New York: Appleton, 1943.

ISEN, A. M. Success, failure, attention, and reaction to others: The warm glow of success. *Journal of Personality and Social Psychology,* 1970, *15,* 294–301.

JARVIK, L. F. Thoughts on the psychobiology of aging. *American Psychologist,* 1975, *30,* 576–583.

JONES, E. E., and SIGALL, H. The bogus pipeline: A new paradigm for measuring affect and attitude. *Psychological Bulletin,* 1971, *76,* 349–364.

JOURARD, S. *Disclosing man to himself.* New York: Van Nostrand, 1968.

KELLEY, G. A. *The psychology of personal constructs.* (Vols. 1 and 2). New York: Norton, 1955.

———. Man's construction of his alternatives. In G. Lindzey (Ed.) *Assessment of human motives.* New York: Holt, 1958.

LAZARUS, R. S. *Psychological stress and the coping process.* New York: McGraw-Hill, 1966.

———. A cognitively oriented psychologist looks at biofeedback. *American Psychologist,* 1975, *30,* 553–561.

LEEPER, R. W. Some needed developments in the motivational theory of emotions. In D. Levine (Ed.), *Nebraska Symposium on Motivation.* (Vol. 13). Lincoln: University of Nebraska Press, 1965.

LENNEBERG, E. H. On explaining language. *Science,* 1969, *164,* 635–643.

MACGREGOR, F. C. Social and cultural components in the motivations of persons seeking plastic surgery of the nose. *Journal of Health and Social Behavior,* 1968, *9,* 287–298.

MADDOX, G. L., BACK, K. W., and LIEDERMAN, V. R. Overweight as social deviance and disability. *Journal of Health and Social Behavior,* 1968, *9,* 287–298.

MISCHEL, W., EBBESEN, E., and ZEISS, A. Selective attention to the self: Situational and dispositional determinants. *Journal of Personality and Social Psychology,* 1973, *27,* 129–142.

MONTGOMERY, K. C. Exploratory behavior as a function of "similarity" of stimulus situations. *Journal of Comparative and Physiological Psychology,* 1953, *46,* 129–133.

———. The role of exploratory drive in learning. *Journal of Comparative and Physiological Psychology,* 1954, *47,* 60–64.

ORNSTEIN, R. *The psychology of consciousness.* San Francisco: Freeman, 1972.

PAVLOV, I. P. *Conditioned reflexes.* London: Oxford University Press, 1927.

SELIGMAN, M. E. P. On the generality of the laws of learning. *Psychological Review,* 1970, *77,* 406–418.

SHELDON, W. H. *The varieties of temperament: A psychology of constitutional differences.* New York: Harper, 1942.

SKINNER, B. F. *Beyond freedom and dignity.* New York: Knopf, 1971.

SPERRY, R. W. A modified concept of consciousness. *Psychological Review,* 1969, *76,* 532–536.

TINBERGEN, N. *The study of instinct.* Oxford: Oxford University Press, 1951.

TOLMAN, E. C. *Purposive behavior in animals and men.* New York: Appleton, 1932.

UNDERWOOD, B. J. Individual differences as a crucible in theory construction. *American Psychologist,* 1975, *30,* 128–134.

CHAPTER 3

The Biological Side of Human Nature

Explanations of behavior sometimes invoke concepts such as human nature especially if the behavior in question seems unchangeable. More often than not, this type of account is used to excuse some type of human frailty or misdeed. Acts of heroism, altruism, or wisdom seem to be attributed less frequently to human nature.

What is the essence of human nature? If there is indeed some intrinsic aspect of humanity, it should appear universally. It might seem that biologically given factors should be the major determinants of any such universal tendencies. These natural tendencies would presumably be those that inevitably manifest themselves despite the social and cultural factors that exist to counteract them.

A major difficulty in the determination of any universal human behaviors is the fact that the human ability to learn from experiences and modify behavioral tendencies is substantial. Variations in expressions of the same motives in different cultures are made possible by the ability to learn from experience. Consequently, the identification of biologically based universals of behavior is quite difficult, and there has been a tendency to focus on the capacity of humans to be influenced by environment. American psychology has denied or downplayed the role of innate mechanisms such as instincts in favor of adaptive processes such as learning.

Important as the learning capacity is to human behavior, it must be recognized that it too is subject to certain constraints or restrictions of a biological nature. Just as physical factors determine that we can walk and run but not fly, physical or biological factors affect the limits of learning. The basis for this selectivity lies in the evolutionary history of our species.

The assumption that selective factors are involved in limiting the kinds of learned behaviors is a relatively recent development, at least among American psychologists. In the past it has been common to assume precisely the op-

52

posite and to regard one stimulus to be as good as the next insofar as it could be associated with some response.

Since behavioristic learning theorists emphasized the role of environmental influences, they ignored or ruled out the possible effect that biological history might have on learning. Theories of conditioning and learning from the early efforts of Pavlov and Thorndike, through the era of Clark Hull and Kenneth Spence in the 1940s and 1950s, and continuing today in formulations such as those of Skinner have generally ignored biological factors that might restrict learning. Instead, learning theorists were concerned with identifying the general laws of the learning process, laws that might apply across species and individuals within species. The identification of the factors influencing acquisition, extinction, stimulus generalization, and other processes associated with learning, which would apply to all stimuli and responses, was the aim of this approach. Because biological factors were considered less important as a source of individual differences, there was no reason to suspect that some types of associations might be more readily formed than others, specifically those that had survived the pressures of evolution and served some survival function for the species.

The Ethological Approach

In direct contrast to the approach just described, ethologists, led by Konrad Lorenz and Nikko Tinbergen, did acknowledge the important effect of biological evolution on behavior. Their approach involved a renewed emphasis on the role of instinct in behavior. Unlike the circular definitions of instinct prevalent at the turn of the century, ethologists were careful in using the term *instinct* as a description rather than as an explanation. Meticulous and painstaking naturalistic field observations of animal behavior were undertaken by ethologists in order to describe the conditions associated with instinctive behaviors such as mating, aggression, or establishment of territory. Instinct was defined as a *species-specific* behavior pattern, which was present because it had served to ensure the survival of the species against the pressures of natural selection. Instinctive behavior, then, was not learned within the lifetime of a single organism, although environmental experiences do influence the occurrence of instinctive behaviors.

Ethologists such as Lorenz (1957) and Tinbergen (1951) assume that the nervous system generates energy to activate behavior and that each action pattern has its own specific source of energy. Each time an instinctive behavior occurs, its energy supply is consumed and must be replenished before it can occur again. It is also necessary for some environmental stimulus to be present to release the energy for a given response. Different instinctive responses are assumed to be under the control of different *releaser stimuli* that act as keys to unlock the *innate releaser mechanism* that controls the energy for that instinct.

If the organism does not encounter the appropriate releaser stimulus, the accumulated energy for a particular instinct may eventually overflow, activating the response even though the situation is inappropriate. Ethologists use this assumption to account for *vacuum activity,* in which an instinctive response occurs in the absence of a suitable stimulus.

The term *fixed action pattern* (FAP) is used by ethologists to refer to instinctive behavior, because it conveys the stereotyped and invariant aspect as well as the fact that instincts involve a sequence or pattern of responses rather than a single response.

TINBERGEN'S STUDY
OF STICKLEBACK FISH

A specific example may be useful in illustrating the approach of ethology. Tinbergen (1942) observed the mating behavior of the three-spined stickleback fish. He identified the sequence shown in Figure 3–1 in which the con-

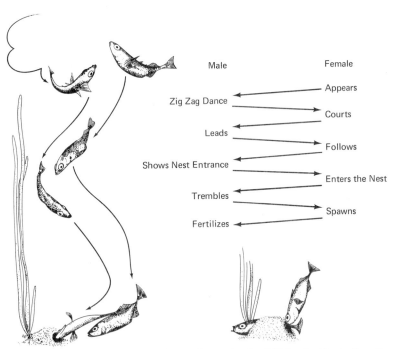

FIGURE 3–1. Courtship behavior of the three-spined stickleback, illustrating the mutually releasing actions of the male and the female. [From N. Tinbergen, *The Study of Instinct,* London: Oxford University Press, 1951. Copyright 1951 by Oxford University Press. Reprinted by permission.]

dition of cues signifying springtime, such as green vegetation plus the sight of a female stickleback with a swollen belly, activates the male into establishing a territory and building a nest. To lure the female into its nest, the male performs a zigzag dance in which it swims alternately between the female and the nest. Once the female enters the nest, the male touches its (the female's) tail with a quivering motion. This action serves to stimulate the female to deposit eggs and then exit. In response, the male enters the nest and fertilizes the eggs.

This complex sequence of behavior involved a number of responses by each member to environmental releaser stimuli as well as to cues produced by the other fish. Without these releasers, the fixed action pattern should not occur, unless the stored energy overflows, such as what may occur when too long an interval exists before a sexual partner arrives.

In determining the specific nature of the releaser stimulus, ethologists may perform controlled experiments in addition to making naturalistic observations. Thus, Tinbergen made dummy stickleback fish varying in shape and coloration, which he then presented to fish in order to determine the critical aspect of the visual stimulus. For example, what is the cue that provokes a male stickleback to defend its nest from another approaching male? By varying the features of dummy models as shown in Figure 3–2, Tinbergen determined that the red coloration of the belly of the male during mating season is the crucial stimulus that elicits attack in order to protect territory. The model *N,* which was realistic except in its lack of a red belly, was less often attacked than were the four red-bellied models, *R.*

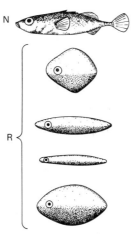

FIGURE 3–2.   Stickleback models. *N* is a form- and color-true imitation of a stickleback without a red belly, which is less frequently attacked than the four simple red-bellied models of series *R.* [From N. Tinbergen, *The Study of Instinct,* London: Oxford University Press, 1951. Copyright 1951 by Oxford University Press. Reprinted by permission.]

THE ISOLATION PARADIGM

Another type of experiment conducted by ethologists is aimed at demonstrating the unlearned nature of FAPs. In these studies young offspring are separated and reared in isolation in order to show that there is no impairment of the instinctive behaviors. These experiments have not always been supportive, as some impairment has been obtained, which suggests that environmental factors also influence the operation of instinctive behaviors. However, these findings are not accepted as valid by some ethologists (e.g., Eible-Eiblesfeldt, 1975).

Consider, for example, the question of whether nest building is instinctive in rats. Rats isolated shortly after birth so that no opportunity is available for direct learning or observation of nest building should be unable to build nests themselves when appropriate unless this behavior is instinctive.

A study by Riess (1954) apparently demonstrated that the behavior involved learning since rats reared in isolation did not know how to build nests out of paper strips provided in their cages. Eible-Eiblesfeldt (1975) criticized this study on the grounds that the rats were tested in cages other than their familiar home cages and that the competing tendency to explore novel environments interfered with the nest-building behavior. Consistent with this criticism was his finding (Eible-Eiblesfeldt, 1963) that no impaired nest building was found when rats reared in isolation were tested in their home cages.

Isolation of birds has been demonstrated to affect the acquisition of their species bird songs by some species. Thorpe (1961) showed that if the chaffinch is reared in isolation during its first year of life, it will not develop its natural bird song.

Isolation rearing may also have delayed effects, as demonstrated in Harlow's (1958) classic studies on mother love with rhesus monkeys who were reared either with wire or terry cloth mothers. Although the original purpose of these studies did not concern the adult sexual behavior of the infant monkeys, it was later (Harlow, 1962) discovered that severe impairment of sexual capacities existed among these isolation-reared monkeys.

One difficulty in evaluating deprivation or isolation studies is the identification of precisely what is being deprived. A period of isolation may deprive the infant of opportunities to experience a variety of events besides the one intended. Furthermore, the isolation also adds something in the form of aversive experience, which itself may alter normal functioning in the infant.

The isolation or deprivation paradigm, therefore, can justify only conclusions about what is not learned. If a response pattern occurs despite the organism's isolation, we may conclude that it was not learned. However, if impairment does occur, we may not infer that necessary learning was prevented (Lorenz, 1965).

Early behaviorists and ethologists disagreed strongly about the determinants of behavior, with the former favoring learning processes occurring during the life of an organism and the latter preferring instincts formed in the species over generations of natural selection. Lorenz (1965) takes both ethologists and behaviorists to task for regarding the two processes as mutually exclusive. There is at present greater acceptance of the view that early experiences can interact with innate factors, and Hess (1973) believes that the gap between ethology and behaviorism will continue to narrow.

The difference in theoretical orientation has also led to different methods of study. Whereas behaviorist relied primarily on laboratory studies, ethologists emphasized studies in natural habitats. Moreover, behaviorists focused on the use of simpler organisms such as the albino rat in order to better control the situation. Because learning theorists were not concerned about species differences and felt that the laws identified with one species could apply to other species, their approach is understandable. In contrast, ethologists assumed that patterns of behavior were species-specific and it was thus imperative that they study a wide range of species. Some psychologists (e.g., Lockard, 1971) have tried to encourage the use of a greater variety of species by comparative psychologists in recent years.

New Directions among Behaviorists

Over the past decade there has been growing recognition among behaviorists of the need to consider the role of biological factors, especially in the learning process (Seligman, 1971; Seligman and Hager, 1972).

TEACHING TRICKS TO ANIMALS

Breland and Breland (1961) revised their earlier thinking and provided a fascinating report of their conversion. A decade earlier they had great success applying operant learning principles in shaping and modifying the behavior of many animals from a wide variety of species. Much of this work involved the teaching of tricks to animals for their appearances in television programs.

These early successes led Breland and Breland (1951) to attempt more complex skill training, which frequently met with failure. They described their attempt to train a pig to pick up large wooden coins and deposit them in a piggy bank. It was necessary for the pig to carry the coins several feet in order to deposit them. At first, it was rather easy to train the pigs, but as time passed, difficulties arose. The behavior became slower and slower, and according to Breland and Breland, "instead of carrying the dollar and depositing it simply and cleanly, he (the pig) would repeatedly drop it, root it, drop it again, root it along the way, pick it up, toss it up in the air, drop it, root it some more, and so on."

Similar seditious acts occurred with porpoises and whales that would swallow items such as inner tubes, with cats that refused to leave the feeding area, and with rabbits that would not approach the food box. Breland and Breland (1961) admitted dismay, "for there was nothing in our background in behaviorism to prepare us for such gross inabilities to predict and control the behavior of animals with which we had been working for years."

They attributed these disruptions of conditioned behavior to the influence of *instinctive drift*. That is, conditioned responses may have conflicted with instinctive tendencies, which eventually asserted themselves and undermined the conditioned response. In the example of the trained pig, the rooting response, which the pig naturally uses to dig for food, dominated so that it disrupted the trick response the Brelands were trying to form.

Innate response tendencies also interfered in an attempt to teach chickens to play baseball. By pulling a wire loop, the chicken would cause a bat to hit a ball. If the ball hit the back fence, the chicken automatically received food if it ran in the direction of first base. This project proved unsuccessful for the chickens would chase the ball wildly all over the field instead of heading for first base. When one considers the fact that chickens naturally eat food by scratching and pecking about the ground in a somewhat erratic pattern, it becomes clear that this tendency was responsible for the difficulty the Brelands had in teaching the chickens to run in a straight line.

The misbehavior of organisms, then, demonstrates the importance of innate factors in setting the limits within which new behaviors can be acquired. Their experiences in fourteen years of conditioning thousands of animals convinced

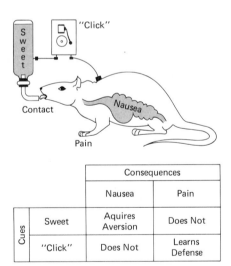

		Consequences	
		Nausea	Pain
Cues	Sweet	Aquires Aversion	Does Not
	"Click"	Does Not	Learns Defense

FIGURE 3–3. The effects of pairing a gustatory cue or an auditory cue with external pain or internal illness. [From "Natural Responses to Scheduled Rewards," by J. Garcia, J. C. Clarke, and W. G. Hankins in *Perspectives in Ethology*, by P. P. G. Bateson and P. H. Klopfer (Eds.), New York: Plenum Press, 1973. Copyright 1973 by Plenum Press. Reprinted by permission.]

Breland and Breland that behavior cannot be "adequately understood, predicted, or controlled without knowledge of its instinctive patterns, evolutionary history, and ecological niche."

Despite this striking testimonial to the necessity of examining instinctive factors in analyzing behavior, overnight acceptance of the Brelands' message was not forthcoming. Eventually, however, as evidence from laboratory studies increased, it was no longer possible to ignore the role of biological constraints in learning.

LEARNING TASTE AVERSIONS

The work of John Garcia and his colleagues, for example, which was concerned with aversion conditioning in rats, clearly showed that all stimuli are not equally capable of serving as conditioned stimuli for aversions. Instead, as shown in Figure 3–3, evidence indicated (Garcia and Koelling, 1966) that gustatory or taste cues such as the sweet taste of saccharin-flavored water could readily be conditioned to forewarn the organism about nauseous internal consequences such as food-poisoning effects, whereas they were ineffective as signals to forewarn the organism of the pain of foot shock. The opposite situation was found when auditory and visual cues such as click sounds and bright lights were used. They were easily conditionable to serve as signals of impending foot shock but were ineffective in alerting the organism to stimuli related to upset stomachs. These findings are in accord with observations noted long ago by Thorndike when he coined the term *belongingness* to refer to the fact that some stimuli seem to go better with some responses than other stimuli do.

Not only did these results demonstrate the specificity of stimuli for different types of situations but the particular pattern of results just described was interpreted to be consistent with the demands of evolutionary influences. Perhaps animals that could readily associate tastes with visceral consequences survived because they were able to learn to avoid ingesting foods or liquids that made them mildly ill. There is a natural relationship between the taste of a food and its subsequent effect, whereas the visual or auditory stimuli associated with the ingestion of nausea-inducing foods is apt to be arbitrary. In fact, it may be maladaptive for the animal to avoid the place at which it ingested the poisoned food as opposed to the food itself. That same location might be the future site of edible food.

Another interesting aspect of the fact that animals can associate taste with the aversive effects of food is the very long delay between the cue and the consequence. Traditional views of reinforcement would hold that it would be unlikely for associations to be formed over such long intervals. But, as Garcia, Ervin, and Koelling (1966) demonstrated in laboratory studies, it is indeed possible to induce conditioned taste aversions over intervals of several hours.

SPECIES-SPECIFIC DEFENSE REACTIONS

Other evidence of the critical influence of innate tendencies of organisms on learning occurs in the area of avoidance conditioning, where the task is to learn a response that will enable the organism to avoid painful consequences such as shock. In laboratory experiments a stimulus such as a light or tone may precede foot shock by a brief interval; if the organism succeeds in pressing a bar or turning a wheel during that interval, it can avoid the shock.

However, these responses are arbitrarily determined by the experimenter and are often not dominant or existent in the natural defense tendencies of the organism. In general, animals survive threats from predators by responses such as immobility, flight or running, or threat displays. Such reactions occur whenever novel stimuli are encountered and do not depend on previous association with pain or some conditioned stimulus such as the lights or tones that precede shock in an experimental situation. Unlike learning experiments, natural situations are not designed to give second chances to targets of prey and as Bolles (1970) aptly describes it, "No owl hoots or whistles just as the mouse gets away so as to reinforce the avoidance response. Nor will the owl give the mouse enough learning trials for the necessary learning to occur. What keeps our little friends alive in the forest has nothing to do with avoidance learning as we ordinarily conceive of it or investigate it in the laboratory."

Bolles (1970) has argued persuasively that each species has its own *species-specific defense reaction*. This innate pattern of reacting to threat is the outcome of the species' struggle against natural selection processes over the course of evolution. It is possible, of course, for an organism also to learn avoidance tendencies to specific stimuli such as those encountered in laboratory experiments conducted by behaviorists. Sometimes these experiments have required organisms to acquire avoidance responses that conflict with natural avoidance reactions and such conditioning has proved difficult or impossible. Recognition of these species-specific defense reactions illustrates the importance of innate factors that limit what can be learned.

In the light of these developments, Seligman (1970) has suggested that instinct and learning might be regarded as opposite ends of the same dimension rather than as a dichotomy. When associations between a stimulus and response are rapidly acquired, instinctive processes are probably involved, whereas if numerous learning trials are necessary, the learning process is implicated. The biological preparedness of the organism for rapidly acquired or instinctive responses is based on the evolutionary background of the species.

Because humans are also a biological species that has evolved, it should be apparent that similar biological restraints govern the process of human learning, whether it be the acquisition of habits, cognitions, attitudes, motives, or emotions. This implication suggests that a study be made of the biological nature of human nature and should be distinguished carefully from a more common and somewhat similar argument. Specifically, the case is often made that because humans are also biological organisms it should be possible to generalize the results of studies of lower animals to humans. Furthermore, because lower animals are more readily available for experiments and certain ethical issues are absent or minimized by using them, it is attractive to focus on their study.

There can be no denying that some findings from these studies can certainly be applied validly to humans, but it is suggested here that more often than not such generalizations are misleading and, worse, mistaken. Our preceding discussion of species-specific biological factors should direct us toward the determination of which unique biological antecedents govern the human learning capacity. To generalize freely from studies of lower animals to humans is to ignore the significance of the discovery of species-specific biological factors.

The Example of Aggressive Behavior

The aggressive battle for survival between predator and prey as well as confrontations among members of the same species for territory, mates, and food has frequently been used to support the contention that human nature is also aggressive. Our animal nature has been held responsible for homicides, riots, and wars; some theorists see aggressiveness as destructiveness and fear for the survival of humankind.

Society is regarded as an attempt to impose some restraints on our tendencies toward mutual destruction. Pessimists fear that the controlling influence of society is limited and that occasional outbreaks of aggression and violence are inevitable manifestations of our animal side.

In the past decade anthropologists have made great advances in studying aggression in our closest relatives on the evolutionary scale, other primates such as chimpanzees, howler monkeys, baboons, and macaques. Several widely read popular accounts of this research such as Konrad Lorenz' *On Aggression* and Robert Ardrey's *Territorial Imperative* have freely generalized from such studies to draw implications about the role of instincts in human aggression. Critics of such interpretations (e.g., Alland, 1972) charge that they are gross oversimplifications and of dubious validity.

In order to evaluate the implications of aggression among primates for the understanding of human behavior, we will now describe some of the ethological and anthropological studies. First, we should recognize that problems exist in the comparison of different species, because the definitions of the same concept may not be comparable. Jay (1968), for example, points out that territoriality, the tendency of organisms to stake out and defend their own living space, cannot be as rigidly defined for primates as it can be for birds, because the former occupy space in more complex ways than do the latter.

Among primates it is necessary to differentiate among such categories of territory as habitual, core, defended, shared, group, and individual.

A similar problem exists with the concept of aggression. Washburn and Hamburg (1968) caution that if we must generalize from lower species to humans we should stick to primates that are more closely related to humans. Even these comparisons are difficult, because humans lack the physical structures that other primates employ in displaying threats such as erecting hair, colored skin, or dramatic ear position. Humans rely more heavily on hand gestures and language to display threats.

Despite such obstacles to valid comparisons, numerous attempts have been made to draw conclusions about human aggression from the study of the aggressive or *agonistic* behavior of lower species, especially nonhuman primates. One influential study by Zuckerman (1932) involved the observation of hamadryas baboons in the London Zoo. Based on his observations that dominant males were accorded greater privileges in food and sexual opportunities with females, Zuckerman concluded that the primary function of dominance patterns was to regulate these two types of behavior. Because dominance was established by the widespread use of aggression among these baboons, it was concluded that the typical behavior of baboons involved substantial aggression in order to gain the privileges of rank.

Unfortunately, as later studies demonstrated, Zuckerman's findings were limited, because they were obtained under the highly artificial environment of zoo captivity. The restricted space and high density of concentration is not similar to the situation in the wild, so that the behavior observed there was no more typical of baboons than the behavior of inmates in a prison is of humans. Dominance plays a far wider role than merely governing access to food and sex partners. Hall (1964) indicated that dominant members of a group act to prevent serious fights within the group, protect mothers with infants from other group members, defend the group against predators, threaten an alien of the same or similar species, and exercise leadership. It is hardly surprising that Zuckerman did not observe these functions of dominance.

Furthermore, there are considerable differences among primates in the nature of dominance patterns, which are highly conspicuous among baboons and rhesus monkeys but virtually absent among species such as chimpanzees. These differences must be explained in terms of other ecological factors such as variations in food gathering, sheltering and resting, avoiding predators, and seasonal birth and mating. The latter factor, for example, may produce incompatible conclusions in studies that fail to take observation samples at different times throughout the year.

The view that social coherence of monkey and ape groups may stem primarily from sexual motivation, as sometimes suggested, is also questioned by Hall (1964) who pointed out that the macaques, which show the clearest evidence of seasonal mating, have no greater occurrence of seasonal differences in grouping patterns than do the baboons, which mate throughout the year.

In contrast to Zuckerman's study of baboon social behavior in a zoo, Carpenter conducted studies of howler monkeys for several years during the early 1930s on Barro, Colorado, an island near the Panama Canal. He was unable to observe much aggression within clans despite his meticulous and lengthy naturalistic observation of their behavior. The conclusion one might draw about aggression from these studies (Carpenter, 1934) is quite different from one based on Zuckerman's observations.

Jane Goodall's (1965) well-known studies of chimpanzees in the Gombe Stream Reserve also show little agonistic behavior. She patiently observed over one hundred chimpanzees at close range and provided a detailed description of their social behavior. Dominance is less clearly delineated among chimpanzees. This loosely organized social arrangement allows different members of a group to occupy the dominant position, because the social rank depends on the composition of the group at any given moment, a situation that is continually in flux as members come and go. As with other primates, threats are observed more frequently than are actual aggressive combats. Various responses are used to communicate threat and dominance such as glaring, throwing sticks or stones, arm raising accompanied by a soft bark, or branching, which involves grabbing a branch and shaking it toward other animals.

In response to threats from a dominant chimpanzee, Goodall noted that the subordinate conveyed its submission in a variety of ways. Presenting or turning the rump toward the male is a common response of a sexually receptive female; this response occurs in other primates as well, in sexual as well as nonsexual situations. Bobbing slowly, bowing, and crouching accompanied by soft panting also are effective in appeasing the dominant member.

In return, the dominant male may often reassure the submissive subordinate by reaching out to touch or pat it. Embracing, kissing, grooming, and mounting are also forms of reassurance that serve to calm the submissive chimpanzee.

Terrestrial patas also display little aggression (Hall and DeVore, 1965). Although these monkeys live in savannas similar to those inhabited by the more aggressive baboons and should face similar problems of survival, other factors may account for their lesser degree of aggression. Patas are smaller than baboons and travel in groups with a smaller proportion of males than do baboons, so that it is more difficult for them to fight off predators. On the other hand, patas are perhaps the fastest primates and rely on speed, silence, concealment, and dispersion to thwart predators. Similarly, the langur of India is poorly equipped to fight predators and has been reported (Hall, 1964) also to exhibit less aggression within its own groups.

Thus, although aggression is sometimes observed among baboons, rhesus macaques, and Japanese macaques (Hall and DeVore, 1965), other primates engage in very little aggression within their own troops or clans. Furthermore in species, such as baboons, in which aggression is reported, strong patterns of dominance keep overt aggression and even threat displays to a minimum.

Hall and DeVore found that once dominance patterns are established, they reduce the need for threat display, because subordinates prefer to avoid the dominant male and keep their distance. Baboon behavior in situations such as zoos where threat displays cannot generate adequate distance keeping did foster aggression (Zuckerman, 1932), but in the natural world the survival function of threat display is able to operate.

What are we to make of the wide variety among primate species with respect to agonistic behavior? Hall (1964) emphasized the point that ecological factors as diverse as physical environment, group size and composition, food supply, and season of the year can affect the extent to which aggression is necessary. Because these conditions differ for various species, it should be no surprise that there is no single pattern of aggression for all species. Aggression can be viewed as one means of adapting to environmental demands. It can serve the positive function of promoting the survival of the species by promoting the dispersal of different groups of the same species, which prevents the too rapid exhaustion of food supplies or too rapid extinction by predators. Far from being a destructive process, aggression is a necessary response for coping with the environment. It is used sparingly and only when other mechanisms such as threat fail. Hall (1964) noted that "probably the most important point to emphasize is that the inhibitory control system of baboon social organization is so effective that the lethal fighting potential is rarely released."

Implications for Views of Human Aggression

To what extent are the findings regarding aggression among nonhuman primates applicable to human behavior? Is it appropriate to explain human aggression and violence of such diverse forms as homicide, suicide, genocide, or war as instincts that reside in our biological make-up?

Tedeschi, Smith, and Brown (1974) conclude that the analogy is misleading and they emphasize the social nature of human aggression. "Whereas dominance hierarchies among primates are determined by size, strength, sex, and biochemical factors, social structures among men are determined by economic wealth, social skills, geographical locations, and many nonbiological factors. In addition, human hierarchies must be rationalized and legitimized if they are to be effective in regulating behavior" (Tedeschi et al., 1970, p. 546).

Predatory or attack behavior between different species is often cited as evidence of the widespread nature of aggression. Field studies have not provided support for this image (Washburn and Hamburg, 1968), as it has been observed that species as widely diverse as baboons, waterhogs, impala, wildebeest, elephants, and rhinoceros can coexist peacefully about the same water hole. This is not to argue that interspecies aggression never occurs but rather that it is not as common as generally thought.

More important is the fact that the concern about human aggression is focused primarily on intraspecies aggression and it is dangerous to generalize from interspecies aggression studies. The latter aggression often stems from biological necessity such as when predator attacks prey, but the aggression of human against fellow human has no corresponding biological survival value.

An examination of agonistic behavior within the same species reveals some important differences between human and animal aggression, factors that led Scott (1970, p. 570) to conclude that ". . . no direct analogies (of agonistic behaviors) from any other species to man are justified." For example, whereas humans may aggress against other humans for purposes of inflicting pain or even death, lower animals appear satisfied when their actions successfully defend their territory.

Although it has been argued (Ardrey, 1966) that humans also stake out territory and fight to defend it, there are important differences between the nature and functions of human and animal territories. The ownership of private property and its defense is not necessary for human biological survival so much as it is for social and economic status. Furthermore such acquisitiveness is by no means universal in human societies.

There is no question but that human behavior may parallel some forms of instinctive behavior of lower animals, but it has to be kept in mind that humans have a greater capacity than lower animals to adapt behavior to environmental demands. The diversity of human societies, in contrast to the stereotyped behavior among lower species, attests to the significance of learning as a determinant of human behavior.

Human nature is not firmly set or determined by biological necessity. As Alland (1972, p. 23) observed, "What kind of behavioral system emerges must conform to man's biological capacities, but since these are wide, the capacities alone tell us little about real systems undergoing the selective process." Alland, an anthropologist, soundly criticizes writings such as Ardrey's *Territorial Imperative* and *African Genesis* and Lorenz' *On Aggression* as oversimplications, which confusingly equate similar behaviors caused by instinct among lower species but by cultural learning among humans.

Ethology and Human Behavior

Thus far we have presented evidence that suggests that biological givens determined over the course of evolution may play an important role in human motivation and emotion. Then a criticism was raised about the loose overgeneralizations frequently made between behaviors of lower species and humans. What is needed, in our view, is the study of *human* behavior as it might be affected by *human* evolution.

Rene DuBos, the noted biologist, made these observations in his Pulitzer Prize winning book *So Human An Animal,* "Many aspects of human behavior which appear incomprehensible or even irrational become meaningful when interpreted as survivals of attributes that were useful when they first appeared during evolutionary development and that have persisted. . . ." (DuBos, 1968, p. 75).

ATTACHMENT

Although the need is not unique to humans, it is necessary that human infants receive sufficient attention from parents. Due to the longer period of physical dependence of human offspring, the precise mechanisms of infant-mother *attachment* may be different from the process known as *imprinting,* which occurs in species, such as ducks, which are physically able to follow their mothers soon after birth. Crying is an unlearned response to physical discomforts such as cold, hunger, or pain, which readily elicits the attention and concern of the mother. Later in the relationship the infant develops the smiling response, an expression that attracts and insures the attention of the mother. During the period of high dependency, the infant forms a bond or attachment to the mother or caretaker that may influence subsequent social responsivity. Bowlby (1973) has discussed the significance of the attachment process for the emotional well-being of the infant. Although attachment may occur because organisms incapable of forming ties did not survive, the precise course of its development can be modified by environmental factors. Ainsworth (1967), in comparing the age at which attachment was formed among American and Ugandan infants, noted that earlier attachments were formed among the latter, possibly due to the continual presence of the mother as mothers often worked in fields with their infants strapped to their bodies. This flexibility of the temporal aspects of human bonds is in marked contrast to the limited "critical period" time during which imprinting occurs.

Separation, temporary or permanent, from the person to whom the infant forms an attachment has been observed to produce profound depression (Bowlby, 1973) and grief-like reactions. This reaction is understandable in view of the survival value of having the presence of the caretaker.

Bowlby regards attachment as an innate process, although it also requires the occurrence of certain early experiences between the organism and other species members such as the mother. There is survival value for the species if separation from the source of attachment creates anxiety, because the organism will then attempt to maintain proximity to the mother. Risks of predators and other dangers to survival could be reduced if young organisms had this tendency to stay close to their mothers. *Separation anxiety,* which occurs whenever the mother is absent, is not so childish or irrational process as it might appear to the casual observer.

Moreover, although specific learning experiences may modify the reactions to separation, Bowlby does not believe that all fearful reactions to separation can be accounted for by learned associations. He observed, "Examination shows, indeed, that, so far from being irrational or foolhardy, to rely on the naturally occurring clues to danger and safety is to rely on a system that has been both sensible and efficient over millions of years" (Bowlby, 1973, p. 139).

There also appears to be a biologically innate mechanism by which adults tend to favor young members of the species with attention and nurturance. Lorenz (1943) speculated that all infants, compared to older species members, have certain features perceived as cute by adults and tend to elicit protection and caretaking. These features include a large head relative to the body, a protruding forehead, which is large relative to the rest of the face, large eyes, short, thick extremities, a rounded body shape, soft, elastic body surfaces, and round protruding cheeks. In addition, behavioral tendencies such as clumsiness exist among the young. These features make most adults want to "mother" the young, which in turn should help the attachment process occur.

Also related to the phenomena of attachment and separation is the occurrence of *stranger anxiety,* a state of tension and distress created by the appearance of strangers, especially if the mother is absent. Tinbergen and Tinbergen (1972, pp. 29–30) described observations of facial expressions and other nonverbal reactions of young children when confronted by strangers, "Usually such a child will start by simply looking intently at the stranger, studying him guardedly . . . Very soon the child will stop studying one. It will approach gingerly, and it will soon reveal its strong bonding tendency by touching one—for instance by putting its hand tentatively on one's knee. This is often a crucial moment: one must *not* respond by looking at the child (which may set it back considerably) but by cautiously touching the child's hand with one's own."

The function of stranger anxiety is adaptive in that it enables the child to test the safety of new acquaintances. The process, however, can go awry (Tinbergen, 1974) and possibly be the genesis of what are termed autistic children. The general reactions to strangers, however, is strikingly similar for both normal and autistic children.

EMOTIONAL EXPRESSION

Charles Darwin (1872) was impressed with the similarity between the emotional expressions of lower animals and those of humans. Although his theory has met with numerous criticisms (Izard, 1971), it was an influential factor in directing attention to the functions of emotional expression. Building on this groundwork, Andrews (1963) emphasized the possibility that emotional expressions that served to communicate intentions and emotional states survived through natural selection. Thus, threats or glares at rivals were communications of threat and may have been adequate to insure population dispersal so that these mutants survived, whereas members lacking these expressions became extinct.

A study of human emotional expression that could demonstrate universal features might support this type of evolutionary analysis. Eible-Eiblesfeldt reported a fast motion camera filming technique he used with Hass. This technique enabled them to compress lengthy behavior segments into smaller viewing times so that regularities of emotional expression might be more readily detected by the observer. Eible-Eiblesfeldt (1975) concluded that their studies showed a high similarity in a variety of emotional expressions across many cultures.

LANGUAGE

Human communication is not limited to emotional expression but can be reported by language. Lenneberg (1969) proposed that language is a species-specific behavior, which humans possess as a consequence of evolution. The human brain is qualitatively different from that of other animals and enables humans to use a different type of cognition, one that is heavily affected by language. Lenneberg ignored the wide differences among human languages and tried to identify universal features. Although some theorists would argue that there are no language universals, Lenneberg regarded all languages as involving rules expressing relationships among words. Human language involves syntax and is not merely a vocabulary or set of labels representing objects.

PHOBIAS

Another area in which the influence of biological factors may be important is that of phobias. Unlike other situations that are aversive, phobias involve associations that are often learned in one trial but are extremely resistant to extinction or elimination. They are strong fears that probably involve stimuli related to situations or objects associated with threats to survival, according to Seligman (1971), such as predators, darkness, and uncertainty. In addition, it is difficult to counteract phobias with intellectual resources such as asking someone who is afraid of snakes to pick up a nonpoisonous one. Seligman argued that phobias are probably fears of stimuli for which our biological make-up predisposes us.

SOCIAL BONDS

Finally, we will mention the hypothesis proposed by anthropologist Lionel Tiger in *Men in Groups*. Speculating that males tend to form bonds or groups with other males because of humankind's background as hunters, Tiger suggested that evolution alone is responsible for such diverse consequences as male secret societies, political dominance by males, and male aggression.

Male bonding is regarded by Tiger as a species-specific tendency that had survival value in hunting societies. Females were not sufficiently strong, especially when they were pregnant, and any group that allowed females to join the hunting would probably not have survived long. Hence, argued Tiger, males originally bonded together with other men for hunting purposes only, but this tendency is responsible today for other forms of "For Men Only" attitudes and practices.

Tiger felt that this predisposition may account for males as well as females rejecting female leaders and males rejecting female colleagues. Women rarely achieve political office except by succession through marriage to a male leader, according to Tiger, who concluded, "Thus, that females only rarely dominate authority structures may reflect females' underlying inability—at the ethological level of "pattern releaser" behavior—to affect the behavior of subordinates" (Tiger, 1969, p. 74).

Tiger does not mention alternative hypotheses or evaluate sociological and historical arguments. His theory is not presented because of its conclusiveness or validity but as another example of the current trend toward invoking biological and evolutionary mechanisms to explain or describe human nature.

Although he does not venture as far as Tiger, DuBos (1968, p. 75) also emphasized the possibility that our social behavior stems from our past, "All social stimuli that man experiences elicit physical and mental processes which in their turn condition his responses to the situations that evoke them."

We have provided only examples that come readily to mind and probably other aspects of human behavior and experience have been greatly influenced by our evolutionary past. It is possible that we can sometimes override these influences but often at great expense in terms of time, effort, and stress. Greater attention to the study of the nature of the selective influence of biological predispositions on our motives and emotions is needed.

It is important that this goal not be confused with the question of the nature of the physiological processes underlying behavior. This is a legitimate and important area of investigation but it does not necessarily involve the examination of evolutionary factors. The frequent tendency of comparative and physiological psychologists to ignore species-specific response patterns and generalize freely among species testifies to this point. Our identification of several aspects of human behavior that seem to involve species-specific mechanisms is an attempt to emphasize the need for the study of human ethology in order to understand the manner in which human evolution may affect human behavior and experience.

Summary

Behaviorism has emphasized the role of environmental factors while directing less attention to innate or inherited biological determinants of behavior. It is assumed that humans acquire most of their behaviors through the process of learning about the environment. Nonetheless there are biological limitations to the learning process, with some forms of associations being easier to acquire than others.

The work of ethologists who study naturalistic behavior has influenced new trends in the thinking of psychologists about the importance of biological factors. Ethologists have discovered that the behavioral patterns typical of various species have been selected through the process of evolution. These instincts or fixed action patterns predispose the organism to act in ways reflective of evolutionary pressures.

These findings have led some psychologists to recognize the biological boundaries of learning and to discover the inherited biases that restrict the range of behavior among laboratory animals as well as humans. The fact that different species may have different biological boundaries means that generalizations between species must be carefully reconsidered.

The example of generalizations about human aggression based on studies of rat and primate aggression in either the laboratory or field situations is relevant. Evidence showed that even among nonhuman primates no single pattern of aggression exists. Analogies between human aggression and similar behavior among other primates are deceptive, because these behaviors may have different causes and functions in human and nonhuman species.

It was suggested that it is necessary to examine the role of innate biological factors in human behavior, but that evidence of such factors be obtained from humans rather than nonhumans. An ethological approach toward identifying the survival value of affection, attachment, emotional expression, language, and phobias, among other processes, was seen as worth pursuing to determine how inherited predispositions related to them affected human behavior.

References

AINSWORTH, M. D. S. *Infancy in Uganda: Infant care and the growth of love.* Baltimore: Johns Hopkins, 1967.

ALLAND, A., JR. *The human imperative.* New York: Columbia U. P., 1972.

ANDREWS, R. J. Evolution of facial expression. *Science,* 1963, *142,* 1034–1041.

ARDREY, R. *The territorial imperative.* New York: Atheneum, 1966.

BOLLES, R. C. Species-specific defense reactions and avoidance learning. *Psychological Review,* 1970, *77,* 32–48.

BOWLBY, J. *Attachment and loss.* (Vol. 2). *Separation, anxiety, and anger.* New York: Basic, 1973.

BRELAND, K., and BRELAND, M. A child of applied animal psychology. *American Psychologist,* 1951, *6,* 202–204.

———. The misbehavior of organisms. *American Psychologist,* 1961, *16,* 681–684.

CARPENTER, C. R. A field study of the behavior and social relations of howling monkeys (*Alouatta palliata*). *Comparative Psychology Monographs,* 1934, *10,* 1–168.

DARWIN, C. *The expression of emotions in man and animals.* London: J. Murray, 1872.

DUBOS, R. *So human an animal.* New York: Scribner, 1968.

EIBLE-EIBLESFELDT, I. *Ethology: The biology of behavior.* Second Edition. New York: Holt, 1975.

———. Angeborenes und erworbenes im verhalten einiger sauger. *Zoologie Tierpsychologie,* 1963, *20,* 705–754.

GARCIA, J., ERVIN, F. R., and KOELLING, R. A. Learning with prolonged delay of reinforcement. *Psychonomic Science,* 1966, *5,* 121–122.

———, and KOELLING, R. A. Relation of cue to consequence in avoidance learning. *Psychonomic Science,* 1966, *4,* 123–124.

———, McGOWAN, B. K., and GREEN, K. F. *Biological constraints on conditioning.* In A. H. Black and W. F. Proksay (Eds.) *Classical conditioning, II: Current research and theory.* New York: Appleton, 1972.

GOODALL, J. Chimpanzees of the Gombe Stream Reserve. In I. DeVore (Ed.), *Primate behavior: Field studies of monkeys and apes.* New York: Holt, 1965.

HALL, K. R. L. Aggression in monkey and ape societies. In J. D. Carthy and E. J. Ebling (Eds.), *The natural history of aggression.* New York: Academic, 1964.

———, and DeVORE, I. Baboon social behavior. In I. DeVore (Ed.), *Primate behavior: Field studies of monkeys and apes.* New York: Holt, 1965.

HARLOW, H. F. The nature of love. *American Psychologist,* 1958, *13,* 673–685.

———. The heterosexual affectional system in monkeys. *American Psychologist,* 1962, *17,* 1–9.

HESS, E. H. *Imprinting: Early experience and the developmental psychobiology of attachment.* New York: Van Nostrand, 1973.

IZARD, C. E. *The face of emotion.* New York: Appleton, 1971.

JAY, P. C. (Ed.), *Primates: Studies in adaptation and variability.* New York: Holt, 1968.

LENNEBERG, E. H. On explaining language. *Science,* 1969, *164,* 635–643.

———. *Biological foundations of language.* New York: Wiley, 1967.

LOCKARD, R. Reflections on the fall of comparative psychology. *American Psychologist,* 1971, *26,* 168–179.

LORENZ, K. The conception of instinctive behavior. In C. H. Schiller (Ed.), *Instinctive behavior.* New York: International Universities Press, 1957.

———. *Evolution and modification of behavior.* Chicago: University of Chicago Press, 1965.

MASON, W. A. Naturalistic and experimental investigations of the social behavior of monkeys and apes. In P. C. Jay (Ed.), *Primates: Studies in adaptation and variability.* New York: Holt, 1968.

RIESS, B. F. The effect of altered environment and of age on the mother-young relationships among animals. *Annals of the New York Academy of Sciences,* 1954, *57,* 606–610.

SCOTT, J. P. Biology and human aggression. *American Journal of Orthopsychiatry,* 1970, *40,* 568–576.

SELIGMAN, M. E. P. On the generality of the laws of learning. *Psychological Review*, 1970, *77*, 406–418.

———. Phobias and preparedness. In M. E. P. Seligman and J. L. Hager (Eds.), *Biological boundaries of learning*. New York: Appleton, 1972.

———, and HAGER, J. L. *Biological boundaries of learning*. New York: Appleton, 1972.

TEDESCHI, J. T., SMITH, R. B., III, and BROWN, R. C., JR. A reinterpretation of research on aggression. *Psychological Bulletin*, 1974, *81*, 540–562.

THORPE, W. H. Comparative psychology. *Annual Review of Psychology*, 1961, *12*, 27–50.

TIGER, L. *Men in groups*. New York: Random House, 1969.

TINBERGEN, E. A., and TINBERGEN, N. Early childhood autism, an ethological approach. *Advances in Ethology*, No. 10. Supplement to *Journal of Comparative Ethology*. Berlin: Verlag Paul Parey, 1972.

TINBERGEN, N. An objectivistic study of the innate behavior of animals. *Biblioth. Biotheor.*, 1942, *1*, 39–98.

———. *The study of instinct*. London: Oxford University Press, 1951.

———. Ethology and stress diseases. *Science*, 1974, *185*, 20–27.

WASHBURN, S. L., and HAMBURG, D. A. Aggressive behavior in old world monkeys and apes. In P. C. Jay (Ed.), *Primates: Studies in adaptation and variability*. New York: Holt, 1968.

ZUCKERMAN, S. *The social life of monkeys and apes*. London: Routledge and Kegan Paul, 1932.

PART TWO

GENERAL CONSIDERATIONS

CHAPTER 4

At the Choicepoint

Although we are not continually aware of them, we are all influenced by long-term goals, values, and purposes. In our day to day existence we may often behave in ways that are inconsistent or even irrelevant to these major guides, but when we examine our most important behaviors it becomes readily apparent that these criteria exist or are in the process of being formulated.

In this chapter we will examine three broad criteria by which most of us evaluate not only our own actions but also those of others: *rationality, consistency,* and *meaningfulness* or *purposiveness.* These yardsticks are applied by us in planning future behavior as well as in evaluating present or past conduct. These criteria are models or ideals held by most of us, even though we may never or inconsistently achieve such standards.

We aspire to behave in rational, consistent, and meaningful ways and feel dissatisfied when we fall short of these goals. Similarly, our appraisal of the goodness of others is often affected by the degree to which their behavior is perceived as rational, consistent, or meaningful. However, in judging others by these dimensions, we must recognize that we usually impose our own subjective definitions or perceptions of acceptable achievement on these criteria. Thus, although we make cognitive interpretations of behavior, we must recognize that these appraisals are often idiosyncratic or subjective and will thus differ among different observers.

Decisions, Decisions, Decisions

We are continually faced with courses of action from which we must choose. What should you do today? What future career should you engage in? What clothes should you wear to the party? Should you attend a movie or study for a test? Whom should you marry? Some choices are relatively unimportant, whereas others are of the utmost significance to our lives. Out of the welter of complex alternatives that frequently perplex us, we somehow eventually arrive at decisions, for better or worse, about our daily activities, lifelong careers, etc. Sometimes our wisdom prevails and our decisions lead to positive outcomes, whereas at other times we live to regret and suffer the negative consequences and attendant misery of what turned out to be poor decisions.

Much of our behavior, then, involves some rather complex cognitive processes *before* we take action. With experience, however, some decisions become such well-ingrained habits that we are unaware of any conscious reasoning process leading to our behavior, except in an after-the-fact reconstruction of the situation. Even in these instances, we presume that deliberation and evaluation of alternative responses and their consequences were required on earlier occasions before the behaviors became second nature.

Motivated behavior is goal-directed. Thus, when we are attempting to achieve some goal, we often must appraise the available alternative responses or choices in terms of the likelihood of each enabling us to succeed. The perception of the set of alternatives is subjective, varying with the individual's experience and background. Different people in the same situation will identify different possible alternatives. Then, after specifying the alternative behaviors that exist, an individual must also evaluate the likelihood that each alternative will lead to the desired goal.

IDENTIFYING ONE'S ALTERNATIVES

Let us use the choice of a career as an example. Most people recognize the need for some form of gainful employment in order to achieve financial security and fulfill material needs. In addition, many people value personal and psychological need fulfillment and hope that the career or occupation they select will also meet this goal.

One person may define his available choices as medicine, law, or pharmacy. These careers may be the only ones that appear rewarding to this individual, or it may be that his or her parents are pressuring him or her into one of these fields. Another person may consider his or her choices as limited to salesperson, accountant, or clerk because of his or her particular level of education, interests, or opportunities.

Can we ascribe more motivation to one person than to another on the basis of occupational choice? Although such conclusions are sometimes made, it should be noted that situational constraints such as financial or personal factors, rather than motivational ones, may determine career choice. Each person chooses only from the set of alternatives that he or she thinks are available.

George Kelley (1955) proposed the concept of *personal constructs*, referring to the notion that each person has subjective categories and ways of perceiving the world. As a result, persons with different constructs may experience difficulty communicating with each other. Kelley (1962) gives an example of a man who despises "capitalism." You and I, on the basis of our personal constructs, might infer that he would have to be a communist or a fascist, because these are the alternatives to capitalism for some people. But he might merely mean that he dislikes all forms of government in which the consent of the governed is required. Kelley argues that we must know the issue at stake in the cognitive system of a particular individual before we can decide what the person meant.

Actually, Kelley had in mind a citizen of the country of Georgia, one of the Soviet Republics, where capitalism refers to the situation in which land-owners regard the education of farmers as useless. Although some American capitalists may hold the same attitude, we do not generally find this attitude to be a key part of the American concept of capitalism.

As Kelley (1962, p. 87) observed, "Understanding a man's construct system is, then, the first, and most important, step in understanding what is commonly known by that vaguest of psychological terms, 'motivation.' " Thus, our first step in understanding a person's behavior is to determine how he or she construes reality. Insofar as each person has a unique set of personal constructs, it is not possible to understand fully one person's behavior in terms of another person's cognitive views of reality.

This point is illustrated by another example cited by Kelley of an East German couple whom he met not long before the Berlin Wall was imposed. At that time it was still possible for this couple to escape the depressing and gloomy atmosphere of East Berlin, at least for a few hours, and enjoy the excitement and prosperity of the brightly lit shopping areas of West Berlin.

When he asked them why they did not attempt to flee East Berlin, they admitted in effect that although West Berlin was a "nice place to visit, they would not wish to live there." Despite the abject and solemn surroundings of East Berlin, they felt secure there, especially because of the provision of medical care for their family.

A casual observer might question the couple's motives and feelings, as-suming that they lacked drive, courage, or intelligence. Yet, in terms of the background and experiences of the couple, the choices that appeared to them were not the same as those that might appear obvious to you or me. Their behavior made sense to them as they defined the situation.

Similar misunderstandings frequently occur when tourists visit foreign countries and fail to understand how the customs and values of other nations lead to different behavior and attitudes among the inhabitants of those coun-tries. Thus, the value of saving face rather than cowardice, as we define it, may be the motive for withdrawal from interpersonal conflict for members of a culture that emphasizes shame. Generally speaking, the ethnocentrism that prevents one nation's people from understanding the behavior of another's is further illustration of the personal nature of constructs of social reality.

HEADS OR TAILS?

Once we have defined our options, how do we make our choices? That is the second question we must deal with in order to understand human motivation. Situational factors play a significant role in our selection among available alternatives. If we are hungry, we may value food over sleep, or vice versa if we have been deprived of sleep. And if we have been satiated with food and sleep, we may prefer to attend a movie. In short, the immediate state of the organism influences the hierarchial arrangement of our needs at any given moment.

In addition to these short-term situational determinants, our present choices are governed by long-range goals, values, and needs. Although it may be true that sometimes we ignore our long-term needs in favor of highly attractive immediate goals, such as spending junior's college education savings for a new sports car, we are generally influenced by long-term goals in our everyday decisions.

Our values and ideals such as security, achievement, loyalty, power, and honesty, are acquired at an early age but continue to change and develop throughout life. Smith (1963) maintains that values are an individual's conception of what is desirable. They are standards by which a person can evaluate the goodness or badness of his or her own behaviors as well as those of others. Self-values, as Smith prefers to call them, can be acquired by modeling and imitation of peers and adults, but a more direct factor is the evaluative feedback a child receives about his or her behavior from other persons, parents in particular.

Whereas some formulations of values equate them with motives, Smith argued that although values can instigate motivated activity, his conception regards values as cognitive standards of what is deemed desirable behavior. Values are related to motives, such as when discrepancies are detected between actual behavior and internal standards. In such circumstances motivated behavior often is generated as a consequence, but the motive is to reduce the discrepancy and is not the same as the value per se.

The manner in which behavior is affected by values is not always simple and, in many instances, rival or competing values may exist, leading to indecision or choices lacking in conviction. Finding a wallet with money in it produces conflict in most people, because their value of honesty may clash with their need for money and the things it can buy.

Sometimes our conflicts are between satisfying our own goals and thwarting the goals of others. Should I spend another $10 on myself or should I donate it to charity so that less fortunate people can benefit? What factors determine when we begin to value giving aid to others, even at some expense or inconvenience to ourselves, over immediate self-gratification?

At other times our conflicts are within ourselves, such as between eating a delicious piece of cake and avoiding excess calories. We are often at war with ourselves concerning immediate versus delayed gratification, such as in saving our money or spending it immediately.

In view of the obvious complexity of the factors that influence our motivated behaviors, it is not surprising that psychologists have often preferred to deal first with simpler situations in developing models and theories about human decision making.

This conception of human motivation emphasizes the cognitive nature of the processes that are frequently necessary before specific actions are undertaken. At the same time, affective factors are implied, because the set of alternative choices an individual may perceive as viable will depend on his or her values. Goals that are compatible with positively charged values may be approached, but goals that are associated with negative values will be avoided.

In this chapter we will examine several assumptions about the manner in which humans attempt to integrate their actions in accord with their total behavior. These integrative models, *rationality, consistency,* and *meaning* or *purpose,* are cited as three examples and are not the only frameworks by which individuals order their behavior. It will become evident that each model discussed could be viewed as a guiding principle that influences the choice of action made by an individual throughout his or her life. In a sense, these criteria could be regarded as values in themselves against which other values and actions are judged.

Concepts such as rationality, consistency, and meaning are difficult to study because they are often defined in subjective terms. Attempts to provide objective definitions of these terms have been made and provide some baseline against which behavior can be judged. Nonetheless, as we shall see shortly, objective criteria are inadequate in evaluating the extent to which an individual uses these models as guides for action. An action that by objective standards might be deemed irrational or nonrational by observers might still be based on the individual's own sense of rationality.

A Rational Approach

Humans may not be rational animals in the strictest meaning of the term, but it may be worthwhile to adopt this concept as a reference point or guide against which to compare human decisions. If we could reach agreement on what would be a rational decision in a hypothetical case, we could then test individuals and compare their decisions with those meeting our definition of rationality. Although this strategy might appear simple, in most everyday situations we find it difficult to agree on rational behavior. Because we have already noted that our personal constructs differ, it is reasonable to expect that each of us will consider different responses to be available to us. We would probably differ in the relative importance we attach to our alternatives, as well as in the perception of the likelihood that each alternative would be successful. Consequently, we would undoubtedly often disagree about what constitutes rational behavior in a given situation.

However, if we restrict ourselves to situations that lend themselves to quantification, such as gambling or investment, as a number of investigators have done, it is possible to reach fairly clearcut accord on the definition of *rationality*. Thus, with a fair coin we can expect each outcome, Heads or Tails, to appear equally often over the long run. Or if we draw a single card from a deck of playing cards, the odds that it will be a face card are much smaller than the odds it will be a card with a number on it. In short, probability of outcomes in these situations can be objectively defined.

One problem, however, is that although probability can be defined objectively, it is not always construed that way by everyone. The so-called gambler's fallacy will attest to the need for a concept of *subjective probability*. For example, most people will expect a fair coin to be more likely to come up Heads on the tenth toss if the preceding nine outcomes had all been Tails than if only half had been Tails. We say that Heads is long overdue; however, it is overdue only to us, because the coin itself has no memory of its previous outcomes and the objective probability of each outcome is still 50 percent on each toss.

Situations dealing with monetary outcomes also have the advantage of quantification. We can all agree that the monetary value of $5,000 is greater than that of $1,000; in fact, it is five times as great numerically. This feature of monetary outcomes is useful in testing models of rational decision making.

However, as with the concept of probability, we must also recognize that value cannot be defined entirely in objective terms. $5,000 does not mean the same thing to everyone; a pauper will see it as more significant probably than will a millionaire, all other things being equal. In short, subjective value, or what is also termed *utility,* of an outcome must also be considered in studying decision making.

Let us now consider a simplified example of decision making. Suppose a man has $5,000. For illustration, assume that he can think of only three alternatives for using his money: investing, spending, or giving it away. The alternative he selects will depend on some combination of short- and long-term factors or needs.

Suppose that in general our hypothetical man with $5,000 valued the excitement of risk taking more than spending the money on a new sports car or donating it to charity. This preference could stem from many factors, such as upbringing or direct experiences in the past. We would then expect him to invest his money. However, short-term factors might counteract the long-term ones. For example, suppose he had no car but wished to impress his dates with his affluence. A new sports car would be more suitable for these purposes than would 100 shares of some speculative mining stock. Or if he were a millionaire with several sports cars, he might think that the immediate and positive social recognition obtained by a $5,000 donation to charity would be more gratifying than an additional $5,000 investment.

In addition to these types of considerations, our hypothetical man would be influenced by the probability of success for each alternative. To what extent would each choice be likely to achieve the envisioned goal? What is the risk of failure of the investment? Or what is the likelihood that the new car will not impress his friends, or that the charitable donation will not produce the favorable image desired?

Thus, the chance that a given choice will lead to the expected outcome must be considered along with the subjective value of each choice. The alternative with the best combination of likelihood of success and degree of preference might then be determined and used as a possible criterion of rational decision making.

Suppose that our hypothetical man regarded investing as his most desirable alternative but it was also the choice with the lowest expected chance of success. If one of the less preferred choices had a higher expected chance of success that sufficiently counteracted its lower attractiveness, we might conclude that our man would choose that alternative. To paraphrase a familiar saying, one less desired goal that is attainable is worth more than two more desired but unreachable goals.

Our example has emphasized the complex nature of decision making in which several pieces of information must be simultaneously processed and evaluated according to some arbitrary decision rule. But even though we have simplified the situation, it is still unsatisfactory for precise analysis. The values of the outcomes are not precisely quantifiable, nor are the probabilities of success of the outcomes easily measured. To avoid these difficulties, tests of models of decision making have usually restricted themselves to situations, such as hypothetical gambling or betting situations, in which one can provide some objective and quantifiable indices of probability of success and value of outcomes.

Edwards (1953, 1954, 1955), for example, has studied aspects of decision making in risk situations in the laboratory. Hypothetical bets are presented in pairs to subjects who must choose between them.

For example, a choice might be offered between Bet A, which has a 60 percent chance of winning $75 or a 40 percent chance of losing $100, and Bet B, which has a 25 percent chance of winning $120 and a 75 percent chance of losing $30. The rational decision, presumably, would be the one that pays off the best in the long run, according to mathematical expectancies. Which bet would you select? Because the expected value for Bet B is higher ($.25 \times \$120 + .75 \times -\$30 = +\$7.50$) than that for Bet A ($.60 \times \$75 + .40 \times -\$100 = +\$5.00$), the rational choice is Bet B.

In an actual experiment, subjects make decisions about a series of bets and their choices are then compared with those that are rational, mathematically speaking. Results of experiments suggest that by this definition human decisions are not perfectly rational. One reason for this failure is that these mathematical models ignore personality differences and idiosyncratic biases (Kogan and Wallach, 1964). However, other models (Edwards, 1955) emphasize subjective definitions of probability and value such as subjective probability and utility, respectively. Although these models more aptly reflect the subjective nature of human decision making, they still fall short of predicting human risk-taking choices accurately.

As already pointed out in an earlier example, real-life decision situations do not usually permit precise quantifiable definitions of value and probability of outcomes. Nor does the decision maker in real life usually have access to all the necessary information that is available in most experiments. For example, in buying a car or investing in real estate, most people find it necessary to investigate and collect information before arriving at a decision.

Furthermore, the laboratory studies may not be generalizable to similar real-life situations, because trivial incentives are usually employed in experiments. Even when monetary rewards are offered for good performance, the subject does not stand to lose his or her own money, because he or she is usually provided with funds at the outset of the test session. Thus, the subject can be no worse off financially at the end of the session than when it started.

Another difference between the laboratory situation and real life is the fact that in the former the subject is required to gamble or take risks, whereas in reality the individual must first decide whether or not he or she even wishes to gamble before choosing among the alternative choices. Moreover, the conclusions of laboratory studies are based on a broader sample than those derived only from risk takers in naturalistic settings who represent a more select sample.

Not all our risks involve monetary consequences or material outcomes. We are engaged in risk taking when we make many intellectual or cognitive judgments where the only reward for being correct is self-satisfaction or the opportunity to say, "I told you so," and the punishment is the embarrassment of being wrong. Prediction of tomorrow's weather and other future events are examples of this type of risk taking.

Mathematical models do not imply that the subjects understand or employ statistical concepts such as expected value or probability in arriving at their choices. The exact process of human reasoning is not a major concern of these models, which are the creations of theorists. The purpose of the model is to determine if it can predict closely the actual choices, not to describe the actual cognitive processes. With such an emphasis, it is possible to overlook individual differences in reasoning. For example, some subjects might place more weight on the probability of outcomes, whereas other subjects might assign more importance to the payoffs of outcomes (Slovic and Lichenstein, 1968).

In summary, a conception of human decision making as rational does not accurately depict much human behavior. This is not to say that humans do not intend or attempt to be governed by rational processes and factors at times. However, the sheer information overload of numerous factors may tax the memory and reasoning abilities such that decision makers do not properly use the available information. At the same time, it should be noted that numerous emotional and idiosyncratic factors influence human decisions. Biases such as the gambler's fallacy have already been cited, and other biases such as lucky numbers and superstitions also affect human choice. For example, John Cohen (1964) has shown that subjects will prefer a gamble in which the chance of winning is nine out of ten over one in which it is ninety out of one hundred. Even though the objective probability of winning is exactly the same in the two instances, it appears that some subjects reason that in the former case you only have one chance of losing, whereas there are ten in the latter case. The operation of these factors also serves to reduce the success of theories that emphasize only rational factors.

One of the major difficulties in evaluating models of rationality is the problem of definition. As we have noted, subjective factors must be considered in determining how people assess situations in which they are confronted with decisions. Attempts to prove that humans are rational have, in effect, further illustrated the necessity of emphasizing the personal and subjective nature of cognitive factors that influence human motivation.

Perhaps, as suggested by Simon (1957), the human is a "satisficer," being content or satisfied so long as some subjective minimal level of aspiration is attained. It is not necessary to choose the alternative with the maximal payoff, at least not in every situation, and one may be satisfied because the payoff received is adequate for one's needs.

Even if it were possible to determine the alternative that provided the maximum payoff, it might be time consuming and expensive for the information to be gathered and evaluated. It may not be within the intellectual capacity of most persons to judge the maximal return in situations in which there is too much information. Like an administrator in an organization, most of us seek simple rules of thumb to increase our efficiency. Like the business person, we may be satisfied as long as we get an adequate profit or our share of the market even if it falls short of some theoretical maximum.

The Hobgoblin of Consistency

If not rationality, what other criteria might serve as a basic guide for our behavior? Although Carlyle disparaged it as the "hobgoblin of simple minds," consistency has been regarded as an influence on much of our behavior. Not only is it assumed that humans are logical, but it is also generally thought that humans strive for consistency or seek to avoid the tensions associated with inconsistency. Whereas a person who is consistent in his or her actions may be viewed as reliable or stable, an inconsistent person may be perceived as undependable, untrustworthy, and perhaps even unintelligent.

Consistency, as used in the above example, emphasizes reliability of behavior over time or on different occasions. Another aspect of consistency, however, refers to the harmony, congruity, or balance between attitudes toward X and Y, between attitudes and behavior toward X, or between behaviors X and Y. For example, if you like Democrats, you probably dislike Republicans. If you say that you like Brand X toothpaste, you probably brush your teeth with it. And, if you drink low-fat milk, you are unlikely to eat ice cream, if you can control yourself. Otherwise, there would appear to be inconsistencies in your attitudes and behaviors.

Why should consistency be such a concern that we attempt to make our attitudes and behaviors achieve this rapport? As suggested above, consistency is regarded by others as a virtue, whereas inconsistency is seen as a character defect. Consequently, we need consistency to promote a desirable image of ourselves to others. Our past behavior is an anchoring habit or tradition from which we are reluctant to deviate for fear of appearing inconsistent. In other instances, we may use our past behavior as a guide or precedent in order to simplify or eliminate the need for complex decisions to be made again in present or future situations. We simply do as we did before, so that the net result is consistency of behavior. Judicial officials similarly rely heavily on the criteria of consistency with precedents in arriving at decisions in new cases. We reduce informational overload on our cognitive processes by taking the route of least resistance, consistency. Inconsistency is a situation that lacks closure and the individual is in a state of unresolved tension or arousal until the imbalance is eliminated.

A number of psychological theories assume that there is a tendency for humans to seek cognitive consistency (Abelson, 1968; Feldman, 1966). Although the concepts of balance, consistency, and dissonance vary in detail, the basic notion is that departures from a homeostatic level create a motivating or arousing state, which leads the organism to attempt to restore the state of cognitive equilibrium. It is possible for some maladaptive responses to occur, such as repression or reluctance to think about the situation. Bolstering and selective attention may also occur in which the individual seeks evidence that supports his or her own view and denies or overlooks contradictory evidence. For example, the smoker faced with alarming statistics about the danger of smoking—might think of greater dangers, such as the risks encountered by freeway commuters. Another stratagem is differentiation, a technique by which inconsistencies càn be resolved by refining one's cognitive categories. Thus, a bigot who finds that he or she likes a black professor might revise the category of blacks into educated versus uneducated blacks and maintain his or her prejudice only against the latter category.

Perhaps the consistency theory that has received the most attention is Festinger's (1957) theory of *cognitive dissonance*. When someone has two or more discrepant facts or beliefs, the theory postulates that a state of dissonance, which is unpleasant, exists. Consequently, there is an attempt, consciously or unconsciously, to restore the balance or consistency of views.

One could, for example, achieve this goal by changing an original attitude.

Because more experimental research has been generated by the theory of cognitive dissonance than any of the other consistency theories, we will limit our discussion of such theories to this influential formulation. The theory deals primarily with attitudinal change as a means of reducing cognitive dissonance, but it can also apply to changes in behavior. One type of situation covered by the theory is post-decision conflict, such as in the case of a man who buys a car, but then has second thoughts about his choice. Dissonance is aroused if he hears that his model is a poor one or that some rival make is a better value. In order to reduce dissonance, our consumer might exercise selective attention and ignore the bad reports.

Another type of setting handled by cognitive dissonance theory is termed *forced compliance,* referring to situations that are just short of coercion but in which more than friendly persuasion is involved. Usually we do not freely enter into behaviors we do not believe are correct or ethical unless we are pressured or coerced. Some of us are willing to do some of these unpleasant things, but at a price. In either case, balance is maintained because we see no inconsistency between our actions and our attitudes if we feel there are either extenuating circumstances or sufficient justification.

But what if we were forced to do some behavior and received little or no compensation or justification. Dissonance theory assumes that this discrepancy would produce high dissonance; one means of reducing such dissonance might be to change one's original attitude toward the situation. Instead of viewing that reluctant behavior as unpleasant, we might subsequently regard it as not being so bad after all, especially since we did perform that behavior ourselves.

One well-known study by Festinger and Carlsmith (1959) tested the idea that forced compliance with insufficient justification would lead to greater dissonance and consequently more attitude change than would forced compliance with adequate justification. Students were tested on a series of boring tasks during the experiment after which they were offered either low ($1) or high ($20) justification if they would aid the experimenter in maximizing the cooperation and motivation of the next subject because the assistant who usually served this function was absent. To be specific, they would have to tell a white lie to the next subject by claiming that the tests had been very interesting, which they certainly were not. A summary of the experimental procedures is shown in Table 4–1.

Because most subjects have been taught to avoid behaving in ways that make them appear foolish or dishonest, it was assumed that this white lie would create some dissonance. Since they themselves had been bored, how could they be consistent by telling someone else that it was interesting? According to dissonance theory, if they had high justification such as $20, this ulterior motive would lessen the amount of dissonance experienced, because they could reason that the large sum of money, and not their liking of

TABLE 4–1.   Summary of the Festinger-Carlsmith (1959) Experimental Design and Predicted Outcomes.

Condition	Interaction with Confederate	Predicted Change in Attitude Toward Boring Task
1. Control	None	None
2. $1 (Low Justification; High Cognitive Dissonance)	Comply with experimenter and tell confederate that boring task was "interesting"	More positive attitude in order to reduce cognitive dissonance
3. $20 (High Justification; Low Cognitive Dissonance)	Same as in $1 condition	Little change in attitude since cognitive dissonance was low

the task, led to the claims that it had been interesting. On the other hand, the low justification group would not have this ulterior motive, so that their dissonance would be higher.

It was predicted that one way for dissonance to be reduced by the low justification group might be to change their attitude toward their own prior experience in the experiment. That is, if they were asked what they thought of the experiment, it might not appear as boring as it had at first. By re-evaluating the experiment as interesting after all, there would be less inconsistency, for they would be telling the next subject the task had been interesting. In summary, the low justification group, which experienced high dissonance, should paradoxically, according to dissonance theory, have a more positive attitude toward the task. In contrast, common sense, as well as learning theory, which assumes that performance is directly related to incentive magnitude, would predict the high justification ($20) group to be more favorable in its attitude toward the task.

Festinger and Carlsmith cleverly arranged for an accomplice to interview subjects after the experiment as part of an alleged departmental survey of all research projects so that they did not realize the interview was actually part of the main study. Subject ratings of the experiment showed that the high dissonance (low justification) group did in fact have a more positive rating of the experiment than did the low dissonance (high justification) group.

Although the results appeared to confirm the dissonance theory explanation, the study has received criticism, as have many of the other dissonance experiments (e.g., Chapanis and Chapanis, 1964). Rosenberg (1965), for example, argued that the extremely high justification of $20 for such a simple task probably aroused the suspicion of the high justification group, so that they may have viewed the study as a measure of honesty. In line with this possible perception, subjects would then be more prone to "tell it like it is" and rate the task as boring when interviewed after the experiment.

Whether this specific alternative hypothesis is correct or not, it illustrates one of the general criticisms of dissonance studies, namely that there are often several alternative explanations of the data besides the one derived from dissonance theory. In general, it can be suggested that whenever discrepancies are presented to a person, reasons other than the need to reduce aversive dissonance could be responsible for the ensuing attitude change. For example, discrepancy may bring new information to the attention of the individual and thus lead him or her to reorganize his or her interpretation of the situation; thus, attitude change in this example is from enlightenment, not necessarily from fear of dissonance.

Moreover, Rosenberg's (1965) study failed to confirm the findings of Festinger and Carlsmith. His results showed that higher incentives led to greater attitude change in writing essays counterattitudinal to the subjects' own opinions on the topics. This finding is what one would expect on the basis of learning theory, namely that higher incentives would produce greater change.

Carlsmith, Collins, and Helmreich (1966) also found evidence that greater attitude change under forced compliance does not always occur with the smaller incentive. They had subjects perform a dull task, followed by either a face-to-face interaction with another subject who was the experimenter's accomplice or an opportunity to write an anonymous essay. In either situation they were to discuss how interesting the task had been. When the face-to-face situation was involved, the results supported the dissonance prediction of greater attitude change with smaller incentives; in contrast, when anonymous essays were involved, the incentive effect of greater attitude change with higher incentives was obtained. The Carlsmith et al. results demonstrated that the effect of incentive size on attitude change depends on the type of situation involved.

Aronson (1966) suggested that the public face-to-face situation may have created dissonance, because more commitment to their attitudinal position occurred in subjects in that situation compared to those in the anonymous condition.

Although such a process may have occurred, Collins (1969) suggested that a more important factor may have been the realization by the subjects in the face-to-face situation that their communication had consequences for the other subject in the situation. On the other hand, subjects in the anonymous condition had been told that only the experimenter would read their essays so they would not expect their arguments to hold consequences for others.

It should not be assumed, however, that private conditions necessarily involve lesser consequences than face-to-face conditions. Collins (1969) pointed out that the subject does not fear retaliation from the subject who received the misleading communication that the dull task was enjoyable; rather, the subject still has to live with himself or herself and the knowledge of what he or she did. Collins also argued that most subjects will feel a sense of personal responsibility for their actions. Such feelings should exist regardless of whether the behavior was public or private as long as the consequences were sufficiently serious.

In order to test the role of two factors, consequences and personal responsibility, in the effect of incentive size and attitude change under forced compliance, Collins and Hoyt (1972) required male subjects living in a university residence to write a 5 minute anonymous essay arguing against the policy of open visitation in the dormitories. Subjects were led to believe that their essays either would affect policy (high consequences) or would not affect policy (low consequences). Half the subjects within each condition were told they were personally responsible and half were told they were not personally responsible for their essays.

As predicted, more attitude change occurred with the low incentive if the subject expected high consequences and high personal responsibility. This dissonance effect lasted over a two-week interval. However, there was no evidence for the opposite prediction that low consequences and low personal responsibility would generate a positive relationship between incentive size and attitude change. Collins and Hoyt (1972) speculated that the incentive size may have been insufficient to produce changes. In any case, their study illustrates the complexity of the forced compliance effect and provides evidence of some of the additional factors that must be considered. The extent to which we strive to achieve cognitive consistency is limited. The dissonance effect reported by Festinger and Carlsmith (1959) occurs only under certain conditions.

APPARENT INCONSISTENCY

One of the difficulties in evaluating the degree to which one person's behaviors and attitudes are consistent is that the observer's criteria, information, and perspective are often different from those of the actor. In other words, some cases of inconsistency are only in the eyes of the beholder.

Thus, an observer finds it odd if a Democrat voted for a Republican, a banker favored welfare, or a communist attended church. He or she assumes that all Democrats vote straight tickets, all bankers have the same capitalistic social values, and all communists are atheists. His or her stereotypes are so fixed that he or she believes each member of a category thinks and feels the same way that the majority of that group does.

But if our observer had more finely differentiated concepts, he or she might have perceived no inconsistency at all. For example, the observer would realize that the Democrat who voted for a Republican may have been conservative rather than liberal. From the perspective of this conservative Democrat, he or she would have felt no inconsistency whatsoever in voting for a Republican. It should also be emphasized that when we categorize a person in one dimension, for example, party affiliation, we tend to overlook the obvious fact that the person can be simultaneously classified in other dimensions such as age, sex, education level, occupation, and other affiliations. One or more of these other characteristics may be more critical than nominal party preference in determining voting behavior. For example, the person may consider himself or herself a Democrat simply because his or her family had been Democrats for generations. But the person's voting behavior may have been influenced more by a personal philosophy of conservatism, occupation, for example, a merchant, or other affiliations, for example, Kiwanis Club.

Inconsistency may also be more apparent than real because, as Kelman (1974) has noted, observers often are unaware of situational factors that constrain the behavior of an individual. Discrepancy between an expressed attitude and actual behavior may stem from outright lying, tactfulness, or socially desirable responses to the interviewer about attitudes.

If I say I like X, even though I really do not, it might be due to the fact that I do not want to hurt X's feelings in case he or she finds out, especially if that person has power over me. Yet if you observed my behavior, you might notice that I generally avoid having anything to do with X. Conversely, I might tell you that I dislike X, but in a social setting my behavior might appear otherwise because social etiquette calls for avoiding public embarrassment or because I have ulterior motives in giving the appearance of getting along with X. In either case, the observer might conclude there was inconsistency between my attitudes and my actions.

Apparent inconsistency can also appear when growth or change takes place in the cognitive organization of an individual. This change may be temporary or permanent, gradual or rapid, subtle or dramatic, but in any case the net result may be what appears to an observer to be an inconsistency. Adolescents blossom into adults, adults reach middle age, and the middle aged eventually attain old age. The hierarchy and set of goals and values will undergo change and modification over the life cycle. In addition, specific incidents, such as religious experiences, deaths of friends and relatives, changes in occupation or income level, marriage or divorce, parenthood, may cause a restructuring or reordering of priorities. As a consequence, behavior and attitudes may undergo radical change and give the semblance of inconsistency.

A NEED FOR COMPLEXITY?

All the preceding arguments that inconsistency is sometimes an illusion do not deny the real existence of inconsistencies that perplex, frustrate, and confuse us. Society is full of conflicting messages. We are taught to be honest, but we see that dishonesty seems to be necessary for survival. We are taught to love and help our fellow beings, but on the other hand we learn to be aggressive and competitive in the daily rat race. We are taught to avoid wastefulness, but we are also encouraged to buy new products before the old ones wear out. And so forth. It can be argued that real inconsistencies such as these can be tolerated, at least for limited periods of time. Furthermore, inconsistency may even be sought after since it may function to challenge our problem-solving ability in a manner similar to how brain teasers, riddles, and paradoxes taunt us.

McGuire (1966) preferred to refer to this characteristic of behavior as a need for complexity rather than as evidence of inconsistency. In other words, some facts may appear inconsistent only because we interpret them through an oversimplified set of constructs. Complexity may serve to generate arousal and interest, and the mastery and understanding of complexity may produce feelings of competence (White, 1959) or achievement. We will discuss a number of related phenomena in Chapter 10, such as the search for incongruity, variety, and novelty. These basic goals could be regarded as support for the view that humans do not always prize consistency over complexity.

Apparently, other humans can cope with inconsistencies better than many psychological theorists can. After all, the world is complex and understanding is difficult to achieve. Humans may have to learn to accept or tolerate a certain amount of inconsistency simply because it cannot be wished away or ignored readily. On the other hand, the scientist tries to follow the law of parsimony, attempts to discover basic laws, and generally hopes to find some simple principles that govern more complex situations. In short, the scientist is oriented toward simple answers and whenever exceptions and paradoxes are found, he or she attempts to find some means of explaining this cumbersome complexity. Kepler, it will be noted, felt that the orbits of the planets were elliptical. This view met with great resistance, partly because it was felt that circular paths were simpler as well as more aesthetically appealing.

It is interesting to note that theorists have argued as if the evidence for consistency was in conflict with the evidence for inconsistency, that the answer had to be in terms of one or the other. A different conceptualization, which views motivation as involving a temporal sequence of consistency, inconsistency, consistency, and so on, would imply no contradiction whatsoever. Thus, it could be argued that consistency may become boring and monotonous. Complexity or apparent inconsistency might then be sought for its intrinsically arousing properties. Eventually, when the complexity is resolved, consistency would again be attained. Then the motivational cycle would begin anew as we seek another activity at an even higher level of complexity to challenge us.

Meaning and Purpose

Thus far, we have examined two basic criteria that might be regarded as factors underlying much human behavior. We have seen that rationality and consistency are ideals rather than criteria that most behavior actually follows. We have also noted the difficulty of reaching accord on the definition of either criterion since objective and idiosyncratic factors are involved in both concepts. This subjectivity is especially apparent in the third and final criterion of behavior we will examine, meaning or purpose.

Perhaps it might be instructive to imagine how life would be without any meaning, if such a situation could exist. If we could imagine a situation in which life was perceived as totally meaningless, what would such an existence be like? Would people work? Would people plan ahead? Would they write poems, plays, or novels? Would they engage in wars, attend schools, or go to church?

Although we engage in many activities out of habit, conformity, or without much conscious awareness of intentions, it is safe to say that all of us have some goals that we consider immensely important. Some of us value being happy, whereas others seek fame, and still others want fortune. But all of us want some thing or some goal. None of us can imagine ourselves without any interest whatsoever in goals. If we can define meaning in terms of our values and goals, then it would appear that meaning is an essential guide in all our lives.

What goals are meaningful to an individual? Obviously the values that govern one person's behavior will not have the same significance for another person. In fact, as we noted earlier the same values will be different in importance for the same person as he or she grows and changes. Whereas one person will find significance and meaning in art, another person will seek business interests. Independence may be of value to a younger person but as he or she reaches middle age, security may assume new and more important meaning. Meaningful activities, goals, and values, then, are subjective and must be examined from the view of the actor.

Are there any universal values or meanings? One might think that life itself might be such a universal. We hear of instincts for survival that suggest that life, itself, is meaningful. Yet, we also know that throughout history idealists, martyrs, and patriots have sacrificed their lives, endured torture, and suffered ridicule in pursuit of some lofty abstract goal. Slogans such as "better dead than Red" aptly illustrate the fact that ideology may be more valued by some people than life itself. Or consider the act of suicide by which many have escaped life and its frustrations, disappointments, and agonies.

Throughout the ages there has been a search for the meaning of life. Even though we may never discover this ideal, it appears that everyone needs to define some goals, purposes, and values to serve as their meaning of life. Work, family, fame, fortune, and religion represent some of the varied sources of meaning in life for most people.

Despite the centrality of meaning, as Maddi (1970) has noted, psychologists have not studied it sufficiently, ". . . being apparently content either to leave it to the philosophers or to chip away at the smallest corner of it with the rudimentary tools of memory drum and semantic differential."

LACK OF MEANING

Maddi's approach is to describe the consequences of the lack or loss of meaning he terms *existential sickness*. He distinguishes three types, varying in degree of severity: *crusadism, nihilism,* and *vegetative.*

Crusadism involves the relentless pursuit of a cause; almost any cause will do, because it is primarily a means toward achieving some apparent meaning to life. Hard core activists who, as conformists of a sort, join any cause for the sake of having some purpose are included in this category.

Nihilism is almost the opposite variety, wherein the person has a cynical and negativistic outlook on life. To this person, God is dead, life is absurd, and there is no meaning to life. The search for meaning, therefore, is itself meaningless and one should merely live until the inevitable event of death occurs.

Finally, the most extreme variety of existential sickness termed *vegetative* by Maddi involves chronic boredom, malaise, and apathy in all aspects of life, including cognitive, emotional, and behavioral dimensions.

Without purpose and meaning, there is no sense in making plans for the future, obtaining education, working and saving money. In short, why do anything? Maddi notes that the most frequent symptoms encountered by psychotherapists in recent years involve meaninglessness of some sort, with its attendant malaise, indifference, and aimlessness.

The root of the crisis, in Maddi's view, is the tendency of many persons to conform to the values of society uncritically. By arbitrarily accepting the meaning of life defined by society, a person leaves himself or herself vulnerable to stresses that can disconfirm this meaning structure. Once this structure has crumbled, some type of existential sickness in the form of apathy or aimlessness may develop.

Every social movement, however worthy its cause, such as war protest, an ecological crusade, or the hippie life, attracts a large number of conformists who are joining the bandwagon, not so much from their own convictions as because it is the latest fad. These conformists are the ones who will suffer most when the movement dies out, for they must hastily find another cause to embrace.

In recent years we have witnessed a succession of issues and crusades against a variety of social problems: environmental pollution, overpopulation, racism, sexism, and discrimination against homosexuals, to name a few. On another level, we have seen movements of a religious, mystical, and philosophical nature.

The disaffected look to each new movement as if it were the cause to end all causes, or the cause that will finally give purpose and direction to their lives. But the fulfillment is only temporary and when one movement peaks, another must be sought to replace it. Consequently, fads change in social movements, just as in the world of fashion.

The important role of the human need for meaning is also emphasized by

Klapp (1972), a sociologist, who attributed social change not so much to economic or political factors but to what she terms *banality,* a term very similar to meaninglessness. Although the powerless may still strive for economic and political avenues to power, those already in comfortable positions are afflicted with a lack of meaning or banality of existence, according to Klapp. Consequently, we see the rise of social movements as alternative life styles to the predominant existing culture. These movements are in search of new meanings to serve as guides for their members.

New movements often provide meaning through the development of an ideology or intellectual foundation. Before long, followers are referred to as adherents of a new "ism," a philosophy that, as Klapp (1972, pp. 362–363) aptly noted, may be quite different from any view held by the founder. "Often there comes a point at which, if the author could be brought back, he would repudiate the doctrine that has grown up in his name." Marx, for example, is reputed to have claimed that he was not a Marxist.

Not only do social movements promote a philosophy, but often a charismatic leader is singled out to be a male or female hero, who might provide a personal image and symbolize some specific human traits. Movements based on martyrs are especially likely to capitalize on the use of a human symbol such as Joan of Arc, Gandhi, or Martin Luther King.

The development of special terms, jargon, and lingo also is present in many social movements. Witness the use of such phrases as "freaking out," "doing your own thing," or "turning on" during the recent enchantment of youth with drugs and the hippie life style. It helps promote a sense of oneness and distinctiveness from nonmembers. This group identity helps to promote a sense of purpose or meaning.

We also have seen in recent years the development of symbols for various social movements, such as the clenched fist salute of the Black Power movement, the peace symbol of the anti-Vietnam War movement, and the distinctive green flag of the ecology movement.

In addition to symbols as a means of focusing attention on a movement, various social institutions have developed complex rituals of behavior, which become as important as the goals themselves to some believers. Initiation ceremonies, baptisms, and similar rites of passage are conducted with special decorations, incantations, and other embellishments. The sheer beauty of the ceremony promotes moving affective experiences in the participants, and the ceremony itself acquires meaning. Advocates may even literally defend symbols such as the cross, the flag, or the dollar as much or more than the things the symbols represent. The rituals and the symbols are revered even when the ideas and values underlying them are forgotten or abandoned.

MEANING AND THE INDIVIDUALIST

Although Maddi regards many adherents of social causes as crusaders who are desperately conforming to give meaning to their existence, he regards the individualist as one who supplies his or her own meaning by his or her own choices. The individualist is changing throughout life as he or she tries to change and improve society. He or she is like Rotter's (1966) internally controlled person who thinks that he or she has some control over destiny. Henry David Thoreau, who renounced conventional ways and retreated to a solitary existence in the woods around Walden pond, might fit this model. As did the narrator in Frost's poem "The Road Not Taken," Thoreau pursued the less traveled route and that was what made the difference in his life.

Considerable conflict exists for the individualist who defies the traditions and customs of the established order. Suppose, for example, social conventions and rules are perceived as unjust, dehumanizing, and repressive, and a point is reached beyond which the victims are unwilling to endure. Although we are taught the necessity for rule of law and respect for authority, we may find that blind obedience to laws that appear to violate our sense of humanity is no longer acceptable. Still, most of us would continue to obey laws or perhaps try to circumvent them surreptitiously rather than directly confront the authorities.

Part of our reluctance stems, no doubt, from fear that makes us cowardly and unable to stand up for what we believe. But, in addition, we have been conditioned to accept without question the legitimacy of the authority of our parents, elders, and officials of the government. We learn that what they tell us is morally right or wrong, but we rarely fully understand any rational basis for such moral judgment. Take the value of honesty. Most children learn to be honest in order to avoid punishment or that it is wrong to be dishonest. Piaget (1948) maintained that it is necessary for children to learn the social necessity of values such as honesty if they are to develop a true sense of morality. Thus, if a child could consider the social consequences of everyone lying, he or she would appreciate the fact that honesty is necessary for a society's survival and not merely an arbitrary convention. Merely punishing a child for dishonesty does not teach him or her the real necessity of honesty, but rather leads him or her to try to find ways of avoiding punishment.

Because most of us do not learn the underlying basis for moral values, we are frequently unable to question the views of those in authority. Mistakenly, we assume such rules to be part of the natural order. Obeying laws per se is a value that assumes more importance than the determination of whether or not specific laws are themselves desirable. Kohlberg (1963) has termed the first type of morality *conventional* and suggests that only a few individuals achieve a higher post-conventional morality in which defiance and violation of unjust laws may be regarded as moral behavior. For example, espionage, sabotage, and other seditious acts are generally regarded as high crimes against the state. Yet, revolutionaries and patriots have frequently committed these crimes when they felt that the established government was unjust or immoral. The actions of colonists against the British during the American Revolution is a good example. Kohlberg would regard these actions as examples of *post-conventional morality*. These behaviors expose their perpetrators to death, torture, or imprisonment, a risk they are prepared to take because their values give meaning to their existence. The immortal words of Patrick Henry, "Give me liberty or give me death," as well as those of Nathan Hale, "I only regret that I have but one life to lose for my country," are vivid examples from our own history of the importance of ideology as a determinant of actions that could otherwise be seen as immoral violations of laws.

A more recent example is the case of Daniel Ellsberg who was responsible for stealing secret documents about government policy regarding the Vietnam war from the Pentagon and releasing them to the *New York Times*. For this act, which led to the eventual publication of the so-called Pentagon Papers, Ellsberg was indicted for high crimes against the government. Subsequently, his name received additional publicity in connection with alleged break-ins of his psychiatrist's office by agents of then President Nixon. Ironically, there is a similarity between these two crimes, because each was justified by those who committed them as necessary actions to preserve our form of government.

Ellsberg viewed the role of our government in the war as immoral and based on deception, lies, and secrecy and felt that his illegal act of defiance could help convince the public of these facts and quicken the end of the war. In a similar manner, but from an opposing ideological stance, many of Nixon's aides in the Ellsberg incident, as well as in the Watergate affair, maintained that they felt Nixon's re-election was essential to the welfare of the country. In both cases, men were willing to undertake technically illegal actions in order to achieve goals they considered desirable. As Barry Goldwater proclaimed in his 1964 presidential campaign, "Extremism in the pursuit of liberty is surely no vice."

The Ellsberg case and the related break-in are clearly two actions based on different and conflicting ideologies. Yet, from the point of view of the participants, they were doing what they genuinely felt was necessary to protect the best interests of the country. Could both parties be justified in their actions? Did not belief in a higher concern prompt violations of existing laws in both cases? How do we decide whether Ellsberg's violations or those of Nixon and his associates are more justified, because both claim patriotism as justification for illegal actions?

Meaning sometimes undergoes a dramatic change in the lives of people, often because of sudden and significant events that may enlighten, disillusion, or even confuse them about their current value system. Religious and spiritual conversions are an excellent example, although examples can be found in other spheres of activity. Prior to conversion, the individual is either lacking in meaning or finds former meaning unfulfilling. Dramatic events awakened St. Augustine and St. Paul to the futility of their lives at that moment and led them to dedicate themselves to a new purpose, in these instances, religious goals. With the commitment to a purpose, a new enthusiasm and zeal permeated the lives of these men as well as those of other converts.

A modern example of a dramatic rededication of purpose is Albert Schweitzer, the great humanitarian who devoted most of his life to caring for the medical needs of the natives of the jungles of the Belgian Congo. Prior to this career, Schweitzer was a successful and creative master of many skills as a theologian, musician, philosopher, and organ builder. Most people would have been satisfied with the position and accomplishments and certainly would not suddenly abandon them to undergo medical training for several years, let alone go to Africa to provide medical attention for the natives there.

But, Schweitzer's perception of life was such that, "It struck me as incomprehensible that I should be allowed to lead such a happy life, while I saw so many people about me wrestling with fear and suffering" (Schweitzer, 1933, p. 84). Even at this point the details of his commitment to humanitarian causes were not formulated, but ". . . one thing only was certain, that it must be directly human service, however inconspicuous the sphere of it." Only after unsuccessful attempts to become involved in humanitarian activities in Europe did he finally decide to go to Africa. After many years of this dedication to humanity, Schweitzer observed, "Let a man once begin to think about the mystery of his life and the links which connect him with the life that fills the world, and he cannot but bring to bear upon his own life and all other life that comes within his reach the principle of Reverence for Life, and manifest this principle by ethical affirmation of life."

Of course, Schweitzer was a rare individual. Although his life may serve as an example and source of inspiration to many people, it is obvious that humanity has seen far more individuals whose purpose in life has been to achieve personal power, achievement, and success at the expense of others.

We cited Schweitzer as an example of how commitment to an ideal can provide a direction and enthusiasm to a life's work; but, it should be clear that ignoble, destructive, and selfish motives have guided the actions of far more individuals throughout history with similar commitment. In contrast, lack of meaning and values, good and evil, has produced no significant achievement. Instead, an apathetic, listless, and unresponsive attitude seems to result, without the presence of meaning of some sort.

It is inevitable that everyone, during moments of despair and frustration at least, must sometimes wonder if life has any meaning or whether it is merely an absurdity. Philosophers and writers have debated this issue for centuries. Perhaps the most influential writer on this theme in recent times has been Albert Camus. In his stories, he emphasizes the struggle of human existence against natural events such as plague, against other humans, and against despair and acceptance of defeat. In his writings, he tries to depict the uncertainty of life, the frustration of suffering, the absurdity or evil of tragedy, brutality, and inhumanity, all of which must humble even the strongest.

How should we respond to the human condition? Camus rules out resignation or suicide and imbues his heroes with a defiant spirit of rebellion at the absurdity of existence. In *The Plague,* Dr. Rieux leads the fight against insurmountable obstacles. Faced with death constantly, one could give up in despair, but Dr. Rieux is portrayed as one whose life's meaning is to continue the struggle. In marked contrast, the central figure of Camus's *The Stranger* is a lonely and isolated person. Unable to express or feel sentiment or emotion, Meursault is the personification of nihilism and meaninglessness. He is defeated and downtrodden, whereas Dr. Rieux is determined and dedicated despite considerable adversity. The difference between Rieux and Meursault is the difference produced by the existence of purpose and meaning.

RELIGION AND MEANING

Over the ages a traditional source of spiritual meaning for most people has been religion. Religion involves a complex blend of beliefs about cosmology, ethics, and life after death. Although religion encompasses more than supernatural beliefs, this aspect is particularly relevant to the present discussion. Out of despair, humans seek aid from someone who is stronger. Who would be a better source of comfort then than an almighty deity? In dark moments, humans are likely to feel the need for a belief in a superhuman deity who can provide deliverance. This attitude is well depicted by the well-known observation that there are "no atheists in foxholes."

Whether the oppression comes from other humans or natural causes, such as illnesses or disasters, the feeling of helplessness fosters a need for divine intervention. The poor, the aged, and the ill, among others, are especially likely to recognize the need for the good graces of the Almighty.

However, our daily lives are fortunately not constantly filled with hopelessness, disaster, and danger. Still, the lives of many people are more or less influenced and guided by concepts such as good and evil or sin. Behaviors that are considered immoral or unethical are frowned on, and we are made to experience guilt at the mere thought of committing such behaviors. Many religions teach that good and virtuous lives will be rewarded in the afterlife by admittance into Heaven, Nirvana, or the Happy Hunting Ground, whereas those who live wicked, evil, and sinful lives will be eternally damned to Hell.

These promises and threats are effective because of the uncertainty and anxiety surrounding the nature of life. Science holds that all living forms must some day die. Most people, even those suffering from depression, unhappiness, disease, and fear, want to live. But life is an uncertain and unpredictable set of events and at some time, it must end. Yet, exactly how, we rarely can predict or control. Much as we would like to think that we can control our destinies through our own efforts, factors beyond our control can affect the end of our lives in dramatic ways. Consider your own death. When and how will it occur? Short of suicide, fatal illness, or a specific threat against our life, most of us cannot predict the circumstances of our own deaths. It is difficult to say whether we will die in peace with dignity, suffer a slow painful death, such as through torture or illness, experience an unexpected accident, be murdered, or die through dozens of other circumstances. We hear of the abrupt and unexpected ends of others in the headlines of our newspapers everyday. Thus, we cannot escape the realization that someday we must all die, and that most of us cannot predict when or how we will die.

Given these uncertain conditions of life, some philosophers have noted the absurdity of life, especially when the "good die young" or in an unjust manner. All through history humanity has recognized this aspect of life but still persisted in pursuing causes, purposes, and goals that have provided some meaning. Religion has been the leading answer to this quest in the past.

Religious beliefs are accepted on faith and do not require scientific proof to those who believe in them. This aspect of religious conviction enables advocates to ignore or accept what otherwise might be viewed as absurd, unjust, or arbitrary. By interpreting events as representing the "will of God," the conflicts can be resolved without undue depression, anger, or frustration at life's disappointments and tragedies. The bitter pills of life are easier to swallow, if we regard them as tests of our faith and we view our own lack of comprehension as human frailty, for God has His ways and divine purpose.

Without attempting to discuss the validity of various religious concepts at a naturalistic level, we have focused our attention on the subjective reality of religious feeling, experience, and sentiment. As has been aptly observed by Voltaire, "If God did not exist, it would be necessary to invent Him." In fact, some views of religious concepts transpose a Christian tenet and maintain that man created God in his own image, replete with human emotions and motives. William James cautions us to worry less about theories of religion for, ". . . to grasp (religion's) essence, you must look to the feelings and the conduct."

Religious conviction can serve many functions such as inspiration, devotion, and the achievement of peace of mind. For our purposes, we have emphasized the direction and purpose it can bring to the person for whom life has no meaning. Such despair has many causes, but there is usually a state of real or perceived helplessness and a tendency to give up. By providing hope and social or moral support, religious convictions can inspire the helpless to feel a sense of strength by association with the Almighty. In turn, a missionary zeal is imparted to the initiate so that he or she may convert or save others from their sense of meaninglessness.

Religious belief should not be viewed as if it were the same experience for everyone. Personality differences among people exist such that the religious experience varies. In his classic work *Varieties of Religious Experience,* William James (1961) distinguished between the healthy minded and the sick soul as disparate approaches to religion. The former individual is able to ignore and minimize evil, whereas the latter regards evil as the essence of life and consequently overburdens himself or herself. The healthy minded view religion and the rest of life in the most positive light, feeling happy about things, even to the point of being blind to opposing facts. James noted (p. 85) that, "To the man actively happy, from whatever cause, evil simply cannot then and there be believed in." In contrast, the sick soul is melancholic and lacks interest in life's values and meaning. He cited the great Russian novelist Tolstoy as an example. In his confessions, Tolstoy related that he knew not "how to live" during his religious melancholy and even contemplated suicide. Of course, eventually Tolstoy did "see the light" again and was able to produce creative works.

PSYCHOLOGY VERSUS RELIGION?

Although traditional forms of religious belief such as organized religion still affect large numbers, they are also experiencing challenges from other alternatives. The rise of science, for example, has repeatedly raised questions about the literal validity of many religious concepts. Changing conceptions about human nature, social institutions, and morality are also making traditional religion unacceptable to large numbers.

Critics such as Freud regard the religious as escapists at best and point out the correlation between religiousness and mental disorder. But Allport (1950) suggested that when people are psychologically disturbed they do grope about desperately for aid. Religion may not be the cause of disorder, but it is a source of refuge sought by those with psychological disorder. Loneliness, alienation, fear, depression, etc. may increase the likelihood that a person will embrace religious views as a way to achieve meaning and purpose.

But although science and a rapidly changing society, with its increased educational level, greater mobility, higher technology, etc., have rendered religion obsolete for many people, no alternative avenue to meaning and purpose has been provided. Consequently, alienation and depression are frequently the outcome. In times of stress or even boredom, what do people turn to in lieu of religion?

Psychotherapy has been viewed as a modern form of religion, one without the theological aspects, which can supply meaning and purpose (Allport, 1950; Fromm, 1950). Most forms of psychotherapy deal with problems similar to those encountered by persons undergoing religious conversion. There is first despair and hopelessness, followed eventually in successful cases by a conversion or cure. The individual then achieves a new hope, enthusiasm, and purpose to his or her life.

Allport (1950) has pointed out the similarity between psychotherapy and religion. Listening, encouragement, advice, and the relationship of transference are found in both modes of dealing with problems of personality. Even the confessional ritual of the church is similar to the process of disclosure during therapy. Allport (1950, p. 86) recognized that, ". . . the vocabulary of religion and modern science differ markedly, though their meanings are essentially the same."

Although psychotherapy is a new challenger to religion as a means of treating psychological problems, it appears that it has been highly accepted.

Allport attributed this acceptance to the preference of most people to seek physical causes, rather than psychological defects, as explanations for their flaws.

On the other hand, Allport insisted (1950, p. 82), "Religion, we conclude is superior to psychotherapy in the allowance it makes for the affiliative need in human nature." Religion places more focus on love of God, which Allport suggested is needed to make life "seem complete, intelligible, right." Psychotherapy is inadequate to deal with the human need for affiliation, perhaps because of its focus on scientific and objective analysis. Moreover, psychology focuses on negative emotions such as fear and hate rather than love or affiliation.

In his analysis of the similarity of religious and psychotherapeutic experiences, Frank (1973) noted that there is invariably a high state of emotional arousal, usually unpleasant, prior to conversion or successful therapy. In religious conversion, there may be despair, anger, and depression prior to conversion, just as in the case of the client seeking psychotherapy.

The phenomenon of religious healing is worth examining. Miracles, such as the faith cures at the famous shrine at Lourdes, are infrequent, but the belief is still unshaken among the faithful advocates. What are some psychological explanations for the persistence of such beliefs? What psychological processes contribute to the success of the cures that do occur?

The desperate and the doomed, persons who have been chronically ill and unresponsive to medical treatment and who have nothing to lose, are more likely to be the ones to take arduous pilgrimages to distant shrines. The lengthy and tiring travel itself, as well as the preparations for the trip, help build an emotional state of anticipation. The prayers and social support of friends and the large expenditure of funds for travel also contribute to the emotional investment. At the shrine itself, there is the social context of thousands of other hopefuls participating in the rituals and ceremonies. Even if no dramatic cures occur, the entire proceding may be a spiritually uplifting experience for the pilgrims, because of these factors alone.

Another illustration of the role of emotional arousal is the fire and brimstone approach of evangelists such as John Wesley, who incorporated fear and vengeance as a means of converting people to religion. Sargant (1957) described some of the techniques of such revivalists and pointed out how the arousal of group emotion can also be a powerful factor in affecting beliefs. Wesley's fiery preaching left the congregations in a state of emotional exhaustion. Wesley aroused fear and anxiety by his emotionally charged threats of eternal Hell, then his offer of salvation for confessions and repentance was more eagerly accepted, especially since the love and grace of God was the reward for religious conversion.

In summary, it appears that religious conviction was often promoted and instilled through the arousal of intense emotional states. The individual's acceptance of religion enabled him or her to avoid such suffering, on the one hand, whereas love was offered as a positive consequence on the other. The contrast between the opposite emotions probably enhanced the effectiveness of the technique.

In a similar manner, according to Frank, psychotherapy, the modern alternative to religion for many people, also involves comparable processes. First, Frank noted (1973, p. 205), "Successful psychotherapy is always an emotionally charged experience, and the emotions are more often unpleasant than pleasant." He also pointed out that, ". . . massive, intensive, emotional reactions sometimes seem to be followed by marked relief of certain forms of distress." For example, in nondirective therapies, there is considerable ambiguity in the situation. The therapist provides no explicit direction so that the ambiguity forces the client to seek his or her own meaning and enhance awareness of himself or herself. Ambiguity leads to considerable anxiety, especially for someone seeking therapy, and Frank feels that this ingredient may foster greater susceptibility to influence in the client. Similar ambiguity is a key feature of group therapies in which a person must discuss his or her problems before strangers.

Other therapies also employ emotional arousal to a large degree. Directive therapists, for example, may arouse emotion by having the client talk about personal fears. Techniques of emotional flooding may involve sudden fright. Even pioneers of psychiatry, such as Pinel and Benjamin Rush, used techniques that seem cruel by modern standards, in hopes that extreme fear could cure madness.

Thus, we can see that emotional arousal is involved in both religious and psychotherapeutic experiences if they are to be successful, although such arousal in itself may not guarantee success. Frank concludes (1973, p. 330), "The role of emotional arousal in facilitating or causing psychotherapeutic change is unclear. One can only note that it seems to be a prerequisite to all attitudinal and behavioral change."

This digression into the similarity of processes underlying religion and psychotherapy is not at all unrelated to the issue of the quest for meaning in life. Because the individual undergoing religious or psychotherapeutic experiences is often depressed and lacks meaning in his or her life, it might be hypothesized that the emotional arousal is a prerequisite because it gets the individual intensely involved and enables him or her to attend to other stimuli. In other words, a depressed person will remain that way, unresponsive to new information, unless he or she can first be goaded into paying attention. The use of fear or guilt, as in many religions, is also a component of many psychotherapies. Such arousal may serve the function of snapping the person out of the depression or withdrawal long enough for other messages to register. Schein (1957), in describing apathy and withdrawal responses among POWs subjected to brainwashing during the Korean war, found that one way to instigate involvement might be to insult or physically attack a fellow POW. By getting the POW angry enough to care about something, it was possible to prevent him from giving up.

The emotional arousal may, figuratively speaking, jolt the person out of his or her rut. Moreover, in the case of religious conversion, the fear aroused may also facilitate the person's adoption of the religious beliefs, because conversion can relieve the present fear as well as provide meaning to the individual's future life. In the case of psychotherapy, the fear aroused may encourage the client to be more receptive to the help offered by others.

For some people, religion may be more effective than psychotherapy in bringing about the acquisition of purpose, whereas the reverse may hold for others. In either case, the central importance of meaning should be apparent. This is not to say that all meanings and values are equally vivid, but from the perspective of each individual, his or her own set of values and beliefs are of the utmost significance, for they provide the most important goal, meaning in life.

Summary

Intentional behavior involves the choice among several alternative actions. Even when the choice is limited to doing something or *not* doing it, we have to make a decision. Each person, depending on his or her set of personal constructs for perceiving the world, may define alternatives in a given situation in a different way.

Three aspects of such choice among alternatives were examined: rationality, consistency, and meaning. The concept of rationality implies that the individual is able to not only determine but also act in accord with choices that provide the maximum combination of likelihood of occurrence and magnitude of payoff. In other words, one would weigh the chances of success of each alternative behavior with the reward attached to it and then select the behavior that yielded the highest combination or expected value.

Out of chaos, humans like to create order according to the view that consistency is important. Imbalances between attitudes and behavior are regarded as unpleasant, so either the attitude or the behavior in a discrepant situation should change toward harmony. Although a number of instances can be identified where consistency seems to be a goal, it also appears that decisions that complicate matters are often made, suggesting that humans can tolerate complexity and even seek it out. It is also the case that different personal constructs may exist for an observer, which would lead him or her to see apparent inconsistency in the behavior of someone else. The actions may seem highly consistent to the individual performing the behavior.

Choices are also affected by the criterion of meaning. Our personal values serve as a guide in our decision making so that we strive to select choices that fulfill our personal meanings and goals. The absence of meaning or the loss of conviction in one's values often produces apathy and inactivity. The decision is made *not* to decide.

A discussion of two major sources of meaning, traditional religion and psychotherapy, indicated the similarity between them. Both are frequently turned to in times of personal crisis, unhappiness, and doubt, and both involve the substantial use of emotional arousal in order to transform or convert the individual from aimless wanderings to a life of direction, purpose, and meaning.

References

ABELSON, R. P. Psychological implication. In R. Abelson, E. Aronson, W. McGuire, T. Newcomb, M. Rosenberg, and P. Tannenbaum (Eds.), *Theories of cognitive consistency: A sourcebook.* Chicago: Rand McNally, 1968.

ALLPORT, G. W. *The individual and his religion.* New York: Macmillan, 1950.

ARONSON, E. The psychology of insufficient justification: An analysis of some conflicting data. In S. Feldman (Ed.), *Cognitive consistence.* New York: Academic, 1966.

CARLSMITH, J. M., COLLINS, B. E., and HELMREICH, E. L. Studies in forced compliance: I. The effect of pressure for compliance on attitude change produced by face-to-face role playing and anonymous essay writing. *Journal of Personality and Social Psychology,* 1966, *4,* 1–13.

CHAPANIS, N. P., and CHAPANIS, A. C. Cognitive dissonance: Five years later. *Psychological Bulletin,* 1964, *61,* 1–22.

COHEN, J. *Behavior in uncertainty.* New York: Basic, 1964.

COLLINS, B. E. The effect of monetary inducements on the amount of attitude change produced by forced compliance. In A. C. Elms (Ed.), *Role-playing, reward, and attitude change.* New York: Van Nostrand, 1969.

————, and HOYT, M. F. Personal responsibility-for-consequences: An integration and extension of the "forced compliance" literature. *Journal of Experimental Social Psychology,* 1972, *8,* 558–593.

EDWARDS, W. Probability preferences in betting. *American Journal of Psychology,* 1953, *66,* 349–364.

————. Probability preferences among bets with differing expected values. *American Journal of Psychology,* 1954, *67,* 56–67.

————. The prediction of decisions among bets. *Journal of Experimental Psychology,* 1955, *51,* 201–214.

FELDMAN, S. (Ed.) *Cognitive consistency.* New York: Academic, 1966.

FESTINGER, L. *A theory of cognitive dissonance.* Evanston, Ill.: Row, Peterson, 1957.

————, and CARLSMITH, J. M. Cognitive consequences of forced compliance. *Journal of Abnormal and Social Psychology,* 1959, *58,* 203–210.

FRANK, J. D. *Persuasion and healing: A comparative study of psychotherapy.* Baltimore: Johns Hopkins, 1973.

FROMM, E. *Psychoanalysis and religion.* New Haven: Yale University Press, 1950.

JAMES, W. *The varieties of religious experience.* New York: Crowell-Collier, 1961.

KELLEY, G. *The psychology of personal constructs.* (Vols. 1 and 2). New York: Norton, 1955.

————. Europe's matrix of decision. In M. R. Jones (Ed.), *Nebraska Symposium on Motivation.* (Vol. 10). Lincoln: University of Nebraska Press, 1962.

KELMAN, H. C. Attitudes are alive and well and gainfully employed in the sphere of action. *American Psychologist,* 1974, *29,* 310–324.

KLAPP, O. E. *Currents of unrest: An introduction to collective behavior.* New York: Holt, 1972.

Kogan, N., and Wallach, M. *Risk-taking: A study in cognition and personality.* New York: Holt, 1964.

Kohlberg, L. The development of children's orientations toward a moral order: 1. Sequence in the development of moral thought. *Vita Humana,* 1963, 6, 11–33.

McGuire, W. J. The current status of cognitive consistency theories. In S. Feldman (Ed.), *Cognitive consistency.* New York: Academic, 1966.

Maddi, S. R. The search for meaning. In W. J. Arnold and M. M. Page (Eds.) *Nebraska Symposium on Motivation.* (Vol. 18). Lincoln: University of Nebraska Press, 1970.

Piaget, J. *The moral judgment of the child.* New York, Free Press, 1948.

Rosenberg, M. J. When dissonance fails: On eliminating evaluation apprehension from attitude measurement. *Journal of Personality and Social Psychology,* 1965, 1, 28–42.

Rotter, J. B. Generalized expectancies for internal versus external control of reinforcement. *Psychological Monographs,* 1966, 80 (1, Whole No. 609).

Sargant, W. *Battle for the mind: A physiology of conversion and brainwashing.* New York: Harper, 1957.

Schein, E. H. Reaction patterns to severe, chronic stress in American Army prisoners of war of the Chinese. *Journal of Social Issues,* 1957, 13, 21–30.

Schweitzer, A. *Out of my life and thought.* Translated by C. L. Campen. New York: Holt, 1933.

Simon, H. A. Administrative behavior. Second Edition. New York: Macmillan, 1957.

Slovic, P., and Lichtenstein, S. Relative importance of probabilities and payoffs in risk taking. *Journal of Experimental Psychology Monograph Supplement,* 1968, 78 (3, Part 2), 1–18.

Smith, M. B. Personal values in the study of lives. In R. W. White, *The study of lives.* New York: Atherton, 1963.

White, R. W. Motivation reconsidered: The concept of competence. *Psychological Review,* 1959, 66, 297–333.

CHAPTER 5

The Feeling of Powerlessness

Alfred Adler (1928), in describing his view of a basic aspect of human experience, wrote

> To be big! To be powerful! This is and has always been the longing of those who are little or feel they are little . . . This goes for the individual as well as for groups, peoples, states, nations. Whatever men are striving for originates from their urgent attempts to overcome the impression of deficiency, insecurity, weakness.

The human condition, according to this view, involves an original state of frailty and powerlessness. As infants and children, we learn how dependent we are on others for our well-being so that a primary goal of our lives becomes a striving to escape feelings of inferiority. We long to have control over what happens to us. A variety of avenues exist for achieving this personal power: education, wealth, social status, influential friends, etc. Some means of acquiring control such as self-improvement are generally regarded as virtuous, whereas other means such as domination of others by force, deception, and similar methods are frequently condemned as immoral.

In this chapter we will focus on the condition of powerlessness to influence the important aspects of one's life. We will not speak specifically of power over others but be more concerned with one's power or control of one's own fate even though there is some overlap of the two areas.

We think that feelings of power or control, or the lack of them, are essential considerations in understanding many aspects of human motivation. Even though a given situation may offer two individuals the same objective chance of success, differences may exist between them in their subjective appraisal of their chances of success. Such feelings, which may be related to their self-perceptions in a dimension of power/powerlessness, may, in turn, influence their actual likelihood of success. Thus, knowledge of the way in which a person perceives himself or herself as a causal agent can help us improve our understanding of that person's behavior.

As we argued in Chapter 2, we cannot assume that knowledge about the objective aspects of a situation is sufficient to enable us to predict behavior. The perceptions of that situation might vary as a function of the individuals's past history of success or failure in controlling outcomes. Knowledge of such past histories may also be inadequate in explaining behavior. Someone who usually succeeds may have an unusually high ambition. It is likely that he or she still sees himself or herself as a relative failure and might even give up. Conversely, an habitual failure who experienced relative improvement might regard these outcomes as successes and develop an optimistic attitude enabling him or her to persist.

Despite the difficulties of accurate assessment of subjective feelings such as these, we think it is vital to include the study of such self-perceptions in the analysis of the determinants of human behavior.

In this chapter we will examine some of the psychological research that explores the causes and effects of states that are highly similar to what we are calling the dimension of power/powerlessness. In particular, we will discuss two influential approaches developed by Rotter (1954, 1966) and Seligman (1968, 1974, 1975). Rotter's approach to the study of the locus of control of reinforcement emphasized the correlational study of individual differences in the perception of the determinants of behavior. These differences in cognition were assumed to be due to differences in earlier histories of reinforcement encountered by individuals but the evidence for this assumption is indirect.

The work of Seligman on learned helplessness attacked the phenomenon from a different direction, focusing on laboratory experiments with dogs primarily, although other species including humans have been studied. By manipulating the treatments received by the dogs, differences in learned helplessness were created experimentally. The question of individual differences is of little importance in this research strategy.

The research of these investigators and their students deals with similar phenomena, even though the labels used and the types of methods and questions are dissimilar. In a sense the approaches of Rotter and Seligman complement each other, with Rotter assessing already existing differences in perception of causality and trying to work backward to discover the causes and Seligman varying the factors assumed to produce differences in learned helplessness.

Individual Differences in Self-Perception of Power: Rotter's Locus of Control of Reinforcement

Rotter (1954, 1966) and his associates have postulated the concept of internal versus external locus of control of reinforcement, which refers to the perceived source of causality of one's behavior by an individual. The person who feels *internal* control believes that he or she is primarily able to influence what happens, whereas the person with a belief in *external* control tends to regard factors beyond his or her control as the major influences on behavior.

This formulation, based on Rotter's social learning approach, assumes that past reinforcement histories will generate corresponding tendencies for individuals to hold expectancies about the locus of control of future events. The individual who has been able to determine his or her behavior in the past should expect similar internal control in most future situations of a similar nature, whereas external control will be expected in future situations by the individual who has perceived the causes of past behavior to lie in forces external to himself or herself.

Expectancies or cognitive factors are only one of the factors that will affect behavior. In addition, one must consider the value or incentive a given situation holds for the individual at a given moment. Value is affected by the current motivational state of the individual. The combined effect of expectancy and value should determine the course of behavior.

Furthermore, Rotter argued that individuals tend to form generalized expectancies about future situations on the basis of their past experiences. Individuals whose own efforts have been influential in the past will expect similar internal control in the future, whereas individuals whose outcomes have been due to external factors such as luck, chance, or other persons will expect continued external control in the future. Expectancies may operate in a self-fulfilling manner so that positive thinking like the "I think I can" attitude of *The Little Engine That Could* will likely succeed in comparison to the defeatist attitude of "what's the use of trying."

THE ROTTER I-E SCALE

The primary research generated by Rotter's formulation has centered on the development of a personality scale to measure the extent to which individuals believe that what happens to them is due to internal or external factors. Rotter (1966) developed an objective paper and pencil inventory to measure internal versus external (I-E) orientation, which consisted of twenty-nine statement items that described various situations. The individual has to choose one of two alternatives in each item, one reflective of internal and the other of external control orientation, that describes his or her beliefs. An example might be an item with the pair of statements, "Many people can be described as victims of circumstance" versus "What happens to people is pretty much of their own making."

CORRELATIONS WITH THE I-E SCALE

Scores on this scale have been found to be related to a variety of real-life behaviors in ways that appear to validate the theoretical conception of internal and external locus of control beliefs. For example, a comparison (Battle and Rotter, 1963) of black and white school children showed a greater tendency toward internal control beliefs among whites, especially when the comparison involved lower socioeconomic samples. This finding has been confirmed in a number of studies summarized by Lefcourt (1972) and apparently reflects the social reality in which blacks have traditionally been subjected to greater external control due to their lack of economic, political, and social power.

The scale has also been used to measure differences within a minority group, which appeared consistent with individual differences in social activism. Gore and Rotter (1963) tested a sample of blacks on the scale and reported that more internality was obtained among persons who signed up to take part in social protest activities such as freedom rides and the 1963 March on Washington for civil rights.

ARE POWER BELIEFS UNIDIMENSIONAL?

Subsequent research has questioned the generality of the internal-external dimension and suggested that it may be more accurate to distinguish between several areas of control. Gurin, Gurin, Lao, and Beattie (1969), based on responses by a sample of blacks to the test, distinguished several dimensions, including Rotter's personal control and also a dimension concerned more with ideological beliefs about the extent to which society can be changed.

A study by Lao (1970) offered evidence both for and against Rotter's views. On the one hand, correlations between scores on personal control and academic achievement were in line with Rotter's formulation, showing higher achievement for internals. In contrast, it was the externals rather than the internals on the ideological control factor who were more active in social reform and protest. Those blacks who blamed the social system were more active than those who blamed themselves for what happened to them.

Collins (1974) has also questioned the meaning of scores on the I-E scale. He suggested that other factors are involved in the subject's interpretation of the statements on the scale. For example, a person might disagree with the statement, "Sometimes I can't understand how teachers arrive at the grades they give," which is scored as an external response by Rotter's conception. However, Collins argued it is possible for both externals and internals to take exception to that item for entirely different reasons.

Thus, disagreement with this item by a person who is internal in orientation reflects a belief that effort or ability determines grades. But disagreement with this same item by a person external in orientation might stem from his or her belief that professors give good grades to people who complain about their test scores.

A determination of the factors involved in the statements on the I-E scale was made by Collins (1974) with a new format of the scale, which required that subjects indicate their agreement with all the alternative items instead of choosing the member of each pair that most closely matched their beliefs. He then examined the pattern of responses by a statistical procedure known as *factor analysis*. Briefly, this correlational technique identifies subsets of items that subjects tend to answer in the same way, producing high inter-correlations among them. It also distinguishes one cluster of items from other subsets that would have low correlations between them. For example, consider the person who strongly believed that fate was an important determinant of one's behavior. He or she would likely agree with items such as "Most of the unhappy things in people's lives are partly due to bad luck" and "In the long run the bad things that happen to us are balanced by the good ones." In contrast, he or she would disagree with a set of items such as "When I make plans, I am almost certain that I can make them work," "What happens to me is my own doing," and "Most misfortunes are the result of a lack of ability, ignorance, laziness, or all three."

The results suggested that in addition to the underlying theme of internal versus external control, the I-E scale items could be broken down into four additional dimensions that Collins termed: difficult-easy world, just-unjust world, predictable-unpredictable world, and politically responsive-unresponsive world.

These dimensions are unrelated or independent; yet, the same response might be made to an item on the scale by individuals differing in these four dimensions. Suppose someone indicated agreement with the item "There's no point in trying; it wouldn't make any difference if I did." Rotter's formulation would view this person as externally controlled, but Collins' analysis suggests that any one of four different subtypes would agree with that item. The person who believed that the world was a difficult one, the person who thought the world was unjust, the person who believed events were random and unpredictable, and the person who thought that government was un-responsive—any one of these quite different persons would all answer that item in the same manner and all of them would be seen as externally oriented on that item by Rotter.

These distinctions between several different dimensions in which individuals may feel variations in the extent to which they have control illustrate the problems of constructs that are too broadly defined. The idea that degree of control in all aspects of one's life is a reflection of the sum total of past experiences is overly simplistic. A professional athlete, for example, with superb control of outcomes of competitive athletic events may be totally inept in financial affairs. Similarly, a renowned scholar who has mastered his or her discipline may turn out to be incompetent in social interactions. It is as if specialization in one area implies weakness in another endeavor.

It may also be worthwhile to examine the role of beliefs in supernatural allies, especially among individuals who would be judged externals. If an individual felt he or she had little or no personal influence on his or her life, but held substantial faith in divine aid, we would expect his or her behavior to differ from that of an externally oriented person who did not have this belief. God can deliver us from our enemies, even if we ourselves are powerless to do so. Indeed, as contrasted with some overly prideful internally oriented individuals who are smug and complacent, greater accomplishments might be attained by externals who believe that God is on their side.

No apparent consideration of this type of distinction is made among externals in the formulation of Rotter, but it would appear to be worth investigation.

Considered overall, the research on locus of control suggests that individuals vary in the extent to which they feel that they have internal control or power over their lives. Those persons who perceive external factors to be the main determinants of what happens to them might be regarded as feeling powerless.

AGE DIFFERENCES

Although Rotter assumed that previous experiences with the environment shape a person's tendency to be internal or external in orientation, little direct evidence is offered for this view. Some indirect support of the role of past experiences might be argued if one accepts age differences in scores in this dimension. Using a children's form of the scale, Crandall, Katkovsky, and Crandall (1965) found that younger children were more external, presumably due to the fact that younger children are more subject to parental control, which gradually diminishes as the age of the children increases. Curiously enough, the optimal level of internality was among tenth graders, with a lower level among twelfth graders. Crandall et al. offered an ad hoc explanation for this unexpected finding, which suggested that impending high-school graduation produced a slight reversal in orientation as the students anticipated greater uncertainty about their lives after leaving high school.

In any case, this type of study deals with average age differences rather than individual differences among students within a given age, the primary fact to be explained. The approach used by Rotter of studying persons who already differ in perception of locus of control does not permit us to identify the causes of such differences as well as does Seligman's work on learned helplessness, which we will now discuss.

"Learned Helplessness": Experimental Studies

Seligman (1974, 1975) has proposed that a state of helplessness can be created if repeated attempts to control outcomes of events are unsuccessful. The experimental evidence for this concept of *learned helplessness* originally came from laboratory studies of avoidance conditioning in dogs, although some recent work has been done with humans.

In the typical avoidance conditioning paradigm, an animal is placed in one side of a two compartment apparatus known as a shuttle box. After a signal such as a tone, an electric shock is given and the animal tries to escape. It will readily learn to leap over a barrier from one side to the other, provided this response will prevent or terminate these painful electric shocks. Seligman and his associates (Overmeir and Seligman, 1967; Seligman and Maier, 1967), however, observed that this adaptive response could be modified under certain conditions. In these latter studies, it was necessary to place the dogs in a restraining harness prior to testing them in the shuttle box. While the dogs were so confined, tones were presented and followed very shortly afterward by shocks. The original question of concern was whether or not these tones associated with shocks could transfer their significance to the shuttle box situation and function as danger signals there.

To their surprise, Seligman and his colleagues found that the tones did not act as warnings that produced evasive action but rather led to passive whining and apathetic acceptance of the shocks. This outcome was interpreted as helplessness, which was learned during the earlier period in which the confined dogs received inescapable shock. In that situation the dogs struggled in vain, because shocks always followed the tones. Perhaps helplessness created in one context generalizes to others.

In order to provide better evidence for this explanation, Seligman and Maier (1967) performed another study to rule out the possibility that stress or physical exhaustion alone might account for the failure of the dogs to avoid shock in the shuttle box in the second part of the experiment. Three groups of dogs were employed. One group was able to terminate shocks received while in the restraining harness by pressing a panel with their noses. A second group consisted of dogs that were yoked with the first group so that for each dog in the first group, there was a corresponding dog in the second group that received the identical pattern, duration, intensity, and number of shocks. The only difference lay in the fact that dogs in the second group could not terminate the shocks themselves, because they were controlled by the experimenter. Finally a third group received no shocks. This basic *triadic design,* as it was termed by Seligman, has been used in many studies of learned helplessness and is diagrammed in Table 5–1.

The next day the three groups were tested in the shuttle box, where all of them received shocks. The group that had previously been able to exert control over the shocks while in the harness readily learned to avoid the shuttle box shocks, as did the control group. On the other hand, the dogs that could not control the shocks while in the harness were much poorer in jumping the barrier of the shuttle box to avoid shocks.

Other studies by Seligman have confirmed and extended the generality of this effect in dogs under a variety of shock parameters and apparatuses, regardless of whether or not shocks are preceded by signals. Research with other lower species such as rats, cats, and fish has revealed similar effects.

TABLE 5–1.   The Basic Triadic Design to Demonstrate Learned Helplessness.

	Pretreatment	Main Task
Group 1	Controllable Outcome, e.g. Escapable Shocks	Same for All Three Groups: Subject placed in situation different from the first one. Aversive stimulation administered and subject can escape or avoid the shock.
Group 2	Uncontrollable Outcome, e.g. Inescapable Shocks Matching Those Received by Group 1	
Group 3	No Pretreatment	

Hiroto (1974) has obtained parallel effects with human subjects. He compared three basic conditions, one in which subjects received escapable noise, one in which subjects received the same pattern of noises as inescapable events, and one in which there were no noise stimuli. Following this procedure, which was aimed at inducing learned helplessness in the condition with inescapable noise, all three groups were tested with a two-way shuttle box containing a knob that could be moved from side to side in order to allow subjects to escape from noises presented to them.

All groups were instructed that "whenever you hear the tone come on, there is something you can do to stop it." As Figure 5–1 indicates, the group that had previously encountered inescapable noises was poorest in learning how to terminate the noise when it was possible to escape it in the shuttle box situation. The superior performance of the other two groups was essentially equal.

Hiroto also included two other variables in his study. Half the subjects in each of the three conditions described were high and half were low scorers on a variant of the Internal-External locus of control dimension. Evidence suggested that persons who saw themselves as externals were also more helpless in the noise escape task.

A second way of examining the effect of expectancies was to instruct half the subjects in each group that the task involved skill and to tell the others that it was a matter of chance. The prediction that chance-instructed subjects would be slower in learning how to escape was upheld. An expectancy that one lacks control again leads to inadequate coping with a situation.

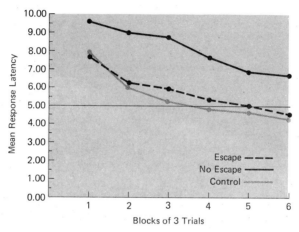

Blocks of 3 Trials

FIGURE 5–1.   Mean response latencies of the six escape-avoidance trial blocks for the three treatment groups. [From "Locus of control and learned helplessness," by D. S. Hiroto, *Journal of Experimental Psychology*, 1974, *102*, 187–193. Copyright 1974 by the American Psychological Association. Reprinted by permission.]

The deleterious effects of the experience of uncontrollable aversive stimulation are not limited to traumatic tasks. Hiroto and Seligman (1975) had college students exposed to either escapable noise, inescapable noise, or no noise as a pretreatment to an anagram-solving task. Performance on this cognitive task was poorer by those who had received prior inescapable noise.

Nor is it apparently necessary for the uncontrollable preliminary experience to be highly traumatic, such as in the case of receiving shocks. Hiroto and Seligman (1975) reported that college students given unsolvable discrimination learning tasks showed greater impairment than subjects given solvable or no problems on a subsequent hand shuttle task in which they had to move their hands to escape loud noises.

One qualifying factor does exist, however, in the Hiroto and Seligman studies. Since subjects encounter both tasks, the traumatic as well as the nontraumatic one, within the same experimental session, the subjects may have shown greater transfer or carryover between the tasks than if the two tasks were received in unrelated sessions. Expectations of the subjects may have led them to suspect that the purpose of the first task was to influence their behavior on the second task.

The more general question of how learned helplessness acquired in one context carries over to other aspects of a persons' life has yet to be studied extensively (Maier and Seligman, 1976). Although the theory implies that such transfer will occur so that experiences in one situation can affect behavior in another context, it is vague about the boundary conditions or limits of situations in which it is applicable. Seligman (1975, p. 59) acknowledged the problem in these words, "Since we all experience some uncontrollability, why aren't we always helpless?"

WHY LEARNED HELPLESSNESS MAY NOT GENERALIZE

Seligman (1975) offered three mechanisms that might offset the transferabilty of learned helplessness: immunization by contrary experience, immunization by discriminative control, and differential relative strengths of outcomes.

The first process deals with the beneficial effects of prior opportunities to control a situation that serves to offset the deleterious effects of later experiences with uncontrollable situations. Although such immunization may occur, a similar question exists here as with the issue of transferability of learned helplessness. What determines which controllable situations will be able to counteract a given type of uncontrollable outcome? The ability to earn a high salary is an example in which the individual exerts control but will this specific experience immunize successfully against academic incompetence?

Discriminative control is a term that merely describes the fact that individuals may be able to detect differences among situations, that is, that one's office is different from one's home. According to Seligman, such discrimination will prevent the transfer of helplessness learned in one of these contexts to the other. But what determines which situations can be differentiated from each other? In the example of the office versus the home, it is not clear that all types of experiences will not transfer between them. Thus, if the inability to control interpersonal interactions occurs in one context it may readily transfer to the other situation, despite the discriminability of the two situations.

Finally, Seligman speculated that helplessness may generalize from an important situation to a trivial one but not vice versa. However, it is not always possible to distinguish between some situations in terms of their importance, especially because large individual differences in values may exist.

For example, a student who is helpless in mathematics may also experience adverse carryover to achievement in psychology even though he or she may have little interest in mathematics and not care. Nevertheless, poor performance in mathematics may lower the student's overall academic self-esteem, which in turn may harm his or her performance in psychology. On the other hand, the inability to control learning in an academic subject of great importance may fail to generalize to some other part of the student's life such as athletic prowess if he or she regarded the latter skills as relatively unimportant.

These examples do not disprove the notion that helplessness in important spheres of a person's life is more likely to generalize to less vital areas than vice versa, but they should illustrate the difficulty in testing this assertion.

ALTERNATIVE EXPLANATIONS: MOTOR FREEZING

The laboratory demonstrations of learned helplessness have not gone unquestioned by other investigators. Seligman's interpretation of the phenomenon emphasizes the cognitive appraisal of the contingencies between response and outcome by the individual. Since the two are independent initially in Seligman's paradigm, the individual learns in effect that nothing can be done to affect the outcome.

In contrast, two different noncognitive counterexplanations have been offered, which focus on the notion that the individual acquires learned responses that are incompatible with escape. Bracewell and Black (1974) suggested that the pretreatment period may involve the punishment of struggling so that the dogs in Seligman's studies learn to hold still, a response clearly incompatible with escape in the later part of the experiment when the dogs are no longer confined to inescapable shocks. A similar view by Anisman and Waller (1973) holds that the dogs might learn to freeze in reaction to inescapable shock in an effort to reduce its impact, a response that would also decrease the subsequent learning of escape responses.

Maier and Seligman (1976) dismiss these motor response theory alternatives primarily on the grounds that the effects of punishment of movement are small compared to those of inescapable shock of restrained animals. Observations of dogs as well as humans in the learned helplessness studies show no indication of any freezing responses. Finally, Maier and Seligman reject these explanations on logical grounds arguing that even if punishment or freezing hampered escape in the preceding studies, it does not follow that these same factors operated in reducing escape tendencies in the learned helplessness studies. It is conceivable that more than one mechanism exists for the production of a given effect.

ALTERNATIVE EXPLANATIONS: PHYSIOLOGICAL DEPLETION

A final rival explanation, the motor activation deficit hypothesis, will be briefly considered here. Although it is also concerned with motor rather than cognitive factors, this explanation differs further in that it emphasizes physiological mechanisms. Miller and Weiss (1969) observed that learned helplessness created in one session with dogs dissipated over a forty-eight hour period, suggesting that some neurochemical substance may be depleted during the heightened stress of inescapable shock. This depletion might account for the lower activity shown when the dogs are tested for learned helplessness shortly thereafter. However, after the substance is replenished (say, after forty-eight hours), the impaired escape behavior no longer is observed.

Norepinephrine is one of the neurotransmitter substances released when there is nervous system activity. It has been shown to decrease temporarily after increased activity but its level is eventually restored. Thus, there is plausibility to this physiological hypothesis. If the primary basis for the phenomenon were cognitive, it should persist even forty-eight hours later rather than show up only with immediate tests.

In rebuttal, Seligman and Groves (1970) found that the learned helplessness effect was long lasting if the dogs received four, rather than one, sessions of inescapable shock training. Furthermore, the test for learned helplessness was delayed until seven days after the last pretreatment session with inescapable shock. If the norepinephrine hypothesis were tenable, learned helplessness effects should be absent when the test is delayed that long. The Seligman and Groves study supports the cognitive view just as strongly as the Miller and Weiss study upholds the physiological interpretation.

Seligman (1975) suggested that the Miller and Weiss finding that learned helplessness disappears after forty-eight hours could be due to *proactive interference,* a type of forgetting process, in which memories of prior events eventually reappear some time after they were impaired by more recent events. Thus, if we assume the dogs had some prior experiences with *controlling* outcomes *before* they were subjected to the inescapable shock training, we see that it is possible that the memory of these cognitions recovered forty-eight hours after the aversive experience and counteracted the more recent experience with helplessness.

Although holding that a cognitive theory accounts for more aspects of the research findings than do rival explanations, Seligman (1975) recognized that cognitive, motor, and physiological theories can be viewed as complementary rather than competing accounts. Learned helplessness may involve all three components, but Seligman maintains that the cognitive factor is the first step in a sequence that then leads to the behavioral and physiological expressions of this state.

Naturalistic Evidence

The concept of learned helplessness has been applied by Seligman to many real-life situations in which the individual lacks control. The phenomenon of more rapid deaths occurs among helpless individuals or groups such as the chronically and terminally ill, shipwreck survivors awaiting rescue, or jail prisoners. The sudden loss of fortune or reputation, the death of a loved one, and disillusionment with life are also reportedly antecedents of premature or sudden deaths.

Seligman (1974) cited a study of 4,500 widowers, for example, which showed higher than expected mortality during the six months immediately following the deaths of their spouses. A study (Schmale and Iker, 1966) of fifty-one healthy women showed that those who recently underwent some psychological loss were more prone to develop cancer.

How does the concept of learned helplessness apply to these dramatic cases? One common feature may be that the victims all experienced helplessness in their plights. Because many of the examples involved prolonged periods of helplessness, they have have become despondent at their hopeless situations.

Exactly how such cognitive and emotional states produce death is not clear. The widowers, for example, probably did not literally die from broken hearts. Perhaps they lost their purpose in life and no longer had a will to live, but such explanations are more poetic than scientific. It is possible that the process is indirect, with the cognition of helplessness leading to impaired health and lowered resistance to disease and eventual death.

The helplessness that accelerates the occurrence of death in the examples cited above is real. However, phenomena such as voodoo deaths illustrate the key role of cognition. Unless one believes in magic, voodoo deaths appear to stem from the extreme fear and stress induced among believers condemned to die. The victim is not helpless in the same sense that the prisoner in a concentration camp is, but rather he or she is a helpless prisoner of his or her system of beliefs.

Seligman offered these parallels from naturally occurring examples as speculative evidence of the operation of helplessness, but one should be cautious in assuming that the processes that produced laboratory varieties of learned helplessness are the same as those involved in producing the dramatic instances cited from real life.

Origins of Powerlessness: Cognitive and Individual Difference Factors

Cognitive factors may be more important in determining behavior than even Seligman's theory would suggest. In his learned helplessness paradigm, the cognitive appraisal of helplessness is based directly on the objective reality of genuine helplessness. In Seligman's experiments, the shocks are inescapable and no behavioral control of the shocks is possible. It is assumed that if the organism did have control of the situation, it would not feel or act helpless.

There is some evidence that even in situations in which the organism *cannot* control outcomes, it is possible to maintain unimpaired performance despite stress so long as the organism can detect a pattern in the aversive stimuli. This type of control, cognitive rather than behavioral, may enable the organism to brace itself for each aversive event before it occurs.

Glass, Singer, and Friedman (1969) designed a laboratory analog of the stresses of urban noise. In one study, different groups received either random or predictable series of noises while they performed simple visual search or addition tasks. In a second phase of the study, the noise was eliminated while a proofreading task was performed.

Impairment on the proofreading task was greater in the group that had previously encountered the random series of noises. Glass et al. suggested that unavoidable aversive stimuli such as these noises may have been more stressful when unpredictable. Perhaps subjects were less startled if they had cognitive control, that is, a predictable regular pattern of disruptive noises, even though they had no behavioral control of the noises.

A second study by Glass et al. (1969) involved creating the impression of control in half the subjects by telling them that the noise could be ended if they pressed a button. Despite the fact that none of the subjects actually used the button, this group performed better than the group without this potential control. Apparently, the mere knowledge that one can control a situation, if need be, is sufficient to prevent performance from deteriorating due to stress.

It is important to add, however, that these results do not necessarily mean that actual stress is reduced when the individual has a sense of control. The preceding studies only demonstrate that the quality of performance is enhanced when the person feels in control of the situation.

Another study, however, does suggest that individuals with a sense of control will also experience less stress. Geer, Davison, and Gatchel (1970) led one group of subjects to think that they could control the duration of electric shocks they would receive. Actually the shocks were entirely under the control of the experimenter and these subjects received shocks equal in number and duration to those administered to a control group of subjects, which was not led to believe they had any control over the shocks. The results showed that galvanic skin response, a measure assumed to reflect stress reaction, was lower in the condition in which subjects thought they had some control over the shock durations.

Averill (1973) has reviewed the conflicting state of evidence regarding the influence of having control. There is no clearcut basis for concluding that such control will lessen actual stress. In those cases in which it does seem to alleviate stress, it appears that a more important factor than control may be the reduction of the uncertainty of the stress. If a person receives shock from which escape is possible, stress will still occur. If these noxious events occur in a predictable as opposed to a random pattern, stress apparently is lower. The predictable pattern, having less uncertainty, may enable the person to prepare himself or herself for the inevitable onslaught. Such bracing is not possible with a random pattern, and such uncertainty may heighten the stressfulness.

Individual differences in stress reactions often occur. For example, Averill and Rosenn (1972) found reduced psychophysiological stress in most subjects who could avoid electric shocks by reacting quickly to a warning signal, but a sizable minority showed increased stress. One factor that may contribute to such differences is the way in which a stressor is interpreted by the individual. A passenger in an automobile accident might wish he or she had been driving, feeling that he or she could have averted the collision, whereas a different passenger may be thankful that someone else was driving and had to face the stress of trying to avoid the danger.

The operation of such cognitive factors is probably minimized in most laboratory studies, which often use electric shock as the stressor so that it would be unlikely for individuals to hold widely different appraisals of the significance of events.

The meaning of the response by which we control outcomes must also be considered. To run from danger may be a sign of cowardice in everyday life, whereas escape from electric shock in an experiment by discovering the correct switch is viewed as an index of intelligence. As Averill (1973, p. 301) observed, about the kinds of arbitrary responses assigned in experiments to serve as the correct means of avoiding stress, "Although such responses may be convenient from the experimenter's point of view, they probably have little inherent significance for the subject."

The type and amount of information or knowledge about an impending stressor may also serve as a means of cognitive control, which determines the level of experienced stress. Someone who is uncertain about the future may fear the worst, expecting consequences far worse than what actually lies in store. If so, information can act as a corrective and provide the individual with a truer picture. Even if the event is worse than expected, the information does remove uncertainty, which in itself is stressful, and may enable the person to mobilize adequate coping responses to deal with the threat.

Egbert, Battit, Welch, and Bartlett (1964), for example, found that surgery patients who were provided adequate information prior to surgery about the procedures and possible aftereffects showed faster recovery. Less anxiety may have occurred when postoperative reactions occurred for which proper forewarning had been provided.

Other Consequences of Powerlessness

The phenomenon of learned helplessness illustrates a situation in which certain previous experiences diminish the organism's capacity to initiate be-

havior that is appropriate to a given situation. These response deficits may
be described as motivational effects insofar as the behavior seems to be
within the ability of the organism but there is an apparent lack of incentive
to perform it.

INABILITY TO LEARN IN NEW SITUATIONS

In addition to this motivational impairment, Seligman also noted deficits
of both cognitive and emotional processes. If an organism first experiences
uncontrollable outcomes, there appears to be difficulty in recognizing later
outcomes due to their own efforts. Maier and Seligman (1976), in summarizing their work, noted that dogs that first had inescapable shock, followed by a period in which their jumping over a barrier led to successful
escape, would still revert to passive acceptance of shock in later trials.

Similarly, in experiments with humans in problem-solving tasks, Hiroto
and Seligman (1975) found a similar negative cognitive set induced by a
prior encounter with uncontrollable loud noises. This experience made the
subjects aware of their lack of control in that context. When the subjects
were given subsequent problems to solve, this prior negative expectancy impaired their ability to detect the contingencies between their responses and
the outcomes.

This example aptly illustrates a basic theme of this book. An individual's
behavior is more strongly influenced by his or her self-evaluation or subjective appraisal than by his or her real ability or capacity. A talented person
with a defeatist attitude will often be less successful than a less gifted person
who is confident.

DEPRESSION

Initial exposures to uncontrollable aversive stimuli in the learned helplessness situation creates heightened emotional reactions such as frantic struggling in the case of the dogs. Eventually, however, the emotional reaction
becomes subdued to the extent that it involves depression or a state of
apathetic indifference and inactivity, according to Seligman.

Thus, it might be conjectured that the despair and hopelessness of those
who continually face lack of control in their everyday lives may turn to
depression eventually. There should also be a lack of initiative or an attitude
of "what's the use of trying." Behavior that might be viewed as irrational
in some sense might also occur, reflecting the impairment of cognitive
processes by prolonged helplessness.

REAL-WORLD REACTIONS

In the laboratory experiments, the variety of available reactions to uncontrollable outcomes is limited. It is unlikely, for example, that the subjects can or will leave the situation or attack the experimenter either physically or verbally. In the real world, however, powerlessness can produce many different effects ranging from withdrawal to suicide and aggression at the individual level. At the societal level, the oppressed may be docile and apathetic under some conditions but hostile, belligerent, and intransigent under other circumstances.

The specific example from recent American history of the civil rights issue illustrates this point. The subjugation of blacks throughout most of this country's history certainly involves a state of prolonged helplessness for them. Passive acceptance of this state was for many decades the only alternative available. However, with the development of recent social changes that on the one hand improved their lot relative to the past but on the other hand created dissatisfaction with their status relative to white society, blacks developed other types of responses to their lack of control.

In the mid-1960s American society was plagued by numerous civil disturbances as increasing numbers of blacks became militant in their demands for social reform to ensure their civil rights. Confrontation with police often led to physical violence and large scale destruction of property.

Another example comes from working conditions on assembly lines in factories. These tedious mechanical jobs often prove unsatisfying to the worker with the possibility that forms of subtle sabotage, such as work slowdowns, absenteeism, and the production of faulty products, occur.

An even deadlier counterattack termed *fragging* (Linden, 1972) is made by enlisted soldiers who are otherwise powerless against the authority of tyrannical officers. Episodes have been reported in which an officer will apparently be killed accidentally by one of his own men or by a hand grenade from an unidentified source. The incidence of such fraggings increased dramatically during the Vietnam war and experts have attributed this increase to the futility and apparent meaninglessness of that conflict to many soldiers. As Linden phrased it, ". . . the grunts and rear-echelon draftees often feel that they are helpless, that they have no avenue of redress of grievances, that the structure of the Army is stacked against them, and that they were railroaded into Vietnam at a time when we have admitted it is a horrible mistake and are pulling out." In contrast, many of the officers who were victims of fragging were strict disciplinarians who enjoyed the combat as if it were a game.

The preceding examples might be judged irrational insofar as these actions often fail to solve the predicament and sometimes expose their perpetrators to even greater costs. In the case of the blacks, it might be their own community that is devastated by violence. The auto worker who is detected trying to sabotage the assembly line process may lose his or her job, and the soldier who commits fragging may be imprisoned. The risk of such negative consequences does not deter these irrational behaviors, because they may be the only perceived means that powerless individuals have for striking back at the boss, the company, or the system.

The Acquisition of Power

As long as individuals continue to feel helpless, they will continue to accept living under the control of external factors. How does one escape the doldrums of despair? What factors instigate the powerless to seek redress or overthrow forces that control them? Is there some point of no return beyond which those who are helpless become rebellious? Will a brief glimmer of hope be sufficient to motivate the downtrodden to rise up and fight the forces that control them?

One plausible source of evidence might lie in historical analyses of major social and political revolutions. Unfortunately, historical events are highly complex, and analyses of their causes are postdictive rather than predictive. They tell us why something happened *after* the event has occurred. Such analyses are often highly selective and biased siftings of evidence to identify those facts that are consistent with what happened. Often the same event has conflicting explanations, but it is not possible to conduct additional experiments to collect further evidence to help choose among rival accounts.

The causes of historical events cannot be limited to psychological factors, important as they are, but must also involve economic, political, social, and historical factors, for example. The particular complex of such factors responsible for a given political revolution may not operate for other revolutions, so that it may be difficult to formulate a theory of revolutions in general.

A PSYCHOLOGICAL ANALYSIS: RELATIVE DEPRIVATION

If we limit ourselves to the psychological level of analysis, one important concept is that of *relative deprivation*. This concept refers to feelings of dissatisfaction that arise from comparisons of one's own situation with that of certain other persons, usually similar to oneself in some relevant way. It appears that this state of dissatisfaction, relative deprivation, may be the essential psychological ingredient in activating the powerless to try to acquire greater control over outcomes affecting them.

In a classic study of American soldiers during World War II, Stouffer, Suchman, DeVinney, Star, and Williams (1949) observed that dissatisfaction over nonpromotion was less among the military police than among airmen. Inasmuch as promotion was relatively slow for military police, this finding seemed somewhat paradoxical. It was conjectured that the airmen, accustomed to expect rapid promotion, experienced greater frustration if they did not get promoted. On the other hand, the military police, relatively speaking, did not feel as deprived when not promoted because as a group they expected slow promotion rates.

The concept of relative deprivation requires that an individual make social comparisons between himself or herself and others in order to arrive at a judgment about his or her relative status or lack of it. Festinger (1954) formulated a more systematic model of the process of social comparison, which suggests that we restrict such comparisons to those who are similar to ourselves.

A state of relative deprivation should occur even if one's situation actually improves but there is even greater gain for those whom one considers it appropriate to compare oneself with. Comparisons of one's present status with one's prior condition may also engender relative deprivation, if the expectations based on past experiences are not reached. Thus, a worker who received gradually larger pay increases each year might still experience relative deprivation if the current increment was smaller than that of the past years.

Several theorists (Davies, 1969; Gurr, 1970; Runciman, 1966) have proposed broad accounts of the role of relative deprivation as a causal factor underlying social change and revolution. For instance, Davies has noted that revolutions have often occurred when a society has encountered economic setbacks after a period of prosperity has occurred. These types of broad interpretations entail much more than psychological factors and will not be considered here. A model of relative deprivation (Crosby, 1976) that is more amenable to our purposes is one that can be tested against evidence collected under better controlled conditions.

In her model Crosby first identified five preconditions necessary for the deprived person (e.g., a person lacking X). All five must be present if relative deprivation is to be experienced. (1) The individual must first notice that someone else has X. But this is not enough. (2) He or she must also desire X. (3) In addition, he or she must feel entitled to X. (4) He or she must also see it as feasible to obtain X. (5) Finally, according to Crosby, the person must not feel personally responsible for not having X.

Crosby regarded all of these preconditions as necessary factors before one feels deprived. Merely lacking X is not a sufficient basis for dissatisfaction. However, large differences in the extent to which relative deprivation occurs can still exist even under the same set of objective, external preconditions. Personality differences, recent past experiences with X, social factors, situational determinants, social values, and biological significance can affect the level of relative deprivation. Crosby cites a large number of studies, mostly dealing with worker productivity and satisfaction or with ethnic and social class differences in civil rights activism, that illustrate how these factors affect the level of relative deprivation. Although most of these studies were conducted without specific reference to the concept of relative deprivation, their findings can be applied usefully to Crosby's model.

Turning to the implications of relative deprivation for behavior, Crosby's model attempts to predict the factors leading to several alternative ways of coping with relative deprivation. Whether nonviolent or violent reactions against society occur or whether positive or negative reactions of an inward nature prevail depends, according to Crosby's model shown in Figure 5–2, on several factors.

First, a personality dimension of intro- versus extrapunitiveness is considered. Does a person tend to react to stress by keeping to oneself or does he or she tend to take it out on others? If he or she is intropunitive and opportunities to alleviate relative deprivation are blocked, the model suggests that he or she will suffer stress symptoms. If, however, some chance to

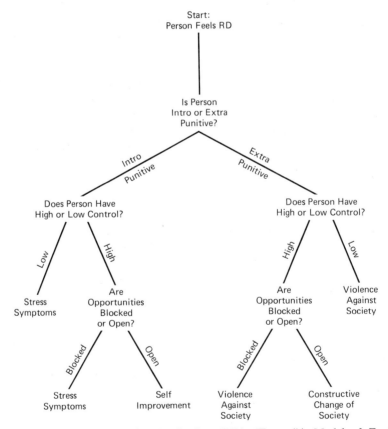

FIGURE 5–2. Results of relative deprivation (RD). [From "A Model of Egoistical Relative Deprivation" by F. Crosby, *Psychological Review,* 1976, *83,* 85–113. Copyright 1976 by the American Psychological Association. Reprinted by permission.]

eliminate the deprived condition is open, and the person has a high ability to control matters, the outcome may be that of some form of self-improvement.

On the other hand, suppose the individual is extrapunitive. If he or she lacks control, there may be use of violent measures under relative deprivation. Such violence may also occur in extrapunitive persons with high control when opportunities for redress are blocked. Finally, extrapunitive persons with high control may initiate constructive social reforms if the opportunities to do so are open.

Thus, there is no single response to the experience of relative deprivation, according to Crosby. It is necessary to at least consider the nature of the individual's personality (intro- versus extrapunitiveness), ability to control events (high or low), and situational factors (open versus blocked opportunity).

The postulation of additional factors that moderate the response to relative deprivation is a worthwhile aspect of Crosby's model. Although little direct evidence has been obtained to test these specific variables, the predictions can readily be evaluated empirically. The wide variability of predicted reactions to relative deprivation as a function of personal and situational factors again illustrates the importance of considering the cognitive appraisal of the individual in predicting his or her response under given circumstances. The same state of relative deprivation may lead to markedly divergent behavior in individuals who assess the situation differently. Social change may require that relative deprivation be experienced by some of those who are powerless, but such a condition is no guarantee that social change will be pursued or achieved.

A CASE HISTORY: THE BLACK MOVEMENT

A vivid example from our own recent history can be used to illustrate how an oppressed and relatively powerless group gradually created a major social revolution. The social status of blacks in America over the past twenty-five years or so has certainly undergone a major transition from a position of powerlessness to one that is more equitable.

A perspective on the situation can be gained by using Pettigrew's (1969) example of a twenty-year-old black male in 1968. When he was born, school segregation was widespread and generally unquestioned, but by the time he was six and entering school, *de jure* segregation had been outlawed. By the time he was nine, the Little Rock battles over school integration were being fought; when he was twelve, the sit-ins and nonviolent protests of Martin Luther King and his supporters had begun. He was fifteen at the time of the historic 1963 March on Washington for civil rights, and by the time he was seventeen a march was made in Selma, Alabama to protest the bombing of black churches, which had resulted in the killing of children.

Viewed in absolute terms, it might be argued that the conditions of life for blacks improved substantially during this period even though there was still much left to be desired. However, at the same time the lot of the white society was improving. The living conditions of blacks did not improve as rapidly as did those of whites. The fact that gains led to rising expectations coupled with the unfulfillment of them made matters worse for blacks. Relative deprivation, accompanied by societal blocking of avenues toward the elimination of such deprivation, eventually led to actions aimed at either reforming or destroying society. Crosby's model does not deal with variables such as social status but focuses on personality differences such as intro- and extrapunitiveness or high versus low control. Her model does suggest that the degree to which opportunities are blocked or opened will determine for some types of persons whether or not violent or constructive means will be used to change society.

The Paradox of Power

From what we have asserted about the destructive nature of powerlessness, one might conclude that powerfulness was the panacea and that those with power would be free to be creative, humane, and fulfilled. Although this potential may exist, power does not automatically bestow these blessings on its holders. As the old cliche goes, power corrupts, often bringing out the worst in terms of arrogance and snobbery.

Clark (1971) refers to the "pathos of power" in describing the situation in which the exercise and possession of power is ambiguous, arbitrary, or disproportionately intense and rigid in spite of consequences. His comments are directed primarily at social power, but also have implications for individual feelings of powerlessness. If those in power use it to interfere with the needs of others rather than to benefit them, the consequences are frequently disastrous, leading to intergroup tensions, violence, and aggression.

Those in power look with condescension toward the powerless. For example, the middle class members who have economic power regard themselves as virtuous self-made individuals and regard the members of the lower class as unmotivated and even immoral. This "arrogance of power" has been analyzed at the level of international relations between our government and the world by Senator Fulbright (1966). In the case of foreign aid, as in any donor-recipient relationship, the donor may adopt a "stronger than thou" attitude. In turn, this posture creates resentment in the recipient, especially because the lending nation expects servitude and deference in return, not to mention economic or military favors such as favorable trade agreements or military bases.

Evidence based on interviews with foreign aid officials of poor countries that receive aid confirms these views (Gergen and Gergen, 1974). Suspicion of the donor's motives is widespread, and this factor affects the attitudes of the recipients. The success of foreign aid appears to depend in large measure on the extent to which the recipient is allowed to maintain its self-esteem and save its face. As Gergen and Gergen note, "Dollars are not simply dollars; they carry a host of implications for the recipient's self-esteem, feelings of obligation, and evaluation of us as donors."

Although each situation has unique features, certain similarities exist in relationships between two parties, one with power relative to the other, whether it be parent-child, black-white, student-teacher, man-woman, young-old, rich-poor, etc. For example, DeCharms (1970) has discussed the problems of motivation in the classroom. He has been attempting to find ways to develop the feeling of internal motivation among students in elementary schools. In the usual student-teacher relationship the student is treated as a pawn who is externally controlled, whereas the teacher is perceived as the origin. In order to teach the teachers how to help the students become origins rather than pawns so that they would feel more internally controlled, a paradoxical situation exists for the psychologist. If the psychologist comes into the school system as the expert and treats the teachers as pawns, he or she is apt to provoke defensiveness and resentment from the teachers.

The strategy employed by DeCharms (1972) in his field experiment with an inner city black school was to respect the teachers as origins on the assumption that only by this means could they in turn effectively encourage the development of origin feelings in their own students. Thus, the teachers who received training did not receive indoctrination from the expert psychologist about how to motivate the children. Instead each teacher helped the psychologist develop techniques based on his or her classroom experience, which he or she then applied to the students. Teachers were excited and highly cooperative. They were not threatened by the expert who did not treat them as pawns by telling them exactly what to do. If such had been the case, the power of the expert, paradoxically, would probably have created a barrier and restricted the influence of this power in the sense that the teachers would have resisted suggestions.

Students with teachers who had received origin training were presumably also encouraged to be origins by their teachers. Scores on projective story tests for these students suggested that they had more internal control and feelings of self-confidence and personal responsibility. Furthermore, as can be seen in Figure 5–3, they also had higher scores on a standardized academic achievement test than did untrained students in sixth and seventh grade classes. It should also be noted that untrained students in the school district in which this study was conducted tend to fall further behind national norms with each successive year. In contrast, the trained students who learned to be origins showed stabilization of their achievement scores relative to such norms.

The findings of this study along with those described earlier are consistent with the view that subjective feelings in some dimension of personal power

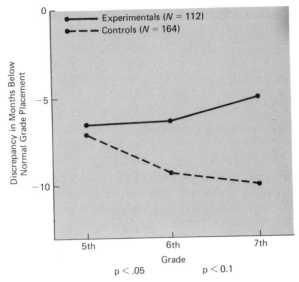

FIGURE 5–3.   Mean discrepancy in months from normal grade placement on the composite Iowa Test of Basic Skills. [From "Personal Causation Training in the Schools" by R. DeCharms, *Journal of Applied Social Psychology,* 1972, 2, 95–113. Copyright 1972 by Scripta Publishing Company. Reprinted by permission.]

such as internal versus external locus of control or origin-pawn are important determinants of behavior. The individual who thinks he or she can do something, just like *The Little Engine That Could,* can achieve some formidable feats. Those with defeatist attitudes, on the other hand, seem to contribute to their own inadequacies. The important task is to discover methods of breaking this vicious circle and redirecting cognitive orientations of the powerless so that they too can control their outcomes.

Summary

   The subjective feeling of control, or the lack of it, is an important experience that may influence our behavior. Loss of hope and the feeling that one's life is under the external control of other persons or factors such as luck may sometimes lead to withdrawal, apathy, and lack of effort. Behavior that may appear irrational or deviant to others is often the consequence of the feeling of powerlessness.

   Rotter's concept of internal versus external locus of control of reinforcement assumes that past reinforcement histories of success and failure are responsible for an individual's perceived level of control of his or her own life. Studies were cited that provide some support for Rotter's view that individual differences in such perceptions are correlated with variations in behavior.

The concept of learned helplessness, developed by Seligman, is a related idea that suggests that the repeated inability to influence outcomes will instill a state of passivity in an organism. When confronted with situations requiring the individual to acquire some response in order to escape danger, for example, the helpless individual will not try or will readily give up. Seligman maintains that a cognitive view of this phenomenon rather than a physiological or neurochemical account is more tenable. Prior experience with helplessness is assumed to create an expectancy of lack of control, which can generalize to a variety of other situations. Learned helplessness also weakens motivation to perform as well as creates emotional disruption that may eventually become depression.

When an individual does control outcomes, behavior is more efficient. However, control of outcomes does not always imply lowered stress, per se. One factor may be the increased stress created by the vigilance, responsibility, and decision making required when it is possible for the individual to control outcomes. In addition, the definition of what represents stress may vary with individuals, depending on the nature of each person's cognitive assessment of the meaning of the situation and his or her appraisal of the means for coping with it.

Relative deprivation is a concept that may be useful in accounting for the process by which previously powerless groups or individuals break out of the apathy and indifference of this condition. Social comparison among individuals is a natural process. When such comparison reveals that similar persons are better off than oneself is, a state of relative deprivation may arise. It is also assumed, among other things, that one envies the better condition of other persons and wants to achieve that status.

In Crosby's model of relative deprivation, personality factors and the degree of opportunity for gaining the desired state play important roles in determining the actual responses made under relative deprivation. The recent history of the black movement in the United States was used to illustrate how relative deprivation might account for the transition of a very powerless group to one that is highly active and successful in achieving gains in all aspects of living conditions.

Finally, a brief consideration was made of some of the adverse effects of power. It does not follow that power is good because lack of power is bad. Those with power are often arrogant and deal with the powerless in a contemptuous and demeaning manner. Such attitudes may paradoxically topple the powerful from their lofty status in the long run.

References

ADLER, A. The psychology of power. *Journal of Individual Psychology,* 1966, *22,* 166–172.

ANISMAN, H., and WALLER, T. G. Effects of inescapable shock on subsequent avoidance performance: Role of response repetoire changes *Behavioral Biology,* 1973, *9,* 331–355.

AVERILL, J. R. Personal control over aversive stimuli and its relationship to stress. *Psychological Bulletin,* 1973, *80,* 286–303.

———, and ROSENN, M. Vigilant and nonvigilant coping strategies in stress reactions during the anticipation of electric shock. *Journal of Personality and Social Psychology,* 1972, *23,* 128–141.

BATTLE, E., and ROTTER, J. B. Children's feelings of personal control as related to social class and ethnic groups. *Journal of Personality,* 1963, *31,* 482–490.

BRACEWELL, R. J., and BLACK, A. H. The effects of restraint and noncontingent pre-shock on subsequent escape learning in the rat. *Learning and Motivation,* 1974, *5,* 53–69.

CLARK, K. B. The pathos of power: A psychological perspective. *American Psychologist,* 1971, *26,* 1047–1057.

COLLINS, B. E. Four components of the Rotter I-E Scale: Belief in a difficult world, a just world, a predictable world, and a politically responsive world. *Journal of Personality and Social Psychology,* 1974, *29,* 381–391.

CRANDALL, V. C., KATKOVSKY, W., and CRANDALL, V. J. Children's beliefs in their own control of reinforcement in intellectual-academic achievement situations. *Child Development,* 1965, *36,* 91–109.

CROSBY, F. A model of egoistical relative deprivation. *Psychological Review,* 1976, *83,* 85–113.

DAVIES, J. C. The J-curve of rising and declining satisfactions as a cause of some great revolutions and a contained rebellion. In H. D. Graham and T. R. Gurr (Eds.), *Violence in America.* New York: Signet, 1969.

DeCHARMS, R. Personal causation training in the schools. *Journal of Applied Social Psychology,* 1972, *2,* 95–113.

EGBERT, L. D., BATTIT, G. E., WELCH, C. E., and BARTLETT, M. K. Reduction of postoperative pain by encouragement and instruction of patients. *New England Journal of Medicine,* 1964, *270,* 825–827.

Festinger, L. A theory of social comparison. *Human Relations,* 1954, *7,* 117–140.

FULBRIGHT, J. W. *The arrogance of power.* New York: Vintage, 1966.

GEER, J. H., DAVISON, G. C., and GATCHEL, R. I. Reduction of stress in humans through nonveridical perceived control of aversive stimulation. *Journal of Personality and Social Psychology,* 1970, *16,* 731–738.

GERGEN, K. J., and GERGEN, M. M. What other nations hear when the eagle screams. *Psychology Today,* 1974, *8,* June, 52–58.

GLASS, D. C., SINGER, J. E., and FRIEDMAN, L. N. Psychic cost of adaptation to an environmental stressor. *Journal of Personality and Social Psychology,* 1969, *12,* 200–210.

GORE, P., and ROTTER, J. B. A personality correlate of social action. *Journal of Personality,* 1963, *31,* 58–64.

GURIN, P., GURIN, G., LAO, R., and BEATTIE, M. Internal-external control in the motivational dynamics of Negro youth. *Journal of Social Issues,* 1969, *25,* 29–53.

GURR, T. G. *Why men rebel.* Princeton, N.J.: Princeton University Press, 1970.

HIROTO, D. S. Locus of control and learned helplessness. *Journal of Experimental Psychology,* 1974, *102,* 187–193.

———, and SELIGMAN, M. E. P. Generality of learned helplessness in man. *Journal of Personality and Social Psychology,* 1975, *31,* 311–327.

LAO, R. C. Internal-external control and competent and innovative behavior among Negro college students. *Journal of Personality and Social Psychology,* 1970, *14,* 263–270.

LEFCOURT, H. M. Recent developments in the study of the locus of control In

B. A. Maher (Ed.), *Progress in experimental personality research.* New York: Academic, 1972.

LINDEN, E. The demoralization of an Army. Fragging and other withdrawal symptoms. *Saturday Review,* Jan. 8, 1972, 12–17; 55.

MAIER, S. F., and SELIGMAN, M. E. P. Learned helplessness: Theory and evidence. *Journal of Experimental Psychology: General,* 1976, *105,* 3–46.

MILLER, W., and WEISS, J. M. Effects of somatic or visceral responses to punishment. In B. A. Campbell and R. M. Church (Eds.) *Punishment and aversive behavior.* New York: Appleton, 1969.

OVERMEIR, J. B., and SELIGMAN, M. E. P. Effects of inescapable shock upon subsequent escape and avoidance learning. *Journal of Comparative and Physiological Psychology,* 1967, *63,* 28–33.

PETTIGREW, T. F. Racially separate or together. *Journal of Social Issues,* 1969, *25,* 43–69.

ROTTER, J. B. *Social learning and clinical psychology.* Englewood Cliffs, N.J.: Prentice-Hall, 1954.

————. Generalized expectancies for internal versus external control of reinforcement. *Psychological Monographs,* 1966, *80* (1, Whole No. 609).

RUNCIMAN, W. G. *Relative deprivation and social justice: A study of attitudes to social inequality in twentieth-century England.* Berkeley: University of California Press, 1966.

SCHMALE, A., and IKER, H. The psychological setting of uterine cervical cancer. *Annals of the New York Academy of Sciences,* 1966, *125,* 807–813.

SELIGMAN, M. E. P. Chronic fear produced by unpredictable electric shock. *Journal of Comparative Physiological Psychology,* 1968, *66,* 402–411.

————. Submissive death: Giving up on life. *Psychology Today,* 1974, *7,* (12) 80–85.

————. *Helplessness. On depression, development, and death.* San Francisco: Freeman, 1975.

————, and MAIER, S. F. Failure to escape traumatic shock. *Journal of Experimental Psychology,* 1967, *74,* 1–9.

STOUFFER, S. A., SUCHMAN, E. A., DEVINNEY, L. C., STAR, S. A., and WILLIAMS, R. M. *The American Soldier: Adjustment during Army life.* (Vol. 1). Princeton, N.J.: Princeton University Press, 1949.

PART THREE

SOME SPECIFIC MOTIVES

CHAPTER 6

Individual Motivation: Achievement

Most of our behaviors are generally evaluated or judged against some criterion of quality or excellence of performance. We are not content merely to perform tasks, but rather we strive for certain standards of mastery, accomplishment, and achievement in doing them. The musician, just like the athlete or craftsman, practices in order to attain some ideal state of perfection.

Some of the incentive for the dedicated pursuit of achievement comes from social factors such as prestige, and the recognition and admiration of other people. It should be noted that such admiration frequently comes from people who themselves value and might wish to achieve equal feats. Their acclaim and the admiration of those who are successful is one indication that society values such accomplishments. In addition to social factors, achievement is also rewarded by motivators such as money and other material benefits.

However, even if these extrinsic sources of gratification were unavailable, it could be argued that humans are capable of receiving satisfaction from the successful accomplishment of tasks without regard to the external consequences. Few of us are satisfied with failure or mediocre levels of accomplishment; rather we continually strive to achieve at high levels. The pride of accomplishment must serve as an intrinsic reward, which motivates behavior in and of itself. By pride, we are referring to the gratification one experiences when one realizes one's potentials by scaling new and greater heights of performance, whether it be in the climbing of a mountain, the writing of a poem, or the making of a great scientific discovery. Of course, excess pride may turn to arrogance, and, as the classical Greek playwrights cautioned, such hubris may be the tragic cause of an individual's downfall. Our use of pride here is restricted to the feelings of satisfaction that accompany the successful completion of challenging tasks.

Attainment of these goals is considered to be intrinsically rewarding, but it is not always apparent that such is the case because successful achievements are also generally followed by extrinsic rewards such as social approval or material rewards. Even if these extrinsic rewards are not primary factors leading the individual to take risks in pursuing achievement tasks, they are consequences that must eventually affect subsequent motivation.

Consider academic motivation. We like to think of the scholar as being engaged in intellectual pursuit because of an intrinsic interest in solving a problem. We assume that a sort of intellectual Mount Everest exists and challenges the scholar. Similarly, we often assume that the student will be motivated by the sheer intellectual beauty of the problem. The scholar is affected by the lure of fame and a small merit raise in addition to his or her quest for knowledge. In the same way the student is as much concerned with the grade he or she will receive, if not more so, than with the intellectual challenge. Some students will readily admit that the grade is all that they are concerned about and that they will work only as much or as little as needed in order to get the desired grade.

In view of this predicament it is difficult to test adequately the view that some behaviors are performed solely for intrinsic reasons. Perhaps the best place to look for human behavior that is relatively unaffected by the influence of extrinsic motives would be in the behavior of young infants: This analysis offers some clearer instances of the intrinsic motivation inherent in the development and mastery of new skills. Thus, infants will persist in simple motor tasks such as swatting a mobile, climbing stairs, or spoon feeding themselves. Despite frequent frustration and failure, the young infant generally perseveres to achieve new levels of mastery. Such ambitious endeavors are not undertaken without frequent crying and whining, as most parents will attest, but it all seems worthwhile when success is accomplished. Even if the parents did not offer encouragement and approval, for many parents do not, the infant will nevertheless pursue the attainment of competence in mastering the complexities of coping with his or her environment.

Play and the Development of Achievement Motivation

INTRINSIC ASPECTS OF PLAY

All forms of play might be regarded as intrinsically motivated. Whereas, the term *work* carries the connotation of serious and productive effort, *play* generally conveys the impression of frivolous, useless, or nonproductive activity. This unfortunate distinction is based primarily on the fact that activities that are considered to be work involve extrinsic rewards, such as money, *but* those activities that are regarded as play do not. Yet, the activity itself cannot be judged as being work or play without considering whether it is done for its own sake or for some reward. Thus, essentially the same behavior, such as singing a song or playing football, is viewed as play when done for fun only, but is considered work when a salary is involved.

An alternative view of play emphasizes its role in the mastery and attainment of new levels of competence. The infant who plays with mechanical toys is acquiring perceptual motor skills, which will be useful in coping with environmental demands. A child who learns to talk is playing with sounds while achieving new levels of linguistic ability In contrast, many forms of work involve little or no intrinsic incentive and are performed primarily for extrinsic rewards such as money.

Play, then, is not useless or trivial but essential to the growth and development of the child. It has been regarded as preparation for the roles of adulthood, as can well be illustrated by some forms of play in which children imitate adult roles. Less obvious in function, perhaps, are fantasy and make-believe through which the child experiences cognitive and emotional growth. Through play, the child learns about the nature of physical, social, and moral reality. Play also provides opportunities for the child to become aware of and learn to deal with emotions, such as fears, anxieties, and frustrations.

One of the salient characteristics of play that has been noted by many observers of children is its highly repetitive nature. Although both Freud and Piaget considered repetition an important aspect of play activities, their theoretical interpretations were different in some respects. Piaget regarded repetition as an example of "practice makes perfect," so that it served as the means by which the child formed new concepts and response patterns termed *schemas*. The degree of repetition exhibited by children in mastering new skills might appear excessive to the observing adult, but this apparent overlearning is assumed to be necessary to ensure the assimilation of new cognitive developments by the child.

Freud places more emphasis on the emotional consequences of what he called the repetition compulsion. Repetition, by leading to mastery of a problem, was a means of reducing anxiety and tension. Pleasure may also be derived from repeated execution of well-learned behaviors, as can be seen by the occurrence of many ritualistic forms of behavior throughout life. Despite different emphases, Freud and Piaget both recognized the importance of the repetitive nature of play in enabling the child to achieve mastery. This is not to say that the child is aware of the future benefits of play. As far as the child is concerned, play is an activity for its own sake, so to speak. Play is interesting to the child, because it offers him or her activities to master.

One of the most significant consequences achieved through the young infant's play is the realization that one is able to act as a causal agent. This important discovery of cognitive development comes from the frequent association between certain responses of the infant and their consequences. The infant forms expectancies about the future and learns that his or her own behavior can be a cause of certain consequences. To use Rotter's internal and external control of reinforcement ideas discussed in the previous chapter, the child is learning to be an internal in the I-E dimension. The child comes to believe that he or she is able to influence and control the environment, albeit to a limited extent.

With the development of causality experiences and cognitions somewhere near the midpoint of the first year, it is then possible to speak of intentionality on the part of the infant. Being able to anticipate consequences of actions, an infant may deliberately choose to make a certain response, because he or she knows what the consequences will be. Although Piaget's (1952) concepts about the development of causality and intentionality are speculative, they suggest the crucial role that playful activities serve. By playing with a mobile, for example, the infant may learn that it is his or her own arm movement that is causing the mobile to move. At first, the infant may not believe his or her own power and may decide to test the hypothesis by reaching out again and swinging at the mobile to double check. Of course, this description is somewhat speculative, but it should serve to convey the process by which the infant acquires the beginnings of the awareness of its ability to affect the environment.

EXTRINSIC ASPECTS OF PLAY

Although play is uncontaminated by extrinsic motivation in the very young infant, by the time he or she forms social attachments in the last half of the first year the approval or disapproval of other persons begins to play an increasingly greater role in the motives for various activities. Even young infants quickly learn to do the things that produce the greatest smile, laughter, or edible rewards from adults.

Furthermore, with increasing age, a child comes to realize that society places importance not so much on what an individual can do but on how well he or she does it relative to other persons. As an infant, it was sufficient that the child learn to walk, run, talk, etc., but, as he or she gets older, other people such as parents take these accomplishments for granted. Now they take pride only if his or her skills are outstanding relative to those of his or her peers. It is not a question of whether or not the child can run, but can he or she run the fastest? It is not a question of whether or not the child can read, but can he or she get the highest score on the reading test? In other words, evaluation of achievement gradually is shifted from absolute criteria to relative ones in which one's performance is compared with or pitted against that of others. Achievement now involves competition against others rather than against some fixed standard or one's own previous accomplishments. The importance attached to competitive achievement can hardly be overstated, because it is often a prime factor in many spheres of life, such as business, sports, and academics.

Whereas the young child is praised if he or she can insert the round and square shapes into the correct openings of a toy, the older child receives approval only if he or she can do it faster than everyone else. The older child is taught games that involve competition and produce winners and losers. The male child, in particular, is encouraged to engage in sports activity, which also places a premium on winning and not merely on playing the game for fun. Play, then, is increasingly affected by extrinsic rewards and punishments until the goal of winning becomes more important than the play itself. The legendary professional football coach, Vince Lombardi, aptly described the situation thusly, "Winning is not everything. It's the only thing."

During his brief service as Vice President, Gerald Ford, who himself was an outstanding college athlete, made these observations (Ford, 1974) about the significance of competition, ". . . competing is always preferable to not competing, whether you win or not." He regards "few things more important to a country's growth and well-being than competitive athletics" because, in his words, ". . . athletics as in most other worthwhile pursuits, first place is the manifestation of the desire to excel, and how else can you achieve anything?"

Thus, competition is prized, because it is thought to bring out optimal effort among competitors. Greater pressure and tension is often generated by competitive situations, but it is questionable whether it always brings out the best performance. Performance can also be disrupted, when arousal is too great. In athletics, the pressure of competition is often the cause of choking up, such that performers do less well than they are capable of achieving.

Winners of competitions receive the glory, admiration, and attention, but what are the effects of losing on subsequent motivation and performance? Losers not only fail to win trophies and awards, but also lose self-esteem and self-confidence. Because there must invariably be more losers than winners, an evaluation of the effects of competition must direct more attention to the possible harmful effects of defeat on losers, especially repeated losers.

Losers are rejected and avoided by the majority for as we all know, "everyone loves a winner." Therefore, it is not surprising that the pressure to win at all costs sometimes leads to cheating and other fraudulent practices to achieve victory.

Academic success in the form of high grades often assumes greater significance than actual learning. Students realize that professional success depends on going to a reputable graduate school, which in turn depends on high undergraduate grades. Hard work and diligent study sometimes are insufficient to enable a student to attain academic success, and large scale cheating is often the result.

Similar pressures abound in all other areas of achievement. Two recent instances in the field of science received substantial publicity in 1974. An investigator at a prestigious research laboratory claimed to have been able to graft skin from black rats to white rats. Photographs of rats with both black and white spots were available as evidence, but when other investigators were unable to replicate the findings, suspicions were aroused. It turned out that the ambitious investigator had merely painted black spots on white rats and had tried to pass them off as evidence for his accomplishment (*New York Times,* April 18, 1974).

A few months later it was reported (*Time,* August 26, 1974) that the director of an important laboratory on extrasensory phenomena had manipulated equipment to produce data that suggested the existence of psychokinesis in rats. This incident was unrelated to the first, but they are similar in that the apparent motives to commit fraudulent and unethical deeds stemmed from the tremendous pressures to publish new discoveries. Of course, competition for prestige and advancement can be a positive factor, which can motivate investigators. An example of this situation is described by Watson (1968) who reports the case history of the attempts to develop a model of DNA-RNA genetic codes. But in the two examples described here, the same pressures ended in tragedy because deception and fraud were committed in hopes of advancement and fame. Scientific achievements involve a considerable amount of intrinsic motivation or disinterested curiosity, but extrinsic factors such as recognition and acclaim also play significant roles.

INTRINSIC AND EXTRINSIC COMPONENTS OF ADULT BEHAVIOR

Since most human activity is affected by a combination of intrinsic and extrinsic rewards or incentives, it would be difficult, if not impossible, to study the effects of each type of motive separately, except in the youngest of infants. However, a major research program of over thirty years has been carried on by David McClelland and John Atkinson and their associates to examine the intrinsic motivation present in risk taking and achievement behavior. These investigators feel that extrinsic motives are minimal in their laboratory tests of the factors underlying human achievement-oriented behavior in risk-taking situations. Aside from personality factors that are also involved, they regard aspects of the task itself to hold intrinsic motivation. A factor such as task difficulty, for example, is an important determinant of motivation for achievement against some standard of performance. In using the term *intrinsic,* achievement motivation theorists are not referring to qualitative aspects of the task but rather to the level of incentive associated with tasks as a function of their expected difficulty. It is assumed that incentive and difficulty are directly related such that the more incentive that is present, the more difficult the task is.

This definition of the intrinsic features of a task is quite different from that which is found in studies of motivation in industrial or work situations that will be discussed in detail in the next chapter. Our present concern will be the kind of achievement emphasized in laboratory studies in which extrinsic factors such as pay, promotion, and fringe benefits are not involved. However, even in the case of laboratory studies of achievement motivation, it is not possible to rule out completely the existence of some minimal levels of extrinsic motivation such as social approval, or at least, the desire to cooperate with the experimenter's instructions. Hope or expectancy of extrinsic rewards in the future if one performs well on an immediate task with no apparent rewards other than intrinsic ones may also influence achievement performance.

Once a new level of performance is achieved, most individuals are not content to rest on their laurels. Given an opportunity, some people would not feel satisfaction in merely repeating the tasks they had previously mastered but would seek the excitement and challenge of even higher hurdles. Continued performance of now routine and simple tasks is boring and provides no satisfaction, whereas new challenges continue to provide a source of motivation to many individuals.

Of course, some element of risk is involved whenever one undertakes a more difficult task, charts an unplotted course, or becomes a trailblazing pioneer. The safe and comfortable solution is to stick to the tried-and-true; but this approach denies one the opportunity for the excitement of attempting the achievement of new goals. The avoidance of risk, however, also protects one from exposure to the failure, shame, or embarrassment that may occur if one fails to succeed. Uncertainty of outcomes in new situations, then, may be a key factor in risk situations and affect an individual's decision to take the safe or the risky alternative.

The concept of *competence* has been proposed by Robert White (1959). Competence is relevant to the present discussion, because it refers to the idea that a central motive underlying behavior is to provide the organism with the capacity to interact effectively with the demands of the environment. Unlike biologically based models of motivation in which the goal is seen as the maintenance of homeostatic equilibrium, the concept of competence suggests that behavior is motivated toward growth or the acquisition of an ever increasing repertoire of behaviors that enable the individual to deal successfully with the environmental events it will encounter.

Competence motivation is regarded as an intrinsic aspect of living organisms; it does not require extrinsic rewards or incentives. The curiosity and exploratory behavior of young organisms, for example, is not taught. These tendencies are *intrinsic;* they serve to provide the young with opportunities to learn about the environment and how to cope successfully with it. In a sense, the state of competence is the very opposite of the condition of helplessness or powerlessness discussed in the preceding chapter. The two constructs might be viewed as the two extremes of a dimension—a dimension that reflects the relative control of the individual versus the environment.

The Atkinson-McClelland Formal Model of Achievement Motivation

The achievement motivation theory developed primarily by John Atkinson and David McClelland (Atkinson, 1957; McClelland et al., 1953) is a detailed and analytical model that attempts to quantify the contribution of several factors toward achievement-oriented activity. In the formulation proposed by Atkinson (1957), two factors involve the characteristics of the individual and two factors deal with the properties of the task to be accomplished. Working together, these four factors are postulated to be the major determinants of risk-taking achievement in a given task.

MEASUREMENT OF MOTIVES

The two dispositional or personality factors, need for achievement (n Ach) and anxiety over failure, are assumed to be relatively stable and long lasting. The Thematic Apperception Test (TAT), a series of pictures of ambiguous scenes involving one or more persons, is used to assess the n Ach of an individual. The person is asked to make up a story describing what is happening in each stimulus picture in this projective test.

The basic assumption underlying this approach is that fantasies and imaginary stories will provide clearer information about a person's needs than will some more direct approach. Whereas direct verbal interrogation is limited due to factors such as lack of awareness or a reluctance to divulge some types of feelings, it is assumed that techniques based on fantasy permit unconscious feelings and needs to express themselves more fully. The content of the stories is scored for achievement imagery or themes reflecting striving and risk taking.

The second trait, anxiety over failure, is measured with a paper and pencil inventory known as the Test Anxiety Questionnaire (Mandler and Sarason, 1956), which measures anxiety over evaluation in situations such as midterm examinations.

DEFINITION OF BASIC TERMS

Major attention has been directed toward two types of individuals depicted in Table 6–1, those who were high in one dimension but low in the other one. One such type is high in the need for achievement but low in anxiety over failure. These individuals were assumed to have a high motive for success achievement (M_S) but a low motive to avoid failure (M_{AF}). The other extreme type is the person who is low in M_S but high in M_{AF}. These individuals were dominated by their anxiety, whereas the other type had an excess of the motive to achieve.

Psychologists have focused on the study of achievement motivation in these two extreme types, because individuals who possessed the two traits in roughly equal amounts would have offsetting qualities, since M_S and M_{AF} work against each other. Individuals with High n Ach were expected to show achievement-oriented activity, because their anxiety over failure was relatively small. But Low n Ach individuals were predicted to engage in little or no achievement activity due to lack of n Ach and to the presence of substantial anxiety about failure.

TABLE 6–1. Two Main Types of Individuals in Achievement Motivation Research.

Type	Need for Achievement Level	Anxiety over Failure Level
$M_S > M_{AF}$	High	Low
$M_{AF} > M_S$	Low	High

In addition to these two personality factors, two situational or task variables must be considered. The expected probability of success on the task (P_S), which refers to the subjective or perceived difficulty of the task, is one determinant of risk taking. To be sure, this expectancy could be determined by an individual's own abilities, but the typical procedure used in experimental tests has minimized this influence. Fake norms concerning past performance of other samples were used to induce different expectancies about the difficulty levels of tasks offered to subjects.

The second task factor affecting performance is task incentive for success (I_S), which refers to the intrinsic interest each task holds for a subject. Note carefully that I_S refers to motivating aspects of the task difficulty level, per se, and not to the content of the task, which might be regarded as yet another determinant of intrinsic incentive, one the theory ignores.

In Atkinson's formulation, I_S was defined in relationship to task difficulty. To be specific, I_S was assumed high when task difficulty was high; when the task was easy, I_S would be low. Atkinson argued that very difficult tasks should hold high incentive since everyone would consider it quite an accomplishment to succeed where everyone or almost all had failed previously. But a very easy task, on the other hand, should contain little incentive. There is little satisfaction to be gained if one succeeds in a task that almost everyone can do. In fact, there is also the risk of great embarrassment if one should happen to fail.

THE ORIGINAL FORMAL MODEL

Atkinson (1957) provided precise equations summarizing the relationship of the described factors to achievement tendency. The tendency for success (T_S) and the tendency to avoid failure (T_{AF}) each refer to a hypothetical potential. Each factor has three determinants, one that is a function of the individual and two that deal with the task. The factor T_S is the product of these three factors, $M_S \times P_S \times I_S$, so that whichever task leads to the highest combination of these three factors will be the one that offers the highest opportunity for achievement.

In a similar manner, three factors are postulated to determine T_{AF}, which is a tendency not to undertake achievement risks. A parallel equation linking the three factors is: $T_{AF} = M_{AF} \times P_F \times I_F$. The combination of these factors determines the overall tendency for avoiding achievement-oriented tasks.

Next, Atkinson combines these opposed potentials, T_S and T_{AF}, to derive his final prediction based on the resultant difference, $T_S - T_{AF}$. If the tendency to achieve exceeds the tendency to avoid it ($T_S > T_{AF}$), we end up with risk-taking achievement, but if the opposite situation exists ($T_S < T_{AF}$), we will not observe achievement-oriented behavior.

The model (see Figure 6–1) further predicts that when $M_S > M_{AF}$, there will be a preference for tasks of intermediate difficulty level, those near .5 P_S, whereas those tasks at either extreme, such as .1 or .9, will be avoided. It is not surprising to expect these subjects seeking achievement to avoid very easy tasks (.9), but it may seem odd that they would not attempt very difficult (.1) tasks. The explanation lies in the fact that High n Ach subjects

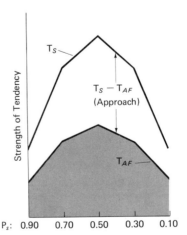

P_s: 0.90   0.70   0.50   0.30   0.10

FIGURE 6–1.   Resultant achievement-oriented tendency ($T_S - T_{AF}$) when the motive to achieve is dominant in the individual, i.e., $M_S > M_{AF}$. [From "The Mainsprings of Achievement Motivation," by J. W. Atkinson, in *Learning and the Educational Process* by J. D. Krumboltz (Ed.), Skokie, Ill.: Rand McNally, 1965. Copyright 1965 by Rand McNally. Reprinted by permission.]

are realistic; although they would like to succeed on very difficult tasks, they realize that it is improbable. Since successful achievement is desired, these subjects realize they would be better off with realistic choices, where success is more probable, and thus avoid very difficult tasks.

In contrast, when the individual's M_{AF} exceeds M_S, the situation is just the opposite, such that moderate difficulty tasks (.5) are avoided, and the very easy (.9) or very difficult (.1) tasks are selected, according to the model. Actually, there should be a reluctance for the Low n Ach subject to engage in even these tasks, because the anxiety about failure is dominant. However, inasmuch as there is invariably some form of *extrinsic* motivation in the situation, defined by Atkinson as social approval, instructions from an authority, or plain curiosity, some attempt to engage in achievement-oriented activity will occur. The tasks that will be least resisted, according to the model (see Figure 6–2) are the very easy or very difficult ones.

Again, we have no problem understanding why an individual who fears failure would select the very easy (.9) task, but why would he or she also be inclined to choose the very high difficult one (.1)? Atkinson (1957) holds that although failure is likely to occur, it is *sure* failure and consequently less anxiety will be aroused. If you know for sure that you are going to lose, you do not tend to get your hopes up, nor is the outcome uncertain. If there is anything the Low n Ach individual cannot tolerate, it is uncertainty. This same factor is assumed to be responsible for the avoidance of moderately difficult tasks (.5) by the Low n Ach person. There is too much uncertainty involved here; it is a 50–50 chance that success or failure will occur and this situation generates too much anxiety.

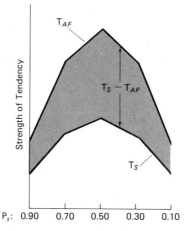

FIGURE 6–2. Resultant achievement-oriented tendency $(T_S - T_{AF})$ when the motive to avoid failure is dominant in the individual, $M_S < M_{AF}$. [From "The Mainsprings of Achievement Motivation" by J. W. Atkinson, in *Learning and the Educational Process,* by J. D. Krumboltz (Ed.), Skokie, Ill.: Rand McNally, 1965. Copyright 1965 by Rand McNally. Reprinted by permission.]

EXPERIMENTAL VERIFICATION

In laboratory tests (e.g., Atkinson and Litwin, 1960; McClelland, 1958) of the theory's predictions, a commonly used procedure has been to have subjects play a ring toss game in which they choose the distance, between one and fifteen feet, from the goal that they feel is appropriate for themselves to stand. As expected, High n Ach subjects prefer intermediate distances relative to the Low n Ach subjects, who select very small or large distances from the goal as shown in Figure 6–3.

Another type of situation has been to examine reactions to continued failure. Feather (1961) gave subjects an unsolvable mental problem, which he described to them as being either very easy or very difficult. They were told that if they wished to, at any time, they could switch to an alternate task. The question of interest was whether individual differences in persistence with the unsolvable first problem will be related to differences in n Ach.

Since the achievement motivation theory assumes that High n Ach subjects prefer intermediate difficulty level tasks, it was predicted that continued failure on a difficult task would lead to the expectancy that the task was

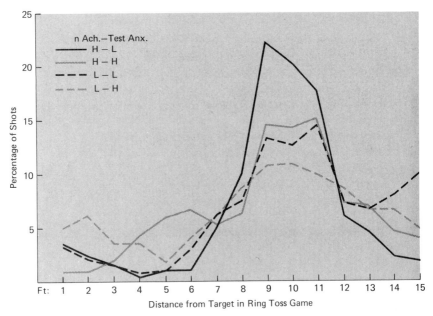

FIGURE 6–3. Percentage of shots taken from each line for subjects classified as high or low simultaneously in need achievement and test anxiety. [From "Achievement motive and test anxiety conceived as motive to approach success and motive to avoid failure," by J. W. Atkinson and G. H. Litwin, *Journal of Abnormal and Social Psychology,* 1960, *60,* 52–63. Copyright 1960 by the American Psychological Association. Reprinted by permission.]

indeed extraordinary in difficulty. The High n Ach subject would then "rather switch than fight," because he or she would soon realize that he or she would not achieve gratification on this extremely difficult task.

In contrast, Low n Ach subjects who prefer very easy or very difficult tasks were predicted to persist longer in the face of failure in difficult tasks. Such failure would be assumed merely to confirm their expectation. There would be certain failure so anxiety or uncertainty would be absent.

Exactly the opposite prediction was made for initial tasks perceived to be easy. High n Ach subjects were expected to persist longer in the face of failure in this type of task, because continued failure would lead them to revise their perceptions of the task from easy to intermediate difficulty. Of course, with continued failure, the task would eventually be seen as too difficult by the High n Ach subjects. In contrast, the same effect of failure on an easy task would reduce persistence in Low n Ach subjects, because the continued failure would lead to the perception that the task was of intermediate rather than of low difficulty, which would activate anxiety.

A different type of support comes from a study of vocational aspirations among college men (Mahone, 1960). Clinicians were asked to judge whether a student's vocational choice was realistic in view of data provided about the student's ability and college performance. Among High n Ach subjects, 75 per cent of the men were judged as having made realistic choices, whereas this was true of only 39 percent of the Low n Ach subjects. These results are interpreted as analogous to the laboratory findings that High n Ach subjects are more realistic in selecting tasks of intermediate difficulty, whereas Low n Ach subjects often unrealistically choose very difficult tasks. It should be noted, however, that if one considered subjects who were low in fear of failure as well as low in n Ach, the percentage of realistic vocational choices was also quite high, 68 per cent.

The effects of success and failure in achievement situations may also depend on the level of n Ach. One would expect that motivation in a task or similar tasks would generally increase following success but decrease after failure, as early studies of level of aspiration demonstrated (Lewin, Dembo, Festinger, and Sears, 1944). However, when individual differences in achievement motivation are taken into consideration, one also discovers a typical reaction such as the lowering of level of aspiration after success or the raising of it after failure.

Mouton (1965) had subjects choose from among three tasks alleged to be very easy, of intermediate difficulty, or very difficult. Regardless of his or her stated choice or level of aspiration, all subjects then received a task described as being of intermediate difficulty.

Mouton manipulated the outcome so that half the subjects experienced success and half failure on this first task. Then each subject was allowed to choose one of the two remaining tasks, very easy or very difficult, to work on.

The results in Table 6–2 showed that all but one of the subjects of High n Ach who normally select tasks of intermediate difficulty chose the

TABLE 6–2. Number of Subjects Making Typical and Atypical Shifts in Level of Aspiration in Relation to n Achievement and Test Anxiety.

n Achievement	Test Anxiety	Typical Shift	Atypical Shift
High	Low	30	1
Low	High	20	11

Note: "Typical" means raising following success and lowering following failure. "Atypical" means the opposite. *Source.* From "Effects of Success and Failure on Level of Aspiration As Related to Achievement Motives" by R. Mouton, *Journal of Personality and Social Psychology,* 1965, *1,* 399–406. Copyright 1965 by the American Psychological Association. Reprinted by permission.

difficult alternative if they had succeeded on the first task but selected the easy task if they had failed on the first. In contrast, about a third of the Low n Ach subjects did the opposite, preferring the easy task after success but choosing the difficult task after failure on the first task.

Thus, the effects of success and failure are quite different, depending on both the original difficulty level of the task and the individual's n Ach level. To the extent that the outcome leads the High n Ach subject to see the task as being of intermediate difficulty, his or her level of aspiration will increase, whereas it will drop if prior experience leads him or her to regard the task as being very easy or very difficult. Exactly the opposite situation exists for the Low n Ach individual. Regardless of whether the outcome is success or failure, if it leads to the revised assessment that the task is of intermediate difficulty, the level of aspiration will decline. However, if the outcome makes the task appear very difficult or very easy, level of aspiration will rise for the low n Ach individual.

NATURALISTIC AND CORRELATIONAL

In addition to laboratory investigation, McClelland has proceeded to gather data from the natural environment to support his theory. Examination of global processes, such as the economic development and achievement of entire nations, has been conducted in *The Achieving Society* (McClelland, 1961).

ECONOMICS AND ACHIEVEMENT. McClelland was influenced by *The Protestant Ethic and the Spirit of Capitalism,* published in 1904 by Max Weber, a famous German sociologist. Weber observed that capitalism and economic prosperity seemed to flourish in the Protestant countries of Europe rather than in the Catholic countries and this led him to attribute economic achievements to religious factors. He later expanded his study and argued that the absence of certain values fostered by Protestant religions was also responsible for the lack of capitalism in non-Western countries.

The critical factor, according to Weber, was what he called "inner-worldly ascetism" or a concern with affairs of this world, rather than with those of some afterlife. Whereas Catholics were called on to devote their lives entirely to God and to withdraw from this world, the Protestants were taught that they could not purchase salvation merely by the accumulation of good works. Calvin and Luther taught that good works could not guarantee entry into Heaven, for in fact God had already made His selections. How could one determine if he or she was so predestined? Weber felt that only by behaving well in every respect, exercising self-control, saving, working hard, etc. could a Protestant convince himself or herself that he or she was among the selected few to escape damnation. This constant fear among Protestants was what Weber felt was responsible for the drive for achievement in the realm of economic endeavors.

This interpretation was highly controversial when it was first proposed but still very influential. McClelland based his key hypothesis (see Figure 6–4) on Weber's arguments of the relationship between religion and economics.

Specifically, McClelland sought to show how processes at the psychological level mediated the correlation noted by Weber. Religious beliefs were assumed to encourage certain differences in child-rearing practices, with Protestants emphasizing achievement and risk taking, hard work, and thrift among their sons. The resulting high levels of achievement motivation would have then led to the eventual growth of capitalism in Protestant countries.

McClelland (1961) went to great lengths to assemble historical data about the economic aspects of many countries. In one study, for example, he showed that the kilowatt hours of electricity consumed, which is a good index of economic prosperity, was greater in Protestant countries than in Catholic ones. Furthermore, at the level of individual behavior, Weber had reported that Protestants worked harder, saved money for long-range goals, and wasted little money on self-indulgences.

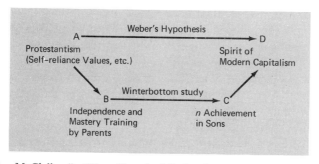

FIGURE 6–4. McClelland's "Key Hypothesis" showing the effects of the Protestant Reformation on need achievement. [From *The Achieving Society* by D. C. McClelland, Princeton, N.J.: Van Nostrand, 1961. Copyright 1961 by Van Nostrand. Reprinted by permission.]

CHILD REARING AND N ACH. These findings led McClelland to conclude that Protestant values led to child-rearing methods that instilled higher achievement needs, with the eventual consequence being greater economic growth and productivity in Protestant countries. It would be impossible to prove this hypothesis conclusively, but McClelland offered some evidence about American child-rearing practices associated with differences in achievement motivation as confirmation of his hypothesis.

Considerable weight was attached to a study by Winterbottom (1958), who interviewed women of twenty-nine years of age who were mothers of eight- to ten-year-old boys who varied in n Ach levels. She discovered that mothers of High n Ach boys *recalled* beginning independence training at an earlier age than did the mothers of Low n Ach boys. Furthermore, they reported that they showed more encouragement and reinforcement of such independence than did the mothers of Low n Ach boys, who had been more restrictive of their sons.

Rosen and D'Andrade (1959) created a situation in which they could directly observe parental behavior while their sons attempted the difficult task of building a tower of blocks while blindfolded. The parents were allowed to talk to their sons but not, of course, physically aid them. Parents of High n Ach boys gave higher predictions about their sons' achievement and these expectancies were fulfilled. High n Ach boys asked less frequently for help from their fathers and they received more warmth and approval from their mothers when successful.

Some criticism of the hypothesis that independence training, per se, contributes significantly to achievement comes from Smith (1969) and Zigler (1970) who point out that an independent person may often achieve little. Independence may be a prerequisite, but not a guarantee of achievement, which may also necessitate traits such as assertiveness or initiative. Achievement training in which the child is taught how to evaluate his or her performance against standards may also be more crucial than the development of independence.

Furthermore, dependency is difficult to measure, because its form of expression may become more subtle at older ages. A child who manifests no signs of dependency, such as separation anxiety, may still be highly dependent. Dependency, itself, might even be considered a goal to be achieved by some children. This situation is likely to occur, because social approval is a frequent consequence of other forms of achievement, so that high achievers may also be highly dependent on others. It is conceivable that truly independent individuals, such as nonconformists, may also be low in achievement.

Finally, there is the problem of the interpretation of correlations between aspects of childrearing and achievement motivation. The observed relationships may not reflect the influence of the mother on the child so much as the opposite. That is, mother's warmth may be higher in response to high achievement children, rather than serve as the cause of this characteristic in their children.

OTHER EVIDENCE. Other historical evidence is cited by McClelland (1961) as further support. In ancient Greece, need for achievement was highest in the early period in the growth of this great civilization but declined as the society decayed. Similar conclusions were reported for Spain and England. Of course, these retrospective analyses had to make inferences about levels of achievement motivation, because it would obviously have been impossible to make direct assessments. The analyses are imaginative and intriguing, but other explanations cannot be ruled out.

Subsequently, DeCharms and Moeller (1962) sampled children's readers used between 1800 to 1950 and measured the amount of achievement imagery, or the extent to which the content of the books stressed themes of

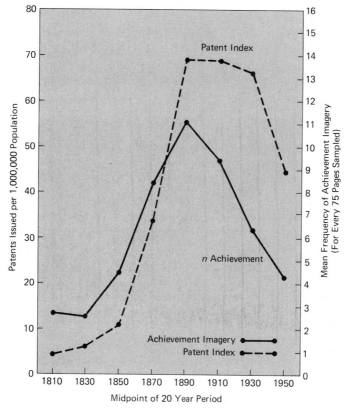

FIGURE 6-5. Mean frequency of achievement imagery in children's readers and the patent index in the United States, 1800-1950. [From "Values expressed in American children's readers: 1800-1950" by R. DeCharms and G. H. Moeller, *Journal of Abnormal and Social Psychology*, 1962, *64*, 136–142. Copyright 1962 by the American Psychological Association. Reprinted by permission.]

achievement and striving. Patent office records were searched for the same period to provide some index of achievement in the society during that time. A high correlation was obtained between the two indices, with both rising between 1800 and 1890 before showing a decline, as can be seen in Figure 6–5.

A similar content analysis of children's readers (McClelland, 1961) for the period between 1920–1929 was conducted for twenty-three different modern societies. Correlations of achievement imagery for this decade were found with an index of economic growth, based on kilowatt hours of electrical consumption, during the period 1929–1950. It was concluded that the antecedent condition of achievement training of children was the cause of the subsequent economic development and growth.

These analyses are more speculative than the laboratory studies and are subject to many alternative explanations. Correlations are always suspect when used to draw causal inferences. It is difficult to obtain complete or adequate data when dealing with past historical periods, especially for whole societies. Nonetheless, McClelland has produced an intriguing overall set of findings about the factors that influence a particular type of achievement, economic or entrepreneurial behavior. Risk taking is clearly involved in this type of activity as is delay of immediate gratification, planning for the future, and striving to achieve or excel against some standard of performance. Whether or not economic achievement is sufficiently similar to other forms of human achievement is difficult to say. Greed, dominance, and materialism often are associated with economic goals and may be absent in other forms of achievement, for example, intellectual, artistic, or spiritual endeavors. On the other hand, economic achievement shares the goals of improvement, striving, and risk taking, which are typical of most spheres of human achievement.

Reformulation of the Original Model of Achievement Motivation

The original approach to the theory of achievement motivation (Atkinson, 1957) was based on a view of behavior as a reaction instigated by the presentation of a stimulus. The emphasis was on the determination of the factors that led to a particular behavior in a given situation without concern for the interrelationship of that behavior with other competing behavior tendencies.

Atkinson and Raynor (1974) have presented evidence based on the work of their associates and other investigators that not only extends the original theory but also challenges its adequacy. Instead of looking at behavioral episodes in isolation, Atkinson and Birch (1970) called for an approach emphasizing the "dynamics of action" in which behavior is seen as a continuous stream of successive actions. Humans are active rather than passive in their behavior. When one behavior ends, another one must necessarily begin. It is not necessary to wait in limbo, so to speak, for a stimulus before new activity will occur.

The Atkinson-Birch model is too lengthy and complex to summarize here, but some of its implications can be presented. Atkinson and Birch believe that this formulation of motivation, whether it be of achievement, affiliation, or whatever activity, calls for an analysis of how an individual distributes his or her time engaging in the various alternative types of activities available. A taxonomy or anatomy of behavior would include a description of the relative frequency of occurrence of the alternative behaviors, the duration or total time spent on each activity, and the operant level or rate of occurrence of each behavior.

The focal question that can be addressed with this approach is, what are the causes of changes in activity? Consider the example of a student who is studying one moment but then joins his friends in social conversation. Two competing rival motives of achievement and affiliation are involved, and the problem is to analyze the factors responsible for the change in activity. This approach differs markedly from the original orientation of achievement motivation theory described earlier, in which only the factors related to achievement in a given task were considered.

An experiment by Brown (1974) illustrates the new approach. Subjects worked on two types of tasks, an achievement situation involving an anagram solution and a nonachievement task in which ratings or opinions of different trait words were made. On the achievement task, feedback was given so that success or failure was experienced after each anagram.

As subjects worked, a signal would occur informing them to switch from their ongoing task to the alternative task. The time required by the subject to deposit his or her work on one task into a compartment in front of him or her before switching to the alternative task was recorded.

When the ongoing task involved achievement, deposit times were longer if failure had occurred. In addition, deposit times were a function of the type of subsequent task expected, being briefer if the next task also involved achievement than if it was nonachievement.

Work time on the nonachievement task was also measured when it was the ongoing task. Differences were small but suggested that less time was spent if the subsequent task called for achievement activity.

Brown's study clearly indicates that persistence on an achievement task is not only a function of the success or failure there but is also influenced by the type of expected subsequent task. Similarly, persistence on the non-achievement task appeared to be affected by the nature of the subsequent task too.

Although Brown dealt with only two alternative tasks, it should be apparent that the analysis could be extended to include a larger number of alternatives. His study fits the reformulation suggested by Atkinson and

Birch for the study of the dynamics of the interrelated factors involved in motivation.

Another aspect of achievement motivation research related to the Atkinson-Birch reformulation involves the extent to which performance on an immediate task is perceived to be related to future achievement opportunities. Raynor (1969) presented an elaboration of Atkinson's (1957) model by adding the assumed contribution of possible future consequences of immediate success or failure on an achievement task. He pointed out the ambiguity in some of the original studies (e.g., McClelland et al., 1953), which demonstrated that achievement imagery in a story-writing task was greater under ego-involving instructions that described the task as a type of intelligence test than when neutral instructions were employed. Raynor argued that these results may not be entirely due to differences in arousal of intrinsic needs to achieve because subjects also received tests that allegedly reflected future leadership potential. Thus, according to Raynor, it is possible that subjects perceived some future consequences of successful achievement on the immediate task.

Even though performance on an immediate task may reflect an intrinsic need to achieve, often the level of achievement on that task has consequences for the future attainment of other achievement opportunities, social rewards and punishments, and material rewards and punishments. Thus, a child may find it challenging to take an intelligence test for no apparent extrinsic motives, but his or her performance clearly has significant implications for his or her future. If the child perceives this contingency between present and future consequences, his or her behavior will be different from that expected if he or she saw no contingency. It is not so much a matter of whether or not there is an actual contingency but rather what the individual's perceived degree of instrumentality is between present behavior and future consequences.

Raynor (1970) illustrated the significance of future orientation on academic performance by assessing the perceived instrumentality of getting a good grade in introductory psychology toward success in the future careers planned by students. Among students with High n Ach but low anxiety over failure, actual grades achieved were higher by students who had previously indicated early in the semester that the course grade was important for their future careers. Less conclusive differences were obtained for students of Low n Ach and high anxiety over failure. Raynor predicted these students should obtain lower grades if the course is perceived to be of high future instrumentality but argued that other incentives might exist that could promote achievement despite the inhibitory effects of high anxiety over failure.

An experimentally controlled test (Raynor and Rubin, 1971) of the influence on future orientation of achievement in a series of arithmetic problem tasks provides clearer support for the prediction of differences between high n Ach and low n Ach subjects. In the contingent condition, male college students were told that in order to have the opportunity to perform a series of four tests they had to reach a certain level of success in each prior test. Other male students were tested in the noncontingent condition in which they were told they could attempt all four tests, regardless of their performance. All subjects were led to believe that the tests were about .5 in difficulty based on past group norms. After the first test consisting of twenty-five problems was completed, the session was ended and no further tests were given.

As predicted and shown in Table 6–3, High n Ach ($M_S > M_{AF}$) subjects attempted and succeeded on more problems in the contingent condition where it appeared that immediate performance determined future opportunity. The opposite was true for Low n Ach ($M_{AF} > M_S$) subjects who attempted fewer problems and were less successful in the contingent condition compared with the noncontingent condition.

TABLE 6–3.   Mean Number of Attempted and Mean Number of Correct Problems As A Function of Motive Group and Contingency Condition.

Motive Group	No. Problems Attempted		No. Problems Correct	
	Condition		Condition	
	Contingent	Noncontingent	Contingent	Noncontingent
$M_S > M_{AF}$	18.43	15.63	17.43	13.00
$M_{AF} > M_S$	8.38	14.14	7.00	11.86

Source. Based on Data Presented by Raynor and Rubin, 1971.

By examining the relationship between achievement on an immediate task and the subject's perceived consequences for the future, Raynor's work has broadened the original model proposed by Atkinson (1957) along the lines pursued by Atkinson and Birch (1970). It is clearly more appropriate to view behavior as continuous rather than to examine isolated episodes of behavior.

The predictions generated by adopting a broader view of the determinants of behavior can be quite different from those based on the analysis restricted to the immediate situation. For example, the original model proposed by Atkinson predicted that High n Ach individuals would prefer risks of intermediate difficulty, whereas Low n Ach persons would choose extremely easy or difficult tasks.

In contrast, Raynor's (1969) revision of the model holds that where there is a perceived contingency between immediate task performance and future outcomes, High n Ach persons will actually prefer easy tasks, whereas Low n Ach persons will prefer difficult tasks. By choosing relatively easy tasks, the achievement-oriented person increases his or her chances of continuing through the successive hurdles along the path to the future goal. The person who is overwhelmed with anxiety over failure can drop out of this sequence and avoid additional confrontations with such anxiety by choosing very difficult tasks early in the game.

Although unpublished research by Raynor (described in Raynor, 1974) does not clearly support these predictions, they are presented here to illustrate the important differences in behavior that might be expected under the old and new versions of Atkinson's approach to the analysis of achievement motivation.

Evaluation of the Atkinson-McClelland Model

The achievement motivation theory, as noted earlier, deals with achievement as an intrinsic motive. Intrinsic motivation or incentive to perform the laboratory tasks is defined only in terms of perceived or expected task difficulty and ignores any qualitative factors affecting interest. The omission of the assessment of the role of extrinsic motives lends to the artificiality of the studies, because most real-life achievement situations are tied to some mixture of intrinsic and extrinsic motives.

THE QUESTION OF GENERALIZABILITY

The term *achievement motivation* is confusing, because it conveys different ideas to different people. McClelland dealt only with those achievement situations in which there is some striving against a standard of excellence and some uncertainty of success. The layperson, however, is apt to regard other types of activities in which goals are accomplished but where there is little or no risk involved, as examples of achievement. Thus the attainment of a Ph.D. or the running of a four-minute mile may, for some talented individuals, not involve much risk of failure and would not be viewed as reflective of achievement motivation by McClelland.

Although the theory was intended to deal with achievement in general, it has found its greatest success in dealing with entrepreneurial or economic risk situations. The theory has limited generalizability in dealing with other important realms of human achievement, such as in science, literature, arts, and humanities. Perhaps it would be useful to rename the phenomena studied by Atkinson and McClelland and use a less inclusive term.

The laboratory tests of the theory are based on a narrow range of unexciting tasks. For example, the ring toss or shuffleboard games, which have often been used, are quite remote from most risk situations. With other tasks, the procedure of using fictitious norms to convey task difficulty to the subject may not always be credible.

FAILURE TO STUDY ACHIEVEMENT MOTIVATION OF WOMEN

Another limitation of the research has been its excessive reliance on male subjects. Although it is true that sex roles are being re-examined and modified, the majority of women today, and certainly during the time the theory was being developed, probably hold different definitions of achievement. Stein and Bailey (1973) have examined factors that affect achievement motivation in women and concluded that the child-rearing practices that foster the traditional feminine sex role are often incompatible with those characteristics needed for encouraging achievement motivation, as conceptualized by McClelland and his associates.

DO WOMEN FEAR SUCCESS? Furthermore, the specific behaviors associated with achievement such as aggressiveness or competitiveness are often contrary to the traits considered appropriate to the feminine role in our society. When placed in an achievement situation, females appear to be more cautious. Moreover, it is possible that women may even avoid success because their sex role socialization has instilled such an attitude.

Horner (1969) administered a projective test in which women were asked to complete sentence stems such as, "After first term finals, Anne finds herself at the top of her medical school class. . . ." Content analysis of the endings led Horner to conclude that about two thirds of the women avoided success. In contrast men generally completed the sentence stems in ways that suggested positive feelings about a hypothetical male who had achieved success.

Horner concluded that fear of success is more prevalent in the motivation of women than in men in our society. This fear arises because social values have traditionally relegated the female to situations offering less opportunity for achievement in risk-taking situations. The woman who succeeds in the male-dominated world of business, for example, may experience hostility, rejection, and condemnation as someone who is lacking in femininity. As a consequence, according to Horner, she may have ambivalence about success, because of this bind wherein successful achievement dooms her to criticism about her competence as a female.

In her study, Horner required subjects to work on verbal and arithmetic tasks either alone or paired against an opponent of either sex. The results showed that women who scored high on fear of success worked better when alone than in competition. Subjects, male or female, who were low in fear of success performed better under competitive pair testing than when tested alone. The overall findings led Horner to argue that those women who were high in fear of success showed deficits in performance when competing with another, regardless of whether the person was male or female.

Morgan and Mausner (1973), however, did not completely confirm Horner's results. Using a similar projective test, they found fear of success was more prevalent among their male subjects. However, actual behavior of subjects when paired together in male-female teams to solve hidden figure perceptual tasks did show the kinds of sex differences postulated by Horner. Whereas males tried harder and acted assertively when they were informed that their scores on a pretest were lower than that of their female partner, females reacted quite differently. Females with low ability in this type of task readily accepted their inferior scores, whereas those with high ability either lowered their efforts while working with their male partners or showed obvious signs of tension. The results on the behavioral tests used by Morgan and Mausner are in agreement with the possibility that women might have learned roles that restrict their efforts during competition with males. However, their results on the fantasy test suggest that the process by which these sex differences occur is not one of greater fear of success on the part of females as proposed by Horner.

One unresolved question in these studies is whether competition, per se, or competition with males is the critical factor undermining the achievement of females. Horner's study suggested that competition per se is sufficient to weaken performance, because her results showed no difference as a function of the sex of the opponent. Morgan and Mausner's findings, on the other hand, seem to argue that males and females working together in teams react quite differently to success and failure. However, because they did not include male-male or female-female teams, it cannot be assumed conclusively that the mixed sex composition of the pairs was responsible for the contrasting reactions found between males and females.

A study by House (1974) provides more conclusive evidence that women perform less well under competition regardless of the opponent's sex. In this study, which involved anagram tasks, women competed against other women, against men, or worked alone. Similarly, men competed against other men, against women, or worked alone. All subjects were initially asked to predict their performance, indicate their minimal goal levels (MGL) of aspiration, and state their degree of confidence that they would achieve their expected levels of performance.

House's results presented in Table 6–4 show that women were adversely affected by competition, whereas men were not. For rivals of either sex, women who had to compete had lower expectancies of achievement, lower confidence, and lower minimal aspirations in comparison to women working alone. Such findings concur with Horner's view that women may avoid success opportunities. House's study also showed that such effects were absent among males as these measures were essentially the same for men regardless of whether they were competing or working alone.

SEX DIFFERENCES IN ACHIEVEMENT GOALS?   Research on achievement has not used women subjects much, but the available evidence shows that the predictions of achievement motivation theory may not apply to women. In part, this outcome may be because the situations used are more suitable to males in our society. The same types of tasks may not arouse equal motiva-

TABLE 6–4.   Mean Performance Expectancies, Confidence Scores, MGLs, and Actual Number of Anagrams Correctly Solved by Males and Females Alone and in Competitive Conditions.

	Females			Males		
Variable	Alone (27)	Competing Against Males (34)	Competing Against Females (25)	Alone (26)	Competing Against Males (33)	Competing Against Females (34)
Expectancy	57.59	53.44	46.68	55.19	55.33	60.76
Confidence	64.63	52.15	49.00	63.27	60.91	64.85
MGL	47.96	45.26	38.88	44.81	44.48	52.00
No. correct	47.48	46.79	43.60	49.85	40.42	43.18

Note. Numbers in parentheses designate *N*'s per group.
Source. From "Actual and Perceived Differences in Male and Female Expectancies and Minimal Goal Levels as a Function of Competition" by W. C. House, *Journal of Personality*, 1974, *42*, 493–509. Copyright 1974 by Duke University. Reprinted by permission.

tion in both sexes. Women are not necessarily less achievement oriented, but it is likely that the areas in which they have been encouraged to develop achievement interests are different. For example, acceptable areas for women to seek accomplishments in our society tend to be those emphasizing social skills.

Stein and Bailey allowed that interpersonal relations are often important areas of achievement for women; however, they disagree with other views (e.g., Crandall, 1963) that female achievement is instigated by affiliation rather than achievement motives. Veroff (1969) also suggested that adult female achievement is dependent on external or social cues, although at younger ages both sexes are similar. Stein and Bailey hold that these views have no clearcut evidence; instead, they maintained that women, like men, strive in their performance to meet a standard of excellence, but that the specific areas of attainment for women are different (for example, social skills) from those for men. To some extent, the issue is a semantic one, but it is clear that men and women have been socialized to seek different goals.

FAILURE TO STUDY ACHIEVEMENT IN INTERPERSONAL COMPETITION

Another limitation of the McClelland conception of achievement motivation is that it deals only with the individual who is competing against his or her own standards or the norms attained by others. The theory ignores achievement in which direct competition with others is involved, a commonplace situation in all types of endeavors.

Aside from the risk inherent in a given task, there is the added stimulation in competitive situations of the uncertainty of the performance of rivals.

Comparison of performance among competitors is inevitable and contributes to the complexity of the situation. How does it feel to be No. 1? Does being No. 2 really make you try harder? What effect does being last have on one's motivation and performance?

This distinction between noncompetitive and competitive achievement situations is the focus of an interesting theory concerning the developmental sequence of achievement motivation. Veroff (1969) has distinguished between two types of achievement motivation: *autonomous* and *social achievement*. The former is more similar to the situation that McClelland emphasizes, whereas the latter resembles the competitive situation.

Autonomous achievement involves the child's motivation to compare and evaluate performance against his or her own levels of ability and accomplishment. This self-evaluation is absent in infancy, but as the child develops a sense of competence and the ability to influence the environment, he or she comes increasingly to evaluate the quality of his or her own performance. This development is likely to occur around one and one-half to two and one-half years, when language is acquired, which helps the child reflect on his or her performance and evaluate its competence. As a child acquires new levels of skills, he or she may set higher levels for himself or herself. Veroff believes that the successful accomplishment of what a child was previously unable to do is the goal of autonomous motivation. Play activities in which there is intrinsic motivation could be regarded as in the category of behaviors considered to involve autonomous achievement.

Veroff measured autonomous achievement motivation by first having children perform different tasks involving different degrees of failure. Then they were asked to choose to repeat one of several tasks that varied in difficulty, as defined by each child's own prior successes and failures in the first part of the experiment. Younger children, up to about the second to fourth grades, preferred tasks of intermediate difficulty. Tasks that the child previously has barely accomplished or failed to accomplish appear to be attractive because they enable the child to strive for mastery of new skills relative to his or her own ability. Older children scored lower in autonomous motivation, reflecting perhaps the development of social achievement motivation. Thus, older children are more concerned about the social comparison of performances among peers than they are about achievement relative to themselves. This type of achievement clearly involves competition and the role of extrinsic factors such as recognition and social approval for success is apparent.

Measures of social achievement motivation were obtained by asking the child to choose among tasks that they had never tried before and that were asserted to be of varying difficulty, as defined in terms of fictitious norms about how other children had fared on them. It was found that younger children preferred easy tasks, whereas older children selected those that were challenging and of intermediate difficulty. Veroff concluded that as children get older they learn that the easy choice is socially disapproved and, furthermore, that the increased concern about social comparison leads to the choice of more difficult tasks. The child wants to know how well he or she can do relative to others and is not content merely to select tasks that everyone can do. Scores on social achievement motivation increased directly with the age of the child.

The attempt to distinguish between the two types of achievement motivation by Veroff is a valuable refinement. One implication of his theory is that the work of McClelland and his associates on what is essentially autonomous achievement should have been more concerned with young children rather than with a college age population. For among this latter group, the social achievement motivation is probably more important, although both forms are assumed by Veroff to exist, even beyond childhood. McClelland, in effect, has frequently been testing his theory on the wrong age group, if Veroff's developmental theory is valid.

Despite these limitations, the work on achievement motivation is impressive for its volume and for its systematic approach to the topic. It is not possible to cover this research adequately here, and we have only presented an overview.

Weiner's Attribution Theory Reanalysis of Achievement Motivation

The Atkinson-McClelland model uses cognitive terms such as *expectancy* and *value* as intervening variables. This approach does not attempt to assess directly the nature of cognitive processes involved in achievement motivation. Achievement behavior is seen to be a function of objectively defined aspects such as task difficulty and task incentive along with the level of the individual's need for achievement.

Weiner and his associates (e.g., Weiner, Frieze, Kukla, Reed, Rest, and Rosenbaum, 1971) have proposed an attribution theory reanalysis of the major findings predicted by the Atkinson-McClelland model. Attribution theory, it will be recalled from Chapter 1, is concerned with the process by which individuals analyze the causes of behavior. Weiner et al. suggest that the cognitive appraisal or interpretation made by an individual when confronted with an achievement task is an important determinant of the individual's willingness to undertake the task.

Attributions about a task can be placed in two independent dimensions, according to this model. Locus of control, internal or external, is one type of attribution we make about what is involved on a given task. If we think ability or effort is required, the attribution is internal, but if we believe all that is involved is the task difficulty or luck, the attribution is external. The causal factors that we postulate also vary in a dimension of stability. Ability is relatively stable, whereas effort fluctuates even though both factors are internally located. In external causes of task performance, the level of task difficulty is stable, whereas chance factors are highly variable.

Weiner et al. summarized evidence that the causal attributions made by persons differing in level of achievement motivation are not similar. They argued that such differences in attributions can explain why high and low need for achievement persons produce different behavior in achievement situations.

For example, why do High n Ach subjects tend to approach achievement opportunities, whereas Low n Ach subjects avoid them? One possible explanation might be the greater tendency of High n Ach persons to attribute any success to internal factors such as effort or ability. Kukla (1970) gave subjects an achievement task in which they had to predict whether a 0 or 1 would be the next digit in a series. The digits were actually random, but it is plausible that subjects could have perceived their performance as affected by any of the factors of ability, effort, task difficulty, or luck.

A comparison of High and Low n Ach subjects showed that successful predictions were later attributed to internal factors such as ability or effort by the High n Ach subjects but to the external factor of low task difficulty by Low n Ach subjects. These results provide a cognitive explanation of the greater tendency of High n Ach subjects to approach achievement situations. Because they believe their success stems from their ability and effort, achievement is apt to be more rewarding to them.

Greater persistence of High n Ach subjects in the face of repeated failure can also be accounted for in terms of differences in the causal attributions of subjects varying in n Ach. Kukla (1970) found that Low n Ach subjects see failure as stemming from lack of ability, a stable factor that is unlikely to change quickly. It is not surprising, then, that they give up. In contrast, High n Ach subjects tend to perceive their failures in terms of lack of effort on their part, a factor that can readily be remedied. As a result, they are willing to persist despite repeated failure on the task. They may believe that once they really start trying they will succeed.

As a final example of the value of examining attributions of the causes of performance, consider the differences in risk preference described earlier in which High n Ach subjects prefer tasks of intermediate difficulty, whereas Low n Ach subjects avoid them in favor of extremely easy or difficult tasks.

Weiner et al. pointed out that failure in very difficult tasks and success in very easy tasks are readily attributed by observers to the task itself. Such outcomes reveal little about the contribution of the individual's ability or effort. In contrast, performance outcomes in tasks of intermediate difficulty may more readily be assumed to reflect these internal factors. If one goes on to assume that High n Ach subjects want to attempt tasks that can help them learn about their ability and amount of effort, whereas Low n Ach subjects prefer to avoid such situations, one would make predictions about task preferences that would be confirmed by studies by Atkinson and his associates.

These attributional reinterpretations of the results of achievement motivation studies are not in conflict with the Atkinson-McClelland model. In the examples cited, both approaches yield essentially the same results. The work of Weiner and his associates tackles the same problems from a different perspective, one that is explicitly cognitive and interested in analyzing the processes of causal attribution used to explain our own behavior as well as that observed in others.

Summary

Many aspects of human behavior involve striving to achieve a given level of quality of performance. We are not content merely to perform certain responses, but instead we compare our performance against some measure of excellence. If we surpass these criteria, we feel successful.

One view of this striving nature of human motivation is that it reflects an intrinsic aspect of living organisms. In order to interact successfully with the environment, an organism must develop competence by acquiring skills, responses, and knowledge. Curiosity and exploratory behavior, for example, are methods by which an organism develops such competence through continued growth from interactions with the environment.

It is difficult, however, to rule out the operation of extrinsic motives such as social approval, prizes, material rewards, or academic grades, in analyzing the causes of human behavior. Unless one is studying very young infants, any form of behavior that might be argued to be motivated intrinsically is affected by extrinsic incentives as well. Thus, play activities in very young children might be viewed as stemming from intrinsic tendencies toward learning about the environment and the development of competence. However, as children increase in age their play activities are influenced increasingly by extrinsic factors such as praise rather than by any intrinsic interest.

The achievement motivation theory stimulated by the views of Atkinson and McClelland implies that a sense of accomplishment is a basic motive in humans. Success in a challenging task is assumed to be intrinsically rewarding. In laboratory studies of achievement motivation, extrinsic incentives are excluded.

Atkinson's model of achievement motivation includes personality factors such as the need for achievement and anxiety over failure as well as task factors such as difficulty and incentive. Incentive in this case does not refer to any extrinsic reward but rather to the intrinsic appeal of a task according to its perceived level of difficulty. The assumption is made that intrinsic incentive is greater, the more difficult the task, for individuals striving for a sense of achievement.

These three factors are combined in the model to produce predictions about such varied factors as the level of aspiration, persistence in the face of repeated failure, preferences for tasks of varying difficulty, and the effects of success and failure. In addition to these laboratory experiments, McClelland has made more speculative correlational analyses based on historical evidence, literature, and cross-cultural comparisons of economic growth, which he presents in support of his theory about the effects of achievement motivation on individual risk taking and achievement.

The original conceptualization of achievement behavior that focused on the determinants of performance in an immediate task without concern for the interrelationship of that situation to others has been abandoned. The adopted view of behavior as a continuous stream of activity places greater emphasis on the determinants of change in activity and the individual's distribution of time in a variety of alternative behaviors.

This reformulation is especially useful in drawing attention to the influence of the future orientation of the individual as an additional determinant of present achievement motivation, a determinant that was ignored by Atkinson's original model. In real-life situations often the success or failure in an immediate task with no apparent extrinsic consequences holds significance for access to future opportunities to achieve where extrinsic incentives do exist.

Individuals with High n Ach will strive harder if they perceive a contingency between present achievements and future consequences. The opposite effect has been found with Low n Ach persons whose overriding anxiety over failure leads them to be less successful when tasks are seen as being instrumental toward future consequences.

The inclusion of factors such as future orientation as a determinant of achievement may lead to improved predictions about behavior. The causes of behavior are not limited to those present at a given moment but also include the individual's perceptions and plans about future goals and consequences.

Among the criticisms of achievement motivation research is the fact that most of work has been limited in generalizability. The definition of achievement is narrow, being closely related to economic and business types of risk taking while ignoring other types of achievement. The laboratory studies have tended to use highly artificial and simple tasks. Social factors such as competition against other individuals are often involved in real-life achievement settings and do not play a major role in laboratory studies. Moreover, most of the early studies dealt only with male subjects. Until recently, the question of the nature of achievement motivation in women has been ignored.

Although the Atkinson-McClelland formulation used cognitive terms such as *expectancy,* the research carried out by them and their associates has not been directly concerned with the cognitive processes involved in achievement risk taking. Weiner's attribution theory approach has compared the types of inferences about the factors affecting performance on tasks made by High and Low n Ach subjects when confronted with different types of information. This approach has offered some interesting interpretations of the same results obtained under the Atkinson-McClelland approach, which show the usefulness of analyzing the individual's cognitions in understanding his or her behavior.

References

Atkinson, J. W. Motivational determinants of risk-taking behavior. *Psychological Review*, 1957, *64*, 359–372.

———. The mainsprings of achievement motivation. In J. D. Krumboltz (Ed.), *Learning and the educational process*. Skokie, Ill.: Rand McNally, 1965.

———, and Birch, D. *The dynamics of action*. New York: Wiley, 1970.

———, and Litwin, G. H. Achievement motive and test anxiety conceived as motive to approach success and motive to avoid failure. *Journal of Abnormal and Social Psychology*, 1960, *60*, 52–63.

———, and Raynor, J. O. *Motivation and achievement*. Washington, D.C.: Winston, 1974.

Brown, M. Some determinants of persistence and initiation of achievement-related activities. In J. W. Atkinson and J. O. Raynor (Eds.), *Motivation and achievement*. Washington, D.C.: Winston, 1974.

Crandall, V. C., Katkovsky, W., and Crandall, V. J. Children's beliefs in their own control of reinforcement in intellectual-academic achievement sets. *Child Development*, 1965, *36*, 91–109.

DeCharms, R., and Moeller, G. H. Values expressed in American children's readers: 1800–1950. *Journal of Abnormal and Social Psychology*, 1962, *64*, 136–142.

Feather, N. T. The relationship of persistence at a task to expectation of success and achievement-related motives. *Journal of Abnormal and Social Psychology*, 1961, *63*, 552–561.

Ford, G. *Sports Illustrated*, July 8, 1974.

Horner, M. Fail: bright women. *Psychology Today*, 1969, *3*, (6), 36–38; 62.

House, W. C. Actual and perceived differences in male and female expectancies and minimal goal levels as a function of competition. *Journal of Personality*, 1974, *42*, 493–509.

Kukla, A. Cognitive determinants of achieving behavior. *Journal of Personality and Social Psychology*, 1972, *21*, 166–174.

Lewin, K., Dembo, T., Festinger, L., and Sears, P. S. Level of aspiration. In J. McV. Hunt (Ed.) *Personality and the behavior disorders*. (Vol. 1.) New York: Ronald, 1944.

Mahone, C. H. Fear of failure and unrealistic vocational aspiration. *Journal of Abnormal and Social Psychology*, 1960, *60*, 253–261.

Mandler, G., and Sarason, S. B. A study of anxiety and learning. *Journal of Abnormal and Social Psychology*, 1952, *47*, 166–173.

McClelland, D. C. Methods of measuring human motivation. In J. W. Atkinson (Ed.), *Motives in fantasy, action, and Society*. New York: Van Nostrand, 1958.

———. *The achieving society*. New York: Van Nostrand, 1961.

———, Atkinson, J. W., Clark, R. W., and Lowell, E. L. *The achievement motive*. New York: Appleton, 1953.

Morgan, S. W., and Mausner, B. Behavioral and fantasied indicators of avoidance of success in men and women. *Journal of Personality*, 1973, *41*, 457–470.

Mouton, R. Effects of success and failure on level of aspiration as related to achievement motives. *Journal of Personality and Social Psychology*, 1965, *1*, 399–406.

New York Times. Charge of false research data stirs cancer scientists at Sloan-Kettering. April 18, 1974.

PIAGET, J. *The origins of intelligence in children.* Translated by M. Cook. New York: International Universities Press, 1952.

RAYNOR, J. O. Future orientation and motivation of immediate activity: An elaboration of the theory of achievement motivation. *Psychological Review,* 1969, *76*, 606–610.

————. Relationships between achievement-related motives, future orientation, and academic performance. *Journal of Personality and Social Psychology,* 1970, *15*, 28–33.

————, and RUBIN, I. S. Effects of achievement motivation and future orientation on level of performance. *Journal of Personality and Social Psychology,* 1971, *17*, 36–41.

ROSEN, B. C., and D'ANDRADE, R. C. The psychosocial origins of achievement motivation. *Sociometry,* 1959, *22*, 185–218.

SMITH, C. P. The origin and expression of achievement-related motives in children. In C. P. Smith (Ed.), *Achievement-related motives in children.* New York: Russell Sage, 1969.

STEIN, A. H., and BAILEY, M. M. The socialization of achievement orientation in females. *Psychological Bulletin,* 1973, *80*, 345–366.

Time, Aug. 26, 1974. Psychic scandal.

VEROFF, J. Social comparison and the development of achievement motivation. In C. P. Smith (Ed.), *Achievement-related motives in children.* New York: Russell Sage, 1969.

WATSON, J. D. *The double helix.* New York: Atheneum, 1968.

WHITE, R. W. Motivation reconsidered: The concept of competence. *Psychological Review,* 1959, *66*, 297–333.

WINTERBOTTOM, M. The relation of childhood training in independence to achievement motivation. In J. W. Atkinson (Ed.), *Motives in fantasy, action, and society.* New York: Van Nostrand, 1958.

WEINER, B., FRIEZE, I., KUKLA, A., REED, L., REST, S., and ROSENBAUM, R. M. *Perceiving the causes of success and failure.* New York: General Learning Press, 1971.

CHAPTER 7

Individual Motivation: Work

Because money does not grow on trees, it is necessary for most adults in our society to engage in activities commonly referred to as *work*. Although the characteristics of the wide variety of jobs, occupations, and professions are quite different, the common feature of work is that some form of economic return to the worker is involved. However, it would be overly simplistic to assume that the only or primary motivation for work is economic. Work may also provide meaningful psychological consequences to the individual. The intrinsic aspects of a job may fulfill an individual's needs for creativity, achievement, or involvement. Other jobs may enable an individual to supervise others or to manage a complex organization, thus challenging interpersonal skills or logical planning abilities.

In this chapter we will examine research concerned with the underlying motivation of work activities. In real-life work situations, it is difficult to separate intrinsic and extrinsic factors that might affect performance. Because the worker is receiving a salary, this extrinsic factor makes it difficult to evaluate the degree of intrinsic motivation a given task holds. Experimental research on work motivation, however, has attempted to vary one type of factor while holding the other one constant. After first examining the effects of attempts to vary the intrinsic features of work situations and the determination of these roles, we will present research aimed primarily at the study of the effect of pay on work performance. Finally, the possible interaction of the two types of incentives will be assessed.

The Nature of Work

Until recent times much of adult human activity was concerned with the struggle for sheer physical survival. Sufficient food, clothing, and housing had to be provided. Physical safety from natural disasters, predators, and other human aggressors had to be established. Only after the basic necessities had been ensured, did humans have the freedom to indulge in the pursuit of leisurely activities.

In the past, the terms *work* and *labor* have been used to note activities directed toward the achievement of either the necessities of life or the economic means of attaining them. Since no one person or family could produce enough to fulfill the variety of needs required for survival, it was necessary for an exchange system to be developed by which one party could exchange surplus goods or provide skills in return for needed goods and services from others.

Work was the major activity of most people until the Industrial Revolution. There was insufficient time for the development of recreation, arts, and other leisure activities. Workers toiled from dawn to dusk, and the distinction between work and play was not necessary. With the advent of mass production made possible by the invention of modern machinery and the development of production processes, economic abundance became possible for many societies. When this change freed the worker from an entire life at a craft or trade, it had the potential of allowing him or her to pursue activities of noneconomic importance.

THE DISSATISFIED WORKER

At the same time, work lost its significance in other ways. Jobs, especially for the unskilled or semiskilled, became routine, boring, and mechanical processes. These forms of employment provided salaries that enabled the worker to obtain goods and services, but they also deprived many workers of interesting and challenging occupations. For example, the assembly line typical of the modern factory places the worker in the position of being a specialist in one small area of the total process. They do not see or understand the other processes nor do they participate in the production of a product from beginning to end.

A report entitled *Work in America* issued by the Department of Health, Education, and Welfare in 1973 concluded that workers are alienated from their work and lack control or "ownership" of the nature of their work. The report criticized the lack of intrinsic meaning in most forms of work.

Although this description might be applicable to many white-collar workers, Schrank (1974) questions its relevance for many blue-collar workers. Since more than twenty million workers live on subsistence level incomes, they are less likely to be concerned about opportunities for self-actualization and more apt to be highly motivated by wage considerations and job security. Another important but overlooked factor, according to Schrank, that affects the blue-collar worker is the lack of nonwork activities and amenities in the work place. Whereas white-collar workers can move freely about the plant or office, take extended lunches, and combine socializing with work, the blue-collar worker is tied to the assembly line. Schrank feels that the equalization of blue-collar and white-collar worker avenues to these nonwork aspects of jobs is more important than the chance for the blue-collar workers to plan their own work, be creative, or have more autonomy within their work, per se.

Not only may boring jobs and poor working conditions reduce motivation but they apparently may lead to incidents of sabotage and retaliation by workers. Frustrated and resentful assembly workers have been suspected of deliberately producing inferior products, a suspicion that may partly explain the high rate of recalls among automobiles.

Intolerable work conditions can sometimes lead to imaginative solutions by employees for ways to make their work more enjoyable, as well as profitable. Zeitlin (1971) suggests that many employees find ways to beat the system and invent schemes by which they commit petty larceny against their organizations. Whether such practices are motivated primarily by chance of material gain or the need to make the job more interesting is debatable. Zeitlin describes one ingenious bridge toll collector who purchased a commuter book of tickets and occasionally substituted one of these discounted tickets when a cash-paying motorist appeared, thus profiting from the difference in fares. Certainly this scheme had financial motives, but it can be argued that it also livened up an otherwise dull and mechanical job. Zeitlin concludes that this type of petty larceny is a small price to pay, if it makes otherwise dull jobs tolerable. When bridge authorities instituted greater surveillance (at added cost) of toll collectors, this abuse decreased, but the rate of employee turnover rose sharply. Although we might wish to condemn even this form of petty larceny, we should also consider the inhumanity involved in many types of jobs. In order to earn an income, many employees must suffer boring, tiring, and even degrading jobs.

Various transgressions occur in industry in which employees steal from the company's time, supplies, and equipment. Dalton (1959) cited several cases such as an office worker who wrote letters during company time on the company letterhead and mailed them at company expense or a hospital technician who stole food and justified it on the grounds that his salary was too low. Dalton suggested that these forms of behavior, which many would consider petty thievery, are actually forms of rewards, which the company may tacitly endorse as a means of allowing the worker to be adequately compensated.

Because work is often devoid of satisfaction to the worker, he or she views the job as merely a necessary means toward other ends but has no involvement in or commitment to his or her activity. Even the connotation of the word *work* has often been one of drudgery, precisely because of the lack of intrinsic meaning in the activities that most occupations entail. If people did not need money in order to obtain desired and necessary goods and services, it is questionable whether anyone would be motivated to perform the duties entailed in some types of jobs.

EXTRINSIC MOTIVATION

The Industrial Revolution improved the means of production of economic commodities, but in the process of emphasizing efficiency, economy, and productivity it created work in many cases that failed to provide any pride, satisfaction, or sense of accomplishment. Instead of correcting the unfulfilling nature of many jobs, corporations have attempted to motivate employees by methods such as providing larger salaries or better working conditions. In other words, it is assumed that extrinsic incentives are an adequate substitute for intrinsic motivation.

Ever since the classic studies were conducted at Western Electric Company to see how environmental factors affected the productivity of workers on an assembly line (Roethlinberger and Dickson, 1939), there have been attempts to improve working conditions in hopes that greater productivity might be achieved. These studies, which gave rise to a phenomenon called the *Hawthorne effect* revealed that a wide variety of changes in lighting, and so on improved performance. Even changes such as reduced illumination, which should impair performance, were found to have benefits on performance. The conclusion finally reached was that the improvements in productivity were not specific to any particular change but were due perhaps to worker morale being boosted by the feeling that management was taking an interest in their welfare.

Many studies were conducted that directed no attention to the characteristics of the job tasks, per se, but rather emphasized the effects of working conditions. This approach was dominant despite the overlooked fact (Lawler, 1973) that these studies also gave evidence that pay was a major determinant of performance.

Motivational Factors Inherent in Work

A major redirection of emphasis in attempts to motivate work has come about with a concern about human relations since McGregor (1960) made the distinction between two views of work motivation: Theory X and Theory Y. If one assumed that humans had to be driven by extrinsic factors to work, one held Theory X, but if one believed that humans worked because they found fulfillment and satisfaction in their work, one subscribed to Theory Y. McGregor, influenced by views such as Maslow's (1943) proposal of work as a means of achieving self-actualization, was promoting the conception of Theory Y as the appropriate view of work motivation.

An influential study by Herzberg, Mausner, and Snyderman (1959) provided evidence that seemed to support this view of work motivation. Using semistructured interviews of 200 engineers and accountants, they made indirect assessments of factors affecting job satisfaction. Workers were asked to describe critical work incidents that had made them either very happy or unhappy. The results led Herzberg et al. to distinguish between two categories of factors, satisfiers and dissatisfiers, that affected work. Dissatisfiers were not merely the absence of satisfiers but were considered to be represented by totally different factors.

Five satisfiers affected job satisfaction: achievement, recognition, the work itself, responsibility, and advancement. They were much more frequent in the high than in the low job attitude incidents. These factors are what motivates the worker, according to Herzberg et al. Without them, a job might be tolerable but the work will not be positively motivated. A second set of factors including pay, company policies, working conditions, and interpersonal relations were identified as dissatisfiers; they dominate the low job attitude incidents and play little part in the high job attitude incidents. They were important, but only in a negative way. If they were satisfactory or adequate, they did not necessarily produce job satisfaction, because this was assumed to be a function of the first category of factors. However, if these extrinsic aspects of the work situation were deficient, it was argued that they would result in job dissatisfaction. Satisfiers were generally reported as more important and the factor of pay, a dissatisfier, was ranked only sixth.

Herzberg (1966) observed that the modern industrial organization focuses only on the needs of the employee in the context of the job setting and fails to consider other needs. Consequently, creativity is impeded and absenteeism, turnover, and failure frequently occur. Herzberg (1966) argued that organizations must deal with the motivator needs and psychological growth of personnel rather than only with what he terms the "hygiene" needs such as working conditions or pay. He maintained that "to the institution it seems easier to motivate through fear of hygiene deprivation than to motivate in terms of achievement and actualizing goals" (Herzberg, 1966, p. 172). As a result, the opportunities for initiative and achievement by the worker are restricted or eliminated. Overconcern with hygienic variables such as interpersonal relationships is criticized by Herzberg. Although he admitted that improving human relationships is important, he discredited the assumption that once this goal is achieved, motivation will be facilitated or improved. Motivation must be based on the nature of the job, per se, rather than in the fringe benefits or working conditions. Important as these latter factors may be in preventing dissatisfaction, they should not be misconstrued as being sufficient to bring about job satisfaction per se. That is, although inadequate pay would undoubtedly create dissatisfaction among workers, the provision of more than adequate pay would in no way guarantee more productive or creative employees.

Other research has corroborated the findings of Herzberg et al. In a provocatively titled book *Where Have All The Robots Gone?,* Sheppard and Herrick (1972) presented the results of interviews they conducted with several hundred young workers. They also found an increasing disenchantment and dissatisfaction with the nature of work, especially the dehumanizing and monotonous work in factories.

The findings of Herzberg et al. were also confirmed in a survey commissioned by the U.S. Department of Labor and conducted by the Survey Research Center of the University of Michigan on a nationwide sample of 1,533 workers in 1969. The factor of "enough pay" was ranked fifth in importance, whereas the highest ranking factor was interesting work.

CONTRADICTORY EVIDENCE: THE ROLE OF PAY

On the other hand, a number of critics have objected to Herzberg's formulation and numerous studies have been conducted to test further his distinction between satisfier and dissatisfier factors. Although some studies support this distinction, many of them suggest that the factor of pay can be a source of both satisfaction and dissatisfaction. House and Widgor (1967) concluded that Herzberg et al. (1969) were probably correct in concluding that pay is a source of dissatisfaction when it is perceived to be unfairly low but they hold that high pay can serve not only as a hygienic factor, to use Herzberg's term, but also as a means of providing recognition and to the worker enhancing self-esteem, thus acting as a satisfier.

Lawler (1973) reviewed over fifty studies published since Herzberg et al. made their report and found that pay was ranked higher in many studies than it was in the Herzberg et al. study. One reason for the discrepant findings, suggested by Vroom (1964), is the fact that Herzberg et al. relied only on self-reports, and respondents may not have wished to appear greedy and so ranked money as less important than it really was.

Despite these criticisms, the Herzberg formulation has obviously had much influence. As a consequence largely of views such as those of Herzberg (1966) and McGregor (1960), increased attention has been given to modifying the work situation to provide more opportunities for workers to fulfill their higher order needs.

JOB ENRICHMENT

What are some solutions being attempted to improve the nature of job tasks? Ford (1969) reported an American Telephone and Telegraph program of job enrichment that attempted to enlarge the scope of tasks assigned to workers and allow them more initiative. Not only did performance improve but absenteeism and turnover decreased. Another job enrichment program instituted among employees in a British company was evaluated by Paul, Robertson, and Herzberg (1969), and they too reported encouraging consequences with technicians, supervisors, engineers, and salespersonnel.

In recent years it has been suggested that the work week itself should be modified. Four-day work weeks, for example, have been recommended not only for possible benefits in worker productivity but also for economic reasons. The total work hours per week would still be forty, because each work day would be expanded to ten hours. Nord and Costigan (1973) reported positive benefits with the modified work week, and workers seemed to have positive attitudes toward it. A survey of over 1,000 companies by the American Management Association disclosed that 143 companies had some form of work week involving less than five days, and most of them reported beneficial effects, according to Jones (1972).

A number of other innovations have been tried and reported (*Time,* October 30, 1972). Several Swedish automobile manufacturers, for example, have reduced the use of assembly line operations, allowing workers more interesting jobs involving a variety of tasks. In a West Germany company, employees were allowed to set their own hours so that they put in forty hours at various times during the week rather than strictly from nine to five.

Most of the reported innovations have apparently been successful, but this outcome is partly due to the fact that failures are not always reported. Another reservation is the well-known fact, established in the Western Electric studies, that some of the beneficial effects may not be specific to the particular innovation per se. Novelty, the excitement of being studied, the awareness that the company cares about you, and other similar factors could produce short-term benefits that will wash out with time. These words of caution are not meant to imply that the innovations are not valid or desirable, but that the innovations must be carefully evaluated to determine their real effects.

SATISFACTION AND PRODUCTIVITY

Although many companies have become increasingly concerned about worker satisfaction, it should be noted that it is not clear that increased satisfaction will increase worker productivity. If anything, there is little relationship between the two variables (Vroom, 1964). Nevertheless, the trend to find ways to increase worker satisfaction continues.

Lawler and Porter (1967) suggested that the expectation that greater job satisfaction will enhance performance is erroneous and argued that the reverse relationship is more tenable. That is, workers who perform better will be the ones who are more satisfied, especially because they may receive greater pay for their better performance.

On the other hand, we must ask what produces better performance at the outset of a worker's employment? Is it greater ability, better motivation, or higher pay? Some factors must be present initially to produce the differences in performance that Lawler and Porter see as the antecedents of eventual differences in satisfaction. The interrelationship between satisfaction and performance may be a two-way street.

Even if the relationship between satisfaction and productivity per se is ambiguous, other factors that are important consequences of satisfaction may need to be considered. For example, absenteeism and turnover are clearly lower, even if productivity is unaffected, with greater job satisfaction. In the long run, an organization would benefit from the enhanced job satisfaction of workers for these reasons. Finally, judged in the broad social context of human values, we may argue that satisfied workers may reduce the social costs of unhappy and alienated individuals. The best interests of society as a whole may require that we encourage organizations to promote job satisfaction even though they may not immediately or directly reap any benefits for their expenditures. A happy worker may not be a better worker, but he or she may be a happier and better member of society.

Despite the disagreement about the *relative* effect of intrinsic and extrinsic factors on work, the factor of pay does have some influence, and we now turn to a more detailed examination of this issue in terms of psychological theories.

Work Motivation and Pay: Research and Theory

What extrinsic factors will motivate an employee to perform well on a job? Employers have invested substantial time, effort, and money to answer this question. If we were to try to find an answer based on achievement motivation theory, we would likely be disappointed. According to that theory, as we have pointed out in Chapter 6, knowledge of the individual's need for achievement, anxiety about failure, probability of success, and the intrinsic incentive of success on the task should enable us to predict the individual's achievement behavior. No attention is given to the influence of extrinsic motives beyond the minimal amount needed to engage low achievement individuals in experiments.

In contrast, extrinsic incentives are assumed to play a key role in performance in the world of work. Salary, fringe benefits, promotions, and status are factors that are extrinsic to the job task, per se, but have substantial impact on motivation to engage in work no matter how intrinsically interesting the job may be.

This important difference between the situation represented by achievement motivation experiments and the real world of work limits the extent to which one can generalize from the former to the latter. In trying to understand how extrinsic motives affect work performance, we must study work itself. We now turn to an examination of the influence of the specific factor of pay on work behavior.

EXPECTANCY THEORIES

One major theory accounting for the effects of pay on work is similar to the expectancy theories proposed for other types of behavior (e.g., Atkinson, 1957; Lewin, 1936; Rotter, 1954; Tolman, 1932). In these expectancy theories, behavior is assumed to depend on two factors: expectancy or the probability of occurrence of an outcome such as money and the value or valence of that outcome. Both factors are defined in subjective terms according to the perceptions of the individual rather than in objective terms. These two factors combine to determine behavior and if either factor is absent motivation should not occur. Thus, if expectancy of an outcome is high but it is not valued, there will be no motivation. Similarly, if the payoff is highly valued but the probability of receiving it is perceived as zero, there should also be no motivation. Motivation, then, should be higher, the greater the combined product of expectancy and value, as the theory assumes that individuals wish to maximize their outcomes.

In the matter of the effect of pay on motivation, expectancy theories (e.g., Lawler and Porter, 1968; Vroom, 1964) assume that motivation will be higher, the greater the expectancy of receiving pay and the greater the valence of the pay. Consider a worker paid on a piece-rate basis. If he or she produces larger quantities of products, he or she maximizes his or her total pay. But workers do not always perform this way, perhaps because of strained relationships with fellow employees who may fear that high productivity may have negative consequences such as unemployment or lowered piece rates. Or perhaps the worker's health might be adversely affected if he or she strives too hard. If we assume that the worker values good health and cordial peer relationships, we see that the worker will not work as hard as he or she might otherwise. Is this incompatible with the assumption of expectancy theory that the worker will try to maximize pay? By stressing the *perceived* value of pay rather than the objective value, expectancy theory attempts to explain why the worker in this example does not maximize objective pay. Less than maximal performance occurs because the worker has a lowered valence associated with pay due to its conflict with cordial peer relationships.

To argue that workers do not become rate busters because the valence of pay is lowered is an explanation of limited usefulness, unless some independent measurement of valence can be developed instead of inferring it only *after* we observe less than maximal production.

Another difficulty if we define expectancies in such loose terms lies in the difficulty of identifying all the factors an individual considers important. We need to specify these factors in advance if we are to generate predictions from the theory instead of explaining behavior after we observe it by adding additional assumptions about the values of the worker.

Lawler (1971, p. 105) admits that one difficulty of expectancy theory is its vagueness about the determinants of valence. We are not clear how the individual determines what the consequences are for the set of possible alternative responses in a situation. Yet, expectancy theory just assumes that such valences exist and influence motivation. Furthermore, individual differences may have to be considered. For example, some workers may not consider peer ostracism a deterrent to rate busting performances, whereas others would be very much inhibited by such a concern.

EQUITY THEORY

In contrast to expectancy theory, Adams (1963) proposed an intriguing theory of equity. This formulation was borrowed from social psychology and stressed the notions of just and fair exchange between parties involved in social interaction. A person may decide to give in proportion to what he or she receives from the other party in order to maintain harmonious and equitable relationships. In the instance of wages, equity theory would imply that a worker who felt overcompensated for work would attempt to work harder to restore balance to the exchange. But if the worker felt underpaid, he or she would work less effectively in return in order to balance matters. Judgments about equity involve a comparison between one's own ratio of inputs to outputs with that of some standard, either internal such as an expectancy one has acquired or external such as in the form of a coworker's pay.

Another factor that must be considered is whether pay is on a piece-rate or an hourly basis. It was predicted that workers on a fixed amount of pay per unit time would perform as described previously, producing more goods of higher quality when overpaid but fewer products of lower quality when underpaid. When piece-rate pay scales are involved, overcompensation was predicted to lead to *less* work because each extra unit produced would only serve to add to the inequity created by the already excessive piece rate. However, the quality of products might improve. Finally, undercompensated piece-rate work was expected to lead to more work, but of lower quality, in order for the worker to achieve an equitable exchange between pay and work.

These predictions are summarized in Table 7–1, along with the predictions based on expectancy theory. It may be noted that expectancy theory predictions generally disagree with those based on equity theory except for the quality of products in the piece-rate situation, which both theories predict will increase with overpayment and decrease with underpayment.

In one experiment (Adams and Rosenbaum, 1962) designed to test equity theory, subjects were hired to conduct interviews. One group of subjects was overcompensated, whereas a second group was paid equitably. The method

TABLE 7–1. The Predictions of Equity and Expectancy Theories Regarding the Effects of Over- and Underpayment on Work Productivity.

	Equity Theory				Expectancy Theory			
	Quantity		Quality		Quantity		Quality	
	Hour	Piece	Hour	Piece	Hour	Piece	Hour	Piece
Overpaid	↑	↓	↑	↑	O	↑	O	↑
Underpaid	↓	↑	↓	↓	O	↓	O	↓

used for producing a feeling of overcompensation involved explicitly informing subjects that for their level of experience, they should *not* be receiving the high salaries they would be getting. Because people with the desired qualifications were unavailable, it was alleged that the subjects were hired despite their lack of experience.

Half the subjects within each group were paid on a piece-rate basis, the other half were paid on an hourly basis, so there was a total of four different treatment conditions.

The predicted results were obtained, with inequity created by overpayment leading to more productivity when pay was on a time basis. However, when a piece-rate basis was used, overcompensation led to lower productivity compared to that of the equitably paid group. Furthermore, the work quality improved with overcompensation.

The overpaid piece-rate results are somewhat paradoxical or counterintuitive, inasmuch as the piece-rate pay basis has generally been assumed to generate higher performance, because it would maximize the worker's pay. Why, then, should overpayment of piece-rate work actually lead to lowered productivity?

Equity theory proponents would interpret these findings as evidence that overcompensated piece-rate workers were attempting to restore equity to the situation. Reduction of quantity of production while improving quality enables the worker to give more in exchange for overcompensation and thus establishes equity.

An alternative explanation for these findings has been offered by Lawler (1968) who argued that the overpaid workers may have felt insecure, because the method of inducing feelings of overcompensation involved telling workers that they were unqualified. As a consequence, they may have concentrated on producing high quality work, at the expense of quantity, as a means of proving themselves adequate and qualified.

This need to prove oneself competent might vary depending on whether one's work performance is tied to future consequences such as being rehired. Adams and Jacobson (1964) overpaid subjects to correct page proofs. Half of them were told that chances for additional employment were high; the other half were led to believe that future employment prospects were minimal. It was felt that job insecurity could not be a factor influencing the performance of the latter subjects because they had little chance of additional employment. If insecurity was in fact important as a determinant of performance, the two groups should perform differently. However, the results, presented in Table 7–2, indicated that, regardless of the chances for future employment, overpaid subjects still produced less work but work that was more accurate compared to that produced by the equitably paid comparison groups.

TABLE 7–2. Mean Quantity (No. Pages Corrected) and Mean Quality (No. Errors Detected).

| | Future Employment Prospects | | | |
| | High | | Low | |
Payment	No. Pages	No. Errors Detected	No. Pages	No. Errors Detected
"Overpaid"	8.70	7.87	7.70	7.98
"Equitably Paid"	11.70	4.90	12.80	4.03

Source. Adapted from "Effects of Wage Inequities on Work Quality" by J. S. Adams and R. R. Jacobsen, *Journal of Abnormal and Social Psychology,* 1964, *69,* 19–25. Copyright 1964 by the American Psychological Association. Reprinted by permission.

Adams and Jacobson (1964) concluded that their results supported the equity theory. Although these results are clearly consistent with equity theory, Lawler (1968) contended that the test was inadequate, because the same technique of inducing feelings of overcompensation was used, namely telling subjects that they were unqualified. Lawler maintained that even without the prospect of future employment, subjects may still be motivated to demonstrate personal competence.

The same criticism is applicable to the finding (Adams and Rosenbaum, 1962) that overpaid hourly workers produce more work than equitably paid workers. It can be explained by both equity theory and Lawler's view that workers who are told they are unqualified may try to prove otherwise.

Pritchard, Dunnette, and Jorgenson (1972) created feelings of inequity with a somewhat different technique. When male subjects responded to advertisements promising either a fixed hourly rate or a modified sliding piece rate for temporary clerical assistance, they told some subjects that there had been an error and that the true rate was either higher or lower. In addition, some of the subjects received the advertised rate. There was no implication that the underpaid subjects were less qualified. Their results showed strong support for the equity theory with hourly underpayment leading to the least amount of work and underpayment leading to the highest productivity when the modified piece-rate scale was used.

Furthermore, after three days of work, all groups were switched to the alternative pay basis. In effect, this shift provided a means of studying naturally occurring inequity, because some of the subjects encountered over- or underpayment compared to their initial pay basis. For example, a worker who was highly productive on an hourly basis stood to earn more for the same amount of units produced when switched to the sliding piece-rate scale. It was predicted that he would experience overpayment feelings and would therefore increase his output to restore equity. In contrast, a worker who was a low producer on the hourly scale would receive lower pay for that same amount of production when switched to the sliding pay scale. He would experience underpayment feelings so that he would produce fewer units to achieve equity. Similar effects of over- and underpayment feelings were predicted for the shift in the opposite direction from the sliding pay scale to an hourly one, which also creates overpayment for some workers but underpayment for others. The high-productivity sliding-pay-rate worker would experience underpayment when switched to the hourly basis, whereas the low productivity worker would feel overpaid on the hourly basis.

The results during this second half of the study also upheld the predictions of equity theory. Because Lawler's (1968) criticism of the method for inducing feelings of inequity used in early studies by Adams cannot be applied here, the case for equity theory is strengthened by these findings.

Additional support for equity theory was obtained by Garland (1973) who also employed a procedure for inducing over- and underpayment feelings in workers that avoids Lawler's criticism. Students were hired for a one-hour proofreading task and paid either $.15, $.30, or $.60 per page. By allowing each subject to interact with a confederate who was presented as another subject being paid $.30 per page, it was possible to create feelings of underpayment, equitable payment, or overpayment in the $.15, $.30, and $.60 per page conditions, respectively.

Performance was scored in terms of the number of pages read and the proportion of errors detected to provide indices of quantity and quality of performance. In line with equity theory, overpayment produced less work of higher quality, whereas underpayment led to more work of lower quality.

Because the subjects in Garland's experiment were able to compare their pay directly with that of other subjects, it is not possible to argue that their feelings did not match the extent to which they were over- or undercompensated. How would expectancy theory incorporate these findings that clearly support equity theory?

The probable response would be similar to that of Lawler (1968) who resorted to the argument that overcompensated workers might attach lower valence to the high and unjustified amounts of money they were receiving. If, in fact, this were the case, their motivation would decrease, since valence is a major determinant. This assumption would help account for the reduced work quantity found in studies of overpayment. With respect to underpaid piece-rate situations in which high productivity results, Lawler (1971) suggested that money might have high valence. Because the underpaid worker has less money than the overpaid worker for the same amount produced, Lawler holds that additional money should have greater valence to the underpaid worker. Consequently, he or she should be more highly motivated and produce more.

By making this simple assumption that perceived valence or attractiveness differs for over- and underpayment, Lawler (1968) maintains that equity theory findings can be accommodated by expectancy theory. But as pointed out earlier, these assumptions about the value of pay are circular. To say that someone values money more because we observe him or her working harder and to say that someone else values money less because we see him or her working less diligently gets us nowhere.

Rather than attempt to stretch expectancy theory to a point of extreme vagueness so that it can incorporate the otherwise incompatible findings of equity theory, as Lawler has done, it seems more useful to examine the case for equity theory more closely. Certainly, from an intuitive level, it does not appear that many workers consider themselves overpaid, even if they are, because they would rationalize and view their overpayment as recognition of their true ability. Someone who receives an undeserved promotion or salary increase is likely to attribute it to his or her own industry, initiative, and achievements rather than to an error of judgment by a supervisor. This tendency to feel overpayment is acceptable is especially likely to occur when a third party such as the company is perceived as the source of pay rather than the foreman or supervisor (Pritchard, 1969). The analogy between social exchange between individuals and the situation existing between an employee and his or her company is somewhat strained. Workers are prone to see the impersonal and inanimate company in a different light from that in which they deal with fellow employees or direct supervisors.

Furthermore, factors other than monetary pay may enter the equation. An underpaid worker may not feel underpaid if he or she receives other valued forms such as fringe benefits, pleasant working conditions, job security, or desirable working hours. It is difficult to assess the effects of equity of pay when so many other factors also operate. The same difficulties prevent a clearcut test of expectancy theories, which, as already noted, have found it necessary to recognize the role of subjective, rather than objective, definitions of compensation.

Effect of Extrinsic Incentive on Intrinsic Motivation

Studies of the influence of pay on work motivation tend to ignore the impact of the intrinsic nature of the job just as research on the effects of the latter factor neglects the importance of extrinsic factors. Clearly, both factors must be considered, and a complete analysis must examine the relative contribution of each factor. For example, the importance of one factor may depend on the level of the other. If intrinsic interest is adequate, pay level may not have much influence within a wide range, but if intrinsic interest is low, the factor of pay may assume greater importance.

To complicate matters more, it is possible that the two factors may interact such that extrinsic motivators may actually reduce the degree of intrinsic motivation for a task. Thus, if the salary is too high, the employee may attribute his or her work to being motivated primarily by pay considerations rather than by an intrinsic interest in the job. Deci (1971, 1972) has proposed a cognitive evaluation theory that predicts such an effect. The overpaid worker thinks, in effect: "I'm working for the money," rather than "I'm working because I like the job." Furthermore, the worker who thinks he or she is working mainly for the money is apt to conclude that the task must be rather uninteresting.

This theory contrasts with equity theory, which would predict that an over-compensated worker would attempt to restore the balance between salary and work by either working to produce more products or products of higher quality. Deci's theory would attribute the observed reduction in performance to the lowering of intrinsic motivation by the presence of extrinsic incentives.

Deci based his generalizations on laboratory tasks, which are quite dissimilar to real work situations. In one study (Deci, 1972), subjects worked on a difficult puzzle called SOMA, which consisted of seven different pieces, each of which looked as if it was comprised of several cubes. The task called for subjects to construct reproductions of the pieces shown in several drawings. After the allotted time, the experimenter left the room to analyze the results and the subject was told to do whatever he or she liked for a few minutes.

On the table with the puzzle were several recent popular magazines. Unknown to the subjects, an observer recorded the amount of time the subject spent working on the SOMA puzzles again, reading magazines, or doing other activities. The assumption was that any time spent working on the puzzles during this eight-minute free period must reflect intrinsic interest in the task.

The basic comparison in this study consisted of an examination of the time spent during this free period working on the puzzles by groups that received money or no money for puzzles solved during the first part of the session.

Two additional factors were considered by Deci: the temporal point at which subjects got paid and the presence or absence of verbal praise from the experimenter for puzzle solutions. Although Deci's theory holds that receiving money should weaken intrinsic motivation for performing a task, he argued that an offsetting factor may exist if subjects get paid *before* the free choice period. He reasoned that subjects would feel overcompensated if paid $1 for each puzzle solution because they might earn $3 or $4 for just thirty minutes activity. Therefore, according to equity theory, subjects might try to work harder to restore equity. This tendency is more likely to occur in subjects who receive money if they are paid before rather than after the free choice period.

In his study, Deci (1972) compared these two types of money conditions with a control group that received no money. The left side of Table 7–3 presents the results. As measured by the amount of time spent on the puzzles during the free choice period, it does appear that intrinsic motivation is reduced by pay given at the end of this period. However, the results also uphold the prediction that more time would be devoted to the puzzles during the free choice period by the group paid just prior to this time period. Intrinsic motivation is still assumed to be reduced in this condition; however, time on the puzzles is not reduced accordingly, because it is assumed that this group is trying to offset feelings of inequity created by being paid generously for their efforts.

TABLE 7–3.   Mean Number of Seconds Spent by Subjects on Puzzles in the 8-Minute Free Choice Period.

Condition	No Verbal Reinforcement		Verbal Reinforcement	
	Females	Males	Females	Males
Money after	151.6	65.6	240.4	219.9
No money	292.4	124.4	142.5	197.8
Money before	346.0	248.0	384.4	392.9

Source. From "Intrinsic Motivation, Extrinsic Reinforcement, and Inequity," by E. L. Deci, *Journal of Personality and Social Psychology,* 1972, *22,* 113–120. Copyright 1972 by the American Psychological Association. Reprinted by permission.

Deci's experiment also examined evidence for another aspect of cognitive evaluation theory, which holds that extrinsic rewards should reduce intrinsic motivation only if it tends to lead the recipient to change attributions about motives in performing the task. Thus, if one gets a lot of money for doing something one enjoys, one might assume eventually that the primary motive for performing the task was the money. On the other hand, extrinsic rewards also serve an informative function by providing feedback about the quality of one's performance. If this is the main effect of an extrinsic motive, then Deci predicts that it may actually increase rather than impair intrinsic motivation. Verbal praise and encouragement, for example, often serve mainly as informative cues and should enhance intrinsic motives.

In Deci's study, three conditions similar to those described were used with the addition of verbal reinforcement from the experimenter for success. The right side of Table 7–3 provides support for Deci's prediction when male subjects are involved but not for female subjects. Exactly why a sex difference should occur is not clear. Deci speculated that it may be an artifact created by the use of an attractive male experimenter. He may have provided social reinforcement for the females but not for the males; the net effect of this factor would be to reduce any possible difference between the presence or absence of verbal reinforcement conditions for female subjects. It should be clear, however, that this account is merely a conjecture.

The question of how extrinsic motives affect intrinsic motivation is an important one, but it is difficult to know how generalizable Deci's situation is. Pushed to its logical end, Deci's argument would suggest that if we provide intrinsically interesting work, we could and should dispense with any extrinsic incentives.

No matter how much intrinsic interest one has in one's work, it is necessary for most of us to be concerned about economic matters. Some form of extrinsic reward must also be provided for our labors, if we are to pay our bills.

Contrary to Deci's hypothesis, a worker who receives high extrinsic reward for work that he or she also enjoys may feel that he or she has his or her cake and can eat it too. The money does not make the work per se any more or less interesting. The work may or may not be interesting, but the amount of compensation is a different dimension. Contrariwise, workers with boring but well-paid jobs probably still regard their jobs as boring but feel that the money is their real incentive for continuing. In other words, the added money should not make the worker perceive the job as being any more or less interesting than it actually is. Its function is to keep the worker from quitting the job, perhaps, but the worker still knows the boring job for what it is.

Deci's hypothesis concerning the reduction of intrinsic motivation by the presence of extrinsic rewards may be applicable in nonwork situations such as the one he used. Using similar situations, others (e.g., Kruglonski, Alon, and Lewis, 1972) have replicated the effect. Furthermore, Levine and Fasnacht (1974) argued that it may extend to clinical situations involving the use of extrinsic tokens, such as in behavior modification.

A discussion of the relative role of intrinsic and extrinsic motivation would not be complete without some consideration of the activities of the average housewife. Although times have changed, many married women are still employed as housewives. Discussions of workers have pertained primarily to men or single women, thus ignoring a sizable percentage of the adult population.

Few women would argue that most domestic chores are intrinsically interesting or intellectually challenging. Nor is there any form of financial reward for such activities. Domestic duties seem to be motivated by a sense of obligation or a need to avoid social disapproval. Women have been socialized traditionally to fulfill the role of housewife and the execution of these duties is assumed to be satisfying. To the extent that a woman never questions what she is taught, these roles may be fulfilling because they provide her with what society has taught her to expect and accept: a husband, children, and a home. But women today can find fulfillment in other ways, ways that heretofore were limited to men. The traditional roles set aside for women, other than the function of childbearing, which is biologically limited to females, do not include duties that anyone would find intrinsically rewarding. (Child rearing, in contrast to childbearing, can be performed by men as well as it can be done by women.) Instead, these duties are done to avoid negative extrinsic motives, such as criticism and ridicule or to fulfill social role demands. Analyses of human motivation have generally failed to consider the bases for this major type of behavior and further study of the motives for housework is needed.

CONCLUSIONS

Generalizations about work in general have been based on studies of blue-collar workers, especially in assembly-line situations. It is easier to measure number and quality of products in such situations, but it is more difficult to find comparable indices for many supervisory and managerial occupations. On the other hand, the likelihood of creative opportunities for imagination and innovation are greater among the latter situations than among the former.

More attention needs to be directed to the identification of individual differences in the values and abilities of workers. Whereas the nature of the work may be more crucial than the pay, within limits, for some workers, the opposite may hold for others.

Vroom and Deci (1971) make the distinction between three main types of arrangements regarding extrinsic motivators such as pay within work settings. In the *paternalistic* approach, the goal is to satisfy all workers on the assumption that this factor will maximize motivation and performance. Pay is not contingent on performance. However, if everyone gets paid the same, regardless of their level of performance, it may prove discouraging to better workers who may quit.

On the other hand, the *scientific management* approach emphasizes the need to make pay contingent on performance so that better and greater productivity leads to higher payoffs. Unfortunately, it is not always easy to define objective criteria for evaluating performance. Lawler (1973) holds that worker dissatisfaction may occur if soft criteria such as human relations are used in determining pay levels. On the other hand, workers can accept the validity of contingency arrangements between pay levels and productivity if there are publicly known objective criteria for evaluating work.

Finally, the *participative management* approach places the emphasis on intrinsic aspects of the work. Jobs designed to suit human needs for responsibility, challenge, variety, and sense of accomplishment are emphasized with this approach. Workers are encouraged to participate in making decisions that affect their working lives.

Lawler (1973) regards the latter two systems as superior to the paternalistic approach, but feels that they have weaknesses. Neither the scientific management nor the participative management philosophy seems to recognize or allow for individual differences among workers.

All workers are not primarily interested in pay. Some workers consider the intrinsic aspects of the work as more important. On the other hand, not all workers wish to get involved in decision making, and not all jobs can readily be redesigned or enlarged. In view of the highly individualistic needs and motives of different workers, Lawler concludes that no one approach will be satisfactory to account for the work motivation of all workers. He argues in behalf of the need to work toward the ideal of identifying the idiosyncratic needs of each worker. For those workers who are primarily interested in lower needs, he recommends that extrinsic rewards be provided so that higher pay is given for better performance. On the other hand, a focus on job enrichment and other intrinsic rewards should be used for workers who value higher order needs.

Consistent with these recommendations are the findings of Hulin and Blood (1968) whose review of previous studies revealed that enrichment programs had differential effectiveness. Whereas workers who held traditional work values preferred complex jobs that offered challenge, workers who were alienated from the importance of work did not respond favorably to job enrichment. Blue-collar workers are more likely to be in the latter category, whereas white-collar workers respond more favorably to enriched jobs.

Sandler (1974) calls for a cafeteria system in which several alternative work patterns would be available, even patterns that management might not believe in, for workers to choose among. This system will enable all workers to find something that suits their personal needs. Failure to provide such an opportunity does not prevent the employee from trying to achieve personal needs nonetheless and, according to Sandler (1974, p. 772), "It is likely that the result will be either covert attempts at constructive satisfaction, or covert attempts at destructive satisfaction through increased waste, downtime, sabotage, etc."

Summary

Many modern work tasks have been condemned as dull, dehumanizing, and unfulfilling. Accordingly, one major goal of research has been to discover means of improving work in order to enhance worker morale. Attempts to increase productivity by improving extrinsic rewards such as salary and fringe benefits or by improving the work environment and physical surroundings have been criticized by Herzberg. His findings have suggested that job *dissatisfaction* may be reduced or removed by such procedures, but that changes are not necessarily sufficient to bring about job *satisfaction*. Satisfaction is assumed to stem from intrinsic features of the job tasks themselves.

Although conflicting results have been obtained about the influence of extrinsic factors such as pay, Herzberg's contention that it is a relatively low factor in determining job satisfaction is highly influential. Consequently many attempts have been made to restructure the nature of work tasks, work hours, and worker participation in decision making in the hope that such changes will improve not only the satisfaction but also the productivity of workers. The relationship between job satisfaction and productivity, however, is ambiguous. Absenteeism and turnover do appear to decrease as satisfaction rises, but these gains do not mean that productivity per se is any higher.

A more extended examination of the effects of pay on work motivation centered around two major theories: expectancy and equity. Expectancy theory predicts greater motivation when the expectancy of receiving pay and the value of pay to the individual are high. Equity theory assumes that the worker's feelings of over- or undercompensation, which he or she forms by comparing his or her pay with that of other workers or some internal standard, is the key factor. If the worker feels underpaid, he or she will work less effectively, whereas the opposite is predicted if the worker feels overpaid. A number of studies attempted to test the two theories but the overall findings are equivocal. In part this situation is due to some vagueness in the concepts of expectancy and equity and also because factors other than pay affect the individual's work performance. Clearcut tests between the two theories have not been achieved.

Some studies have tested Deci's theory that performance of an intrinsically interesting task can be weakened by providing extrinsic incentives, suggesting that the individual changes his or her perception of motives for engaging in the task. Instead of assuming that he or she is performing the task simply because he or she likes it, the worker who receives extrinsic rewards may come to think that he or she is doing it for these latter incentives. Later, if the external rewards are terminated, we might expect to find less willingness to perform because the original intrinsic appeal of the task has been undermined.

Whether or not this intriguing theory is applicable to real-life work situations is unknown as most of the tests have dealt with laboratory situations. The worker may be able to separate the dimension of pay from his or her evaluation of the intrinsic appeal of the job so that the former does not affect his or her judgment of the latter.

Finally, it was suggested that greater attention be given to the nature of individual differences in determining work motivation. Whereas some workers may be attracted more by extrinsic considerations such as pay, other workers may consider the intrinsic aspects of the job more vital.

References

ADAMS, J. S. Toward an understanding of inequity. *Journal of Abnormal and Social Psychology*, 1963, *67*, 422–436.

———. Inequity in social exchange. In L. Berkowitz (Ed.), *Advances in experimental social psychology*. (Vol. 2.) New York: Academic, 1965.

———, and JACOBSEN, P. R. Effects of wage inequities on work quality. *Journal of Abnormal and Social Psychology*, 1964, *69*, 19–25.

———, and Rosenbaum, W. B. The relationship of worker productivity to cognitive dissonance about wage inequities. *Journal of Applied Psychology*, 1962, *46*, 161–164.

ATKINSON, J. W. Motivational determinants of risk-taking behavior. *Psychological Review*, 1957, *64*, 359–372.

DALTON, M. *Men who manage, fusions of feeling and theory in administration.* New York: Wiley, 1959.

DECI, E. L. Effects of externally mediated rewards on intrinsic motivation. *Journal of Personality and Social Psychology*, 1971, *18*, 105–115.

———. Intrinsic motivation, extrinsic reinforcement, and inequity. *Journal of Personality and Social Psychology*, 1972, *22*, 113–120.

FORD, R. N. *Motivation through work itself.* New York: American Management Association, 1969.

GARLAND, H. The effects of piece-rate underpayment and overpayment on job performance: A test of equity theory with a new induction procedure. *Journal of Applied Social Psychology*, 1973, *3*, 325–334.

HERZBERG, F. *Work and the nature of man.* New York: Crowell, 1966.

HERZBERG, F., MAUSNER, B., and SNYDERMAN, B. B. *The motivation to work.* Second Edition. New York: Wiley, 1959.

HOUSE, R. J., and WIDGOR, L. A. Herzberg's dual-factor theory of job satisfaction and motivation: A review of the evidence and a criticism. *Personnel Psychology*, 1967, *20*, 369–390.

HULIN, C. L., and BLOOD, M. R. Job enlargement, individual differences, and worker responses. *Psychological Bulletin*, 1968, *69*, 41–55.

JONES, J. A. Try it, you'll like it, say the four-day week firms. *Los Angeles Times*, April 9, 1972.

KRUGLONSKI, A. W., ALON, S., and LEWIS, T. Retrospective misattribution and task enjoyment. *Journal of Experimental Social Psychology*, 1972, *8*, 493–501.

LAWLER, E. E., III. Equity theory as a predictor of productivity and work quality. *Psychological Bulletin*, 1968, *70*, 596–610.

———. *Pay and organizational effectiveness: A psychological view.* New York: McGraw-Hill, 1971.

———. *Motivation in work organizations.* New York: Wadsworth, 1973.

———, and PORTER, L. W. The effect of performance on job satisfaction. *Industrial Relations*, 1967, *7*, 20–28.

LEVINE, F. M., and FASHACHT, G. Token rewards may lead to token learning. *American Psychologist*, 1974, *29*, 816–820.

LEWIN, K. *Principles of topological psychology.* New York: McGraw-Hill, 1936.

MASLOW, A. H. A theory of human motivation. *Psychological Review*, 1943, *50*, 370–396.

McGREGOR, D. *The human side of enterprise.* New York: McGraw-Hill, 1960.

NORD, W. R., and COSTIGAN, R. Worker adjustment to the four day week. *Journal of Applied Psychology*, 1973, *58*, 60–66.

PAUL, W. J., ROBERTSON, K. B., and HERZBERG, F. Job enlargement pays off. *Harvard Business Review,* 1969, *47,* 61–78.

PRITCHARD, R. D. Equity theory: A review and critique. *Organizational Behavior and Human Performance,* 1969, *4,* 176–211.

———, DUNNETTE, M. D., and JORGENSON, D. O. Effects of perceptions of equity and inequity on worker performance and satisfaction. *Journal of Applied Psychology,* 1972, *56,* 75–94.

ROETHLINBERGER, F. J., and DICKSON, W. J. *Management and the worker.* Cambridge, Mass.: Harvard University Press, 1939.

ROTTER, J. B. *Social learning and clinical psychology.* Englewood Cliffs, N.J.: Prentice-Hall, 1954.

SANDLER, B. E. Eclecticism at work, approaches to job design. *American Psychologist,* 1974, *29,* 767–773.

Schrank, R. Work in America: what do workers really want? *Industrial Relations,* 1974, *13,* 124–129.

SHEPPARD, H. L., and HERRICK, N. Q. *Where have all the robots gone? Worker dissatisfaction in the '70s.* New York: Free Press, 1972.

Time, Oct. 30, 1972. Is the work ethic going out of style?

TOLMAN, E. C. *Purposive behavior in animals and men.* New York: Appleton, 1932.

VROOM, V. H. *Work and motivation.* New York: Wiley, 1964.

———, and DECI, E. L. *Management and motivation.* Baltimore: Penguin, 1971.

W. E. Upjohn Institute for Employment Research. *Work in America: Report of a special task force to the Secretary of H. E. W.* Cambridge, Mass.: M.I.T.

ZEITLIN, L. R. A little larceny can do a lot for employee morale. *Psychology Today,* 1971, *5,* (1) 22; 24; 26; 64.

CHAPTER 8

Social Motivation: Winning Friends and Influencing People

A book written in 1936 by Dale Carnegie, entitled *How To Win Friends and Influence People,* was one of the most successful how-to-do-it books of all time. Written simply, it was a practical guide of tips and advice for success in our daily social interactions. Because it dealt with a basic concern or motivation, Carnegie's book received a wide audience. This chapter will examine some of the reasons people are so highly motivated to find ways to win friends and influence people.

The basic social nature of the human condition is well captured in the immortal lines of John Donne: "No man is an island, entire of itself; every man is a piece of the continent." From the moment of birth, humans are highly dependent on the protection and nurturance of other humans in order to survive physically. Studies by Bowlby (1969) of infants and Harlow (Harlow, 1958; Harlow and Zimmerman, 1959) of primates clearly indicate the need for the formation of vital social and affectional bonds between young offspring and adults. Thus, not only is the infant dependent on others for physical needs but in the process acquires psychological attachments and dependency. This tendency may exist because it has proved necessary for the survival of the species over the long course of evolution.

As the individual matures, the degree of dependence may give the impression of being reduced as socialization goals demand that some amount of independence be developed. Although it is undeniably true that there is a reduction in the physical and psychological dependence between the child and parent, a different dependency takes over, namely dependency on peer group members. The child may become less emotionally dependent on his or her parents but may develop a dependency on other children or adults. Needs for affiliation, social approval, aid, etc. still exist and lead us to seek interactions with other people. The present chapter is concerned with such social motivation—why we affiliate and with whom.

Why Do We Affiliate?

The tendency to affiliate is inherent in the nature of human needs. We could not survive without the assistance of others. Out of this situation, we develop a generalized motivation or need for affiliation, even when our physical survival is not in jeopardy. By association, our early experiences teach us that affiliation with other humans is a positive situation. Erikson (1968) refers to this outcome as basic trust and suggests that negative early social interactions could lead to a basic mistrust of others in later years.

Throughout life, one finds oneself in one association or another with other people. A child attends school with classmates. He or she joins clubs and activity groups with others who share common interests. Later the adult works with associates and colleagues. Friends are joined for companionship during leisure and social activities. In short, most human activity is socially based.

As one of the author's students observed when reflecting on her motives for joining groups during high school, not joining became a type of deviant behavior because joining was a familiar behavior. In fact, she reported that she felt anxious when she considered not joining groups on one occasion. Her earlier conditioning to affiliate consequently led her to yield and join groups as she had so often in the past.

ANXIETY AND AFFILIATION

Anxiety, in general, may be a basic antecedent of affiliation. This anxiety is not limited to that generated by the act of not joining as in the example described. Instead, it is likely that any type of anxiety can lead to affiliation.

One reason is that there may be safety in numbers so that danger or threat can sometimes be confronted better by a group than by an individual. Even if the group cannot counteract the adversary, there may be some comfort to be gained by affiliating with fellow victims, just as chickens huddle together as they are about to be attacked by a fox. Perhaps knowing that one is not alone in one's suffering serves to mitigate the pain or stress.

Schachter (1959) reports evidence from anecdotal sources and autobiographical accounts of the unpleasant nature of prolonged isolation. People who are imprisoned, lost, or otherwise prevented from normal social contact typically report extreme anxiety and discomfort at their plight.

Schachter recognized that this evidence may be biased in that only those persons who found isolation to be aversive might have recorded their experiences. In his own pilot studies, Schachter paid volunteer college students to live in isolation for a short period and found that a few subjects experienced no discomfort whatsoever. This evidence was considered inconclusive because the subjects, unlike prisoners or persons lost in the wild, suffered little stress due to the uncertainty of whether they would ever be saved or released. Moreover, these college students were volunteers for an experiment and therefore a rather biased sample.

Does the anxiety observed in naturalistic observation of persons who have experienced prolonged isolation imply that social contact and affiliation is necessary to alleviate the anxiety created by isolation? This is one possible inference, but it should be kept in mind that these people were accustomed to social contact, and the changed circumstances rather than isolation per se may have created the anxiety. If persons who were generally isolated throughout their lives were then subjected to prolonged isolation, the adverse effect might be absent or reduced. It might also be suggested that for the latter individuals, a shift to heightened social contact might be a stronger source of anxiety than isolation.

In a well-known study by Schachter (1959), one group of women was told that they would receive painful shocks (high anxiety) and another group was led to think that they would receive mild shocks (low anxiety). While waiting for the study to begin, they filled out anxiety questionnaires. Then they were given the choice of waiting alone or with other women who were also waiting for the shock apparatus to be set up.

Twice as many women in the high anxiety condition elected to wait with other women than to wait alone. Moreover, not only does misery love company, but the company must also be experiencing misery too. Schachter found in a second study that if women expecting shock were given a choice of waiting alone or with women who were merely waiting to see their advisors, none of them wanted company but preferred to suffer alone.

Schachter's study demonstrated that greater anxiety led to greater affiliation. In a similar manner, other forms of anxiety also promote affiliation. Farmers fearing crop failure might form cooperatives, workers fearing exploitation might form unions, and small nations fearing war with a stronger enemy might form a pact.

On the other hand, there are limits to the kinds of aversive states that could foster affiliation. For example, shame or embarrassment is aversive but hardly a condition that would tend to promote affiliation. As Sarnoff and Zimbardo (1961) have shown, these aversive states are better borne in solitude than in companionship. Using male subjects, they replicated Schachter's results when subjects expected to receive shock. But when subjects had to suck a pacifier, instead of receive shocks, they preferred to wait alone.

Returning to the finding that affiliation is increased when fear or anxiety is aroused, what are the underlying processes? Do individuals feel stronger and more capable of coping with danger? Although this process could occur in some situations, it is not possible for affiliation to prevent the impending shock in Schachter's study. Perhaps affiliation allows group conversation to occur and thus distracts members from thinking about the impending pain. Schachter, himself, hypothesized that a process of social comparison occurs in the group such that each member compared her own level of anxiety with that of the others. Social comparison among group members is a means by which a person can identify his or her relative standing (Festinger, 1954) and this process is common. But exactly how social comparison can act to reduce anxiety in Schachter's situation is unclear. Although it undoubtedly might occur, the effect would be that some subjects would find that they were above average and others would find that they were below average in anxiety. But how would this knowledge provide the women with any better means of coping with the shocks they were awaiting?

On the other hand, the information about one's relative characteristics obtained from the social comparisons permitted by affiliation has been found to affect some behaviors such as risk taking (Kogan and Wallach, 1964). It is reported that individuals will advocate bigger risks after a group discussion of hypothetical everyday decision-making situations. Apparently, the opportunity to learn the views and reasoning of others as well as the tendency to avoid appearing overly conservative might produce this *risky shift,* as the phenomenom is termed. Although there have been recent questions about the validity of the concept (e.g., Cartwright, 1973), it does serve to focus on the important question of how social comparison affects behavior (Brown, 1974). Thus, charitable behavior has been found to vary as a function of opportunities for social comparison (Blake, Rosenbaum, and Duryea, 1955). Pledges were obtained for donations to buy a gift for a secretary of a psychology department. Persons approached were shown a list of what others had allegedly donated. The list values varied, being higher on the average for one-half the subjects. Donations tended to approach the means of the list that the donors were shown, demonstrating clearly how social comparison affects generosity.

Another consequence of affiliation during adversity may be an increased cohesiveness. After surviving an ordeal, members may discover that they like each other better because of their shared or common fate. Naturalistic accounts of survivors of shipwrecks, natural disasters, and other stressful events suggest such an outcome. In Schachter's study, the attitudes of the women toward each other could not be assessed inasmuch as the other girls were confederates. Furthermore, the stressful event was very brief and would not have provided much time for a group of strangers to get acquainted.

The example of initiation ceremonies such as those typical in college fraternities and sororities is a stressful event for the initiate, which presumably makes him or her value membership more highly after surviving the ordeal. Unfortunately, some of the ordeals have tragic endings because the prank selected was unduly dangerous and the initiate actually died. Tiger (1969, pp. 146–47) described some of the humiliating and stressful stunts used for initiations in fraternal as well as military organizations. Frequently, an attempt at exposing the initiate to some form of sexual embarrassment or harassment is involved.

An experimental study (Aronson and Mills, 1959) of the effects of the severity of the initiation on the initiate's liking for the group employed such a situation. The study required college women to say taboo words as a screening test in order to join a discussion group that would deal presumably with sexual topics. Then they got a chance to listen in on their group discussion, which turned out to be rather dull. Compared to a control group that did not undergo the embarrassing pretest, the initiates who suffered indicated a greater liking of the discussion group, boring as it was. The implication of the experiment is that we appreciate those things for which we have had to work hard.

The situation we have been describing is one in which we are assessing the byproducts rather than the anticipated or planned consequences of affiliation. In contrast, we will now consider situations in which affiliation is sought deliberately for the express intention of winning friends and increasing one's likeableness.

THE IMPORTANCE OF BEING LIKED

Even when there is no pressing need for aid or assistance from others, most people enjoy and seek the company of friends and acquaintances. In return, we also like it when others seek our companionship as it is testimony to our own importance and popularity when other people need and like us. Thus, we affiliate not only because we need other people but because we hope that others will reciprocate by accepting, liking, and seeking our presence. On the other hand, if no one is attracted to us or calls upon us for help or mere companionship, our self-concepts may suffer devaluation. We enjoy being popular and being liked by others. Of course, individuals differ widely in the extent to which they need the social approval of others, and these generalizations will not apply equally to everyone.

Our behavior is heavily influenced by the approval or disapproval of other people. Indeed, many actions are deliberately selected to enhance the receipt of social approval. Although the search for social approval is not identical with the need for affiliation, a close relationship may exist. Long-term affiliations such as friendships are based on interpersonal liking, which would be difficult to achieve usually without some degree of approval of each other by members of the friendship. Furthermore, although it is not clear, it is possible that anxiety about one's own adequacy may be associated with a higher need for social approval. Being unsure of one's own abilities, approval of others serves as a powerful social source of feedback about oneself. Thus, social approval needs and affiliation needs may have similar origins. In fact, one consequence of the need for social approval may be affiliation, and it is possible that the continuation of an affiliation depends on whether or not social approval comes from the affiliate.

INDIVIDUAL DIFFERENCES. Crowne and Marlowe (1964) developed a paper and pencil personality scale to assess individual differences in the need for social approval. Items that they felt were untrue of most persons but represented admirable qualities were used as well as items that were probably true of most persons but reflective of socially undesirable behaviors and attitudes. An example of the first type might be "I always tell the truth," whereas "Sometimes I drive after I've had a drink or two too many" illustrates the second type of item.

Answers of true to the first type of item and false to the second variety were scored as indicative of a need for social approval. In other words, claiming that socially desirable statements that are true of almost no one are applicable to oneself may reflect a need for social approval as does denying the validity of socially undesirable statements that are generally true of most people.

Several validation studies were conducted to see if persons who differed on the social approval need test scores also differed in expected ways in actual behavior. In one study, subjects were assigned a boring spool packing task in which they had to fill a box with empty thread spools, empty it, refill it, and so forth. Then subjects were asked to rate the enjoyableness of the task. Because it had been boring, a candid answer would be to rate the task low in this dimension. However, it was assumed that the socially desirable response would be to claim that the task had been enjoyable. It was therefore predicted and found that higher ratings were obtained from subjects scoring high in need for approval.

Other validation studies included tests of conformity and verbal conditioning. Using a task in which a number of confederates gave false responses on perceptual judgments prior to the real subject making his or her judgments, greater conformity to group pressure was obtained with high need for social approval subjects. Verbal conditioning was assumed to be susceptible also to the influence of social cues. In this task, the subject must construct sentences or name words, while the experimenter reinforces a subset of the responses with a subtle response such as "mmhm hmm." All sentences starting with "We" or all plural nouns might be used as the subset, for example. The results showed greater verbal conditioning, that is, an increase in the frequency of the reinforced response subset among subjects who were high in the need for social approval.

Crowne and Marlowe's scale provides us with one means of identifying individuals differing in social approval need, but it does not tell us how such differences come about. It would appear that social approval is related to affiliation inasmuch as one motive for affiliation may be the opportunity to gain social approval. For some people, the achievement of social approval may be an end in itself. It is desirable, because it enhances one's self-esteem to realize that one is valued and popular among others. It is conceivable that persons low in self-esteem develop high needs for social approval precisely in order to enhance self-esteem.

LIKING AND ULTERIOR MOTIVES

Being popular and well liked is not without its liabilities. Those who are sought for social interaction and companionship are not always popular merely, or even at all sometimes, because of their charming and delightful personalities. Instead, especially if they are influential, powerful, and prestigious persons who are able to make or affect decisions with important implications for others, they may be the targets of ingratiators who seek ulterior goals by first securing their friendship and approval.

Ingratiation refers to the process by which a person seeking special treatment and vantage from a more powerful person attempts to increase his or her likeableness to that person. Being liked is assumed to lead to favoritism and preferential treatment from those with power and influence. Consequently, those who lack ability, resources, or power may resort to ingratiation tactics in dealing with those who can bestow favors.

Affiliation, then, can also be a means toward an end rather than a goal itself. Ulterior motives underlie the attempts to be liked in which ingratiation is involved, whereas the need for social approval, which also leads to affiliation, is a goal in its own right.

Tactics of Ingratiation. The process of ingratiation is a subtle and complex one, because the intent of the ingratiator is something that must be disguised. There is the danger that the target of ingratiation may be suspicious or even detect the true basis for the ingratiator's fawning and servile attempts to endear himself or herself. Since the would-be ingratiator, by definition, is not already in the high esteem of the target person, how can he or she reduce the distance between them?

Jones (1966) and Jones and Wortman (1973) summarize the major tactics of ingratiation. The ageless strategy of flattery is a technique by which one might attempt to gain the liking of the target. A different approach is to determine how to present oneself in the most favorable light, even if misrepresentation is necessary. Offering favors to the target person might succeed in gaining the liking of the target so that he or she might reciprocate on some later occasion. Finally, opinion conformity might be employed in which the ingratiator tries to agree with the views of the target. The assumption is that most people like those who hold views that are similar to their own and that opinion conformity will foster liking by the target.

Effectiveness of Ingratiation. Jones (1966) reported a number of studies with his colleagues in which he attempted to assess the degree to which these tactics succeeded in increasing the attraction of the ingratiator in the eyes of the target person. The basic paradigm in these experiments

called for confederates of the experimenter to use various tactics in an interaction with the subject who represented the target person. Comparisons of
the subjects' liking of the different confederate behaviors provided an assessment of the effectiveness of the different ingratiation tactics.

Without going into detail about the outcomes of the specific experiments,
a number of general points are worth making. The degree to which an ingratiator will be successful in generating attraction depends largely on how
credible his or her behavior is. For example, a lower status person who
flatters a higher status person may be suspect, because the latter may perceive the possibility that he or she is being buttered up. Consequently, the
superior may disregard the compliment or may even retaliate at the real or
imagined attempt to ingratiate by punishing or at least, disliking, the subordinate.

Jones and Wortman (1973) also discuss the possibility that under some
conditions praise may have negative effects, because it places the recipient
in an awkward or embarrassing position. To the extent that this occurs, the
skillful ingratiator must avoid this unintended consequence if he or she is to
achieve his or her goals.

Use of favorable self-presentation may fail to ingratiate if the image is too
positive, because it appears as boastful conceit. Sometimes modesty is the
better policy, because it is less likely to arouse suspicion. Even here, however, there are dangers as, for example, in the case of a person who actually
does have positive qualities that must be played down in order to avoid
the appearance of ingratiation.

Another aspect of Jones's work has focused on a laboratory investigation
of the other half of the picture, the actual behavior displayed by persons
placed in a situation in which the use of ingratiation on their part is likely.
The basic paradigm in these studies varies the degree of dependence the
subject has on other persons within the experiment. In the experimental or
ingratiation condition, subjects might be told to interact with another subject
who is actually a stooge. He or she is told that compatible pairs of subjects
will be selected for a subsequent study in which monetary prizes may be rewarded. Thus, there is an incentive for the subject to attempt ingratiating tactics when interacting with the stooge. Subjects in the control condition also
interact with another subject, but they are instructed that their task is to aid
clinical psychology graduate students in their training in judging people.
They are told to present their "true selves." Comparison of the interaction
between the subject and confederate under the two situations provides a
measure of the nature of the ingratiation process.

In an illustrative study (Jones, Gergen, and Jones, 1963), pairs of college
Naval R.O.T.C. students were tested, with one member of each pair being a
freshman (low status) and one an upperclassman (high status). During the
first year of the study, all subjects were instructed to try to get the other pair
member to like them, so that they could be assessed more accurately for
leadership potential. Ingratiatory tactics were expected, because each subject

stood to benefit if he was liked. Pair members had to communicate via written messages, because they were isolated from each other so that the experimenter could intercept their messages. He substituted his own messages in order to standardize the input received by all subjects. For example, in one task subjects had to exchange opinions on various topics, some related to the navy, others to academic matters, and some to miscellaneous subjects. A measure of conformity was obtained by comparing the similarity of each subject's message with those inserted and manipulated by the experimenter but which each subject thought was coming from the other pair member.

In the control condition, pair members were instructed to be as accurate as possible in presenting information about themselves during this part of the study. It was assumed that subjects should have little or no reason to ingratiate or try to improve their likeability under these instructions.

More opinion conformity was obtained under the ingratiation condition, as predicted. Figure 8–1 shows that whereas high status (HS) subjects conformed more on items irrelevant to the Naval dimension in which status differences existed, it was precisely this area in which the low status (LS) subjects conformed the most. Thus, high status subjects wanted to appear more approachable by agreeing on non-Naval topics but also maintain their status by not conforming on Naval topics. The opposite attitude exists in the low status subjects who deferred to their partners on Naval topics.

It should be pointed out that the use of ingratiation in real life is usually done without the full awareness or realization of the ingratiator. Years of deliberate flattery in order to gain advantages result in such strong habits that a person may come to exercise ingratiatory tactics without even being conscious of any exploitative strategy or intention. And even if a person has

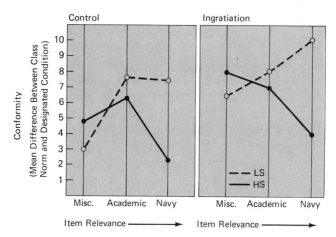

FIGURE 8–1. Conformity as a function of issue relevance. [From "Tactics of Ingratiation Among Leaders and Subordinates in a Status Hierarchy" by E. E. Jones, K. J. Gergen, and R. G. Jones, *Psychological Monographs,* 1963, *77* (3, Whole No. 566). Copyright 1963 by the American Psychological Association. Reprinted by permission.]

genuine motives in offering a compliment, some of the time such flattery will produce the consequence of enhanced status in relationship to the recipient.

ADVANTAGES OF BEING LIKED

Does one increase the chances of receiving benefits and favors if one is liked? Are people more willing to help those whom they like? Certainly this assumption is made whenever we attempt to ingratiate ourselves with others.

But even if no ingratiation is involved, such as when a recipient of favors does not know the benefactor, it is likely that an unexpected dividend of being likeable is the receipt of favors, preferential treatment, etc.

Equal Status Relationships.   One study (Baron, 1971a) demonstrated that a favor is more likely to be done for more likeable persons, especially if the requests are more demanding. In Baron's study, a confederate interacted with a subject and exchanged information with him about their attitudes on several topics. One group of subjects learned that the confederate shared many similar attitudes and had given a favorable rating of the subject, whereas a second group learned that the confederate had many attitudes that were different from their own and also had given them an unfavorable rating. As one might expect, the first group gave the confederate higher ratings on likeableness.

As the experiment ended, the confederate then requested a favor such as returning a library book or checking out a book and holding it until the confederate could claim it. More subjects granted the favor that was more demanding when they liked the confederate, but there was little difference in response to the trivial request.

A related question is whether we are more inclined to like or at least help those who aid us. Do we feel obliged to reciprocate even if the original aid to us was given with no strings attached by our benefactor? Berkowitz (1973) has suggested that a norm of social reciprocity exists that leads us to want to return favors to those who help us. Quite possibly our liking of our benefactors may also increase. This prediction assumes, however, that we do not perceive the favors as manipulative attempts to win our attraction.

The situation involving the confirmation hearings in late 1974 of Nelson Rockefeller as Vice President of the United States illustrates the situation. During the hearings, Governor Rockefeller revealed that he had made generous gifts over the years to important and influential persons. We do not know exactly what his motives were in making these gifts, but let us assume, for sake of argument, that his intentions were honorable. Even so, there would always be the possibility that some of the recipients of his gifts might feel obliged to return political favors to him whenever possible. To what extent such reciprocation would be due to a sense of obligation versus an increased liking of the benefactor would be difficult to separate.

SOCIAL MOTIVATION: WINNING FRIENDS **199**

UNEQUAL STATUS RELATIONSHIPS. In addition to liking between friends who are more or less on an equal basis, liking may also exist between a subordinate and a superior, such as when one person is under the control of another. The factors that affect liking in these situations are not the same as those underlying equal status friendships.

We have already cited the ingratiation situation in which a person of lower status or power tries to get a more influential person to like him or her. In this case the lower status person must appear likeable to the higher status member of the dyad, but it is not usually important that the target of the ingratiation be likeable. In fact, it is easier for the ingratiator to justify his or her exploitation of the higher status person if he or she is unlikeable.

The ingratiator neglects criteria such as likeability in selecting a target person and focuses on those persons with the power and ability to help him or her achieve goals. The ingratiator even associates with detestible, obnoxious, or contemptible persons if he or she really wants the benefits that he or she thinks the target person can grant.

Freud's concept of *defensive identification* is a related concept that emphasizes the role played by likeability in gaining the favor of those with more power. Freud held that the male child is in conflict with the father for the mother's affection. This rivalry known as the *Oedipus complex* creates considerable anxiety in the child, because he knows that his foe is more powerful. In order to attain the good graces of his father, the child emulates his values and personality traits. The assumption is that the father would be less hostile toward a child who was highly similar to himself. Just as with ingratiation, defensive identification leads to behaviors that foster liking between the more powerful person and the weaker one.

Another psychoanalytic concept known as *identification with the aggressor* also illustrates the assumed benefits of being liked. If a more powerful foe can be induced to like you, he or she may be less likely to attack you. Consequently, a defensive tactic for one lacking in power would be to ingratiate oneself with the enemy. Bettleheim's (1943) classic study of Nazi concentration camp inmate behavior is frequently cited as an example. Some of the inmates emulated the behavior, mannerisms, and even the dress of the Nazi guards and were often more brutal in their treatment of fellow inmates than were the guards. Bettleheim regarded this behavior as an illustration of identification with the aggressor.

Studies in which jury decisions have been simulated have confirmed what most people already believe, namely, that the attractiveness or likeability of a defendant can influence the jury's judgments. Landy and Aronson (1969) described an automobile accident that resulted in a death. The defendant in the case was described to three different subgroups: attractive, unattractive, or neutral. In addition, they included another variable of little interest to us here, the attractiveness of the victim.

The subjects were all told that negligible automobile homicide could carry a sentence from one to twenty-five years imprisonment. Their task was to consider the case and render a sentence according to their personal judgment. Results showed a mean sentence of 11.75 years for the unattractive defendant, significantly longer than the 8.58 years recommended for the attractive defendant, or the 8.22 years for the neutral defendant.

Mitchell and Byrne (1973) used a student disciplinary case in their experiment on the effects of attractiveness. Subjects read about a student who was charged with the theft of an examination. They also received a personal description of the defendant who was depicted as being totally similar or dissimilar to the subject in five topics on which subjects had given their own attitudes earlier in the semester.

Finally, subjects saw a statement by the defendant in which he admitted his guilt. They then made their recommendations about possible punishment ranging from reprimand, probation, suspension, to expulsion. The results indicated that less stringent punishment was recommended by a subject if there was a high similarity of attitudes between the subject and the defendant.

These results should not be interpreted to mean that attractiveness is a major determinant of jury decisions, because the laboratory situation is greatly simplified compared to an actual courtroom situation. Kalven and Zeisal (1966) conducted a study of factors influencing actual judges and juries. Based on close to 1,000 cases in which judge and jury disagreed, judges indicated that about 11 percent of these disparities were due to the impression made by the defendant on the jury. In the majority of the cases, other factors must be operative such as the actual merits of the case, as seen by the judge and jury. Perhaps attractiveness becomes important as a determinant of decisions only when there is ambiguity in the evidence.

In summary, a less powerful person is motivated to be liked, because he or she stands to benefit from being attractive to those who hold the power over him or her. More benefits (or less harm) is the reward for being likeable, in everyday situations, prison camps, or courtrooms.

Criteria for Choosing Friends

Thus far, we have discussed factors that might favor affiliation without examining factors that might determine the kinds of persons who are sought for association. Excluding involuntary associations such as military organizations, for example, we usually like to select our own acquaintances. In forming a car pool, bridge group, or discussion group we may be relatively indiscriminate, but in fulfilling goals of marriage, close friendships, etc., we are apt to be choosy.

Generally speaking, we prefer affiliating with people whom we like or at least respect, whereas we reject associations with persons whom we dislike, feel contempt for, or disagree with on important issues. By selecting associates who are similar to ourselves in background, beliefs, and values, mutual reinforcement and minimal conflict exists. Similar people are apt to provide more social approval for each other, a goal that is important to many people, because it provides some measure of self-worth.

THE ROLE OF SIMILARITY

The argument that attraction is a function of similarity can be vague, unless one can specify in which dimensions similarity is important. Although everyday observation suggests that similarity of race, religion, political views, age, and social economic status might foster attraction, it is less clear whether similarity of some personality traits is necessary or desirable. As long as two persons do not clash in their attitudes and traits, it seems possible for persons with complementary but different characteristics to be attracted to each other.

ATTITUDINAL SIMILARITY. Byrne (1969) has summarized a decade of research on the factors influencing attraction or liking. In most of his studies (e.g., Byrne, 1961, 1962; Byrne and Nelson, 1965), subjects first complete an attitude survey on a number of topics such as smoking, drinking, public school integration, university grading practices, and political parties. Later they are presented with the responses of a hypothetical stranger to the same topics and asked to rate the attractiveness of the individual in dimensions such as intelligence, morality, knowledge of current events, and adjustment. In addition, they are asked explicitly about their personal feelings toward the person and whether or not they would like to work with the person in another experiment.

Variations in the degree of similarity between the stranger's attitudes and those of the subjects are manipulated by Byrne. Figure 8–2 indicates that there has generally been a direct relationship between the percentage of topics on which there was agreement between the stranger and the subject and the extent to which the stranger was judged attractive.

The research of others can also be viewed as consistent with Byrne's findings. Newcomb's (1961) naturalistic study of the process by which strangers get acquainted and friendships develop is a good example. In this study, seventeen male students agreed to live together and participate in a project during which they would complete numerous questionnaires throughout the academic year in exchange for free rent in a house they shared.

Each week they completed questionnaires concerning their interactions with the other participants and rated their attitudes toward each other. Because the subjects were initially strangers to each other, ratings of friendships were low at the beginning of the year; with each successive week, some ratings began to reflect the development of friendships.

An examination of the close friendships that had been formed by the end of the study revealed that those persons who shared similar values and atti-

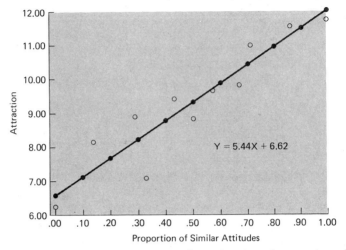

FIGURE 8–2. Attraction toward stranger as a linear function of proportion of similar attitudes. [From "Attraction As a Linear Proportion of Positive Reinforcements" by D. Byrne and D. Nelson, *Journal of Personality and Social Psychology*, 1965, *1*, 659–663. Copyright 1965 by the American Psychological Association. Reprinted by permission.]

tudes on a variety of topics such as ethnic relations, religion, and sex at the time the study began were more likely to be close friends than were subjects who had dissimilar initial attitudes.

PHYSICAL SIMILARITY. Why do people tend to affiliate with those of the same skin color or ethnic background? Is physical similarity the major basis for prejudice? Rokeach, Smith, and Evans (1960) suggested that prejudice is not so much based on skin color or religion, etc., as it is on the fact that people *assume* that the beliefs and attitudes of peoples of other backgrounds are different from their own. They presented descriptions of hypothetical persons and their attitudes on topics such as socialized medicine or communism. Subjects rated these stimulus persons on friendship scales. Earlier the subjects had already been tested for their own attitudes on the same issues.

The results suggested that similarity in attitudes rather than race was more critical in determining friendship ratings. Thus, Rokeach et al. found that black persons whose attitudes were similar to those of the white subject were more liked than white persons whose attitudes were dissimilar.

Triandis (1961) felt that Rokeach's results were limited, because the ratings dealt only with friendship judgments, which is a limited aspect of interpersonal interaction. Prejudice often deals with strangers and persons you do not interact with except on superficial terms. He presented descriptions of hypothetical persons varying in four dimensions: race, socioeconomic status, religion, and personal life philosophy.

Measures of social distance based on preferences for interaction in a variety of situations other than friendship were obtained; although all four factors affected these judgments, race was the largest factor in Triandis' study. The white subjects preferred associating with the stimulus person of the same race for a variety of types of social interaction.

Stein, Hardyck, and Smith (1965) used the paradigm of Rokeach et al. in which subjects were presented with the attitudes of four fictitious stimulus persons, two black and two white. Within each race, one of the persons held views similar to those of the real subject, whereas the other one had dissimilar attitudes. White teenagers were asked to examine the information about the stimulus persons and indicate how much they liked them and whether or not they would associate with them.

Similarity of beliefs seemed to be a stronger factor than similarity of race. Subjects liked persons who shared their beliefs even if they were not white. However, some results also showed how race factors affected judgments. Blacks were more likely to be rejected as candidates to "invite home to dinner" or "date my sister" even when their attitudes were similar to those of the subjects. In short, it appears that both belief and race similarity influence attraction, although the relative strengths of the two factors may depend on the type of interaction involved.

These findings, however, come from an artificial situation in that the stimulus persons are hypothetical descriptions and there is no real face-to-face interaction with the subjects. Such realism would be difficult to study, because it would be impossible to standardize the stimulus person's behavior, which would be altered by that of the subject's own behavior. However, somewhat greater realism could be achieved by using standardized but contrived films of stimulus persons interacting with other persons.

Using a live interaction between the subject and four confederates, two white and two black, Rokeach and Mezei (1966) had one stooge of each race agree and one disagree with the subject's view in a discussion. Subsequent measurements of liking showed that subjects preferred those whose beliefs were similar to their own rather than persons of their own race.

Hendrick, Bixenstein, and Hawkins (1971) modified this procedure in order to standardize the group interaction. They had four stooges participate in a videotape discussion that the subject viewed. Again two of the stooges were white and two were black, with one stooge of each color agreeing and one disagreeing with the subject's views. As in the study by Rokeach and Mezei (1966), the subject preferred the stooges who shared the subject's beliefs. In general, the evidence suggests that attitude similarity rather than physical similarity is the more important factor in liking.

DO OPPOSITES ATTRACT? THE CASE OF ROMANTIC ATTRACTION

Despite the evidence showing that similarity is related to attraction, there is another view worth considering, namely, that opposites attract. This folk wisdom is based on anecdotal evidence and frequently is used to describe mate selection. It may not extend to same-sex friendships or opposite-sex friendships of a nonromantic nature.

NATURALISTIC STUDIES. Winch (1955), for example, interviewed twenty-five married couples and concluded that there was evidence for a complementarity of needs view of attraction. There is not necessarily a contradiction between Winch's and Byrne's views, according to Marlowe and Gergen (1969) who argued that people may like those who are similar to themselves but nonetheless also need others with views and traits different from their own.

Or it may be that for certain needs, we seek those who are similar but for other needs, opposites attract. Thus, a need to be with others may lead a person to like people with the same need, whereas a need to be dominant will lead to a choice of someone who is submissive. Furthermore, needs and attitudes are not the same and people with similar attitudes may have different but compatible needs.

Murstein (1961) was unable to confirm the complementary needs hypothesis of Winch, and he criticized it as being too vague. Murstein (1970) has emphasized the importance of examining different stages in a romantic relationship, because different factors may vary in importance at different points in time. During the initial contract or *stimulus stage,* the physical features of the object of romance should take precedence. Murstein predicted and found high correlation of physical attractiveness for dating couples. This matching is assumed to occur, because an unattractive male would not be likely to risk being rejected by courting a very attractive female nor would an attractive male date unattractive females because although he would probably be accepted he would not consider it much of a "conquest."

As courtship continues and the couple exchanges ideas about values, etc., Murstein sees similarity of values assuming greater importance. His study of engaged or "going steady" couples revealed greater than chance similarity of values concerning marriage. During this *value stage,* apparently those couples with dissimilar values abandon their relationships and do not proceed to the third stage identified by Murstein as the *role stage.*

During this final stage preceding marriage, Murstein posits that the couple considers role compatibility or "fit." Unlike the two previous stages, similarity here is not necessarily desirable and could even be detrimental. If the roles the partners wish to assume conflict with the goals of one or both partners, difficulties may ensue.

In selecting a mate we seek someone who matches our image of the *ideal spouse.* We also develop a concept of the *ideal self* as we grow up. Both ideals are strongly affected by cultural values and, according to Murstein, they should be similar. However, individual differences exist in the extent to which persons are able to approximate their ideal selves as diagramed in Figure 8–3. To the extent that there is a small gap between one's actual self and ideal self, Murstein predicted that there will also be a small discrepancy between a

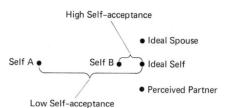

FIGURE 8–3. A, whose self and ideal-self concepts are far apart (low self-acceptance), will see his or her partner as unlike him- or herself, whereas B, whose self and ideal self are close together (high self-acceptance), will see his or her partner as highly similar to the self. [From "Stimulus—Value—Role: A Theory of Marital Choice" by B. I. Murstein, *Journal of Marriage and the Family,* 1970, *32,* 465–481. Copyright 1970 by National Council on Family Relations. Reprinted by permission.]

person (*B* in Figure 8–3) and his or her perception of spouse. In contrast, someone (*A* in Figure 8–3) with a large disparity between actual self and ideal self will show a large gap between actual self and perception of spouse. This difference stems from the fact that in selecting a spouse the person tried to match an ideal-spouse concept, one that, however, is quite different from the actual self for a person who is unable to match his or her own ideal self. A study of ninety-nine engaged or "going-steady" couples (Murstein, 1967) showed support for these predictions, in that men with high self-acceptance showed a higher correlation between their self-concepts and their perceptions of their women friends than was true for low self-acceptance men.

In summary, Murstein's model emphasizes the importance of considering the stage of a romantic relationship in analyzing the effect of similarity. Whereas *physical* similarity is crucial when couples first meet, *value* similarity is more important during the intermediate stage of acquaintance. Finally, the last stage is complex, and high similarity of *roles* for the couple seems to exist only in cases in which there is a small self versus ideal-self discrepancy. Low similarity of roles of the male and female seems to exist when the male has a large gap in self versus ideal-self concept.

LABORATORY STUDIES. Unlike Murstein's correlational studies, most laboratory studies of romantic attraction do not deal with *real* couples who are attracted to one another. Instead, fictitious or *hypothetical* stimulus persons are presented for ratings on romantic appeal. Do results from these two approaches agree?

In one such study similarity of attitudes on topics such as those assessed by Byrne has been shown (Strobe, Insko, Thompson, and Layton, 1971) to contribute to the attractiveness of a hypothetical person as a potential date or prospective marriage partner. Thus, in the case of date or mate compatibility, it may be necessary for similar attitudes to be shared concerning topics such as religion, politics, and sex. This finding does not preclude the possibility that a couple may be dissimilar in other dimensions, because the couple may still need to complement each other in areas such as needs for dominance or attitudes about the sharing of domestic responsibilities.

Some Important Differences Between Romantic and Nonromantic Liking. Romantic liking is a topic that has proved elusive to researchers (e.g., Rubin, 1970: Walster, 1971) and findings for it may be different than those for nonromantic liking. And why not? For the person who is loved is someone extra special, enchanting, and fascinating, according to the Western concept of romance. No one else will suffice, poets and love balladeers tell us. The special person is even recognizable by the effect produced on us such as the ringing of bells, flashing of lights, and so forth. As Robert Louis Stevenson wrote: "Falling in love is the one illogical adventure, the one thing which we are tempted to think of as supernatural, in our trite and reasonable world."

Small wonder then that psychologists have not really been able to make much headway in understanding the factors underlying romantic choices ("What does she see in him?").

Whatever it is, it is something different from what she sees in other men. Whatever it is, it may or may not actually be present in him. In other words, romantic love attributes to its target that which we fervently wish and hope it possesses but, alas, hoping cannot make it so, if it is not already true. Such is not the basis for ordinary or nonromantic liking.

In nonromantic friendships, one is free to have as many friends as one wishes, but with romantic relationships one seeks only one person and also hopes that he or she will be the other's exclusive romantic interest as well. The importance of this attitude may account in part for men's attraction to the woman who is hard to get. Since she is regarded as a challenge, she is also attractive. A man's belief that he alone will be able to win her affection fulfills his romantic conception of the exclusive attention of the hard-to-get woman.

Walster, Walster, Piliavin, and Schmidt (1973) simulated a computer date matching situation in order to test some of the common beliefs about the attractiveness of the hard-to-get woman. Male subjects were told that the computer had matched them with dates. They were given the opportunity of examining the folders describing the backgrounds of five prospective dates and asked to choose one. For three of the dates, information was also available about how the potential date had evaluated the male's attractiveness as a date along with similar ratings of four other males matched with her. Actually, all the information was contrived and none of the information was valid.

One date appeared uniformly easy to get, because she rated all of her matches, including the subject, as attractive dates. A second date was uniformly hard to get and rated all of her matches as minimally attractive, and a third was selectively hard to get. She rated the subject as attractive and the other four matches as unattractive. Finally, there were two dates for whom no such information was available.

It was hypothesized that the selectively hard-to-get date might be the most desirable date. The uniformly hard-to-get woman might be seen as too inaccessible, unfriendly, and lukewarm, whereas the uniformly easy-to-get woman might be perceived as someone desperate for a date and someone who might be difficult to get rid of.

The results indicated that the most popular date was indeed the selectively hard-to-get woman, with forty-two of seventy-one of the men choosing her. Table 8–1 shows that she is rated the highest as a likeable date. It should be pointed out that a different description of the selectively hard-to-get woman was presented to different subjects, as was true for all the other types of dates. By this procedure one can assume that the choices reflect attractiveness of the date's attitudes toward her potential dates rather than her actual description. Furthermore, all the hypothetical dates were described in similar terms, more or less.

The remaining men spread their choices fairly evenly over the other four dates, with only six choosing the uniformly hard-to-get and five choosing the uniformly easy-to-get date. The other eighteen men split their choices between the two dates for whom no information was available about their ratings of their matches.

The findings show that romantic choices, at least for a computer-matched first date, are governed by the perceived attitudes of the prospective dates toward the men. They seemed to want to date the woman who was hard to get for other men but easy to get for themselves, but it is possible that women who are selectively hard to get but prefer one of the rivals might prove even more attractive since she would be a challenge. However, Walster et al. did not include this type of women in their study.

Walster et al. hypothesized that the basis for this choice lies in the assumptions that the men made about the selectively hard-to-get date. She would be perceived as having all the desirable features of the hard-to-get woman but none of her liabilities. Similarly, she would be seen as having the positive qualities of the easy-to-get woman but none of her disadvantages. In other words, this ideal of romantic perfection would be perceived as a composite of the best features of both extreme types of dates, the uniformly easy- or hard-to-get woman.

Table 8–1 shows that the selectively hard-to-get date was rated highest on selectivity and popularity, qualities that the uniformly hard-to-get woman probably has. She is also rated highest on friendliness, warmth, and easygoingness, qualities generally ascribed to the uniformly easy-to-get woman.

Romance, then, is a special type of attraction situation characterized by the need for a feeling of exclusiveness, for that feeling of "You're the only one for me" on the part of the partners. Walster, et al. study provides clear evidence about the role of this factor, at least from the male's perspective.

Another essential aspect of romantic attraction, which is probably less critical for nonromantic liking, is that of physical attractiveness, beauty, or handsomeness. This factor may be more important during early stages such

TABLE 8-1. Men's Reactions to Various Dates.

Item	Type of Date			
	Selectively Hard to Get	Uniformly Hard to Get	Uniformly Easy to Get	No Information
Men's Liking for Dates	9.41[a]	7.90	8.53	8.58
Evaluation of Women's Assets and Liabilities				
Selective[b]	5.23	4.39	2.85	4.30
Popular[b]	4.83	4.58	4.65	4.83
Friendly[c]	5.58	5.07	5.52	5.37
Warm[c]	5.15	4.51	4.99	4.79
Easy-going[c]	4.83	4.42	4.82	4.61
Problems Expected in Dating	5.23[d]	4.86	4.77	4.99

[a] The higher the number, the more liking the man is expressing for the date.
[b] Traits we expected to be ascribed to the selectively hard-to-get and the uniformly hard-to-get dates.
[c] Traits we expected to be ascribed to the selectively hard-to-get and the uniformly easy-to-get dates.
[d] The higher the number the *fewer* the problems the subject anticipates in dating.
Source. From "Playing Hard to Get": Understanding an Elusive Phenomenon" by E. Walster, G. W. Walster, J. Piliavin, and L. Schmidt, *Journal of Personality and Social Psychology,* 1973, *26,* 113–121. Copyright 1973 by the American Psychological Association. Reprinted by permission.

as in dating preferences than it is as a determinant of mate selection where the factors of attitude similarity and need complementarity must also be considered.

Walster, Aronson, Abrahams, and Rottman (1966) staged a "Computer Dance" and presumably partners were matched according to their personalities by the computer. Actually, they were randomly paired, with the restriction that the male partner always be taller than the female. Ratings of their partners during the dance intermission showed that the key factor affecting liking was physical attractiveness, especially in ratings by the male subjects. Similar strong effects of physical attractiveness of persons judged from photographs were found in subjects' preferences for dates and mates in the aforementioned study by Stroebe et al. (1971). Romance, then, is truly not blind, at least not to physical appearances. This tendency was strongest among subjects who were themselves physically attractive. Apparently lower levels of aspiration were held by less attractive subjects, possibly due to greater fear of rejection from very attractive persons.

Given that physical attractiveness is such a potent factor underlying romantic attraction, what is the basis for this effect?

In the first place, one of the first aspects one learns about another person is how that person appears visually. If first impressions based on physical attraction are positive, they may favorably bias one's assessment of subsequent input about the person. Sometimes one receives information about a person before actually having a live encounter, and in that situation the effects of physical attraction may be different. But in those cases in which the first information is physical appearance, these first impressions may influence subsequent interpretations of conversations or observations.

Why should first impressions of an attractive person be biased in a favorable direction? Bersheid and Walster (1974) point out the possibility that previous social learning may have taught one to value the attractive person. In addition, they refer to the "rating and dating complex" in which one can enhance one's prestige among one's peers by being out on a date with an attractive person. Other persons may hold you in higher esteem if you are seen with an attractive person because they infer that you must have special qualities. Sigall and Landy (1974) actually had subjects rate a man who was observed to be in the company of a female whose appearance was contrived to be either attractive or homely. Ratings of the man's qualities were higher when he was in the company of the attractive female.

Finally, the attractive person may be sought because of attributes that person is assumed to possess. Dion, Bersheid, and Walster (1972) found that both men and women subjects held similar stereotypes of attractiveness for either sex. Attractive males and females were generally thought to be sexually warm and responsive, sensitive, kind, strong, sociable, and they were expected to have a better future in life. Given such great expectations, it should be no surprise that attractive persons are so highly sought after.

Theories of Attraction

A REINFORCEMENT VIEW

Byrne (1969) proposed a reinforcement model to account for the general finding that we tend to like those who are similar to ourselves in their attitudes. This formulation argues that attraction to another person should be a linear function of the ratio of rewards and punishments associated with that other person. Thus, as similarity of attitudes increases between two persons, the greater should be the number of rewards each receives from the other person. Agreements of attitudes are reinforcements, inasmuch as they tell us we are right, whereas disagreements act as punishments by contradicting our own views.

In general, the evidence is consistent with Byrne's model. We do seem to like those who are similar to ourselves. But is this relationship indeed due to the availability of more reinforcement from similar persons? Are there other reasons we like persons similar to ourselves?

A dissenting view has been raised by Aronson (1969) who suggested that the usefulness of a reward or reinforcement theory of liking is limited by the difficulty of specifying rewarding events in advance. On intuitive grounds, for example, it might seem that we would like competent persons better, because our affiliation with them should produce more benefits for us. However, Aronson reviewed some research that shows that the most capable members of problem-solving groups are not the best liked, contrary to expectations from a reinforcement view of attraction.

Aronson also argued that it is possible that we might like someone who disagrees with us more than someone who always agrees because the former may help us learn how to improve. This situation is also incompatible with Byrne's theory, unless one considers long-term benefits of association with persons who are somewhat dissimilar from ourselves.

COGNITIVE THEORIES OF ATTRACTION

Attraction has also been explained in terms of cognitive balance (Heider, 1958; Newcomb, 1956), as illustrated in Table 8–2. If we have two persons A and B, both of whom like X, we have a balanced situation if A and B like each other. The term X can refer to another person or some object, issue, or topic. The prediction in this example is no different from that in reinforcement theory but the terminology is different. When A and B share a common attitude toward X (even if it should be negative), a balanced situation exists when A and B dislike each other, as when they hold dissimilar attitudes about X.

Some situations, however, are unbalanced, and cognitive theories suggest that an attempt will be made to restore balance, consistency, or consonance. For example, if A and B disagree in their attitudes toward X, the cognitive theories suggest that an imbalance would exist if A and B were to like each other. Something has to change so that balance can be restored. For example,

TABLE 8–2.   Attractiveness of Person B to Person A
As a Function of Their Attitudes Toward X.

B's Attitude Toward X

		+	−
A's attitude Toward X	+	Balanced so A likes B	Unbalanced so A dislikes B
	−	Unbalanced so A dislikes B	Balanced so A likes B

Note. When both A and B share the same attitude, positive or negative, balance exists and A should like B. Imbalance exists if they do not share the same attitude, and one consequence may be that A will dislike B.

A and B might change their views of each other or one or both of them might change their attitude toward X.

Balance theories are more applicable to *changes* in attitudes over time than are reinforcement theories. Changes are predicted whenever unstable relationships exist among attitudes in order to restore balanced or stable relationships among the elements A, B, and X. However, both balance and reinforcement theories oversimplify the situation and ignore important aspects of attraction. They deal with the situations marked in Table 8–3, which involve the liking of similar persons and the disliking of dissimilar persons. Yet, people are frequently known to share similar attitudes with someone whom they nevertheless dislike intensely. Or they may find themselves attracted to someone who does not share similar attitudes with them.

TABLE 8–3. The Predicted Relationship Between Similarity of Attitudes Between Two Persons and Likeability Based on Balance and Reinforcement Theories.

		Other Person	
		Similar Attitudes	Dissimilar Attitudes
Your Attitude Toward Other Person	Like	Predicted	—————
	Dislike	—————	Predicted

Although it may be the case that we like those who are similar to us, the opposite does not necessarily follow. That is, everyone who is similar to us need not be attractive to us. Failure to recognize the asymmetrical relationship between liking and similarity creates problems in both theories. If I like one psychologist because I am also a psychologist, it does not follow that I should like all other psychologists.

Does similarity even act as the major determinant of attraction? Perhaps attraction between two persons must occur first, after which selective attention leads them (as well as us) to notice their similarities, as diagramed in Figure 8–4. Consistent with this assumption is the fact that Newcomb (1968), a major balance theorist, has pointed out that if A dislikes B to begin with, it may be irrelevant whether or not they share similar beliefs and attitudes toward X. Thus, if I dislike a particular psychologist, it matters little whether we share similar attitudes about psychology. Furthermore, because I dislike him or her and do not interact with him or her, there is less opportunity to discover whether or not we share attitudes.

CONCLUSIONS

Where does this leave us? If neither reinforcement from others nor a balanced relationship of our attitudes and that of others is the cause for attraction, what is? Perhaps some global or general factors account for

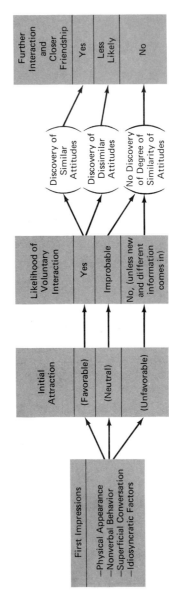

FIGURE 8–4. A model of the sequential relationship between attraction and similarity of attitudes between two persons.

liking, at least in general situations. First impressions can affect initial attraction even when no knowledge of other people's attitudes is available. People who are friendly, polite, or helpful might be best liked during early stages of acquaintance or in superficial relationships. The factor of physical attractiveness, discussed earlier in the context of romantic liking, is also applicable here. But people who are honest, reliable, or supportive might be preferred at a later stage or in a closer relationship. The characteristics that favor likeability may also depend on the nature of the situation.

The problem in discovering what leads to attraction is that people vary in countless dimensions, some of which are salient or important to us in one context but not in another. Laboratory studies testing balance and reinforcement theory must necessarily limit the number and type of attitudes and topics on which subjects must judge another person. This limitation is a particular shortcoming of balance theories, which generally deal with only three elements and their interrelations. The attitudes of two persons toward only one person or topic is presumed to determine their liking for each other.

Thus, balance theory expects A to like B if he or she learns that both of them like or dislike C. But in real life, C may not be very important to A. He or she may also be interested in B's attitudes toward D, E, F, and G. He or she might like B even if they disagree because he or she thinks B can be converted or changed.

Cognitive balance theories also err in expecting logic to govern liking. A subject can tell you that if $A > B$, and $B > C$, then $A > C$. This balanced situation of transitivity is a logical one. But a subjective dimension such as liking is often illogical. The attempt to apply predictions based on logic to interpersonal relationships is ill-founded.

Finally, balance or consistency is perhaps not as essential for everyone as cognitive theories suggest. Some people are able to not only handle but may even seek out complexity. The misleading analogy between homeostatic balances of a physiological nature and affective states in social relationships is of limited value.

RECIPROCITY AND FRIENDSHIP

Genuine friendships are two-way streets involving reciprocity. If someone befriends me, even if his or her attitudes are dissimilar from my own, it is likely that I will try to return the friendship. The notion of balance in the sense of equity in social exchange (Adams, 1965; Homans, 1961) suggests that we will strive to achieve equitable exchanges in our dealings with others. This tendency, rather than similarity per se, could account for the observed relationship between attraction and similarity. We may prefer to associate with persons holding similar attitudes, but that is not sufficient to produce friendships. In addition, and more importantly, the other person must initiate or reciprocate gestures of friendship such as doing favors, rendering aid, or being cordial. Norman Vincent Peale (1952) pointed out the importance of this concept in his influential guide *The Power of Positive Thinking* by advising readers to, "Build up as many people as you can. Do it unselfishly. Do it because you like them and because you see possibilities in them. Do this and you will never lack for friends" (p. 244). Similar advice was the essence of Dale Carnegie's (1936) recommendations for winning instant friends. His last rule was, "Make the other person feel important—and do it sincerely." Some of his other rules suggested the use of smiles, genuine interest in others, listening to the other person talking about himself or herself, and talking in terms related to the other person's interests when talking about oneself as ways of making someone else feel important. Usually persons with similar attitudes will be the ones who will engage in such activities, but occasionally someone with dissimilar attitudes will employ these techniques so that strong friendships can occur between persons even when attitudes are quite different.

People who like us, even if they are dissimilar in attitudes, make us feel significant so it is hardly surprising that we should like them in return. Of course, if we suspect that the liking is insincere or an attempt to gain favors by first securing our good graces, we are likely to resent and look with contempt upon the would-be ingratiator.

THE GAIN-LOSS HYPOTHESIS.   A study by Aronson and Linder (1965) suggests that we like those who express liking toward us better than we like persons with unfavorable feelings toward us. Moreover, they hypothesized that an additional and more potent factor is a *change* from negative to positive attitude toward us. This gain in esteem may be more rewarding than a positive attitude that remains constant. An adverse change in attitude from an initially positive to a negative reaction to us, on the other hand, may be more negative than a consistently negative attitude.

Aronson and Linder (1965) employed an elaborate deception paradigm in which two female subjects had a chance to converse briefly before serving in an experiment. One girl was a confederate of the experimenter. However, the real subject was led to believe the confederate was to be tested on a verbal conditioning task by the experimenter with the assistance of the real subject who was hidden from the confederate's view. Verbal conditioning involved the experimenter providing verbal reinforcements for certain types of verbal statements by the subject. The procedure called for the confederate who was presumably unaware that the real subject was present during this part of the study, to answer questions about what her impressions had been of the real subject.

Four types of impression conditions were used so that real subjects heard one of these four patterns of evaluation of themselves by the confederate, always positive; first positive, then negative; always negative; first negative, then positive.

Finally, after the experiment was supposedly over, it was necessary to find out how the real subject felt about the confederate without arousing suspicions about why this information was necessary. The experimenter told the real subjects that unintentional bias can occur in verbal statements. Therefore, it was necessary to know their attitudes toward the confederates, because they may have biased their verbal reinforcements toward them. It was also alleged that the experimenter had correction formulas that could be used to "eliminate" these biases from the data.

The results shown in Table 8–4 supported the gain-loss hypotheses of Aronson and Linder, showing that gains or a shift in the confederate's attitude toward the subject from negative to positive led to greater liking of the evaluator than if the attitude had been always positive. Conversely, losses or a shift of the confederate's attitude toward the subject from positive to negative produced a greater dislike of her than if her attitude had always been negative. It should be added, however, that subsequent studies have not been as successful in replicating the Aronson-Linder results, especially for the negative shift or loss effect.

TABLE 8–4.   Mean Liking of Confederate by Subject.

Condition	Liking
Negative–positive	+7.67
Positive–positive	+6.42
Negative–negative	+2.52
Positive–negative	+0.87

Source. Adapted from "Gain and Loss of Esteem As Determinants of Interpersonal Attraction," by E. Aronson and D. Linder, *Journal of Experimental Social Psychology,* 1965, *1,* 156–171. Copyright 1965 by Academic Press printed by permission.

The gain-loss hypothesis illustrates how the other person's attitudes toward *us,* rather than his or her attitudes toward other persons or topics, can influence our reactions to them. It may be the positiveness of the actions and attitudes of others toward us, rather than their sharing similar attitudes with us that is responsible for creating our attraction to those whom we like.

We can not adequately understand why people like each other if we limit ourselves to the study of the end product. It is necessary to examine the process of interaction that occurs over a period of time as people get to know each other.

Summary

Beginning as early as the infant-mother association and continuing throughout life, we depend on our contact with other humans for physical and psychological well-being. It is possible that the strength that stems from affiliation with others may be a basic condition that leads us to seek the comfort of others whenever we are faced with anxiety and threat. Being alone for extended periods is itself very stressful, perhaps due to our helplessness in isolation.

Experiments have shown that anxiety will promote affiliation among strangers with a common fate or problem. After the threat is dealt with successfully, there may be greater liking of group members who suffered common stressful experiences.

Even when there is no apparent threat or anxiety produced, humans seek and prefer the company and companionship of others from time to time. A number of learned motives may be involved in this goal. We learn that being popular is gratifying and has certain benefits. One way to facilitate one's own popularity is to show others that we like them, because a norm of reciprocity governs much human social behavior. If you scratch my back, I'll return the favor for you sometime.

Due to the high premium many of us place on being liked and having the social approval of others, we are susceptible to the influence of those whom we would like to give us their approval. Ingratiatory tactics such as favorable self-presentation, flattery of others, and opinion conformity or agreement may also be employed in order to gain liking.

Leaving aside more powerful or prestigious targets whom we assume are likely to bestow favors if we can gain their good graces, the persons we are more likely to prefer affiliating with are those who share with us some common interests, attitudes, and backgrounds. In this way there can be mutual reinforcement of values rather than conflict. The importance of similarity of beliefs in determining affiliation does not rule out the possibility that persons with dissimilar personality traits may be attracted to each other or even compatible with one another. As in marriages, complementariness rather than similarity of personality may be desirable and can exist side by side with high similarity of beliefs and attitudes by the couple on ideological issues.

The research of Byrne and his colleagues has documented the important role of attitude similarity and attraction. Byrne assumes that the greater the similarity between two persons, the more mutual reinforcements they administer to each other.

Other theorists have raised the possibility that in other situations, opposites may attract. Situations such as romantic relationships may also involve more complex effects, especially because physical attractiveness has been found to be a potent determinant of romantic attraction, at least initially. Attractive persons are highly regarded by others and tend to be held as models of perfection. Romantic attraction also differs from other forms of interpersonal attraction in that we may value someone who seems to prefer us over rivals, perhaps because this feeling of exclusivity elevates our self-esteem.

Whereas Byrne's reinforcement theory of attraction emphasizes the importance of rewards coming from the similar person as the basis for our attraction, cognitive balance theories look at the degree of consistency between our liking of persons and the extent to which we share attitudes with them. These theories assume that we prefer consistency in the relationships among our evaluations of others and the extent to which our attitudes on various issues are shared with others. For example, consistency theories would predict that A and B should not like one another if they disagreed on their attitudes toward some issues. If this disagreement persisted, the attraction between A and B should eventually deteriorate in order to restore balance.

An alternative view, however, is that attraction, for whatever reasons, may precede our awareness of the similarity or dissimilarity of attitudes shared with someone else. Once we like the other person, we increase our interaction and learn more about the other person's attitudes and the extent to which they are similar to our own. If they are highly different, we may revise our opinion and lower our liking, but only after we have formed an initial attraction based on other criteria.

If our attraction to someone else is to continue or to increase, it may be necessary that some reciprocation occur from the other party. Even if we like someone initially because common attitudes are shared, that fact is insufficient to sustain a friendship and we do not end up liking everyone who shares common attitudes with us. Only that subset that additionally renders favors, gives us praise, and otherwise actively rewards us will be likely to be regarded as friends to whom we would in return reciprocate.

References

ADAMS, J. S. Inequity social exchange. In L. Berkowitz (Ed.), *Advances in experimental social psychology.* (Vol. 2). New York: Academic, 1965.

ARONSON, E. Some antecedents of interpersonal attraction. In W. J. Arnold and D. Levine (Eds.), *Nebraska Symposium on Motivation.* (Vol. 18). Lincoln: University of Nebraska Press, 1970.

————, and LINDER, D. Gain and loss of esteem as determinants of interpersonal attraction. *Journal of Experimental Social Psychology,* 1965, *1,* 156–171.

————, and MILLS, J. The effects of severity of initiation on liking for a group. *Journal of Abnormal and Social Psychology,* 1959, *59,* 177–181.

BARON, R. A. Behavioral effects of interpersonal attraction: Compliance with requests from liked and disliked others. *Psychonomic Science,* 1971, *25,* 325–326.

BERKOWITZ, L. Reactance and the unwillingness to help others. *Psychological Bulletin,* 1973, *79,* 310–317.

BERSHEID, E., and WALSTER, E. Physical attractiveness. In L. Berkowitz (Ed.), *Advances in experimental social psychology.* (Vol. 7). New York: Academic, 1974.

BETTLEHEIM, B. Individual and mass behavior in extreme situations. *Journal of Abnormal and Social Psychology,* 1943, *38,* 417–452.

BLAKE, R. R., ROSENBAUM, M., and DURYEA, R. Gift-giving as a function of group standards. *Human Relations*, 1955, *8*, 61–72.

BOWLBY, J. *Attachment and loss.* (Vol. 1). New York: Basic, 1969.

BROWN, R. Further comment on the risky shift. *American Psychologist*, 1974, *29*, 468–469.

BYRNE, D. Interpersonal attraction and attitude similarity. *Journal of Abnormal and Social Psychology*, 1961, *62*, 713–715.

———. Response to attitude similarity-dissimilarity as a function of affiliation need. *Journal of Personality*, 1962, *30*, 164–177.

———. Attitudes and attraction. In L. Berkowitz (Ed.), *Advances in experimental social psychology*. (Vol. 4). New York: Academic, 1969.

———, and NELSON, D. Attraction as a linear proportion of positive reinforcements. *Journal of Personality and Social Psychology*, 1965, *1*, 659–663.

CARNEGIE, D. *How to win friends and influence people.* New York: Simon and Shuster, 1936.

CARTWRIGHT, D. Determinants of scientific progress: The case of research on the risky shift. *American Psychologist*, 1973, *28*, 222–231.

CROWNE, D. P., and MARLOWE, D. *The approval motive: Studies in evaluative dependence.* New York: Wiley, 1964.

DION, K., BERSHEID, E., and WALSTER, E. What is beautiful is good. *Journal of Personality and Social Psychology*, 1972, *24*, 285–290.

ERIKSON, E. H. *Childhood and society.* Second Edition. New York: Norton, 1963.

FESTINGER, L. A theory of social comparison processes. *Human Relations*, 1954, *7*, 117–140.

HARLOW, H. F. The nature of love. *American Psychologist*, 1958, *13*, 673–685.

———, and ZIMMERMAN, R. R. Affectional responses in the infant monkey. *Science*, 1959, *130*, 421–432.

HEIDER, F. *The psychology of interpersonal relations.* New York: Wiley, 1958.

HENDRICK, C., BIXENSTINE, V. E., and HAWKINS, G. Race versus belief similarity as determinants of attraction: A search for a fair test. *Journal of Personality and Social Psychology*, 1971, *17*, 250–258.

HOMANS, G. C. *Social behavior: Its elementary forms.* New York: Harcourt, 1961.

JONES, E. E. *Ingratiation: A social psychological analysis.* New York: Appleton, 1966.

———, GERGEN, K. J., and JONES, R. G. Tactics of ingratiation among leaders and subordinates in a status hierarchy. *Psychological Monographs*, 1963, *77* (3, Whole No. 566).

———, and WORTMAN, C. *Ingratiation: An attributional approach.* Morristown: N.J.: General Learning Press, 1973.

KALVEN, H., JR., and ZEISEL, H. *The American jury.* Boston: Little, Brown, 1966.

KOGAN, N., and WALLACH, M. A. *Risk-taking: A study in cognition and personality.* New York: Holt, 1964.

LANDY, D., and ARONSON, E. The influence of the character of the criminal and his victim on the decisions of simulated jurors. *Journal of Experimental Social Psychology*, 1969, *5*, 141–152.

MARLOWE, D., and GERGEN, K. J. Personality and social interactions. In G. Lindzey and E. Aronson (Eds.), *Handbook of Social Psychology*. (Vol. 3). Reading, Mass.: Addison-Wesley, 1969.

MITCHELL, H. E., and BYRNE, D. The defendant's dilemma: Effect of jurors' attitudes and authoritarianism on judicial decisions. *Journal of Personality and Social Psychology*, 1973, *25*, 123–129.

MURSTEIN, B. I. The complementary need hypothesis in newlyweds and middle-aged married couples. *Journal of Abnormal and Social Psychology*, 1961, *63*, 194–197.

————. Empirical tests of role, complementary needs, and homogamy theories of marital choice. *Journal of Marriage and the Family,* 1967, *29,* 689–696.

————. Stimulus—value—role: A theory of marital choice. *Journal of Marriage and the Family,* 1970, *32,* 465–481.

NEWCOMB, T. M. The prediction of interpersonal attraction. *American Psychologist,* 1956, *11,* 575–586.

————. *The acquaintance process.* New York: Holt 1961.

————. Interpersonal balance. In R. P. Abelson, E. Aronson, W. J. McGuire, T. M. Newcomb, M. J. Rosenberg, and P. H. Tannenbaum (Eds.), *Theories of cognitive consistency: A sourcebook.* Skokie, Ill.: Rand McNally, 1968.

PEALE, N. V. *The power of positive thinking.* Englewood Cliffs, N.J.: Prentice-Hall, 1952.

ROKEACH, M., and MEZEI, L. Race and shared belief as factors in social choice. *Science,* 1966, *151,* 167–172.

————, SMITH, P. W., and EVANS, R. I. Two kinds of prejudice or one? In M. Rokeach, *The open and closed mind.* New York: Basic, 1960.

SARNOFF, I., and ZIMBARDO, P. G. Anxiety, fear, and social affiliation. *Journal of Abnormal and Social Psychology,* 1961, *62,* 356–363.

SCHACHTER, S. *The psychology of affiliation.* Stanford, Calif.: Stanford University Press, 1959.

STEIN, D. D., HARDYCK, J. E., and SMITH, M. B. Race and belief: An open and shut case. *Journal of Personality and Social Psychology,* 1965, *1,* 281–290.

STROEBE, W., INSKO, C. A., THOMPSON, V. D., and LAYTON, B. D. Effects of physical attractiveness, attitude similarity, and sex on various aspects of interpersonal attraction. *Journal of Personality and Social Psychology,* 1971, *18,* 79–91.

TIGER, L. *Men in groups.* New York: Random House, 1969.

TRIANDIS, H. C. A note on Rokeach's theory of prejudice. *Journal of Abnormal and Social Psychology,* 1961, *62,* 184–186.

WALSTER, E., ARONSON, V., ABRAHAMS, D., and ROTTMAN, L. Importance of physical attractiveness in dating behavior. *Journal of Personality and Social Psychology,* 1966, *4,* 508–516.

————, WALSTER, G. W., PILAVIN, J., and SCHMIDT, L. "Playing hard to get": Understanding an elusive phenomenon. *Journal of Personality and Social Psychology,* 1973, *26,* 113–121.

WINCH, R. F. The theory of complementary needs in mate selection: A test of one kind of complementariness. *American Sociological Review,* 1955, *20,* 52–56.

CHAPTER 9

Social Motivation: Tooth and Nail

Among the many problems that have confronted human societies throughout history, perhaps none has been more challenging than that of aggression. Its very nature has repeatedly threatened societal harmony and survival. What are the causes of this pervasive behavior? Is it possible to prevent, reduce, or redirect aggressive energies into more socially desirable activities? Or is aggressive behavior an inevitable, necessary, or even desirable form of activity? These basic questions have concerned human societies for countless generations.

Defining Aggression

Aggression has proved to be a difficult concept to define. Definitions that emphasize only the observable *consequences* of aggression to the victim are inadequate; they ignore the important factor of *intention*. Table 9–1 summarizes four possible situations based on the presence or absence of two factors, intent and harm to the victim. Without taking intent into account, accidental cases of harmful consequences will be perceived as equivalent to premeditated actions that cause harm. It is also important to determine intentions, because the absence of harmful effects does not rule out the possible existence of intentions to create harm. The behavior may be inhibited by situational constraints or attempts to do harm may be misdirected or unsuccessful. Of course, it is difficult to detect aggressive intentions if no consequent harm is observed, but it is not uncommon for inferences, sometimes erroneous, to be made from situational factors about the existence of unrealized aggressive intentions.

It is similarly difficult to prove that intentions did not exist when accidental harm occurs. Again, indirect evidence is generally used to draw inferences

TABLE 9–1. The Definition of Aggression Depends on
The Presence of Both Intent and Harm.

		Intent	
		Yes	No
Harm	Yes	Premeditated and Successful Aggression	Accidents
	No	Inhibited Aggression, Abortive Efforts	Other Behavior

that no intentions or awareness of consequences existed in the mind of the harm-causing agent.

The definition of aggression is further complicated by the fact that the intentions of the aggressor must be inferred by others, either observers or the victim himself or herself. Whether or not we blame or hold the agent of harm responsible for the consequences obviously depends on our conclusions about the presence or absence of his or her intentions. Although victims may sometimes act in the same manner as third party observers would toward the aggressor, for example, retaliate if the act was perceived as intentional but forgive or punish lightly if the act was interpreted as accidental (e.g., Greenwell and Dengerink, 1973; Nickel, 1974), victims and observers may not agree in their assessment of the intentionality behind a given harmful act.

Biases also affect the classification of harmful acts by different observers. Frequently the actions of those we dislike are condemned, whereas the very same types of behaviors by our friends and ourselves are accepted and approved. Harmful actions of our enemies are termed vicious and immoral acts of aggression, whereas the same actions committed by our friends are justified as self-defense, provocation, or revenge.

In addition to causing harm to someone, the aggressor often gains other benefits such as praise, respect, or material consequences. In other instances it appears that the only goal of the aggressor is to harm the victim, such as in revenge cases. Some (e.g., Berkowitz, 1965; Buss, 1961) make a distinction between the two situations, terming the former *instrumental aggression* and the latter *hostile aggression*. Most of the time the two types occur together and are difficult to distinguish.

The form in which aggression is expressed can vary widely, ranging from verbal means such as sarcasm and profanity to actual physical violence. Factors such as the situation or the relative physical strengths of the adversaries may affect the exact manner in which aggression occurs. In fact, if the foe is too formidable, the aggression will be completely inhibited even though the intent may be strong but undetectable to the observer. This variety of forms of expression makes it difficult to pin down the concept of aggression for scientific purposes. If we predict that aggression will occur in a given situation, and it does not, it is possible that the intent was present but that the aggression was expressed in a different and probably more subtle form. If one cannot physically attack a stronger foe, one may be able to make clever sarcastic or satirical comments that run less risk of physical retaliation. But this situation does not allow us any chance of refuting our hypotheses, a condition that is essential to meet scientific standards.

Even aggression of an intentional nature does not always reflect the same motive. In his analysis of seventy-five prison inmates, Toch (1969) distinguished between different types of aggressors. There were some men for whom aggression served to boost self-images of manliness and fearlessness. Fights are initiated to prove one's mettle. Other men became aggressive primarily as a defense, such as when they felt insulted or felt that they had to defend their masculinity. Men who had been gang leaders, on the other hand, used aggression to command respect and control the gang. Another type was the norm enforcer who acted as a police officer and used violence whenever he felt that norms were being violated. The pressure remover type used force as a solution to problems because this was the only method he knew.

Other types identified by Toch tended to treat others as objects rather than as people. Exploiters, bullies, self-indulgers, and catharters are not as concerned with elevating their own images as they are with applying force toward others. Exploiters take advantage of others by the use of violence, the bully enjoys frightening the victim, the self-indulger expresses tantrums through aggression, and the catharters use aggression to release pent-up emotions.

Toch's taxonomy is based on a small sample of a select population, which is not representative of the normal population. The distinctions are probably overdrawn, but they do serve to illustrate the importance of considering the various functions that essentially the same behavior serves for the individual. Even though the consequences of a form of aggression may be the same for the victim, the motives of the aggressor may differ markedly from person to person.

In view of the many varieties of aggression, it is difficult as well as misleading to study aggression as if it were a unitary phenomenon. It would be wiser, Bandura (1973) suggests, to study the factors influencing specific aggressive responses and not assume that the identified factors necessarily apply to all other forms of aggression.

The disadvantage of Bandura's approach is that it ignores the motives underlying the harmful act. As Tedeschi, Smith, and Brown (1974) noted, the aggression observed in laboratory experiments is intentional in the sense that it is not accidental, but the subject does not necessarily intend to create harm, because experimenters do not assess the subject's motives. Tedeschi et al. (1974, p. 542) suggested that, "Since there are no ubiquitous effects or topographical features of responses that allow one to identify them unambiguously as aggressive, researchers make independent phenomenological judgments about classification." As an alternative to defining aggression only in terms of all nonaccidental responses that cause harm, Tedeschi et al. proposed that aggression be viewed as coercive power, a concept that places more emphasis on the interpersonal nature of aggression in which one person attempts to force another person to act in a certain manner. Usually, coercive power is a tactic used only after gentler methods such as persuasion have been tried unsuccessfully.

Viewed in this light, an important research question becomes one of determining the conditions that lead one to use coercion. Laboratory studies of aggression cannot address themselves to this issue, because they typically have involved paradigms in which the subjects are *required* to deliver shocks to the other subjects. The only alternatives subjects have is how much or how little shock to use. Factors such as the motives of the subject, as perceived by himself or herself, are ignored in these paradigms, but they are important factors that determine whether or not subjects will resort to coercive aggression. The subject's values, perception of the other person's intents, and the context must be used in judging whether or not a specific behavior is aggressive.

Theories of Aggression

Our discussion of the ethological view of aggression will be brief since it was presented in detail in Chapter 3. This study of the survival function of aggression among various species has emphasized the biological and instinctive determinants of aggression. Because humans are also a biological species that has emerged from the course of evolution, it is reasonable to examine the survival function of aggression in humans. Generally, however, ethological studies of other species have been used to explain human aggression and such extrapolations are of questionable validity. The role of sociocultural factors plays a key role in human aggression, and a proper study of human behavior requires greater focus on studies of aggression in humans.

ETHOLOGICAL VIEWS

One important aspect of ethological theory, shared by other views as well, is the concept of *catharsis*. It is assumed that the occurrence of aggression consumes energy so that aggressive tendencies are lessened immediately after its occurrence. Eventually the energy reservoir is replenished, so that aggression can occur again under appropriate circumstances.

The other important aspect of aggression, as viewed by ethologists, is its instinctive nature. Learning is not necessary for it to occur, because inherited tendencies for aggression exist. These tendencies can be modified and even reduced by certain experiences that prevent normal development. Under natural conditions, however, it is assumed that appropriate conditions will elicit aggression without any direct learning.

Despite the popular view of lower animals as vicious and savage aggressors and the attempt to imply that humans must therefore be the same, ethological findings actually reveal the positive survival role of aggression. The display of threat rather than actual aggression is often sufficient to signal hostility among members of the same species so that combat is not inevitable. Furthermore when combat does occur, victors do not kill their rivals but accept their signals of defeat gracefully. For the survival of the species, aggression and threat serve to insure adequate population dispersal, which protects the overexploitation of feeding areas or eradication by predators. Some human forms of aggression involving destruction and annihilation such as homicide or war seem to serve the selfish goals of the aggressor and are quite different from the positive forms of aggression within species at lower levels of the evolutionary scale.

PSYCHOANALYTIC VIEWS

The psychoanalytic view of aggression bears some similarity to the ethological inasmuch as instinct and catharsis is concerned, but psychoanalysts such as Freud and Menninger regard aggression as primarily destructive in nature. Death instincts have been postulated to account for the presence of many forms of aggression such as war or suicide—behaviors that are uniquely human, we might add. It is not surprising then that the attitudes toward aggression are quite dissimilar for ethologists and psychoanalysts.

Freud originally regarded aggression in relation to libidinal (sexual) energies. When the sexual instinct was blocked, aggressive behavior was the consequence unless it too was inhibited. The blockage of aggression toward a specific target was assumed to lead to displacement in which case aggression occurred but was directed to a different target from the one originally planned. The occurrence of aggression was assumed to be cathartic or tension reducing, so that it would be less likely to be repeated soon after its occurrence.

The destructiveness of World War I, among other factors, led Freud to revise his views and postulate a death instinct as an explanation for aggression. He felt it was necessary that society provide avenues by which such destructive energies could be discharged and released without harming others. It was thought that if they were pent up and inhibited, these destructive tendencies would produce self-destructive behavior.

Such sweeping loose explanations may represent colorful metaphors but they have little scientific value. There is no way to test Freud's theory of aggression, which is circular. Alternative explanations such as those that emphasize the role of learning processes as determinants of aggression, for example, cannot be ruled out.

FRUSTRATION-AGGRESSION HYPOTHESES

An influential view of aggression that received its inspiration from Freudian views was proposed by Dollard, an anthropologist, and his behavioristic psychology colleagues (Dollard et al., 1939). According to this approach, which came to be known as the *frustration-aggression hypothesis,* there were no instinctive factors. Instead, it was postulated that all frustration generates an unlearned source of drive or motivational energy, which activates the organism to seeks its reduction. In particular, frustration was assumed to lead always to aggression against the source of frustration. The infliction of harm serves to allow a catharsis or lowering of the tendency for future aggression, as the drive is assumed to be reduced.

Shortly after its formulation, some of its proponents (Miller, 1941; Sears, 1941) modified the theory in recognition of the fact that frustration does not always produce aggression, as shown in Figure 9–1, and that aggression can be produced by direct learning with no need for prior frustration.

Actually instrumental learning is involved even when frustration leads to aggression, because it may be due to the fact that the aggressor feels better or obtains some other benefit as a consequence. Displaced aggression that occurs when the frustrator is too powerful may similarly produce benefits for the aggressor. A classic example (Hovland and Sears, 1940) of the displacement of aggression as a response to frustration is the correlation of lynchings of blacks in the American southern states with the economic conditions. During the span from 1882–1930, such aggressive atrocities were higher generally in periods of economic hardship. Presumably, the frustration due to one source increased the likelihood that aggression would be taken out on a weaker target to reduce one's feelings of frustration.

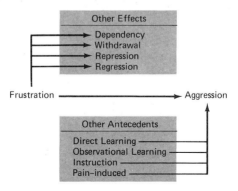

FIGURE 9–1.   Frustration is only one possible cause of aggression; frustration produces other effects besides aggression.

Even when frustration cannot be identified, learning plays a role in the acquisition of aggressive tendencies. In our society the pushy salesperson, the intimidating bully, and the outspoken critic often get what they want, whereas the nonaggressive do not. Our society admires and rewards the aggressive football player, the pugnacious boxer, or the hostile and sarcastic comic. In every instance, aggressive behavior is reinforced directly by admiration, approval, and material benefits and there is no need for frustration to occur in order to produce such aggression.

These qualifications about the generality of the assumed causal relationship of frustration to aggression do not mean that the hypothesis is totally wrong. For example, some studies (e.g., Ulrich and Azrin, 1962) suggest that pain produced through foot shocks may instigate aggression between a pair of rats confined to a small chamber. However, it is also possible that some of the fighting tendency may stem from coincidental association of fighting with shock termination even though there is no causal relationship. In any event, many of the situations previously interpreted as evidence for a frustration-induced aggression can also be accounted for by instrumental learning explanations.

As Bandura (1973, p. 38) has noted, "Since drive theories viewed aggression as impelled by the action of an aggressive drive, a number of important processes, including the conditions governing the acquisition of injurious modes of behavior, the powerful influence of response consequences in regulating behavior, and symbolic activities that enable people to hurt others without experiencing self-contempt, were essentially ignored."

LEARNING THEORY VIEWS

The conditions and techniques of aggression toward others are not instinctive, according to learning theory, but are acquired in the same way as other cultural customs whether they deal with altruism, achievement, or affiliation. Learning by means such as trial-and-error experience, moral teaching, specific instruction, and vicarious experience by the observation of others serves to teach modes of responding to the individual. He or she also learns the conditions under which various forms of behavior are acceptable or unacceptable by learning the consequences of performing or not performing specific responses.

Whereas psychoanalytic and drive theories emphasized internal forces that governed behavior, learning theories shifted the focus to the role of external or situational factors such as reinforcement contingencies. The shift was somewhat extreme and internal processes such as cognitive regulation by values, morals, and attitudes were disregarded but it did serve to redirect attention to the neglected role of external factors.

The work of Berkowitz (1962, 1965a, 1965b, 1970) and his colleagues illustrates how aggression can be analyzed in terms of the learning principles of classical conditioning. Because aggression originally occurs in the context of some types of stimuli, it is possible that future occurrences of these stimuli can serve as cues that elicit aggressive feelings and thoughts. For example, we learn that guns are instruments of aggression, so that when we see guns, we may have aggressive thoughts aroused, *provided* other conditions, such as a state of anger, also exist. Berkowitz (1965b) argued for a revision of the frustration-aggression hypothesis that requires a state of readiness involving anger such as that generated by frustration before aggression will occur. In his version, frustration does not automatically produce aggression but is only a factor that prepares the individual for aggression.

Given the presence of such readiness, previously conditioned stimuli for aggression are likely to elicit aggressive feelings that may lead to overt aggression. An additional factor that increases the likelihood of overt aggression is the observation of aggressive behavior by others, especially if it is perceived as justified.

A number of experiments have been performed by Berkowitz and his associates using one basic paradigm with some minor variations in procedure. College males are either insulted or treated in a neutral manner by the experimenter or a stooge pretending to be another subject. Then they are shown film segments of the movie *Champion,* in which Kirk Douglas portrays a boxer who receives a serious beating in a prize fight. Half the subjects watch this aggressive modeling, and the other half are shown a nonaggressive but exciting film such as one about the running of a four-minute mile by a track star.

Then pairs of subjects, one of whom is a stooge, are tested in a situation in which the real subject indicates his evaluation of the quality of the stooge's performance in some task such as designing plans for a house. A somewhat unusual method is used for such evaluation: the subject is asked to select one of a graded series of electric shock intensities, which would be felt by the stooge as a feedback cue regarding his performance. Actually the stooge, who is isolated in another room, does not receive the shocks. Although such a procedure may strike the subject as odd, Berkowitz devised it as a means of measuring aggressive tendencies as a function of anger state and type of model observed. It was predicted that those subjects who had been angered at the outset of the session and had watched the boxing film would administer higher levels of shock to the stooge. Frustration led to anger and the observation of an aggressive model served to disinhibit aggressive tendencies. It is important to note that the subject does not (and cannot) produce the same type of aggression he observes, but such experience facilitates the expression of a form of aggression appropriate to the experimental situation. As we shall see shortly, modeling of specific responses can also occur so that the observer acquires new aggressive responses by observing a model's behavior.

The ability of the viewed aggression to disinhibit aggression is affected by the extent to which it is perceived to be justified. Berkowitz and Rawlings

(1963) told half of the subjects who saw the *Champion* fight scenes that Kirk, the victim, was a heel and deserved the beating; the remaining half were told that he did not deserve such a beating. When given the chance to shock the stooge, higher levels were administered by subjects who saw justified aggression.

Whereas the studies of Berkowitz have consistently shown that the observation of aggression by the model leads to increased aggression by the observer, Feshbach (1961, 1970) has argued that under some conditions there can be a cathartic effect of modeled aggression such that the observer's aggression is lowered. The important difference between Feshbach's (1961) procedure and that of Berkowitz was the former's use of indirect measurements of aggression, which was inferred from word associations. After subjects were angered or treated neutrally, half of each group watched a neutral film while half saw the fight film. The word associations produced by subjects who were angered and watched the neutral film were more aggressive than those of the other group. Confidential ratings of the subjects' attitudes toward the experimenter revealed greater hostility toward the experimenter who had angered them when the neutral film had been seen.

These results led Feshbach to conclude that the subjects who watched the aggressive film underwent catharsis and were subsequently less aggressive toward the experimenter and during the word association test. Ratings toward an insulting experimenter were also collected in the Berkowitz and Rawlings (1963) study cited above. The ratings, collected by a second experimenter, did not support the catharsis notion as subjects who saw the aggressive film, especially when it was seen as justified, gave the lowest ratings to the first experimenter who had angered them.

One of the problems in demonstrating the cathartic effect, according to Berkowitz (1962), is the fact that a frustrated person may sometimes show less overt aggression simply because of inhibition induced either by fear or guilt. Reduction of aggression due to these factors should not be interpreted as reflective of a cathartic effect.

Buss (1961) hypothesized that one of the critical factors in determining whether or not catharsis should occur is the emotional arousal of the person. If the would-be aggressor is not angry, for example, there would be no opportunity for observed aggression to be catharted. Thus, it may be necessary for subjects to be angry before catharsis can occur, according to Buss.

A study by Hartmann (1969), however, does not support this view, unless one holds that anger is a necessary but not sufficient condition for catharsis to occur. Hartmann (1969), in any case, found that angered as well as non-angered delinquent boys who observed aggressive filmed models showed greater aggression toward peers who had angered them earlier than boys who saw neutral films. However, it is possible that catharsis is difficult to demonstrate in any experiment, because subjects inhibit their anger, knowing that they are in an experiment.

In addition, it is important to note that the boys in Hartmann's study witnessed aggression that did not involve as victims those who had angered them. If they had observed aggression toward their tormentors, a cathartic effect may have occurred. Doob and Wood (1972) obtained evidence that suggested that subjects who are annoyed will undergo catharsis if those who annoyed them are observed to suffer.

In this study a confederate of the experimenter deliberately insulted or treated subjects in a neutral manner. Each of the two groups was divided into three subgroups, one that had a chance to give painful shocks to the confederate, one that merely observed the experimenter shocking the confederate, and one that neither administered nor watched shocks to the confederate. The rationale for giving shocks was to provide feedback to the confederate who was trying to learn a concept task.

TABLE 9–2. Mean Numbers of Shocks Delivered on the "Creative Association" Task.

Condition	Subject Shocks	Experimenter Shocks	No Shock
Annoy	6.80	7.60	10.67
No annoy	8.07	9.73	6.60

Source. From "Catharsis and Aggression: The Effects of Annoyance and Retaliation on Aggressive Behavior" by A. Doob and L. Wood, *Journal of Personality and Social Psychology,* 1972, 22, 156–162. Copyright 1972 by the American Psychological Association. Reprinted by permission.

In the next part of the experiment, all subjects had a chance to shock the confederate as a means of evaluating the creativity of his responses on a word association test. The results, presented in Table 9–2, indicate that if the subjects were initially annoyed by the confederate there is a cathartic effect with the chance to give or view the confederate getting shocked in the first part of the study. The reduction in shock given by annoyed subjects in the second part of the study was greater for those who got to give shocks to the confederate than for those who merely got to watch. In contrast, if subjects had not been annoyed by the confederate, there was more shock given in the second part of the study by subjects who either gave or watched shocks during the first part. It would appear then that catharsis can occur, provided subjects are first annoyed or angered and then get to see their annoyer shocked.

We will return to the issue of possible cathartic effects of viewing aggression when we deal specifically with the effects of aggression on television and in movies. First, however, we will examine social learning theories of aggression, which are highly relevant to an understanding of the acquisition of aggression.

SOCIAL LEARNING VIEWS

Social learning approaches such as that of Bandura and Walters (1963) emphasize the influence of the observation of the behavior of others on the acquisition and performance of aggressive behavior. Aggression is regarded as a learned behavior rather than a biologically driven pattern of responding. Much human learning, aggressive or otherwise, stems from the observation of models who have the responses in their behavioral repertoires. If aggressive models can be shown to increase the amount of aggression in the observer, it would have significant implications for future policies aimed at reducing human aggression.

Outspoken critics of the high incidence of aggression in our society attribute much of it to entertainment media such as movies and television, which contain many scenes of violence. It is assumed that viewers of such violence, especially young children, are more likely to acquire aggressive tendencies after witnessing aggressive models in the media. A rival hypothesis that under some conditions such viewing might actually be cathartic and lower aggressive tendencies has also been proposed, but it generally has found fewer proponents. In view of the implications that social learning theories of aggression have for affecting the content of entertainment programs, it is not surprising that considerable controversy has been generated in recent years not only between governmental commissions and the television industry but also among psychologists.

Albert Bandura (1973), a prominent psychologist who recently served as President of the American Psychological Association, has vigorously argued that televised aggression is a major source for learning aggression. His own research with young children has shown how aggressive models can increase the observing child's imitation of the model's behavior in the laboratory. In most of his experiments, the basic procedure uses a live or filmed model who is physically or verbally aggressive. Later the children are placed in a situation in which they have a similar opportunity to express aggression. Those who observed an aggressive model are more aggressive than control subjects who watched a neutral model, especially if the children were frustrated by the experimenter just prior to the test for aggression.

An early study (Bandura, Ross, and Ross, 1961) presented nursery school children with adult models who were physically and verbally aggressive toward an inflated Bobo the clown punching bag. To rule out the chance that the child already knew some forms of aggression that would then not be attributable to the model's influence, the model employed unusual behavior. Bandura (1973, p. 72) reported, "In the general procedure, after addressing the figure belligerently, the model pummels it on the head with a mallet, hurls it down, sits on it and punches it in the nose repeatedly, kicks it across the room, flings it into the air, and bombards it with balls. These physically assaultive behaviors are accompanied by distinctive hostile remarks."

Compared to control subjects who did not see the aggressive model, the children displayed significantly more of the novel aggressive behaviors they had watched the model perform.

Furthermore, a single experimental session produces effects remembered as long as eight months later (Hicks, 1968b), a finding that Bandura (1973) finds striking. However, considering the fact that these young children would be apt to regard any unusual experience, such as serving in a psychological experiment, with awe, this recall is not as dramatic as Bandura would suggest.

Hicks (1968b) did not find that the children exposed to the aggressive model, compared to a control group that watched a neutral model, were actually more aggressive eight months later. Aggressive behavior was substantially reduced compared to that exhibited in the initial test session, but when the children were explicitly instructed to reproduce the aggressive responses modeled for them eight months earlier, they were able to recall much of them. These results illustrate an important distinction between learning and performance or between knowing what to do and wanting to do it. The children did not perform, unless explicitly asked to, the imitated aggressive responses on the delayed test, although it appears that they had learned them and could remember them.

Bandura (1973, p. 77) interprets these results as indicative of the power of a single modeling experience to produce lasting effects, but it is also possible to argue that even though the children could remember what they had seen they did not want to perform these responses. They may have felt such behavior was undesirable and rejected these responses until Hicks asked if they remembered them.

Another study (Bandura, 1965) that illustrates the learning-performance distinction involved children who observed an aggressive filmed model who was either rewarded, punished, or received no obvious consequences for his behavior. When the children were given an opportunity to employ the modeled aggression, those who had seen the model punished showed the least amount of aggression, especially the girls in the group. The question may arise whether or not these latter subjects failed to learn the model's behavior or learned them but were inhibited from performing them.

In the next part of the same study all the children were offered rewards for performing the aggressive responses they had witnessed earlier. As shown in Figure 9–2, the previous differences in performance were eliminated and all groups showed the same amount of aggression regardless of the consequences that they had seen the model receive. Thus it would appear that observation of a punished model does not block the learning of the aggression, although it does inhibit its performance. Since the observed behavior does become a part of the subject's repertoire, it will occur later if reward becomes available for its performance. One might draw the implication then that viewing violence and aggression in the movies or on television might not

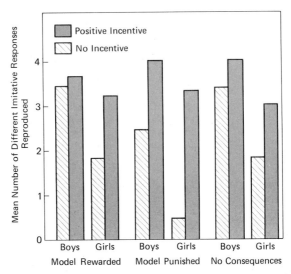

FIGURE 9–2. Mean number of different matching responses reproduced by children as a function of positive incentives and the model's reinforcement contingencies. [From "Influence of Models' Reinforcement Contingencies on the Acquisition of Imitative Responses," by A. Bandura, *Journal of Personality and Social Psychology*, 1965, *1*, 589–595. Copyright 1965 by the American Psychological Association. Reprinted by permission.]

necessarily produce immediate effects on performance, but that the tactics of aggression are learned and stored until a suitable opportunity to perform them arises.

NATURALISTIC CASES OF MODELING. Although most studies have concentrated on the acquisition of the specific responses displayed by the model, Bandura (1973, pp. 85–6) also holds that general tactics, attitudes, and values regarding aggression can be instilled in children by observational learning.

Innumerable naturalistic cases suggest the learning of aggressive behaviors from mass media models. The more dramatic cases are publicized daily in our newspapers and on television. These media serve not only to report news but often, unfortunately, to enlarge the audience for learning these behaviors. Bandura (1973, pp. 102–107) summarizes some of the more recent examples such as the epidemic of air hijackings (see Figure 9–3), urban disorders of the 1960s, and political kidnappings. Modeling effects are not limited to violent behaviors, of course, and the same process leads to the rapid spread of fads such as streaking, telephone booth stuffing, and similar light-hearted antics.

Berkowitz (1970) provided an explanation of "contagious" violence in less cognitive terms, which suggested that media publicity regarding sensational violent crimes acts as a conditioned stimulus that may trigger aggressive tendencies under certain conditions. He presented crime statistics collected

FIGURE 9–3.   Incidence of hijacking over a span of twenty-five years. The rise in the foreign hijackings during the 1949–50 period occurred in Slavic countries at the time of the Hungarian uprising and the second flare-up between 1958–61 was comprised almost entirely of Cuban hijackings to Miami. A sudden widespread diffusion of hijacking that occurred between 1969–70 eventually involved airliners from a total of fifty-five different countries. (Plotted from data furnished by the Federal Aviation Administration.) [From *Aggression: A Social Learning Analysis*, by A. Bandura, Englewood Cliffs, N.J.: Prentice-Hall, 1973. Reprinted by permission of Prentice-Hall, Inc., Englewood Cliffs, New Jersey.]

in forty American cities between 1960–1966, as shown in Figure 9–4. Aggressive crimes appear to have risen dramatically over this eighty-four month period according to this illustration, which shows the deviation between each month's index of violent crimes and the total mean for the corresponding calendar month over the entire seven years.

Noting that two particularly sharp increases occurred shortly after the assassination of President Kennedy in 1963 and the Speck murders of eight Chicago nurses in July, 1966, Berkowitz argued that this data showed how an epidemic of violence can be generated by the public awareness of key incidents of violence.

It is possible that the threshold for violence may be lowered in a person on the verge of aggression by exposure to information about sensational acts of violence. This mechanism need not be at odds with Bandura's explanation of modeled aggression, because there may be more than one type of learning situation. Modeling deals more with the role of observation in the acquisition of new responses and may be the process that occurs when the observer imitates a specific form of violence.

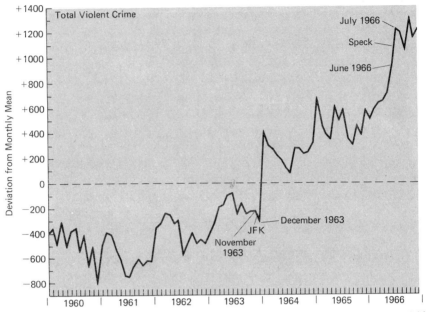

FIGURE 9–4. Deviations from monthly mean for sum of violent crimes, 1960–1966. [From "The Contagion of Violence: An S-R Mediational Analysis of Some Effects of Observed Aggression," by L. Berkowitz in *Nebraska Symposium on Motivation* (Vol. 18) by W. J. Arnold and M. M. Page (Eds.), Lincoln: University of Nebraska Press, 1970. Reprinted by permission of University of Nebraska Press.]

The possibility that processes such as those suggested by Berkowitz and Bandura increase aggressive violence is not limited to real incidents but could operate in fictional situations as well.

In some bizarre crimes the perpetrator was inspired by the plot of a movie or television program. So that we will not be guilty of (or accused of) spreading diabolical ideas to would-be culprits, we will not cite specific examples. These incidents are also cited as evidence of the harmful ways in which modeled aggression and violence can instill similar responses in viewers. But before accepting these conclusions based on the findings of laboratory experiments such as those of Berkowitz and Bandura, let us examine some criticisms and limiting factors associated with these studies.

LIMITATIONS OF LABORATORY AGGRESSION. As Singer (1971) has commented on the generalizability of experimental studies, they "smell of the laboratory." In the studies with college students, for example, it is possible that the *demand characteristics* of the task may influence the subjects to behave in ways atypical of their ordinary modes. Orne (1962) has coined this term to refer to the fact that the subject in an experiment often tries to determine the purpose of a study and to behave in ways that make him or her appear to be a good subject in order to help the experimenter. If deceptions are not effective, and the subject figures out the purpose of a study, his or her cooperativeness may produce an apparent confirmation of the experimenter's hypothesis.

Consider, for example, the possible demand characteristics in a study by Berkowitz and LePage (1967) in which pairs of males are supposed to take turns evaluating each other's performance of a task by shocks. One of the subjects is a stooge and he is always chosen to be first in evaluating the real subject. In half the subjects, high shocks are used to create anger; in the other half, low shocks are used to create nonangry subjects. Then the roles are reversed and the real subjects evaluate the stooge. Three subgroups are formed, two of which see a gun and a rifle on the table next to the shock apparatus. As if to reassure the subjects, the experimenter makes sure that they are noticed by asking them to disregard the weapons, telling half of them that they belong to the stooge who is using them for another study and the other half that they belong to another experimenter. No guns are present for the remaining subgroup. Finally, an additional group that served as a control group was also angered (received high shocks) by the stooge; when it was their turn to shock the stooge, badminton equipment was next to the shock machine.

The purpose of these props was to test the idea that the presence of weapons, because they are associated with violence, might elicit more aggression from subjects. The results showed that such was the case for the angry subjects, those who had received the high shocks, but not for the nonangry subjects.

An obvious question is whether or not demand characteristics might have biased the results. A perceptive subject might have figured that the weapons were really part of the study and that they were supposed to be more aggressive toward the stooge.

Berkowitz and LePage interviewed their subjects after the study and dismissed the possibility that such artifacts occurred. Furthermore, the nonangry subjects did not show the weapons effect, as one might expect if the demand characteristics of the props were acting to enhance aggression.

Page and Schiedt (1971), however, felt that a more careful postexperimental interview than the one used by Berkowitz and LePage might disclose that subjects had been influenced by their awareness and suspicions about the purpose of the study. Although they did show that the weapons effect might be due to demand characteristics with subjects who had been in an earlier deception study, it is also possible that the postexperimental interview itself biased the subjects, according to Berkowitz (1971).

A subsequent study (Exp. 5) by Buss, Booker, and Buss (1972) attempted unsuccessfully to replicate the original study of Berkowitz and LePage. In fact, more aggression was shown by the angry subjects when there were no weapons present. The conclusion that guns, by their presence, can instigate aggression in angered subjects is open to question. First, the findings of a weapons effect could stem from the influence of demand characteristics in experiments. In addition, later studies show conflicting results.

Although the laboratory study of aggression, as with other phenomena, is more efficient than natural observation insofar as you can create the situations at your convenience, too much reliance has been placed on the teacher-learner paradigm developed by Buss (1961). It is an implausible, elaborate, and circuitous method for obtaining feedback on a learning task from the subject's perspective. Moreover, how can the aggressive and evaluative functions of the shock levels chosen by subjects be identified? A high shock may not reflect aggression entirely but may mean that the subject's opinion of the learner's performance is rather low.

A similar criticism has been raised by Tedeschi, Smith, and Brown (1974, p. 541), "Laboratory studies of human aggression almost never establish the intentions of subjects, they often rationalize actions to subjects through cover stories so that delivering shocks to others will be interpreted as beneficial to the victim or to science, and frequently involve neither harm doing nor intent to do harm."

Furthermore, Tedeschi et al. point out that if we distinguish between legitimate and illegitimate aggression, as defined by the norms of a specific group, the latter variety rarely occurs in the laboratory so that "subjects simply do not harm others in the laboratory for no reason" (p. 542). In our society defensive retaliation is generally accepted as legitimate, and thus subjects insulted in an experiment may consider their subsequent aggression legitimate.

With respect to the studies of Bandura and his associates dealing with the initial acquisition of aggressive responses by imitation, Tedeschi et al. also question whether intent to do harm exists. Although the child admittedly intends to perform the modeled behavior such as strike the inflated clown punching bag or shoot a toy gun, it is not clear that the child intends harm or regards his or her behavior as bad, especially since the experimental session is presented as a play session.

WHEN WILL AGGRESSIVE MODELS BE IMITATED? It may be helpful at this point to diagram some of the many factors that might affect the likelihood of a specific modeled aggressive response being used against a source of anger. As Figure 9–5 shows, once a specific aggressive response is displayed by a model and learned by the observer, its performance will still depend on some other learned aspects of the modeled behavior. Whether or not the observer perceived the act as intentional, justified, or instrumental to other goals may affect performance. The severity of the reactions of the victim, not always observable, may also be important. The affective state of the observer must also be considered.

Even Bandura (1973, p. 129) allows that factors such as self-evaluative responses to one's own behavior and to anticipated social and other external consequences will affect the tendency to imitate the model. Indiscriminate copying of modeled aggression does not occur because the observer's values and cognitive interpretation of the situation also are important.

In contrast, the subject who observes a neutral model is assumed to learn

Some Other Factors Affecting Likelihood That Modelled Aggression
Will Be Imitated By Observer

Observe Behavior of Model	Make Cognitive Appraisal of Model's Behavior	Observe Consequences of Model's Behavior	Motivational Factors
Aggressive Behavior	Was it intentional? Was it justifiable?	Does victim suffer, show signs of pain, etc.?	Opportunity for Aggression
			Perceived Risks and Rewards
			Emotional State of Observer

FIGURE 9–5.   Some of the factors that can alter the likelihood that observed aggression of a model will be imitated by the observer. The observed aggression may be learned, but it is evaluatively interpreted in terms of intentionality, justifiability, and instrumentality. Performance of learned aggression that is positively evaluated still depends on appraisal of the situation in which the observer is presented with an opportunity to aggress.

no new aggressive responses and should not perform aggressively, unless he or she employs previously learned modes.

Returning to the behavior of the observer of an aggressive model, we note that other factors, not shown in Figure 9–5, could affect the likelihood of imitation. The presence of an audience, the similarity of the model's background to that of the observer, and the ability of the model to influence the observer, for example, might be important factors.

Furthermore, although the effects are not simple, it appears that characteristics of the model's personality affect the degree to which an observer will imitate him or her (Bandura, Ross, and Ross, 1963). In addition, negative statements by a co-observer about modeled aggression at the time it occurs have been found to markedly reduce its imitation (Grusec, 1973; Hicks, 1968a).

The significance of these qualifying factors is that they suggest that many of the conclusions about the adverse effects of the observation of aggression, especially on television, may be gross overstatements. This is not to say that no danger is involved but that the effects of such viewing have been exaggerated. Moral attitudes, alone, probably counteract the tendency to imitate much of the aggression we observe. As implied by the Grusec and Hicks studies, parental values expressed while a child is observing aggression may have a great influence on the effects of such observation.

Without these counteracting factors, it would not be a question of why we have so much aggression, as social critics lament, but why we do not have even more. For all of us are continually bombarded with countless opportunities to observe aggression, at least in the media and movies, but not all of us run amok. One problem in determining the true effects of observed aggression on actual aggression is that we have no good baseline measure of the level of aggression that would exist if we never had a chance to observe aggressive models.

Television and Aggression

In contrast to laboratory studies of modeling and aggression in which processes assumed to be similar to those that occur during the viewing of television are examined, a number of studies have dealt more directly with the relationship between actual television viewing and aggression.

CORRELATIONAL STUDIES

A controversial report was made by the U.S. Surgeon General's Scientific Advisory Committee on Television and Social Behavior (e.g., Comstock and Rubenstein, 1972). The overall findings of these studies concluded that a modest relationship exists but acknowledges that third factors such as parental or familial upbringing and environment may be involved. There may no simple direct causal effect between viewing aggression and being aggressive and the report states ". . . neither individually nor collectively are the findings conclusive," as illustrated by the cartoon in Figure 9–6.

Most of the studies in the report (e.g., McIntyre and Teevan, 1972; Robinson and Bachman, 1972) show correlational evidence only. The aggressiveness shown in favorite programs has had modest correlations with adolescent aggressiveness and delinquency in the McIntyre and Teevan and the Robinson and Bachman studies. As with earlier correlational studies in this area (e.g., Eron, 1963; Himmelweit, Oppenheim, and Vince, 1958), it is not possible to determine whether these correlations mean that the violence viewed is the cause of aggressive behavior or whether aggressive individuals prefer watching violent programs. Nor is it possible to rule out the possibility that some third factor(s) are involved.

There is undoubtedly much aggression and violence displayed on television, but there is also much violence in the everyday world. A child could learn aggressive behavior from either source or from both. Factors also inhibit the translation of what is learned by observation into action, as we have already discussed. It may be that the viewed fictional aggression can be kept distinct from reality in the minds of most children, and that this ability may also reduce any adverse effects of viewing aggressive content. Consistent with this view is the fact that Feshbach (1972) found that children who watched the same film of a campus riot were more aggressive later toward the experimenter if the film were described as a newsfilm than if it were depicted as a Hollywood dramatization of a college disturbance.

One correlational study (Eron, Lefkowitz, Huesmann, and Walder, 1972), which does permit stronger inferences about causality, involved a comparison

"OUR STUDIES SHOW <u>CONCLUSIVELY</u> THAT TV DOES NOT CAUSE VIOLENCE... EXCEPT WHEN IT DOES."

FIGURE 9–6. The "relationship" between viewing television violence and aggressive behavior. [From *American Psychological Association Monitor,* 1972, *3,* (3), 1. Copyright 1972 by the American Psychological Association. Reprinted by permission.]

of the relationship between viewing habits and aggressiveness in the same sample at two different ages. No correlation was found between the two variables during the third grade, but a correlation was found between third-grade viewing behavior and thirteenth-grade aggressiveness, at least in males. The more they viewed aggression at the earlier age, the more aggressive they were at the later age. This finding, showing a correlation between viewing habits of an earlier point in time with behavior at a much later time, is a stronger indication that the viewing habits could have been a cause rather than a mere correlate of the later aggressive behavior. Still, third factors such as parental attitudes could have caused both the viewing habits and the aggressive behavior. These findings were not obtained with females, suggesting that additional factors must operate in conjunction with modeled aggression in order to produce the increase in males.

EXPERIMENTAL STUDIES

A direct study of the effects of television viewing was conducted in a field setting by Feshbach and Singer (1972). They were able to perform a rare controlled experiment in which the viewing diet of adolescent boys was assigned by the experimenters rather than freely selected by the boys themselves. This procedure has both advantages and disadvantages. Boys can be randomly assigned to either an aggressive or nonaggressive set of programs for viewing so that any behavioral differences cannot be attributed to self-selection factors such as more aggressive boys tending to prefer viewing aggressive programs. But the external regulation of viewing content can and probably did create some hostility and resistance, as illustrated by the strong protest by the boys who were in the nonaggressive program control group when they realized they could not watch *Batman,* which was in vogue at the time of the study. It was necessary for the experimenters to compromise and allow them to have that one exception.

It was possible to achieve the level of control described because Feshbach and Singer had access to boys attending private boarding schools. The experimental group was restricted to aggressive programs such as *FBI Story, Gunsmoke,* and *Bonanza,* whereas the control group was allowed to watch only nonaggressive programs such as *Lawrence Welk, Meet the Press,* and *Walt Disney,* to cite a few examples. The programs were not always appropriate, especially those watched by the control group, and in some cases some could be classified both ways, for example, *Walt Disney.*

The viewing conditions were also artificially regulated insofar as all boys had to watch a minimum of six hours per week. The study was concluded after six weeks of regulated viewing. The results showed that the aggressive fare led to less verbal aggression toward peers, although it did not affect physical aggression. Feshbach and Singer concluded that a cathartic effect had occurred, because the boys who viewed aggression were less aggressive than those who watched the nonaggressive programs.

A number of criticisms of the study have been raised. One question that has not been mentioned is whether or not the greater sacrifice made by the control group insofar as they probably encountered the larger shift from their usual viewing habits might have created more frustration. In addition, the inappropriateness (e.g., *Lawrence Welk Show*) of some of the options for this group might have also engendered resentment leading to more aggression in the control group. Thus, catharsis need not be invoked to explain the relatively lower aggression in the aggression-viewing group at all.

A more subtle and unobtrusive procedure was devised by Milgram and Shotland (1973) to study the effects of violence seen on television on real life behavior. With the cooperation of a major television network, it was possible to film a sequence displaying antisocial violence incorporated as part of a popular television program, *Medical Center.* The segment deals with a young hospital attendant named Tom who quits his job but soon finds himself in serious need of money. While watching television, he sees his former employer, Dr. Gannon, who is on a telethon appealing for public donations to a charity. Due to his frustrating situation, Tom makes a couple of abusive calls to the telethon and then goes on a rampage, smashing open a donation box for that charity in the bar in which he is watching the telethon. Then he is seen going to other parts of town and smashing several other donation boxes and taking their contents.

The purpose of including this segment in the *Medical Center* program was to see if the incidence of similar aggression among some of the viewers would be greater than it had been during a baseline period just prior to the airing of this program. Several different procedures were used in order to establish the effect of the viewing of the antisocial segment.

In the first study, subjects were recruited to attend a preview showing of a television program at the studio and promised a free gift of a transistor radio for attending. They were to claim their gifts by appointment at a local warehouse a day or two later. However, when the subjects arrived there, no one was present and a sign indicated that the supply of radios had been exhausted and no more would be given away. The deserted waiting room contained a breakable charity donation box similar to the one Tom had smashed and money was clearly visible in it.

The question, obviously, was whether or not the frustrated subjects would imitate Tom's act of aggression. Three different subgroups in the study saw different endings to the film segment. One group saw the program end with Tom being arrested and jailed, whereas a second group observed Tom successfully fleeing to Mexico. A third group watched Tom's temptation but saw him restrain himself and even donate some money himself. Finally, a fourth control group observed a totally different film about a love story in which neither violence nor antisocial behavior was shown during the preview.

The study, conducted on a large sample of several hundred participants, disclosed no significant differences in antisocial behavior as a consequence of their experiences. Although a few subjects in each group did break into the donation box at the office where their efforts to claim their gift were frustrated, there were no differences as a function of the type of ending or story they observed. Finally, it should be added that as the subjects left the office and passed a door that was obviously part of a different company, they received their free gifts from someone who was allegedly substituting for the company supposed to distribute the gifts. Actually he was part of the research team.

In another field study the program featuring Tom was actually broadcast on television but only in the New York area. A program without the violent segment was shown one week, whereas the aggressive behavior was associated with punishment during the showing one week later.

Since viewers watched the program at home, it was necessary to mail invitations to a sample of homes asking viewers to report to a local office if they wished to claim a free gift. The procedure at the office was similar to that used in the previous study. Hidden television cameras recorded the subjects' reactions and behavior in the empty office with the donation box. Again, no differences were found between those who watched the antisocial film with the punishment ending and those who saw the neutral version. A replication of this study used the nonpunished version of the antisocial scene in St. Louis, again the program content had no apparent effect on the subjects' tendency to commit similar thefts.

Milgram and Shotland resorted to the use of telephone calls from viewers as an index of antisocial expression in another study. In the film segment, as you may recall, Tom made several abusive calls to Dr. Gannon right after he saw him deliver his appeal on the telethon. In this study, the local television station ran a public service message right after *Medical Center* ended. A young woman appealed for donations to a real charity and gave a phone number for viewers to call if they wished to pledge.

It was expected that the viewing of Tom's aggression might lead to similar aggression by viewers in the Detroit and Chicago areas where the program was aired. Milgram and Shotland felt that this technique might generate a larger sample of subjects than usually possible. Any small effects of televised content on antisocial behavior might be better detected if the sample size was enlarged to the thousands.

Very few calls were in fact received at all, and the abusive ones were primarily those of a sexual nature bearing no similarity at all to the type of verbal abuse used by Tom in the film segment.

All in all, the Milgram and Shotland study provides no support whatsoever for the contention that the viewing of this type of antisocial behavior will produce similar behavior in viewers. Although they acknowledge some of the limitations of their studies, Milgram and Shotland suggest that some investigators have been too facile in arguing that the viewing of aggression is readily imitated.

The studies in themselves are unique in dealing with the assessment of the effects of a very specific type of behavior shown on an actual network program on the behavior of viewers in a natural setting. The studies employed large samples and were conducted under highly controlled conditions, especially for this type of problem. Milgram and Shotland do admit that their research cannot be considered definitive. For one matter, the cumulative effects of year in and year out watching of televised aggression cannot be assessed. A single observation of the kind of highly reprehensible behavior modeled in these studies may be insufficient to induce imitation. Not only is stealing involved, but it is stealing from a charity, which is quite different from physical or verbal aggression directly against an adversary. The latter can often be justified or rationalized as appropriate, whereas it is more difficult for most of us to defend stealing from charity. Perhaps the use of a less-contemptible form of antisocial activity may have generated a larger modeling effect.

INDIVIDUAL DIFFERENCES

AGE DIFFERENCES.　The likelihood of demonstrating that the observation of aggressive models on television leads to imitation may be greater with young children than with older subjects, in which additional factors such as moral values and critical judgment may offset blind imitation of observed behaviors. Liebert and Baron (1972) showed brief three and one-half minute segments of a popular television program involving aggressive scenes to five to six and eight to nine year old children. A comparable amount of viewing of scenes from a nonaggressive track race occurred with control groups.

The children then went to another room and were seated before a panel with two buttons, one labeled "help" and one labeled "hurt." They were informed that another child was in an adjacent room trying to win a prize by turning a handle. They could either help or hurt the other child, depending on which button they pressed each time a ready signal was presented. If they pushed the "help" button, the other child was more likely to win as the handle would be easier to turn. But whenever they pressed the "hurt" button, the other child would be less likely to win because the handle would become too warm to hold. These instructions were a deception and there was no other child in the other room.

The results of the Liebert and Baron study showed that children of either age group were more likely to press the "hurt" button if they had viewed the aggressive film segments just prior to the chance to help or hurt the other child. It should be noted that the subjects had not been angered or frustrated by either the experimenter or by the other child, who did not in fact exist. It would appear that the brief exposure to aggressive models is sufficient to increase the likelihood of harmful responses toward other persons by young children. Note that the specific harmful response available to the children was not the same as that shown in the film aggression, so it was not simply a case of copying a particular response.

Whether or not the children fully understood the harmful consequences of their actions is not clear. They do not see actual harm to the hypothetical child. Why they would want to harm the other child is also unclear. Nonetheless, if the consequences are harmful to another person it may be less important to know why the responses were made than to know that observed aggressive responses are likely to reduce inhibitions against harming others.

PERSONALITY DIFFERENCES. Individual or personality differences should also be considered. Stein, Friedrich, and Vondracek (1972) conducted a naturalistic experiment with children to examine the effects of television viewing for one month on aggression. They found that watching violent cartoons did increase aggression for some children, namely those who were already above average in aggressiveness.

SEX DIFFERENCES. Although some studies have compared sex differences and generally found less aggression among girls (e.g., Bandura, 1965; Eron et al., 1973), it has been common for critics of television to ignore this difference and focus on male aggression. A study of which environmental factors, if any, serve to insulate girls from modeling aggressive models might be a useful approach to finding how to reduce imitation by males. In any event, the existence of individual differences such as those just described may serve to obscure some of the factors that do favor imitation of aggressive models. Future studies need to further identify the individuals who are more susceptible to the adverse influences of aggressive models.

ADDITIONAL CONSIDERATIONS

In general, the available evidence has been used to argue that the viewing of televised aggression can be either detrimental, ineffective, or beneficial. Most of the conclusions, however, have been of the first category and television has borne the brunt of responsibility for societal violence in the eyes of some observers. Yet, the available evidence is not so unambiguous that firm conclusions are possible, as suggested by the U.S. Surgeon General's Scientific Advisory Committee on Television and Social Behavior report.

Unfortunately, political factors seem to have influenced the selection of the membership of this select committee, and two of the leading critics of television practices regarding violence, Leonard Berkowitz and Albert Bandura, were excluded. This deplorable practice creates suspicion in the minds of many about the objectivity of the committee report, which is unfortunate in our opinion because we feel that their conclusion is nevertheless a fair assessment of the existing evidence.

Bandura's (1973) otherwise excellent summary of the research findings relevant to a social learning theory analysis of observed aggression effects is marred by an extended attack on the television industry (pp. 266–87), because the evidence does not support his arguments firmly. This is not to say that we condone or approve of the amount of video violence, for we would join others in deploring the sterility of the "vast wasteland" that television programming has come to be called. We are not so much frightened that the viewed violence will be the major cause of viewer violence as we are concerned about the potential of this medium lost in the monotonous, stereotyped, formula plots used in these displays of aggression. More to the point, however, is that our defense of television programming is only a defense of it from *unfair* criticism based on inadequate studies that are simplistically applied to far more complex situations.

Some critics imply that the very fact that advertisers pay to sponsor programs proves that television content affects viewer behavior. And if commercials on television sell products, then aggression on television obviously also sells violence to the viewer. The logic is that if some television content (commercials) changes some viewer behavior (buying), it follows that other television content (e.g., aggression) will also change other viewer behavior (e.g., aggression).

For one matter, some question exists whether commercials are as successful as generally assumed. And, for those that are effective, is the mechanism merely one of brand name exposure and familiarity or is it the often exaggerated and emotional sales pitches that sell the customer? Ignoring this issue, one also sees that the logic is weak in assuming that the same processes must operate in selling products, services, and ideas. Solely on logical grounds, one notes that it is possible for commercials to affect consumer behavior without violent programs necessarily increasing viewer aggression during interpersonal interactions.

OTHER SOURCES OF MODELED AGGRESSION.   Television has its faults, but it should not be the scapegoat for societal violence that stems from numerous factors. The adequacy of the behavioral examples of parents and role models as well as the moral guidance of parents and other socializing agents should be examined before attributing blame to secondary sources such as television. Prior to the widespread opportunity to view television, the scapegoat was books, especially comic books in the case of children and adolescents. It may be true that such books contributed to the effect, but it seems that the basic conditions may have already been present because so many readers somehow seemed to escape the evil influences of such books.

POSSIBLE SOLUTIONS.   What types of solutions are viable for reducing even the secondary effects of aggressive television? Attempts to censor and control content create additional problems in restricting freedoms. Furthermore, where does one draw the line? If television is edited for aggression, do we do the same for comic books, fiction, and true stories involving aggression? The philosophy that aggressive comic books should end with an outcome showing that crime, violence, and aggression do not pay was adopted in hopes that the impressionable young reader would not copy undesirable models. Is this a viable solution?

Leaving aside for the moment the important issue of censorship as a justified means to achieve a socially desirable goal, one sees other problems associated with this strategy for preventing the anticipated adverse effects of viewed aggression. It is apt to be transparent to the average child who can readily see that in real life illegal and aggressive actions do sometimes unfortunately succeed. Fortunately this same sense of reality in children should enable them to realize also that fictionalized presentations are fantasies and not reenactments or portrayals of real life. In short, it is not necessary to regulate fiction so that the good guys always beat the bad guys. Children with a sense of social morality probably are inoculated and will not readily incorporate antisocial behavior into their lives merely because they saw it portrayed as a successful tactic in a movie or on television.

Unfortunately, one hears of instances in which some child (or adult) is impressed by an antisocial incident shown on television and imitates it in real life, often with tragic consequences. A recent example, although it does not involve violence, of the modeling effect is Evel Knievel's well-publicized and exploited 1974 attempt to jump the Snake River in his rocket. Reports indicated a spate of imitations by children, many of whom sustained injuries in their efforts.

But would these very children have been the same ones who would have found some other way to take risks if Knievel did not exist? Children who lack good judgment, common sense, and moral judgment may be more prone to engage in behaviors that are apt to injure themselves or others. This possibility is overlooked when a model for their behavior can be found and we can assign all of the blame to it.

THE CHILD'S INTERPRETATION OF TELEVISED AGGRESSION. Much of the preceding defense of televised aggression is admittedly speculative and aimed at showing alternative hypotheses, because the evidence against television is not as strong as some critics hold it is. One study (Snow, 1974) that does suggest that the effects of fictional violence are less harmful than laboratory experiments would imply involved an interview of preadolescent children regarding their perceptions of televised content. Most previous studies have defined aggression in adult terms and have ignored the child's perspective. Snow hypothesized that make-believe violence is accepted by children as precisely that, make-believe, and that they do not usually confuse it with real life. His results suggested that make-believe violence is not regarded as violence by the children themselves. In fact, they reported that they would not engage in similar activities themselves. Although the answer to the last question may be biased by the fact that the interviewer was present, Snow's findings do point out the value of determining how events are interpreted by the child.

EMOTIONAL REACTIONS TO TELEVISED AGGRESSION. Aside from the question of whether or not viewed television aggression increases actual aggression, there is another generally ignored issue. It is conceivable that even if observers were not themselves more or less aggressive as a consequence of what they view on television, they may become less alarmed or upset by the observation of violence. Emotional response to violence may become blunted and the anxiety over the harm done to others may be reduced with repeated exposure to viewed aggression. Goranson (1970), in evaluating the evidence for such a process, concluded that it is likely that this type of desensitization or adaptation to viewed aggression does occur.

If observers are less disturbed at witnessing violence, they may be more likely to resort to, or at least condone, aggression. At the same time, Goranson is careful to add that observing media violence and real violence may not produce the same effects. Habituation to television violence may not desensitize the observer to the emotional effects of witnessing live violence, because the former is presented in an antiseptic manner. Usually there is no blood or guts spilled on television as is sometimes true in real life.

EFFECTS OF PAIN CUES FROM VICTIM. Lorenz (1966), a noted ethologist, observed that animals inhibit their aggression when they observe suffering in their victims. A similar process, termed a *revised catharsis hypothesis* by Goranson (1970), may occur among humans such that observation of the gory or painful consequences of violence may reduce its chances of being imitated. According to this view, catharsis does not come about, as suggested by psychoanalytic theory, because of the observer's vicarious experience of aggression but because of the chance to learn about the nature of the consequences of aggression for the victim. It is assumed that if the average person could see the suffering inflicted on the victim, he or she would hesitate before acting aggressively.

Laboratory studies (Baron, 1971; Geen, 1970) provide some support for this view as subjects, angered as well as those not angered, reacted less aggressively toward potential victims who appeared to be suffering pain. In these studies the subjects administered shocks to confederates who were supposedly making errors on a learning task. Subjects received feedback about how much pain was experienced by the confederates and results suggested that less shock was administered, the more apparent pain was suffered by the victim.

On the other hand, it would seem that in real life greater aggression may be triggered by signs that the victim was suffering. The sight of blood, the cries of anguish, and other cues of pain might stimulate the aggressor to finish the "kill." Cases of revenge or retaliation might also provoke greater aggression when the victim shows suffering.

EMOTIONAL STATE OF THE AGGRESSOR. One factor that may be important in determining whether pain cues from the victim lead to more or less aggression is the emotional state of the aggressor. Anger, as Buss (1961) has suggested, may be a state that influences aggression. Feshbach, Stiles, and Bitter (1967) hypothesized that the observed suffering of a victim might reduce aggression if the aggressor is not angry, but that the opposite effect would occur if the aggressor was angry.

In Feshbach et al.'s study, female subjects were first angered or not angered by a confederate. Then they observed the confederate perform a task supposedly without the latter's knowledge. The task of the subjects was apparently to rate the confederate's emotional level. They were also told that in order to prevent successive ratings from contaminating each other, a filler task would be inserted between judgments in which they were to make up sentences starting with a personal pronoun and containing a verb to be chosen by the experimenter.

Unknown to the subjects, this latter task involved verbal conditioning such that the experimenter arranged for the confederate to receive shock after each sentence that the subject made starting with a specific pronoun arbitrarily designated. The control group subjects' performance did not lead to shock of the confederate but produced a light that appeared behind the confederate. In other words, the performance of the subjects on the verbal conditioning task determined whether or not the confederate received shock in the experimental condition and whether or not a light appeared behind the confederate in the control group. In neither case were the subjects informed about this contingency.

Feshbach et al. concluded that anger is necessary before observation of the victim's pain will lead to more aggression, because the performance of the experimental group surpassed that of the control, if subjects had been angered by the stooge. Performance by the nonangered groups, on the other hand, was poorer under the experimental condition and suggested that observation of the victim's pain reduced the aggression of the subjects toward them.

The evidence appears to conflict but it should be noted that the teacher-learner shock paradigm used by Baron is quite different from the complicated procedures of the Feshbach et al. study. In the former situation it is clear that subjects know they have the power to cause pain or to show mercy toward the victim, whereas in the latter context the subjects are unaware that their verbal behavior is the basis for the consequences that befall the victim.

Clearer evidence along the lines of the Feshbach et al. conclusion is available from a subsequent study (Baron, 1974) using a less ambiguous paradigm. After subjects were either angered or not angered by the stooge, a second part of the study involved having one subject shock the other ostensibly to study the effects of punishment on physiological reactions. It was suggested that the stooge who had had the chance to shock the real subject during the first part of the study should now receive the shock.

The subject and the confederate were in separate rooms but fake feedback about the confederate's experience of pain was presented on an instrument alleged to be a psychoautonomic pain meter, which measured physiological reactions to pain. The results indicated that angry subjects gave more shock when the meter indicated the victim was experiencing higher pain levels; the opposite was found with nonangry subjects who gave less shock when alleged victim pain was high. Baron concluded that anger is an important factor that modifies the effect of pain cues on the behavior of an aggressor. He attributed his earlier (Baron, 1971) contradictory results to the possibility that subjects in that study were not sufficiently angered.

It may also be important to consider personality differences in the response to pain cues emanating from a victim. Presence or absence of witnesses could also be important. The answer to this significant question about the factors affecting aggression is not yet clearcut.

Situational Determinants of Aggression

Throughout the preceding discussion of aggression, the implication has been that it is a disposition or characteristic of the individual. The problem of situational versus trait formulations of behavior was already discussed at length in Chapter 1, and it is relevant to the present section.

The level of aggressive behavior is obviously affected by situational factors. On the one hand, we may find that inhibitions exist against the expression of aggression in some contexts. Fear of reprisal or ostracism from more powerful and influential persons may restrain us from aggressive actions. The presence of an authority figure, be it teacher, parent, or police officer, can act to dampen our tendency toward aggression.

Situational factors may also operate in the opposite direction and enhance the likelihood of aggressive behavior. An individual who may feel aggressive may be too timid to act alone, but the presence of others with similar feelings may encourage the overt expression of aggression. The example of mob violence comes readily to mind. The presence of an audience may also serve to bring forth aggressive behavior as a means of showing off or impressing others.

Although situational factors may function both as inhibitors and as releasers of aggression, we will focus on the latter situation since it is more likely to create problems for society.

Consider, for example, acts of extreme aggression, which are often cruel, senseless, and irrational. Most of us would regard the perpetrators of such misdeeds as barbarians or lunatics. We could not imagine ourselves knowingly committing acts of torture, brutality, and harm toward others, especially if they were innocent children or animals. Whenever we hear of these horrible incidents, we are apt to attribute them to sadistic and demented individuals.

Some research, however, has raised the possibility that persons who commit these actions do not always do so because of any motive or trait but rather as a consequence of certain aspects of the situation in which they find themselves. The frightening implication of such findings is that we moral, law-abiding, good people may someday find ourselves in similar situations in which we act in ways that we consider to be highly reprehensible.

ANONYMITY AND DEINDIVIDUATION

Zimbardo's (1969) analysis of deindividuation suggests how "good" people may be transformed into "evil" ones. Anonymity is a factor common to many varieties of inhumane and aggressive actions. Anonymity enables a person to escape individual responsibility for his or her actions. It is not surprising that Klu Klux Klan members wear hoods when performing their violent misdeeds. Zimbardo cited the practice in some states of having several executioners, each of whom pull a switch simultaneously but only one of which actually closes the circuit. Thus, each executioner can avoid personal responsibility, guilt, and anxiety somewhat, because he does not know for sure that he was the true executioner.

A more rigorous test of the anonymity hypothesis by Zimbardo (1969) involved a laboratory experiment. College women were tested in groups of four, either anonymous (wearing hoods) or identifiable (wearing name tags).

The alleged purpose of the study was to assess their empathetic tendencies. They were to listen to a brief taped interview with a woman who was portrayed as either nice and sweet or as just the opposite, obnoxious, conceited, etc. The deindividuated group was told that since facial cues could bias the other subjects, they would be asked to wear hoods. As soon as the tape was over, they all rated the woman on a number of traits.

In addition, the subjects had to administer electric shocks to the woman they had rated. The rationale for the shock was that the interviewed woman was also being paid to be in a conditioning experiment; it would be economical to employ these shock trials in the present study whose alleged purpose included comparing empathy as a function of active versus passive involvement with the target. To create active and passive involvement, two of the women were told to press a button on each trial, while the other two merely watched passively.

The subjects watched the victim being interviewed by the experimenter through a one-way mirror. When a shock was supposed to be given, the target who was an accomplice of the experimenter merely faked pain. Each of the two women who were told to press the button were informed that as long as one of them pressed, a shock would occur and that it would not be any stronger if they both pressed. Thus, even if one or both women failed to press on some trials, they always got the impression that the other one did since the target reacted as if in pain on every trial.

Although almost all of the women followed orders to give shock, as demonstrated in a somewhat similar study by Milgram (1963) to be described shortly, the women in the deindividuated group pressed almost twice as long. However, there was not as much pressure to obey as in Milgram's study, especially since each woman could have allowed the other one to do the job. Moreover, whereas women with name tags gave longer shocks to the obnoxious women, it did not seem to make any difference to the hooded subjects whether the target person was nice or obnoxious.

The significance of this involved deception study lies in the demonstration of the deindividuating effect of anonymity on behavior that produces a release from conventional restraints. Zimbardo feels that similar factors operate in producing real incidents of senseless destruction or aggression. One common category of such behaviors is vandalism or the wanton destruction of buildings, parks, and other property.

The women who served in Zimbardo's study were college students and not particularly likely to be future Eichmanns. Yet the situation seemed to be a potent factor in bringing about behavior that involved apparent pain for others. On the other hand, it is possible that these effects are exaggerated, because the subjects realized that it was an experiment and really did not believe the pain was as bad as it appeared, or they may have suspected that a deception was involved.

Although it seems plausible that anonymity per se fosters irrational and impulsive deindividuated behavior, it would seem that additional factors such as personality may affect these behaviors. Merely putting on a mask should not provoke everyone into antisocial behavior. One factor that may produce even greater disinhibiting effects than anonymity may be a feeling of helplessness or powerlessness. Individuals who have been treated by society in a dehumanizing manner may seize the cloak of anonymity to perpetrate destructive acts of retaliation with less fear of being apprehended or identified. Zimbardo did briefly discuss dehumanization, but emphasized it as a process by which those in power degrade others. The present analysis focuses on the reactions of the victims of that process of dehumanization and suggests that deindividuated behaviors are one of several possible responses, others including reactions such as apathy and withdrawal.

Situations in which humans are just numbers also might contribute to less than humane treatment. Feelings of helplessness are generated in people by highly efficient but impersonal computerization.

BLIND OBEDIENCE TO AUTHORITY

The weight of authority, with its attendant threat of punishment or criticism, also can induce persons to engage in cruel and dehumanizing actions toward victims. Children learn to respect the authority of parents, employees obey the orders of their employers, and soldiers follow the commands of their officers. Such obedience is often desirable for the mutual benefit of both parties in a relationship, but what are the limits of obedience to authority? We will often obey orders that we dislike either from fear of reprisal from those in power or because we believe in the value of obedience to authority. Nonetheless, at some point we may feel that an order is unjust or that we are being exploited or overworked and we may resist or even actively rebel.

The determination of this breaking point was one of the goals of a series of well-known and controversial studies by Stanley Milgram (Milgram, 1963, 1974) on obedience to authority in a laboratory setting. His studies demonstrated that apparently normal and moral college males would yield to the orders of the experimenter and create apparent suffering for another person.

Subjects in the experiment met another subject when they first arrived. It was explained that one subject would be the learner and the other would serve as the teacher in a memory task. A rigged drawing was held to determine the roles, so that the other subject, in reality a confederate of Milgram, would serve as the learner. The real subject was instructed that the study dealt with the effects of punishment on learning and that he was to administer ever-increasing levels of shock after each error made by the learner who was seated in an adjoining cubicle. Although the subjects were unable to see each other during the learning trials, it was possible to hear the fake screams and cries of pain from the confederate as he supposedly received his shocks for his learning errors. Anytime the real subject hesitated or questioned the experimenter about the propriety of continuing to give shocks, the experimenter urged him on. Eventually, the nonexistent shocks apparently received by the stooge reached a level at which no further sounds were heard from the stooge. Although some subjects were upset and wanted to stop, the

TABLE 9–3.   Distribution of Breakoff
Points.

Verbal Designation and Voltage Indication	Number of Subjects for Whom This Was Maximum Shock
Slight shock	
15	0
30	0
45	0
60	0
Moderate shock	
75	0
90	0
105	0
120	0
Strong shock	
135	0
150	0
165	0
180	0
Very strong shock	
195	0
210	0
225	0
240	0
Intense shock	
255	0
270	0
285	0
300	5
Extreme intensity shock	
315	4
330	2
345	1
360	1
Danger: severe shock	
375	1
390	0
405	0
420	0
XXX	
435	0
450	26

Source. From "Behavioral Study of Obedience"
by S. Milgram, *Journal of Abnormal and Social Psychology,* 1963, *67,* 371–378. Copyright 1963 by the
American Psychological Association. Reprinted
by permission.

experimenter ordered them to continue and over half of them (26 of 40) proceeded to complete the experiment until they administered the highest possible shock level, 450 volts. In fact, as shown in Table 9–3 the lowest maximal shock for any subject was labeled 300 volts and marked Intense Shock, whereas Milgram had not expected most subjects to go beyond shock levels labeled Very Strong Shock.

Milgram argued that the situational demands such as the orders of an authority rather than the immortality of the subjects led to the infliction of apparent pain to others. In his words (Milgram, 1965, p. 74), "With numbing regularity good people were seen to knuckle under the demands of authority and perform actions that were callous and severe."

Would the subjects in these experiments have followed orders to shock another person if they did not realize that it was an experiment? Orne and Holland (1968) argue that the demand characteristics of the situation led the subjects to trust the experimenter so that they probably did not really believe that real harm was being inflicted. Milgram, however, was able to replicate his study in an off-campus setting, where there was less likelihood that the prestige of a university setting might operate to allay subjects' doubts about the adverse consequences to the victim learners.

Parallels have been drawn between real life cases of inhumane actions involving blind obedience to authority such as the actions of Adolf Eichmann toward the Jews in concentration camps and Lt. Calley during the My Lai massacre in Vietnam. Although most of us are sure than none of us would have committed such atrocities, Milgram's findings suggest that placed in situations in which strong authority existed, we might obey orders that involve considerable suffering for others.

This evidence suggests that it is the situation, more than the individual, that leads to the failure to keep violence under control. Kelman (1973) and Opton (1971) suggest that aggression toward groups who are not themselves threats to the aggressor can occur among persons who are otherwise normal. However, their restraints against violence that ordinarily exist can be overruled by the force of authority as in the Milgram studies, by routinization in which certain automatic habits are performed, or by the process of dehumanization in which the victim is debased so that the aggressor can justify his or her actions.

THE STANFORD PRISON EXPERIMENT

What happens when a person is placed in a situation in which he or she has near total control or power over someone else? The relationship between a prison guard and the inmates comes close to being such a situation. A dramatic simulation of this relationship and its effect on the behavior of normal college men was made in the so-called Stanford Prison Experiment (Haney, Banks, and Zimbardo, 1973). Ads placed in newspapers solicited volunteers for a study of the psychological effects of prisons and offered pay of $15 per day. Twenty-four white male college students were selected after careful screening.

The experiment "began" abruptly one Sunday morning with the subjects who were to act as prisoners being arrested by real police officers. Without any forewarning, the officers arrested them early in the morning and took them to a makeshift prison in a squad car with its sirens on. The full procedure of fingerprinting, stripping, and delousing prisoners occurred.

Other volunteers were arbitrarily assigned the role of guard and given uniforms, billy clubs, whistles, and silver-reflecting sunglasses. Whereas the prisoners were locked up continuously in the basement of a university building, the guards worked in eight-hour shifts and, as in real life, were free to go home after the completion of their shifts.

Prisoners were awakened at 2:30 a.m. for a head count. Punishment in the form of pushups was meted out for rule infractions. By the second day, the prisoners held a rebellion, which so upset the guards that they reacted with brutality and harassment. Then the guards resorted to psychological tactics of control such as granting special privileges to the least rebellious prisoners.

The experiment proved to be so realistic that it was terminated after only six days, because some of the prisoners found the experience too harrowing and the guards were too zealous in playing their roles with hostility and brutality. Although this study was only an experimental demonstration, it did suggest that the situational characteristics of prisons are such that disturbing consequences occur for both prisoners and guards. When one group is totally helpless and at the mercy of another group, which is highly powerful, it is possible for apparently normal persons to undergo radical transformations in behavior.

The results imply that the role of guard, rather than the characteristics of the person who is the guard, is responsible for the brutal and abusive actions toward the prisoners. Although this role analysis has some merit, it should be kept in mind that in real prisons the guards are not randomly selected from the general population. It is possible that the kind of person who becomes a real prison guard is more likely than the average person to take advantage of the powerful role. This criticism does not deny the importance of situational determinants in behavior but warns against generalizing from the simulated prison to real prisons.

A different reservation concerns the extent to which the students were merely acting to fulfill their expectations. Their previously learned stereotypes of prison guards may have influenced their conduct in the experiment. Banuazizi and Movahedi (1975) used a questionnaire that enables respondents to role-play the Stanford Prison Experiment procedures. The results led them to conclude that demand characteristics such as cues provided by the experimental context and setting (the prison was located on campus in the basement of a psychology building) encouraged the subjects to act in ways to meet the expectations of the experimenters. Subjects, after all, knew that they were in an experiment. These critics question whether the results are valid inferences about the processes that occur in real prisoner-guard relationships. Their analysis also questions whether the simulated effects are valid in themselves as evidence of the role of situational factors in behavior.

Summary

The definition of aggression must take into account both the factors of intent and harm. Both aspects are necessary before an act can be considered aggressive. However, it is often difficult to infer intentions accurately and some forms of accidental harm are misclassified as aggressive behavior. Similarly, many intentions to do harm get inhibited or displaced, which also makes the accurate interpretation of aggressive behaviors difficult.

The mode of aggressive expression can take a variety of forms ranging from verbal to physical means, depending on situational factors. The same form of expression may not reflect the same underlying motives in different instances. These factors add to the difficulty of studying an already elusive concept.

Laboratory studies of aggression are often of limited validity in understanding natural aggression, especially because the subjects in many experiments are required by instructions to engage in some form of aggression, unlike the situation in the real world.

Ethological theories of aggression emphasize innate factors and regard aggression as necessary for biological survival. To be more precise, the threat of aggression is the key feature of aggression, because it usually suffices to ensure adequate warning is given to rivals of the same species so that territory can be established without a fight to the finish. Psychoanalytic views are similar and emphasize instinctive mechanisms for aggression. A cathartic model of aggression is used in which it is assumed that the buildup of energy for aggression must be released eventually or it may overflow; overt aggression serves to deplete the reservoir of energy temporarily.

Earlier learning theory regarded aggression as a learned response that served to reduce the frustrative drive energies created when the goals of the organism were blocked. This frustration-aggression hypothesis was soon revised in the light of shortcomings, as it was noted that frustration has other nonaggressive effects and that aggression may occur without any apparent antecedent frustration.

Learning theory denied the role of instinct and suggested that aggressive behavior can be acquired by a variety of means as can any other learned response according to the principles of reinforcement. Berkowitz' formulation stressed the role of classical conditioning and suggested that stimuli become associated with aggressive responses when they occur. On later occasions, the presence of these stimuli increase the chances that aggression will occur if other conditions such as anger also exist. Laboratory tests conducted by Berkowitz and his colleagues first involved the experimenter in arousing the subject's anger by insulting or belittling him. Next subjects watched either an aggressive or nonaggressive film and were then given an opportunity to evaluate a confederate's performance of some laboratory task by administering shock as feedback to the stooge. The results generally show that subjects who are both angered and have a chance to witness a filmed aggressive model tend to inflict higher levels of shock.

In contrast, the studies of Feshbach have usually supported the concept of catharsis, as subjects who witness modeled aggression tend to be less aggressive. Whether this cathartic effect is genuine or merely due to inhibition of aggression by the subjects is uncertain.

Additional evidence arguing for the view that observation of aggression increases such behavior comes from social learning studies such as those of Bandura with young children. Such findings have obvious implications for the mass media, because it is possible that the models of aggression shown on television and the movies may increase the aggression of children. Critics, however, contend that the laboratory studies are artificial and that the types of aggression observed there may not extend to real life behavior. Subjects in experiments may also behave in ways that they think are expected of them by the experimenter.

The observation of modeled aggression may not automatically lead to imitation, as some social learning theorists seem to imply, but can be watched without causing imitation because of numerous inhibitory factors such as the interpretation of the justifiability of the observed aggression, the consequences of aggression, and one's moral values.

Television, movies, and comic books have often been blamed for a number of undesirable behaviors in children, and although they probably do have some harmful effects, the case against them seems overstated. Conclusive evidence that these media are primary causes of learned aggression is not available.

Extended observation of aggression may diminish our sensitivity and concern about the suffering of victims of aggression. The evidence for this issue is also equivocal. Some studies suggest that aggressors ease up when it is obvious that their victims are in pain, but this observation may hold only if the aggressors are not angry.

Correlational studies as well as experiments dealing more directly with televised aggression and its effects do not provide conclusive evidence that viewed aggression causes similar behavior in observers. Differences among viewers in the original levels of aggression may lead to high correlations between aggressive viewing habits and aggressive behavior, so that the evidence would merely be a reflection rather than a cause of aggressive tendencies. One field study involving an experimental design suggested that viewing aggressive television fare actually had a cathartic effect and reduced aggression in adolescent males. Another large scale naturalistic experiment was unable to show any modeling influence of the observation of a highly specific single episode of antisocial aggression.

Some of the conflicting evidence might be resolved if greater attention was directed toward investigating the role of individual differences in personality or sex in the effects of observed aggression.

Most analyses view aggression as the reflection of tendencies on the part of the individual. Situational factors, however, can also affect the expression of aggression. At times, situational factors inhibit aggression, while at other times it serves to generate or release it. Studies of the deindividuation process, obedience to authority, and situations in which one group has total power over another are examples in which aggression is strongly affected by situational factors.

References

Bandura, A. *Aggression: A social learning analysis.* Englewood Cliffs, N.J.: Prentice-Hall, 1973.

―――. Influence of models' reinforcement contingencies on the acquisition of imitative responses. *Journal of Personality and Social Psychology,* 1965, *1,* 589–595.

―――, Ross, D., and Ross, S. A. Transmission of aggression through imitation of aggressive models. *Journal of Abnormal and Social Psychology,* 1961, *63,* 575–582.

―――, Ross, D., and Ross, S. A. Imitation of film-mediated aggressive models. *Journal of Abnormal and Social Psychology,* 1963, *66,* 3–11.

―――, and Walters, R. H. *Social learning and personality development.* New York: Holt, 1963.

Banuazizi, A., and Movahedi, S. Interpersonal dynamics in a simulated prison: A methodological analysis. *American Psychologist,* 1975, *30,* 152–160.

Baron, R. A. Aggression as a function of magnitude of victim's pain cues, level of prior anger arousal, and aggressor-victim similarity. *Journal of Personality and Social Psychology,* 1971, *18,* 48–54.

―――. Aggression as a function of victim's pain cues, level of prior anger arousal, and exposure to an aggressive model. *Journal of Personality and Social Psychology,* 1974, *29,* 117–124.

Berkowitz, L. *Aggression: A social psychological analysis.* New York: McGraw-Hill, 1962.

―――. Some aspects of observed aggression. *Journal of Personality of Social Psychology,* 1965, *2,* 359–369. (a)

―――. The concept of aggressive drive: Some additional considerations. In L. Berkowitz (Ed.), *Advances in experimental social psychology.* (Vol. 2). New York: Academic, 1965. (b)

―――. The contagion of violence: An S-R mediational analysis of some effects of observed aggression. In W. J. Arnold and M. M. Page (Eds.), *Nebraska Symposium on Motivation.* (Vol. 18). Lincoln: University of Nebraska Press, 1970.

―――. The "weapons effect," deviant characteristics, and the myth of the compliant subject. *Journal of Personality and Social Psychology,* 1971, *20,* 332–338.

―――, and LePage, A. Weapons as aggression-eliciting stimuli. *Journal of Personality and Social Psychology,* 1967, *7,* 202–207.

————, and RAWLINGS, E. Effects of film violence: An inhibition against subsequent aggression. *Journal of Abnormal and Social Psychology*, 1963, *66*, 405–412.

BUSS, A. H. *The psychology of aggression.* New York: Wiley, 1961.

————, BOOKER, A., and BUSS, E. Firing a weapon and aggression. *Journal of Personality and Social Psychology*, 1972, *22*, 296–302.

COMSTOCK, G. A., and RUBENSTEIN, E. A. (Eds.), *Television and social behavior.* (Vol. 3). *Television and adolescent aggressiveness.* Washington, D.C.: Government Printing Office, 1972.

DOLLARD, J., DOOB, L. W., MILLER, N. E., MOWRER, O. H., and SEARS, R. R. *Frustration and aggression.* New Haven: Yale University Press, 1939.

DOOB, A. N., and WOOD, L. Catharsis and aggression: The effects of annoyance and retaliation on aggressive behavior. *Journal of Personality and Social Psychology*, 1972, *22*, 156–162.

ERON, L. D. Relationship of TV viewing habits and aggressive behavior in children. *Journal of Abnormal and Social Psychology*, 1963, *67*, 193–196.

ERON, L. D., LEFKOWITZ, M. M., HUESMANN, L. R., and WALDER, L. O. Does television violence cause aggression? *American Psychologist*, 1972, *27*, 253–263.

FESHBACH, S. The stimulating versus cathartic effects of a vicarious aggressive activity. *Journal of Abnormal and Social Psychology*, 1961, *63*, 381–385.

————. Aggression. In P. H. Mussen (Ed.), *Carmichael's manual of child psychology*, (Vol. 2). New York: Wiley, 1970.

————. Reality and fantasy in filmed violence. In J. P. Murray, E. A. Rubenstein, and G. A. Comstock (Eds.), *Television and social behavior.* (Vol. 2). *Television and social learning.* Washington, D.C.: Government Printing Office, 1972.

————, and SINGER, R. D. *Television and aggression: An experimental field study.* San Francisco: Jossey-Bass, 1971.

————, STILES, W. B., and BITTER, E. The reinforcing effect of witnessing aggression. *Journal of Experimental Research in Personality*, 1967, *2*, 133–139.

GEEN, R. G. Perceived suffering of the victim as an inhibitor of attack-induced aggression. *Journal of Social Psychology*, 1970, *81*, 209–215.

GORANSON, R. E. Media violence and aggressive behavior: A review of experimental research. In L. Berkowitz (Ed.), *Advances in experimental social psychology.* (Vol. 5). New York: Academic, 1970.

GREENWELL, J., and DENGERINK, H. A. The role of perceived versus actual attack in human physical aggression. *Journal of Personality and Social Psychology*, 1973, *26*, 66–71.

GRUSEC, J. E. Effects of co-observer evaluations on imitation: A developmental study. *Developmental Psychology*, 1973, *8*, 141.

HANEY, C., BANKS, C., and ZIMBARDO, P. G. Interpersonal dynamics in a simulated prison. *International Journal of Crime and Penology*, 1973, *1*, 69–97.

HARTMANN, D. P. Influence of symbolically modeled instrumental aggression and pain cues on aggressive behavior. *Journal of Personality and Social Psychology*, 1969, *11*, 280–288.

HICKS, D. J. Effects of co-observer's sanctions and adult presence on imitative aggression. *Child Development*, 1968, *39*, 303–309. (a)

————. Short and long-term retention of affectively varied modeled behavior. *Psychonomic Science*, 1968, *11*, 369–370. (b)

HIMMELWEIT, H. T., OPPENHEIM, A. N., and VINCE, P. *Television and the child.* London: Oxford University Press, 1958.

HOVLAND, C. I., and SEARS, R. R. Minor studies of aggression: Correlation of lynchings with economic indices. *Journal of Psychology*, 1940, *9*, 301–310.

KELMAN, H. C. Violence without moral restraint. *Journal of Social Issues*, 1973, *29*, 25–61.

SOCIAL MOTIVATION: TOOTH AND NAIL **259**

LIEBERT, R. M., and BARON, R. A. Some immediate effects of televised violence on children's behavior. *Developmental Psychology,* 1972, *6,* 469–475.

LORENZ, K. *On aggression.* New York: Harcourt, 1966.

MCINTYRE, J., and TEEVAN, J. Television violence and deviant behavior. In G. A. Comstock and E. A. Rubenstein (Eds.), *Television and social behavior.* (Vol. 3). *Television and adolescent aggressiveness.* Washington, D.C.: Government Printing Office, 1972.

MILGRAM, S. Behavioral study of obedience. *Journal of Abnormal and Social Psychology,* 1963, *67,* 371–378.

————. Some conditions of obedience and disobedience to authority. *Human Relations,* 1965, *18,* 57–76.

————. *Obedience to authority: An experimental view.* New York: Harper, 1974.

————, and SHOTLAND, R. L. *Television and antisocial behavior: Field experiments.* New York: Academic, 1973.

MILLER, N. E. The frustration-aggression hypothesis. *Journal of Experimental Psychology,* 1941, *48,* 337–342.

NICKEL, T. W. The attribution of intention as a critical factor in the relation between frustration and aggression. *Journal of Personality,* 1974, *42,* 482–492.

OPTON, E. M., JR. It never happened and besides they deserved it. In N. Sanford and C. Comstock (Eds.), *Sanctions for evil: Sources of social destructiveness.* San Francisco: Jossey-Bass, 1971.

ORNE, M. T. On the social psychology of the psychological experiment: With particular emphasis to demand characteristics and their implications. *American Psychologist,* 1962, *17,* 776–783.

————, and HOLLAND, C. H. On the ecological validity of laboratory deceptions. *International Journal of Psychiatry,* 1968, *6,* 282–293.

PAGE, M. P., and SCHIEDT, R. J. The elusive weapons effect: Demand awareness, evaluation apprehension, and slightly sophisticated subjects. *Journal of Personality and Social Psychology,* 1971, *20,* 304–318.

ROBINSON, J. P., and BACHMAN, J. G. Television viewing habits and aggression. In G. A. Comstock and E. A. Rubenstein (Eds.), *Television and social behavior.* (Vol. 3). *Television and adolescent aggressiveness.* Washington, D.C.: Government Printing Office, 1972.

SEARS, R. R. Non-aggressive reactions to frustration. *Psychological Review,* 1941, *48,* 343–346.

SINGER, J. L. The influence of violence portrayed in television or motion pictures upon overt aggressive behavior. In J. L. Singer (Ed.), *The control of aggression and violence.* New York: Academic, 1971.

SNOW, R. P. How children interpret TV violence in play context. *Journalism Quarterly,* 1974, *51,* 13–21.

STEIN, A. H., FRIEDRICH, L. K., and VONDRACEK, F. Television content and young children's behavior. In J. P. Murray, E. A. Rubenstein, and G. A. Comstock (Eds.), *Television and social behavior.* (Vol. 2). *Television and social learning.* Washington, D.C.: Government Printing Office, 1972.

TEDESCHI, J. T., SMITH, K. B. III, and BROWN, R. C., JR. A reinterpretation of research on aggression. *Psychological Bulletin,* 1974, *81,* 540–562.

TOCH, H. *Violent men.* Chicago: Aldine, 1969.

ULRICH, R. E., and AZRIN, N. Reflexive fighting in response to aversive stimulation. *Journal of the Experimental Analysis of Behavior,* 1962, *5,* 511–520.

ZIMBARDO, P. G. The human choice: Individuation, reason, and order versus deindividuation, impulse, and chaos. In W. J. Arnold and D. Levine (Eds.), *Nebraska Symposium on Motivation.* (Vol. 17). Lincoln: University of Nebraska Press, 1969.

PART FOUR

SOME AFFECTIVE FACTORS

CHAPTER 10

Variety Is the Spice of Life

Boredom and monotony are feelings all of us have encountered and have tried to avoid and escape. At the other extreme, we show curiosity and interest in situations that we would like to maintain. But the same situation that is of interest to us at one moment may soon become one that is boring. We then seek a change.

When we face uncertainty, we often experience tension or anxiety and attempt to resolve the doubts or escape the situation. But at other times we deliberately seek uncertainty and risk, because we enjoy the excitement. Gambling, in particular, and risk taking, in general, are examples of situations that are appealing precisely because outcomes are not certain or determined in advance.

On some occasions we enjoy the novel, the complex, or anything that is different from that which we expect. At other times, we take comfort or refuge in the familiar, simple, or predictable situation. Variety seems to be our goal, in the long run.

Consider some everyday examples. When people are bored, they may attend an exciting and thrilling movie or take an exhilarating roller coaster ride, whereas people under continual stress and tension may prefer to take calm walks along the beach, to relax or meditate, or listen to soothing music.

Young children are noted for their curiosity and interest in exploring and manipulating novel objects and toys. But as they master and control these objects with repeated exposure, children often seek other objects to sustain their interest. At other times, children seem to retreat from new stimulation as if too much excitement were unpleasant. On these occasions the child often seeks the comfort of familiar objects and environments such as a security blanket or teddy bear.

How do we explain this apparent need for stimulus variation, sometimes for more and sometimes for less intense, novel, complex, or predictable stimuli? What roles do affective states play in determining how behaviors vary as a function of stimulus conditions? And, how do affective states themselves differ as a consequence of various stimulus conditions? These basic questions will be the major focus of this chapter. In order to answer them, it may be useful first to examine some neuropsychological concepts.

The Concept of Arousal

What usually happens when a novel stimulus is encountered? If a tone, for example, is presented to an organism, an orienting reflex (Sokolov, 1960) or reaction will occur and attention will be focused on the novel stimulus. At the subjective level, we may speak of the "raw feeling" or sensation that we experience as arousing or alerting. Neuropsychological theories of arousal (Hebb, 1955; Malmo, 1959; Lindsley, 1951) have been developed to account for the nonspecific or generalized activation of the total organism by incoming stimuli. Without describing any details of these mechanisms, suffice it to say that all stimuli, in addition to affecting a specific modality such as audition or vision, contribute to increased general alertness or arousal via an area of the brain stem known as the *reticular formation*. The passage of all nervous impulses to and from higher cortical areas of the brain through this area is assumed to affect the overall activation of the organism.

If we assume the stimulus is neutral and not associated with any other consequences, we will note that interest in the novel stimulus will wane or habituate gradually. As our exposure to it increases, we eventually no longer notice it. Physiological reactions such as changes in heart rate, blood pressure, or galvanic skin response, which we felt when the stimulus was first introduced, gradually return to normal levels.

If we were to be presented with the same stimulus in the near future, we would show less awareness or arousal, because that stimulus would no longer be novel. Furthermore, if we were confronted with a situation in which the same stimulus was presented over a long period we would experience boredom, daydream, and even possibly fall asleep or at least become drowsy. For example, if we were to hear someone repeatedly pronounce a given word, say *psychology,* the meaning of the word would be altered or weakened by a process called semantic satiation (Amster, 1964). Or if we were to gaze at a visual object such as a light or a picture for a prolonged period, we would also experience changes in what we saw and felt. At the physiological level, we would assume that similar changes in responsiveness were occurring and that arousal was diminishing with gradual satiation to a stimulus.

SENSORY DEPRIVATION AND AROUSAL

An even more extreme situation that involves invariant stimulus conditions is the sensory deprivation or restriction paradigm, which has been studied extensively (e.g., Bexton, Heron, and Scott, 1954; Schultz, 1965; Zubek,

1969). When the individual receives an impoverished and constant sensory environment for several days, unpleasant affect and discomfort is generally reported. In addition, hallucinations, cognitive distortions, and impairments of performance of perceptual motor tasks are found.

In the study by Bexton et al., volunteers were recruited to "sit around and do nothing" for $20.00 a day. They were confined in a small chamber containing a bed on which they could rest. They had to wear translucent goggles and what amounted to, in effect, a spacesuit. In short order, many of the subjects were bored by the monotonous environment and lack of sensory or cognitive stimulation.

It should be noted that not all studies have found such severe impairment. Using airmen at a training station, Zubek (1969), for example, has even found an absence of the intellectual deficits obtained by Bexton et al. with college students, although he confirmed the affective disruption. It is conceivable that effects may differ in individuals. Moreover, the instructions to subjects may influence their perceptions of the experiment and their reactions to it.

Orne and Scheibe (1964) studied the influence of having a "panic button" in the confinement cubicle, because it was considered likely that subjects in sensory isolation experiments might expect dire effects because of their knowledge of the effects of real prison camps, solitary confinement, and dungeons. By telling subjects that if they wished to terminate their participation in the study because of undue stress, they could press the "panic button," it is possible that the power of suggestion or demand characteristics of the task might contribute substantially to the observed effect.

Orne and Scheibe (1964) conducted a sensory deprivation experiment with two groups, one of which was given an extensive medical check-up in the presence of impressive-looking first aid equipment and medicines prior to serving in the experiment. They also signed a release form relieving the investigators of any responsibility for possible ill effects. The other group served as a control group and, in fact, was told precisely that.

Actually both groups received identical confinement for four hours. Sensory input was not reduced as substantially as in most sensory deprivation studies; in fact, the subjects were placed in a small room where they could hear outside sounds so that the procedure was more one of social rather than sensory isolation. As predicted, more negative affect and cognitive impairment occurred for the group led to expect something bad to happen.

It is not suggested that all the results of sensory deprivation studies showing adverse effects are attributable to demand characteristics, but this factor does appear to play some role. Suedfeld (1969) allowed that such factors may occur but argued that they may not always lead to *adverse* effects because some subjects may not know what is "supposed to happen." On the other hand, experiments might underestimate the negative effects of sensory deprivation, because it is difficult to convince a volunteer for such an experiment that the danger in a sensory deprivation study is as real as that of, say, solitary confinement in a prison. The two tendencies may be somewhat off-setting factors.

CURIOSITY AND AROUSAL

Fortunately, we are ordinarily not compelled to suffer such severe conditions of monotony for periods as long as those employed in these studies (even the worst college lecture is over within one hour). If the book, movie, or person we are with is too boring, we can usually find some means of choosing an alternative that promises more interest. We are free to modify our environment until some more agreeable affect is achieved. Our curiosity leads us to seek more interesting or exciting situations.

The phenomena of curiosity, exploration, and spontaneous activity have been observed to serve as their own rewards. This is not to say that they might not also lead to other consequences. In fact, it could be argued that if exploration of new objects and environments have led to positive reinforcements in the past, the organism may have a generalized habit of exploring whenever novel circumstances are present. However, it is likely that the organism has also encountered aversive conditions while exploring novel conditions. This combination of positive and negative past experiences might explain why organisms are ambivalent about novel situations, attracted by curiosity yet repulsed by fear.

The importance of behaviors such as these can hardly be overstated. Unless the individual is severely deprived of biological needs, goals such as curiosity and exploratory behavior are exceedingly important to most individuals. As Charles Dickens observed in *Barnaby Rudge,* "Curiosity is, and has been from the creation of the world, a master-passion. To awaken it, to gratify it by slight degrees, and yet leave something always in suspense, is to establish the surest hold that can be had, in wrong, on the unthinking portion of mankind." Although Dickens was emphasizing the negative aspects of curiosity and intrigue in the unknown and mysterious that enable some to exploit others for their own benefit, it should be noted that many of the greatest achievements of humankind are also due to this same propensity to seek the new, the different, and the unexpected.

The suggestion that curiosity may be part of intrinsic motivation certainly makes sense to anyone who has observed young infants and toddlers closely for even a brief period. With no apparent ulterior motives or other reinforcement, young children entertain themselves (and their observers) for long periods by manipulating, exploring, and investigating the properties of new objects, environments, etc.

The process of such interaction with the environment involves the informational exchange or comparison of the present stimulation with past experiences. These comparisons may occur in a number of dimensions, referred to by Berlyne (1967) as *collative,* such as intensity, complexity, novelty, or uncertainty. This process of collation or comparison leads to the identification of similarities and differences, such as in the discovery of conceptual distinctions, and could be regarded as an essential aspect of cognitive growth.

Implications of the Effects of Sensory Variation

What are the implications of these and related phenomena? As noted in Chapter 2, in the 1950s it was commonly assumed that activity, curiosity, and exploratory behaviors were based on drives similar to those based on tissue deficits such as hunger or thirst. The recognition of these behaviors was impeded by the tendency to study need-deprived organisms that were less prone to engage in them. Because there did not appear to be any biological deprivation involved in activity, arousal, or exploratory behavior, reinforcement theories based on drive-reduction principles were especially challenged by these phenomena in which, if anything, organisms appeared to be seeking *increased* stimulation.

One approach to the interpretation of these behaviors was to regard them as responses that had been reinforced by primary reinforcers in the past; for example, exploration may have led to food, so that it became a generalized habit. However, although this can occur, it appears that infants and animals display curiosity reactions very early in life with no apparent opportunity for such learning to precede them. Another explanation (Bronson, 1968) is to assume that some basic process such as fear of novelty is the basis for the increased activity and exploration usually observed in animals placed in new environments. This fear would be unlearned, but dependent on some previous experiences against which new stimuli would be judged to be novel. It is not specific to a particular stimulus, but rather to all novel situations. There is biological survival value in this type of cautious curiosity on the part of organisms to new situations until more information about them can be obtained.

White (1959) in discussing the concept of *competence,* which was introduced in earlier chapters, also emphasizes the functional significance of curiosity, exploratory, and other spontaneous activities that serve no immediately obvious goals. According to his view, the organism is mastering the environment and acquiring competence, in the broad sense of the word, in coping with it.

Similarly, Piaget's (1952) analysis of the repetitive nature of children's play suggests that behaviors that appear to have no direct or immediate goals may be important for cognitive growth and mastery. At the subjective level, the gains in mastery achieved with succeeding repetitions of a complex task may be assumed to be a source of pleasure. Although Freud's emphasis on the ritualistic and compulsive nature of repetition is different, it does share with Piaget the belief that the consequences of repetition are pleasurable.

A view similar to that of White and proposed by Hunt (1965) holds that behaviors such as curiosity may have intrinsic motives. They serve to facilitate interaction between the organism and environmental stimuli, so that comparisons can be made between past experiences and incoming stimuli. The searches for novel stimuli on one occasion and for familiar ones on another occur because the organism needs variety of stimulation to prevent boredom on some occasions and overstimulation on others. The term *intrinsic motive* may be redundant, but the implication is that living organisms, by their very nature, engage in certain activities without need of any extrinsic rewards or punishments. It is not necessary to postulate separate drives for each type of behavior that serves this general purpose of achieving variation such as exploration or curiosity.

As Fiske and Maddi (1961, p. 55) concluded, "There is a biological utility in perceiving and reacting to such new stimulation. Yet even when new stimulation imposes no demands upon the organism, it utilizes such stimulation to sustain its internal processes and its activity. For this purpose it is the stimulation, as stimulation, which is important, whatever its specific quality or significance. But in addition to the utilization of new stimulation for its internal economy, a higher organism and especially a human being may seek to experience varying stimulation almost as an end in itself."

Incongruity and Arousal

Incongruity or discrepancy between past experiences and current stimulation is a key factor in several formulations dealing with arousal. In dealing with incongruity, we have a situation that is not directly based on learning, but does indirectly involve past associations and expectancies, which are compared with a given situation. Hunt assumed that if past expectancies formed through past learning are disconfirmed or unfulfilled, the incongruity between expectancies and current stimuli will produce an affective response such as arousal.

Whenever we speak of being surprised, pleasantly or unpleasantly, we are referring to an affective response to an outcome that violates our expectancy. In an old study by Tinklepaugh (1928), monkeys were taught a discrimination task in which food was placed under a lid on either the left or right side of the test situation. They got to see where the food was placed but were restrained for a few seconds before being allowed to approach the food containers. In some trials, Tinklepaugh deftly replaced the food that the animals had seen placed in the container with a different food. When the animals lifted the top, their reactions were quite emotional, as if expectations had been violated, and they refused to eat the substituted food, which pretests had shown was palatable.

Attention to incongruous stimuli has been measured and found to exceed the visual inspection time allotted to congruous stimuli. Berlyne (1958) showed human subjects a set of pictures of animals such as elephants or birds with either normal or distorted or illogical features such as an elongated elephant or a bird with elephant-like legs. Results showed more attention was directed to the more incongruous figures.

If we were to analyze works of art, we would find that we have learned to expect certain rules or norms in each art form. Thus, as Berlyne (1971) points out, most symphonies contain a "fast first movement, a slow second movement, a minuet or scherzo, and a final fast movement." Likewise poetry, novels, painting, and other forms of art follow certain conventions and patterns, although there are variations for different time periods. Most of the time these norms are followed; if an artist were to violate these expectations, we would experience some arousal. In fact, if the break with tradition is too great, reaction is usually negative. As time passes and the new movement is given more exposure, it may grow on us and we begin to like it. The history of art has many examples that support this analysis.

Perhaps nowhere in everyday life is the role of incongruity and the unexpected so pervasive as in the area of humor. Although there are other elements of humor such as aggressiveness and superiority, such as that present in ethnic jokes, moron jokes, mother-in-law, wife, or women jokes, most of these examples also include an element of surprise in the punch lines. Puns, riddles, and other intellectual forms of humor also rely heavily on incongruity and surprise.

The important role of incongruity in capturing and holding interest and attention is well recognized, at least intuitively, by successful writers, painters, and musicians. Take for example, the classic short story by O. Henry, "The Gift of the Magi," about a couple without any money but each anxious to buy a Christmas present for the other. The husband has one prized possession, a valuable watch, but he has no chain for it. His wife has no material possessions of value, but does have beautiful long hair, which is her pride and joy. In order to give gifts to each other, they both sacrifice the one thing of value which each of them has; the husband pawns his watch and the wife cuts her hair and sells it.

The unexpected twist at the end of the story is in the gift each bought for the other. Ironically, the wife bought a chain for the husband's watch, whereas he bought an expensive comb for her hair. Perhaps the story is too contrived, but it is a touching tale that has been very popular.

Or consider a short story entitled "Next Door," by Kurt Vonnegut, Jr., in which a young boy is home alone one evening when he hears a violent argument next door between a man and a woman despite the fact that they have their radio on full blast. While listening to the neighbor's radio, which is tuned to a program on which the disc jockey plays telephone requests, he gets an inspiration that he thinks will pacify the quarrelers. He decides to call in and request a romantic song for Mrs. X from Mr. X, telling the disc jockey to preface it with, "I love you! Let's make up and start all over again!" Shortly afterward, the disc jockey fulfills his request; as soon as he makes the announcement, the argument next door abruptly stops. The boy is relieved and feels pleased with his ingenuity in resolving the domestic squabble next door.

A cute story thus far, but that is not how it ends. Instead, there is suddenly a sound of gunshots. The frightened boy rushes out of his apartment and bumps into a blonde woman who is hastily making her exit from the next door apartment. A few minutes later a taxi rushes up, a different woman jumps out and rushes up to see Mr. X, exclaiming that she heard his song request and dedication and that she is ready to come home and make up.

Although these events are implausible as facts, the story is delightful as fiction because of the incongruous and surprising conclusion. We think the story is over at one point and achieve closure, and then we are hit with a totally different ending. Uncertainty, surprise, and incongruity are all factors that enhance the tension, interest, and suspense found in works of the best writers.

Is There an Optimal Level of Stimulation?

OPTIMAL LEVEL OF INCONGRUITY

Not only is incongruity assumed to play a major role in determining arousal, but Hunt (1965) also postulated that there is an optimal level of incongruity. The preferred stimuli in a given situation would depend on the extent to which they differed from or were incongruous with the stimulus expected on the basis of past experience. Apparently there must be some incongruity but not too much or too little.

Another way of looking at this view is to suggest that the attempt of the organism to raise or lower its level of arousal will depend on the extent to which the present stimulation and the expected stimulation is discrepant. When the incongruity equals the postulated optimal level, an equilibrium may be assumed and no further change in activity will occur. On the other hand, if the incongruity is either insufficient or too great, the arousal will also be less than or more than, respectively, the assumed optimal level, and the organism will engage in behaviors aimed at changing the situation in order to achieve stimulation that is optimally incongruous with expectations.

Consistent with this view are a number of studies showing a curvilinear or inverted U-shaped relationship between affect and incongruity. Figure 10–1 provides a hypothetical example of this function, showing how arousal first increases, reaches a peak, and then drops with increasing levels of stimulus incongruity. In a later section of this chapter similar results will be reported showing the relationship between affect and stimulus complexity, which could be viewed as a specific instance of incongruity. Material that is either

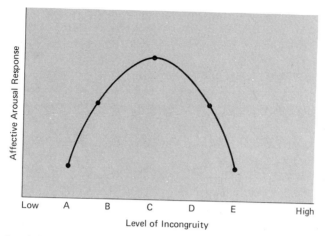

FIGURE 10-1. A hypothetical inverted U-shaped functional relationship between affective response and degree of incongruity between stimulation received and the level expected on the basis of past experience.

more or less complex than what you expected on an exam, for example, would represent incongruity.

There also appears to be an optimal level of incongruity associated with the capacity of humorous materials to elicit positive affect. We consider jokes that have either too much or too little incongruity to be poor jokes, as a rule. We say, "We don't get it," and fail to smile or laugh. Consider the story about the man whose three sons went out West to earn a living raising cattle. They had a difficult time agreeing on a name for their ranch, but finally selected the name "Focus." When the puzzled father wrote to ask why they selected that unusual name, they replied, "because that's where the sons raise meat!" This joke or triple pun comes across better when it is told than when it is read. Most people do not get the point because it is too cute, too clever, and too contrived.

In contrast, consider the joke told about the three little boys, ages six, seven, and eight, who were playing near a neighbor's house. The six year old happened to glance in the window. He quickly called his playmates over, "Come see the big fight between a man and a woman." The seven-year old looked and laughed at the six year old, "Silly, they're not fighting, they're making love." Upon which the eight year old, being wisest of all, noted, "Yeah, and badly."

Another theorist who has dealt extensively with the relationship between incongruity and arousal is Berlyne (1960, 1967, 1971). In his earlier works (Berlyne, 1950, 1955), he adhered to a drive reduction approach in which the goal of behavior was seen as reducing arousal. His views evolved during the 1960s as increasing evidence indicated that behavior often seems directed toward the increase of arousal. Berlyne (1960) referred to the interaction between the organism and the environmental input as *collation,* a term referring to the comparison of incoming stimuli with past experiences. Those stimuli that were novel, complex, or incongruous relative to past experiences were regarded as capable of increasing arousal.

Whether or not an organism seeks out or avoids stimuli with collative properties such as novelty or incongruity is not unrelated to the state of the organism but rather depends on its level of arousal at that time. Berlyne's theory also assumes there is an optimal level of arousal so that if one is already above that level, attempts will be made to reduce arousal or avoid stimuli that increase arousal, and vice versa, if one's arousal is below that level. His approach is highly similar to that proposed by Hunt (1965) in emphasizing the information processing of environmental input by the organism as a type of intrinsic motivation. Berlyne's formulation is broader, however, in that he does not limit the occurrence of arousal to the presence of incongruity in stimuli.

OPTIMAL LEVEL OF AROUSAL

An influential view of arousal proposed even earlier by Hebb (1955) stressed the role of an optimal arousal level rather than an optimal level of incongruity. However, as with the optimal incongruity view, Hebb argued that organisms will strive to achieve optimal levels of arousal at which behavior or performance will be most efficient. If arousal is too low, the person may be sluggish or apathetic, but if it is too high, such as in an emergency, panic and incoherent behavior will result. The predicted relationship is identical to that shown in Figure 10–1 and by changing the label on the abscissa or horizontal axis to "Level of Stimulation" we can use this diagram to illustrate Hebb's position (see also Figure 11–1).

A reconciliation of the optimal arousal (Fiske and Maddi, 1961; Hebb, 1955) and the optimal incongruity (Berlyne, 1960, 1967; Hunt, 1965) might subsume the latter as a special case of the former. That is, arousal can be created by a number of factors, with incongruity being only one type. Arousal can exist without any discrepancy or incongruity, but the opposite situation is not possible.

Because Hunt's (1965) usage of *incongruity* is quite broad and includes virtually all differences between past and present stimulation, the difference between the optimal incongruity and optimal arousal views may be more apparent than real. There does not appear to be any clearcut evidence that one view is more valid than the other.

Another proposal by Deci (1975) suggests that arousal refers to the physiological level, whereas incongruity reflects the psychological experience. Deci also attempted to relate arousal and incongruity theories of motivation with competence (White, 1959) or personal causation (DeCharms, 1968) theories, which maintain that organisms strive to achieve mastery or control over their environments. Deci suggested that the way in which one can experience a feeling of self-control is by seeking moderate levels of arousal. If an individual is not challenged by a situation, he or she gets no feeling of accomplishment; on the other hand, if an individual is overwhelmed by a task, he or she will probably be frustrated.

Limitations of Optimal Level Concepts

AD HOC NATURE

Returning to the concept of an optimal level of either arousal or incongruity, we should note that although a number of phenomena appear to be handled by these formulations, one limitation of an optimal level hypothesis is that it is often invoked after the fact to explain results. There is no independent means of defining the optimal level. If there is no inverted U-shaped function obtained between behavior and arousal, then it is tempting to suggest that the test conditions did not include a sufficiently low or high level of arousal. Suppose we selected three levels of punishment to use in teaching a skill to a group of children. Referring back to Figure 10–1, and relabeling the stimulus dimension "Level of Punishment" and the response dimension "Learning Performance," suppose we happened to use values corresponding to A, C, and E. Our results would confirm our hypothesis of an inverted U function and support the optimal arousal theory.

If, however, we sampled values A, B, and C we would find that the higher the punishment, the better the performance on the learning task. Now if we already knew that the effect was curvilinear, we could argue that if we had sampled higher levels of punishment an eventual decline in the response curve would occur. However, if we are trying to test a hypothesis, we cannot assume it is right and explain away any discrepant results. Similarly, if we happened to choose punishment levels C, D, and E our findings would reveal an inverse effect, with lower punishment leading to the best learning. If we were wedded to our optimal level of arousal view, we could argue after the fact that had we included some lower values of punishment, our overall curve would show an inverted U shape. In order to test the optimal arousal theory we need to find some method of predicting in advance the range of stimuli that will yield the optimal arousal, so that failures to confirm the view cannot be attributed to the choice of an inadequate range of stimuli.

ORGANISMIC VARIABLES AND AROUSAL

Even if we developed theoretical predictions about the particular stimulus values that would be optimally arousing, it would be difficult to test them. At least three sets of factors combine with present stimulation to affect arousal level. First, biological differences may exist in the extent to which individuals need stimulation. Next, differences in past experience in situations similar to the one under study can affect the arousal created by a given stimulus. Third, the present internal state of the individual such as the level of hunger, wakefulness, or fatigue, will affect his or her reaction to a given stimulus. Zuckerman (1969) felt that other factors such as age, task demands, and diurnal cycles were also factors in producing individual differences in optimal level of stimulation.

Let us consider the role of biological differences in more detail. Pavlov (1927) first suggested that there might be constitutional differences in the strength of the nervous systems of organisms. His observations of his dogs showed that differences in excitability existed when he attempted to produce conditioned responses in them. Following Pavlov's theory about cortical excitatory and inhibitory mechanisms and the balance between the two opposed states, Eysenck (1955) proposed that extraverts have greater need for excitation, whereas introverts function better under lower stimulation. He also presumed that these differences reflected constitutional differences. Petrie (1967), whose work will be discussed in Chapter 13 in relationship to pain tolerance, also held that individual differences exist in the way a given level of stimulation affects organisms.

More recently, Sales (1971) has expanded on Petrie's work using kinaesthetic judgments as the criterion for classifying augmenters and reducers. Augmenters tend to overestimate stimulus magnitudes so that they need less stimulation to produce a given effect, whereas the opposite is true for reducers. Sales reasoned that the augmenters have "weak" nervous systems, whereas reducers have "strong" nervous systems. His comparisons showed that reducers preferred more complex stimuli, attended more closely to verbal communications, showed more activity when isolated, and talked more in group discussions.

A later study (Sales, Guydosh, and Iacono, 1974) followed the same issues but used an auditory threshold test to classify their augmenters and reducers. Subjects were tested for twenty minutes in a situation in which they could press buttons for simple or complex auditory and visual stimuli. Reducers, subjects who had a high threshold on the auditory test, appeared to need more stimulation as they were more readily bored than the augmenters by simple stimuli.

The possibility that individual differences in need for stimulation exist and that such differences are biologically determined is intriguing. It not only complicates the empirical specification of the optimal level of arousal for a given stimulus situation, but it also could account for the similarity of the individual differences found for many phenomena such as smoking, drinking, or using psychoactive drugs. The proposal of genetic factors for such differences does not deny the operation of learning differences that might enhance them.

Past learning experiences can affect the optimal level of arousal. As Zuckerman (1969) suggested, repeated exposure to a given stimulus can produce adaptation, thus shifting the value of the optimal level upward or downward, depending on whether past experience involved gradual increases or decreases, respectively, in stimulation. Another factor that may complicate matters is that the optimal levels of arousal vary with the state of the organism. One arousal view (Fiske and Maddi, 1961) that directs attention to these organismic factors suggests that no specific level is optimal. Thus, a given situation such as constant stimulation from the environment might be sleep-inducing in a person who was physically fatigued, but might prompt a search for varied stimulation in someone who was just awakened.

LOW INTERCORRELATIONS OF PSYCHOPHYSIOLOGICAL INDICES

In addition, the measurement of arousal is difficult insofar as the commonly used psychophysiological indexes are not highly intercorrelated, so that results from a study using one index of arousal may not be compared legitimately with a study using a different one. Lacey and Lacey (1958) maintained that indexes such as heart rate, for example, will sometimes increase and sometimes decrease in the same situation in different individuals. Furthermore, Lacey (1959) has found that the same individual will display different directions of heart rate change as a function of the type of task. If he or she is attending to internal stimuli such as mental addition, heart rate goes up; on the other hand, if he or she is attending to external stimuli such as looking at pictures, heart rate goes down. However, despite opposite heart rate changes in the two situations, another autonomic index, skin resistance, seems to increase in both situations. Lacey is critical of the usefulness of the arousal concept, because of measurement problems such as these when psychophysiological indices are involved.

INADEQUACY OF VIEWS OF ACTIVATION AS UNITARY DIMENSION

The formulation of activation as a single dimension in which the level of energy of an organism can vary may be too simplistic. Thayer (1976) has proposed that it may be more fruitful to consider the existence of at least two different activation dimensions. He noted situations that are difficult to explain in terms of a unidimensional view of activation but that can be accounted for by his multidimensional model.

For example, when we are very tense and anxious we often feel sleepy and tired at the same time. When we look at the same phenomenon from the other side, it seems that we experience the most anxiety from personal problems when we are tired and sleepy (e.g., after stresses or late at night when bodily resources are depleted). Another inconsistency observed by Thayer is the increases in energy and vigor, often produced by moderate physical exercise, which appear to alleviate tension and anxiety, at least temporarily. In contrast when we sit around doing nothing, we often feel tired although we apparently have expended little physical effort.

Thayer proposed a model of activation consisting of two states, A and B, where we will describe briefly. State A varies from sleepiness and tiredness to energy and vigor. It varies over the course of the day, starting low, peaking at late morning or early afternoon, and then declining throughout the rest of the day. There may also be secondary peaks and troughs such as those we experience as midafternoon "blahs" and early evening energy. State A corresponds in many respects to the type of activation dimension that previous single-dimension views have emphasized.

The second dimension postulated by Thayer, State B, deals with stressful responses such as reactions to defense and emergency situations. It varies from placidity and quietness to a state of tension. Thayer hypothesized that these two states, A and B, tend to covary and have similar behavioral effects in the middle ranges of the dimensions. At low levels of both states, the effect is the reduction of both types of activation.

The interesting suggestion concerns the interaction of the two states when they are both at high levels. It is assumed by Thayer than an opposing or offsetting effect occurs there such that a high level of one counteracts the effects of a high level on the other dimension. Thus, high state A (vigor, energy) can reduce state B (tension). Similarly, high state B (tension) can reduce state A (vigor, energy).

The Nature of Affective Feeling

DEGREE OF INCONGRUITY AND AFFECT

At the subjective level, the individual experiences affective feeling ranging from positive through neutral to negative states. McClelland, Atkinson, Clark, and Lowell (1953) have investigated the role of the discrepancy or incongruity of present and past stimulation as a determinant of the nature of affective responses.

Using the concept of adaptation level (Helson, 1947) to refer to the level of stimulation encountered by the organism in the past, McClelland et al. predicted that small departures from this adaptation level of stimulation would lead to positive affect. Additional discrepancies from the adaptation level, however, would produce a reversal, or negative affect. As shown in Figure 10–2, small to moderate changes above or below the stimulus level to which the organism is adapted will cause positive affect, but larger discrepancies will produce negative affect.

McClelland et al. further maintain that these affective states may be the basis for the hypothesized optimal incongruity effect. Thus, when discrepancy is small and affect is positive, the organism may seek to increase this feeling by seeking larger discrepancies in stimulation. On the other hand, if the discrepancy is so great that negative affect occurs, the organism will attempt to reduce it by seeking smaller levels of stimulus change. Somewhere in between is a level that is just right, at least momentarily.

Haber (1958) had subjects place both hands in a bucket of water until they reported feeling neutral affect, that is, no thermal sensation. Next, each hand was placed in different containers with water of differing temperatures and the subject was instructed to withdraw the hand that felt less pleasant within three seconds. A number of trials were given using different test combinations of water temperatures. Results indicated that small discrepancies up to one degree Centigrade above or below the adaptation level of the first container were pleasant, but as the water temperature increased or decreased beyond that point, it was judged less pleasant. These results fit the so-called butterfly model shown in Figure 10–2.

DeCharms (1968) pointed out some limitations of McClelland et al.'s discrepancy theory when the stimuli have been associated with extrinsic meaning. For example, consider academic grades. A student who on the basis of past achievement expected a grade of C would not be happier with a small discrepancy in his grade (B) than with a large one (A). The main point of DeCharm's comment is that different principles may hold when extrinsic reinforcers are involved rather than primary sensory stimuli, but it does not question the validity of the model for the latter type of stimuli.

Berlyne (1967) pointed out that a nonmonotonic relationship between

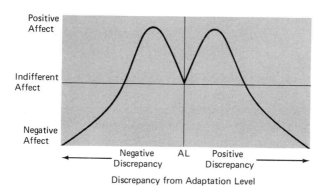

FIGURE 10–2. The "butterfly curve." [From "Discrepancy from adaptation level as a source of affect," by R. N. Haber, *Journal of Experimental Psychology*, 1958, *56,* 370–375. Copyright 1958 by the American Psychological Association. Reprinted by permission.]

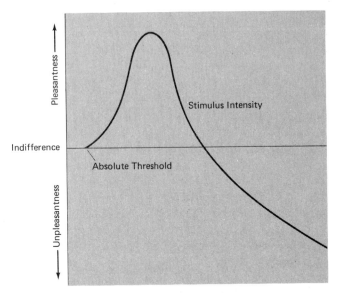

FIGURE 10–3. Wundt's curve of the relationship between affect and stimulus intensity. [From "Arousal and Reinforcement" by D. E. Berlyne, in *Nebraska Symposium on Motivation* (Vol. 15) by W. J. Arnold (Ed.), Lincoln: University of Nebraska Press, 1967. Reprinted by permission of University of Nebraska Press.]

affect and stimulation had been postulated back in 1874 by the founder of experimental psychology, Wilhelm Wundt. The shape of this curve (See Figure 10–3) shows increasing positive affect as factors such as stimulus intensity, novelty, or complexity increase up to some point, then a drop and reversal to negative affect.

It should be noted that Wundt's curve is identical to the right-hand side of McClelland's model for discrepancy and affect. By adding the mirror image of the curve to the left side, Wundt's curve can account for discrepancies in either direction from the adaptation level as McClelland et al.'s curve does.

STIMULUS COMPLEXITY AND AFFECT

One example of evidence supporting this model is provided by Munsinger and Kessen (1964), who conducted several studies in which they demonstrated a U-shaped relationship between stimulus complexity and affective response. In one experiment they presented a series of word strings or sequences that varied in the degree to which they approximated the statistical properties of normal English. In another study, they gave subjects nonsense geometrical polygons, which varied in number of sides from three to forty. In both cases, preferences showed the U-shaped relationship between complexity and liking.

Using twenty-second sequences of tones, which varied in complexity of the pattern of loudness, frequency, and duration of individual tones in the series, Vitz (1966) also obtained an inverted U-shaped function between pleasantness ratings and the amount of stimulus variation.

In addition, both Munsinger and Kessen (1964) and Vitz (1966) compared reactions of subjects varying in specialized training in art or music, because the stimuli they used were distantly related to materials that might be encountered in fields such as the fine arts. It was assumed that training could raise the lowest level of stimulus variation that would be judged pleasant, because it would not then be perceived as being complex compared to how it would be perceived by the untrained eye or ear. Thus, Munsinger and Kessen found that the U function obtained for visual stimuli was limited to non-art students, whereas art majors showed a higher liking the more complex the stimuli. A real life example in the case of music might be the preference of the layperson for Tschaikowsky over Bach, whereas the opposite would hold for the person with the trained ear.

Berlyne (1970) has also provided evidence that the relationship between preference and exposure depends on the complexity of the stimuli. Using black and white reproductions of complex (many human figures) and simple (one human figure) paintings, as well as pictures that were nonrepresentational and varied in complexity (as measured by the number of elements), he found that there was no difference in preference on the first exposure. However, after ten exposures, a preference had developed for the more complex stimuli.

A number of experiments have found U-shaped curves between judgments of pleasantness and complexity with auditory, visual, and verbal stimuli. An extensive review is provided by Berlyne (1971) who has related this evidence to an arousal analysis of aesthetic preference. Although most of the laboratory studies have used simple and artificial stimuli, Berlyne feels that similar principles may affect judgments of artificial stimuli and aesthetic works of art.

REPETITION AND AFFECT

What is the influence of repeated exposure to the same stimulus on affect? According to optimal level of arousal theory, one would expect liking or preference to first increase to a point, and then decrease as frequency of exposure increased. In other words, when stimuli are novel or infrequently encountered, they should be less preferred than if they are somewhat familiar. However, if the frequency of contact is too great, they should be less well liked, or boring.

Some evidence on this question is available from the studies by Zajonc and his colleagues (Zajonc, 1968; Zajonc, Shaver, and Tavris, 1972; Zajonc, Swap, Harrison, and Roberts, 1971) who have examined the effects of frequency of mere exposure to neutral stimuli on liking or attraction. *Mere* exposure refers to the fact that the stimuli are not presented in association with rewards or punishments; instead a series of neutral or meaningless stimuli such as Chinese ideographs, Turkish words, or photos of unfamiliar faces are presented at various frequencies in random order. It is necessary sometimes to disguise the purpose of the task by instructing subjects to do some irrelevant task such as rating the pronunciability of Turkish words, although for some of the stimuli such as the faces they are merely told to pay close attention.

The results shown in Figure 10–4 suggested that repeated exposure to unfamiliar objects tends to increase liking for them. However, when familiar stimuli have been used, the curves relating exposure frequency and liking may differ. Maddi (1968) obtained results with familiar objects that even suggested the relationship is curvilinear and that a type of satiation occurs with overexposure that causes a downturn in liking.

Just as there might be an optimal level of discrepancy for arousal, there

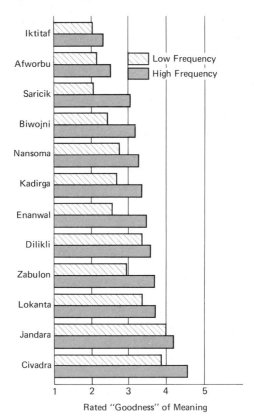

FIGURE 10–4. Average rated affective connotation of nonsense words exposed with low and high frequencies. [From "Attitudinal Effects of Mere Exposure," by R. B. Zajonc, *Journal of Personality and Social Psychology Monograph Supplement,* 1968, *9* (2, Pt. 2), 1–27. Copyright 1968 by the American Psychological Association. Reprinted by permission.]

may be an optimal frequency of exposure for liking. Using reproductions of nonrepresentational paintings, Zajonc, Shaver, Tavris, and Kreveld (1972) varied the exposure from 0 to 25 for a set of reproductions of twelve paintings. Results showed a curvilinear relationship with liking at its highest level after one or two exposures, not only for those paintings that were generally liked, but also for those that were disliked.

In contrast, when Zajonc et al. used other stimuli such as photos of male faces or nonsense syllables, linear relationships were found, such that the more frequent the exposure up to twenty-five trials, the greater the liking. In the study by Zajonc, Swap, Harrison, and Roberts (1970), a similar failure to show satiation of liking was found with Chinese ideographs, even with as many as eighty-one exposures.

Zajonc et al. (1972) suggested two reasons why results varied as a function of the type of stimulus used. First, perhaps the number of exposures used was insufficient in those studies that did not show a satiation or leveling off of the exposure effect. As pointed out earlier, this is an after the fact argument that could be made for many studies that fail to show an hypothesized downturn. However, Zajonc et al. rejected it on other grounds, arguing that even eighty-one exposures did not lead to a downturn with the Chinese characters, whereas only two exposures did with the abstract paintings. This argument is not convincing, because the exact number of exposures needed to cause changes in liking may vary with the type of stimuli. Whereas paintings are perceived as potential aesthetic experiences, this is not the case for Chinese ideographs, except possibly for lovers of calligraphy.

The second alternative is that a linear relationship is the general rule, and that the finding of a curvilinear relationship with art stimuli is an exception. If this is the case, it would conflict with the optimal arousal theory, which would predict a curvilinear relationship. Part of the discrepancy may stem from the fact just mentioned that Zajonc et al.'s (1972) evidence for a direct relationship between liking and exposure is based on neutral and even meaningless stimuli, for the most part, whereas the curvilinear relationship was obtained when aesthetic stimuli were used.

The role of the initial affective nature of the stimuli is recognized by Zajonc (1970), who admitted that in some situations increased exposure could even lead to increased *dislike,* such as when the initial attitude toward a stimulus is negative. Ordinarily, people avoid increased contact with stimuli of negative value, so that if one examined the correlation between *voluntary* exposure and liking, a positive relationship should exist. If we could impose exposure of negative-valued stimuli on individuals, we might get greater disliking, the more frequent the contact.

Some evidence is available to support this conjecture. Burgess and Sales (1971) asked subjects to memorize pairs of nonsense syllables and words that were exposed at different frequencies. Some words were positive, others negative, and some neutral in affective meaning. Later ratings of the likeability of the nonsense syllables were obtained. Those syllables that had been paired with positive words showed a positive relationship between liking and frequency of exposure. The opposite was true for nonsense syllables paired with negative words, and no relationship was found for those paired with neutral words.

In another experiment (Perlman and Oskamp, 1971) ratings of photographs of a black or white male in one of three contexts were made. The model was clothed in a positive (clergy attire), negative (prison garb), or neutral (street clothes) context. Increased liking was obtained with higher exposure for positive contexts, whereas the opposite was true for negative contexts. Again, neutral contexts did not produce a frequency effect. Furthermore, results were similar for both the black and white stimulus person.

In summary, it is still useful to predict that liking should bear a U-shaped relationship to frequency of exposure. The findings of Zajonc that disagree with this formulation may be special cases limited to the meaningless stimulus materials employed.

THE TEMPORAL COURSE OF AFFECT

Another aspect of affective response that bears examination is the temporal course of feeling. Solomon and Corbit (1974) have noticed that a number of affective reactions, positive or negative, show a rapid peaking, followed by a drop to a steady state (State A). Then, if the stimulation is abruptly ended,

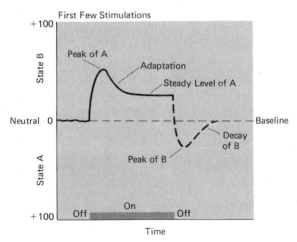

FIGURE 10–5. The manifest temporal dynamics generated by the opponent-process system during the first few stimulations. [From "An Opponent-process Theory of Motivation: I. Temporal Dynamics of Affect," by R. L. Solomon and J. D. Corbit, *Psychological Review*, 1974, *81*, 119–145. Copyright 1974 by the American Psychological Association. Reprinted by permission.]

there is generally an affective reaction (State *B*) in the opposite direction, which also quickly peaks and then slowly dissipates. (See Figure 10–5.) In studying this illustration one should be careful not to think that the baseline is the same as that for the McClelland et al. curve. Whereas that baseline represents the degree of disparity between two levels of stimulation, the Solomon-Corbit model deals with the temporal course of affective feeling in relation to the onset and offset of a stimulus.

Another interesting aspect of affective reactions noted by Solomon and Corbit is what happens in future exposures to the same situation. The re-action (State *A'*) to the onset of stimulation becomes weaker over repeated encounters, whereas the reaction (State *B'*) to the offset is enhanced in strength and duration (See Figure 10–6).

This temporal course of affective response is found in a number of situations such as those listed in Table 10–1. For example, a dog receives un-avoidable shocks (Solomon and Wynne, 1953) while strapped in a restrain-ing harness for a number of trials before it is suddenly released. The model indicates that the onset of shock produced a rapid increase of negative affect, which peaks and then drops before leveling off. As soon as the dog is re-leased, the opposite affect of excitement, tail wagging, etc., occurs. Further-more, during the future trials there is less intense negative affect to the shock but even greater positive affect to the release from the shock situation.

Another example can be found in the work of Epstein (1967) on stress seeking in chutists. On the first few jumps, the initiate is anxious and scared. After landing safely, the novice takes a few seconds to regain his composure

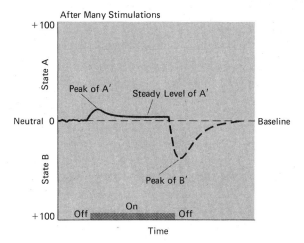

FIGURE 10–6. The manifest temporal dynamics generated by the opponent-process system after many repeated stimulations. [From "An Opponent-process Theory of Motivation: I. Temporal Dynamics of Affect, by R. L. Solomon and J. D. Corbit, *Psychological Review*, 1974, *81*, 119–145. Copyright 1974 by the American Psycho-logical Association. Reprinted by permission.]

TABLE 10–1. Selected Examples of Hedonic-Affective Phenomena Illustrative of the Opponent Process Theory.

Example	First Few Stimulations		After Many Stimulations	
	State A (input present)	State B (input gone)	State A' (input present)	State B' (input gone)
Dogs in Pavlov harness, 10-second shocks, gross behavior	terror, panic	stealth (subdued, cautious, inactive, hesitant)	unhappy (annoyed, anxious, afraid)	joy (euphoric, active, social), happy
Dogs in Pavlov harness, 10-second shocks, electrocardiograph responses	large cardiac acceleration	slow deceleration, small overshoot	small acceleration or none	quick deceleration, large overshoot
Epstein's parachutists, free fall, gross behavior, physiology	terror, autonomic nervous system arousal	stunned, stony-faced	tense, eager, expectant	exhilaration, jubilation
Opiate users, intravenous injection, moods and feelings	euphoria, rush, pleasure	craving, aversive withdrawal signs, short duration	loss of euphoria, normal feeling, relief	intense craving, abstinence agony, long duration
Dogs and M & Ms, gross behavior	pleasure, tail wagging, chewing	tenseness, motionless	—	—
Love, interpersonal stimulation, moods, feelings	ecstasy, excitement, happiness	loneliness	normal, comfortable, content	grief, separation syndrome, long duration
Imprinting, the attachment of creatures to their "mothers"	pleasure, cessation of fear, no distress	loneliness, distress cries, short duration	pleasure, no cries	loneliness, intense cries, long duration

Source: From "An Opponent-Process Theory of Motivation: I. Temporal Dynamics of Affect" by R. L. Solomon and J. D. Corbit, *Psychological Review,* 1974, *81,* 119–145. Copyright 1974 by the American Psychological Association. Reprinted by permission.

and experience pleasure. On later jumps, there is a weakening of the pre-jump anxiety to a mild level of tension, followed by greater exuberance after the successful completion of the jump.

A final example deals with reactions to the use of psychoactive drugs. First, after the use is habitual there is a rush of pleasure, followed by a weakened euphoria that later becomes painful craving. As use of the drug is repeated, the pleasurable aspect weakens, while the subsequent aversive aspect of withdrawal symptoms becomes more intense and longer lasting. The eventual outcome is the well-known fact that users become "addicted" to these substances at least in a psychological sense and it is quite difficult to terminate usage without suffering strong negative affect.

To account for these observations, Solomon and Corbit (1974) developed an opponent processes model, following the example by Hurvich and Jameison (1957) in the area of perception. They suggest that for most strong affects, there is a rebound of an opposite affect. This second aspect of the cycle is termed a *slave process* in the sense that the first reaction must occur before the opponent process will ensue. Furthermore, the opponent process is automatic and involves no conditioning. It seems to be what Solomon and Corbit refer to as an offsetting cost of the primary affect, serving to bring affect back to equilibrium. They suggested that addiction in which one affect is inevitably followed by an opposite feeling state might be regarded as a model for all acquired motives.

Affects, according to this model, are similar to drives in their homeostatic tendencies, so that changes in one direction from neutrality lead to feelings in the opposite direction as soon as the stimuli for the first state end. Solomon and Corbit allow that this process may depend on there being a rapid termination of the initial stimulus and that if it is gradual the opposite process may not occur.

In many respects, the concept of arousal jag (Berlyne, 1960) is similar to the sequence of affects described by Solomon and Corbit when the negative state occurs first. It has been noted that people seek thrills, excitement, and even danger because they feel so good when safety is achieved. It is like the kid who bangs his head on the wall because it feels so good when he stops.

One reason the first state should diminish in magnitude over repeated occasions, which is not discussed by Solomon and Corbit, is the role of expectancy. The organism learns eventually that the first state is temporary; anticipation of the change could then eventually produce the opposite affective state. Therefore, bad events will be more tolerable because termination is known to be imminent; likewise, good events are less enjoyable because their cessation is expected soon.

The question also arises whether or not all of the second or opposite states should become enhanced with practice, as the model suggests. In the case of the chutists, the model predicts that relief and euphoria should occur after the completion of the first few successful jumps. However, repeated successes should also increase confidence and competence so that the chutist will feel less anxiety and will come to expect success. If this is the case, successful completion of additional jumps should provide no further elation. This consequence is probably the reason individuals seeking achievements and risks shift their goals upward to maintain a sense of challenge. In this respect, Solomon and Corbit's model is applicable since the choice of a greater challenge again raises anxiety that leads to strong positive affect if success is achieved.

Summary

Feelings as diverse as boredom, calmness, and excitement influence our behavior in varied ways. Sometimes we seek increased stimulation, whereas at other times we try to reduce it. Our analysis of these aspects of behavior has focused on the concept of arousal, a construct usually defined and measured in terms of psychophysiological activation. Indices such as heart rate, respiration rate, and skin conductance, to name a few, are measured and used to infer the level of a general state of alertness or activity in the organism.

Not only does an organism seek arousal states that vary in intensity, but it appears that qualitative aspects must be considered, because positive states are sought in preference to negative ones. The two dimensions are difficult to separate, because it is assumed that direction of affect, positive or negative, is tied integrally to the intensity dimension. It is hypothesized that there is an optimal level of arousal, one that is best for efficient functioning, and that arousal levels above or below this optimum yield poorer performance. Furthermore, our past experience gives us expectations about what stimulation will occur in many situations. If the stimulus is similar to expectation or only moderately discrepant, we may feel positive affect, but if the incongruity is too great we will feel negative affect.

This view of arousal suggests that we act to alter our stimulation in order to achieve the optimal level whenever possible, trying to increase arousal if it is too low and lower it if it is too high. Variety of stimulation is sought over the course of time, because the optimal level of arousal is not a fixed value but one that can change as a function of our past experiences and our fluctuating internal states. What is interesting at one moment may shortly become tedious and tiresome; what is frightening and anxiety provoking at one moment can later become enjoyable and pleasurable if we can learn how to deal with it.

It is also possible that biological and constitutional differences exist among individuals in the level of stimulation that is optimal in a given situation. These differences might be related to the differences in tolerance and reactions to stressful events and involve nervous and endocrine system activity differences.

Although the individual measures of different psychophysical responses may be precise, the theoretical construct of activation or arousal that builds on them is somewhat ambiguous, especially the notion of an optimal level. In part this vagueness is due to the simultaneous operation of several factors in the individual: past experience, biological differences, present internal sources of arousal, and present environmental sources of stimulation. Thus, for two individuals with assumed identical optimal levels for arousal due to biological make-up, the specific environmental optimal stimulus can be quite different, because there may be marked differences between them in either internal arousal states such as wakefulness or in past experience with the type of stimulus situation involved. Due to this multiplicity of determinants and the difficulty of identifying all of them in a given situation, experimental tests of the optimal level of arousal concept are often conflicting or inconclusive so that its status remains more an assumption rather than an established fact.

The feelings or affects experienced by the individual may be viewed as the subjective basis for the fact that behavior often corresponds to predictions based on the idea of an optimal level of incongruity. A number of studies have found that affective responses go from neutrality to positive and then become negative as the degree of incongruity from expectancies increases.

Affect is also a function of repeated exposure to stimuli. In stimuli of neutral affective value, there appears to be a direct relationship between amount of exposure and liking. However, with familiar objects and for aesthetic stimuli there seems to be a U-shaped function in which there is an optimal frequency of exposure associated with liking.

When intense affects are aroused but abruptly ended, an automatic occurrence of opposite affects has been noted in a number of situations. As this cycle increases in frequency, the strength of the initial affect is weakened, while its opposite feeling becomes more intense. This process appears not to involve learning.

References

AMSTER, H. A. Semantic satiation and generation: learning? adaptation? *Psychological Bulletin*, 1964, *62*, 273–286.

BEXTON, W. H., HERON, W., and SCOTT, T. H. Effects of decreased variation in the sensory environment. *Canadian Journal of Psychology*, 1954, *8*, 70–76.

BERLYNE, D. E. Novelty and curiosity as determinants of exploratory behavior. *British Journal of Psychology*, 1950, *41*, 68–80.

———. The arousal and satiation of perceptual curiosity in the rat. *Journal of Comparative and Physiological Psychology*, 1955, *48*, 238–246.

———. The influence of complexity and novelty in visual figures on orienting responses. *Journal of Experimental Psychology*, 1958, *55*, 289–296.

———. *Conflict, arousal, and curiosity.* New York: McGraw-Hill, 1960.

———. Arousal and reinforcement. In W. J. Arnold (Ed.), *Nebraska Symposium on Motivation.* (Vol. 15). Lincoln: University of Nebraska Press, 1967.

———. *Aesthetics and psychobiology.* New York: Appleton, 1971.

BRONSON, G. W. The fear of novelty. *Psychological Bulletin*, 1968, *69*, 350–358.

BURGESS, T. D. G., JR., and SALES, S. M. Attitudinal effects of mere exposure: A re-evaluation. *Journal of Experimental Social Psychology*, 1971, *7*, 461–472.

DeCHARMS, R. *Personal causation: The internal affective determinants of behavior.* New York: Academic, 1968.

DECI, E. L. *Intrinsic motivation.* New York: Plenum, 1975.

EPSTEIN, S. M. Toward a unified theory of anxiety. In B. A. Maher (Ed.), *Progress in experimental personality research.* (Vol. 4). New York: Academic, 1967.

EYSENCK, H. J. Cortical inhibition, figural aftereffect, and theory of personality. *Journal of Abnormal and Social Psychology,* 1955, *51,* 94–106.

FISKE, D. W., and MADDI, S. R. *Functions of varied experience.* Homewood, Ill.: Dorsey Press, 1961.

HABER, R. N. Discrepancy from adaptation level as a source of affect. *Journal of Experimental Psychology,* 1958, *56,* 370–375.

HEBB, D. O. Drives and the c.n.s. (conceptual nervous system). *Psychological Review,* 1955, *62,* 243–254.

HELSON, H. Adaptation level as a frame of reference for prediction of psychophysical data. *American Journal of Psychology,* 1947, *60,* 1–29.

HUNT, J. MC V. Intrinsic motivation and its role in psychological development. In D. Levine (Ed.), *Nebraska Symposium on Motivation.* (Vol. 13). Lincoln: University of Nebraska Press, 1965.

HURVICH, L. M., and JAMEISON, D. An opponent-process theory of color vision. *Psychological Review,* 1957, *64,* 384–404.

LACEY, J. I. Physiological approaches to the evaluation of psychotherapeutic process and outcome. In E. A. Rubenstein and M. B. Parloff (Eds.), *Research in psychotherapy.* Washington, D.C.: American Psychological Association, 1959.

————, and LACEY, B. C. Verification and extension of the principle of autonomic response stereotypy. *American Journal of Psychology,* 1958, *71,* 50–73.

LINDSLEY, D. B. Emotion. In S. S. Stevens (Ed.), *Handbook of Experimental Psychology.* New York: Wiley, 1951.

MCCLELLAND, D. C., ATKINSON, J. W., CLARK, R. A., and LOWELL, E. L. *The achievement motive.* New York: Appleton, 1953.

MADDI, S. R. Meaning, novelty, and affect: Comments on Zajonc's paper. *Journal of Personality and Social Psychology Monograph Supplement,* 1968, *9* (2, Pt. 2), 28–29.

MALMO, R. B. Activation: A neuropsychological dimension. *Psychological Review,* 1959, *66,* 367–386.

MUNSINGER, H., and KESSEN, W. Uncertainty, structure, and preference. *Psychological Monographs,* 1962, *78* (9, Whole No. 586).

ORNE, M. T., and SCHEIBE, K. E. The contribution of nondeprivation factors in the production of sensory deprivation effects: The psychology of the "panic button." *Journal of Abnormal and Social Psychology,* 1964, *68,* 3–12.

PAVLOV, I. P. *Conditioned reflexes.* London: Oxford University Press, 1927.

PERLMAN, D., and OSKAMP, S. The effects of picture content and exposure frequency on evaluations of Negroes and whites. *Journal of Experimental Social Psychology,* 1971, *7,* 503–514.

PETRIE, A. *Individuality in pain and suffering.* Chicago: University of Chicago, 1967.

PIAGET, J. *The origins of intelligence in children.* Translated by M. Cook. New York: International Universities Press, 1952.

SALES, S. M. Need for stimulation as a factor in social behavior. *Journal of Personality and Social Psychology,* 1971, *19,* 124–134.

————, GUYDOSH, R. M., and IACONO, W. Relationship between "strength of the nervous system" and the need for stimulation. *Journal of Personality and Social Psychology,* 1974, *29,* 16–22.

SCHULTZ, D. P. *Sensory restriction: Effects on behavior.* New York: Academic, 1965.

SOKOLOV, E. N. Neural models and the orienting reflex. In M. A. B. Brazier (Ed.),

The central nervous system and behavior. New York: Josiah Macy, Jr. Foundation, 1960.

SOLOMON, R. L., and CORBIT, J. D. An opponent-process theory of motivation: I. Temporal dynamics of affect. *Psychological Review,* 1974, *81,* 119–145.

SOLOMON, R. L., and WYNNE, L. C. Traumatic avoidance learning. *Psychological Monographs,* 1953, *67* (4, Whole No. 354).

SUEDFELD, P. Theoretical formulations II. In J. P. Zubek (Ed.), *Sensory deprivation.* New York: Appleton, 1969.

THAYER, R. E. Toward a psychological model of multidimensional activation (arousal). *Motivation and Emotion,* 1977, In press.

TINKELPAUGH, O. L. An experimental study of representative factors in monkeys. *Journal of Comparative and Physiological Psychology,* 1928, *8,* 197–236.

VITZ, P. C. Affect as a function of stimulus variation. *Journal of Experimental Psychology,* 1966, *71,* 74–79.

WHITE, R. W. Motivation reconsidered: The concept of competence. *Psychological Review,* 1959, *66,* 297–333.

ZAJONC, R. B. Attitudinal effects of mere exposure. *Journal of Personality and Social Psychology Monograph Supplement,* 1968, *9* (2, Pt. 2), 1–27.

———. Brainwash: Familiarity breeds comfort. *Psychology Today,* 1970, *3* (9), 33–35; 60–62.

———, SHAVER, P., TAVRIS, C., and KREVELD, D. V. Exposure, satiation, and stimulus discriminability. *Journal of Personality and Social Psychology,* 1972, *21,* 270–280.

———, SWAP, W. C., HARRISON, A. A., and ROBERTS, P. Limiting conditions of the exposure effect: Satiation and relativity. *Journal of Personality and Social Psychology,* 1971, *18,* 384–391.

ZUBEK, J. P. (Ed.), *Sensory deprivation.* New York: Appleton, 1969.

ZUCKERMAN, M. Theoretical formulations I. In J. P. Zubek (Ed.), *Sensory deprivation.* New York: Appleton, 1969.

CHAPTER 11

Getting Emotional About It

Think about some recent experience in which you were angry, afraid, joyful, or disgusted. Can you still almost feel some of the bodily sensations such as heart palpitations, dryness in the throat, sweaty palms, or rapid breathing? Emotional experiences such as these are frequent and highly significant aspects of our lives.

Despite the obvious importance of such experiences, the scientific understanding of emotions leaves much to be desired. For one matter, the fragile and transitory nature of many emotions has rendered the laboratory investigation of them rather difficult. The subjective and idiosyncratic nature of emotional experiences has discouraged many investigators from probing this area. Furthermore, the interaction of emotional processes with other processes such as learning and perception has also been ignored by those who investigate other aspects of psychology. Whenever emotion has been approached by researchers, the emphasis has been limited to behavioral and physiological aspects and the subjective and phenomenological side of emotions have generally been dismissed.

The concept of emotion is closely associated with the inner feelings stemming from physiological activation and bodily reactions. Our awareness of these feeling states is what constitutes the vibrancy, spice, or turmoil associated with many of our experiences. In order to achieve a scientific understanding of these states, however, we must go beyond the experiential level. The identification of the factors that elicit, control, and modify emotions is needed. The discovery of the manner in which emotions influence other aspects of our behavior and experience is another important goal. In this chapter we will present evidence dealing with these aspects of the study of emotions.

Basic Problems in Studying Emotions

Part of the difficulty in the study of emotion stems from the lack of agreement among investigators about the definition and use of basic terms. The terms, *emotion, feeling,* and *affect* are treated as interchangeable and synonymous by some, whereas others see them as distinct processes. Some workers emphasize behavioral aspects, whereas others focus on subjective experience. Still others prefer dealing with emotion only at the physiological level. Of course, all these approaches are legitimate, because emotions, like other psychological processes, have physiological, behavioral, and phenomenological aspects.

The study of emotions has focused on strong emotions such as fear or anger, which also involve negative feeling states, whereas less attention has been directed toward positive feeling states such as joy, happiness, or love. Earlier interpretations of the role of emotion emphasized the disruptive and disorganizing consequences of emotion (Young, 1943). This conclusion is hardly surprising if only the intense negative emotions were being considered. However, Leeper (1948, 1965, 1970) has repeatedly championed the view that emotions primarily serve to promote organized behavior. He maintains that the disorganization is more apparent than real and although emotion may redirect ongoing behavior into another activity, this rechannelling itself is organized and purposive. Just as a person who is reading may seek food if he or she is hungry, a person who is reading might flee the room if it catches fire. One would not consider the first case to be one involving disorganized behavior but as one in which another motive became dominant. Similarly, Leeper would argue, the second instance would not constitute disorganization on the grounds that the reading was interrupted. As long as the exit from the room was purposeful and organized, we could argue that the emotion operated in a manner similar to that of the motive of hunger in the first example.

It is not clear why the history of the study of emotion has taken the course that it has but Leeper (1965) suggested that the history of investigation of many processes has shown that the more palpable or tangible processes receive prior attention. Thus, the stronger emotions and the ones that have the more salient effects on human interaction, such as fear and anxiety, may be the ones that get studied first, especially if they were associated with clinical problems.

Another aspect of how emotion is viewed is the frequent contrast between it and reason. Part of the age-old distinction between reason and emotion may stem from the fact that extreme emotions can disrupt reasoning. Leeper (1965) has questioned the distinction and has attempted to show that perceptual-cognitive factors are a necessary component of emotions. Thus, emotions and perceptions are not regarded as mutually exclusive and separate processes with the former being less advanced or complicated. Leeper held that cognitive factors influence both emotions and perceptions. As we shall see shortly, other important investigators are also emphasizing the vital role of cognitive factors in emotions.

The reason-emotion dichotomy has also played a role in the contrast between humans and infrahuman species. The assumed superiority of humans is due, in part, to the belief that humans are not governed merely by base emotions as are the lower animals. Instead, humankind is assumed to be able to control emotional tendencies with the aid of rational processes, at least most of the time.

But are humans really so less capable of emotional expression and influence than lower animals? Hebb and Thompson (1968) speculated that this view is questionable in view of the highly protective societies that humans have created to prevent emotional experience. Institutions such as education, for example, can be regarded as a means of creating a protective societal context in which emotional insulation is possible. Ironically, Hebb and Thompson noted, this protection will not only fail to reduce *susceptibility* to emotional disturbance, but it might increase it, because the slightest deviations from the conventional might be more capable of eliciting emotional reactions.

Charles Darwin's concern with the continuity of biological species in his famous studies of evolution also extended into a similar search for continuity between humans and lower animals at the behavioral level. His less well-known study of *Expression of Emotions in Man and Animal* (1872) might be viewed as an important stimulus to the scientific study of emotion. One of the principles formulated in this study, that of "once serviceable habits," held that emotional expressions such as postural and facial cues that previously played important social functions in lower animals were less vital or functional for humans. Thus, lower animals snarl and bare their teeth when faced with an adversary. To some extent, humans make similar facial expressions when angry or expressing insults but they do not literally bite into their foes.

Although Darwin's explanation of the transmission of emotional expressions from lower animals to humans via evolution has generally been ignored, his work did direct attention to the description and observation of emotional behavior rather than experience. This shift aided the development of scientific studies of this topic. His emphasis on the continuity of emotional expression across species draws attention to the biological bases of emotion. We will discuss more recent views of the significance of emotional expression later.

The Experience of Emotion: The James-Lange Theory

A good point of departure for the discussion of current views of emotion is the so-called James-Lange theory, which was independently proposed about the same time by William James (1884) and Carl Lange (1885). James felt that emotion could be defined in terms of the conscious experiences of bodily reactions encountered during emotions. Consider the example of a person who suddenly is confronted by a bear in the woods. Whereas common sense would say that we would run out of fear, James' explanation was just the opposite. That is, his interpretation would be that the fear we experience is due to the fact that we ran. Such running led to increased heart rate, faster breathing, and changes in other visceral responses; the consciousness of these bodily reactions constitutes our feelings of emotion.

CRITICISMS OF THE JAMES-LANGE THEORY

Critics of James have focused on his statement that ". . . the emotion is nothing but the feeling of the reflex bodily effect. . . ." Although James seems to take this position insofar as conscious experience of bodily reactions is concerned, he does appear to give more attention to cognitive factors than his critics recognize. Thus, he acknowledged the role of the perception of the stimulus that precedes the bodily changes in the person. In the example of the bear, James does not explicitly state why a person would run in the first place. Presumably it is due to past direct or indirect learning about the danger involved. This cognitive appraisal enables us to "know" that we should be afraid. Then we run or take other appropriate action, the conscious experience of which, according to James, is the emotion. The necessity of considering the cognitive appraisal as a prior condition to the autonomic arousal becomes obvious if we consider our reaction to meeting a bear as we suddenly round a corner in a zoo. It is doubtful that the sight of this bear either behind bars or separated from us by a pit would cause us to run or tremble or to experience fear.

In saying that emotion is nothing but the experience of bodily reactions, James is emphasizing the determinants of our subjective feelings of emotion, but it does not seem fair to say that he felt that cognitive factors, or perceptions, are not necessary antecedents.

The most notable critic of James' view was the famous physiologist, Walter B. Cannon, whose objections have been repeated by subsequent critics. Cannon (1927) presented five major criticisms as well as his own alternative thalamic theory of emotion, which placed more emphasis on the role of higher brain centers. First, he noted that total separation of the viscera from the central nervous system, such as in sympathectomies in which the connections between higher and lower nervous systems are surgically disrupted, does not alter emotional behavior. For example, sympathectomized cats still show superficial signs of rage when presented with a barking dog. They hiss, snarl, bare their teeth, and raise their paws to strike. Only the erection of the hairs is noticeably absent. Cannon, readily admitted, however, that there is no real proof that *felt* emotion occurred. Due to prior learning, the animals "knew" that the dog was a threat and assumed a defensive posture even though they may not have "felt" emotion. This criticism does not seriously weaken James' view.

Consistent with this argument is a study of paraplegics by Hohmann (1966). He found that they reported a reduction in felt or experienced emotion compared with their experiences prior to their spinal cord injuries. However, because they had previous knowledge of emotional experiences, it was still possible for them to act emotionally on the behavioral level, even though there was no physiological basis available.

Cannon also maintained that, contrary to what James' theory might imply, the same visceral changes occur in markedly different emotional states as well as in nonemotional states. Activation of the sympathetic nervous system seems to occur under such distinguishable states as fear and anger as well as under fever, exposure to cold, and difficult breathing. The interpretation of evidence on this matter is controversial even today. Cannon may have been correct in 1927 that no physiological differences could be found between different emotional situations, but since that time some investigators have identified differences (Averill, 1969; Ax, 1953; Funkenstein, King, and Drolette, 1957). However, some writers (e.g., Duffy, 1962; Mandler, 1962) have not fully accepted this type of evidence. In summary, the available evidence is not so convincing that it shows different patterns of visceral response existing for every emotion. One can always argue that refinements in tools and measurement procedures will enable the identification of more subtle physiological differences as a function of different emotions than is presently possible. For the moment, the issue is still under debate, so Cannon's criticism is tenuous.

The third and fourth arguments against James lie in the fact that viscera are relatively insensitive and slow in responding. If emotion were nothing but the reactions of these slow processes, how could we react to emergencies with appropriate behavior as rapidly as we sometimes do? The implication is that cognitive appraisal of danger is necessary and that such activity may occur more quickly than is possible for visceral responses. If one considers an example such as a driver who must suddenly avert a hazard, one might note that trembling, palpitations, and nausea do appear to occur only *after* the adaptive response to the emergency has been completed. Actually James' view did not preclude the role of cognitive factors and his theory allows that even in this example the felt emotion is the awareness of these visceral reactions, slow as they might be. Fehr and Stern (1970) presented a review of evidence that suggested the viscera are not as insensitive as Cannon assumed.

Finally, Cannon noted that the artificial induction of visceral changes, such as by laboratory injections of adrenalin, does not produce emotional feelings. Citing the work of Maranon (1924), it was pointed out that although subjects may have reported an awareness of bodily changes, there was generally an absence of emotional experience. Most subjects felt coldness, although it is important to note that some subjects who had discussed depressing topics with the investigator prior to receiving the adrenalin injection did experience an intensification of these feelings. This incidental finding suggests that the mental state of the individual is an important factor in determining the effect of the induced bodily changes. Because most of the subjects in Maranon's experiment were probably viewing the situation as a scientific experiment, their thoughts probably were of a nonemotional state and thus the injections had no opportunity to intensify any existing emotional feelings. Later studies, which will be discussed in another section, indicate that cognitive appraisals of context do affect the emotional reaction to induced visceral states.

CONCLUSION

An overall assessment (Fehr and Stern, 1970) of the issue suggests that Cannon's criticisms are not well supported by later research. The controversy between James and Cannon dominated the study of emotion for many years. Insofar as James' speculations were based on everyday observation and not on scientific experiment, this focus on discrediting James is somewhat surprising. His view is largely untestable, dealing as it does with the phenomenology of emotion. It did, however, stimulate much research on the peripheral nervous system aspects of emotion. The controversy probably distracted investigators from a more direct study of the nature of emotion. Advances in physiological techniques and instrumentation since then have led to more interest in central nervous system bases of emotion.

Activation Views of Emotion

If you cannot make headway studying emotion, maybe you should abandon the topic. At least this development seemed to occur during the development of activation views of emotion (e.g., Duffy, 1934, 1941, 1962; Lindsley, 1951). Emphasis was on the similarity of emotions to the high end in the dimension known as general activation, which we discussed at length in Chapter 10. Behavior varies in a dimension of intensity of energization, ranging from low levels such as sleep or drowsiness through moderate levels such as wakefulness to high levels such as emotional states like fear or distress. Activation is viewed as a general dimension of energy induced by the total stimulation affecting the organism at a given moment. In emotion that entails high activation, it is largely due to autonomic responses such as heart rate, galvanic skin response, or respiratory rate, all of which serve to stimulate the reticular activating system, an area of the brain stem assumed to produce a general or nonspecific alerting state of the organism when aroused by stimuli.

Activation and arousal are neuropsychological constructs that have been used to account for the relationship between physiological responses and behavioral efficiency. Starting with formulations proposed in the 1930s (Duffy, 1932; Freeman, 1933), the goal of these theories has been to quantify the amount of energy present at the physiological level and correlate it with behavioral outcomes under various stimulus conditions.

Activation or arousal theorists have postulated the existence of a non-monotonic or U-shaped function between arousal and behavior. Thus, Hebb (1955) argued that performance is assumed to be less than optimal under arousal that is either too low (such as under drowsiness) or too high (such as under a panic state), as shown in Figure 11-1. Cognition and perception may be adversely affected by extreme arousal levels, thus producing the lower performances at these levels.

Dramatic evidence illustrating this impairment was obtained in an investigation in which subjects were unaware that they were being assessed (Berkum, Bialok, Kern, and Yagi, 1962). Soldiers on a training mission in a plane heard the control tower instruct the pilot to ditch into the ocean because of engine difficulty. The plane had been rigged so that the soldiers could see smoke streaming from one engine. While the pilot prepared to ditch the plane, a set of emergency forms needed for insurance claims were distributed. These forms were disguised tests of mental functioning, which enabled an assessment of the cognitive impairment produced by very high arousal. Compared with a control group, the stressed group showed more errors and poorer memory on the tests. Needless to add, this study can be criticized on ethical grounds.

Easterbrook (1959) examined the results of a number of studies and found that high arousal and stress is more likely to impair perceptual-cognitive functioning on more complex tasks, which require attention to more numerous stimuli. He suggested that perceptual narrowing or restriction of attention occurs under high arousal, thus disrupting performance.

As noted in Chapter 10, stimulation can also be initiated by the individual in order to modify the incoming arousal sources. If arousal is currently too low, the individual could augment it by various activities such as attending an exciting movie, exercising, or riding a roller coaster. Or if the situation is already too arousing, the level can be reduced by the person's leaving the situation, thinking about other topics, or actively changing the situation.

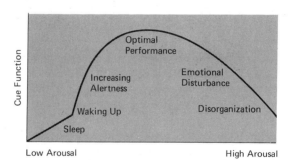

Figure 11-1. Postulated relationship between arousal function and cue function. [From "Drives and the c.n.s. (conceptual nervous system)," by D. O. Hebb, *Psychological Review*, 1955, *62*, 243–254. Copyright 1955 by the American Psychological Association. Reprinted by permission.

CRITICAL EVALUATION OF EMOTION
AS ACTIVATION

THEORETICAL PROBLEMS.   How useful are theories such. as activation for handling phenomena such as emotions? Inasmuch as these attempts look only at a single quantitative dimension of intensity, it is difficult to see how important theoretical and empirical questions about emotion can be addressed, let alone answered. The activation approach is an oversimplified way of studying emotions, allowing no means of differentiating among behaviors that might involve the same approximate levels of arousal. Thus, reading a book, watching a movie, or listening to music might be treated the same way if the arousal level was similar even though the content and meaning of the various activities differed.

Cofer and Appley (1964) have suggested that activation theory is not of theoretical significance in understanding behavior. For advocates such as Lindsley (1951), its main function lies in providing recognition of the physiological role of the reticular formation as a center for nonspecific arousal. For others such as Duffy (1962) and Malmo (1959), activation does have behavioral implications, because these theorists are interested in the inverted U function between arousal level and performance. Just as the concept of drive has been employed as an intervening variable to handle motivation, behaviorists have regarded activation as a similar generalized conceptualization of emotion. Malmo (1959) even argued for the use of arousal in preference to the concept of drive.

We have seen earlier in Chapter 10 that the formulation of U-shaped relationships, which maintain that behavior is optimal at some intermediate level of arousal, is imprecise because it is usually not possible to predict where that optimal point will be. Usually, researchers sample a sufficiently broad range of points in the arousal dimension and hope that the optimal point has been included. In order for any such relationships to be valid evidence for the concept of optimal level of arousal, it would be necessary for some theoretical rationale to exist for the expectation of such a function.

Lazarus, Averill, and Opton (1970) maintained that the activation approach has begged the central questions about the nature of emotion. As mentioned earlier the evidence is still in conflict but since Lazarus et al. held that sufficient evidence exists that physiological differences have been found for different emotions, they regarded the activation theory treatment of all emotions as varying only in intensity as invalid. Of course, activation theory has other applications besides serving as an explanation of emotions and for those purposes it might still be defended.

METHODOLOGICAL PROBLEMS.   But criticisms of activation theory have also been directed at methodological aspects. Measurement of arousal is difficult for a variety of reasons and the validity of many studies is called into question. For one matter, intercorrelations among different measures is not high so that different measures are not interchangeable (Duffy, 1951). Yet comparisons are often made among studies based on a single index that differs from study to study, such as heart rate in one study and galvanic skin response in another. Additional problems arise because individual differences exist among subjects in which index best reflects their arousal states. Lacey and Lacey (1958), for example, found that cardiac measures are better indices of activation for some persons, whereas electroencephalagram responses are better for others. These problems have already been mentioned in Chapter 10 and they create similar problems here.

In summary, it can be noted that the measurement problems in the area of activation theory pose formidable obstacles. Unless they can be satisfactorily handled, the empirical basis of activation theory will remain questionable. Even if these issues can be resolved, activation theory can, at best, offer a limited perspective of emotions. The understanding of the nature of emotion must go beyond the mere analysis of its physiological basis.

Cognitive Factors in Emotion

MISATTRIBUTION OF AUTONOMIC RESPONSES

Perhaps the most influential laboratory study of emotional processes in recent years was conducted by Schachter and Singer (1962). In a sense this study was a replication of the Maronon (1924) study with some interesting additions. Schachter and Singer hypothesized that the cognitive appraisal of the situation in which arousal occurs plays a central role in the subsequent emotional experience. If Maronon's subjects failed to experience emotions when injected with adrenalin in the formal context of a laboratory experiment, perhaps the introduction of social stimuli might modify the experimental context sufficiently so that the induced arousal might lead to emotional arousal.

Volunteers were obtained for what was presumably a study of the effects of a vitamin, Suproxin, on visual skills. In truth, Suproxin turned out to be either adrenalin or a saline placebo injection. There was no interest in tests of visual skills, but subjects were told to sit in a waiting room with another subject until the side effects of the injection wore off before taking the visual tests.

The other subject was in reality a confederate of the experimenters and his role was to act in either of two ways, both unusual for experimental subjects. For some conditions, the stooge displayed euphoria and zaniness by making and flying paper airplanes, playing basketball by tossing wads of crumbled paper into a wastepaper basket, etc. For other conditions, the stooge played the role of the angry and resentful subject. He verbally expressed resentment about the experiment, about the questionnaires that he felt invaded his privacy. In general, he was hostile to the endeavor.

Let us focus first on conditions with the euphoric stooge. It was assumed that this context might induce a similar emotion in the real subject, especially if the adrenalin injection was made without any correct information being given the subject about its side effects. The subject might infer that he was feeling autonomic arousal because his emotion was similar to that of the stooge.

In order to test this hypothesis, one group of subjects received adrenalin injections that were allegedly Suproxin and told nothing about the side effects. A second group received the injections but was given false information about the side effects, being told that they would feel itchy, experience numb feet, and have headaches, none of which are typical reactions to adrenalin. A third group received the injections as well as information that was true, that they might feel flushed, experience tremors, and have increased heart rate. Finally, a placebo group received a saline injection to control for any suggestive effects due merely to the process of injection.

Recall that the rationale for the experiment was to compare the effects of the same physiological state, as induced by the adrenalin injection, on three subgroups that differed only with respect to what they had been told about the nature of the side effects of Suproxin. If physiological factors are dominant, no differences should occur among these three groups because the injections were identical for the three adrenalin subgroups.

On the other hand, Schachter and Singer predicted that the situational factor as defined by the stooge's behavior would affect the behavior and feelings of subjects who received either no information or misinformation about the effects of Suproxin. Because these subjects could not readily attribute their arousal to Suproxin, as the subjects in the correct information group could, it was reasoned that they might conclude that their feelings were similar to those of the stooge.

Not only did ratings of mood provide support for this prediction but the actual behavior of the subjects also reflected euphoria as some of the subjects joined the stooge in his party-like activities. A summary depiction of the situation is shown in Figure 11–2.

Additional support was obtained when the angry stooge was employed. This portion of the study paralleled the euphoria conditions except that the misinformed group was not included. The results also suggested that when subjects could correctly ascribe their feeling states to the injection, they were less influenced by the stooge's behavior. But subjects who were ignorant of the source of their arousal inferred that their feelings were more similar to those of the stooge.

A subsequent study (Schachter and Wheeler, 1962) used a slapstick movie, *The Good Humor Man,* rather than a live stooge. Some subjects received adrenalin; others received chlorpromazine, a blocking agent whose

FIGURE 11–2. The Schachter and Singer (1962) experimental procedures. [From "Emotion," by G. Mandler, in *New Directions in Psychology*. *I*. by T. M. Newcomb (Ed.), New York: Holt, 1962. Copyright 1962 by Holt, Rinehart, and Winston. Reprinted by permission.]

effect is opposed to that of adrenalin. A control group received a saline placebo. All groups were told they were receiving Suproxin to test its effects on vision. Judgments of emotion were based on laughter response to the film. Laughter was highest in the group receiving adrenalin, followed by the placebo condition, and lowest in the chlorpromazine condition. Thus, the situational level of stimulation interacted with the type of injection. As in the prior study, the injection of adrenalin led to emotional experience, provided the background stimulation was arousing.

The Schachter studies are important in that they called attention to the role of cognitive factors in the determination of emotions. However, it must be realized that these laboratory studies artificially reverse the sequence of events that occur under most natural emotional experiences. In real life, we do not receive adrenalin injections nor does our nervous system usually release such substances prior to cognitive assessment of the situation, as was the case in Schachter's experiments.

On the contrary, in real life we must first interpret a situation as dangerous, amusing, or disgusting, *before* our juices will start to flow. In other words, we must first be cognitively aware of our emotions, before we can also experience the bodily expression of our emotions in most instances. One could argue that we are sometimes unconscious or at least unaware of the stimulus that triggered our autonomic arousal. In these cases we would experience our bodily feelings first and then retrospectively attempt to identify the causes. Even in these latter cases, however, some type of cognitive appraisal is assumed to precede and cause the visceral responses.

This conceptual limitation of the Schachter paradigm does not mean that social factors such as the behavior of others may not serve to induce emotional arousal. On the contrary, phenomena such as behavioral contagion or mob panic are examples in which group behavior leads an individual to assess a situation differently from the way he or she might have appraised it alone. In turn, this socially determined cognition leads to physiological arousal. However, this sequence is not the same as that used in the Schachter studies in which the induced arousal comes first via artificial means, and then gets interpreted against the context of the social setting.

MISATTRIBUTION OF FAKE AUTONOMIC FEEDBACK

A different approach to the study of the role of cognition in emotion has been developed by Valins (1966). He provided fake feedback to his subjects about the level of their autonomic activity to see if cognitive factors, alone, could influence affective judgments. No recourse to manipulations of the actual physiological states by injections was employed as in Schachter's studies. Valins assumed that the fake feedback, or what he termed *nonveridical* perceptions, about bodily reactions would be sufficient to influence emotional reactions to external stimuli.

Male subjects were hooked up to an apparatus that allegedly measured heart rate. Subjects were told that because the equipment was outmoded, it also provided amplified feedback of their heart beats, signals the subjects were asked to try to ignore. In reality, the feedback was based on prerecorded fake heart rates designed to either increase or decrease over short intervals. Control group subjects heard exactly the same signals, but they were told these sounds were extraneous signals rather than heart beats. They were told that they were serving in a control condition so that the effects of extraneous noises on autonomic reactions to certain test stimuli could be assessed.

The apparent purpose of the study was to assess the influence of sexual stimuli, ten nude *Playboy* models. For half of the nudes the subject's heart rate appeared to change, whereas it remained more or less constant when the other five nudes were shown. For some subjects, the change in heart rate was an increase, for other subjects it was a decrease.

It was predicted that the misinformation about the heart rate would affect the judgments of arousal or liking of the nude models. Thus, if the heart rate changed either upward or downward, it was assumed that subjects would infer that these models were sexier or more attractive than those models for whom no apparent change was detected. Valins admitted that our stereotype of attraction would call for increased heart rate only; however, given that all the nudes were attractive, he maintained that even *decreases* in heart rate must be interpreted as reflective of greater attraction. This argument is not persuasive and in fact Valins reported that most subjects were startled whenever decreases occurred. Nonetheless, they accepted the false feedback and did not become suspicious about the purpose of the study.

The results presented in Table 11–1 supported Valins' predictions, with higher ratings of attraction occurring for the nudes which had associated or reinforced with heart rate changes in either direction than for the slides associated with no change. Such differences were larger, however, for heart rate increases. Similar effects did not occur for the control group, which heard the identical sounds in association with the same stimuli but were told they were extraneous distractor noises. The right-hand column of Table 11–1 combines the results of control subjects who received increases in sound rate along with those receiving decreases because there were no differences between them.

TABLE 11–1.   Mean Slide Attractiveness Ratings

	Conditions		
Slides	Heart-rate Increase (N = 20)	Heart-rate Decrease (N = 20)	Sound Increase + Sound Decrease (N = 10 + 10)
Reinforced	72.42	69.26	60.86
Nonreinforced	54.11	62.57	63.76
Difference	18.31	6.69	−2.90

Source. From "Cognitive Effects of False Heart Rate Feedback" by S. Valins, *Journal of Personality and Social Psychology*, 1966, *4*, 400–408. Copyright 1966 by the American Psychological Association. Reprinted by permission.

Thus, as long as subjects believe their autonomic systems have reacted to a given stimulus, this cognition can affect the emotional response to that stimulus. It is not necessary to actually alter the subject's physiological state, according to Valins. Postexperimental interviews suggested that subjects often attempted to justify their apparent cardiac response changes by studying the slides more closely and by magnifying the positive assets of the nude. Thus, if a particular nude was only moderately attractive but the feedback disclosed large heart rate changes, the subject might reevaluate his initial judgment and conclude that the nude's features were better than he originally thought.

A study with a similar rationale by Valins and Ray (1967) used false heart rate feedback to alter the emotional responses of subjects who were afraid of snakes. Volunteers observed slides of snakes and slides showing the word *shock,* which were also followed by an actual shock to the finger tips a few seconds later. In the experimental condition, subjects heard sounds which were allegedly their own heart beats. Feedback given to these subjects showed that heart rate increased whenever the slides with the word *shock* appeared, but not when the slides of snakes were presented. Control subjects received the same feedback treatment except that they were not led to believe that the sounds were heart beats. The rationale was that the false feedback would lead subjects in the experimental group to infer that they were less fearful of snakes because their heart rates did not increase when they saw the slides of the snakes.

In the next phase of the study, subjects were asked to perform a series of graded responses ranging from entering a room containing a boa constrictor in an enclosed box, to lifting the box lid, to actually touching and lifting the snake. The dramatic results suggested that mere exposure to the fake feedback was adequate to enable many subjects to overcome their fears sufficiently to perform the requested procedures.

A skeptic must wonder to what extent the subjects may have seen through the deception, assumed the snake was harmless, and performed in a manner to cooperate with what they perceived to be the purpose of the experiment. It would be unusual that years of fear could be undone so easily. Furthermore, even though Valins provided fake feedback, what about the nature of the subjects' actual autonomic activity during the viewing of nudes and snakes? Can we assume that the fake feedback had no influence on the actual autonomic activity? In contrast, as suggested in Figure 11–3, it is conceivable that the fake feedback might induce similar levels of actual arousal, which in turn could have mediated the ratings of attraction or reduction of fear.

DOES BOGUS AUTONOMIC FEEDBACK AFFECT ACTUAL AROUSAL?   Valins (1966, p. 407) felt that, "Although physiological variables were not measured, there is little reason to suspect that the bogus feedback had any direct effects other than cognitive ones." One basis for this conclusion is that the control groups that received the identical patterns of sounds did not show the effect. Still, it might be countered that the belief that the sounds were heart rates may be necessary before this induction of similar genuine autonomic effects would occur. Since the control group was told that the sounds were extraneous noises, there would be no induction of physiological changes in this group which may still have occurred in the experimental group.

In addition, Valins obtained self-ratings of awareness of heart beats during the experiment. Contrary to the view that the experimental group may have experienced more real heart rate changes, there was actually less awareness of heart palpitations reported in the experimental group. Of course, this evidence is indirect and does not tell us exactly what did happen at the

Interpretation A

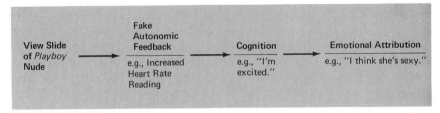

Interpretation B

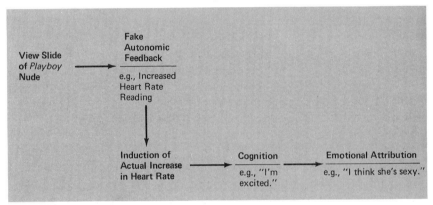

Figure 11–3. Two possible interpretations of the operation of fake autonomic feedback on emotional attributions in Valins' experiment. According to Valins, there is a direct effect of the fake feedback on cognitive appraisal, as shown in **A.** However, other studies support **B,** which suggests that the fake feedback may induce *actual* autonomic changes, which are then used by the subject as the basis for emotional attributions.

autonomic level. The only way to resolve this question would be to record ongoing autonomic responses during the experiment.

Several subsequent studies have used Valins' paradigm but have also recorded psychophysiological responses to the fake feedback. Stern, Botto, and Herrick (1972) found actual heart rate to show increases when subjects received fake sounds alleged to be heart rate. Goldstein, Fink, and Mettee (1972) obtained results showing that bogus increased heart rate feedback induced actual heart rate increases also when nude female slides were shown, but not for nude male slides. Presumably, the male subjects were upset at receiving such stimuli. The effects of fake heart rate feedback also extend to other responses such as the galvanic skin response in a similar manner to its effect on heart rate. Hirschman (1975) found that increases in fake heart rate feedback induces activation of the galvanic skin response. All this evidence casts doubt on the validity of Valins' assumption that his fake feedback does not in itself induce arousal. Consequently, his interpretation of his results as showing the role of cognitive appraisal in identifying affective states is weakened.

WHICH OCCURS FIRST—COGNITIVE APPRAISAL OR AROUSAL?

A criticism raised earlier in connection with the Schachter studies is relevant here with the Valins studies also, namely the fact that ordinarily the cognitive appraisal *precedes* rather than follows the occurrence and awareness of the autonomic responses. Valins, like Schachter, places the cart before the horse, so to speak. They demonstrate what could potentially happen, but what actually does happen in most naturally occurring emotions is not necessarily the same.

One theorist who does emphasize the temporal priority of cognitive appraisal is Lazarus (1966) in his model of stress, diagrammed in Figure 11–4. Although stress situations usually involve longer lasting emotional conditions such as chronic anxiety, disasters, or prolonged illness, his formulation is also suitable for an analysis of emotions of briefer duration. In fact, Lazarus used the term *stress* quite loosely, because it has been used by different investigators to cover a variety of emotion-arousing situations. More

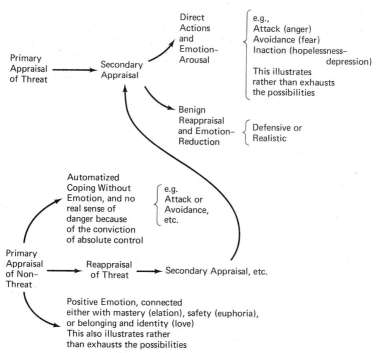

FIGURE 11–4. Outline of theoretical analysis of emotions proposed by Lazarus. [From "Emotions and Adaptation: Conceptual and Empirical Relations," by R. S. Lazarus, in *Nebraska Symposium on Motivation* (Vol. 16) by W. J. Arnold (Ed.), Lincoln: University of Nebraska Press, 1968. Reprinted by permission of University of Nebraska Press.]

recently, Lazarus (1968; Lazarus et al., 1970) extended his model for stress directly to the topic of emotion.

Acknowledging the similarity of his views to the earlier ones of Arnold (1960) concerning cognitive appraisal, Lazarus emphasized the role that primary appraisal or cognitive interpretation of the situation plays in generating autonomic arousal. He held that each emotion involves a different cognition, pattern of physiological changes, and behavioral reaction.

Lazarus (1968) emphasized the need for the study of emotions as adaptive responses. Although he did not deny the usefulness of viewing emotions as intervening variables, he felt that insufficient effort had been directed toward the empirical assessment of physiological and behavioral responses in emotional situations. His own research on stress has focused on recording responses of subjects who view stressful films.

Unlike Schachter or Valins, Lazarus makes no attempt to manipulate autonomic responses via injections or false feedback. In some of his studies, the film provides different soundtracks, which might alter the pattern of psychophysiological response. Thus, some subjects might receive a soundtrack that intellectualizes the stressful scene, whereas another set of subjects might hear a commentary that intensifies the traumatic episode.

In addition to recording a battery of autonomic indices, Lazarus also obtained self-ratings from subjects regarding their reactions to the films. Occasionally discrepancies occurred such that a subject reported feeling no fear or anxiety but his psychophysiological record indicated that he did. Rather than debate which dependent variable is more valid, Lazarus maintained that the discrepancy itself is revealing. In this example, we may be dealing with an individual who relies on denial as a means of coping with stress.

A second part of Lazarus' model, which he termed, *secondary appraisal,* places more emphasis on the effects of emotions on subsequent processes and responses than on the process by which the emotions are initially interpreted (see Fig. 11–4). In other words, primary appraisal is essential for the experience of the initial emotion. The individual, in reacting to this arousal, employs various modes of coping, which Lazarus terms secondary appraisal. It may also refer to a purely cognitive reappraisal of the original situation rather than some specific mode of action to cope with the emotional arousal. If fear is aroused, secondary appraisal might lead the individual to run, scream, or fight, on the one hand, or to a reappraisal of the situation that might entail denial, rationalization, or a realistic reassessment of the situation as being less dangerous than originally appraised.

Lazarus (1974, 1975) has related his cognitive formulations about emotional processes to the general topic of self-regulation. In contrast to the first or first few occasions in which an emotional stimulus is encountered, the individual can anticipate the consequences of such stimuli on later occasions. These expectancies enable the individual to take certain courses of action that enable him or her to cope with the emotion to some extent before it

actually occurs. As Figure 11–5 indicates, the individual can choose preparatory or anticipatory coping responses such as selective attention, cognitive
appraisal, or taking drugs, which can alter the normal impact of the emotional stimulus when it occurs. Most of the time we try to control emotions
by reducing them, but it is logically possible that we can similarly increase
them by the same types of self-regulatory stratagems.

A study by Koriat, Melkman, Averill, and Lazarus (1972) serves to illustrate this discussion. Subjects were shown films of a wood-shop accident,
in which various types of serious injuries to a man are portrayed. After being
shown the film twice to establish baseline reactions to the scene, subjects
watched the film again sometimes under the instruction to detach themselves
from emotion and sometimes with the goal of involving themselves emotionally. No specific instructions were given about how they were to regulate
their emotions, but the subjects were successful, judging both from self-
reports of emotion and heart rate indices.

The most common technique of self-regulation to reduce emotion was a
form of detachment in which subjects reminded themselves that the accident
was a staged one, not a real event. A form of empathy was used most frequently when subjects tried to get involved. They used their imagination and
placed themselves in the role of the victim.

Lazarus (1975) viewed the Koriat et al. study as one that shows how
coping can be anticipatory so that cognitive processes can either decrease or
increase the eventual emotional response. However, coping is not limited to
deliberate and planned strategies such as those observed in the Koriat et al.
study. Lazarus suggested that automatized and well overlearned response
patterns can occur to cues signaling danger. Some reactions may be of a
broad nature, such as a life philosophy of avoidance of confrontations that
involve anxiety.

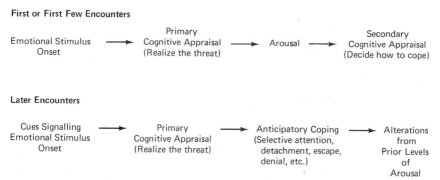

FIGURE 11–5.   Diagram showing difference between early and later encounters with
an emotional stimulus based on Lazarus' views. On later occasions, coping can be
anticipatory and occur *before* the arrival of the emotional stimulus and act to alter
the arousal level previously generated by that stimulus. On early occasions, the coping
occurs primarily *after* the emotional stimulus occurs.

Whether one is dealing with carefully considered coping actions that involve deliberation or with reflex-like conditioned responses that occur without much awareness, these responses alter the course of ensuing emotional arousal. Lazarus (1974) saw such self-regulation as more than merely manipulating the environmental contingencies, as radical behaviorists such as Skinner would. Lazarus argued that "an executive agency within the person" determines what aspects of the environment will be attended or how the environmental cues will be interpreted, which in turn affects the type of emotional response that will occur to a stimulus.

The work of Schachter, Valins, and Lazarus, as well as others, clearly shows the complex interplay between emotion and cognition and should serve to emphasize the artificiality of the distinction between the two categories.

The Nature of Stress

Sometimes emotional arousal is short-lived, either because the arousing stimulus is removed by adequate coping responses or simply because it is of brief duration. Most laboratory studies of emotion deal with a relatively short-term state, because it is easier to work with, raises less ethical problems if it is induced by the experimenter, and is in fact transitory. We may be angry or sad one moment but calm or happy shortly afterward.

On the other hand, in some situations there is continuous and recurring long-term emotional arousal. These situations are more difficult to recreate and study in the laboratory, both for ethical reasons and because realism is difficult to achieve. Although we could continue to speak of emotional arousal in such situations, the term *stress* seems to be used more frequently. Our discussion of research on stress will be brief and aimed primarily at showing the relationship between emotion and stress.

As used in physics or engineering, stress emphasizes the forces or pressures acting on an object or structure. High stress is capable of damaging or destroying a physical structure. This connotation of the term is applicable in describing psychological situations that involve stress. One of the first studies to use the concept of stress (Grinker and Spiegel, 1945) was concerned with the stress encountered by soldiers in combat. The phenomenon of battle fatigue was assumed to be the result of unrelenting and intense levels of stress from war combat.

PHYSIOLOGICAL REACTIONS
DURING STRESS

We have already discussed some of Walter B. Cannon's contributions to the study of emotion in the context of evaluating William James' views on emotion. Many of his ideas can be extended to a consideration of the concept of stress. Cannon, in *The Wisdom of the Body,* was interested in the mechanisms of the body designed to enable the organism to survive physically. He noted the importance of the regulatory processes of the body that made homeostasis or balance of bodily needs possible. For example, we perspire when it is too hot, but our skin constricts its pores when it is too cold and we shiver. These responses help maintain normal body temperature.

At the behavioral level, Cannon applied the physiologically derived idea of homeostasis to the means by which organisms react to intense emotional experiences such as emergencies to life and limb. He studied the physiological basis of the "fight or flight reaction" to emergencies in which survival is achieved either by withdrawal from or confrontation with the threatening stimulus. Cannon's research emphasized the role of the autonomic or involuntary nervous system, which produces responses generally beyond our control such as increased heart rate, stomach contractions, or increased blood pressure. It was seen as adaptive for organisms to have a system that responded reflexively. If one had to rely entirely on voluntary and deliberate responses controlled by the skeletal nervous system, one might not be as fit for survival because of the inability to attend to all incoming stimuli continually.

In his formulation, Cannon placed special emphasis on the part of the autonomic nervous system known as the *sympathetic* nervous system—the part responsible for galvanizing the organism to cope with emergencies or threats to survival. The sympathetic activation leads to the release of importance substances such as *norepinephrine* and *epinephrine* (adrenalin) from the medulla of the adrenal glands. These substances help the body prepare for emergencies by redirecting needed blood and sugar from digestive processes to the muscles, heart, and the brain.

When the emergency has been met, the "wisdom of the body" restores the normal balance of bodily functions through the operation of the *parasympathetic* portion of the autonomic nervous system, which generally affects the functioning of organs in the opposite manner to the sympathetic nervous system. For example, whereas the sympathetic nervous system increases heart rate and breathing, the parasympathetic portion decreases them back to normal levels.

Our description of the body's reactions to emotional threats of brief duration is simplified, but should provide a general idea of the complex interplay of systems required in the body. What happens, however, in situations in which the intense arousal of an emergency is repeated or continued for long periods of time?

Selye, a noted endocrinologist, has studied the body's reactions to long-term stress for many years. In his influential book *The Stress of Life,* Selye (1956) described a model called the general adaptation syndrome (GAS), consisting of three different stages. The first, alarm, is similar to the situation studied by Cannon and deals with the initial shock of the threat. It produces a reaction termed *countershock,* which involves autonomic excitation of the sort studied by Cannon. In addition, later research has shown that emergencies stimulate the pituitary gland located near the hypothalamus to release a hormone into the bloodstream. This hormone, because it acts upon the adrenal gland, is referred to as the adrenocorticotrophic hormone (ACTH). It causes the adrenal cortex, which is near the top of the kidneys, to release other hormones that help the organism maintain a normal blood-sugar level. The hormones released from the adrenal cortex as a result of ACTH action are referred to as glucocorticoids and include such substances as cortisone and corticosterone. These hormones stimulate the formation and storage of glycogen, which is a supply of quick energy; they also have an anti-inflammatory effect on body tissues. It is clear that the adrenal hormone helps the organism adapt to the stressful conditions involved in emergencies.

During the second stage of GAS termed *resistance,* the body makes adaptive responses to cope with the stress. If they are unsuccessful, a third and final stage of *exhaustion* develops in which the body makes one last attempt to counteract the stress. The adrenals pump more ACTH and steroids into the system and recovery may occur. Otherwise there eventually will be irreversible damage to the body in the form of disease and a breakdown in the functioning of glands such as the thymus and lymph glands. The adrenal glands are unable to continue their normal functioning and become enlarged. Various impairments such as ulcers and other so-called psychosomatic disorders can occur as well.

PSYCHOLOGICAL ASPECTS OF STRESS

Stress can occur from a variety of causes, both physical and psychological in nature. Lazarus (1966) recommended the use of the term *stress* to include a variety of related phenomena also referred to by various terms such as *conflict, frustration,* or *anxiety.* If the stress stems from the fact that the individual must choose between several alternatives, usually some positive and some negative, we speak of conflict. Frustration distinguishes those situations in which the stress stems from the person being blocked from achieving a goal, either by physical or psychological obstacles. Anxiety is often used to refer to the unpleasant feelings associated with both conflict and frustration situations. Although some worthwhile distinctions among these concepts can be made, for our purposes we will follow Lazarus' approach and focus on the similarities of these stress situations and regard them all as involving relatively long-term emotional arousal.

Some examples of the wide diversity of situations subsumed under the concept of stress can be found in several conferences on stress research (e.g., Appley and Trumbull, 1967; McGarth, 1970). Sensory isolation, imprisonment, aquanaut training, brainwashing, and parachute jumping, to name a few, have been studied. Sometimes stress involves waiting for and anticipating dreaded or unpleasant events, or it entails enduring actual hardship and duress, or it might involve potential or actual loss of some material, social, or psychological value or object.

Natural events such as emergencies, disasters, floods, and fires have provided much evidence (e.g., Barton, 1969; Drabek and Stephenson, 1971; Wolfenstein, 1957) about behavior under realistic stress, which obviously is difficult to reproduce in laboratory situations. The evidence is often unreliable or idiosyncratic as well as difficult to verify, but it does provide valuable hypotheses and insights about human reactions under stress. We hear of the heroic behavior of those we least expected to be brave or of the cowardice of those we thought would be heroes. We find it hard to predict what we ourselves would have done in the same emergency. Behavior under stress is often irrational and atypical.

Why does stress dramatically alter the behavior of people? The immediate threat of injury, loss, or death apparently disrupts and interferes with normal cognitive processes such as perception, reasoning, judgment, and decision making. The concept of secondary appraisal (Lazarus, 1966) suggests that we have two alternative classes of response to stress: direct action or reappraisal. Direct action may be fighting or it may be fleeing; it is some overt behavior that the person uses to cope with the stress. Reappraisal, on the other hand, is purely cognitive or covert. It involves a reanalysis of the situation to see if the original assessment of the danger was correct. If indeed the danger is real, various mental strategems might be used ranging from denial to rationalization and intellectualization. The actual process of deciding how one will cope is complicated and depends on a number of factors including the individual's own abilities, the immediacy of the threat, the availability of aid, etc.

Lazarus (1966) held that the anticipation and waiting per se is the essence of psychological stress. It may be more harmful than the actual event itself. Although the doctor's needle hurts when you get a shot, that period of dread and anticipation before it is the major source of psychological stress.

We have already described Lazarus' use of stressful films as a means of inducing stress in laboratory situations in order to test hypotheses about coping mechanisms. Psychophysical measures and self-report measures are both obtained as films are observed under a variety of conditions to determine how stress reactions can be altered. Although this approach has advantages, it is of limited generalizability. For one matter, the available coping responses are limited to cognitive responses such as denial or rationalization. There is no opportunity for direct action against the stressful stimulus as might be the case if one were in a tornado, fighting in a war, or making executive decisions.

It may be necessary to rely on evidence of a naturalistic nature to obtain better indications of the human response to stress situations. Lazarus (1975), in fact, has also turned in this direction.

How could one study in the laboratory, for example, the reactions to stress among survivors of a natural disaster? On the other hand, even though the evidence may be biased, the report (Read, 1974) of the reactions of the survivors of a 1972 air crash in the Andes Mountains illustrates the potential of the study of naturalistic stresses. Faced with certain death, a handful of survivors managed to exist for over two months in below freezing weather by finally eating the flesh of those who had died. Only because two of the survivors managed to trek over the snowy mountains for two weeks to seek aid were they rescued at all. The story of the stressful experiences of these survivors could not be obtained readily from a laboratory analog.

The similarities between emotion and stress can be overdrawn, and it is worth considering the differences. A long stressful period is not uninterrupted by intervals of nonemotional states. Ordeals and traumas involve emotional arousal, but they also seem to involve more, especially in life-or-death situations. Much cognitive activity such as a reassessment of values or the meaning of life occurs during prolonged stress along with the affective responses.

It appears worthwhile to distinguish also between different types or aspects of stress. Although Lazarus' contention that a major aspect of stress is the anticipatory period seems valid, the aversive stimulus or event should be seen as another type of stress. Illness, torture, injury, and other sources of physical pain are stresses just as psychological traumas are. Although coping may reduce stress, it entails responsibility that is itself stressful. The uncertainty of the success of coping responses also creates another interval of stressful anticipation of feedback, which is different from the anticipation of the arrival of the stress stimulus, per se.

STRESS SEEKING

Whereas the major emphasis in stress research, as described above, is on the threat and danger of harm to the individual, it should be noted that stress is sometimes deliberately sought and danger is courted by some people (see Figure 11–6). Usually, as Opton (1969) observed, these phenomena are explained in terms of stress being sought because the eventual stress reduction feels so good. Thus, getting scared or excited by adventures, real or vicarious, is assumed to be motivated by the eventual resolution of the situation. Sports parachutists, motorcycle daredevils, or mere roller coaster riders all get a thrill of suspense and danger but eventually reach safety and calm.

Although it may be true that most fictional stress situations such as literary and theatrical suspenses have happy endings and the spectator can expect eventual drive reduction, this formula is less reliable for real-life stresses. If the average person were to fight a duel, walk a circus high wire, or jump off the high diving board, he or she would probably experience an unhappy and painful ending. Opton suggested that in undertaking real-life stresses voluntarily, the individual is able to do so only if he or she appraises the

FIGURE 11–6. Exciting and even frightening experiences that *increase* arousal and stress may be deliberately encountered. [From "Berry's World." Copyright by NEA, Inc., 1974. Reprinted by permission.]

situation subjectively as containing more danger than there is objectively. Riding a roller coaster might be a good example of a situation in which there is not much objective danger but it is exciting because people think it is hazardous.

Opton (1969) took the position that stress seeking is not primarily a case of behavior aimed at escaping boredom or seeking the pleasurable relief experienced after the stress is terminated. Instead, he suggested that the excitement and tension of stress are valued by some individuals. In other words, being stressed and risking danger are thrilling in themselves, above and beyond the social and personal prestige and gratification one might receive for being a daredevil.

Opton's analysis is interesting and certainly suggests the need for the further study of stress seeking. Although there are occasional Eviel Knievels and Harry Houdinis who may court stress with no apparent concern for safety, most of us probably are willing to undergo only those stresses that we inwardly feel are certain to produce safe endings. The stressful event is tolerable only because we know that the danger is only temporary or make-believe. People who are afraid of their own shadows might still be able to watch the scariest horror movie because they know it is not real.

Other Aspects of Emotion

EMOTIONS AS MOTIVES

Most of our prior discussion has viewed emotions as reactions, either phenomenological, physiological, or behavioral, to some stimulus situation that has been appraised as involving some threat, promise, or frustration, etc. In other words, emotions have been seen in their roles as effects or at least, correlates of other stimuli.

However, emotions may in turn serve as motives or causes of subsequent behavior. We know that our anger can lead us to be aggressive or that our fear can produce impaired coordination.

Leeper (1965, 1970), for example, has maintained that emotions and motives are quite similar and argued that emotion might be regarded as a type of motive. In fact, he even went on to point out the role of perceptual-cognitive processes in both emotions and motives, trying to show that the dichotomy between cognition and emotion is invalid.

Although Leeper made some cogent points about the flaws in our constructs, little empirical research has developed from his criticisms. The main value, perhaps, of his argument is to point out the interrelationship among various processes such as perception, motivation, and emotion.

As an illustration, we can examine the manner in which the emotion of guilt can motivate behavior. Several studies have shown how the arousal of guilt feelings increases the likelihood that a person will try to make amends toward the offended party. In one such study (Darlington and Macker, 1966) subjects were misled into thinking that they were responsible for the accidental harm of another subject. After the study was completed, another experimenter unrelated to the first made requests for blood donations to the blood bank. More donations were pledged from the group that was made to feel guilt than from a control group that did not experience this emotion. Presumably, the opportunity to do something socially constructive made the subjects in this experiment feel good. This effect, in turn, helped offset the bad feelings of guilt created by their realization that they had apparently harmed an innocent victim, an obviously socially undesirable behavior.

This example does not imply that guilt is the only or even the major determinant of helping behaviors. The person who is altruistic may be acting to gain some measure of self-gratification in thinking that he or she is beneficent. Charitable appeals often try to provide some token reinforcement to those who make donations by giving badges, buttons, or window stickers recognizing their aid. Even though these gold stars may seem childish, they are important as Dichter (1971, p. 121) noted, "The donor is dissatisfied if he doesn't receive something too. . . . If he's not told that he's a great guy or if he isn't given some concrete symbol of his generosity, he may not give again."

Not only may guilt arousal act to goad helping behavior but the avoidance of expected future guilt feelings may also work to encourage altruistic actions. We are taught the value of helping others, especially those in dire need. This norm of social responsibility (Berkowitz, 1973) is so well ingrained that many of us experience guilt feelings and threats to our self-esteem if we fail to render aid when we are called upon. Thus, we may sometimes help so that we can avoid suffering future pangs of guilt feelings.

THE EXPRESSION OF EMOTION

As Darwin made clear in his study of emotional expression, social communication is a major consequence of such stimuli. One animal can signal its rage, fear, or dominance to another by postural and facial cues, which can provide benefits to the survival of the individual and to the species.

ACTIONS AND THOUGHTS AS MODERATORS OF EMOTION.   In addition to this important benefit, emotional expression may play an essential role in the experience of emotion per se, so that it is more than a mere outer manifestation of the inner experience. Thus, if I am happy, my smile is not just a reflection of that state but may function to intensify that pleasant emotional state.

Darwin himself, although he emphasized the social role of emotional expression for communication, also recognized the possibility that postural cues served to intensify the emotion.

Cognitive factors such as attitudes may influence the extent to which emotion is aroused or suppressed. Our thoughts may alter the way we react to a given situation, because our emotions depend on our perceptions of that situation. William James (1884) similarly acknowledged this process:

Each fit of sobbing makes the sorrow more acute, and calls forth another fit stronger still, until at last repose only ensues with lassitude and with the apparent exhaustion of the machinery. In rage, it is notorious how we "work ourselves up" to a climax by repeated outbreaks of expression. Refuse to express a passion, and it dies. Count ten before venting your anger, and its occasion seems ridiculous. Whistling to keep up courage is no mere figure of speech. On the other hand, sit all day in a moping posture, sigh, and reply to everything with a dismal voice, and your melancholy lingers.

In a lighter vein, the humorist Dan Greenburg (see Figure 11–7) describes how to make oneself miserable by negative thinking.

FACIAL EXPRESSION AS A MODERATOR OF EMOTION.   Many years later, Tomkins (1962, 1963, 1970) proposed a theory of affect or emotion that

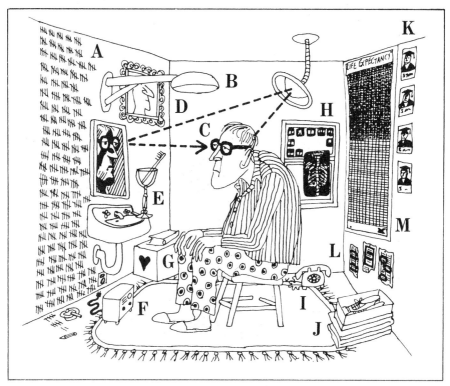

FIGURE 11–7. Essential brooding equipment for advanced practitioners. (**A**) Lifetime tally of cigarettes smoked; (**B**) arc light or sodium vapor light for exaggerating facial blemishes; (**C**) mirrors for observing progress of bald spot; (**D**) optional photograph of self before nose job; (**E**) precariously poised expensive crystal drinking glass; (**F**) unrepaired electrical appliance; (**G**) box of old love letters from someone who rejected you; (**H**) dental and chest x-rays in light-box for intensive scrutiny; (**I**) telephone (see section *The Telephone as an Instrument of Self-Torture*); (**J**) shoes too tight to wear, too old to return, and too new to throw out; (**K**) photos of successful classmates, with estimated annual income; (**L**) obituaries of people younger than you; (**M**) insurance company life expectancy chart with used-up days crossed off. [From *How to Make Yourself Miserable,* by Dan Greenburg with Marcia Jacobs. Copyright © by Dan Greenburg. Reprinted by permission of Random House, Inc.]

places facial expression in the central position. Because the face is more expressive, more finely differentiated, and capable of faster expression relative to the viscera, Tomkins assigned facial expressions the primary role in his theory of affective experience. Facial expressions are regarded as response patterns that reflect variations in the rate and level of stimulation from incoming events. He speculated that innate programs in subcortical brain areas produce different expressions such as raised eyebrows and eye blink when we are surprised or eyes and head lowered when we experience shame or humiliation.

According to Tomkins, the density of neural firing or stimulation is what determines the type of affective experience we will have. As Figure 11–8 shows, prolonged constant levels of high stimulation or neural firing will lead to either anger or distress, depending on how high the stimulation is. On the other hand, decreases in ongoing stimulation invariably result in joy. Finally, increases in stimulation will produce affects such as startle, fear, or interest. The negative affects such as fear are likely if the rate of increase is quite rapid, whereas a more gradual increase is responsible for creating interest in the situation.

Tomkins maintained that each major emotion or affect produces a characteristic facial expression. For example interest or excitement is reflected with eyebrows down, stare fixed or tracking an object, whereas fear or terror is expressed with eyes frozen open in fixed stare or moving away from the dreaded object to the side, along with skin pale, cold, sweating, trembling, and hair erect. Our conscious awareness of these facial cues is assumed to be

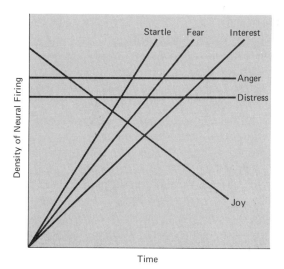

FIGURE 11–8. Graphical representation of a theory of innate activators of affect. [From "Affect As the Primary Motivational System," by S. Tomkins, in *Feelings and Emotions* by M. B. Arnold (Ed.), New York: Academic, 1970. Copyright 1970 by Academic Press. Reprinted by permission.]

the major determinant of the emotional experience. Thus, Tomkins' view is a type of James-Lange theory with the emphasis shifted from the viscera to the face.

As suggested above, James also recognized the role of the voluntary or skeletal responses in the conscious experience of emotion. Angell (1916) also suggested that skeletal muscle tone might differ under various emotions, which might be undifferentiable at the level of visceral responses. Nevertheless most research has examined the role of involuntary or autonomic responses.

One recent exception (Laird, 1974) deals specifically with the role of facial muscle responses in emotions. Assuming that facial expressions such as smiles, frowns, or grimaces might be a source of cues to aid the individual in identifying emotional experiences, Laird performed a laboratory test in which he misled subjects into contracting facial muscles in various ways in order to produce, in effect, smiles or frowns.

Deception of the subjects involved telling them that the study dealt with the effects of muscle tension on perception. In order to justify the assessment of the affective states of subjects they were told that such measures would be taken so that investigators could take into account any emotional arousal that occurred and might contaminate the results.

Pictures of either Ku Klux Klansmen or children playing were shown for brief periods while subjects were assuming the facial expressions equivalent to either smiles or frowns. Then ratings of affect were taken that turned out to be more positive when subjects were "smiling" than when they were "frowning." Laird interpreted these results as indicating that the awareness of the muscle response patterns is one factor in the determination of the nature of emotional experience.

Because this study is subject to the criticism that subjects may have realized that more positive responses should occur for pictures of playing children than for pictures of Ku Klux Klanners, Laird performed a second study using cartoons. Again, subjects assumed either the "smiling" or "frowning" facial expression as each cartoon was presented. The results agreed with those of the first study, showing that facial expression can influence the humor experienced in response to the cartoons.

Laird's findings offer support for James' view as well as the more contemporary theories of Izard (1971) and Tomkins (1962), which emphasize the role of facial expression on emotions. Laird himself prefers attribution theory explanations (e.g., Bem, 1967) that suggest that the facial cues are interpreted by the individual who essentially observes his or her own behavior in order to make inferences about inner states and attitudes. On the other hand, the views of theorists such as Izard and Tomkins imply that the facial cues are *direct* determinants of emotion, which are immediate and invariant. However, Laird allowed that his studies support both types of theories.

CONCLUSION

At this point, we will conclude our examination of theoretical approaches to the complex topic of emotion. We have not attempted to describe all important theories but have tried to summarize representative examples of major types. It should be apparent that much confusion and controversy exists in this field. Conceptual and methodological impasses have contributed to the lack of progress. In principle, theories are useful as guides to further research. Sometimes, however, overconcern with theoretical issues obscures the need for additional empirical research. To some extent this seems to be the situation with respect to the area of emotion. Perhaps when more research findings about the nature of emotion are available, better theories can be constructed. The final sections of this long chapter will examine some empirical research on a few selected specific emotions. Theories about these specific emotions rather than theories about emotion in general will also be examined.

How Many Emotions Are There?

Our language contains hundreds of words that refer to emotional states, but many of them are synonyms and do not refer to differentiable states at the experiential level. If we combined synonymous terms, we would still have many emotions. These terms may refer to distinctions we make on the basis of the behavioral context rather than on the experience of discriminable physiological reactions. Thus anger may be the label we use when someone insults us, whereas disgust may be the term employed if we witness someone belching; yet the physiological reactions we can discriminate in the two situations may not differ appreciably. In other words, cognitive appraisal of the behavioral situation enables us to make distinctions between emotional *cognitions* rather than between emotional *feelings*. The different labels referring to various emotions go beyond the feeling states by including consideration of the context. In a similar manner, differences between emotions such as jealousy and anger, for example, depend on situational factors. One cannot properly be said to be jealous if someone steps on one's foot but one could be quite angry. Yet the emotional feelings, at the physiological level, may be highly similar under the two states.

Additional illustrations of how the circumstances surrounding an experience determine how we label an emotion are based on temporal relationships. Consider positive events. If something good has just happened to you, you feel *happy* or *joyful;* if you are waiting for this good thing to occur, you are said to be *hopeful;* if the anticipated event fails to occur, you are *disappointed.* A similar analysis can be made of negative events. If they have just occurred, you are *sad* or *angry;* if you are waiting for them, you are experiencing *anxiety* or *fear.* Finally, if the expected negative event fails to occur, your experience is said to be one of *relief.*

THE EXAMPLE OF FEAR

The emotion that has received perhaps the greatest amount of study is fear. Fear is known to reduce humans to quivering, cowering creatures. But fear can also mobilize adaptive behavior to cope with and solve problems. There is no paradox involved, because there are different types and sources of fear as well as different intensity levels of this emotional state. Because fear is an intense emotion that is so commonplace and its effects are often incompatible with normal functioning, it has received considerable attention from researchers.

Anxiety is closely related to fear and tends to be equated with it. Some psychologists make a distinction between the two, preferring to use the term *fear* to refer to specific unpleasant states associated with specific situations, whereas *anxiety* is used to refer to similar unpleasant feelings that are more generalized and not limited to a particular stimulus situation. Thus, a person might be afraid of a dog due to past conditioning or association of unpleasant consequences from dogs. Anxiety would be used to refer to uneasy feelings about new situations, strangers in general, or examinations in general.

Not all psychologists make this distinction and the terms are often used interchangeably. Our preference is to speak of *fear* when discussing relatively short-lived experiences and to use the term *anxiety* when talking about long-term feelings such as moods, which will be discussed in Chapter 12. However, this is an arbitrary distinction that will not agree with all usages of these terms by others.

Fears can be viewed as unlearned or innate as well as the product of learning. Many situations involving surprise, unexpected or uncertain events, and novelty are capable of producing fearful behavior such as frenzy, immobility, or agitation. Monkeys that were shown artificial heads of monkeys attached to the ends of sticks, for example, became excited and fearful (Hebb, 1946). Infants are noted for their display of fear of strangers and fear of separation from their mothers during the last half of the first year of life. Although these fears are unlearned, the term *innate* is perhaps misleading insofar as some early experience is necessary to create expectancies so that subsequent fearful incongruities can exist.

Most fears, however, involve specific associative learning. It is assumed that previously neutral stimuli paired with an aversive consequence can acquire the capacity to arouse subsequently fearful anticipation of the negative stimulus. The dog that is subjected to a paired tone and electric shock will, after a few trials, display emotional activity such as whining, agitation, and cringing when the tone occurs, even if the shock is withheld, such as in extinction procedures.

Some theorists, such as Miller (1951), postulate fear or anxiety as an intervening variable and do not concern themselves with its physiological or subjective basis. Obviously, there is increased autonomic arousal in response to the tone, but learning theorists prefer to employ motivational constructs such as drive. *Drive,* according to behavior theorists such as Hull, Spence, or Miller, is a general state of energization that stems from a variety of sources including food deprivation, water deprivation, and the onset of painful and aversive stimuli, as we noted in Chapter 2.

FEAR AND LEARNING.   Like other sources of drive, fear is capable of promoting new learning of instrumental responses. Any behavior that can reduce drive, according to some learning theories, becomes reinforced and learned. In a classic study by Miller (1948), rats were shocked in one half of a two-compartment apparatus. Distinctive color cues were defined by painting the two halves of the box different colors. The fear aroused in the rats when they were placed in the dangerous half of the box led to responses that made escape possible. The apparatus had a wheel that, if turned, enabled the rats to escape to the safe half of the apparatus. The acquisition of this adaptive behavior could be said to be motivated by the reduction of the drive of fear, which occurred when wheel turning led to escape.

In a sense, fear can be viewed both as a response and as a drive state that can aid in the acquisition of other responses. Fear involves heightened activation and autonomic responding. This internal state leads to other responses that which, if successful in reducing the drive, become associated with certain stimuli. Such responses are likely to occur whenever the organism is in that situation in the future.

Although the learning theory conception of fear is a useful and valid one, some types of fear situations are difficult to handle with this model. Not all human fears are of physical pain or harm, some are of conditions such as fear of aging, death, failure, and poverty. Learning is, of course, involved here as well, but of a variety different from that emphasized by Miller.

Fear, as a drive, may also serve to inhibit other behavior. Estes (1944), and others since then, have used the conditioned emotional response paradigm to demonstrate how an ongoing behavior can be suppressed by the appearance of fear-related stimuli. In this situation, rats received pairings of a tone and shock in one part of the experiment; later they learned to press a lever to receive food. Then the tone was reintroduced when the rats were pressing for food. A marked reduction in pressing occurred as the fear aroused by the tone disrupted the responses required to obtain food.

FEAR AND ATTITUDE CHANGE.   Fear is also presumed to influence attitude change, although the experimental research in this field has produced equivocal findings. Advertising relies frequently on fear appeals such as the threat of bad breath; politicians use scare tactics and innuendoes such as implying that sex education will increase promiscuity; health campaigns resort to statistics about illness in their attempts to change behavior such as in the dissemination of findings about the relationship between smoking and lung cancer.

A dramatic illustration of scare tactics occurred in advertisements used in the June 1973 California election by opponents of Proposition 9, a so-called pollution initiative to curb the use of certain chemicals. In part, the ad read: "Who wants to bring back typhoid? Or malaria? Or encephalitis? Only people who love mosquitoes. The sponsors of Proposition No. 9 on the June 6 ballot must love mosquitoes—also termites, cockroaches, and silverfish. Because Proposition No. 9 makes illegal the use or possession of a long list of chemicals, including the only effective pesticides for controlling various pests."

Higbee (1969) suggested that one reason for the lack of accord in different studies about the effects of fear on attitudes is that they do not all deal with the same variety of fear. He distinguished between neurotic anxiety and realistic fear. In the former case there is no reality testing to see if the fear is justified. If the fear appeal creates this condition, denial or repression may ensue with the net result being no attitudinal or behavioral change due to the fear message.

In contrast, fear appeals that provoke realistic fear may motivate the recipient to search for realistic means of avoiding, escaping, or combating the anticipated threat. In Janis' (1967) terms, this reflective fear leads the individual to think or reflect about the potential harm. The old saying that "to be forewarned is to be forearmed" is relevant here insofar as arousal of realistic fear may help the individual plan suitable coping responses. According to Janis, vigilance should increase in order to enable the detection of environmental threats while the individual seeks reassurances. Compromise attitudes that involve a combination of vigilance and reassurance may also develop. Someone who has a serious illness and is sensitive to danger signs may also respond to the reassurance that some remedies exist.

An important factor that determines the reaction to threat is its intensity. Janis (1967) suggested that low threats create only mild fear, which is easy to deny and thus little planning is done. Moderate threat produces sufficient fear to activate vigilance and the need for reassurance with the result that the individual prepares for the danger. Finally, high threat generates strong reflective fear followed by indiscriminate vigilance, high tension, and feelings of high vulnerability. The individual may resort to defensive avoidance strategies by using various forms of denial.

The possibility that there may be a curvilinear or inverted U-shaped relationship between fear and persuasion is one reason there are so many conflicting findings in this area. Small to moderate amounts of fear may succeed in changing attitudes and behavior, but high levels may so overwhelm the individual that he or she ignores or rationalizes the information and does not change. Studies that show that fear produces changes may be sampling from the low to moderate range of fear intensity, whereas studies that demonstrate that higher levels of fear are ineffective may be using levels ranging from moderate to very high. Studies that show no effects of fear could also be using levels from the extremes of the intensity dimension.

As Highbee (1969) has argued, the preceding analysis does not explain the basis for the assumed curvilinear relationship. Unless a plausible theoretical account for the function can be provided, the postulation of an inverted U curve is merely a convenient after-the-fact description of the complex pattern of findings.

Janis (1967) postulated that fear communications have both facilitating and interfering effects on persuasion. The increased vigilance created by fear could promote change, but the disruption of focused attention and cognitive functioning could prevent change. The balance of these opposite effects is assumed to depend on the level of fear. With lower levels, Janis proposed that the facilitative effects are stronger, but as higher levels of threat are used, the interfering effects take command.

To avoid circularity in this argument, one must also identify the conditions that affect the relative balance of facilitatory and interfering processes rather than merely postulate such explanations after the results are observed. Janis suggested that any factor that shifted the balance in favor of the facilitative processes should enable the individual to accept higher levels of fear without resorting to defensive avoidance. For example, suppose a television commercial invoked a certain amount of fear in attempting to persuade us to take a new vitamin to prevent certain diseases. In theory, there is an optimal level of fear arousal for this situation for our acceptance of the recommendation. Fear levels that are less than or greater than this optimal level will not produce as much acceptance. Now suppose the same commercial was given by a respected authority in the field of nutrition rather than by an actor. Janis would argue that this factor should give a boost to one of the facilitative factors affecting persuasion. Therefore we should be able to tolerate a higher level of fear from the authority than from the actor before resorting to defensive avoidance. Even though fear is aroused, the prestige of the authority at least lends some reassurance that the message is credible and not merely the use of a scare tactic by an overzealous advertisement writer.

An important implication of this argument is that there is not just one specific inverted U function relating fear and persuasion but rather a hypothetical family of curves, as depicted in Figure 11–9. The specific optimal level of fear that leads to change will depend on a variety of factors related to such aspects of a communication as the source, content, and situation as well as to personality differences among recipients.

The dimension labeled "determinant of optimal level" in Fig. 11–9 refers to any factor such as source credibility in our example that shifts the balance in favor of facilitative processes. If we could obtain ten different communicators varying in credibility to give a particular communication involving fear arousal, we should obtain a family of ten curves, *A* to *J*, as

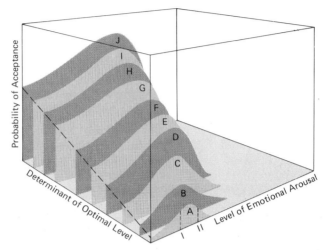

FIGURE 11–9. A three-dimensional model for analyzing effects of emotional appeals varying in emotional arousal. [From "Effect of Fear Arousal on Attitude: Recent Developments in Theory and Experimental Research," by I. L. Janis, in *Advances in Experimental Social Psychology* (Vol. 4) by L. Berkowitz (Ed.), New York: Academic, 1967. Copyright 1967 by Academic Press. Reprinted by permission.]

shown in the diagram. The dimension "determinant of optimal level" in this example would be "level of source credibility," with level *A* being the lowest and level *J* being the highest. Thus, each curve shows a different optimal level of arousal as well as a different probability of acceptance correlated with the level of source credibility. As we proceed from *A* to *J* (increasing source credibility), both the specific optimal level of arousal and the probability of message acceptance increases.

Janis' model has not been completely tested, but it is a useful conception that integrates many findings and suggests additional ones. It also avoids many of the weaknesses of most explanations based on the general idea of an inverted U function, because it attempts to identify underlying processes responsible for the function in terms that can be tested.

A different type of explanation for inverted U functions between fear and persuasion was suggested by Higbee and Heslin (1968), who emphasized that high fear messages are usually less plausible. The fear aroused may be counteracted somewhat by the individual's awareness that the threat is unlikely or implausible.

In other words, although fear is assumed to increase the desire to plan adequate coping responses, messages that generate implausible fear will be discounted and reduce the likelihood of change. This failure to believe that high fear content is likely to occur will offset the tendency of fear to promote change otherwise. The net effect is the inverted U-shaped curve with the optimal point representing levels of fear generated by messages that are still sufficiently plausible to be accepted. Messages that induce even greater fear are rejected not because of emotional reasons, according to Higbee and Heslin, but because of cognitive ones.

Higbee (1969) attributed much of the confusion regarding the effects of fear to a lack of conceptual clarity. For example, different studies measure fear by different means. In some studies the fear involves physical or health dangers whereas in others the concern with social disapproval is studied. A variety of topics are used but the familiarity as well as the importance of the topics to the subjects varies widely. In some studies the effect of fear on attitude or opinion change is assessed whereas other studies deal with stated intentions to change and still others deal with behavioral changes recommended by the communications.

SOME BENEFITS OF FEAR.   In view of these differences among studies, Higbee argued that it is not surprising that results sometimes appear conflicting. One should not be surprised if the effects of fear are dissimilar for widely different situations. Thus, the use of fear-arousing messages to instigate changes in attitude or behavior should not be equated with their use primarily as a means of informing individuals about impending threats which would create even greater fear without such information. A message about the dangers of smoking is aimed at changing behavior, whereas a message about emergency procedures to follow in case of an earthquake is primarily preparatory information. Although both may create fear, the latter is aimed at preventing even greater fear at some later time. An illustration of the beneficial innoculatory effects of fear when used as a forewarning is provided by Janis' (1958) work with surgery patients.

Although it may be intuitively reasonable to see that excessive fear can be maladaptive, it may appear paradoxical to discover that insufficient fear may similarly have adverse effects. Janis (1958), in his classic study of pre- and postoperative stress among surgery patients, found that individuals who showed little or no fear prior to the operation sometimes displayed resentment and anger subsequently. Janis attributed these reactions to the fact that these patients were unprepared for the postoperative pains and discomforts of recovery.

In contrast, patients who were informed about these stressful experiences in advance appeared to cope better. Janis hypothesized that preoperative fear, in moderate amounts, is useful in preparing patients to do the "work of worrying" which helps the patient develop adequate defenses. However, since these observations were correlational, one could argue that personality differences may account for both the differences in preoperative fear arousal and postoperative reactions. Persons who tend to have little fear before the operation might have a greater tendency to react poorly during recovery even if they had been informed as to what to expect.

Evidence is available, however, from a study by Egbert, Battit, Welch, and Bartlett (1964) that supports Janis' view with a more conclusive research design. Two groups of surgery patients were randomly assigned to receive either no information or information about the postoperative pain and discomfort that would occur normally. Armed with this knowledge of what to expect and how to interpret these symptoms, the informed group showed better recovery from surgery.

In this type of situation the communication may have created fear and worry but that was an incidental byproduct of the message which was primarily informational in purpose. The recipients were being prepared to deal with a future threat rather than being subjected to fear arousal for the purpose of changing their attitudes or behavior.

Although we have been discussing fear as if it were a "pure" emotion that operated in isolation from other emotions, it should be noted that like other emotions fear can change rapidly even to the point of being transformed into other emotions. A stimulus that is fear producing one moment may, in the next second, become a source of amusement or embarrassment if the cognitions of the situation suddenly change. For example, someone plays a practical joke such as poking a stick in your back and saying, "your money or your life." Your immediate reaction may be fear but as you turn and confront your giggling friend you may suddenly become angry instead.

Fear, like positive emotions such as hope, involves anticipation of some expected outcome. On the other hand, emotions such as grief, which we will discuss next, deal with reactions to situations that have already occurred.

THE EXAMPLE OF GRIEF

Grief, in various degrees, is a common experience but one that has received less attention than many of the other emotions by researchers. When an individual suffers the loss of some valued person, social status, or material object, he or she experiences feelings that are subdued and depressed in contrast to the agitated state usually associated with fear. Crying, sobbing, and trembling may be involved but more passive forms of sullen withdrawal are also common expressions of grief.

The analysis of grief by Averill (1968) will serve as the major basis for our discussion. He pointed out a paradoxical aspect of grief, especially as it pertains to the death of or separation from loved ones, insofar as the grief response is not adaptive. Whereas fear can motivate instrumental behavior to eliminate the noxious threat, grief cannot restore the loss of the beloved.

OBJECT-LOSS VS. ROLE-LOSS. Averill distinguished between *object-loss* and *role-loss*. Grief appears to stem from the object-loss, i.e., the person or possession lost, but it is maintained that an accompanying role-loss (or change) is usually also involved and it is difficult to separate the role of the two losses on the grief reaction. Thus, the oldest son in the family not only loses his father when he dies but also changes his role in assuming new and greater responsibility. This change itself may be stressful.

Averill suggested that when object-loss occurs without role-loss the grief may be short-lived. For example, a person who sees a tear-jerker of a movie may experience grief at the death of the hero but soon after he leaves the theater, he resumes his normal state as the grief rapidly dissipates. Similar transitory effects occur when other emotions are aroused by artistic means. Movies with messages calling for peace, love, and brotherhood may arouse noble sentiments while they are being shown but the good intentions and feelings are not long lasting after the patrons exit the theater. The film, *Guess Who's Coming to Dinner,* in which Sidney Poitier starred in a story about interracial marriage may have stirred noble sentiments in the theater but probably failed to have much impact on racial attitudes and behavior afterward. In a similar fashion, recovery of people from the loss of John F. Kennedy was faster than recovery from the untimely death of a loved friend or relative because Kennedy's death involved object-loss without role-loss, according to Averill.

SOCIAL VALUE OF GRIEF.   We have already noted that grief cannot restore the loss. What then is the adaptive value of grief? According to Averill, grief has value in producing social cohesion because of the concern instilled in us about the fate of our fellow humans. Societies encourage the expression of grief even though it does little for the individual because it strengthens the social togetherness. Failure to feel or express grief is regarded as virtually immoral behavior as illustrated by Camus' *The Stranger* in which Meursault is depicted as unworthy during his trial for murder by witnesses who noted that he failed to show grief at his mother's funeral.

Averill seems to overemphasize the requirement that all behaviors be adaptive. An alternative view would be to accept the unadaptiveness of grief but to view it as a natural reaction to the loss of objects to which positive associations have been formed. To be sure, cultural factors have modified the manner in which grief is expressed. But grief need be no more adaptive than responses to frustration such as fixation or regression.

We also question whether there is a direct causal link between individual grief and social cohesion. One could argue, as an alternative, that other factors promote the positive value attributed to social cohesion and support such as the fact that emergencies or disasters that strike communities require group action and cooperation or the fact that groups working together can hold off enemies or harvest crops more efficiently, etc. Given, then, that social cohesion is recognized as valuable, it would follow that when an individual suffered a loss and experienced grief, other members of society would want to offer sympathy. Thus, social cohesion does not stem from grief but has independent bases of development. Grief may be regarded as a reflection of that social cohesion.

RELATIONSHIP WITH OTHER EMOTIONS.   What is the relationship of grief to other emotions? Averill pointed out that a loss not only produces grief but also anger or even aggression in some case. A man is killed. In grief, and in anger, his kinsmen seek out the murderer to avenge the victim.

Loss also is followed by anxiety so that the widow is worried about financial security in addition to her feelings of immediate grief. Averill felt, however, that anxiety is limited to the situations in which there is still uncertainty about a loss (miners are trapped several days below the earth's surface) whereas grief is more likely to occur when where the loss is definite (the plane crashed and exploded).

Guilt is sometimes a component of the experience of bereavement, especially if we feel that we have transgressed against the deceased one in the past. We feel that we no longer have a chance to set things right. Even worse, we may think that our own behavior toward the deceased might have contributed to his or her demise, especially in cases of suicide. Or some people might regard the loss as a form of divine punishment against them for their wrongdoings against the victim.

Thus, guilt, anxiety, or anger may be associated with the grief experience. Emotions do not function in isolation but may affect or be affected by other emotional states as well.

Most of Averill's analysis is restricted to grief in cases of death or the loss of loved ones. However, milder forms of grief are also important aspects of experience. Loss of money, reputation, self-respect, for example, may be regarded as traumatic, if not more so, than the loss of loved ones. Instances of suicide are not uncommon reactions to such situations. On the other hand, the grief experienced by persons for misdeeds can have beneficial future effects as illustrated by people who resolve to reform and make amends.

In contrast to the discussion of fear, there has been no mention of experimental research on grief. In part, this reflects the relative ease with which fear can be induced in the laboratory or observed in the real world. The effects are strong and of brief duration usually. It is virtually impossible or unethical to study grief in laboratory settings. Grief and bereavement under natural conditions are also difficult to study intensively because of the private and personal nature of the experience, an experience that often extends over long periods of time. Experimental research tends to be confined to those events that can be observed in a brief time period. Consequently, less is known about the nature of grief except from naturalistic observation and introspective accounts.

CONCLUSIONS

In the last section of this chapter, we have selected two examples of specific emotions, fear and grief, for extended discussion. The study of specific emotional states does not appear to be closely related to theories about emotion in general described in the first part of this chapter. Those theories often tend to treat all emotions as essentially the same and assume that most subjects respond the same way to the same situation. Although there are common features between emotions such as fear and grief, it is also important to recognize their differences.

Izard (1971, p. 184) maintained that overuse of general terms about emotion ". . . confuse us further by treating emotion as though it were a sort of isolated trouble zone rather than one of the interacting subsystems of personality." He called for a recognition of the fact that people "feel happy, angry, fearful, sad, disgusted, or excited, not simply emotional."

The theorist may emphasize the general features of emotions but the layperson as well as the practitioner is more concerned about the different factors influencing the experience of a variety of emotions.

Summary

Emotions have generally been regarded as being in opposition to rational and cognitive processes for many centuries. Psychology has tended to consider them subjective and difficult to study so they have been ignored by researchers studying behavior. Even when attention has been aimed at their study, the negative and intense emotions such as fear and anxiety have captured most of the concern, whereas milder and positive emotions have not been adequately investigated.

The James-Lange theory of emotion, proposed before the turn of the century, places the emphasis on the conscious experience of autonomic nervous system changes during emotional situations. These strong feelings of our reactions to emotional stimuli were equated with the emotion itself. This theory stimulated much research aimed at disproving it and showing that something more than bodily reactions is involved in emotions.

The activation theory is not a theory about the origins of emotions but it provides an empirical specification of the psychophysiological reactions during emotions. It treats all emotions in an intensity dimension, viewing them as states that are usually at the high end of general activation.

Much contemporary research on emotions has centered on the role of cognitive factors, showing that the dichotomy between reason and emotion is not viable. Experiments in which adrenalin was injected in subjects who experienced inexplicable reactions because they were deceived as to the true effects showed that these subjects were strongly influenced in their emotional reactions by the reactions displayed by a confederate of the experimenter. Other studies suggested that fake feedback to subjects about their autonomic arousal influenced their appraisal of external stimuli, again emphasizing the importance of cognition on emotional appraisal.

Although dealing with stress situations, usually involving longer term emotional arousal, Lazarus' studies of psychophysiological reactions to stressful films also show the necessity of cognitive appraisal before a situation will produce stressful reactions. In his analysis of the nature of stress itself, Lazarus emphasized the possibility that anticipation or waiting for the stressor is more arousing than the stressor itself, at least in some situations. It is worthwhile distinguishing between stress stemming from different aspects of a threatening situation, the anticipation period, the stressor itself, and the stress of coping or combatting the stressor.

Stress is often regarded as undesirable and maladaptive, perhaps because it does often lead to serious disorder. On the other hand, it must be argued that there are instances of stress-seekers, individuals who seem to choose deliberately to undertake risky activities for no apparent reason other than the challenge of danger and adventure.

The arousal of inner emotional states is accompanied by outer manifestations such as facial and postural expressions that serve as major factors in aiding others who make inferences about emotions. It is possible that these emotional expressions are not merely consequences caused by emotions but that their occurrence may act to influence the course of emotions. Grimacing or frowning may occur as a consequence of anger but the opposite statement is also plausible, that such expressions may act to intensify or generate emotional arousal.

The number of specific emotions is indeterminate since the degree of semantic distinctions one is willing to or able to make is an important factor in identifying emotions. Emotions are often terms that refer to the context as well as the autonomic arousal so that distinctions between emotions such as shame, disgust, and contempt may not involve differentiable physiological states.

One of the most significant emotions affecting humans is fear. Fear may be both an emotional reaction to a situation and a causal factor which influences other behavior. The effects of fear appear to vary considerably, depending on its level. There appears to be a curvilinear relationship between fear and many forms of behavior. A second emotion, grief, was also discussed. When a loss of an important and valued person or object occurs, a depressive reaction called grief occurs. From an adjustment point of view, one could argue that it is maladaptive since grief cannot restore the loss. However, it could be argued that the experience of grief by individuals has survival value for groups because it helps promote social cohesion.

It is important, despite the similarities of emotional states, to also examine the unique features of each. Such consideration will show that physiological explanations are inadequate and that it is necessary to examine the cognitive aspects of emotional experience as well.

References

APPLEY, M. H., and TRUMBULL, R. *Psychological stress: Issues in research.* New York: Appleton, 1967.

ARNOLD, M. B. *Emotions and personality.* New York: Columbia University Press, 1960. (Vols. 1 and 2)

ANGELL, J. R. A reconsideration of James' theory of emotion in the light of recent criticisms. *Psychological Review,* 1916, *23,* 251–261.

AVERILL, J. R. Grief: Its nature and significance. *Psychological Bulletin,* 1968, *70,* 721–748.

————. Autonomic response patterns during sadness and mirth. *Psychophysiology,* 1969, *5,* 399–414.

Ax, A. F. The physiological differentiation between fear and anger in humans. *Psychosomatic Medicine,* 1953, *15,* 433–442.

BARTON, A. H. *Communities in disaster.* New York: Doubleday, 1970.

BEM, D. J. Self-perception: An alternative interpretation of cognitive dissonance interpretation of cognitive dissonance phenomena. *Psychological Review,* 1967, *74,* 183–200.

BERKOWITZ, L. Reactance and the unwillingness to help others. *Psychological Bulletin,* 1973, *79,* 310–317.

BERKUM, M. M., BIALEK, H. M., KERN, R. P., and YAGI, K. Experimental studies of psychological stress in man. *Psychological Monographs,* 1962, *76* (15, Whole No. 534).

CANNON, W. B. The James-Lange theory of emotion: A critical examination and an alternative theory. *American Journal of Psychology,* 1927, *39,* 106–124.

COFER, C. N., and APPLEY, M. H. *Motivation and emotion: Theory and research.* New York: Wiley, 1964.

DICHTER, E. *Motivating human behavior.* New York: McGraw-Hill, 1971.

DARWIN, C. *The expression of the emotions in man and the animals.* London: J. Murray, 1872.

DRABEK, T. E., and STEPHENSON, J. S., III. When disaster strikes. *Journal of Applied Social Psychology,* 1971, *1,* 187–203.

DUFFY, E. The relationship between muscular tension and quality of performance. *American Journal of Psychology,* 1932, *44,* 535–546.

————. An explanation of "emotional" phenomena without the use of the concept "emotion." *Journal of General Psychology,* 1941, *25,* 283–293.

————. The concept of energy mobilization. *Psychological Review,* 1951, *58,* 30–40.

————. *Activation and behavior.* New York: Wiley, 1962.

EASTERBROOK, J. A. The effect of emotion on cue utilization and the organization of behavior. *Psychological Review,* 1959, *66,* 183–201.

EGBERT, L. D., BATTIT, G. E., WELSH, C. E., and BARTLETT, M. K. Reduction of postoperative pain by encouragement and instruction of patients. *New England Journal of Medicine,* 1964, *270,* 825–827.

ESTES, W. K. An experimental study of punishment. *Psychological Monographs,* 1944, *57* (3, Whole No. 263).

FEHR, F. S., and STERN, J. A. Peripheral physiological variables and emotion: The James-Lange theory revisited. *Psychological Bulletin,* 1970, *74,* 411–424.

FREEMAN, G. L. The facilitative and inhibitory effects of muscular tension upon performance. *American Journal of Psychology,* 1933, *45,* 17–52.

FUNKENSTEIN, D. H., KING, S. H., and DROLETTE, M. E. *Mastery of stress.* Cambridge, Mass.: Harvard University Press, 1957.

GOLDSTEIN, D., FINK, D., and METTEE, D. R. Cognition of arousal and actual arousal as determinants of emotion. *Journal of Personality and Social Psychology,* 1972, *21,* 41–51.

GRINKER, R. R., and SPIEGEL, J. P. *Men under stress.* Philadelphia: Blakiston, 1945.

HEBB, D. O. On the nature of fear. *Psychological Review,* 1946, *53,* 259–276.

————. Drives and the c.n.s. (conceptual nervous system). *Psychological Review,* 1955, *62,* 243–254.

————, and THOMPSON, W. R. The social significance of animal studies. In

G. Lindzey and E. Aronson (Eds.), *Handbook of Social Psychology*. (Vol. 2). Reading, Mass.: Addison-Wesley, 1968.

HIGBEE, K. L. Fifteen years of fear arousal: Research on threat appeals: 1953–1968. *Psychological Bulletin*, 1969, *72*, 426–444.

———, and HESLIN, R. Fear-arousing communications and the probability of occurrence of the threatened consequences. Paper presented at the meeting of the Indiana Psychological Association, French Lick, April, 1968.

HIRSCHMAN, R. Cross-modal effects of anticipatory bogus heart rate feedback in a negative emotional context. *Journal of Personality and Social Psychology*, 1975, *31*, 13–19.

HOHMAN, G. W. Some effects of spinal cord lesions on experienced emotional feelings. *Psychophysiology*, 1966, *3*, 143–156.

IZARD, C. E. *The face of emotion*. New York: Appleton, 1971.

JAMES, W. What is emotion? *Mind*, 1884, *9*, 188–204.

JANIS, I. L. *Psychological stress*. New York: Wiley, 1958.

———. Effects of fear arousal on attitude: Recent developments in theory and experimental research. In L. Berkowitz (Ed.), *Advances in experimental social psychology*. (Vol. 4). New York: Academic, 1967.

KORIAT, A., MELKMAN, R., AVERILL, J. R., and LAZARUS, R. S. The self-control of emotional reactions to a stressful film. *Journal of Personality*, 1972, *40*, 601–619.

LACEY, J. I. Somatic response patterning and stress: Some revisions of activation theory. In M. H. Appley and R. Trumbull (Eds.), *Psychological stress: Issues in research*. New York: Appleton, 1967.

———, and LACEY, B. C. Verification and extension of the principle of autonomic response stereotypy. *American Journal of Psychology*, 1958, *71*, 50–73.

LAIRD, J. D. Self-attribution of emotion: The effects of expressive behavior on the quality of emotional experience. *Journal of Personality and Social Psychology*, 1974, *29*, 475–486.

LANGE, C. On Leudsbeveegelser (original not available; see translation by I. A. Haupt). In K. Dunlap (Ed.), *The emotions*. Baltimore: Williams and Wilkins, 1922.

LAZARUS, R. S. *Psychological stress and the coping process*. New York: McGraw-Hill, 1966.

———. Emotions and adaptation: Conceptual and empirical relations. In W. J. Arnold (Ed.), *Nebraska Symposium on Motivation*. (Vol. 16). Lincoln: University of Nebraska Press, 1968.

———, AVERILL, J. R., and OPTION, E. M., JR. Toward a cognitive theory of emotion. In M. B. Arnold (Ed.), *Feelings and emotions*. New York: Academic, 1970.

LEEPER, R. W. A motivational theory of emotion to replace "emotion as disorganizing responses." *Psychological Review*, 1948, *55*, 5–21.

———. Some needed developments in the motivational theory of emotions. In D. Levine (Ed.), *Nebraska Symposium on Motivation*. (Vol. 13). Lincoln: University of Nebraska Press, 1965.

———. The motivational and perceptual properties of emotions as indicating their fundamental character and role. In M. B. Arnold (Ed.), *Feelings and emotions*. New York: Academic, 1970.

LINDSLEY, D. B. Emotion. In S. S. Stevens (Ed.), *Handbook of experimental psychology*. New York: Wiley, 1951.

MANDLER, G. Emotion. In T. M. Newcomb (Ed.), *New directions in psychology*. *I*. New York: Holt, 1962.

MARONON, G. Contribution à l'étude de l'action émotive de l'adrenaline. *Revue Française d'Endocrinologie*, 1924, *2*, 301–325.

MILLER, N. E. Studies of fear as an acquirable drive. I: Fear as motivation and fear-reduction as reinforcement in the learning of new responses. *Journal of Experimental Psychology,* 1948, *38,* 89–101.

————. Learnable drives and rewards. In S. S. Stevens (Ed.), *Handbook of experimental psychology.* New York: Wiley, 1951.

McGRATH, J. E. (Ed.), *Social and psychological factors in stress.* New York: Holt, 1970.

MALMO, R. B. Activation: A neuropsychological dimension. *Psychological Review,* 1959, *66,* 367–386.

OPTON, E. M., JR. Why do people like stress? Paper presented at Western Psychological Association Convention, Vancouver, 1969.

READ, P. P. *Alive, the story of the Andes survivors.* Philadelphia: Lippincott, 1974.

SELYE, H. *The stress of life.* New York: McGraw-Hill, 1956.

STERN, R. M., BOTTO, R. W., and HERRICK, C. D. Behavioral and physiological effects of false heart rate feedback: A replication and extension. *Psychophysiology,* 1972, *9,* 21–29.

SCHACHTER, S., and SINGER, J. Cognitive, social, and physiological determinants of emotional state. *Psychological Review,* 1962, *69,* 379–399.

————, and WHEELER, L. Epinepherine, chlorpromazine, and amusement. *Journal of Abnormal and Social Psychology,* 1962, *65,* 121–128.

TOMKINS, S. *Affect, imagery, and consciousness: The positive affects.* (Vol. 1). New York: Springer, 1962.

————. *Affect, imagery, and consciousness: The negative affects.* (Vol. 2). New York: Springer, 1963.

————. Affect as the primary motivational system. In M. B. Arnold (Ed.), *Feelings and emotions.* New York: Academic, 1970.

VALINS, S. Cognitive effects of false heart rate feedback. *Journal of Personality and Social Psychology,* 1966, *4,* 400–408.

————, and RAY, A. Effects of cognitive desensitization on avoidance behavior, *Journal of Personality and Social Psychology,* 1967, *7,* 345–350.

WOLFENSTEIN, M. *Disaster, a psychological essay.* New York: Free Press, 1957.

YOUNG, P. T. *Emotion in man and animal.* New York: Wiley, 1943.

CHAPTER 12

In the Mood

Life is full of ups and downs; our feelings change in response to variations in the internal and external events we encounter. We already know that periods of calm are occasionally interrupted by emotional responses. Mood states such as elation or depression can also shake us up at times. Unlike emotions, which are intense but fairly brief feelings, moods are more subtle and more persistent states. They may last hours, days, or weeks.

Fatigue, illness, time of day, state of health, and similar factors can modify physiological variables and thus alter the way a person feels and in turn the way he or she responds. According to popular belief, external factors such as weather, humidity, altitude, physical terrain, and environment may also exert subtle influences on mood.

In this chapter we will examine some of the evidence concerning the nature of moods, their determinants, and their influence on behavior. Mood states are not *motives* in the same sense that we used the word when we discussed hunger or social approval. But they do act as background variables that modulate the influence of motive states.

Moods, like emotions, are difficult to create realistically in laboratory settings when a subject knows that he or she is serving in an experiment. That knowledge can prevent the subject from acting in emotional or affective ways. The subject is more likely to try to distance himself or herself from the situation, to be objective and analytical. Thus, attempts to induce strong affect will be difficult. Although this subject attitude is desirable in other types of experiments, it obviously limits the usefulness of laboratory studies of mood. The long time span needed to observe the nature of moods also creates problems of procedure and of ethics.

Even if one could solve these practical problems and impose conditions that did, indeed, produce genuine moods in subjects over periods of a week or month, one is faced by ethical questions in creating such lengthy interventions in subjects for research purposes. It is hardly surprising then, that very little research on either the causes of mood changes or the effects of moods on other processes is available from laboratory experiments; most of the evidence comes from anecdotal report and clinical settings.

Clinical evidence deals primarily with negative affect such as chronic anxiety or deep depression, because happy individuals are unlikely to seek psychiatric assistance. It is also important to note that conclusions about severe anxiety and depression in patients in psychiatric settings may not be valid in understanding milder forms of negative affective moods, states that the individual is often able to resolve himself or herself or that gradually dissipate over time without any intervention or therapy.

The Mood of Depression

It may be worthwhile here to deal in further detail with a specific mood such as depression. Clinical and psychiatric cases of depression are numerous and appear to be increasing in number. In normal populations, brief periods of mild depression or "blues" also occur frequently in most people. In general, depression involves a pervasive and debilitating mood of listlessness, indifference, and apathy. There seems to be an absence of purpose, direction, or concern, a lack of energy or vitality, and a general sense of nihilism.

SEPARATION AND LOSS AS FACTORS IN DEPRESSION

Freud (1917, 1950), in a paper entitled *Mourning and Melancholia,* noted the similarity between depression and the reactions typically observed in grief and bereavement. Both instances involve a profound negative mood stemming from the loss of a loved person or object of value. Situations such as the loss of a fortune, the loss of self-respect, or the loss of a lover produce a type of reaction in which there is detachment or withdrawal from other aspects of life along with impaired sleep, loss of appetite, and general apathy. Victims of depression are unable to concentrate on other matters; they act as if they were drugged by the depression that spreads over all aspects of their lives. In extreme and prolonged cases, suicides are sometimes the consequences of depression.

Scott, Stewart, and DeGhett (1973) have similarly suggested that one cause of depression is separation, provided it is for a prolonged time period. The results of studies of temporary separation, a milder form of loss, with a variety of species such as dogs (Scott, 1968), monkeys (McKinney, Suomi, and Harlow, 1973), and rodents (Denenberg, 1964) have agreed with those based on humans (Bowlby, 1973). The classic observations of Spitz and Wolf (1946), substantiated by many others both in clinical and experimental settings (Bowlby, 1973), indicate that the human infant undergoes a grief-like reaction involving a form of depression when separated from his or her mother. Furthermore, the permanent loss of parents, such as through death or divorce, also produces a depressive response. Heinicke (1973) reported that adults who suffered the loss of a parent prior to age fifteen were more likely to develop psychiatric problems as adults.

Separation does not immediately produce depression. On the contrary, Bowlby (1973) has observed several parts in the response sequence of human infants to mother separation. First, there is protest in which a child might resist the separation. Then, after the mother has gone, the child may suffer despair and begin to lose hope although he or she remains vigilant for her return. Next, there is a detachment in which the child seems not to care. Finally, if the mother returns after a period that is not excessively long there is a process of recovery of attachment.

The protest reaction is similar to the invigorated reactions of rats when they faced nonreinforcement (Amsel, 1962) or when response patterns were interrupted (Mandler, 1964). This frustration effect, as Amsel termed it, reflects increased arousal. It may be functional in attempts to recover lost objects or it may also lead to aggressive attacks against persons who caused the loss. If such attempts fail in achieving restoration, the organism may give up, become passive, and depressed. Eventually other sources of reinforcement may be obtained and recovery from depression may occur.

The negative affective response of depression can be expected in view of the Solomon and Corbit (1974) analysis of opponent processes of affect discussed earlier in Chapter 10. The loss of a positively valued object, according to this model, should inevitably lead to the opposite feeling state of depression.

Another similar proposal by Klinger (1975) also maps the sequence of reactions from invigoration, aggression, depression, and recovery to the loss or disengagement from positive incentives. He also points out the importance of such a cycle in individual adaptiveness. Although there is value in persistence, it would be unwise for an organism to pursue rigidly an unattainable or unretrievable object indefinitely, especially if viable alternatives existed. The aversive state of depression, then, could serve as a normal process that aids survival by assuring eventual disengagement from lost causes. Klinger even suggested that therapies which reduce depressive states may be undesirable in cases in which the person is prevented from disengagement from a goal that were better abandoned.

There are some interesting parallels between the reactions to the loss of valued objects and persons and behavior in situations in which organisms do not control their fate. As we noted in Chapter 5, Seligman and his colleagues (e.g., Overmier and Seligman, 1967; Seligman and Maier, 1967) observed that animals placed in situations in which they received inescapable shocks were subsequently less proficient at learning in another situation in which they could escape shocks. As a consequence of their helplessness, the animals were passive and slow to learn adaptive behavior.

Seligman (1975) argued that this learned helplessness is analogous to depression, so that it is the lack of control in a situation that produces passivity and apathy. This analysis differs from those emphasizing the importance of the loss of some valued reinforcer.

Klinger's (1975) criticism of this view pointed out that the situation used by Seligman in which subjects have no control of the environment still entails the loss of a valued incentive, namely, comfort and safety. This loss, according to Klinger, causes the depression state. In addition, but secondarily, the cognition that the organism is helpless is formed in the paradigm used by Seligman. Thus, although it is true that animals that know they are helpless are depressed, lack of control is not the primary cause of such depression. Klinger cited the fact that many persons who are in full control of their lives still suffer depression when there is a loss encountered in one aspect of their experience.

Using Klinger's argument, however, one would expect depression among animals subjected to escapable shocks, because such animals would also suffer some loss of comfort and safety. However, such events usually lead to increased activity and arousal, rather than depression. The advantage of Klinger's position is that it is more parsimonious, however, in that a wider range of phenomena are explained by the same mechanism, loss of positive incentives. The disadvantage, however, comes if the definition of positive incentive loss is made so broad as to be useless. The lack of control emphasized by Seligman is essentially the same situation represented by the unsuccessful attempts of an individual to regain lost positive incentives; it would thus appear that Klinger and Seligman are dealing with the same phenomenom even if their terminology differs.

It is not clear exactly how much of the depression resulting from separation is attributable to the loss and how much to the changed situation stemming from the loss being traumatic. Of course, both factors could operate to produce the overall effect. In actual practice, it would be impossible to separate them. Freud emphasized the role of the changed situation rather than the loss per se, because he felt that the child would miss the mother only because his or her needs would now go unattended.

REINFORCEMENT AND DEPRESSION

The behavioristic conception of depression (Ferster, 1973; Lazarus, 1968), on the other hand, places more emphasis on the lost person or object that serves as a reinforcer. There is no recourse to subjective states such as grief in this analysis, which focuses on the external stimuli that were previously available to the individual as reinforcement but are now lost.

Although the terminology is different, Bowlby's (1973) concept of attachment also emphasizes the relationship between the individual and the lost person or object as the primary source of the depression.

Without denying the importance of the loss of reinforcers or the attached object as one source of depression, Costello's (1972) argument suggests that depression is a state in which reinforcers are not necessarily unavailable but are less effective. The morose individual no longer gets the same satisfaction from his or her usual sources of reinforcement. Although he cited no data, Costello noted that depression is not limited to concern over the lost reinforcer but extends to most aspects of the individual's life. Therefore, Costello suggested that the loss represents a break or disruption in the total pattern of behavior, which upsets the individual's receptivity to other available reinforcers.

SOME EFFECTS OF DEPRESSION
ON BEHAVIOR

The apparent disagreement lies in the fact that Costello is describing some of the *effects* of depression, whereas Lazarus (1972) is postulating one of the *causes* of depression. Viewed in this light, both of them could be correct. Depression, like other moods, has antecedent conditions, but it too can produce its own effects on other processes. As we argued in Chapter 2, factors that affect self-concepts can modify the influence of external events such as reinforcements.

A study by Loeb, Beck, and Diggory (1971) illustrates this point. Using depressed psychiatric patients, Loeb et al. manipulated feedback on a card sorting and matching task such that half the subjects experienced success and half suffered failure. Measures of mood and self-evaluation of performance were lower for subjects who failed. In line with Lazarus' view, these results show that lack of reinforcement led to lowered affect.

A second part of the study used a similar but more difficult task. The subjects who previously failed showed lower optimism and aspiration levels as well as poorer performance on the second task. Following Costello's argument, one could say that the reinforcers in this part of the study were less effective for these subjects due to the negative mood they developed from experiencing failure in the first part of the experiment. It should be noted that a control group of nondepressed subjects was also included. The opposite effect was found here, with subjects who failed on the first part performing better on the second task.

Another effect of being depressed is the tendency to distort the interpretation of the instrumentality of one's own actions and thus regard oneself as less effective. Miller and Seligman (1973) compared students who varied in scores on a depression inventory scale on their expectancies for success in a perceptual-motor skill task in which they had to raise a wooden platform by pulling a string over a pulley without causing a ball to fall off.

Using a concealed magnet, the experimenter was able to regulate the success rate (50 per cent for all subjects) without the knowledge of the subjects. In addition to the skill task, all subjects were tested also on a chance task in which they had to predict whether an X or an 0 would appear on a screen

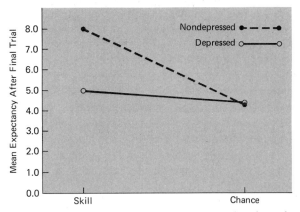

FIGURE 12–1. Mean expectancy after final trial for depressed and nondepressed groups in chance and skill. [From "Depression and the Perception of Reinforcement," by W. R. Miller and M. E. P. Seligman, *Journal of Abnormal Psychology,* 1973, *82,* 62–73. Copyright 1973 by the American Psychological Association. Reprinted by permission.]

for a number of trials. As in the skill task, subjects made statements of their expectancies for success prior to each test.

As shown in Figure 12–1, depressed subjects had lower expectancies of success when the skill task was involved, which suggested that they tend to regard their outcomes as being more independent of their own actions than do the nondepressed subjects. These results are consistent with Seligman's view of depression as involving learned helplessness or the perception that one's own responses are generally ineffective.

SOME DETERMINANTS OF DEPRESSION

It is obvious that wide variations exist in the affective reaction to different situations. In the case of depression when a loss or separation is encountered, variations in the severity of the depression and time to recovery exist. Are these individual differences due to basic biological differences that existed at birth? Evidence from animal breeding experiments and genetic studies of humans suggests that this possibility exists. In contrast to *reactive* depression in which we are dealing with environmental factors that affect this state, *endogenous* depression refers to a state assumed to depend primarily on innate predisposition. Beck (1967) considers the latter variety to be more severe; unlike reactive depression, endogenous depression does not appear to require precipitating events to trigger it.

GENETIC AND CONSTITUTIONAL FACTORS. Studies with dogs (e.g., Fuller and Clark, 1966) suggest that genetic factors are involved in that some breeds are more prone to display depression than others. At the human level, studies of relatives of depressives have shown higher incidence rates within families than that which one would expect in the general population (Winokur, Clayton, and Reich, 1969). In addition the likelihood that both twins are depressive seems to be higher for monozygotic or identical than for dizygotic or fraternal twins. Depression has also been found over successive generations within families.

Although the human studies are cited as supportive of a biological explanation of depression, they are not as conclusive as the animal data. As in similar studies dealing with factors such as intelligence, it is not easy to rule out the role of environmental determinants of the higher correlation within families. Members of a family tend to share similar experiences and environments, so it can be argued whether the similarity in affective mood is due to genetic similarity exclusively.

The idea that biological differences influence temperament or moods is not a new one or one limited to depression. In ancient Greece, Hippocrates proposed his four types of temperament, sanguine, phlegmatic, choleric, and melancholic. More recent distinctions between extraverts and introverts (Eysenck, 1967; Jung, 1923) also held that there may be basic biological differences in reactivity. Sheldon (1942) proposed that constitutional differences in body shape are related to variations in personality. Pavlov (1927) observed that some dogs were more excitable than others and that such differences were associated with variations in conditionability. He hypothesized that the balance between excitatory and inhibitory neural processes might vary in different animals.

These variations in affective responsiveness can be referred to as differences in emotionality. This term should be distinguished from the term *emotion,* which refers to specific affective responses to given situations. *Emotionality* deals with general sensitivity or responsiveness. Individual differences in emotionality are related to, but not limited to, differences in arousal of specific emotions and also can produce differences in longer term affective states such as moods.

Studies of emotionality with animals (e.g., Hall, 1951; Scott, 1962) show correlations between the temperament of parents and offspring in breeding experiments. Many of these studies use behavioral indices such as activity in open field situations or reactions to fearful stimuli as measures of emotionality. Urination and defecation, in addition to freezing or immobility, have frequently been used to measure emotionality. In Hall's study, for example, rats were selectively bred for twelve generations so that the high emotionality animals were bred with other high emotionality animals each time and similarly low emotionality animals were bred with low emotionality animals. Scores of urination and defecation in test situations showed wider differences with successive generations.

It is more difficult to prove the role of genetic factors in the creation of human differences in emotionality. Breeding experiments are out of the question, and the correlational studies within families, as noted above, do not completely rule out environmental factors. Similarly, comparisons of sex differences in emotionality cannot be attributed only to biological factors. The frequently observed differences between men and women in emotional sensitivity and expressiveness as well as differences in emotional disorder such as higher depression among women may be determined by social and cultural factors such as sex roles rather than biological or constitutional factors.

Assume for the sake of argument that biological differences in emotionality do exist. The problem in identifying the nature of such differences is that by the time adult individuals are studied the additional influences of learning experiences and environmental factors may mask the contribution of genetic factors. Evidence demonstrating the role of biological factors should be more likely found if younger individuals are studied, but even here the situation is not as simple as one might hope.

DIFFERENTIAL EARLY EXPERIENCES. It is sometimes difficult to separate constitutional factors from the effects of differential treatment in early experience when assessing the causes of adult differences in emotionality. This problem is by no means unique to emotionality but extends to other areas such as intelligence, sexuality, and eating behavior. Early experiences such as handling and gentling of rats, for example, has been found to influence the emotionality observed later in life (Denenberg, 1964). Apparently the early handling may acclimatize the animals to this type of stress, so that in adulthood they do not experience as much stress as they would if they were being handled for the first time. Anecdotal evidence and naturalistic observation of the taming of wild animals early and late in life also attests to this effect.

Levine (1971) argued that the handling is a stress that influences certain endocrinal responses such as the adrenal gland steroid levels that increase with stress. Such stress experiences early in life alter the organization of the nervous system such that it reacts to later stress in ways different from animals that are not handled early in life.

Scott (1968) described evidence that suggested there may be a critical period for the beneficial effects of early experience. Using dogs, Scott found that puppies displayed distress when stimuli they had encountered during the critical period were removed. Whether or not a specific period is critical for early experience effects, the studies showing that some early experiences affect emotionality of adults suggest that some of the findings attributed to constitutional differences could in fact stem from undetected early experience effects.

It should be pointed out that although early experiences are also important for humans, as demonstrated by studies of infant-mother attachment (Bowlby, 1973), the handling studies with animals such as rats may not be applicable to humans in which adult stress does not involve being picked up by the experimenter!

In addition to noting the possibility that later behavior in humans might be affected by long-lasting neurochemical changes induced by early experiences, one should be aware that cognitive factors such as attitudes and expectancies created by early experiences can also affect later behavior. Stereotypes and overgeneralizations from early experiences are often the basis of racial prejudices. Parental attitudes toward sexual matters may affect the child's subsequent sexual behavior.

The overall evidence suggests that both genetic and early experiential factors may contribute to individual differences in emotionality. These differences may account for differences in arousal of specific short-term as well as longer term affective states. In the case of environmental factors the situation is more complex for humans, because cognitive and cultural factors are more important than the physical stimuli that govern the behavior of lower animals to a greater extent.

Measuring Moods

Now that we have examined the mood of depression in some detail, we can turn to a discussion of moods in general. Many of the same issues are involved for all moods whether it be depression, elation, or anxiety. One would be interested in the causes, genetic or experiential, of each mood, a description of its qualitative nature, and the ways in which each mood affects other behavior.

DIRECT ASSESSMENT WITH ADJECTIVE CHECKLISTS

As mentioned earlier, it is difficult to measure moods in laboratory conditions, because they often require long observation periods under natural circumstances. However, attempts to assess mood states have been made based on the use of verbal self-reports. This direct approach assumes that the person is honest and truthful. In addition, it presupposes that the individual is sensitive or aware of these inner feelings and can verbalize them accurately. It is difficult to prove this latter assumption unless one has some independent basis by which to infer what mood state should occur in a given situation. If we ask subjects to report their own moods under a variety of conditions in which we have good reason to know what moods should occur, we can begin to answer the question of how sensitive individuals are to their feelings, provided they are honest and cooperative.

Nowlis (1970) summarized work conducted by him and his colleagues in which mood was measured with a paper-and-pencil self-report inventory consisting of adjectives descriptive of various moods. The subjects, primarily college students, completed Mood Adjective Check Lists (MACL) similar to the brief form shown in Figure 12–2, marking each adjective to reflect their own appraisal of their current affective states.

Validation studies were conducted in which subjects filled out the MACLs

Each of the following words describes feelings or mood. Please use the list to describe your feelings at the moment you read each word. If the word definitely describes how you feel at the moment you read it, circle the double check (vv) to the right of the word. For example, if the word is *relaxed* and you are definitely feeling relaxed at the moment, circle the vv as follows:

relaxed (vv) v ? no (This means you definitely feel relaxed at the moment.)

If the word only slightly applies to your feelings at the moment, circle the single check v as follows:

relaxed vv (v) ? no (This means you feel slightly relaxed at the moment.)

If the word is not clear to you or you cannot decide whether or not it applies to your feelings at the moment, circle the question mark as follows:

relaxed vv v (?) no (This means you cannot decide whether you are relaxed or not.)

If you definitely decide the word does not apply to your feelings at the moment, circle the no as follows:

relaxed vv v ? (no) (This means you are definitely not relaxed at the moment.)

Work rapidly. Your first reaction is best. Work down the first column, then to the next. Please mark all words. This should take only a few minutes. Please begin.

angry	vv	v	?	no		kindly	vv	v	?	no
clutched up	vv	v	?	no		sad	vv	v	?	no
carefree	vv	v	?	no		skeptical	vv	v	?	no
elated	vv	v	?	no		egotistic	vv	v	?	no
concentrating	vv	v	?	no		energetic	vv	v	?	no
drowsy	vv	v	?	no		rebellious	vv	v	?	no
affectionate	vv	v	?	no		jittery	vv	v	?	no
regretful	vv	v	?	no		witty	vv	v	?	no
dubious	vv	v	?	no		pleased	vv	v	?	no
boastful	vv	v	?	no		intent	vv	v	?	no
active	vv	v	?	no		tired	vv	v	?	no
defiant	vv	v	?	no		warmhearted	vv	v	?	no
fearful	vv	v	?	no		sorry	vv	v	?	no
playful	vv	v	?	no		suspicious	vv	v	?	no
overjoyed	vv	v	?	no		self-centered	vv	v	?	no
engaged in thought	vv	v	?	no		vigorous	vv	v	?	no
sluggish	vv	v	?	no						

FIGURE 12–2. A short form of the mood adjective check list (MACL). [From "Mood: Behavior and Experience" by V. Nowlis, *Feelings and Emotions* by M. B. Arnold (Ed.), New York: Academic, 1970. Copyright 1970 by Academic Press. Reprinted by permission.]

before and after a variety of experiences assumed to induce diverse mood states. A study by Nowlis and Green (1964), for example, employed six different conditions for a group of male college students. The first session involved the completion of the MACL before and after watching a documentary film about Lincoln. The second session required the completion of long and tedious questionnaires and the imposition of a hoax in which the experimenter interrupted them to tell them that the experiment would take longer than expected. Other sessions included the showing of a Harold Lloyd comedy film, a documentary on the Nuremberg trials, a color film of major surgery, and a contest for prizes for the best recall of information shown in a travel film.

Comparisons of the mood ratings made before and after each of the different mood-inducing films revealed that ratings on the MACL seemed to reflect moods appropriate to the different films. Thus, adjectives that reflected aggressive feelings, such as *rebellious, angry,* or *grouchy,* were checked off more often following the aggressive hoax than after such experiences as the Lincoln film or the comedy film. In contrast, adjectives reflective of elation, such as *pleased, overjoyed,* and *refreshed,* increased after viewing the comedy, remained unchanged after the Lincoln film, and decreased after films such as the hoax, Nuremberg trial, surgical operation, or travel film associated with the contest.

The strategy in the preceding type of study is to obtain self-reports of moods under conditions in which one may safely assume what moods are being experienced. Then a comparison of the self-reports with the assumed moods can be made.

A practical problem in the assessment of moods by this approach is determining how many and which adjectives to include in the checklist. It should be obvious that one would like to have a broad range of moods represented so that the subject can report his or her feelings as accurately as possible. Several adjectives reflecting the same mood should be included to see if the subject who checks one tends to check most of the others in the same group.

Instead of using intuition to determine the adjectives that refer to the same mood, an objective method involving correlational statistics known as factor analysis is employed in many studies. As we noted in Chapter 5, this procedure enables one to reduce a large number of variables such as adjectives by categorizing those that are highly correlated or similar into one term or factor. For example, subjects who check *sad* generally tend to also check *sorry* and *regretful.* Instead of viewing each of these states as unrelated, we could combine them under a hypothetical factor arbitrarily named *Sadness.* The adjectives that tend to go together in the judgments of the subjects would produce high intercorrelations with each other. Other items that have low correlations with the items comprising the *sadness* factor measure some other factors. Factor analysis, by identifying these correlations, enables one to identify separate clusters or groups of items, each of which represents a different factor.

The approach of using a list of adjectives describing different mood feelings can thus lead to the identification of some basic underlying factors or dimensions of mood. It should be clear, however, that the resulting description is limited in the sense that it is based on a specific set of adjectives chosen for a given study. In other words, a different study using different adjectives might disclose factors that were not identified in the first study simply because items reflecting those moods were not on the list in that study.

An example of the factor analytic approach can be seen in Thayer's

(1967) study in which subjects checked a list of twenty-eight activation adjectives embedded in a larger list of forty-nine terms. Activation refers to the general level of alertness or arousal discussed in the preceding chapter. The intercorrelations among the items led to the discovery of four factors or sets of items that were highly interrelated within each set and uncorrelated between sets. Set 1, which was given the name *General Activation,* included lively, active, full-of-pep, energetic, etc. Set 2 was named *High Activation* and included clutched-up, jittery, stirred-up, etc., whereas set 3, *General Deactivation,* included still, quiet, calm, and placid. Finally, set 4, which consisted of sleepy, tired and drowsy, was named *Deactivation-Sleep.*

The results showed that the twenty-eight items could be reduced into four subgroups of factors, each of which reflected some level of general activation. Since the scale did not include items so that a subject could express positive versus negative moods such as elation versus depression, it is not surprising that these kinds of distinctions do not show up in the results. As we noted above, studies of self-reported mood can only reveal factors if the relevant items were included in the original set of objectives used by subjects to describe their feelings.

Nelson (1971) was more concerned with qualitative than with intensity dimensions such as activation. In his study of student mood over an academic year, he devised adjective lists which reflected four moods or subscales: *apprehension, resentment, discouragement,* and *cheer.* In addition, two composite indices were used, *disrelish* (the opposite of *relish*), which included all dimensions except *cheer,* and *personal involvement,* which was based on all four subscales.

Students reported their moods at the start of each week over three consecutive academic quarters; the results in Figure 12–3 show that cheer is usually highest at the start of a quarter, whereas the negative moods peak at the end. Moods apparently reflected the types of activities the students engaged in at different temporal points over a term. As exams, assignments, and pressure mounted over the term, moods became more negative.

MEASURING MOOD WITH INFERENCES

In contrast to the direct approach of the assessment of mood by self-report from the individual, it is also possible to infer the existence of different moods from knowledge of the situation in which individuals are placed. For example, in the far northern outreaches of Norway, the inhabitants of Trömso must face twenty-four hours of darkness during each day of winter. During this period, the incidence of hospital admissions for disorders related to depression, insomnia, and hypertension increases dramatically. Although this correlation is not conclusive evidence of a causal relationship between mood and behavioral disorder, it is strongly suggestive. The local inhabitants, themselves, refer to this season as Moerketident or the murky time.

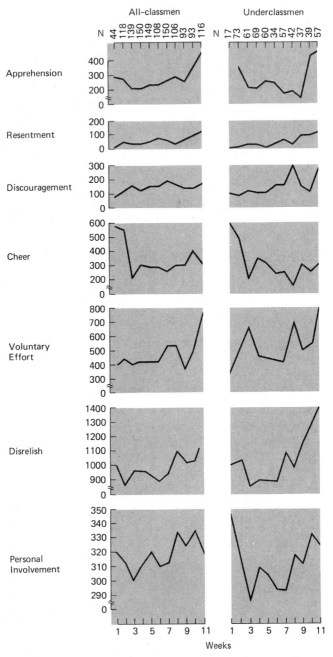

FIGURE 12–3. Medians of six dimensions of mood and *voluntary effort* are given for each of eleven weeks of classes irrespective of quarter. [From "Student Mood During a Full Academic Year," by T. M. Nelson, *Journal of Psychosomatic Research*, 1971, *15*, 113–122. Copyright 1971 by the Pergamon Press, Ltd. Reprinted by permission.]

On a less extreme level, we have all experienced variations in mood depending on whether our climate was sunny, rainy, foggy, or smoggy. We tend to attribute these mood differences to the external factors at least in part. We also have the impression that these moods can affect our motivational levels. Hot and humid weather makes most of us languish, whereas cool brisk weather seems to invigorate. Our activity pace, appetite for food, and ability to sleep seems to fare better with cooler weather.

Determinants of Mood

INTERNAL FACTORS DETERMINING MOOD

BIORHYTHMS. Internal factors also affect moods. Biologists (e.g. Pittendrigh, 1960) have shown that biorhythms or biological clocks regulate levels of activity at different times of the day. These built-in differences in responsiveness to the environment at different periods of the twenty-four-hour day-night cycle are not always apparent in humans whose behavior is strongly affected by social and cultural factors. Examination of the behavior of lower animals or of humans in controlled experiments does reveal the existence of these unlearned or biological mechanisms affecting activity and alertness.

Experiments in which cycles of rest and activity that differ markedly from the circadian pattern have been imposed upon lower animals or humans have shown that behavior is disrupted and irritability occurs. Other evidence that the circadian rhythms are important is the fact that human volunteers who live in caves for extended periods without external time cues nevertheless develop waking-sleep cycles that are closely similar to the circadian cycle. It is difficult, however, to rule out the influence of past experience with day-night cycles. An overview (Luce, 1971) of the findings supporting the concept of biorhythms presents evidence that physical and psychological well-being can be impaired by waking-sleep patterns that are incompatible with those that are biologically innate.

TIME OF DAY. Direct evidence is available concerning variation in mood as a function of time of day. Thayer (1967) had college students complete adjective check lists at different times of the day and found that self-reports of mood differed, depending on the time of day, as can be seen in Figure 12–4. Two factors, General Activation and High Activation, started low but rose to a peak by noon and then steadily declined over the day. Two other factors, General Deactivation and Deactivation-Sleep, dropped from waking levels to bottom out around noon and then increased over the day. Taub and Berger (1974), using similar methods, also confirmed circadian rhythm influences on moods, with positive moods being elevated while negative moods were lowered at noon and late afternoon compared to morning measures.

HORMONES. Internal factors such as differences in hormonal influences

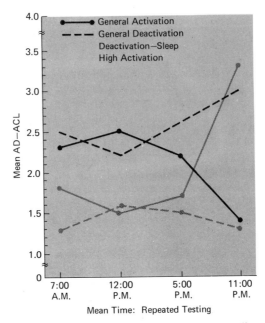

Figure 12–4. Mean scores of four AD-ACL factors at four diurnal periods. [From "Measurement of Activation Through Self-report," by R. E. Thayer, *Psychological Reports*, 1967, 20, 663–678, Monograph Supplement 1–V20. Copyright 1967 by *Psychological Reports*. Reprinted by permission.]

also affect mood. For example, the greater susceptibility of women to mood swings has been attributed to the effect of menstrual cycles. Little and Zahn (1974) found evidence that women suffered more depression just before and during menstrual periods, confirming earlier findings of Dalton (1964). Combined with the findings of Speroff and Vande Wiele (1971) that levels of female hormones such as estrogen and progesterone drop during menstruation, it is plausible that hormonal changes are an important factor in producing the depression observed. Furthermore, similar rapid reduction of progesterone has been implicated as a contributor to the depression and fatigue characteristic of post-partum blues experienced after childbirth, according to Melges (1968). The finding of Somner (1972) that women using contraceptive pills that contain progesterone and estrogen show fewer mood swings during menstrual periods further demonstrates a relationship between hormones and mood.

The precise mechanism by which these hormonal differences generate their effect is unclear. Little and Zahn (1974) found psychophysiological differences in measures such as heart rate, respiration rate, body temperature, and skin conductance in women during menstrual periods. They raised the possibility that the hormonal changes may first affect autonomic nervous system functions, which in turn produce mood effects rather than acting directly.

Social factors may also add to the influence of hormones. One's attitudes about menstruation, the inconvenience, and the physical discomfort can also create depression. In fact, Parlee (1973) has suggested that stereotypical beliefs and expectations about the adverse effects of menstruation may lead women to *report* behavioral fluctuations that may not exist; she suggests women are taught to *say* the mood changes. Her review of past psychophysiological studies purporting to show the ill effects of menstruation points out a number of limitations of research on the menstrual cycle and mood.

EXTERNAL FACTORS DETERMINING MOOD

Our moods may also be affected by a variety of environmental factors as diverse as physical space, weather, architectural design, and social context. Interest in environmental psychology is relatively recent and definitive conclusions about the effects of such variables are not always available.

In some cases the evidence is limited to naturalistic correlations which suggest environmental influences on mood may exist and that these mood fluctuations, in turn, affect behavior. For example, Lieber and Sherin (1972) analyzed murder cases in Dade County, Florida for a fifteen-year period and found that the murder rate seemed to increase in the twenty-four hours prior to the full moon, peak with the full moon, and then drop. Berke and Wilson (1951) noticed that hot months tend to have more social rebellions and uprisings than cooler months. A correlation was found between the number of items lost on streetcars and barometric pressure in Tokyo (Mills, 1942).

In the next section we will examine some evidence showing the effects of several environmental factors commonly assumed to influence behavior. In most of these examples the investigators do not explicitly postulate mood factors as intermediary processes between the environmental variables and the behavioral outcomes. We believe, however, that it is useful to argue that long-term exposure to certain types of environmental conditions induces affective states that, in turn, affect subsequent behavior. After a discussion of the influence of some aspects of the physical and spatial environment on behavior, we will examine the effects of some social environmental variables.

SPACE AS A "HIDDEN DIMENSION." Anthropologist Edward Hall (1966) has referred to the space in which we live as a "hidden dimension"; he argues that space has influences on our behavior *and that we are not usually aware of this spatial influence.* For example, we prefer closeness only with those whom we know and like; proximity to strangers elicits anxiety and discomfort —but we may not realize that it is the fact that the stranger is standing too close that makes us uncomfortable.

Lower forms of animals also display alarm when another animal approaches within a certain distance. From an evolutionary perspective, there is adaptive value in such caution because the invader may be dangerous. Whether or not this tendency of lower animals continues at the human level and thus accounts for similar human tendencies is an interesting question.

Human societies vary in which distance is culturally acceptable so that biological factors cannot be the sole determinant.

Experimental observation has confirmed and extended the work of Hall and others. Sommer has conducted numerous studies in which reactions of target persons were observed as confederates of the experimenter invaded their territory or personal space. For example, in one study (Sommer, 1969) conducted in a college library, confederates occupied the seat next to or the seat separated by one from the target person. Blind ratings (e.g., ratings by observers who did not know the hypotheses) indicated more discomfit by the target person when the invader took the seat adjacent to the target. Moreover, a higher percentage of the targets whose space was invaded left the table within the next thirty minutes compared with control subjects.

One implication of the concept of personal space is that the design and arrangement of our physical spatial environment may influence our feelings of well-being. If seating arrangements for strangers, for example, are too close together or require people to face each other, more discomfort may be experienced. The result may be that people will leave or avoid those settings.

We have all probably noticed that people tend to disperse themselves about an auditorium or classroom when selecting seats rather than bunching themselves together. People seem to respect the personal space of others as well as attempt to obtain their own personal space. Sommer (1969) argued that designers of buildings, rooms, and other spatial environments must recognize such features of human psychology and take them into account when designing spatial arrangements.

Sommer suggested, for example, that a bar environment should be designed to invite people to linger, so external cues are shut out by low illumination and windowless walls to prevent or minimize the patrons' awareness of time and external events. On the other hand, the design of airport or hotel lobbies should discourage unnecessary loitering or relaxing.

The mood created by different seating patterns may influence the learning environment of the classroom. Sommer found that circular and semicircular seating increased class participation. In the traditional arrangements of rows of seats, one after another, everyone is oriented toward one person, the instructor at the head of the room. Although this pattern might be adequate for lectures, it does not seem to be conducive to group interaction because most students are looking at the backs of their fellow students rather than their faces.

The spatial arrangements of religious structures, aside from their symbols and other religious decorations, are usually markedly different in design from secular buildings. Until recently it was common to build tall, imposing cathedrals and churches with sanctuaries having high vaults. Some have suggested that this physical arrangement facilitated the feeling of smallness on the part of the worshipper as he or she gazed toward heaven. Whether this is the actual reason the buildings were so designed or merely one of the consequences of such design, it does suggest that the physical aspect of spatial environments can determine or influence the mood and feeling of the in-habitant.

On the other hand, office buildings are designed for business-like efficiency. With the advent of central air conditioning, many office buildings either have windows that cannot be opened or are windowless. Although the aim was to improve performance by minimizing distraction from events outside the office, it is conceivable that such isolation could have undesired effects.

Most evidence that architectural space influences mood is largely con-jectural and based on opinion. Maslow and Mintz (1956), in contrast, com-pared judgments of facial stimuli by subjects who were tested in surroundings that varied in esthetic appeal. Faces were perceived as holding more "energy" and "well-being" when they were judged in the more attractive surroundings; it is possible that differences in rater mood created by the test conditions may have affected the judgments. Kasmar, Griffin, and Mauritzen (1968), how-ever, could find no differences in self-reports of mood between two groups of psychiatric patients, one tested in a "beautiful" and one in an "ugly" inter-view room. Neither of these studies, it should be emphasized, dealt with the effects of long-term exposure to different physical environments of mood states.

THE EXAMPLE OF CROWDING. Another popular belief is that our moods are affected by crowding, especially with respect to living conditions. This issue is relevant to present concerns about overpopulation. Is there some point at which the degree of population density, even if adequate food and shelter were available, would begin to produce adverse effects such as tension, irritability, stress, or even aggression and violence?

Popular accounts of the dire effects of urban crowding suggest that such is the case. The Kerner Commission (Report, 1968) concluded that one of the causes of the widespread 1967 civil disorders in our large cities was over-crowded living conditions. As we have often repeated however, a correlation is not conclusive evidence. In this example, we cannot be sure that population density per se causes urban strife. Other variables such as socioeconomic status, or racial composition, which may also be correlated with urban strife, are not ruled out as possible causes when correlational analyses are made.

DEFINING CROWDING. A major problem in the study of the effects of crowding is a definitional one. As Lawrence (1974) observed, researchers in this area tend to interchange different constructs such as density, crowding, and overpopulation. This equation is inappropriate because these terms refer to different situations. Stokols (1972) distinguished between crowding as a subjective feeling and density as an objective index of population in terms of the number of persons per unit of space. There is not a 1:1 correspond-ence between the subjective feelings and the objective density. Crowding may be felt even under conditions where density is low; yet it may not be experi-enced in other circumstances where density is high.

Altman (1975) based his analysis of crowding on the significance of privacy to most humans. He suggested that the adverse subjective feeling known as crowding occurs whenever the individual is unable to maintain the desired degree of control over his or her privacy. Altman was speaking of small group situations in which interpersonal interaction is possible. His analysis is less concerned with crowding as it occurs in larger social units such as cities.

One may feel crowded even by the presence of only one other person who invades one's privacy. On the other hand, even though density is high at a concert or ball game, one may not feel crowded or at least not experience unpleasant stress due to such density.

Altman's analysis suggests that when the adverse state of crowding is encountered, the individual tries to cope by finding ways to reduce this unpleasant state such as by achieving privacy from others. If the efforts are successful, it may even appear to an observer that the crowding created no adverse effects. The detrimental costs of crowding are more evident whenever attempts to circumvent crowding meet with failure.

The emphasis of Stokols (1972) and Altman (1975) on the importance of viewing crowding in subjective terms rather than in objective indices such as density makes good sense. As we suggested in Chapter 2, an understanding of behavior often requires knowledge of the actor's subjective view. His or her cognitions may be more important determinants than the external or objective conditions. An individual's interpretation of the density of a situation in which he or she is placed will determine his or her affective reaction. Due to individual differences in past experience, it is likely that the same situation may evoke different feelings with respect to crowding in different people.

Separating (Controlling) Density from Other Correlated Variables in Animal Studies. Because sociological studies of the effects of population density cannot directly rule out the operation of variables correlated with density, evidence has been sought from better controlled studies of either lower animals or humans. These studies tend to equate crowding with density. In a widely cited naturalistic study of sitka deer confined to a small island, Christian, Flyger, and Davis (1960) discovered mysterious occurrences of mortality, which were apparently not due to aggression or starvation. Apparently the population had increased substantially and the stress of crowding presumably led to the increased death rate as well as to a decline in reproduction rate.

Calhoun's studies of the "behavioral sink" (Calhoun, 1962) are also dramatic evidence that crowding due to overpopulation can have disruptive effects. Using an old barn as his laboratory, Calhoun placed a colony of rats in it with ample food and water. Gradually, the colony reproduced and increased the population density to a point that exceeded that which one would expect in natural environments. Aggression increased, infant mortality rose, bizarre sexual behavior occurred, and, in general, there was a breakdown of normal behavior patterns.

One must exercise caution in generalizing these findings to human societies. Some critics of overpopulation ignore differences between species and assume that increased density will produce the same effects in all species. Up to some point, increased population density and size affords the possibility of greater diversity and opportunity for humans, provided there is sufficient food and water. Greater stimulation as well as alienation, anonymity, and loneliness, can occur in large cities.

SOCIOLOGICAL EVIDENCE. A sociological analysis of the relationship between density and social pathology in Chicago was reported by Galle, Gove, and McPherson (1972); they presented alternative hypotheses to the implication of Calhoun's study that density is the direct cause of pathology. For example, some other factor associated with big cities may cause high density as well as social breakdown; it is also conceivable that some other factor first leads to high density, which then produces pathological behavior.

Galle et al. examined five indices of social life, which they felt corresponded somewhat closely to Calhoun's measures: mortality, fertility, public assistance rate, juvenile delinquency, and mental hospital admissions. Because other factors associated with density such as social class or ethnicity might be more direct causes of relationships between density and pathology, Galle et al. used statistical techniques to make comparisons with these factors controlled. Their results at first suggested that no relationship existed between density and pathology.

However, realizing that human living arrangements cannot be properly reflected by density measures that are valid for lower animals, e.g., population per acre, Galle et al. devised new indices that considered factors such as number of persons per room, rooms per house, and type of dwelling such as detached or high rise apartments. In general, when these definitions of density were used, density was strongly related to pathology.

HUMAN LABORATORY EXPERIMENTS. Freedman, Klevansky, and Ehrlich (1971) investigated the effects of density on the performance of simple laboratory tasks involving memory, reasoning, and verbal skills. They attempted to control for other variables usually correlated with density such as reduced air, increased discomfort, restricted movement, and high temperature. Using high school students in groups of five or nine, Freedman et al. placed them in rooms varying in size from 35 to 160 square feet. Each subject was tested under different density conditions; different subjects received the test conditions in different sequences.

The subjects were comfortable, as the rooms were quiet, air conditioned, and equipped with water coolers. It was assumed then that any effects on performance could be attributed to the factor of density per se. The results showed no differences whatsoever as a function of room size for either the five- or nine-person groups. Additional experiments were conducted using fewer tasks to enhance possible boredom. Women subjects of ages twenty-five to sixty were also tested to provide more generality of the findings. In all cases, no detrimental effects of density were obtained.

Freedman et al. concluded that density per se does not impair performance. They admit, however, that the duration of the crowding experience was relatively short and that the subjects knew it would be; these factors could have prevented the occurrence of impairment. It might also be argued that the number of persons as well as their density might be a factor. Freedman et al. used a maximum of only nine persons in a room, and a larger number may have produced impairment.

No effect of crowding on competition was found by Freedman, Levy, Buchanan, and Price (1972). Groups of four males or four females were confined for four hours in either a high-density (5 square feet) or low-density (8.5 square feet) room. They were paid $8 for participation in the study, which required them to perform laboratory tasks while seated and allowed little physical movement.

Freedman et al. themselves pointed out that the experimental context of this study might limit its generalizability. Because the subjects were paid volunteers, knew of the brief duration of the session, and performed innocuous tasks, one should be cautious in assuming that the effects of crowding for months and years on performance would be similar. Nonetheless, Freedman et al. argued that their findings can at least be viewed as evidence that crowding will not always produce negative results.

Freedman (1975) proposed that crowding can intensify any existing positive or negative effects in a situation but that crowding per se is not the cause of the affect. High density, in his view, makes positive situations more positive but renders negative contexts more negative. In support of this hypothesis, Freedman, Heshka, and Levy (1975) had subjects deliver a short speech (written for them) before a small group, which gave either positive or negative evaluations of the speaker. Each condition was tested under both high- and low-density conditions by using small or large rooms, respectively.

As predicted, Table 12–1 shows that a number of measures of subjective experiences about the session were found to be affected by density. High density led to higher or more pleasant ratings, if the situation involved positive evaluations of the speaker. In contrast, high density intensified negative affect for those subjects who received negative feedback about their speeches.

Throughout the studies conducted by Freedman and his associates, crowding has been defined in strictly objective terms. A given number of persons have been tested in rooms of varying sizes, and high density has been equated with crowding. One might object, however, that the participants who served in the high-density conditions did not *feel* crowded. Freedman's (1975) argument that crowded conditions (high density) are not stressful in his studies may merely mean that his subjects did not experience the subjective feeling of being crowded. Furthermore, his definition of high density is a relative one rather than an absolute one and it could be argued that if he were to use even higher densities or confine his subjects for longer durations, they might experience stressful feelings of crowding.

One study (Sherrod, 1974), which is relevant to this point, demonstrated

TABLE 12–1.   Ratings of Group and Session as a Function of Density and Pleasantness.

	Pleasant Condition		Unpleasant Condition	
	Low Density	High Density	Low Density	High Density
Liked other people	2.01	2.22	2.10	1.92
Would participate again	2.38	2.74	2.48	2.21
Learning experience	2.01	2.30	1.70	1.48
Lively	1.26	1.65	1.65	1.22
Liked other speeches	4.50	4.61	3.79	3.63
Be with same people again	2.36	2.54	2.47	2.46

Note: On all scales a higher number is more positive.
Source: From Crowding and Behavior by J. L. Freedman, San Francisco: Freeman, 1975. Copyright 1975 by W. H. Freeman and Company. Reprinted by permission.

that a negative effect of crowding may show up only after a period of time has elapsed since the confinement. Sherrod compared the performances of subjects on a variety of simple and complex tasks for one hour under either crowded or noncrowded conditions. No impairment was obtained in the performance of these tasks due to crowding. However, the performance of a subsequent frustration tolerance task performed under noncrowded conditions was poorer by the subjects who had been subjected to crowding in the first part of the study. Less impairment was found in a third group, which had also been tested earlier under crowded conditions but had been told that they could have moved into a less crowded room if they wished. Sherrod suggested that this group suffered less stress from their crowded experience because they felt some degree of control. This study, as well as one by Glass and Singer (1972) to be described shortly in another context, shows that crowding may have delayed negative effects even when there are no immediate adverse consequences.

The possibility that density does affect behavior in undesirable ways is shown in a study by Griffitt and Veitch (1971) of the effects of density and temperature. Common sense and observation suggest that hot temperatures make us irritable. These moods are blamed for short tempers and various forms of antisocial behavior. For example, analyses of civil strife such as the violent outbreaks in the slums of many major cities during the mid-1960s have shown that hot weather was invariably present. However, again such correlations are not conclusive evidence about causation.

In the controlled experiment by Griffitt and Veitch, temperature was systematically varied, being set at a comfortable 73.4 degrees for half the subjects and a hot 93.5 degrees for the other half. Subjects were tested for forty-five minutes on a set of paper-and-pencil tasks in a chamber that was seven feet wide by nine feet high by nine feet long. In half of the groups there were three to five subjects, whereas there were twelve to sixteen in the remaining half. The latter condition represented the high-density or crowded condition.

Next an adjective check list was administered to assess mood. Finally subjects made judgments of their impressions of an anonymous stranger whose responses to an attitude scale had been shown to them. The stranger's responses were fictitious and rigged in order to create either high or low similarity with those held by the subject.

The results shown in Figure 12–5 indicated that both high density and high room temperature acted to lower self-reported mood as well as reduce interpersonal liking of the hypothetical stranger. At first glance, it might appear that the Freedman et al. studies and the Griffith-Veitch experiment are in conflict, but it should be noted that the former studies involved the assessment of verbal and reasoning task performance, whereas the latter study measured mood and feelings. The use of tasks other than those selected by Freedman et al. might demonstrate impairment due to the effects of density.

It is possible that subjects in the Freedman et al. studies felt irritable moods due to density, but if the tasks used were insensitive no apparent adverse effects of mood would be detected. It should be noted in this regard that Freedman et al. took pains to avoid the imposition of uncomfortable conditions on their subjects precisely because they wanted to obtain a relatively pure measure of the effects of density.

STRESSFUL NOISE AND MOOD. Another factor associated with crowded urban environments that is generally viewed as an adverse influence on mood and behavior is the intense noise level created by the inhabitants of these areas. More factories, automobiles, airplanes, and people simply add up to

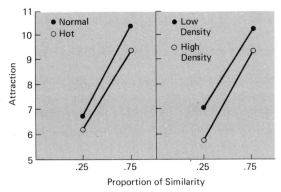

FIGURE 12–5. Attraction toward a stranger as a function of effective temperature and proportion of similar attitudes (left panel) and of population density and proportion of similar attitudes (right panel). [From "Hot and Crowded: Influences of Population Density and Temperature on Interpersonal Affective Behavior by W. Griffitt and R. Veitch, *Journal of Personality and Social Psychology*, 1971, *17*, 92–98. Copyright 1971 by the American Psychological Association. Reprinted by permission.]

more noise. It is often assumed that continual exposure to loud noises will create stress along with greater irritability and tension. Eventually disruption of cognitive functioning, interpersonal harmony, and emotional tranquility is presumed to occur.

Glass and Singer (1972) reported a series of experiments conducted in controlled laboratory conditions aimed at demonstrating these types of impairment from loud noises. We will examine only one study at length, because the basic paradigm was similar in all studies. Glass, Singer, and Friedman (1969) required subjects to perform simple tasks such as addition of numbers or visual search for embedded letters while being subjected to noise distraction. Four different combinations of noise intensity and noise predictability were created by using two levels of each factor. Predictability refers to whether or not the noise appeared at regular or random intervals. The results showed that noise was initially disruptive but that subjects were soon able to adapt so that it no longer impaired performance. Parallel effects may occur in the real world, attesting to human adaptability even to possibly undesirable conditions.

Then subjects received additional tasks such as proofreading. In this phase of the study no distractor noise was imposed. Nonetheless performance did vary among the groups as a function of the type of noise encountered in the first part of the study. If the louder noise had been experienced, performance showed more impairment in the second half of the study. Even greater impairment was found in subjects who received random unpredictable noises compared to those who had regular and predictable noises in the first part of the experiment.

These findings suggest that noise stress may have no *immediate* adverse effects, especially because subjects may try to ignore the distraction. However, adverse effects did show up later. One could argue that the stressful noises created irritable moods slowly over the course of the first part of the study, which then exerted observable impairments of performance in the second part.

SOCIAL ENVIRONMENT AND MOOD.   In addition to the general environmental factors associated with urban living, it also appears that more specific factors such as aspects of the psychosocial and organizational structure of social institutions can affect mood and behavior. Moos (1973a, 1974) has reviewed his work and that of his colleagues in diverse behavior settings such as correctional institutions, classrooms, psychiatric wards, university residence halls, and work milieus.

One study (Moos, Shelton, and Petty, 1973) compared treatment outcomes in relation to the social environment of psychiatric wards. High dropout rates were found in wards perceived as low in involvement, support, order and organization, and program clarity by both staff and patients. It is possible that such conditions weakened confidence and morale, with the result being unsuccessful therapy and eventual dropout from the program.

A study of military company environment (Moos, 1973b) examined the relationship between test scores at the end of basic training, AWOL (absent without official leave) rate, and sick call rate with psychosocial climate. Better performance was found in companies that had officer support and peer cohesion. The possibility that this relationship may have occurred through the development of more positive mood and morale is supported by scores on mood measures, which showed that men in companies without both officer support and peer cohesion reflected more anxiety, depression, or hostility compared to those in companies that had both features.

These two examples do not adequately describe the scope of Moos' goals, which included the development of a system for analyzing and comparing the basic dimensions of a variety of human environments. However, it should serve to illustrate the important role of social structure and organization in affecting mood and behavior.

CONCLUSIONS. Inferences can be made about a number of internal or bodily and external or environmental variables, which produce differences in long-term affective states. These moods can be quite dramatic, such as in the case of clinical depression, but they can often be subtle and go undetected because we can still function without the impairment of many skills and tasks. It may be necessary for additional conditions to exist before some of the effects of moods will be sufficiently great to be noticed. For example, moods created by level of fatigue may not alter performance unless it is also very hot. Similarly, crowding may not change moods enough to provoke aggression unless the person is also angered. In short, moods may often be inadequate to modify behavior, but they can do so if combined with more potent variables. This subtlety may explain why many studies of factors that should alter mood do not also show effects on behavior.

Certain features of laboratory studies may prevent the detection of such subtle effects of moods. Because most experimental sessions are of brief duration compared with the intervals involved in the generation of naturally occurring moods, there may be inadequate opportunity to induce strong moods. Awareness that one is being studied, especially if one is a volunteer, may also serve to mask the effects of any moods involving antisocial feelings or block actions that might present the subject in an unfavorable light. The use of naturalistic or unobstrusive measures may be a more productive method of studying moods and their behavioral effects.

A final explanation for the failure of some apparently adverse environmental conditions to affect behavior is that humans are remarkably adaptive, especially for short time periods. Rene DuBos, a noted biologist, lamented the possibility that this aspect of humans allows us to accept urban pollution, traffic jams, and unesthetic environs. "Man is so adaptable that he could survive and multiply in underground shelters, even though his regimented subterranean existence left him unaware of the robin's song in the spring, the whirl of dead leaves in the fall, and the moods of the wind—even though indeed all his ethical and esthetic values should wither" (DuBos, 1965, p. 279).

Like a mirror image of adaptation to undesirable living conditions in the real world, perhaps subjects in psychological experiments also passively accept the conditions imposed on them as if they were normal or unavoidable circumstances.

Summary

The study of mood has been neglected and there is relatively little research available on the nature and consequences of mood. This chapter has necessarily been more speculative as a consequence. It appears that many behaviors are not readily explained in terms of motives, especially motives based on tissue or need deficits. Instead, subjective states such as moods or morale sometimes alter the general level of responsiveness to other stimuli. For example, extreme physical crowding might induce states of irritability, which could lower thresholds for aggression. Although the crowding would not be considered the primary motive or cause of aggression, it could be viewed as a contributing factor, which might combine with other factors such as frustration, for example. Although moods cannot be regarded as motives in themselves, it appears that the operation of motives takes place against the context of the mood of the person, feeling states induced either by physiological or environmental factors. Thus, hunger will lead to different types of eating behavior in a depressed versus an elated person. This interaction of mood and motives makes it important for us to learn more about the nature and operation of these long-term feeling states.

Depression was cited as a particularly prevalent form of mood that is not limited only to psychiatric cases. Separation from or loss of valued persons or objects appears to produce a series of affective reactions. First, there is a form of protest or attempt to restore the situation to its former state, followed by despair and depression. Aggression and resentment may occur but eventually recovery usually follows. Parallels have been drawn between depressive reactions and the condition of animals placed in situations in which they have no control.

The effects of depression are not limited to the lost object or person but influence most aspects of the individual's experience, suggesting that depression lowers the effectiveness of previous reinforcers that are still available. Evidence shows that persons high in depression level tend to distort their perceptions by underestimating the extent to which their performance in a situation is affecting the attainment of success.

Studies with animals as well as humans suggest that biological differences may predispose some individuals toward depressive reactions. Similar genetic arguments can be made for affective differences in general, as suggested by evidence that emotionality or general reactivity to stimulation can be selectively bred in animal populations. Similar arguments have been made for human differences, for example, sex differences in affectivity, but it is more difficult to rule out cultural factors among humans.

Moods are relatively long-lasting affective states that have been difficult to study in artificial situations. Direct measurement of moods has generally involved the use of self-reports on adjective check lists. Studies of the effects of factors such as the time of day on moods have also employed self-report measures to show how biorhythms are correlated with mood variations. Speculations have suggested that environmental factors such as territory, invasion of privacy, spacing, and architectural design can affect subjective states such as moods.

Investigators differ in their definition of crowding. Some researchers equate density or the number of persons per unit of space with crowding, whereas others feel that this definition is inadequate because it fails to consider the subjective feelings of the persons being studied. It appears more valid to include measures of these subjective states to be sure that the feeling of being crowded is in fact being experienced.

Variations in moods have implications for our behavior in many areas such as performance on mental tasks, motor skills, or group interaction. A popular conception about crowding is that serious disruption of the quality of human life will result. This view sees the densely populated large cities as contributing to social problems such as crime and aggression.

Evidence on the effects of crowding based on animal studies tends to support these dire predictions, but it is debatable how far one can generalize from nonhuman studies to human behavior. A number of laboratory experiments with humans suggests that a wide variety of conditions involving crowding do not appear to produce deficits in either mood or performance. Although these studies are controlled, they are usually short-term studies. Since those who live in crowded cities do so over very long intervals, it may not be warranted to generalize to these situations from laboratory studies. Immediate effects of crowding may show no impairment but as some experiments have found there may be delayed effects.

Finally, it was noted that other aspects of the environment such as noise and social structure can affect mood and behavior. Mood alone may be insufficient to affect behavior and may require additional factors. The effects of mood may not appear immediately or over short periods but show up later.

References

Amsel, A. Frustrative nonreward in partial reinforcement and discrimination learning: Some recent history and a theoretical extension. *Psychological Review,* 1962, *69,* 306–328.

Altman, I. *The environment and social behavior: Privacy, personal space, territory, crowding.* Monterey, Calif.: Brooks-Cole, 1975.

BECK, A. T. *Depression: Clinical, experimental, and theoretical aspects.* New York: Hoeber, 1967.
BERKE, J., and WILSON, V. *Watch out for the weather.* New York: Viking, 1951.
BOWLBY, J. *Attachment and loss. Separation, anxiety, and anger.* (Vol. 2) New York: Basic, 1973.
CALHOUN, J. Population density and social pathology. *Scientific American*, 1962, *206*, 139–148.
CHRISTIAN, J. J., FLYGER, V., and DAVIS, D. C. Factors in the mass mortality of a herd of Sitka deer, *cervus nippon. Chesapeake Science*, 1960, *1*, 79–95.
COSTELLO, C. G. Depression: Loss of reinforcers or loss of reinforcer effectiveness. *Behavior Therapy*, 1972, *3*, 240–247.
DALTON, K. *The premenstrual syndrome.* Springfield, Ill.: C C Thomas, 1964.
DENENBERG, V. H. Critical periods, stimulus input, and emotional reactivity: A theory of infantile stimulation. *Psychological Review.* 1964. *71.* 335–351.
————. Stimulation in infancy, emotional reactivity, and exploratory behavior. In D. C. Glass (Ed.) *Neurophysiology and emotion.* New York: Rockefeller University Press, 1967.
DUBOS, R. *Man adapting.* New Haven, Conn.: Yale U. P., 1965.
EYSENCK, H. J. *The biological basis of personality.* Springfield, Ill.: C C Thomas, 1967.
FERSTER, C. B. A functional analysis of depression. *American Psychologist*, 1973, *28*, 857–870.
FREEDMAN, J. L. *Crowding and behavior.* San Francisco: Freeman, 1975.
————, KLEVANSKY, S., and EHRLICH, P. The effect of crowding on human task performance. *Journal of Applied Social Psychology*, 1971, *1*, 7–25.
————, LEVY, A., BUCHANAN, R. W., and PRICE, J. Crowding and human aggressiveness. *Journal of Experimental Social Psychology*, 1972, *8*, 528–548.
————. HESHKA, S., and LEVY, A. Crowding as an intensifier of pleasantness and unpleasantness. In J. L. Freedman, *Crowding and behavior.* San Francisco: Freeman, 1975.
FREUD, S. *Mourning and melancholia.* Reprinted in *Collected papers* (Vol. 4). London: Hogarth, 1950. (Originally published 1917.)
FULLER, J. L., and CLARK, L. D. Genetic and treatment factors modifying the post-isolation syndrome in dogs. *Journal of Comparative and Physiological Psychology*, 1966, *61*, 251–257.
GALLE, O. R., GOVE, W. R., and McPHERSON, J. M. Population density and pathology: What are the relations for man? *Science*, 1972, *176*, 23–30.
GLASS, D. C., and SINGER, J. L. *Urban stress: Experiments on noise and social stressors.* New York: Academic, 1972.
GLASS, D. C., SINGER, J. L., and FRIEDMAN, L. N. Psychic cost of adaptation to an environmental stressor. *Journal of Personality and Social Psychology*, 1969, *12*, 200–210.
GRIFFITT, W., and VEITCH, R. Hot and crowded: Influences of population density and temperature on interpersonal affective behavior. *Journal of Personality and Social Psychology*, 1971, *17*, 92–98.
HALL, E. T. *The hidden dimension.* New York: Doubleday, 1966.
HALL, C. S. The genetics of behavior. In S. S. Stevens (Ed.), *Handbook of Experimental Psychology.* New York: Wiley, 1951.
HEINICKE, C. M. Parental deprivation in early childhood: A predisposition to later depression? In J. P. Scott and E. C. Senay (Eds.), *Separation and depression: Clinical and research aspects.* Washington, D.C.: American Association for the Advancement of Science Publication No. 94, 1973.
JUNG, C. G. *Psychological types.* New York: Harcourt, 1923.
KASMAR, J. V., GRIFFIN, W. V., and MAURITZEN, J. H. Effect of environmental

surroundings on outpatients' mood and perception of psychiatrists. *Journal of Consulting and Clinical Psychology*, 1968, *32*, 223–226.

KLINGER, E. Consequences of commitment to and disengagement from incentives. *Psychological Review*, 1975, *82*, 1–25.

LAWRENCE, J. E. Science and sentiment: Overview of research on crowding and human behavior. *Psychological Bulletin*, 1974, *81*, 712–720.

LAZARUS, A. A. Learning theory and the treatment of depression. *Behavior Research and Therapy*, 1968, *6*, 83–89.

————. Some reactions to Costello's paper on depression. *Behavior Therapy*, 1972, *3*, 248–250.

LEVINE, S. Stress and behavior. *Scientific American*, 1971, *224*, 26–31,

LIEBER, A., and SHERIN, C. The case of the full moon. *Human Behavior*, 1972, *1*, 29.

LITTLE, B. C., and ZAHN, T. P. Changes in mood and autonomic functioning during the menstrual cycle. *Psychophysiology*, 1974, *11*, 579–590.

LOEB, A., BECK, A. T., and DIGGORY, J. Differential effects of success and failure on depressed and nondepressed patients. *Journal of Nervous and Mental Diseases*, 1971, *152*, 106–114.

LUCE, G. G. *Body time: Physiological rhythms and the social stress*. New York: Pantheon, 1971.

MANDLER, G. The interruption of behavior. In D. Levine (Ed.), *Nebraska Symposium on Motivation*. (Vol. 12). Lincoln: University of Nebraska Press, 1964.

MASLOW, A. H., and MINTZ, N. Effects of esthetic surroundings: I. Initial effects of three esthetic conditions upon perceiving "energy" and "well-being" in face. *Journal of Psychology*, 1956, *41*, 247–254.

MCKINNEY, W. T., JR., SUOMI, S. J., and HARLOW, H. F. New models of separation and depression in rhesus monkeys. In J. P. Scott and E. C. Senay (Eds.), *Separation and depression: Clinical and research aspects*. Washington, D.C.: American Association for the Advancement of Science Publication No. 94, 1973.

MELGES, F. T. Postpartum psychiatric syndromes. *Psychosomatic Medicine*, 1968, *30*, 95–108.

MILLER, W. R., and SELIGMAN, M. E. P. Depression and the perception of reinforcement. *Journal of Abnormal Psychology*, 1973, *82*, 62–73.

MILLS, C. *Climate makes the man*. New York: Harper, 1942.

MOOS, R. H. Conceptualizations of human environments. *American Psychologist*, 1973, *28*, 652–665. (a)

————. *Military company environment inventory manual*. Palo Alto, Calif.: Department of Psychiatry, Stanford University, 1973. (b)

————. *Evaluating treatment environments: A social ecological approach*. New York: Wiley, 1974.

————, SHELTON, R., and PETTY, C. Perceived ward climate and treatment outcome. *Journal of Abnormal Psychology*, 1973, *82*, 291–298.

NELSON, T. M. Student mood during a full academic year. *Journal of Psychosomatic Research*, 1971, *15*, 113–122.

NOWLIS, V. Mood: behavior and experience. In M. B. Arnold (Ed.), *Feelings and emotions*. New York: Academic, 1970.

————, and NOWLIS, H. The description and analysis of mood. *Annals of the New York Academy of Sciences*, 1956, *65*, 345.

OVERMIER, J. B., and SELIGMAN, M. E. P. Effects of inescapable shock upon subsequent escape and avoidance responding. *Journal of Comparative and Physiological Psychology*, 1967, *63*, 28–33.

PARLEE, M. B. The premenstrual syndrome. *Psychological Bulletin*, 1973, *80*, 454–465.

PAVLOV, I. P. *Conditioned reflexes*. London: Oxford University Press, 1927.

Report of the National Advisory Commission on Civil Disorders. New York: Bantam, 1968.

SCOTT, J. P. Critical periods in behavioral development. *Science*, 1962, *138*, 949–958.

————. *Early experience and the organization of behavior*. Belmont, Calif.: Brooks-Cole, 1968.

————, STEWART, J. M., and DEGHETT, V. J. Separation in infant dogs. In J. P. Scott and E. C. Senay (Eds.), *Separation and depression: Clinical and research aspects*. Washington, D.C.: American Association for the Advancement of Science Publication No. 94, 1973.

SELIGMAN, M. E. P. *Helplessness. On depression, development, and death*. San Francisco: Freeman, 1975.

————, and MAIER, S. F. Failure to escape traumatic shock. *Journal of Experimental Psychology*, 1967, *74*, 1–9.

SHELDON, W. H. *The varieties of temperament: A psychology of constitutional differences*. New York: Harper, 1942.

SHERROD, D. R. Crowding, perceived control, and behavioral aftereffects. *Journal of Applied Social Psychology*, 1974, *4*, 171–186.

SOLOMON, R. L., and CORBIT, J. D. An opponent-process theory of motivation: 1. Temporal dynamics of affect. *Psychological Review*, 1974, *81*, 119–145.

SOMMER, R. *Personal space: The behavioral basis of design*. Englewood Cliffs, N.J.: Prentice-Hall, 1969.

SOMNER, B. Menstrual cycle changes and intellectual performance. *Psychosomatic Medicine*, 1972, *34*, 263–269.

SPEROFF, L., and VANDEWIELE, R. L. Regulation of the human menstrual cycle. *American Journal of Obstetrics and Gynecology*, 1971, *108*, 243–247.

SPITZ, R., and WOLF, K. Anaclitic depression. *Psychoanalytical Study of Children*, 1946, *2*, 313–342.

STOKOLS, D. On the distinction between density and crowding: Some implications for future research. *Psychological Review*, 1972, *79*, 275–277.

TAUB, J. M., and BERGER, R. J. Performance and mood following variations in the length and timing of sleep. *Psychophysiology*, 1973, *10*, 559–570.

THAYER, R. E. Measurement of activation through self-report. *Psychological Reports*, 1967, *20*, 663–678, Monograph Supplement 1-V20.

WINOKUR, G., CLAYTON, P., and REICH, T. *Manic depressive illness*. St. Louis, Mo.: Mosby, 1969.

PART FIVE

SOME BIOLOGICAL FACTORS

CHAPTER 13

At the Gut Level: Hunger, Thirst, and Pain

Our physical survival depends on the availability of sufficient supplies of food and water and the avoidance of painful and life-endangering situations. Fortunately most of us are not confronted with extreme threats to our physical well-being so that our concerns are primarily directed toward goals that are not directly related to physical survival. Unless we are facing starvation, lethal aggression, serious bodily harm, and the like, our physical survival is of less urgency to us than our psychological motives such as affiliation with friends, aggression toward enemies, achievement of economic, intellectual, or physical accomplishments, and enjoyment of corporal and aesthetic pleasures.

The pursuit of ideal and lofty principles may lead some to undergo conditions that are serious threats to health and physical safety. Humans throughout history have been willing to fast, endure torture, and sacrifice their lives to defend treasured beliefs and ideals.

Attempts to understand the nature of so-called primary or basic biological needs of humans such as food, water, sex, and physical safety cannot succeed if we limit our study to an analysis of physiological mechanisms, especially those determined in studies of lower species. Although obviously tissue deficits, hormonal factors, genes, peripheral and central nervous system processes, etc. are ultimately involved, we assume that the picture will be incomplete and misleading without a consideration of cognitive and sociocultural determinants of behaviors such as eating or coping with pain.

Biologically based motives can be markedly influenced by nonbiological factors. The cultural beliefs and values of the society in which an individual lives will determine many aspects of behaviors such as eating. Unlike the assumption of homeostasis, which biological approaches emphasize, eating is not merely a response made to restore the equilibrium of food needs. The amounts and types of food, as well as the circumstances under which we eat them, are strongly affected by cultural factors. Psychological beliefs, often of

367

a religious or symbolic nature, influence eating practices. Eating may serve aesthetic needs rather than survival interests. The gourmet has been defined as one who lives in order to eat. Eating makes one feel good and may serve as a compensatory response to life's frustrations or conflicts.

Sexual activities serve the biological function of procreation, thus facilitating the survival of the species. But a study of human sexual behavior suggests that motives such as pleasure or physical gratification are usually more important for most people. According to a strictly biological point of view, painful experiences should be avoided if survival is to be achieved, but humans sometimes actively seek pain. They seem challenged rather than threatened by some painful situations. Suffering is sometimes regarded by humans as a test of character or an opportunity to develop character and to prove one's bravery in defense of some cause.

Our discussion of biologically based needs such as eating, drinking, pain avoidance, sex, and sleep will emphasize cognitive and cultural determinants. The psychological causes and effects of these behaviors will receive the major attention. Some discussion of physiological mechanisms will be included, but this treatment will be minimized.

The approach toward these topics is unlike that of drive theorists such as Hull described in Chapter 2, where the hunger drive was considered to be a source of the motivational energy that activated the organism. Other motives such as affiliation were then presumed to be learned by association with situations leading to reduction of the hunger drive. In contrast, our discussion will simply deal with each behavior in its own right without any interest in its implications for behavior in general.

General Plan of Analysis: Chapters 13–15

Although the precise approach will vary with the specific behavior under discussion, we will generally first emphasize the basic evidence regarding the physiological bases. The role of local or peripheral processes at the receptor level and that of central processes in the brain, particularly in the hypothalamus, will be examined.

We will then proceed to a discussion of how the individual identifies or becomes aware of his or her need state. What processes occur at the cognitive level to enable valid labeling of inner states? The influence of situational or environmental cues, interpersonal and nonpersonal, will be assessed as factors that must be cognitively interpreted by the individual. These external factors can alter the impact of internal physiological cues on the individual's interpretation of his or her motivational state.

How do cultural values and beliefs influence behavior? Can cultural controls modify behavior so that the biological determinants become less important? Thus, to what extent is the pattern of sexual practices in a society the reflection of biological needs and tendencies as opposed to the mores and attitudes of that society?

Finally, we will discuss the functions served by each behavior that do not fit into a strictly biological survival model. One common alternative conception of the purpose of biologically based motives comes from psychoanalytic theory. Although it generally is used to explain abnormal and excessive tendencies, the concept of compensatory gratification in the form of overindulgence can be applied to behavior within the normal range.

Overeating, overdrinking of alcoholic beverages, and even oversleeping might provide gratification and frustration reduction for someone who has been thwarted in some other activity. The acceptance and tolerance of pain can be rationalized as a form of retribution and punishment, which one stoicly endures in order to pay one's debt.

Practices associated with biologically based motives may function to achieve social approval, prestige, status. Whereas dieting or fasting can hardly promote physical survival, it can enhance one's physical or social attractiveness. Other practices such as the avoidance of certain foods may serve symbolic and religious purposes.

Pleasure and hedonistic feelings may motivate certain behavior associated with biologically based needs. The use of alcohol, marijuana, and stronger drugs can produce alterations in consciousness, which can be regarded as pleasurable, at least under appropriate circumstances. None of these affective functions of these behaviors can properly be seen as being necessary for physical survival.

Hunger

LOCAL FACTORS

Generally speaking, we are more likely to experience hunger and want to eat, the longer the interval since we last ate. What processes occur at the physiological level when we have been deprived of food? The stomach should be empty, and awareness of these sensations might stimulate eating. This type of reasoning was behind local theories of hunger such as that proposed by Walter B. Cannon in the 1930s. It was noted (Cannon and Washborn, 1912) that gastric motility, which is greater when the stomach is empty, was correlated with subjective reports of hunger.

On the other hand, clinical evidence showed that persons who have had their stomachs removed surgically still experience hunger. This evidence, however, did not disprove the possibility that stomach cues once played a factor in the past learning of cues for hunger by these patients. These cases did imply that some other processes such as cognitive factors are also involved.

A more direct method of studying the role of stomach distension in eating behavior calls for techniques that generally are limited to animal subjects. By surgical means, it is possible to preload the stomach with nutrients directly so that the mouth is bypassed. In a study by Epstein and Teitelbaum (1962), rats treated in this manner still regulated the amount consumed. Each time a rat pressed a bar, the apparatus delivered a liquid diet directly into the stomach without it passing through the mouth.

Taste and smell, as well as visual cues, associated with the nutrient cannot influence intragastric feeding as they might possibly affect normal oral ingestion. Even when the concentration of the liquid was modified such as by halving or doubling it, Epstein and Teitelbaum found that rats compensated by doubling or halving, respectively, the intake in order to maintain normal weight.

It should not be concluded that taste and smell play no role in maintaining or initiating eating, but this evidence shows that it is possible to regulate eating solely on the basis of local factors associated with the stomach.

CENTRAL FACTORS

It is understandable why attention was originally directed toward local factors, because they corresponded to the individual's direct experiences of hunger. Moreover it was relatively simple to gather relevant data such as indices of stomach contractions, which could be measured by having a subject swallow a balloon that had a recording stylus attached at the other end. In contrast, the identification of central nervous system bases of motivational states was far more difficult. Clinical cases of human pathology supplied the initial hypotheses. It was suspected that the pituitary gland might be involved, because a case of an obese individual with a pituitary tumor was reported in 1840. However, this evidence was only suggestive especially since the hypothalamus is directly above the pituitary.

An important study in 1921 by Bailey and Bremer in which lesions were produced experimentally in laboratory animals in the regions of the hypothalamus provided more substantial proof. Obesity, as well as overdrinking, was observed to occur.

Although the technique was available as early as 1905, attempts to stimulate specific brain nuclei or collections of cells did not become prominent until the 1930s. This technique allowed more precise mapping of the hypothalamus, so that the effects of stimulation of different nuclei could be identified.

Brobeck, Tepperman, and Long (1943) demonstrated over- or undereating in rats as a function of the location of lesions produced in parts of the hypothalamus. Anand and Brobeck (1951) also reported evidence suggesting that a specific area served as a feeding center, whereas a different area functioned as a satiety center. Specifically, when lesions were made in the ventromedial region of the hypothalamus, extreme overeating known as *hyperphagia* was the consequence. It was inferred that the ventromedial center serves as an inhibitor of eating or a satiety center, so that its destruction results in obesity and overeating. On the other hand, lesions placed in the lateral hypothalamus lead the animal to stop eating completely. This result suggests that the intact lateral hypothalamus must function as an initiator of eating or a feeding center.

The overall picture is one of two opposed but interacting hypothalamic control areas, which operate like a system of checks and balances. Additional support comes from studies (Epstein, 1960; Wyrwicka and Dobrzecka, 1960) in which the artificial method of electrical and chemical stimulation of the ventromedial center stops eating, whereas the same treatment of the lateral center stimulates eating.

On the other hand, some evidence challenges this view of the two hypothalamic centers. Krasne (1962) showed that rats with ventromedial lesions not only stop eating but also try to escape. He argued that the stimulation of this area may be aversive, so that the cessation of eating is an artifact. The role of lateral hypothalamic lesions was questioned by Davenport and Balagura (1971) who suggested that weight loss may be due to metabolic impairment caused by stimulation of this area rather than to a motivational deficit.

How do these hypothalamic areas operate to influence eating? Obviously, these higher centers must use some process to detect the consequences of eating. When food is ingested, a number of changes occur including increased blood sugar level, elevated temperature, and stomach distension. It is possible that these as well as other local factors interact with hypothalamic centers to regulate intake. Nature repeats itself by providing several sets of cues: if impairment occurs in the detection of one factor, it can still operate on other factors.

Theories have been proposed suggesting that factors as varied as blood sugar or glucose (Mayer, 1955), temperature (Brobeck, 1955), and stomach distension (Sharma, Anand, Dua, and Singh, 1961) may serve to influence the hypothalamic centers. Briefly, evidence suggests that the ventromedial area that serves as a satiety center is activated when factors associated with food intake such as blood sugar, temperature, and stomach distension increase. In contrast, increased activation of the lateral area, which presumably functions as a feeding center, is associated with decreases in blood sugar, temperature, and stomach distension, as would be the case when the organism has not eaten for a period.

This overview of the physiological bases of eating is a simplified account, because there is conflicting evidence regarding some of the inferences. However, for our present purposes it should provide a general view of the methods and findings of physiologically oriented studies of an earlier era dealing not only with hunger or eating but also with thirst or drinking. Although the regulation of fluid intake is obviously important, research on this topic has been small compared to that on hunger. The fact that parallel developments in the history of the physiological analysis of local and central factors underlying water intake and food intake exist may account for the lesser study of liquid regulation.

GENERALIZABILITY TO HUMANS. Much of the research dealing with physiological mechanisms of motivational states cannot easily or ethically be conducted with humans. Although the findings with laboratory rats are important discoveries about the mechanisms underlying motivation, the question of how generalizable they are to humans is inevitable. The mechanisms may or may not be similar among rats and humans at the physiological level, but there is also the possibility that higher order cognitive factors may override or modify the influence of physiological controls.

One may admire the technological sophistication involved in electrical stimulation, creation of lesions, and use of fistulas and cannulas, but one must bear in mind that in such studies one is dealing with something other than the "normal" intact animal. Electrical stimulation by electrodes is not the natural means whereby an organism is stimulated into eating or ceasing to eat. When one stimulates or produces lesions, what *other* areas may also be stimulated or destroyed? What other functions, perhaps undetected, are being served by the area we stimulate or destroy in our interest to examine the effect on a specific function? Is there more than one route to the same effect so that the causes of over- or undereating in the intact organism may differ from those in the artificially stimulated or lesioned animal?

Despite these problems in generalizing from laboratory experiments with lower species to humans, it must be admitted that a number of striking parallels in the eating behavior of obese laboratory animals and humans exist. Schachter and Rodin (1974), after a comprehensive review of research, noted that the eating behaviors of animals with obesity caused by ventromedial hypothalamic lesions and obese humans are similar in that both appear to be less sensitive to internal physiological cues. On the other hand, initial evidence suggested that they are more responsive to external cues related to food.

These observations led them and their colleagues to conduct further experiments to determine if other similarities could be established between obese animals and humans. Among their findings, it was noted that obese animals or humans, in contrast to normals, eat more, eat more rapidly, and show less activity. The obese are affected by taste and the amount of effort required to obtain food, whereas the normals are not. The obese eat more if the food is tasty, but eat less if it tastes bad. Similarly, the obese eat more if little effort is required, but less when effort is considerable. Schachter and Rodin (1974, p. 40) go so far as to conclude that there may be a malfunction in the hypothalamus of the obese human, as can be demonstrated in rats with experimentally induced lesions in that area.

COGNITIVE FACTORS

Human eating is strongly affected by culturally determined external factors such as time, place, and setting. Social factors such as the presence or absence of other persons who are eating or the degree of social encouragement or discouragement may also affect eating. We usually are unaware of such forces, but if we reflect on the conditions of eating we can usually identify these external factors.

Less apparent to most of us is the manner in which our subjective internal state associated with need for food determines our eating. The sensations from the viscera differ, depending on how recently we have eaten, and could serve to signal us whether or not we were hungry.

CLINICAL EVIDENCE. Both sets of factors, internal and external, are available to all of us, but it appears that some of us may make better use of the internal cues that are more in tune with our actual bodily needs. Hilde Bruch (1973), a psychiatrist who specializes in the study of eating disorders, has hypothesized that young infants must learn to differentiate among different internal states, so that eating should occur only when the feelings of food deprivation are detected. Indiscriminate eating in reaction to other internal states such as fear, anxiety, or sleepiness prevents the proper association between feelings due to food deprivation or hunger and eating. Because the human infant's eating is governed largely by the feeding practices of the mother, it would be important that she facilitate this discrimination learning by feeding the child only when she knows it to be in need of food. Otherwise, according to Bruch, the child will develop eating disorders that could result in later obesity.

Some evidence that this hypothesis is plausible comes from comparisons of normal weight and obese human adults who are asked to judge or rate their hunger at different times, while records of their stomach movements are being made with the use of a gastric balloon they have swallowed. Strunkard and Koch (1964) found that normals were more likely than obese subjects to report feeling hungry when their stomachs were contracting than when they were not. More recently, Strunkard and Fox (1971) have found that the ability of normals to produce reports of hunger in line with gastric motility is not as strong as previously thought.

EXPERIMENTAL EVIDENCE. Behavioral studies of eating in laboratory settings conducted by Stanley Schachter (1967) and his associates provide evidence consistent with Bruch's observations in clinical settings. Schachter and Gross (1968) reasoned that if normals are better at detecting and using internal or physiological cues to govern their eating, obese persons are more likely to rely on external or environmental cues. Under the guise of studying the relationship between physiological reactions and psychological traits, subjects were hooked up to a polygraph, which measured heart rate and sweat gland activity for thirty minutes. The test room was windowless so that subjects could receive no cues about time other than from a clock on the wall

(Schachter and Gross had removed the subjects' watches, ostensibly to protect them from the metal corroding electrode jelly placed on the arms of the subjects to permit physiological recording).

Actually the purpose of the study was to compare the amount of eating by normal and obese subjects, as influenced by faked clock readings on the room clock.

The experimental session began at 5 P.M., as shown in Table 13–1. By the time the physiological recording of thirty minutes was completed, the clock had been doctored to give either a slow reading of 5:20 or a fast reading of 6:05 (the true time being 5:35). At this point in time, the experimenter returned to administer a brief five-minute test of perceptual ability. He brought a box of crackers along and ate some during the test. Then he left the subject a questionnaire to complete and also left the box of crackers, telling the subject to help himself if he desired.

A tenuous assumption was made by Schachter and Gross that most subjects typically ate dinner around 6 P.M. so that half the subjects (slow clock reading of 5:20) were left alone with the opportunity to eat prior to their dinner time and the other half (fast clock reading of 6:10) were left alone with the crackers at a time that was slightly after their usual dinner time. A summary of the procedure and the precise clock (real and false) times for each group is shown in Table 13–1.

The subjects were twenty-two obese and twenty-four normal weight male college students (obesity was defined as 15 percent or more overweight as based on life insurance norms). It was predicted that if external cues such as

TABLE 13–1.   Sequence of Events and Manipulated Clock Time in Schachter and Gross Experiment

True Time	Event	Clock Reading in	
		Slow Condition	Fast Condition
5:00–5:05	Subject arrives, receives experimental instructions, watch removed, electrodes attached.	5:00–5:05	5:00–5:05
5:05–5:35	Period for getting "base line" readings of EKG and GSR. Subject alone in room.	5:05–5:20	5:05–6:05
5:35–5:40	Experimenter brings in box of crackers, administers Embedded Figures Test.	5:20–5:25	6:05–6:10
5:40–5:50	Subject alone with crackers; fills out questionnaire.	5:25–5:35	6:10–6:20
5:50–	Experimenter removes crackers; subject fills out questionnaires.	5:35–	6:20–

Source: From "Manipulated Time and Eating Behavior" by S. Schachter and L. Gross Journal of Personality and Social Psychology, 1968, 10, 98–106. Copyright 1968 by the American Psychological Association. Reprinted by permission.

clock time influence eating, this cue should be more important for obese subjects. Accordingly, more crackers should be consumed by the obese subjects who had the speeded-up clock, as was the case as shown in Figure 13–1. On the other hand, it was predicted that normals who rely more on internal hunger cues should be less affected by the time factor, although the speeded-up clock group should eat a bit more. The prediction failed to be upheld as normals ate less than half as much under the speeded-up clock as under the slowed down clock conditions. Schachter and Gross offered the ad hoc explanation that normals ate so little in the fast clock condition because they realized that they would be eating dinner soon and did not want to spoil their appetite. Another embarrassing result, seen in Figure 13–1, is the fact that the greatest amount was eaten by the normals under the slow clock who consumed more than the obese subjects under the fast clock.

However, other evidence supports Schachter's views regarding the differences between normal and obese persons with respect to the influence of internal and external cues. Schachter, Goldman, and Gordon (1968) examined the impact of level of food deprivation and amount of fear on eating by obese and normal subjects. The apparent purpose of the experiment was to determine how taste is affected by tactile stimulation.

The subjects, all male students, were not allowed to eat the meal just prior to serving in the study, so that half the subjects could be "preloaded" or satiated with food while the other half would not. At the outset of the study, the full-stomach subjects were offered roast beef sandwiches so that everyone's most recent taste experiences would be identical. A cover story was told to encourage them to eat until they were full. The empty-stomach subjects were not offered any food; however, at the end of the study they also received roast beef sandwiches.

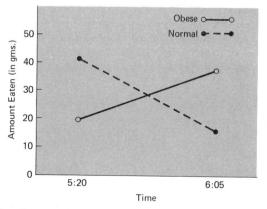

FIGURE 13–1. The effects of manipulated time on eating in experiment by Schachter and Gross (1968). [From "Cognitive Effects on Bodily Functioning: Studies of Obesity and Eating," by S. Schachter, in *Neurophysiology and Emotion* by D. C. Glass (Ed.), New York: Rockefeller University Press, 1967. Copyright 1967 by Rockefeller University Press. Reprinted by permission.]

In the main part of the study, subjects were to taste different flavored crackers and rate them. It was explained that the experimenters wanted to see how tactile factors such as electric shock would affect the taste of the crackers. The high-fear subjects were told that painful but not damaging shocks would be received, whereas the low-fear subjects were told that the shocks would merely tingle or hardly even be detected.

Preshock or baseline ratings of the crackers were then obtained. Observers watched through one-way mirrors and counted the number of crackers eaten. Subjects then expected to receive the shocks but the experiment was completed and the reason for deceiving the subjects into thinking that shock would be received was explained.

In summary, there were four treatment conditions based on the combinations of two levels of food deprivation and two levels of fear. It was assumed that normal subjects would be more able to detect their internal state so that high food deprivation would increase eating whereas high fear would decrease eating. In other words, because normals are assumed to eat only when hungry the presence of fear should not produce the same effect as food deprivation. In contrast, obese subjects are assumed to be relatively insensitive to internal states, either the type or amount, so that eating should not differ much as a function of the four treatments. Figures 13–2 and 13–3 show that the results are very consistent with the hypotheses.

NATURALISTIC EVIDENCE. The laboratory findings are consistent with some fascinating speculations by Goldman, Jaffa, and Schachter (1968) about the eating behavior of obese persons in natural circumstances. For example, in one field survey to determine which Jews would be more likely to

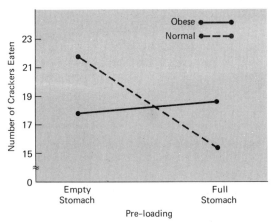

FIGURE 13–2. Effects of preloading on the eating behavior of normal and obese subjects in experiment by Schachter, Goldman, and Gross (1968). [From "Cognitive Effects on Bodily Functioning: Studies of Obesity and Eating," by S. Schachter, in *Neurophysiology and Emotion,* by D. C. Glass (Ed.), New York: Rockefeller University Press, 1967. Copyright 1967 by Rockefeller University Press. Reprinted by permission.]

observe Yom Kippur by obeying the command to fast for twenty-four hours, it was predicted that among the devout there would be more fasting among the obese. Since obese persons, Jewish or otherwise, are influenced by external cues it was assumed that fasting would be easier under circumstances lacking in food-related cues. The devout would spend more time in synagogues, which lack food cues, so it was reasoned that obese, fasting Jews would be more likely to succeed than would normal, fasting Jews who are more strongly affected by their internal states of food deprivation. Whereas about 83 per cent of obese devout Jews fasted, only about 69 per cent of normal Jews fasted, thus supporting the hypothesis.

Another study examined the relationship between obesity and the likelihood of college freshmen dropping out of a dormitory dining hall food contract. Food taste, being an external cue, is assumed to govern the eating of obese persons more than it affects normals. College dormitory food at Columbia University where the study was done was assumed to be similar to that at most other colleges—not very tasteful. It was therefore predicted that obese students would be more likely to withdraw from participation in dormitory dining plans so as to eat off campus. Whereas a third of the normal weight students renewed their food contracts, only about 14 per cent of the obese students did, as predicted by Goldman et al. Another possible explanation, not considered by Goldman et al, is based on another universal feature of dormitory food—small portions. Thus, obese students may have found that they were not getting enough food.

Finally, Goldman et al. examined the effect of jet lag and time changes on the eating behavior of flight crew members of Air France. The time changes probably affect everyone, but these external cues were predicted to be less

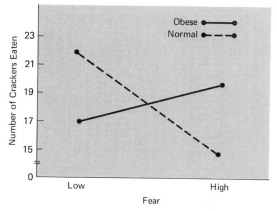

FIGURE 13–3. Effects of fear on the eating behavior of normal and obese subjects in experiment by Schachter, Goldman, and Gross (1968). [From "Cognitive Effects on Bodily Functioning: Studies of Obesity and Eating," by S. Schachter, in *Neurophysiology and Emotion,* by D. C. Glass (Ed.), New York: Rockefeller University Press, 1967. Copyright 1967 by Rockefeller University Press. Reprinted by permission.]

adverse on overweight crew members (given the fact that physical requirements for an air crew are stringent, the range of weight deviation is small).
For example, a flight leaving Paris at Noon requires eight hours to go to
New York, but due to time zone differences it arrives at 2 P.M. New York
time. A person on this flight should be hungry, but it is still several hours
until local dinner time. Data from Air France showed that complaints about
the adverse effects of time changes on eating were significantly greater
among normals. Thus obese flight crew members were less adversely affected
by the discrepancy between their internal states of food deprivation and
eating.

Goldman et al. admit that these field studies are speculative and that alternative explanations are possible but they feel that the attempt to show how
they fit in with their overall theory is worthwhile. They concluded humor-
ously (p. 123), "whatever the eventual interpretation of the three studies, if
one permutes these facts, the implications are unassailable: fasting, fat,
French freshmen fly farther for fine food."

Implications. The research findings of Schachter and his colleagues do
not deny the importance of physiological factors and hypothalamic centers
on the control of eating but place more emphasis on the role of external
stimuli as determinants of eating by obese individuals. However, the situation
may be more complex than originally assumed by Schachter (1967) as later
studies reported by Schachter and Rodin (1974) revealed some exceptions to
the generalization that external cues will govern eating by the obese. For
example, the obese reported eating less often per day, which is contrary to
expectation because the everyday world is abundant with food cues.

Schachter and Rodin modified the external cues hypothesis for obese eating
by adding the requirement that these cues must also be salient. Some support
for this qualification was obtained by Ross (1974) who led subjects to think
that they were having their physiological responses measured during different
types of cognitive activity in which they were asked to think about different
objects that were before them. In addition to the presence of objects such
as marbles, candlesticks, and chessmen, a container with fresh cashews was
placed before subjects who were invited to help themselves to the nuts during
the study. High and low salience was created in two ways, by the amount of
room illumination and by the extent to which the experimenter's instructions
during a period alleged to help adjust the recording equipment emphasized
the presence of the cashews and their tastiness. The results showed that
either method of salience variation led to greater eating of the nuts by the
obese subjects when salience was high. No effect of salience was obtained on
the eating by normals.

If we leave aside for the moment the differences in the determinants of
obese and normal eating, we see that the Schachter et al. research illustrates
the importance of cognitive factors such as the appraisal of taste, time of day,
and circumstances surrounding eating opportunities as influences on eating.
Eating is not an automatic response to food governed only by the level of

food deprivation; indeed it is frequently a behavior that occurs when the individual may have recently received ample food.

DIFFERENCES IN GENERAL SENSITIVITY.   There is also evidence that the differences between obese and normals may not be restricted only to eating but may be evident in sensitivity to stimulation in general. Pliner (1973, a, b), a student of Schachter, demonstrated that obese subjects were more affected by salient external cues than were normals even in tasks that did not involve eating. In one experiment (Pliner, 1973a) the task involved time estimation while the interval was filled with either a loud or soft auditory distractor stimulus. When the loud or salient cue was presented, obese subjects overestimated the time; when the soft cue was used, they did not. In the other study (Pliner 1973b), subjects were instructed to think about a scene that was either verbally or visually depicted before them. During this time period the subjects immersed their arms in a container of ice water, which was painfully cold, because the alleged purpose of the study was to examine the effects of pain on thinking. It was predicted that obese subjects would be more distracted from pain by the more salient visual stimulus than the verbal one. Therefore obese subjects should take longer to report experiencing pain from the ice water, as was the case when the stimulus was salient. In addition, Pliner had subjects estimate how long they had been thinking of the stimulus they had been instructed to concentrate on. Similar results were obtained as the obese subjects reported more time thinking of the scene when it was visually rather than verbally presented, whereas the opposite effect was found in normal subjects.

The two experiments reported by Pliner show that the greater reliance of obese subjects on salient external cues is found even when food stimuli are not involved. These findings suggest that some more general factor may account for the differential responsiveness of individuals to stimulation. A tendency to eat more and become obese is only one of the effects of this differential sensitivity to internal and salient external stimuli.

IS THERE A BUILT-IN REGULATOR OF EATING?   An interesting theory proposed by Nisbett (1972) shifted the emphasis toward internal determinants of eating, so that its explanation of obesity is at variance with Schachter's view. Nisbett suggested that the hypothalamic feeding centers have set points, somewhat akin to speed limits, which regulate eating. Because these base lines or ponderstats, as they have been termed, are determined by biological factors and early nutritional experiences, the theory expects individual differences to exist in the set points.

The implications of this formulation are substantial, for it would suggest that many so-called overeaters merely have a higher set point than so-called normals. Due to the social pressures against obesity, most overweight persons wage a seemingly never ending battle of the bulge. Countless dieting methods are tried in the hope of bringing their weight down to the level considered normal. However, Nisbett contends that the set point of overweight persons may actually be higher than that of normals and that their weight reduction places them below their "physiologically dictated normal body." The effect, as is well known by dieters, is to feel constantly hungry.

Studies of the eating of normal weight individuals who have been food deprived show some interesting parallels with the eating of obese persons. Both show more responsiveness to the taste of food but less reaction to post-ingestional feeding cues. Both show greater emotion but lessened activity in general as well as in sexual behavior. Nisbett speculates that these similarities are consistent with the theory that food-deprived normals and obese persons have different set points, because both behave toward food in the same hungry way.

This provocative theory is a physiologically oriented explanation, not a cognitive theory, which views overeating as stimulated by internal rather than external cues as suggested by Schachter. Additional research bearing on Nisbett's theory will be interesting, because such a conception of overeating would affect some attitudes toward obese persons. Thus, the notion that they lack will power or that they should eat to maintain a weight level considered normal in society will have to be revised if Nisbett's theory is supported.

Movements such as Fat Liberation that advocate the obese person's right to personal dignity may take heart from Nisbett's theory. Some overweight people say that they enjoy their physical condition and resent social standards that force them to try to conform to the slender image admired in our society.

CULTURAL FACTORS

Traditions and customs surrounding eating practices exert strong influences on what, when, and how we eat. Sometimes the reasons may be religious, magical, or superstitious; at other times the reasons may be based on necessity or convenience or may even be founded on nutritional grounds. Most people probably believe that the logic behind their eating is sound, whereas the bizarre and different customs of other cultures, especially primitive societies, are ill-founded.

Pyke (1968), however, has observed that the assumption that a hot breakfast of porridge, bacon, and eggs is rarely questioned by the British (or by Americans, we might say too) as being essential for good nutrition. We would be highly suspicious about the diet of a group such as the Otomi Indians of Mexico who enjoy malva, hediondilla, yucca, pigweed, sorrel, and cactus fruit, among other exotic items. But a nutritional analysis conducted at a leading American university disclosed that the Otomi diet was of superior nutritional quality to that of a group of American townspeople.

In his classic work the *Golden Bough,* noted anthropological pioneer J. G. Frazer recorded the role of magic in determining eating and drinking practices. Many early societies believed that it was possible to cast evil spells over food remaining from a meal that a person did not finish. One social implication of this belief was that one would not share a meal with someone you planned to injure through this magical method. Fraser suggested that harmony among tribes that have shared meals is enhanced by the belief that such socializing protects oneself from possible evil spells cast by an enemy. It is possible that ceremonial events such as diplomatic banquets among statesmen today stem from these ancient beliefs.

Pyke reported that one society in Paraguay eats jaguars, bulls, and stags because they believe this diet will give them strength and speed; hens or tortoises are avoided for fear they would render the eater cowardly or slow afoot. The Aino of Japan omit otters from their food supply, because they think they will become forgetful like the otter if they consume them. We should not forget that Americans have their share of similar beliefs, for example, fish is regarded as brain food.

Of course, some foods are beneficial along the lines suggested by folk myths. However, the benefits are nutritional rather than from the assumed acquisition of the personality or character of the animal eaten. This situation can be illustrated by the example of aphrodisiacs, substances presumed to enhance sexual activity and prowess. The mandrake plant is assumed to possess these properties, primarily because its divided thick roots resemble the two legs of a man. Apparently the mandrake's reputation is warranted due to its ability to serve as a pain killer and antispasmodic agent. Pyke reasons that these qualities might calm timid lovers and facilitate sexual endeavors so that the mandrake earned its reputation over the centuries, but not for the reasons originally assumed.

Superstition played a role in a campaign in the 1940s to improve nutrition among South African Zulus. Infant mortality was substantial along with other consequences of malnutrition, so a campaign was initiated to encourage women to drink more milk. However, the women would not drink milk from cows unless they were fortunate enough to own them. The Zulus believed that cows were adversely affected if menstruating or pregnant women other than their owners passed near them. These beliefs were more influential than any scientific information about the health benefits of milk.

These few examples are sufficient to illustrate the complexity of the cultural factors that influence eating practices. We will now examine some of the motives underlying eating behavior that have little or nothing to do with physical survival.

FUNCTIONS OF EATING

The psychoanalytic view that eating may be a form of compensatory gratification when a person is faced with anxiety, guilt, frustration, or conflict is an intriguing hypothesis. Even boredom can be regarded as a motive that leads to the seeking of the pleasures of eating. Some explanations of obesity focus on this psychological basis of overeating.

Related but somewhat different is the emphasis on the hedonistic pleasures of eating for eating's sake. Good food tastes good and is worth eating even if one is not frustrated. Overlapping with this motive is eating for status or prestige. Exotic delicacies may be sought, not primarily for gustatory pleasures, but because they are expensive status symbols or in Veblen's term, forms of conspicuous consumption.

Social approval affects our eating also, such as when we diet to make ourselves more attractive physically. Finally, some eating practices serve important symbolic and ceremonial functions. Just as primitive societies place a religious taboo on eating their totem or sacred animal, modern religions proscribe the consumption of one type of food or another. Religious fasting, in contrast to political fasting, represents sacrifice and dedication. Bread and wine serve as sacraments to symbolize the body and blood of Christ.

Food, then, functions in many different ways as a means for humans to achieve goals remote from that of physical survival. Hunger strikes and politically motivated fasts directly operate against physical survival but serve to promote the attainment of goals of vast psychological significance. On a more individualistic plane, eating is a refuge, a consolation, or a haven. Thus, the state of our emotions, as well as the state of our stomachs, can affect the extent to which we eat.

Thirst

Without adequate water, we could not survive very long. This fact is often overlooked, because most of us are rarely in danger of extreme dehydration. We are more likely to feel starved to death from lack of food than we are to feel desperate for water.

What factors initiate the ingestion of water? Does some mechanism inform us when our water level is low? And once we gain access to water, what determines when we stop drinking?

HOMEOSTATIC VS. NONHOMEOSTATIC CONCEPTIONS

A homeostatic model of water regulation would suggest that whenever a certain degree of water deficit occurs, sensations tell us we are thirsty and we seek water. Peripheral cues such as parched lips and dry throats might serve to direct our attention to our internal needs. Then once we locate water it might be assumed that we would drink until our deficit was eliminated.

One major problem with this type of model for the understanding of human water regulation is that most human drinking of water is nonhomeostatic in nature. We often drink even when we are not feeling thirsty. Social factors often lead to such nonregulatory drinking among humans, especially of liquids other than water. Kissileff (1973) acknowledged that little is known about the mechanisms underlying nonhomeostatic drinking and recognized the need to distinguish this behavior from homeostatic drinking.

Fitzsimons (1972) has pointed out the role of habitual daily routines in the control of water intake. We learn, for example, to drink water and other liquids along with our meals. This type of thirst is termed secondary by Fitzsimons who recognized the greater role of feeding schedules, oropharyngeal cues, and cognitive factors on drinking that is not based on emergency conditions such as when substantial water deficits exist. He considers the latter type of drinking to be based on primary thirst.

Hedonic or pleasurable consequences are often associated with drinking to relieve thirst. Studies that employ animal subjects cannot measure such affective consequences readily, but this factor should not make us lose sight of the obvious function of affective consequences in the control of human water ingestion (Epstein, 1973).

Interest in the physiological and neurological bases of water regulation has led investigators to prefer working with a variety of nonhuman species such as rats, dogs, and goats. The use of such species has permitted the use of techniques such as electrical stimulation and lesioning of brain sites as well as injections of chemicals directly into areas of the brain assumed to govern water regulation.

Although advantages were gained by this approach, it also meant that most research on water control has been on homeostatic drinking, precisely the type that is relatively infrequent in humans so that the generalizability of results from animal studies to humans may be very limited. With these shortcomings in mind, we will present an overview of research on homeostatic drinking.

LOCAL FACTORS

Whenever we experience a deficit of water, we usually also experience dryness of the mouth and lips. It is not surprising then that many theorists have assumed that these local cues are the basis of the thirst drive and the initiation of drinking. Cannon (1932), for example, emphasized local factors as the basis for thirst just as he focused on local cues when studying hunger.

Studies with clinical cases suggested shortcomings of local theories. If local cues were the primary factors, how could patients without salivary glands experience thirst as they reportedly did (Steggerda, 1941)? Research with dogs that ingested water that never reached the stomach (e.g., Adolph, 1941) because of a surgical bypass procedure also created problems for local theories. The dogs managed to drink amounts of water that matched the amount of deficit even though the water never reached the stomach or the rest of the body after passing through the mouth and throat areas. This result would suggest that past conditioning or learning is involved in telling the dogs how much drinking is necessary to restore the deficits.

Bellows (1939) placed water directly into the stomach and then observed the tendency of animals to drink immediately thereafter. By preloading the animal, so to speak, in this manner it should be possible to speed up the absorption of water into the body. In addition, if stomach distension created by the preload acts as a cue that water has been replaced, there should be little drinking. However, despite this advantage, drinking did not stop any sooner compared to the control condition in which animals did not receive the preload. In terms of the body state with respect to water, one should expect the preloaded animals to stop drinking sooner. However, it may be that the act of drinking is important, because this process helps the animal know when it has had sufficient amounts to drink. Direct placement of water into the stomach may restore deficits in a physical sense, but it may be inadequate to reduce drinking behavior. Interest in local factors decreased as it became apparent that they were not sufficient to explain all the factors related to the onset and offset of drinking. In addition, the development of techniques that permitted better study of central nervous system factors also led to a shift in research.

CENTRAL FACTORS

The hypothalamus appears to contain centers that are important in the regulation of drinking. Various procedures including direct injection of substances such as sodium chloride, electrical stimulation, and electrical destruction with lesions have shown the role of the hypothalamus in governing water balance. Using goats, Andersson and McCann (1955) found that they would start drinking if a small amount of sodium chloride was injected into specific areas of the hypothalamus. They also reported that electrical stimulation of these areas led to drinking, whereas electrical destruction led to a loss of drinking.

The exact manner in which higher centers such as those in the hypothalamus operate in regulating drinking is not clear. When water deficit occurs, a number of simultaneous processes occur. *Extracellular* water is lost first; if deprivation continues, *intracellular* water will also decrease. The fact that one source of water is diminished first means that the balance of water between the two sources, cellular and extracellular, will be disrupted. As diagramed in Figure 13–4, the change in osmotic pressure created by extracellular water deficit will cause cellular water to leave the cells to restore the balance at least temporarily.

One theory (Verney, 1947) about thirst assumes that the hypothalamus contains osmoreceptors, cells sensitive to osmotic pressure changes that occur

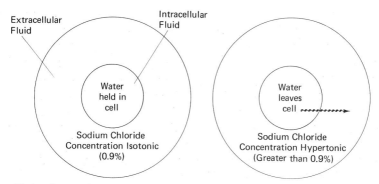

FIGURE 13–4. Intracellular and extracellular fluids. Water is drawn from cells into extracellular fluids when the body has lost water. Appreciable loss of water from the body increases concentration of sodium chloride or NaCl (ordinary "table salt") in extracellular fluids. Increased extracellular sodium concentration draws water from cells by *osmotic pressure*. Loss of water from the body can be simulated by injections of a salt solution that is more concentrated than that found in the normal hydrated condition. A salt solution that is this concentrated is called *hypertonic;* that found in normal hydrated condition (0.9 percent NaCl) is called *isotonic*. [From *On Emotions, Needs, and Our Archaic Brain* by Robert Beverley Malmo. New York: Holt, Rinehart, and Winston, 1975. Copyright © 1975 by Holt, Rinehart, and Winston. Reprinted by permission.]

when water is lost. However, other concomitant changes also occur when water deficits occur. The concentration or viscosity of blood increases, sodium chloride concentrations in the body fluid increase, temperature may rise, and there are also endocrine changes due to the release of antiduretic hormones (vasopressin) by the pituitary and angiotensin by the kidneys to help prevent the further loss of water. Any and all of these changes that occur when there is water deficit may be argued to be vital in the control of drinking. As in the case of hunger, it may be adaptive for us to have multiple regulators, which serve as backup systems for each other. Reliance on a single factor such as feelings of thirst, osmoreceptors, or sodium concentration level may be unwise for survival.

A theory that recognizes the complex interaction of several factors is the *double depletion hypothesis* (Epstein, 1973). This explanation considers the role of both cellular and extracellular water loss in water regulatory behavior. A classic study by Gilman (1937) had shown that thirst involves loss of water from both areas. He injected sodium chloride into dogs so that changes in osmotic pressure forced water to pass from the cells into the extracellular water supply. This procedure, compared to injections of urea (a procedure that does not change osmotic pressure as much), led to increased drinking. It was concluded that thirst requires water loss from both cellular and extracellular sources.

The double depletion hypothesis extends this finding and shows that the mechanism for water control varies with the source of the loss. Hypovolemia or reduced blood volume appears to trigger drinking when extracellular losses occur. In addition, the kidneys activate a hormone system known as renin-angiotensin that serves to stimulate further fluid ingestion through its effects on brain areas that control drinking. In the case of depletion of cellular water there is increased activation of preoptic area cells but no release of hormones. Finally, if both sources of water are reduced, the pituitary is alerted and antidiuretic hormone is released to reduce further loss.

COGNITIVE FACTORS

In addition to the central nervous system mechanisms we are unaware of, cognitive factors at the conscious level can influence our drinking of water. We develop many habits of drinking that are nonhomeostatic in nature. That is, as mentioned earlier, we do not restrict our drinking to the restoration of deficits as a rule. We drink at regular intervals such as at meals. When drinking is due to local cues of thirst such as after eating salty foods or after strenuous exercise, we have gradually learned how much we need to drink to reduce our deficits.

Cognitive control of water regulation is not infallible as we may sometimes be deceived by our expectations. A person who thinks about eating a bag of salted peanuts may begin to feel thirsty even before eating them. The power of suggestion may activate sensory experiences in the absence of the normal stimulus for those sensations.

Cannon (1932) used the term *appetite* to refer to the learned desire for food or water where the purpose is not homeostatic. A person may not be deprived of water but suddenly the idea of a nice tall glass of ice water seems inviting and refreshing. The need is more psychological than physiological in basis.

Eating food, unless it is excessively dry, does not require that water also be consumed. Yet, eating is invariably done in conjunction with the drinking of water or other beverages. It is possible that the act of eating serves to stimulate an appetite for water. In rats, Falk (1961) discovered a similar process he termed *schedule-induced polydipsia*. Rats were trained to press a bar for food on a variable interval schedule of one minute. Access to a tube of water was freely available. This procedure allowed access to food only after intervals of one minute on the average regardless of how often the rats pressed. Under this procedure rats were observed to drink excessively in relation to the amount needed to restore water deficits. One explanation for this phenomenon might be the activation of an appetite for water due to the stimulation of frequent eating.

It should be clear that most human water consumption is not aimed at water balance maintenance. Furthermore, cognitive factors play important roles in the determination of our nonregulatory drinking of water.

Pain

In order to survive, organisms must be able to cope with pain-producing stimuli that threaten bodily harm, injury, or death. The capacity to detect and anticipate agents or factors that cause pain enables the organism to seek the means of escaping present dangers and, if successful, avoiding future encounters with them. The experience of pain, although unpleasant and frequently intense, is of great practical value in the long run. It serves to warn the organism of possibly greater threats to its well-being and thus motivate it to attend to the removal of pain, either by withdrawal, counterattack, or the seeking of aid.

Pain often leads to agitated or frantic disorganized behavior. Motor coordination as well as cognitive integration is disrupted, which may sometimes impede efficient or successful coping with pain. These dramatic effects suggest that the stimuli that produce pain must be quite different from ordinary nonpain-producing stimuli. Yet, frequently the main factor distinguishing pain- and nonpain-producing stimuli is that of intensity, for both types can be found in many dimensions. Sound, light, tactile pressure, warmth, and cold are pleasant stimuli at certain intensity levels; if they are increased, they all can produce painful experiences.

When we attribute to stimuli or situations the capacity to create pain for others in everyday life, we often infer pain from the individual's verbal behavior, facial expression, or general behavior toward or away from the situation. We do not directly observe the painful sensations that another person experiences but must rely on indirect evidence often of limited accuracy. Our language for expressing pain does not permit subtle differentiation, nor are most people able to communicate precisely where it hurts, as many physicians can report from their interactions with patients. Social factors such as the embarrassment of admitting the experience of pain may render our inferences of limited accuracy as to what the person is actually feeling. Our own expectancies, based on our own reactions to a given situation, may bias our observations and inferences about the level of pain someone else is feeling.

These limitations of naturalistic observations are some of the reasons the experimental study of pain in laboratory situations offers some advantages. Under controlled conditions, one can vary the stimulus conditions assumed to produce pain as well as record objective behavioral, as well as physiological, responses. Such laboratory studies, whether with rats, monkeys, or humans, have relied heavily on the use of electric shock as the source of pain. It can be quantified and easily standardized and it can be given in convenient doses over a series of trials and in varying intensity levels, all features that are useful in experimental work. At the same time, many forms of natural pain are not so localized, of as short fixed duration, or of such high intensities as electric shock.

An important distinction exists between experimental pain and clinical pain on other grounds. As Sternbach (1968) has pointed out, the experimental subjects are generally paid volunteers who are not in pain coming to receive it for a brief period that will end at the conclusion of the study, whereas the clinical patients are persons who are already experiencing unwanted pain from which they seek relief.

One obvious difference between these two types of situations, if all else were equal, is the possibility that pain thresholds would be lower in patients. Many experimental volunteers would probably want to show how strong and tough they were by accepting higher levels of pain, whereas the clinical patient feels he or she already is suffering too much pain. The bravery of the experimental subject also is increased by the fact that subjects generally trust the experimenter and assume that he or she will be ethical and not place them under conditions that will actually harm them seriously. Protected by this sometimes tenuous assumption, the experimental subject will react to pain-producing stimuli in ways that may differ from the reactions of the patient who is suffering from chronic pain.

Some evidence that is consistent with these speculations comes from Beecher (1959) who found that morphine and similar analgesics can relieve pain in clinical cases but not in experimental subjects. One reason may be that the latter subjects are not experiencing a level of pain equivalent to that faced by patients. In particular, Beecher argued that anxiety would be greater among patients and that the analgesic agent might not be effective in experimental subjects for this reason.

LOCAL FACTORS

Around the turn of the century, the study of pain emphasized its sensory nature. An attempt was made to identify pain stimuli and pain receptors, paralleling the orientation to the study of other sensory processes such as vision or audition. But, unlike other senses, no specific receptors exist for pain per se, because it appears that the critical factor of stimuli for pain is its intensity. Pain stimuli, in other words, are not in a separate category but may include visual, auditory, or tactile stimuli, if they are intense.

Prior to the development of experimental physiology in the nineteenth century, the common view of the mechanism of pain assumed a specific connection between pain receptors in the skin and brain centers. Descartes, for example, drew an analogy between the ringing of a bell in the church belfry by the pulling of a rope and the stimulation of a peripheral receptor and the experience of pain.

Tests of this type of specificity theory became possible with the development of more powerful physiological techniques and attempts to map the sensory pathways leading from receptors for pain to the brain were undertaken near the turn of the century. For example, von Frey (1895) concluded that the free nerve endings on the skin constituted the pain receptors. Although this sensory approach to the study of pain may be adequate at the physiological level, it was inadequate to account for the psychological experience of pain, especially for some pathological phenomena of pain.

The notion that pain receptors exist suggests that there should be a 1:1 correspondence between sensory input and felt pain, but such does not appear to be the case. Cognitive factors such as expectancies and emotional factors such as fear and anxiety are known to affect the level of pain experienced from a given pain stimulus. Pain, then, is not merely a sensory event but involves the interaction of sensory and central processes such as thinking, attention, emotion, and arousal.

CENTRAL FACTORS

In 1965, Melzack and Wall proposed a totally different theoretical approach to the topic of pain that focused on the critical interplay between sensory, cognitive, and motivational processes rather than dealing only with the sensory aspect as earlier theories did. Numerous phenomena simply were inexplicable by a strictly sensory approach, and Melzack and Wall's formulation was exciting because it was able to deal with these problems by suggesting how cognitive factors interacted with sensory processes to determine the eventual experienced pain felt by the organism.

For example, Beecher (1959) found that the same men who report little pain from battle wounds in war were quite irritable when a vein was ineptly punctured during medical treatment. Studies with dogs (Pavlov, 1927) showed that stimuli associated with earlier painful stimuli could be used to condition salivation for food without them showing signs of fear; yet these same stimuli when applied to other parts of the body would produce howls. In general, some factors such as distraction and suggestion can decrease pain, whereas other factors such as fear, expectancy of pain, or excitement can increase pain.

THE GATE THEORY.   These and related phenomena strongly suggest that central processes such as attention, arousal or activation, and appraisal must somehow modulate the sensory input coming from the source of pain, sometimes increasing and sometimes decreasing its perception. First, it is necessary to describe the gate theory of Melzack and Wall, as it has come to be called. A later version (Melzack and Casey, 1968) provides a simpler diagram that will help us describe the model.

As shown in Figure 13–5, sensory input flows into a gate control system before undergoing a spatiotemporal analysis by the sensory-discriminative system. The input proceeds along two separate routes, the large (L) and faster nerve fibers that also go directly to the higher brain centers and the small (S) and slower fibers that feed into the gate control system to the T fibers, then through the sensory-discriminative system, before finally being projected upward to brain centers where they can affect central control processes. In other words, the stimuli sent along the slower and longer route

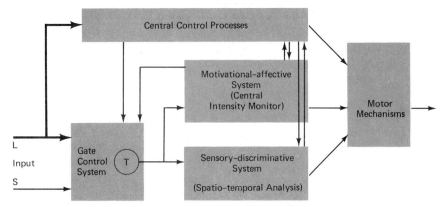

FIGURE 13–5. Schematic diagram showing the three categories of activity involved in pain processes at the brain level: (1) central control processes, (2) activity of the motivational-affective system, and (3) spatiotemporal analysis of input. These three blocks of activity interact with each other and with the Gate Control System, their output impinges on motor mechanisms. [From "Sensory, Motivational, and Central Control Determinants of pain: A New Conceptual Model," by R. Melzack and K. L. Casey, in *The Skin Senses*, by D. Kenshalo (Ed.), Springfield, Ill.: C C Thomas, 1968. Courtesy of Charles C Thomas, Publisher, Springfield, Illinois.]

by the S fibers get analyzed as to location, timing, and intensity on their way to the brain, whereas some of the input also gets to the brain directly over some of the L fibers. This faster route enables past experience, expectancies, suggestion, and other forms of central control processes to feed back downward into the system and influence the operation of the gate control and T cells, sometimes opening the gate more and sometimes closing it, so to speak, and modifying the eventual level of felt pain.

A third component that interacts with the gate control system is the motivational-affective system, which is assumed to involve the brain areas known as the reticular and limbic systems and to be particularly sensitive to the intensity of the pain stimulation. It responds to the total input of stimulation coming from the lower T cells. This system is important in determining whether or not motor mechanisms are activated to produce coping behavior. If the overall firing of the T cells is below some critical level, such actions will not occur and, in fact, the experience may even be pleasant and attractive. However, above that critical level, negative feelings will be experienced such as the sensation of pain. Defensive reflexes, autonomic activity, and previously learned or new responses will be evoked to deal with the threatening situation. This assumption of a critical intensity level would explain why low levels of one type of stimulus, say electric shock, might be pleasant and tingling, whereas higher levels are painful and traumatic.

This brief overview of the model of Melzack and his colleagues (Melzack and Wall, 1965; Melzack and Casey, 1968) does not attempt to describe the physiological evidence they cite to defend it. For our purposes, it is useful to view the model as an indication of the interaction among cognitive and motivational-affective processes with sensory factors in determining behavior and experiences related to pain.

APPLICATIONS OF THE MODEL. An example of the possibility that expectancies can influence our reactions to pain stimuli that also illustrates the application of the Melzack and Wall theory is the phenomenon of acupuncture, which has been sensationalized in the Western world in recent years. With the easing of world political tensions between Red China and the West, numerous Western observers were able to see first-hand the effects of acupuncture (a process in which small needles are inserted in various parts of the body), which enables surgery to take place without modern anesthesia. The patient is conscious and in some instances even watches the operation by means of an overhead mirror.

Wall (1974) was one such observer to describe the process. His analysis repeatedly emphasized the positive attitude and expectancy among acupuncture patients as a key factor in its effectiveness. It should also be pointed out that the location of the needles is considered crucial by practitioners. Certain points are considered vital locations, namely those which release *ch'i,* a Taoist concept of vital or life force; if the needles are inserted at other points, acupuncture is less effective in preventing pain.

Wall, although not explicitly refuting the concept of ch'i, does question the Chinese acupuncture assumption that specific channels or meridians exist for the flow of ch'i on which the determination of the specific points for needling insertion is based. For one matter, schools vary in their beliefs about the location of the meridian points. What does seem to happen in acupunctural needling is the creation of a distracting sensation that may divert the patient's attention from other sources of pain. The inserted needles, themselves, are supposed to produce a feeling of heaviness, swelling and numbness, and soreness. Although Wall does not specifically discuss the gate theory in connection with acupuncture, it is possible that attention to the sensations produced by the needles may help close the gate on the pains associated with the surgery, so that these sensations do not reach the brain in their full intensity.

In addition to this process, which we suggest may occur, Wall emphasized the necessity of other factors such as the relief of anxiety. Unlike the procedure in even the best Western hospitals, the Chinese are careful to reduce the anxiety commonly associated with medical settings, especially those involving surgery. The patient comes to be viewed as part of the medical team treating himself or herself rather than as a passive patient for the doctors to work on. Wall also pointed out that conventional procedures to combat pain such as sedation from barbiturates, intravenous analgesics, and local anaesthetics are also used when acupuncture surgery is performed, although admittedly these procedures are inadequate to explain the phenomena reported under acupuncture.

Suggestion is another key aspect of the process, as evidenced by the fact that children are not treated by acupuncture, because they have not had sufficient training in developing the necessary expectations about the benefits of acupuncture. According to Wall, the biggest problem encountered by the Chinese in using acupuncture on children is that they cry.

Melzack (1973) suggested that acupunctural analgesia is due to the hyperstimulation created by the needle insertion and the twirling of them or passing of electrical current through them as is frequently done. This increased stimulation produces greater activity in a central biasing mechanism located in the brain stem reticular formation, which was postulated by Melzack (1971) as a refinement of the gate control theory. When it is stimulated, it acts to inhibit activity at other levels including the spinal gates so that less pain is experienced.

Other pain phenomena may be similar to acupuncture in that increased and intense pain stimulation, rather than decreased stimulation, produces paradoxical relief from pain eventually. The gate-control theory is better able to incorporate these puzzles of pain than theories that assume that pain is an increasing function of the amount of painful stimulation.

Melzack (1973) pointed out that clinical phenomena such as phantom limb pain, causalgia, and the neuralgias can all be treated by *either* decreasing or increasing the sensory input. Anesthetic blocks can be used to decrease input from the painful area, but relief can also be produced by pain-producing injections. The latter procedure involving counter-irritation is a common folk remedy for pain as can be seen from the use of either cold or hot compresses to relieve painful bruises, for example. Melzack does not believe that suggestion or distraction are adequate explanations for their analgesic effects but maintains that some physiological processes must be considered.

Analgesia produced by hyperstimulation such as creating an intense pain in one area to relieve pain in another is explained by Melzack in terms of the gate-control theory along the same lines used to account for the benefits of acupuncture. The induced pain activates the central biasing mechanism in the brain stem reticular formation, which exerts an inhibiting or blocking influence on sensory input from the source of pain to be treated.

These forms of therapy avoid the necessity for surgical intervention called for by the theory that pain is carried directly from receptors to brain centers. In contrast, the gate-control theory implies that methods that can activate some form of central blockage or closing of the gates can reduce the felt pain encountered by the sufferer.

COGNITIVE FACTORS

The preceding discussion of acupuncture has suggested that cognitive factors such as attention can alter reactions to pain. We will now examine additional evidence illustrating cognitive influences.

Sternbach (1965) conducted a study that illustrates the effect of anxiety on the experience of pain. He administered shock to several groups, which received different instructions as to what to expect. The groups led to expect higher intensity shocks also reported the most pain.

In another experiment (Nisbett and Schachter, 1966), all subjects first received a placebo treatment although they thought the pill they were given would affect their skin sensitivity as measured by their reaction to electric shocks applied to their hands. The drug was alleged to have mild and transitory effects, and one group of subjects was led to believe that they would feel tremor, palpitations, etc., effects that they would in fact feel when shocked later in the study. A second group was misled to expect the pill to make them itchy or numb, effects that neither shock nor placebos create. Half of each of these two groups expected high shocks and half expected low shocks. Subjects were left alone for about ten minutes before the shock stimuli were presented.

Electrodes were then attached to the subject's fingers and he received a series of progressively more intense shocks every fifteen seconds, until he indicated that the shocks were too painful. The group that expected the pill to produce effects similar to those of actual shocks were expected to assign these effects to the pill, whereas those groups expecting the pill to make them itchy or numb would conclude that the shock-produced tremor and heart-rate increases came from the shocks. Nisbett and Schachter (1967) predicted that the group that misattributed the effects of shock to the pill would tolerate more intense shocks as a consequence. The results showed that such was the case, provided the level of expected shocks was low.

The Nisbett and Schachter study demonstrates how cognitive labeling of the source of bodily reactions that stem from pain can affect the experienced painfulness. The unpleasant feelings caused by shock lead subjects who are misled into thinking these effects are caused by the pill to endure higher levels of shock.

The circumstances under which one receives painful stimuli can also influence one's tolerance for aversive consequences. A study by Staub and Kellett (1972) varied the kind of information male subjects were given prior to receiving shocks of brief duration every twenty seconds, which gradually increased in magnitude. One group was informed about the kinds of sensations generally experienced by subjects receiving shocks, such as tingling, tremor, heart rate increase, and faster breathing. A second group was informed about the safety precautions of the equipment. Both types of information were received by a third group, whereas neither kind was provided for a fourth group.

Then the shocks were administered and subjects reported when they first felt anything, first felt uncomfortable, first felt pain, and when they could not tolerate any higher shock level. The results showed that the group that received both types of information was able to accept higher shocks before reporting pain or asking to terminate the session. There was little difference among the other three groups. As might be expected, responses to a post-experimental inquiry indicated that subjects who received neither type of preliminary information reported having the most worry about the effects of the shocks. It seems that the two groups that received one type of information were not any more worried than the group that received both kinds of information. Yet, the reactions to the shocks suggest that subjects who were told only about what effects to expect might still have worried about the safety of the situation because they received no assurances about it. Similarly, the subjects who learned of the safety of the apparatus may have been anxious, because they were not told what sensations to expect from the shock. The fact that the group that was briefed about both aspects of the situation accepted more shock implies that being "forewarned was to be forearmed" and they were less anxious about the situation.

There has been little doubt that numerous cognitive factors can influence the reaction to pain. It is typical to infer that the lowered threshold for pain found when subjects are anxious and uncertain as to what to expect is reflective of greater experienced or felt pain. Similarly, if a placebo is presented as a pain reliever to subjects, as in a study by Clark (1969), they will tolerate higher levels of pain. But does this mean that the placebo has actually reduced the experienced or felt pain? Clark takes exception to this usual interpretation and suggests that the sensitivity to pain is unchanged but that the subjects' criterion or standard for judging a stimulus to be painful has been shifted upward by their expectations. Traditional psychophysical techniques for measuring sensory thresholds do not permit one to determine which of these two alternative explanations is more accurate, but the signal detection theory approach (Green and Swets, 1966) does permit separate indices to be calculated for sensory discrimination and the subjective criterion that the subject uses as a standard for judgment. Clark found that there were no differences in discrimination of thermal pain stimuli between the placebo and nonplacebo conditions but that the placebo condition led to the use of higher criteria for judging a stimulus to be painful.

CULTURAL FACTORS. We need look only at the differences in how parents respond to the reactions of young children to pain to see how cultural attitudes modify and mold our experiences of pain. In our society, as is the case in most, young boys are discouraged from crying or complaining about painful falls or bruises, whereas young girls receive sympathy and nurturance for overt expression of their pains.

It is also likely that different cultures vary in their general attitudes toward pain and its expression. Among Jews and Italians, for example, parents react with sympathy and concern when children experience pain and discomfort. Will these children react differently to pain in later life than children from cultures such as middle class America where there is more emphasis on independence, assertiveness, and courage?

A classic study by Zborowski (1952, 1969) involved open-ended interviews of male patients in a Veteran's Administration hospital representing

Italian, Jewish, and "Old American" backgrounds. Particular attention was directed toward their reactions to pain and the use of pain-relieving drugs. Both Italian and Jewish patients were similar insofar as expressing pain and being intolerant of it, but they differed in acceptance of analgesics. Whereas the Italians readily accepted the drugs and were satisfied when pain was relieved, the Jews were anxious about the medication and afraid it might be habit forming or not really treat the disease. Even if pain was relieved, the Jewish patients still worried about their health being permanently improved. In contrast, the American patients tended to deny or disregard their pains.

FUNCTIONS OF PAIN

Pain is more than aversive stimulation because it also is associated with varied social meanings. Although pain may signal the organism of bodily threat and harm by producing intense and unpleasant feelings at the sensory level, it also conveys some type of more cognitive and sometimes abstract message. On one extreme, due to the frequent associations between pain and punishment that children experience when they are disciplined, the over-generalization may be made that all pain represents a form of punishment. Even if a person stubs his or her toe accidentally and suffers pain, he or she might view it as punishment and conclude, "It serves me right for being careless."

Bakan (1968) argued that adults may tend to construe painful events as punishments even though an objective observer would not interpret the situation in the same manner. Events that others might attribute to chance might be seen by the sufferer of pain as an act of providential retribution and thus find it necessary to offer prayers for forgiveness to God. All kinds of pain— pain caused by impersonal agents such as diseases as well as that caused accidentally by human agents—may generate guilt feelings.

Such attributions of pain to justifiable acts of retribution are not limited to the recipient of pain. It has been common for more fortunate persons to interpret the misfortunes of others as consequences of the misdeeds and short-comings of the latter. Perhaps this interpretation helps insulate the more fortunate from feeling the need to console and assist the sufferers.

In his social history of nineteenth-century cholera epidemics in the United States, Rosenberg (1962) documents the superior and disdainful attitudes of those who escaped the disease. It was commonly believed by the middle and upper classes that poverty itself was a moral rather than a social issue. The wrath of God was assumed to be manifested by the epidemics of cholera, which initially struck the poor because of their less-sanitary living conditions.

Bakan also noted that the experience of pain can be taken to represent a test of character, courage, and fortitude. He used the Biblical story of Job, which chronicled the series of misfortunes that befell him. Because Job was a virtuous and righteous man, these sufferings could hardly be considered punishments from God. Yet Job was able to survive these misfortunes and maintain his religious faith, because he interpreted this series of injustices as tests of his religious conviction. Because the death of Job's children whom he loved dearly was viewed as a call for sacrifice on his part, suffering created no resentment in him.

Pain and suffering may at other times elicit feelings of sympathy and compassion from others. Ability to withstand and endure pain may be regarded by others with admiration. Frequent complaints about real or imagined pains may irritate others. In short, there are interpersonal consequences stemming from our experiences and reactions to pain. Different styles of coping with pain may be learned, so that some people stoically accept pain while others proclaim it conspicuously in order to achieve martyrdom. A learning theory approach would suggest that these diverse styles were learned by the process of differential reinforcement. Persons who received sympathy and attention for expressing intolerance of pain acquired their style of reacting to pain in the same manner as those who were reinforced for inhibiting expressions of pain. Zborowski's previously described ethnic group differences in attitudes toward acceptance of pain are relevant here.

An alternative explanation for individual differences assumes that differences in sensory capacities may exist. Petrie (1967), for example, as noted in Chapter 10 hypothesized that a given pain stimulus may be experienced more intensely by those whom she termed *augmenters* than by those she called *reducers*. These differences were assumed to be correlated with general perceptual sensitivity, so that individual differences in one dimension might be predicted from those found in another.

A kinesthetic figural aftereffect test was devised in which subjects felt an unseen wood block and then had to rely on their kinesthetic memory or aftereffect of its width to identify the corresponding width on a triangular apparatus by touch.

Subjects who overestimated the width of the original stimulus input were termed *augmenters,* whereas those who underestimated it were considered *reducers*. To demonstrate the generality of such differential sensitivity, pain tolerances were determined for these subjects next. It was expected that augmenters would experience a given pain stimulus as more intense than would reducers and consequently show lower tolerances for pain. Presumably these differences reflect some physiological differences in reactivity, although it is still possible for cultural and social factors to exert additional influences on the experience of pain. In any event, her results are consistent with the hypothesis that differences in kinesthetic judgments are correlated with pain tolerance differences. Petrie favored the view that individual differences in pain tolerance reflect only one aspect of more general differences in processing information from the environment.

Even if there are physiological factors responsible for individual differences in pain tolerance, there are also learned differences in the meanings assigned to the experience of pain, learned differences in the extent to which pain can be expressed or acknowledged, and learned differences in methods for coping with pain. In addition to its role in the behavior and experience of the individual, pain also exerts important influence on social interactions. Our attitudes and reactions toward the pain encountered by others can be one of sympathy and aid or one of smug superiority or gloating satisfaction, depending on whether the sufferer is our friend or our enemy.

Pain is an unpleasant and sometimes unavoidable experience interpreted in terms that go beyond the physical sensations themselves. In order to understand the human experience of pain, we must understand its perceived meaning, the learned strategies for coping with one's own pains, and the learned reactions to the pains suffered by others.

Summary

Behavior related to biological needs for survival such as eating or avoiding pain cannot be fully understood when humans are involved if we limit our attention to physiological processes. Cognitive, cultural, and subjective factors play an important part in determining the eventual behavior. For instance, a strictly biological survival view would expect organisms to seek food when deprived and to avoid pain if possible. Yet humans are affected by cultural factors that may lead them to fast either for health or ideological reasons so that food is actually avoided. Similarly, humans may seek to suffer pain to prove their courage or to punish themselves for their shortcomings.

The early studies of eating focused on peripheral factors such as cues from the stomach, but as technology improved, attention turned to the examination of brain centers. Theories were developed suggesting that centers for the control of eating were located in the hypothalamus, which responded to feedback from the body regarding blood sugar level, temperature, or stomach distension.

We placed more emphasis on the role of cognitive factors underlying eating such as taste, temporal cues, and environment as opposed to level of biological need. Undoubtedly, eating can be affected by both external cues and internal bodily cues. In fact, Schachter's views suggest that individual differences in obesity could stem from the fact that obese persons are more strongly affected by external cues, whereas normal-weight persons govern their eating primarily by internal cues. It is also possible, however, that there are biological differences in the setting of the eating center regulator, its being higher in those prone to overweight.

Eating serves functions other than survival in a physical sense. Psychological gratification through eating can also exist, such as when frustration or boredom leads to overeating as a form of compensation. Eating practices are also affected by ideological and religious beliefs.

Physical survival also requires adequate regulation of water needs. Homeostatic drinking refers to the ingestion of water aimed at maintaining the normal levels by replenishing water loss through elimination and perspiration. All human drinking, however, is not homeostatic in nature. Factors such as learned habits or affective consequences of drinking may lead to nonhomeostatic drinking.

Earlier research in this century emphasized the role of local cues such as dryness in the mouth region as a stimulus for the initiation of drinking. Experiments showed, however, that local factors were inadequate to explain drinking.

With the development of more advanced surgical tools and techniques, the role of central factors such as hypothalamic centers were postulated to govern water regulation. Water intake was affected by a variety of procedures involving regions of the hypothalamus such as injections of sodium chloride, electrical stimulation, and lesioning of these areas.

The role of osmotic pressure also became evident. As the balance between the water concentration within cells and outside cells shifts whenever water deprivation occurs, changes in osmotic pressure occur. It is assumed that osmoreceptors in the hypothalamic region detect such changes and signal the need to drink water.

Other changes also occur at the same time such as increased blood viscosity, increased sodium levels, increased temperature, and the release of hormones from the kidney and pituitary. All these factors work together in maintaining the proper balance of water levels. The double depletion hypothesis is one model that illustrates this complex interplay of numerous factors in the control of water balance.

Although pain is an unpleasant experience, it has obvious utility for survival in warning the organism of possibly greater dangers. Cultural values can alter reactions to pain, as in the disapproval of crying in boys whereas it is tolerated in girls. It is unwise to generalize freely from animal studies of pain to humans because such cultural factors are absent for nonhuman species.

Early theories of the physiological basis of pain assumed a point-to-point correspondence between the periphery and brain centers. However, because the experience of pain is not exclusively affected by sensory factors but is also altered by cognitive and emotional factors, it has been difficult to understand the mechanism of pain.

The gate theory of Melzack and Wall incorporated sensory, motivational, and cognitive factors and was able to incorporate many of the puzzling phenomena related to pain. In essence, it showed how attentional processes might diminish or magnify the felt experience of pain coming from a given stimulus. Factors such as expectancies and suggestion, for example, that can alter the level of pain experienced are easily handled by this model, which shows how various neural pathways leading to brain centers might be blocked by competing messages or facilitated by compatible inputs.

The meaning of pain to the individual varies widely, serving as punishment in the sense of retribution for some people even when the source of pain was nonpersonal. The same situation may elicit anger, resentment, or despair in other people. Similarly, there are individual differences in our reactions to others who are suffering from pain. We may or may not feel sympathy depending on the details of the situation. These meanings are culturally learned interpretations of the pain experience, which can influence our ability to endure or tolerate pain. Pain cannot be fully understood if it is analyzed only in terms of the physical properties of the pain-producing stimulus.

References

ADOLPH, E. F. Internal environment and behavior: Water content. *American Journal of Psychiatry*, 1941, *97*, 1365–1373.
————. Thirst and its inhibition in the stomach. *American Journal of Physiology*, 1950, *161*, 374–386.
ANAND, B. K. and BROBECK, J. R. Hypothalamic control of food intake in rats and cats. *Yale Journal of Biological Medicine*, 1951, *24*, 123–140.
ANDERSSON, B., and McCANN, S. M. Drinking, antidiuresis, and milk ejection from electrical stimulation from the hypothalamus of goats. *Acta Physiologica Scandia*, 1955, *35*, 191–201.
BAILEY, P., and BREMER, F. Experimental diabetus insipidus. *Archives of Internal Medicine*, 1921, *28*, 773–803.
BAKAN, D. *Disease, pain, and suffering: Toward a psychology of suffering*. Chicago: University of Chicago Press, 1968.
BEECHER, H. K. *Measurement of subjective responses*. London: Oxford University Press, 1959.
BELLOWS, R. T. Time factors in water drinking in dogs. *American Journal of Physiology*, 1939, *125*, 87–97.
BROBECK, J. R. Neural regulation of food intake. *Annals of the New York Academy of Sciences*, 1955, *63*, Art. 1, 44–55.
————, TEPPERMAN, J., and LONG, C. N. H. Experimental hypothalamic hyperphagia in the albino rat. *Yale Journal of Biological Medicine*, 1943, *15*, 831–853.
BRUCH, H. *Eating disorders, obesity, anorexia nervosa, and the person within*. New York: Basic, 1973.
CANNON, W. B. *The wisdom of the body*. New York: Norton, 1932.
————, and WASHBURN, A. L. An explanation of hunger. *American Journal of Physiology*, 1912, *29*, 441–454.
CLARK, W. C. Sensory-decision theory analysis of the placebo effect on the criterion for pain and thermal sensitivity (d'). *Journal of Abnormal Psychology*, 1969, *74*, 363–371.
DEVENPORT, L. D., and BALAGURA, S. Reevaluation of function in motivated feeding behavior. *Science*, 1971, *72*, 744–746.
EPSTEIN, A. N. Reciprocal changes in feeding behavior produced by intrahypothalamic chemical injections. *American Journal of Physiology*, 1960, *199*, 969–974.
————. Epilogue: retrospect and prognosis. In A. N. Epstein, H. R. Kissileff, and E. Stellar (Eds.), *The neuropsychology of thirst*. Washington, D.C.: V. H. Winston, 1973.

————, and Teitlebaum, P. Regulation of food intake in the absence of taste, smell, and other oropharangyeal sensations. *Journal of Comparative and Physiological Psychology,* 1962, *55,* 753–759.

Falk, J. L. Production of polydipsia in normal rats by an intermittent food schedule. *Science,* 1961, *133,* 195–196.

Fitzsimons, J. T. Thirst. *Physiological Reviews,* 1972, *52,* 468–561.

Frey, M. von. Beitrage zur Sinnesphysiologie der Haut, *Ber. Sachs. Ges. Wiss,* 1895, *47,* 166–184.

Frazer, J. G. *The Golden Bough. A study in magic and religion.* Abridged Edition. New York: Macmillan, 1950.

Gilman, A. The relation between blood osmotic pressure, fluid distribution, and voluntary water intake. *American Journal of Physiology,* 1937, *120,* 323–328.

Goldman, R., Jaffa, M., and Schachter, S. Yom kippur, Air France, dormitory food, and the eating behavior of obese and normal persons. *Journal of Personality and Social Psychology,* 1968, 117–123.

Green, D. M., and Swets, J. A. *Signal detection theory and psychophysics.* New York: Wiley, 1966.

Kissileff, H. R. Nonhomeostatic controls of drinking. In A. N. Epstein, H. R. Kissileff, and E. Stellar (Eds.), *The neuropsychology of thirst.* Washington, D.C.: V. H. Winston, 1973.

Krasne, F. B. General disruption resulting from electrical stimulus of ventromedial hypothalamus. *Science,* 1962, *138,* 822–823.

Mayer, J. Regulation of energy intake and body weight: The glucostatic and the lipostatic hypotheses. *Annals of the New York Academy of Sciences,* 1955, *63,* 15–43.

————. *Overweight.* Englewood Cliffs, N.J.: Prentice-Hall, 1968.

Melzack, R. Phantom limb pain: Complications for treatment of pathological pain. *Anesthesiology,* 1971, *35,* 409–419.

————. *The puzzle of pain.* New York: Basic, 1973.

————, and Casey, K. L. Sensory, motivational, and central control determinants of pain: A new conceptual model. In D. Kenshalo (Ed.), *The skin senses.* Springfield, Ill.: C. C. Thomas, 1968.

————, and Wall, P. D. Pain mechanisms: A new theory. *Science,* 1965, *150,* 971–979.

Nisbett, R. E. Hunger, obesity, and the ventromedial hypothalamus. *Psychological Review,* 1972, *79,* 433–453.

————, and Schachter, S. Cognitive manipulation of pain. *Journal of Experimental Social Psychology,* 1966, *2,* 227–236.

Petrie, A. *Individuality in pain and suffering.* Chicago: University of Chicago Press, 1967.

Pliner, P. L. Effects of cue salience on the behavior of obese abnormal subjects. *Journal of Abnormal Psychology,* 1973, *82,* 226–232.

————. Effects of external cues on the thinking behavior of obese and normal subjects. *Journal of Abnormal Psychology,* 1973, *82,* 233–238.

Pyke, M. *Food and society.* London: Murray, 1968.

Rosenberg, C. E. *The cholera years, the United States in 1832, 1849, and 1866.* Chicago: University of Chicago Press, 1962.

Schachter, S. Cognitive effects on bodily functioning: Studies of obesity and eating. In D. C. Glass (Ed.), *Neurophysiology and emotion.* New York: Rockefeller University Press, 1967.

————, Goldman, R., and Gordon, A. Effects of fear, food deprivation, and obesity on eating. *Journal of Personality and Social Psychology,* 1968, *10,* 91–97.

————, and GROSS, L. Manipulated time and eating behavior. *Journal of Personality and Social Psychology*, 1968, *10*, 98–106.

————, and RODIN, J. (Eds.), *Obese humans and rats*. Potomac, Md.: Erlbaum and associates, 1974.

SHARMA, K. N., ANAND, B. K., DUA, S., and SINGH, B. Role of stomach in regulation of activities of hypothalamic feeding centers. *American Journal of Physiology*, 1961, *201*, 593–598.

STAUB, E., and KELLETT, D. S. Increasing pain tolerance by information about aversive stimuli. *Journal of Personality and Social Psychology*, 1972, *21*, 198–203.

STEGGERDA, F. R. Observations on the water intake in an adult man with dysfunctioning salivary glands. *American Journal of Physiology*, 1941, *119*, 409.

STERNBACH, R. A. *Pain: A psychophysiological analysis*. New York: Academic, 1968.

STRUNKARD, A. J., and FOX, S. The relationship of gastric mobility and hunger, a summary of the evidence. *Psychosomatic Medicine*, 1971, *33*, 123–134.

————, and KOCH, C. The interpretation of gastric motility. I. Apparatus bias in the reports of hunger by obese persons. *Archives of General Psychiatry*, 1964, *11*, 74–82.

VERNEY, E. B. The antidiuretic hormone and the factors which determine its release. *Proceedings of the Royal Society* (London), Series B, *135*, 25–106.

WALL, P. Acupuncture revisited. *New Scientist*, 1974, *64*, (No. 917), 31–34.

WYRWICKA, W., and DOBRZECKA, C. Relationship between feeding and satiation centers of the hypothalamus. *Science*, 1960, *132*, 805–806.

ZBOROWSKI, M. Cultural components in responses to pain. *Journal of Social Issues*, 1952, *8*, 16–30.

————. *People in pain*. San Francisco: Jossey-Bass, 1969.

CHAPTER 14

At the Gut Level: Sleep and Sex

Sleep is a universal process, one generally assumed to be necessary for normal functioning during waking states. We feel tired and irritable if we get inadequate or uncomfortable sleep during the preceding night. Sleep, however, is not the uniform deep trance it is sometimes depicted as being; as we shall see it involves varying degrees of depth. Our approach to sleep will focus on the psychophysiological method, a technique that made it possible to identify the various stages of sleep as well as to discover important facts relevant to our understanding of the functions served by sleep.

We tend to take sleep for granted unless we are denied access to it. In contrast, sexual activities are generally goals we must work to obtain by wooing or being wooed through the courtship process. We can live without sex, physically speaking, but because of its limited or restricted access we sometimes think that we could not survive psychologically without it. Human sexual behavior is intimately associated with social institutions such as marriage and the family and governed by stringent moral and religious beliefs.

Whereas ample objective information is available about sleep because it is relatively easy to obtain volunteers to sleep in the laboratory, similar objective data about the nature of sexual response is difficult to obtain. The interviews about sexual behavior conducted by Kinsey over twenty-five years ago encountered great criticism and resistance and the more recent efforts of Masters and Johnson (1966) to study actual physiological responses during heterosexual intercourse in laboratory situations also generated much objection.

The fact that sleep is not a moral issue whereas sexual behavior is means that our discussion of the two topics must differ in the extent to which empirical evidence can be presented. Cultural factors play relatively small roles in determining sleep compared to their impact on sexual behavior. Our treatment of sleep, then, will emphasize the role of physical factors, whereas our analysis of sexual behavior will concentrate on sociocultural and psychological determinants.

Sleep

We spend about one-third of our lives in sleep, a state that has fascinated and perplexed humans for centuries. Only in the past half-century have precise measuring instruments been available, such as the electroencephalogram (EEG), to permit significant advances in the scientific understanding of this important process. In ancient times, it was not uncommon to believe that the soul departed the body during sleep, especially because of the mysterious process of dreaming that often occurs in sleep. Sleep was regarded as a necessary consequence of fatigue and tiredness developed during waking and was assumed to restore the body for the subsequent waking period. Of course, this conception of sleep's function is also held today by both laypeople and some scientists but there are alternative views. Kleitman (1963), for example, whose sleep laboratory at the University of Chicago was a leading research center suggested that sleep might be the natural state of the organism and that the question should be, what causes wakefulness?

SLEEP DEPRIVATION

Unlike food seeking or pain avoidance, which are obviously intentional and motivated behaviors necessary for survival, sleep is less obviously voluntary or motivated in the same sense. There has even been some question whether it is necessary for survival, even though prolonged sleep deprivation in animals results in death (Kleitman, 1963). Furthermore, our own subjective experiences with sleep loss as well as those of researchers (e.g., Agnew, Webb, and Williams, 1967; Wilkinson, 1965; Williams, Lubin, and Goodnow, 1959) show that irritability, emotionality, and mood disturbances may occur. Impairments in behavioral efficiency in psychomotor tasks, perceptual vigilance, and cognitive operations may also occur, especially if the task requires more than a few minutes to complete.

But are these impairments due to sleep loss or to other factors such as uninterrupted muscular tension, the stress engendered by the procedures used to prevent sleep, or the discrepancy between our circadian time and that imposed by the uninterrupted waking. *Circadian rhythms* refer to a day-night variation in activity levels that has been identified in all forms of living organisms. In humans the period is about twenty-five hours, as determined by experiments in which humans are placed in a controlled environment with no external cues. Because these "free running rhythms" of activity cycles still occur under such conditions, biologists (e.g., Pittendrigh, 1960) consider them endogenous or innate aspects of the organism, although they can be entrained or modified to fit environmental or exogenous conditions such as our twenty-four-hour patterns.

Returning to the problem of the effects of sleep loss, we see that the phenomenon of circadian rhythms raises the possibility that the impairments found with sleep deprivation might be due to the subject being out of phase with his or her biological rhythm by being continuously awake rather than to the loss of sleep per se.

Another aspect of sleep deprivation that suggests that we do not need all the sleep we use is the fact that recovery sleep time is less than the amount deprived. For example, Kleitman (1963) reported that subjects who are deprived of sleep for several nights might require twelve to fourteen hours on the first recovery night but by the next night need only their normal amount of sleep.

Although the sleep deprivation findings are interesting, the data do come from an atypical situation and must be interpreted with caution in making inferences about the necessity of sleep. Human studies of sleep deprivation deal with a period of three or four consecutive days. Highly motivated volunteers for these studies, as well as persons in everyday life who must sacrifice sleep under stress for several days, may be able to do without adequate sleep for these brief periods without undue impairment.

Although speculative, evolutionary arguments would imply that sleep was adaptive and necessary for the survival of primates because it would be dangerous to wander about in the night. Organisms that did not sleep or remain inactive during the night were eliminated by predators and natural calamities (walking off the edge of a cliff, etc.), so that natural selection has left us with variants that require a period of sleep during the dark hours. Nocturnal animals, in contrast, sleep during hours of light but apparently for similar purposes. Thus, rodents are more likely to avoid natural predators such as hawks if they sleep during the day and emerge from their burrows to engage in food-seeking and other behaviors during the dark hours.

Although the question of whether or not sleep is necessary is fascinating, it may be more fruitful for us to focus on some aspects of the nature of sleep, especially because modern research has clearly demonstrated that sleep is not a unitary process but one that involves cycles of two basic varieties. The functions of these two types of sleep appear to differ significantly.

TWO TYPES OF SLEEP

Sleep was difficult to study objectively before the EEG permitted brain waves to be recorded from the scalp of the sleeping subject. Without some technique such as this one, it was difficult to determine whether a subject was, in fact, asleep or merely drowsy. As shown in Figure 14–1, the EEG shows frequent but low amplitude waves (about eight to twelve cycles per

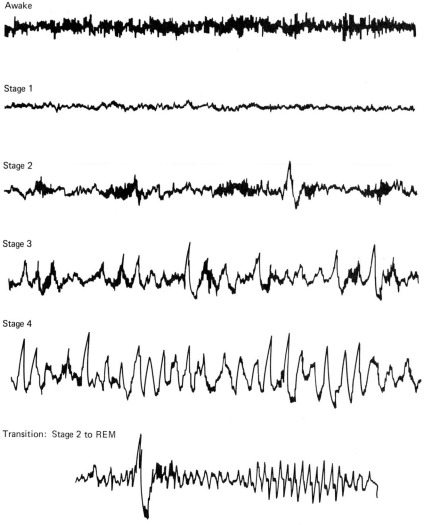

FIGURE 14–1.   Stages of sleep. This figure shows sample EEG tracings that illustrate the typical patterns seen in wakefulness, the four NREM EEG stages, and the transition from Stage 2 to REM sleep. [From *Some Must Watch While Some Must Sleep,* by W. C. Dement, M.D., San Francisco: San Francisco Book Co., 1976. Reprinted by permission of the publisher.]

second) during relaxed waking states; as sleep begins, the patterns go through several types of changes. In the type of sleep later termed NREM (nonrapid eye movement) sleep, four distinct stages were identified. Moreover, Aserinsky and Kleitman (1953) showed that, contrary to popular belief, a person does not proceed from waking to sleep and back again to waking eight hours later but through several cycles of sleep of different depths during the night, as shown in Figure 14–2.

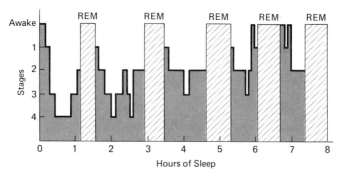

FIGURE 14–2. A plot showing the pattern of REM sleep, NREM sleep, and the four stages of NREM sleep over the course of one entire night of sleep. [From *Some Must Watch While Some Must Sleep*, by W. C. Dement, M.D., San Francisco: San Francisco Book Co., 1976. Reprinted by permission of the publisher.]

Aserinsky and Kleitman also distinguished between two types of sleep, that involving rapid eye movements (REM) and that without them, as described above. The specification of the relationship between these previously observed but unstudied eye movements and EEG patterns revealed a distinctive wave pattern.

This discovery was the impetus that stimulated many investigators to intensify their efforts to study the nature of sleep. As shown in Figure 14–2, REM sleep normally begins each time the four stages of NREM sleep are completed and together these five periods of sleep last about ninety minutes before the next five complete cycles begin. Each successive REM period is usually longer, with the REM period occurring just prior to waking being the longest. The total REM sleep in an eight hour sleep period is about one and one-half hours. In addition to the EEG records, the study of REM required the use of the electrooculogram (EOG) to record eye movements and the electromyogram (EMG) to measure muscle fiber activity, which also greatly increases during REM sleep.

Whereas NREM sleep seems passive and deep, REM sleep is more active. The eyes themselves move to and fro even faster than during waking. Breathing becomes irregular and the pulse quickens. Muscle activity increases and can be seen directly in the form of facial twitches. It would seem likely that such dramatic differences in the state of the organism during REM sleep indicate that it is a different process from NREM sleep.

SLEEP AND DREAMING

Aserinsky and Kleitman (1953; 1955) suspected that the increased activity observed during REM sleep might be reflective of the occurrence of dreams. The obvious test would be to awaken subjects from their slumber when the EEG indicated they were having REM sleep and compare their verbal reports with those produced following awakenings from NREM sleep. Aserinsky and Kleitman found that REM awakenings showed dream recall about 75 per cent of the time, whereas NREM awakenings led to dream recall only about 17 per cent of the time. Summarizing the overall findings by a number of investigators in different laboratories in the mid- to late 1950s, Dement (1974) showed a high correspondence in results with 78.6 per cent of REM awakenings and only 14.0 per cent of NREM awakenings involving dream recall.

The identification of the period during which dreams seem to occur prompted studies of the effects of dream deprivation (e.g., Dement, 1960). Some subjects were prevented from dreaming by being awakened whenever they entered REM sleep on five consecutive nights; a comparable number of awakenings during NREM sleep were made for a control group. Dream-deprived subjects appeared to be more irritable and disrupted by their treatment, suggesting that dreams are an essential activity of sleep. Furthermore, they spent twice as much time in REM sleep on the sleep recovery night as did the control group. The fact that many people cannot recall dreams does not support their claims that they do not, in fact, dream. It is possible that they do dream but are unable to remember them.

Similarly, we should not conclude that no dreams occur at all during NREM sleep. Because it is a deeper sleep during some stages, NREM period dreams may occur but be inaccessible to recall. Furthermore, as Foulkes (1962) has shown, dream recall is possible from subjects awakened from NREM sleep if fragmentary thoughts or ideas are accepted as constituting dreams. As Dement (1974) pointed out, assumptions that all subjects define the term *dream* in the same manner as the experimenter does is unwarranted and may lead to erroneous conclusions.

INTERPRETING DREAMS

Perhaps the most fascinating aspect of dreams to the lay person, and to many scientists, is the meaning of dreams. The psychophysiological approach we have been describing has focused on the identification of the stages of sleep during which dreaming occurs but, with little exception, has not been concerned with the content and meaning of dreams. The monumental contribution of Sigmund Freud (1900/1953) to this aspect of dreaming in his book *The Interpretation of Dreams* emphasized the hidden meanings of dreams. Due to the repression of traumatic experiences and thoughts during waking activity, it was assumed that the less-censored dreaming activities of sleep would permit the expression of these anxiety-producing thoughts. Even dreams, however, had to be represented, according to Freud, in symbolic terms rather than expressed directly.

Freud's contributions to the study of dreams, significant as they were, produced considerable controversy. His interpretations of dreams reported by his clients are difficult to test scientifically; furthermore, his judgments were made with knowledge of other aspects of the client's life history, which may have influenced his interpretations as much or more so than the dream content per se. The meanings he assigned to dreams fit his theory of psycho-neuroses based on sexual conflicts and anxieties to a large extent. The idea that dreams served as a means of wish fulfillment illustrates how the problems of waking life are carried over and sometimes resolved during sleep.

Whether or not a given interpretation of a dream is valid is difficult to demonstrate for the additional reason that such interpretations are sometimes self-fulfilling prophecies. Throughout history, dreams have been regarded as omens and portents of things to come, so that the likelihood of subsequent behavior being influenced by some types of dreams is enhanced. Even when the dream deals with situations over which one can not exert any control such as a dream that a world leader will be assassinated, other interpretations are possible than that of prophetic powers if the event comes true. Our memories are selective and we ignore or fail to notice the prophetic dreams that did not or have not yet come true. And, in the specific example here, we must recognize that the likelihood of such assassination is reasonably high even if no one dreams about it.

Nonetheless, dreams are an important aspect of our lives, because our assumptions about them influence our behavior. Freudian views suggest how waking motives and emotions influence the content of dreams. Recall of these dreams, with or without the aid of a psychoanalyst, can in turn influence subsequent motives during waking states.

OTHER FUNCTIONS OF SLEEP

The two types of sleep may differ in ways other than more frequent dreams during REM sleep. Hartmann, Baekeland, and Zwilling (1972) assessed the characteristics of the sleep of persons whose sleep habits differed from the normal patterns engaged in by most people. Long sleepers who spent over nine hours asleep and short sleepers who always required less than six hours of sleep were compared for eight nights in a sleep laboratory. No differences were found between them or compared with normal sleepers in the amount of the slow wave sleep typical of Stages 3 and 4 of NREM sleep, but the long sleepers spent more time in REM sleep compared to the short sleepers. Hartmann et al. also obtained personality test scores, which suggested that the long sleepers were neurotic and anxious compared to the confident and energetic short sleepers. However, another study (Webb and Agnew, 1970) did not find any such personality differences, although long sleepers were also found to have more REM sleep.

In any case, the finding that the same amount of Stages 3 and 4 NREM sleep occurs for long, normal, and short sleepers and the fact that recovery sleep after several nights of sleep deprivation shows high amounts of this slow wave sleep led Hartmann (1973) to suggest that there is a primacy or greater need for this type of sleep. Combined with other evidence, Hartmann argues that these stages of NREM sleep may play a part in physical restoration.

On the other hand, REM sleep is presumed to restore more specific functions, especially those systems exhausted by worry, depression, stress, uncertainty, or increased cognitive demands. Some indirect evidence for this view comes from two studies (Brewer and Hartmann, 1973; Hartmann et al., 1972) that asked subjects for self-reports of the conditions associated with variations in the amount of sleep they require on different nights. Figure 14–3, from Hartmann (1973), summarizes the findings of the two studies and shows that subjects claim to sleep more following stress, worry, and increased mental or physical activity, whereas they think they need less sleep following "times when everything goes well."

Because Hartmann et al. (1972) established that NREM Stages 3 and 4 sleep is essentially equal for sleepers who differ in their typical amount of

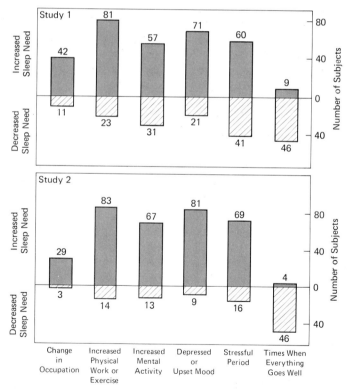

FIGURE 14–3. Number of respondents reporting increased or decreased sleep under various conditions. Study 1 refers to a university population and Study 2 to a random sample of registered Voters. [From *The Functions of Sleep,* by E. Hartmann, New Haven, Conn.: Yale University Press, 1973. Copyright 1973 by Yale University Press. Reprinted by permission.]

sleep, it is possible that the increased sleep reported by subjects following stress or effort is primarily an increase in REM sleep. Thus, Hartmann (1973) concluded that the function of REM sleep is to restore these specific forms of imbalance.

It must be kept in mind that self-reports can be biased and there was no direct assessment of variations in sleep as a function of waking activity in the above studies. However, Hartmann (1973) did report studies by other investigators who have shown increased REM sleep following stress and learning situations in humans and laboratory animals.

In summary, investigators of the nature of sleep are in accord in the belief that there are two distinct types of sleep, REM and NREM, even though the question of the functions of the two types is still debatable. One possibility (Hartmann, 1973) is that REM sleep is the period during which certain biochemical processes depleted during waking are replenished. Specifically, it is hypothesized that substances called *catecholamines,* which are necessary for waking, become resynthesized during REM sleep. When waking activities are particularly stressful, tiring, or effortful, the catecholamines are consumed more readily and more REM sleep time is needed to restore them.

From an evolutionary perspective, an argument can be made for the necessity of two types of sleep. It would not be adaptive for the organism to spend long uninterrupted periods in the deep sleep of Stages 3 and 4 NREM sleep and it has been suggested (Ephron and Carrington, 1966; Snyder, 1966) that REM sleep that occurs periodically during the night serves to place the organism into lighter sleep so that it can detect possible threats from the environment. In this way physical restoration can occur during one portion of sleep, and the organism can periodically tune in to the external world to detect dangers from predators or natural events that threaten it. However, although the EEG pattern during REM sleep might suggest that it is a lighter form of sleep, it is actually rather difficult to awaken an organism during this phase of sleep.

Another theory (Roffwarg, Muzio, and Dement, 1966) focuses on the significance of REM sleep as a means of stimulating cortical development in newborn and young organisms. Hartmann (1967) reported that about half of the seventeen to eighteen hours of sleep of the newborn human infant consists of REM sleep and this percentage drops with increasing age. These facts are consistent with the interpretation that fetuses and newborn infants that need stimulation may receive it during sleep inasmuch as REM sleep activates the cortex.

CENTRAL MECHANISMS

Sleep has often been viewed as a passive state reflecting the absence of stimulation as contrasted to waking, which is associated with the presence of stimulation. The discovery of the functions of the reticular formation (Moruzzi and Magoun, 1949) as a source of general activation or arousal was used to support the view that the degree of alertness of an organism varies directly with the level of reticular formation activity. Sleep was considered to consist of states that involved the absence of stimulation of the reticular formation.

Routtenberg (1968) pointed out evidence that suggests that this view is inaccurate. For example, lesions of the reticular formation (Feldman and Waller, 1962) does not produce somnolence in animals even though the electrocortiogram pattern shows the synchronized waves characteristic of sleep. On the other hand, somnolence was produced by electrical stimulation of either the reticular formation or the pons if lesions had been made in the adjacent posterior hypothalamus. Similarly Jouvet (1961) was unable to eliminate electroencephalographic indices of sleep by making lesions in the reticular formation without damaging the Raphe cells of this area. On the basis of such findings, Routtenberg (1968) felt it necessary to postulate two different arousal systems, one similar to the one based on the reticular formation and one involving a region known as the limbic system. The latter system was assumed to be critical in mediating reinforcement processes. This model was not developed primarily to account for the process of sleep, but it points out the limitations of a single arousal system approach for explaining the neuroanatomical basis of sleep.

Jouvet (1967) described a model of sleep, which also involves other mechanisms in addition to the reticular formation. According to this formulation sleep is not merely the absence of reticular formation activity but rather it may be the result of the operation of brain centers (depicted in Figures 14–4 and 14–5) capable of suppressing the functions of the reticular formation. Using cats in most of his studies, Jouvet proposed a theory about the anatomical and neuroendocrinological bases of two types of sleep, *slow* and *fast,* as measured by brain wave frequencies from the cortex with the electroencephologram. *Light* and *deep* or paradoxical sleep are also used in speaking of slow and fast wave sleep, respectively.

Experiments in which the medial raphe cells along the midline of the brainstem are destroyed revealed that the cats were unable to sleep. Because the Raphe cells are the major source of serotonin in the brain, Jouvet surmised that this neurotransmitter may be important in producing the onset of light (NREM) sleep by inhibiting the activity of the reticular formation.

It is assumed that the normal transition from light into deep sleep requires an additional factor, because other studies with cats in which the brainstem is severed between the pons and the medulla showed that deep or paradoxical sleep disappears. This procedure destroys an area of the pons known as the *locus ceruleus.* This group of cells was proposed by Jouvet as the center for deep (REM) sleep. Furthermore, because it contains noradrenalin (or norephinephrine), it was inferred that this neurotransmitter may be crucial in producing this type of sleep.

It should be noted that this theory is still speculative but it has helped

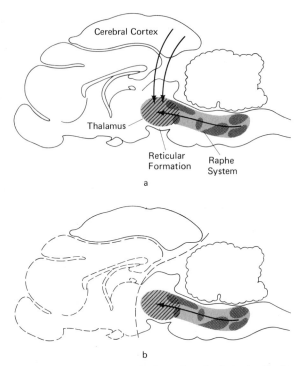

FIGURE 14–4. Brain structures involved in light sleep include the Raphe system, which, by producing the monoamine serotin, serves to counteract the alerting effects of the brain's reticular formation. (a) Jouvet suggests that other nearby structures act to modulate the fast wave pattern of the alert cortex into the slower pattern typical of light sleep. Such slow activity, however, is known to depend on higher as well as lower brain structure (b); when a cat is deprived of its cerebral cortex and thalamus, the wave pattern characteristic of light sleep disappears. [From "The States of Sleep," by M. Jouvet. Copyright © 1967 by *Scientific American, Inc.* All rights reserved. Reprinted by permission.]

integrate many findings otherwise incompatible with prior views of sleep. Hobson (1974) pointed out that the lesions in Jouvet's studies, while suggestive, are not conclusive about the role of these areas on sleep. This warning is especially apt because direct stimulation of either the raphe nuclei or the locus ceruleus does not increase sleep as one would expect on the basis of the theory even though such electrical stimulation of the Raphe system in rats has been shown to release serotonin (Aghajanian, Rosecrans, and Sheard, 1967). Quay's (1966) finding of greater serotonin levels during sleep than in waking activity also fits in with Jouvet's theory.

Hobson also pointed out the nonspecificity of the effects of the lesions created by Jouvet. Insomnia is not the only consequence, because other fibers are also cut when such lesions are made. The animals are also unable to eat as a consequence of these operations and they die in several weeks. It should also be noted that lesions in other sections of the posterior hypo-

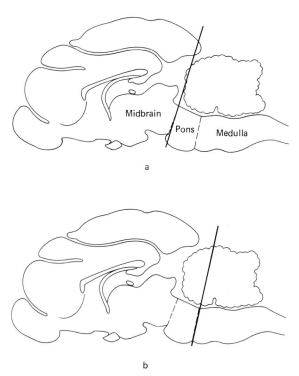

FIGURE 14–5. Paradoxical-sleep structure evidently lies far back along the brain stem. A cat deprived of all its higher brain function by means of a cut through the pons (a) will live for months, alternately awake and in paradoxical sleep. If a cut is made lower (b) along the brain stem, however, the cat will no longer fall into paradoxical sleep, because the cut destroys the brain cells in that region, which produce another monoamine, noradrenalin. [From "The States of Sleep," by M. Jouvet, Copyright © (1967) by *Scientific American*, Inc. All rights reserved. Reprinted by permission.]

thalamus can produce insomnia, so that Jouvet's argument that his studies have established evidence of the existence of specific brain centers controlling sleep can be questioned.

Sexual Behavior

The fact that heterosexual intercourse is necessary by some members of a species in order for that species to survive has mistakenly led some to conclude that sexual behavior is as necessary for the individual organism as food or water is. Nothing could be further from the truth, of course, and many persons live otherwise normal lives without either the opportunity or the inclination for heterosexual intercourse.

The emphasis on the biological nature of sexual activity leads to the idea that some basic physiological mechanisms operate within the genital regions. Certainly, in the final analysis, heterosexual intercourse involves the insertion of an erect penis into a vagina, but as Gagnon and Simon (1973, p. 22) so aptly put it, "What is misleading in this physical description is that it sounds as if one were rubbing two sticks together to produce fire; that is, if only enough body heat is generated, orgasm occurs." A more accurate account must bring psychological factors into consideration.

Thus, the notion that areas such as the genitals are among the erogenous zones that may contribute to sexual arousal by tactile stimulation is a biologically based assertion that needs some qualification. Although the genitals are more highly innervated and sensitive to touch, their stimulation will not automatically or reflexively produce sexual arousal but must be interpreted in the context of the situation. Who is touching me must be considered as well as where am I being touched.

Human sexual behavior has been one of the most difficult aspects of human activity to study, scientifically or otherwise. Not only is it generally regarded as a private and often sacred affair between the participants, but sexual behavior has also been surrounded by an aura of sinfulness or wickedness.

One consequence of this situation has been even greater reliance on the study of lower animals in order to understand sexual behavior. Unfortunately, vast differences exist between the factors responsible for human and nonhuman sexual behavior, and generalizations from studies of the latter to humans are limited. Whereas strong drives based on physiological and hormonal factors govern the occurrence of sexual activity in lower animals, culturally learned beliefs and attitudes can override such factors in determining human sexual activity. Nonetheless it is useful to examine the factors that affect sexual behavior in nonhuman species, because it is less morally objectionable to study it in lower species than in humans. The use of procedures to identify neural and hormonal factors involves surgical interventions such as castration (surgical removal of the gonads) or electrical brain stimulation, which are also unacceptable for use on humans for research purposes.

LOCAL FACTORS

Sex hormones created by the gonads play an important role in the control of sexual capacity and readiness. The male testes produce androgen and the female ovaries generate estrogen and progesterone, which not only contribute to physical maturation of sexual characteristics but also affect sexual behavior. One technique of assessing the role of hormonal influence is to castrate animals and then compare their sexual behavior with control animals. Beach and Holz (1946) varied the age at which male rats were castrated from 1 to 350 days. The age of puberty for this strain of rats was about fifty days. All the rats used were sexually naive. Several months after castration all rats were placed individually with a receptive female rat. The normal male rat typically makes a series of very brief intromissions in which the penis penetrates the vagina but there is no release of sperm. Eventually the vigor of the thrusting movements of the male increases markedly, followed by ejaculation and the release of the semen or sperm. Beach and Holz found an impairment of normal sexual function, as none of the castrated rats ejaculated and few of them even achieved intromission. The age at which castration occurred among these virgin males did not make any difference in the level of sexual activity in this test.

Subsequent tests for copulation were given after the rats received injections of androgen. The sexual capacity of the males improved after this treatment. The results of this study illustrate the importance of hormones in male sexual behavior for this species.

The evidence relating to the effects of castration on adult males with prior copulatory experience is conflicting. Castration impairs sexual performance but there appear to be wide individual differences within species in dogs (Beach, 1970) or cats (Rosenblatt and Aronson, 1958).

When the effects of castration on naive and experienced members of the same species are examined, there appears to be little difference in the impairment of rats (Bloch and Davidson, 1968), but greater impairment among the experienced animals when cats are used (Rosenblatt and Aronson, 1958).

Castration of females causes even greater disruption in sexual behavior. In nonhuman species, the female is receptive to the male only during limited periods of the year. These breeding seasons are controlled by many factors, but the sex hormones are involved (Marler and Hamilton, 1966). Therapy in which injections of hormones such as estrogen or progesterone are given can restore normal sexual behavior in some female mammals.

The degree to which male and female sexual behavior is governed by hormones varies inversely with the phylogenetic status of the species (Beach, 1958), especially in the male. As one ascends the phylogenetic scale, factors such as experience assume greater influence over sexual behavior. There is a corresponding increase in the role of the cerebral cortex with higher species in sexual behavior, especially in the male. Ablation or destruction of the cerebral cortex is more disruptive in male than in female sexual behavior.

CENTRAL FACTORS

The use of a variety of techniques has led to the identification of the role of various brain structures in sexual behavior. Injection of sex hormones into regions of the hypothalamus have produced sexual behavior in castrated rats of either sex (Pfaff and Keiner, 1972). Vaughn and Fisher (1962) employed electrical stimulation of the anterior hypothalamus and obtained sexual behavior in male rats. Yet another technique was used by Sawyer (1956) who made lesions in the ventromedial hypothalamus to disrupt sexual behavior in rabbits.

These examples illustrate the strategy for discovering the nature of higher brain structures involved in the control of sexual behavior. The hypothalamus has been implicated as a major regulator of sexual activity. The ventromedial region probably manifests its influence through its control of hormones released by the pituitary. Destruction of this area with lesions disrupts sexual activity in female cats and rabbits, but the administration of estrogen can counteract this deficit (Robinson and Sawyer, 1957) so that it appears reasonable to infer that this area involves the release of hormones.

In contrast, Sawyer (1969) found that lesions of the anterior hypothalamus impaired sexual behavior but did not at the same time lead to atrophy of the gonads. It appears that the region is responsible for the neural control of the reflexive coordination of sexual activity rather than the hormonal control.

EXPERIENTIAL FACTORS

In addition to physiological and hormonal determinants, specific experiences, especially early ones, assume a role in affecting the sexual behavior of higher species.

Harlow and Harlow (1965) reported that rhesus monkeys reared under conditions in which the natural mother was absent exhibited impaired adult sexual behavior. These findings were not the major purpose of the original studies, which were concerned with the mothering process. However, in order to assess this process, it was necessary to isolate male rhesus monkeys for the first six months of life. This procedure apparently was responsible for the impaired sexual behavior shown by these monkeys when they reached adulthood. It should be noted that lack of maternal contact per se was not the critical deficit, because contact with peers during the first six months as an alternative does not cause impairment in sexual functioning.

Similar findings with monkeys were obtained by Mason (1968) who reared monkeys under conditions affording little social stimulation. At adulthood, these monkeys were unable to mate successfully. Mason hypothesized that the restricted early experience led to the monkeys becoming so aroused in later situations that they could not respond appropriately.

These studies with primates are supported by findings with lower species such as male guinea pigs (Valenstein, Riss, and Young, 1955), dogs (Beach, 1968), and rats (Gerall, Ward, and Gerall, 1967). There are, however, individual differences within a given species as normal copulation does occur among some animals reared in isolation, such as cats (Rosenblatt, 1965).

The detrimental effects of social isolation during early life do not appear to stem from the lack of opportunity for physical contact per se that might involve responses similar to those required for sexual intercourse. Gerall (1963) demonstrated that there was no impairment in the adult sexual behavior of male guinea pigs that were prevented from touching other animals in adjacent cages but could see, hear, and smell them. It seems likely that the restriction produces emotional disturbances that may not be limited to sexual activity. As we noted in Chapter 12, early restricted experience can alter the general level of emotionality or reactivity to stimulation.

This section has focused on the results of studies of sexual behavior in lower species in order to determine how biological factors affect this activity. It was noted that experiential factors become increasingly important with primates. In the case of human sexual behavior, the role of experiential factors should assume even greater importance. Recognition of the fact that learning experiences create attitudes and responses that greatly affect human sexual behavior should not make us lose sight of the fact that humans are still governed by biological considerations.

In the next section we will examine three influential but widely differing approaches to the study of human sexuality, the work of Sigmund Freud, Albert Kinsey, and Masters and Johnson.

THE INFLUENCE OF SIGMUND FREUD

Sigmund Freud is often credited with being a pioneer in the scientific study of human sexual behavior. There is no denying that his theories were so influential and controversial that attention was directed toward research on human sexual behavior. On the other hand, Freud did not study sexual behavior directly in the same sense that Kinsey or Masters and Johnson did many years later. Whereas Kinsey's sociological interviews dealt with actual sexual behavior and Masters and Johnson made direct observations of sexual activities in the laboratory, Freud's contributions were based on his hypotheses about the repression and anxiety centered in sexual conflicts and inhibitions.

Freud's theory of infantile sexuality was revolutionary in suggesting that adult sexual attitudes were shaped during the first few years of life. The ideas that the feeding and toilet training experiences of the infant involved sexual experiences were highly controversial as were his suggestions concerning the sexual attraction of the young child to the opposite sexed parent.

Freud's stages of psychosexual development, which described the sequence of concerns of the developing individual about bodily functions involving the sex organs and erotic relationships with parents, were based largely on retrospective inferences from clinical evidence obtained during therapy of adult clients. His theories of infantile sexuality did not involve the direct observation of children's behavior. They were instead speculative views of the relationship between the psychological and physical development of the individual at the sexual level.

THE KINSEY REPORTS

The first large scale empirical studies of actual sexual practices of "normal" men and women were conducted by Albert Kinsey and his associates (Kinsey, Pomeroy, and Martin, 1948; Kinsey, Pomeroy, Martin, and Gebhard, 1953). In their interviews, Kinsey et al. focused on the orgasm as the basic unit, because it was felt that this experience would be easiest for respondents to identify and report. They also adopted the concept of *total outlets,* recognizing the fact that heterosexual intercourse is not the only means by which people achieve orgasm, although it is the major source for married men or women. Masturbation was found to be a more common outlet for unmarried men and women, and among the men this was especially true, the higher the education level. This latter relationship was not the effect of education per se, but reflected the fact that sexual intercourse was a more frequent outlet for less-educated unmarried men.

In our discussion of human sexual behavior, our focus will be on heterosexual intercourse among married couples, although as Kinsey has shown there are many other outlets. Our choice does not necessarily reflect any value judgment of our own but is based primarily on the fact that this outlet is the one generally held to be the only "normal" and legitimate or moral condition for intercourse. Mores have changed drastically since Kinsey's era and sexual practices have become more varied and open among increasing numbers, but the influence of the "old morality" that proscribes premarital, extramarital, and homosexual intercourse can still be felt. The fact that some forms of sexual activity can be considered immoral or deviant among humans is in contrast to the situation among other species, again attesting to the critical role of cultural and psychological factors in human sexual behavior.

Prior to the pioneering venture of Kinsey and his associates, little empirical evidence was available about the nature of human sexual behavior in the population at large compared to knowledge of clinical cases of deviant or impaired sexual functioning. The details of sexual behavior in the general population were considered private and not a matter for scientific investigation until Kinsey conducted his interviews. How often sexual intercourse occurred, at what age it first began, the number of different sexual partners in one's experience—these and many other questions were asked by Kinsey.

Critics of his research, even those who recognized its importance and quality, were concerned about its questionnable validity. The sampling procedures were criticized, because the respondents were probably highly selective, thus biasing (its) representativeness. Moreover, the use of live in-depth interviews was attacked for it was felt that the honesty and accuracy of the responses were in question.

Be that as it may, even though the studies had such limitations they had a tremendous impact on the sexual attitudes and behavior of the general public. For better or worse, for example, the famous Kinsey Reports, as they came to be called, provided a respected set of normative data against which comparisons of sexual behavior could be made. An example illustrating a positive effect of the availability of such information is a grateful letter to Kinsey from a professional man who was slightly past middle age.

He was the father of three grown children but he had been burdened with a self-image of moral perversion for many years, because he had engaged in a variety of sexual practices during his life, some of which he thought were practiced by so very few people that he felt deviant. After reading Kinsey's research reports, he could write to Kinsey:

Now when I find such a high percentage of others in the same boat, I have been mentally relieved and now can hold my head a bit higher and meet life on a surer basis. (Pomeroy, 1972, p. 271)

Thus, the opportunity to obtain knowledge about normative sexual behavior enabled this man to realize that his behavior was not so rare or unusual after all. Doubtless, many other anxious and guilt-ridden individuals experienced the same relief with the publication of Kinsey's studies.

On the negative side, it was possible for some readers of Kinsey's work to draw the conclusion that Kinsey was promoting his own recommendations about normal sexual conduct, although this goal was far from his aims, which were truly scientific. Nevertheless, his published findings have sometimes been charged with leading to sexual excesses, because many readers may have become less inhibited after learning of them. Thus Kinsey reported data showing that the incidence of premarital and extramarital sexual intercourse was much higher than was commonly assumed. Similarly, his data showed that intercourse with prostitutes and male homosexual behavior were also more frequent than suspected.

Although his work may have had these unintended influences, Kinsey himself took no moral position for or against these behaviors. In the process of pointing out the normality or a variety of sexual outlets, he undoubtedly liberated and encouraged more forms of sexual activity, which previously were less frequent.

THE WORK OF MASTERS AND JOHNSON

Kinsey's classic studies would be considered quite tame in comparison with the sex research of Masters and Johnson (1966). These highly controversial studies of human sexual response focused on measurement of actual physiological indices during sexual activities such as masturbation, artificial coition, and coition. A rather unrepresentative sample of the general population was studied as Masters and Johnson carefully interviewed and screened potential candidates for their research, which was conducted under laboratory conditions. Most of the participants were white married couples from a university community who were concerned about some form of sexual inadequacy so that the research participation was partly motivated by hopes of obtaining therapeutic benefits.

Such a scientific investigation of a highly personalized relationship as sexual intercourse obviously generated much publicity, favorable and unfavorable. This research, based on at least 10,000 orgasms, provided data about aspects of human sexual behavior that was impossible to obtain otherwise.

Their study led Masters and Johnson to identify many similarities between male and female sexual responses. Both sexes appear to have four distinguishable stages of sexual response, *excitement, plateau, orgasm,* and *resolution,* as illustrated in Figures 14–6 and 14–7. It should be emphasized that these illustrations show the typical response but there are wide individual differences among people in the exact nature of their response. The excitement phase involves a period of increasing arousal of erogenous zones of the body due to physical and/or psychological sexual stimulation, which then reaches a momentary plateau of sustained tension, the second phase of the cycle. Then a renewed surge of excitement produces the orgasm phase, which involves ejaculation for the male and intense uterine contractions for the female. Orgasm involves uncontrollable release of the built-up forces. Finally, after orgasm is achieved there is a gradual reduction of arousal during the resolution phase, although it occurs more rapidly in males than in females.

In addition to these similarities of male and female sexual functioning, Masters and Johnson also noted some important differences. The range of variability in sexual response is considerably greater in females than in males. How much of this variability is due to biological differences and how much to psychological factors is not clear.

As Figure 14–6 indicates, the male has a refractory period following orgasm that is absent in the female. This interval refers to the period during which the male is incapable of further responsiveness to sexual arousal

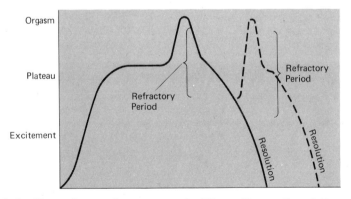

Figure 14–6. The male sexual response cycle. [From *Human Sexual Response,* by W. H. Masters and V. E. Johnson, Boston: Little, Brown, 1966. Copyright 1966 by Little, Brown and Company. Reprinted by permission.]

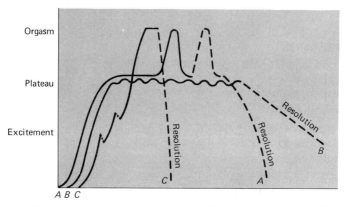

FIGURE 14–7.   The female sexual response cycle. [From *Human Sexual Response,* by W. H. Masters and V. E. Johnson, Boston: Little, Brown, 1966. Copyright 1966 by Little, Brown and Company. Reprinted by permission.]

toward orgasm. The female does not undergo a refractory period following orgasm but rather is potentially able to experience a series of orgasms. This sex difference appears to involve biological factors for the most part, although it should be apparent that psychological factors such as attitudes, emotions, and expectations could also affect sexual responsiveness following the orgasm phase of the cycle.

Although the empirical determination of the physiological nature of human sexual response is an important accomplishment, we must remember that the roles of the psychological and sociological factors that can influence sexual behavior were not originally considered by Masters and Johnson in their research. Their later views (Masters & Johnson, 1975), however, agree that it is important to examine these factors if we wish to understand motivational aspects of sexual activity. The physiological responses that define sexual activity can take place only after a complex set of psychological and sociological variables lead individuals to engage in such activity. For example, sexual attraction must exist before the rituals of courtship, which invariably precede any voluntary sexual intercourse. In the next section we will consider these prerequisites of sexual activity further.

COGNITIVE FACTORS

In our society, as in many Western industrial countries, voluntary heterosexual activities depend on the presence of some important psychological states such as physical attraction, infatuation, and romantic love. With the assumption they are physically capable and sexually mature, a number of nonbiological factors will determine whether or not activities such as petting, kissing, or intercourse will occur between a male and a female who otherwise have the opportunity.

One such precondition is whether or not their attraction is mutual. Physiological analyses of sexual behavior such as the well-known study by Masters and Johnson (1966) can tell us what happens to lead up to and through the sexual act, but it is not possible to predict whether or not a couple will want to, or actually, engage in such activity. Factors commonly termed *sex appeal* or *sexiness* must be considered first.

As Ford and Beach (1951) observed, sexual attractiveness in different cultures depends on different physical attributes. The American ideal of sexual beauty is not universal. One might add that the behavioral or psychological characteristics considered sexually stimulating also vary across cultures. A set of learned mannerisms exists in each culture by which one may attempt to attract sexual partners. The way one walks, dresses, sits, or talks can serve to communicate subtly to others that one is interested sexually in attracting another person.

Once attraction occurs, a form of courtship ritual ensues, which traditionally assigns the male the role of the initiator although the female may sometimes assume this role if she is very subtle. In our society, the expected or learned role of the female is the passive or submissive one, whereas the male is expected to take the more active or dominant role. Similar courtship rituals occur throughout the animal kingdom, but they are more invariant in their patterns whereas wide variations exist in different human societies.

Courtship is a process by which the prospective mates convey their mutual attraction. Humans, like birds, display fancy plumage or attire and engage in sweet talk, poetry, and song to enhance their attractiveness. The female is wooed with gifts, proclamations of love, and constant attention. Even the male road runner usually offers some prey such as a small lizard when courting its fair road runner (Ford and Beach, 1951). In response the female "begs" and copulation commences. Only then does the male relinquish its present, unlike human males who present their gifts before consummating the act, if ever at all.

During courtship the female role entails modesty, shyness, or coyness. One consequence of this technique is that the pursuing male becomes more highly attracted and motivated by the challenge. This type of sexual gamesmanship is not universal, however, and among the Bali, for example, the direct approach may be taken by members of either sex without the need for either party to make a pretense of reluctance. Playing hard to get is more important in our society where being too eager for sexual activity is seen as a moral defect in women by a large part of society.

Nevertheless, the result of the apparent reluctance of the female even when she is willing activates in the male what Beach (1956) termed the sexual arousing mechanism (SAM). The greater arousal is prior to sexual activity, the more pleasurable will be the sexual act when completed, so that it can be argued that the process of courtship is an essential rather than superfluous element of sexual activities.

Preliminary sexual foreplay during courtship may lead eventually to consummation. These activities also serve to heighten sexual arousal so that more intimate behavior can follow. However, Gagnon and Simon (1973) hold that the basis of foreplay is socially determined and that foreplay itself does not facilitate physiological processes directly. These sociologists, who were previously associated with Kinsey, emphasize the influence of socially learned roles or *scripts* in governing sexual behavior. We have taken the scripts for granted and often confused them with biological processes.

The aforementioned active role of the male and passive role of the female throughout sexual involvements is one example of a script. The apparent naturalness of the sequence of physical intimacy is another. Holding hands progresses to kissing, to fondling the breasts of the clothed female, to touching the breasts under the clothing, to touching her genitals. Yet, according to Gagnon and Simon, these behaviors and their sequence are not biologically determined or invariant but rather reflect the learned scripts or roles of our society. Kissing on the mouth, for example, is more prevalent among the middle classes, although there is also a tendency not to drink from the same glass for fear of germs. The opposite preferences seem to hold in the lower socioeconomic class. Young children who are amused or repulsed by the sight of kissing between lovers become infused with this expectation so that by the time they become adolescents a kiss can generate high emotional excitement and pleasure.

Sexual arousal and attraction is by no means limited to the influence of overt gestures, verbal expressions, physical movements, attire or lack of attire, and physical caresses and touching. Cognitive processes involving imagination and fantasy occur frequently in sexual encounters and may stimulate and enhance sexual excitement. Romance and infatuation in themselves involve favorable distortions of reality, which may be seen as fantasies of a sort.

Interviews with married women by Hariton and Singer (1974) disclosed that fantasies and daydreams occur frequently during sexual intercourse. Moreover some women used these fantasies as a means of enhancing sexual arousal. They also suggested that it may act to reduce some of the passivity that some women experience during sexual relations. According to this view, male fantasies during sexual relations would probably serve a different function.

CULTURAL FACTORS

Human sexual behavior is profoundly affected by cultural values. Ford and Beach (1951) described the wide variety of sexual practices and attitudes found in a number of primitive societies as well as in the United States. They focused on heterosexual intercourse because it is the only variety that can lead to offspring, but they also examined so-called deviant sexual activities such as masturbation, homosexuality, and pre- and extramarital sexual intercourse. Even though heterosexual behavior was favored in most of the societies examined, it was found that about half of them tolerated homosexual activities, unlike our own society.

Monogamy was rarely found either among these societies or among various subhuman species. The official belief or ideal in our society may be monogamy but there seems to be an increasing tolerance of successive monogamy as individuals marry, obtain divorces, and remarry periodically. Even among monogamous individuals, extramarital sexual relations are common. Even back in 1948, Kinsey et al. found that about one-third of the married men in their sample reported such activities and the majority of them expressed desires for such outlets.

Along with the ideal of monogamous sex, our society has traditionally subscribed to the philosophy of premarital virginity, at least in females. Reiss (1960) conducted national probability sample surveys that showed that these beliefs were still prevalent about twenty years after Kinsey's famous reports, although the extent to which such ideals are being followed has weakened considerably, especially among college students.

What determines values such as those that deal with sexual practices? Why is sexual intercourse formally denied prior to some form of marriage in most societies? What is the purpose of placing taboos on certain forms of sexual behavior under all circumstances? Why is sex generally a taboo topic even in the confines of matrimony?

One contributing factor toward restraint of sexual activity has been the Protestant Ethic, which emphasized hard work, thrift, and sacrifice, in contrast to leisure, pleasure, and self-indulgence. Sexual activity has also been downgraded as a base, animal, and demeaning activity that involves the loss of control and can only be tolerated for purposes of procreation. In general, the Judeo-Christian philosophy has been the major force in molding our moral heritage toward sexual activity. The Catholic belief that sexual activity could be engaged in only for the natural purpose of reproduction favored restraint, bans against contraception, and restriction of sex within the holy state of matrimony. In medieval times, sex was seen as a necessary evil for purposes of reproduction, but chastity was regarded as more virtuous because it involved self-control, discipline, and asceticism. The traits that served to regulate sexual activity to a necessary minimum are also assumed by the famous German sociologist Max Weber to have contributed to the rise of modern capitalism and economic growth.

Despite the rapid liberalization of sexual attitudes and practices of the 1970s, the religious tradition still affects many aspects of social attitudes toward sexual matters.

The concern that erotic and pornographic material may erode moral character as well as fears that they may cause epidemic outbreaks of illicit sexual practices illustrate this influence. Similar fears that sex education in the schools will promote sexual experimentation and moral decay also reveal the attitude held by many that sexual motives for physical pleasures will destroy interest in our traditional values.

One indication that some change in basic attitudes is generally occurring is the advocacy of situation ethics by an Episcopalian, Joseph Fletcher (1966, 1967), who justified any form of sexual activity, provided it is motivated by love. Premarital sex between a loving couple, according to this criterion, can be ethical just as marital sex by a couple for purposes other than love may be unethical. The morality of a sexual act depends on the motives of the participants and the situation, not on any absolute rules.

Similar changes are reflected in the United Presbyterian Church, which recommends that the ban against premarital sex be replaced with a sliding scale of permissible premarital sex (*Time,* Dec. 13, 1971).

Whatever the future may bring in the way of new sex mores, it should be clear that human sexual activity is unique in that it is highly influenced by such abstract factors and cannot be regarded as merely a biological process or as Katchadourian (1974, p. 25) phrased it, ". . . is in no sense a private affair between the genitals."

FUNCTIONS OF SEXUAL BEHAVIOR

Viewed strictly as a biological function, sexual activity serves the function of procreation. Although this goal is necessary for the survival of the species as a whole, sexual activity is not biologically necessary for the individual organism, certainly not in the same sense that eating or avoiding pain is. Unless humanity were reduced to only two survivors, one male and one female, there would still be the chance that the species would survive if some members did not produce offspring.

Consequently sexual activity fulfills many functions other than that of procreation for most people at some time or other. Indeed, with the spectre of overpopulation and food shortages and the elimination of major contagious diseases that might decimate populations on a large-scale basis, there is significant discouragement of sex primarily for procreative purposes. In addition, technological advances and scientific discoveries leading to better methods of contraception have also promoted changes in contemporary attitudes and motivations for sexual activity.

We will identify some of the functions served by sexual activity other than procreation. The list will not be exhaustive probably and some of the motives may overlap or occur simultaneously. Most of the motives will be more generally applicable to heterosexual rather than homosexual activities.

Heterosexual sex has generally assigned a dominant role to the male and a submissive role to the female, although such differences also have their biological or hormonal bases.

The battle of the sexes is portrayed as a type of war with the aggressive male out to conquer or dominate the female, although usually by wily and seductive techniques rather than brute force. Conquest is used in a metaphorical sense. Although the courting and wooing process may culminate in sexual union, the process of seduction may become more important to some males than sexual intercourse itself. The great lover Casanova who bragged about his prowess and sexual adventures is a classic example of how the excitement of new conquests can motivate sexual activity.

The submissive female who is either captured or plays the role of the vanquished may be motivated in a complementary fashion to see how frequently she can entice, seduce, and beguile male partners. Again, although sexual union may result, the primary motive may lie in proving one's attractiveness and irrepressible charm.

To engage in battles of any sort, romance included, is to risk rejection, ridicule, or defeat. The courtship and wooing process is stimulating for many reasons, not the least of which is the uncertainty and risk involved. Will you be attractive and successful? What kind of rivals must you compete against? As in other forms of competition, excitement and tension permeate the encounters between prospective sexual partners.

Although sex is no longer as taboo and restricted as it was a generation ago, some element of sin is still associated with many aspects of sexual activity and carries over even to morally acceptable forms of sexual activity. Restrictions on the availability of sexually explicit materials to minors generates curiosity and determination to taste the forbidden fruits. The moral ambiguity that surrounds sexual activity is exploited by commercial interests. Books, movies, and other forms of entertainment capitalize on the situation by providing vicarious opportunities for sexual arousal beyond the types and amounts that could be legitimately defended on artistic or literary grounds. Sex and sex appeal is exploited by sellers of commercial products ranging from toothpaste to liquor to automobiles on the one hand to flying on specific airlines or drinking milk on the other.

In short, the repressive attitudes toward sex that has traditionally existed in this society has created a situation that has been commercially exploited to such an excessive extent that sex itself tends to be viewed by many as a product. Just as one might trade last year's car for a newer or higher status model, one might perceive sexual partners as mechanical and nonhuman devices that can be discarded in favor of the latest models. By being seen with an impressive looking sexual partner, one can enhance one's own self-esteem in much the same way affluence can produce this effect by enabling one to purchase material products such as clothes, cars, and houses that are admired and envied by all.

The heralded sexual revolution of today replaces the restrained Puritanical attitude with an hedonistic emphasis on the fun and pleasure to be derived from sex. Sex without guilt and fear of pregnancy because of better contraceptive methods has fostered sex as a form of recreation instead of only a means of procreation. Numerous books, many explicitly illustrated, have appeared in the past decade to instruct the reader in ways to increase the joy and sensual delights of sex. The tone is far different from the detached and objective air of some marriage manuals of the past.

Our list of the uses of sex is not intended to be complete but is offered to indicate the limited perspective gained when sex is viewed primarily as a biological means for reproduction. At the same time, we do not intend to ignore this important motive. People do engage in sexual intercourse in order to have children for such various reasons as an expression of love, a means of prolonging the family line, or a symbolic means of achieving immortality. Even here we observe the interaction of other motives besides that of reproduction per se as the rationale for sexual intercourse.

Much personal unhappiness and tragic consequences are created by many of the motives that govern our sexual behaviors. The over-emphasis on sexual prowess, generated in part by the restrictive attitudes of society toward sex, is, as Freud observed, the cause of much anxiety, anguish, and destruction of personal lives.

Summary

Although sleep and sex sometimes occur closely together in time, and on that basis might go well together in one chapter, it is also important to emphasize important differences between them. Whereas sex is not necessary for the biological survival of the individual, without sleep there is severe disruption of human behavior. Although cultural factors influence sleeping habits to some extent, such factors have a considerably greater effect on sexual behavior, especially with respect to moral values.

The development of precise recording instruments has greatly facilitated the understanding of the neurophysiological nature of sleep. Laboratory studies of sleep deprivation as well as normal sleep have enabled researchers to obtain evidence about the function and nature of sleep. The issue of whether or not sleep is really necessary, at least in the amounts commonly found in humans, has not been conclusively answered. Recovery time sleep has been found to be less than the amount of sleep lost in deprivation experiments but these studies are rather atypical situations involving highly motivated volunteers.

Sleep involves five levels of depth or stages, which each reoccur five times each sleep night. Four of these stages do not involve rapid eye movements, whereas a fifth stage, which is implicated in the process of dreaming, does. The rapid eye movement sleep stages seem to be more active, as other psychophysiological indices show increases.

The discovery of the rapid eye movement stages of sleep enabled studies of dream deprivation to be conducted such that subjects were awakened during either rapid or nonrapid eye movement stages. The effects of such awakenings led to more irritability if they occurred during the stage associated with dreams and suggests that dreaming may be a necessary part of sleep.

Some evidence suggests that the restorative function of nonrapid eye movement sleep is basic for physical processes, whereas the role of rapid eye movement sleep may act to restore imbalances stemming from stress, worry, or effort.

The existence of two types of sleep has also been used to provide explanations of survival against environmental dangers. The deeper stages of nonrapid eye movement may be necessary to repair physical processes, whereas the lighter sleep of the rapid eye movement stages enable the organism to periodically be responsive to threats from the environment during sleep.

The study of human sexual behavior, like sexual behavior itself, is complicated by the attitudes of society, moralistic restrictions, etc. As a consequence, it was often necessary to rely on studies of sexual behavior of lower animals, which unfortunately are of limited generalizability to human behavior. Human sexual behavior is strongly influenced by culturally learned expectations and values and is less dominated by biological factors, such as in the case of lower organisms. Social and psychological variables such as love, sex appeal, marriage and family, and desire for children must also be considered in analyzing human sexual motivation. The guilt and anxiety that humans often have in relation to sexual behavior is absent among lower organisms, which are not burdened by moral considerations.

Although his insights were based on clinical inferences rather than scientific experiments, the theories of Freud about the significance of sexual activities were very influential in directing attention to this behavior.

The Kinsey studies of human sexual behavior were a landmark in the empirical study of the nature of this important aspect of human experience. Although his questionnaire and interview procedures were frequently criticized as inadequate or invalid, his findings have generally been accepted and have had much influence. The pioneering efforts of Kinsey and his colleagues also opened the door for other investigators.

Masters and Johnson, who based their conclusions on actual observation of physiological reactions of couples engaged in intimate sexual activities, distinguished four stages of male and female sexual response—excitement, plateau, orgasm, and resolution. Females showed greater individual differences in sexual response.

References

AGNEW, H. W., JR., WEBB, W. B., and WILLIAMS, R. L. Comparison of stage four and 1-REM sleep deprivation. *Perceptual and Motor Skills*, 1967, *24*, 851–858.
ASERINSKY, E., and KLEITMAN, N. Two types of ocular motility occurring in sleep. *Journal of Applied Physiology*, 1955, *8*, 1–10.

————, and KLEITMAN, N. Regularly occurring periods of eye motility and concomitant phenomena during sleep. *Science,* 1953, *118,* 273–274.

BEACH, F. A. Characteristics of masculine sex drive. In M. R. Jones (Ed.), *Nebraska Symposium on Motivation.* (Vol. 4). Lincoln: University of Nebraska Press, 1956.

————. Coital behavior in dogs: III. Effects of early isolation on mating in males. *Behaviour,* 1968, *30,* 218–238.

————. Coital behavior in dogs: IV. Long-term effects of castration upon mating in the male. *Journal of Comparative and Physiological Psychology Monograph,* 1970, *70,* Part 2.

————, and HOLZ, A. M. Mating behavior in male rats castrated at various ages and injected with androgen. *Journal of Experimental Zoology,* 1946, *101,* 91–142.

————, and JAYNES, J. Effects of early experience upon the behavior of animals. *Psychological Bulletin,* 1954, *51,* 240–263.

BLOCH, G., and DAVIDSON, G. Effects of adrenalectomy and experience on postcastration sex behavior in the male rat. *Physiology and Behavior,* 1968, *3,* 461–465.

BREWER, V., and HARTMANN, E. Variable sleepers: When is more or less sleep required? Report to the Association for the Psychophysiological Study of Sleep, San Diego, 1973.

DEMENT, W. C. *Some must watch while some must sleep.* San Francisco: San Francisco Book, 1976.

EPHRON, H. S., and CARRINGTON, P. Rapid eye movement sleep and cortical homeostasis. *Psychological Review,* 1966, *73,* 500–526.

FORD, C. S., and BEACH, F. A. *Patterns of sexual behavior.* New York: Harper, 1951.

FELDMAN, S. M., and WALLER, H. J. Dissociation of electrocortical activation and behavioral arousal. *Nature,* 1962, *196,* 1320–1322.

FLETCHER, J. F. *Situation ethics: The new morality.* Philadelphia: Westminster Press, 1966.

FLETCHER, J. F. *Moral responsibility: Situation ethics at work.* Philadelphia: Westminster Press, 1967.

FOULKES, W. D. Dream reports from different stages of sleep. *Journal of Abnormal and Social Psychology,* 1962, *65,* 14–25.

FREUD, S. *The interpretation of dreams.* London: Hogarth, 1953. (Originally published 1900.)

GAGNON, J. H., and SIMON, W. *Sexual conduct.* Chicago: Aldine, 1973.

GERALL, A. An exploratory study of the effect of social isolation variable on the sexual behaviour of male guinea pigs. *Animal Behaviour,* 1963, *11,* 274–282.

GERALL, H., WARD, I., and GERALL, A. Disruption of the male rat's sexual behaviour induced by social isolation. *Animal Behaviour,* 1967, *15,* 54–58.

HARITON, E. B., and SINGER, J. L. Women's fantasies during sexual intercourse: Normative and theoretical implications. *Journal of Consulting and Clinical Psychology,* 1974, *42,* 313–322.

HARLOW, H. F., and HARLOW, M. K. The affectional systems. In A. M. Schrier, H. F. Harlow, and F. Stollnitz (Eds.), *Behavior of Nonhuman Primates.* New York: Academic, 1965.

HARTMANN, E. *The functions of sleep.* New Haven, Conn.: Yale University Press, 1973.

————. *The biology of dreaming.* Springfield, Ill.: C. C. Thomas, 1967.

————, BAEKELAND, F., and ZWILLING, G. Psychological differences between long and short sleepers. *Archives of General Psychiatry,* 1972, *26,* 463–468.

HOBSON, J. The cellular basis of sleep cycle control. In E. M. Weitzman (Ed.), *Advances in sleep research.* (Vol. 1). Flushing, N.Y.: Spectrum, 1974.

JOUVET, M. Telencephalic and rhombencephalic sleep in the cat. In E. W. Wolstenholme and M. O'Conner (Eds.), *The nature of sleep.* London: Churchill, 1961.

————. The states of sleep. *Scientific American,* 1967, *216,* February, 62–72.

KATCHADOURIAN, H. *Human sexuality: Sense and nonsense.* San Francisco: Freeman, 1974.

KINSEY, A. C., POMEROY, W. B., and MARTIN, C. E. *Sexual behavior in the human male.* Philadelphia: Saunders, 1948.

————, POMEROY, W. B., MARTIN, C. E., and GEBHARD, P. H. *Sexual behavior in the human female.* Philadelphia: Saunders, 1953.

KLEITMAN, N. *Sleep and wakefulness.* Second Edition. Chicago: University of Chicago Press, 1963.

MARLER, P., and HAMILTON, W. J., III. *Mechanisms of animal behavior.* New York: Wiley, 1966.

MASON, W. Early social deprivation in the nonhuman primates: Implications for human behavior. In D. C. Glass (Ed.), *Environmental influences.* New York: Rockefeller University Press, 1968.

MASTERS, W. H., and JOHNSON, V. E. *Human sexual response.* Boston: Little, Brown, 1966.

————, and JOHNSON, V. E. *The pleasure bond. A new look at sexuality and commitment.* Boston: Little, Brown, 1975.

MORUZZI, G., and MAGOUN, H. W. Brain stem reticular formation and activation of the EEG. *Electroencephalography and Clinical Neurophysiology,* 1949, *1,* 455–473.

PFAFF, D. W., and KEINER, M. Estrdiol-concentrating cells in the rat amydala as a part of a limbic-hypothalamic hormone-sensitive system. In B. Eleftherious (Ed.), *The neurobiology of the amydala.* New York: Plenum, 1972.

PITTENDRIGH, C. Circadian rhythms and the circadian organization of living systems. *Cold Springs Harbor Symposium on Quantitative Biology,* 1960, *25,* 159–184.

POMEROY, W. B. *Dr. Kinsey and the Institute for Sex Research.* New York: Harper, 1972.

QUAY, W. B. Regional and circadian differences in cerebral cortical serotin concentrations. *Life Sciences,* 1965, *4,* 379–438.

REISS, I. *Premarital sexual standards in America: A sociological investigation of the relative social and cultural integration of American sexual standards.* New York: Free Press, 1960.

ROBINSON, B. L., and SAWYER, C. H. Loci of sex behavioral and gonadotropic centers of the female cat hippocampus. *Physiologist,* 1957, *1,* 72.

ROFFWARG, H., MUZIO, J., and DEMENT, W. Ontogenetic development of human sleep-dream cycle. *Science,* 1966, *152,* 604–618.

ROSENBLATT, J. S. Effects of experience on sexual behavior in cats. In F. A. Beach (Ed.), *Sex and behavior.* New York: Wiley, 1965.

————, and ARONSON, L. R. The influence of experience on the behavioral effects of androgen in prepuberally castrated male cats. *Animal Behavior,* 1958, *6,* 171–182.

ROUTTENBERG, A. The two-arousal hypothesis: Reticular formation and limbic system. *Psychological Review,* 1968, *75,* 51–80.

SAWYER, C. H. Effects of central nervous system lesions on ovulation in the rabbit. *Anatomy Reviews,* 1956, *124,* 358.

————. Regulatory mechanisms of secretion of gonadotropic hormones. In W. Haymaker, E. Anderson, and W. J. H. Nanta (Eds.), *The hypothalamus.* Springfield, Ill.: C. C. Thomas, 1969.

SNYDER, F. Toward an evolutionary theory of dreaming. *American Journal of Psychiatry*, 1966, *123*, 121–136.

Time, Dec. 13, 1971. The new commandment: Thou shalt not—maybe.

VALENSTEIN, E. S., RISS, W., and YOUNG, W. C. Experimental and genetic factors in the organization of sexual behavior in male guinea pigs. *Journal of Comparative and Physiological Psychology*, 1955, *48*, 397–403.

VAUGHN, E., and FISHER, A. E. Male sexual behavior induced by intracanial electrical stimulation. *Science*, 1962, *137*, 758–760.

WEBB, W. E., and AGNEW, H. W., JR. Sleep stage characteristics of long and short sleepers. *Science*, 1970, *168*, 146–147.

WILKINSON, R. T. Sleep deprivation. In O. G. Edholm and A. L. Bucharach (Ed.), *The physiology of human survival*. New York: Academic, 1965.

WILLIAMS, H. L., LUBIN, A., and GOODNOW, J. L. Impaired performance with acute sleep loss. *Psychological Monographs*, 1959, *73* (14, Whole No. 484).

CHAPTER 15

At the Gut Level: Drinking and Smoking

Smoking and drinking are among the most fascinating aspects of human behavior. Despite strong moral condemnation in some quarters against the use of such substances, which have been shown to represent health hazards and serve no nutritional function, these visceral vices are widespread. Even where their consumption is accepted for adults, minors are generally forbidden to partake of their enjoyment. Excessive use, particularly of alcohol, produces tragic personal and social consequences. Nonetheless, smoking, drinking, and in recent years, the use of hard drugs do not seem to be seriously diminished.

The nature of the motivation for such behavior should be of prime interest to psychologists, not merely because of the social significance but because of the unique features of this behavior. Only humans voluntarily partake of these substances, and attempts to produce alcoholic laboratory rats and monkeys are generally unsuccessful. Once these behaviors are established in humans, they are highly resistant to extinction, as learning theorists term it, or to therapeutic intervention or cure, as the clinician and layperson refer to it. Prevention, even in the face of criminal penalties in the case of drugs other than alcohol, has proved elusive, and these forbidden fruits have managed to retain their enticing and alluring images for each succeeding generation of users.

Alcohol Drinking

This chapter will focus on alcohol drinking, but many of the same statements will be shown to be applicable to the use and abuse of other substances. The fact that smoking and drinking are legal, whereas the use of other drugs is not, affects some of the generalizability among substances.

Marijuana occupies an interesting situation due to its yet unresolved legal status.

Most discussions of human drinking in motivation texts deal with the ingestion of water, which is necessary for biological survival. However, humans are rarely depleted of water and unless they are lost in the Mohave desert in the middle of a summer day, or otherwise in dire need, they are rarely motivated to seek water. Many people never drink straight water, but obtain it in some adulterated form by mixing it with other substances such as coffee, tea, or scotch. Fruits, soups, and other liquids provide sufficient liquid to most people, so that dehydration is rarely a serious problem of survival.

In contrast, many people, most of whom would not be considered alcoholics, are clearly motivated or goal oriented toward alcoholic beverages. On a *psychological* level, alcohol may be perceived by many people as more essential than water for survival. And in alcoholics, it may even supplant the priority of food. Our discussion in this chapter will focus on normative or social drinking, which actually covers a wide range, and will generally exclude the consideration of alcoholism per se. Although the estimate is probably too low because of the stigma associated with alcoholism, there are about five to ten million alcoholics in America. About half of the adult population is estimated to drink alcohol occasionally (at least once a month), according to a national survey of American drinking practices conducted in 1964–5 (Cahalan, Crossley, and Cisin, 1969), as shown in Figure 15–1. Thus, numerically speaking, the larger problem to answer is that of the motives of normal rather than of excessive drinking.

Of course, it cannot be denied that the larger social and personal costs occur among alcoholics, although some tragedies such as automobile accidents occur frequently with the mild use of alcohol by nonalcoholics. Most of our research efforts have been directed (misdirected?) toward alcoholics, in part perhaps because of the desire of normal drinkers and nondrinkers to stigmatize the alcoholic. But because future alcoholics must start somewhere, it may be useful to get some understanding of the motives for social drinking. That is to say, if we want to treat alcoholics it may be useful to know what motivates drinkers who are less advanced. In view of the lack of real progress in curing the alcoholic by professionals, there is all the more reason to study the origins of drinking on the theory that "an ounce of prevention is worth a pound of cure."

For example, as we shall see more fully later, there is good reason to suspect that the use of fear and moralizing, as well as the very attempt to alter the alcoholic's drinking, could be precisely the wrong strategy. For those alcoholics who drink to escape, to enhance self-esteem, or to feel more powerful, the aforementioned strategy may be the best way to insure that he or she continue.

Finally, aside from possible implications for therapy, we must seek an understanding of the socially acceptable uses of alcohol, especially in view of its widespread consumption in most societies throughout history. Many of

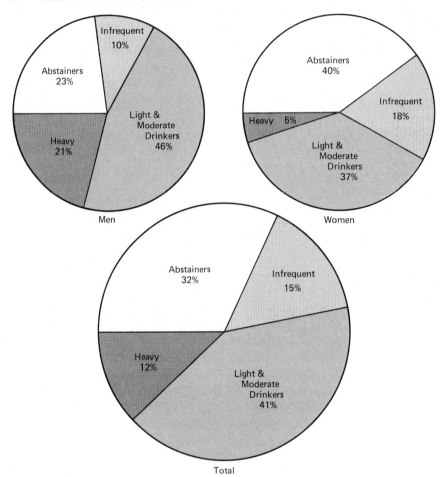

FIGURE 15–1. Per cent of abstainers and types of drinkers among adults (age 21+) in U.S.A., 1964–1965, based on findings of the American Drinking Practices study by Cahalan, Cisin, and Crossley (1969). Degree of drinking was classified according to a rather complex combination of the quantity of alcohol consumed per occasion and the frequency of drinking. *Heavy drinking:* Drink nearly every day with five or more per occasion at least once in a while, or about once weekly with usually five or more per occasion. *Moderate drinking:* Drink at least once a month, typically several times, but usually with no more than three or four drinks per occasion. *Light drinking:* Drink at least once a month, but typically only one or two drinks on a single occasion. *Infrequent drinking:* Drink at least once a year but less than once a month. *Abstainers:* Drink less than once a year or not at all. [From U.S. Department of Health, Education, and Welfare, *First Special Report to the U.S. Congress on Alcohol and Health*, 1971.]

the functions that alcohol serves for the individual user may help us understand the motives for the consumption of other drugs because they may be similar. Whether it be the smoking of cigarettes or marijuana, the drinking of coffee, or the use of hard drugs, one common factor is the existence of prohibitions of varying degree against usage. Sometimes the restrictions are limited to one's age and sometimes the boundaries are legal, but in either case, there is some form of external sanction against usage. A second common feature of these substances is that their ingestion alters sensory, perceptual, motor, and cognitive functions to some extent. These alterations can be highly pleasurable, a fact which is partly responsible for the moralistic attitudes held by some against users of such substances.

The existence of these common features is not to argue that all drugs are similar, because there are obvious important physiological differences in their effects. However, noting common features of drug use may help us understand the basic motivation for their consumption.

PHYSIOLOGICAL EFFECTS OF ALCOHOL

Subjective reports from alcohol users generally indicate a loosening of inhibitions. People become more outgoing, vivacious, and gregarious at parties, for example. Sometimes they even become rowdy or obnoxious and quite different from their normal sober selves.

Although these effects do occur, the pharmacological effect of alcohol on the central nervous system is that of a depressant rather than a stimulant (Mello, 1968). Alcohol's very rapid effect on the central nervous system is a major reason for its popularity among users. Alcohol is readily absorbed from the stomach into the circulatory system, where it works its way toward the brain. If the amount consumed is small, the liver may be able to metabolize or decompose it so that its effect on behavior and subjective experience is negligible. But if the amount and rate of consumption overloads the capacity of the liver to transform the alcohol, the concentration that eventually reaches the brain will be sufficient to alter cognitive functions such as judgment, reasoning, and thinking. Social inhibitions may weaken and the individual may behave in a more extroverted fashion. However, as we shall point out later, social expectations and beliefs about the effects of alcohol or any other mild drug are important determinants of our reactions to their ingestion. Alcohol does not have the physiological ability to produce gregarious outgoing behavior per se.

These relatively mild effects of light to moderate use of alcohol are widespread and for most drinkers they are sufficient. Although moralists may hold that any use of alcohol is undesirable, the prevalent view in our society is that light to moderate drinking is not only acceptable, but desirable in certain contexts. Indeed, our society regards the abstainer in a worse light than it views the social drinker.

Unfortunately, some drinkers go to excess and consume quantities of alcohol that produce more dramatic effects on their nervous systems, their behavior, their interpersonal relationships, and society. Higher concentrations of blood alcohol content created by excessive drinking impair voluntary motor coordination and control and can eventually block breathing, producing coma and death. Furthermore, the chronic use of alcohol produces *tolerance,* a condition such that it requires greater amounts of alcohol to produce a given effect that formerly required smaller amounts. By the time this condition develops, the nervous system may have adapted to alcohol so that the sudden discontinuance of the use of alcohol will lead to *withdrawal* reactions such as delirium, tremulousness, and convulsions.

COGNITIVE BASES OF DRINKING

The drinking of alcoholic beverages serves no function insofar as promoting biological survival, although some avowed imbibers will attest to the contrary. Alcohol drinking is universally found throughout the world and dates well back into antiquity. Despite the risk of some members of a society becoming alcoholics, some form of moderate drinking is accepted in most, but not all, societies.

But whereas the pharmacological effects on the nervous system must be identical, it appears likely that the psychological interpretation of these effects can vary considerably. McAndrew and Edgerton (1969), proposed the idea of drunkenness-as-an-excuse. This concept suggests that drunkenness is a role that is a learned expectation associated with the excessive use of alcohol. As we stated above, alcohol has no universal specific behavioral effect. McAndrew and Edgerton compared the effects of the use of alcohol in different primitive societies and reported wide variations. Drunkenness did not always produce disinhibition and extroverted behavior but sometimes had the opposite effect leading to a withdrawal from social interaction.

Drunkenness-as-an-excuse suggests that each society tolerates or condones some forms of behavior that it might ordinarily reject or condemn, if it appears to be the consequence of the use of some drug such as alcohol. In our society, an employee could not insult the boss at work with impunity but at an office Christmas party, he or she might get away with it, provided he or she had had three or four drinks. Everyone would excuse the employee because "he [or she] didn't really know what he [or she] was saying." We would attribute the out-of-character comments to the alcohol, not the person.

Thus, within limits societies find it useful to allow individuals opportunities to avoid the strict rules and norms of everyday sobriety. The time-out periods provide changes of pace that enable us to survive the serious business of everyday routines.

Since we have all grown up in a society in which alcohol use has been widespread for a long time, it is less obvious to us that the behavioral effects of alcohol are so strongly affected by our learned expectancies. An analysis of the effects of marijuana smoking is more instructive. Howard Becker (1953), a sociologist, analyzed the process of learning to be a marijuana smoker well before it became commonplace on college campuses. He pointed out that the uninitiated often fail to experience or show awareness of the physiological effects of smoking marijuana. Even when the effects are detected, it is necessary for the user to believe that they are positive in order to enjoy the experience. In other words, the effects are not intrinsic to the pharmacological ingredients but also depend on the expectations of the smoker. In the same sense, the effects of alcohol that we have learned to identify from either direct experience or hearsay are strongly determined by our original expectations.

Our expectations about the effects of alcohol also depend on the context or circumstances in which we drink. Drinking at a party may produce different effects from drinking alone just as whether we are happy or sad when drinking can influence its effect. Kalin (1972) compared the amount of alcohol consumed as well as the content of fantasy under different settings. Parties, either wet or dry, were held for college males in an apartment setting with an attractive female folk singer present or absent. In addition, wet parties were conducted in a classroom setting, with or without the female folksinger. Unlike most social gatherings there were no other females present in any of the conditions.

Alcohol consumption was lower under the classroom setting. The presence of the attractive woman led to greater drinking only in the apartment setting. Fantasy, as measured by the use of the Thematic Apperception Test consisting of a series of stimulus picture cards depicting people in various situations to which the subject makes up a story, was also affected by the drinking environment. The inhibiting context of the classroom produced fewer sexual fantasies than that which occurred in the apartment situation when the female folksinger was present. Kalin's findings illustrate the possibility that different learned expectancies about alcohol and its effects may occur in different contexts.

CULTURAL FACTORS

Although alcoholic beverages are consumed throughout the world, the circumstances governing their use vary considerably. Whereas some religious beliefs such as those of the Hindu or Mormon faiths prohibit its use, alcoholic beverages may be incorporated within religious observances of other beliefs such as in the Jewish faith. The extent to which alcoholic beverages are a part of meals as opposed to being the center of attention also widely varies. In other words, the integration of alcohol drinking into the total life pattern depends on beliefs and values of different cultures. When it is excluded such as by moral taboo, or regarded as an occasion in its own right, alcohol drinking takes a different social meaning from that which it has when it is regarded as a normal part of everyday life.

In the Jewish culture, for example, alcohol plays a religious function and is integrated into daily activities, which may account for the low incidence of alcoholism in Jewish families (Snyder, 1958). When alcohol use is frequent but a part of everyday life, such as a beverage associated with meals, its abuse seems to be minimized, such as among Italians. In contrast, another country where wine is an essential part of the culture, France, suffers pronounced alcoholism problems. It has been noted that wine is imbibed throughout the day by the French, not merely with meals, and this difference may account for much of the difference in effect between Italy and France (Lolli, Serianni, Golder, and Luzzato-Fegiz, 1958).

In societies such as the American Indian and Eskimo cultures, alcoholism has had epidemic proportions. Unlike most cultures, which have had centuries in which to evolve social norms and meanings that controlled alcohol abuse, neither the Indian nor the Eskimo cultures had much previous experience when alcohol was introduced to them. As a consequence, they did not have the social means of controlling or limiting excess use. When finally faced with the threats from white settlers, the increased anxiety and stress led to increased use of alcohol.

Barry, Buchwald, Child, and Bacon (1965) conducted cross-cultural comparisons of problems with alcohol in a number of primitive societies. In accord with the hypothesis first proposed by Horton (1943) that anxiety can lead to increased reliance on alcohol, it was noted that hunting societies, as opposed to farming cultures, had more drinking problems. The assumption was made that greater insecurity and uncertainty of survival exists when one must hunt prey instead of grow crops for survival.

In a related study, Bacon, Barry, and Child (1965) found that those societies that placed high emphasis on achievement seem to have more problems with drinking than those without achievement drive. The stress created by such values is presumably relieved by turning to alcohol. In addition, Bacon et al. observed that more problems existed with alcohol in those cultures in which children were not indulged during infancy. This deprivation is assumed to leave a high need for dependency, but because the society may emphasize independence and achievement, considerable conflict may occur. Drinking alcohol can act to relieve this conflict and also fulfill some of the need for indulgence.

Whether one accepts the validity of these types of psychodynamic explanations for drinking, it is indisputable that societies vary widely in the extent to which alcohol is used. The values of the culture, which are determined in part by geography and economics, can influence child-rearing attitudes, which, in turn, might possibly affect drinking practices. However, these types of explanations are speculative and difficult to prove. Other factors, unrelated to child rearing, might affect attitudes toward alcohol more directly.

As a final illustration of the cultural context as a factor in drinking practices, we will describe a specific case in somewhat more detail.

The Example of Drinking in Rural Greece.   Let us examine the role of alcohol in several rural communities of Greece and contrast it with American beliefs and attitudes. Blum and Blum (1969) interviewed and observed Greek villagers and concluded that the common factor underlying alcohol

drinking there was the importance of drinking as part of some social interaction with friends and family. Drinking was limited to meals, excluding the
morning one, the taverna, family celebrations, festivals, religious functions,
and medical uses. It was never regarded as an end in itself.

The socialization of drinking practices begins earlier there than in most
American families, usually by adolescence and even before the age of ten
in many cases. Drinking for the male, as in many cultures, is important but
drunkenness per se is a mark of disgrace. A male must achieve *philotimo*
(love of honor) and this manliness must be defended from shame or doubt.
If one becomes drunk, one leaves oneself vulnerable and one's *philotimo* is
questioned. Consequently, although drinking is accepted, Blum and Blum
suggest that men must learn to be "inventive nondrinkers" and resort to
stratagems such as covering one's glass when refills are being poured around
the table.

Alcohol is not expected to alter one's behavior, especially the small quantities consumed at meals or religious rites. Although alcohol may liven social
gatherings, the behavior is not always attributed to alcohol per se but rather
to the attitudes of the participants.

Nonetheless heavy drinking can occur, leading to undesirable behavior
such as quarrels, shouting, fighting, amorous activities, passing out, or loss of
coordination, just as in our society. These effects are attributed to alcohol.

Blum and Blum identify several factors that govern rural Greek drinking
practices. There is no forbidden aspect associated with either drink or food
as both are provided to children as rewards for good behavior but never are
withheld as forms of punishment for bad behavior. In addition, beliefs in the
magical aspects of alcohol promote the use of caution in use of alcohol. It
also serves important religious use as a symbol of blood. Next, the value of
moderation also serves to regulate the use of alcohol. Finally, there is an
absence of the tendency to drink in order to produce altered states of consciousness.

Despite these cultural forces, there are some cases of excess drinking, but
they are rare. There is a notable lack of the diagnosis of alcoholism, even
though some individuals exist who could probably be termed alcoholics by
American criteria. For one matter, the lack of physical facilities for treatment would discourage such diagnoses by physicians. More important, however, is probably the fact that such individuals create no social problem, given
the values of rural Greeks. The responsibility of caring for deviant drinkers
is assumed by the families of the excessive drinkers and creates no imposition
on the resources of the community. The ability of the families to cope with
the problem, aside from experiencing some mild distress and humiliation, is
generally adequate so that social strain is prevented. It is likely that other
societies, which handle the problem in ways that impose more demands on
community resources, would regard the problem of alcoholism more seriously.

FUNCTIONS OF ALCOHOL DRINKING

In view of the rather unpleasant taste associated with most alcoholic beverages for the beginning drinker, it is obvious that the motivations for acquiring the habit must be potent. Otherwise, one would think that one taste would be sufficient to deter any further consumption. Later, as physical ill effects and psychological problems develop with excessive prolonged use, it is still difficult to alter the drinking habits associated with alcohol. These aspects of alcoholic drinking attest to the powerful incentives the use of this substance holds for many people.

If sensory pleasures are not involved in the *initial formation* of such a habit, why does drinking persist long enough so that it eventually becomes a strong habit that apparently produces sensory and gustatory pleasures? Perhaps the most significant factor at the outset is social, rather than physiological, in nature. Since adolescents imitate adult behavior, one function of alcohol drinking is to achieve adult status and the feeling of being grown-up. Closely related but different is the motive of rebellion from parental fiat or authority. Because it is typical in our society for parents to forbid their children to drink until they reach adulthood, the clandestine use of alcohol by adolescents is one way of expressing independence from control of authority. In addition, drinking becomes the object of curiosity and intrigue by the very fact that it is forbidden to youths.

The approval, admiration, and encouragement of peers also plays an important role in promoting the adoption of alcohol; failure to drink is seen as a sign of fear or immaturity. The reinforcement from peers is powerful, because it must counteract the physical reactions to alcohol, which are generally negative for the initiate.

With practice, the drinker learns how to drink in the sense that physical tolerance develops. Sipping rather than gulping of drinks may begin to occur. The nausea or queasiness some new drinkers experience no longer occurs; at the same time the expectations about the benefits of alcohol as well as social reinforcements take over to reinforce its use. The physical and psychological experiences under alcohol such as giddiness, relief from anxiety, and greater social openness lead to the continued and often increased use of alcohol.

Altered states of consciousness such as "highs" become valued effects of alcohol especially when the individual encounters stress, depression, or boredom. These personal effects of alcohol drinking reduce tensions and enable one to think that one is functioning more adequately, especially in social situations. In their studies of the nature of male fantasies under the influence of alcohol, McClelland, Davis, Kalin, and Wanner (1972) concluded that men drink to enhance their feelings of power or personal control of situations. Using similar measures of fantasy, Wilsnack (1974) argued that women experience greater feelings of femininity as a consequence of drinking alcohol. Even though sex differences may exist in motivating drinking, both hypotheses imply that the alteration of conscious experiences is a major reason for drinking.

Whether or not the feelings produced are accurate is another question, one that may or may not be important. If a male drinker feels more competent after a few drinks, it may be beneficial if he relaxes and can interact better with others. But if this altered feeling leads him to take excessive risks such as by driving recklessly, the consequence can be detrimental and tragic. The fact that over half the traffic accidents involving deaths also involve a drinking driver (Borkenstein et al., 1964) attests to the fact that some forms of performance can be markedly impaired by alcohol.

PERSONALITY DIFFERENCES. There are individual differences in the motives that underly drinking. Mulford and Miller (1960) assessed the reasons why people drink and identified two basic categories: personal effects and social motives. Personal effects such as the experience of "highs" or the relief of depression were also associated with higher amounts and frequencies of drinking compared with social motives such as drinking to celebrate an occasion or to join in the spirit of conviviality at a party. Apparently then alcohol can serve different functions for different drinkers. Nonetheless, a frequent question is whether or not there is some fundamental difference between drinkers, considered as a whole, and nondrinkers or abstainers. A related question is the nature of personality differences between excessive drinkers or alcoholics and light to moderate social drinkers.

The problem with findings (e.g., Conner, 1962; Williams, 1965, 1967) showing that heavy drinkers are impulsive, immature, and feel inadequate, among other things, is how to interpret these differences. Alcohol drinking may have caused these personality differences, but it is also conceivable that these differences were already present to some extent before drinking even began. In the latter case, the differences in drinking patterns would be regarded as an effect, rather than the cause, of personality differences.

Several longitudinal studies fortunately shed some light on this issue. Jones (1968) was able to demonstrate that middle-aged men who differed in their drinking patterns could be differentiated on the basis of assessments made on them when they were in junior and senior high school. The original purpose of this life-span developmental study, known as the Oakland Growth Study, encompassed a much broader scope than the study of alcohol drinking. Because the data were available concerning the conditions existing prior to the onset of drinking, Jones was able to provide some useful information about the probable relationship between personality and levels of alcohol drinking.

A summary of the differences existing during senior high school years for persons who differed in their levels of middle age drinking is shown in Tables 15–1 and 15–2. For example, she found that male problem drinkers had been undercontrolled, assertive, and rebellious *as teenagers,* traits that also are found among adult ages. They also showed difficulty in dependency relationships, in agreement with McCord and McCord's (1960) idea that alcoholics have conflicts over dependency. The characteristics of the problem drinkers

TABLE 15–1.   Senior High School *Q*-Sort Ratings on
Which Problem Drinkers Have High Scores.

Trait	Mean		
	Problem[a]	Moderate[b]	Abstainer[c]
Undercontrolled	7.2	4.2	2.7
Rebellious	6.4	4.2	3.8
Direct hostility	6.1	4.1	2.2
Pushes limits	5.8	3.7	2.3
Manipulative	4.9	2.95	3.3
Self-indulgent	5.6	4.1	2.3
Rapid tempo	7.6	4.8	2.2
Expressive	5.9	4.9	3.99
Assertive	6.99	5.1	3.5
Masculine	6.9	6.4	2.5
Proffers advise	5.2	3.7	3.7

[a] *n* = 6.
[b] *n* = 17.
[c] *n* = 2.
Source: From "Personality correlates and antecedents of drinking patterns in men" by M. C. Jones, *Journal of Consulting and Clinical Psychology*, 1968, *32*, 2–12. Copyright 1968 by the American Psychological Association. Reprinted by permission.

TABLE 15–2.   Senior High School *Q*-Sort Ratings on
Which Problem Drinkers Have Low Scores.

Trait	Mean		
	Problem[a]	Moderate[b]	Abstainer[c]
Overcontrolled	3.7	5.3	6.8
Emotionally bland	3.6	4.95	5.5
Dependable	3.99	6.3	6.8
Objective	4.9	6.2	5.3
Calm	3.1	5.4	5.5
Accepts dependency	3.4	5.4	5.3
Arouses nurturance	3.8	4.3	5.2
Evaluates motives	3.8	4.7	5.5
Socially perceptive	3.4	4.4	5.3
Aware of impression	3.4	4.5	5.3
Productive	3.8	6.1	4.8
Esthetic	4.1	5.2	6.8
Verbally fluent	4.7	5.5	6.99
Aloof	4.1	5.4	6.8
Considerate	4.4	5.2	7.3

[a] *n* = 6.
[b] *n* = 17.
[c] *n* = 2.
Source: From "Personality correlates and antecedents of drinking patterns in men" by M. C. Jones, *Journal of Consulting and Clinical Psychology*, 1968, *32*, 2–12. Copyright 1968 by the American Psychological Association. Reprinted by permission.

when they were teenagers also show some differences from those of adult deviant drinkers. For example, the isolation, self-pity, and destructiveness sometimes found in adult alcoholics were not apparent during the teen years of her problem drinker sample.

Jones concluded that her findings reveal the existence of personality traits prior to the onset of problem drinking that may contribute to the subsequent excessive use of alcohol. Because the data involved a longitudinal comparison, it is not plausible to argue that personality differences observed were the effects of alcoholic drinking.

A similar study (Jones, 1971) examined the relationship between alcohol drinking and personality among women and found that the differences between normal and excessive women drinkers are even greater than those found in men. In accord with the male study, problem drinkers were more impulsive, unstable, and unpredictable, but in addition women problem drinkers differ from other women drinkers in being more depressive, self-negating, and distrustful. A somewhat surprising finding was that problem drinkers and abstainers were similar in that both seemed to lack adequate coping devices and were pessimistic, self-defeating, and withdrawn as well as more anxious and irritable. But whereas problem drinker women were also submissive as youths, the abstainers were responsible, conventional, and more emotionally controlled.

Because these differences existed prior to the development of the differential drinking histories, it is reasonable to conclude that such differences may have been causes rather than effects of drinking. Additional corroboration of the kinds of differences found by Jones has been provided by Jessor, Collins, and Jessor (1972) who administered a battery of measures to adolescents before they began drinking. A follow-up study only a year later enabled them to contrast those who did or did not start drinking during the year. The initiates differed from nondrinkers in many ways other than alcohol use, showing more personal problems, less concern for academic achievement, more alienation, less religiosity, and greater tolerance of deviant behavior in general.

A longitudinal study of drinking levels of college students over a one-year period conducted by the author (Jung, 1977) showed greater increases in drinking for students who had a large number of motives for drinking, such as loneliness, tension, boredom, and a desire to escape. Because these motives were present at the beginning of the observation period, it is possible to conclude that they were causes rather than effects of heavier drinking.

Genetic Differences.   The possibility that genetic factors might contribute to tendencies for heavy use of alcohol also exists. The findings just described show that personality differences between heavier users and nonusers are present prior to the use of alcohol and could reflect the effects of early environmental influences but might also stem from genetic factors. Goodwin (1971), in summarizing research using family histories, noted that sons of alcoholics have rates of alcoholism ranging from 25 to 50 per cent, far greater than that of the general population. Although this type of evidence is consistent with a genetic hypothesis, it is not conclusive, because the home environment is not controlled.

More powerful evidence, however, is available for a genetic view in the form of studies of alcoholism among adoptees separated from their parents before the sixth week of life. Goodwin et al. (1973) made a comparison of fifty-five male adoptees who had at least one biological parent who was an alcoholic and who had been adopted by nonrelatives with seventy-eight male adoptees who had no biological parents with alcoholism and who were adopted by nonrelatives. This study was conducted in Denmark, where extensive records on adoptions are maintained.

Greater problems with alcohol were found among the adoptees who had a biological parent with alcoholism. These *probands,* as they were termed, showed four times the alcoholism rate found in the controls. Furthermore, the probands required psychological treatment more frequently for other types of emotional problems. Divorce was three times as likely among probands.

Studies of ethnic differences in autonomic reactivity to alcohol administered to infants also suggest a genetic factor. Wolff (1972) compared the degree of facial flushing in response to alcohol among Japanese, Korean, Taiwanese, and Caucasian infants. Whereas almost all of the noncaucasian infants were affected, only six percent of the caucasian infants showed increased facial flushing.

These findings are not conclusive proof that genetic transmission of alcoholism exists, but they do suggest the possibility. It is also possible that prenatal factors can contribute to biological differences that affect subsequent reactions to alcohol. Jones, Smith, Streissguth, and Myrianthopoulos (1974), for example, suggest that the higher incidence of maldeveloped infants born to alcoholic mothers may stem from damage to the fetuses from alcohol in the blood of the mother.

It is possible that these types of differences whether genetic, prenatal, or learned, which already exist before drinking begins in earnest, can also lead to more frequent problems in general. If the potential problem drinker is more outgoing, extroverted, impulsive, etc., as many studies indicate, he or she is apt to take more risks, encounter more problems, and have more emotional upheavals. Drinking alcohol may be one means of coping with these situations but it may also represent one means of enhancing one's experiences, having fun, or experimenting. Furthermore, if alcohol is used for these reasons, it should be likely that other agents or substances capable of altering one's conscious experiences dramatically will be tried. Smoking cigarettes, marijuana, and other substances as well as the use of hallucinogenic drugs, stimulants, depressants, and tranquilizers may reflect similar motives. This is not to say that all alcohol users will try all forms of pills and drugs, but that similar reasons may underly the use of many of these substances.

A more extended discussion of evidence that supports the preceding analysis will be presented after we examine some similarities between the drinking of alcohol and the smoking of tobacco cigarettes. Some of these commonalities will also be applicable to the smoking of marijuana and the use of drugs such as the hallucinogens and other illicit substances.

Smoking Cigarettes

The smoking of tobacco is a topic of great concern because of the evidence linking it to health dangers. Lung cancer, heart disease, emphysema, and bronchitis are the most commonly mentioned ailments attributed to cigarette smoking.

The widespread dissemination of information about the grave risk associated with cigarette smoking has had scarcely any impact toward the reduction of smoking by Americans, at least among those who were already smoking when the Surgeon General's Office released its 1964 report linking cancer with cigarette smoking. Perhaps the influence on *potential* smokers may have been stronger, but cigarette sales figures still suggest that many new smokers are recruited each year. It is estimated that about eighty billion cigarettes were sold in 1970 and that over half of the males and over one third of the females in this country smoke cigarettes.

Obviously there are some powerful incentives for engaging in behavior that "is dangerous to your health," as the warning labels required on cigarette packages suggest. What factors act to maintain the persistence of smoking despite the health hazards? Does the effort to alter smoking actually boomerang and produce a greater reluctance to quit?

Why do people smoke in the first place? As with alcohol drinking, one powerful motive is peer approval for engaging in a behavior for which minors are disapproved. The desire to assume adult status by imitating the smoking of adults is another factor. Like drinking, smoking also provides an opportunity for the adolescent to rebel against the restrictions imposed by parents.

Kaplan (1970) in his discussion of the issue of marijuana smoking considers the battle between conflicting generational values and life styles to be the crux of the struggle on the legality of marijuana use. Smoking of marijuana is more controversial than the smoking of tobacco. Whereas the older generation can accept tobacco use as being a bad habit at worst, because many of its members use it, marijuana is seen as a vice of the younger generation, which is apt to lead to moral and spiritual decay, lack of initiative, and an excess of pleasure seeking. Legal sanctions have been imposed against the use of marijuana accordingly, but, as in the case of the prohibition of alcohol, they have not been sufficient to deter widespread use. For that matter, around the turn of the century a number of states had laws that completely banned tobacco cigarette smoking. Possession of tobacco then, like marijuana now, could lead to a fine or imprisonment, according to a 1915 Michigan law, for example (Neurhring and Markle, 1974).

The smoking of tobacco is also productive of affective states that reduce tension and anxiety. It gives the smoker something to do with his or her hands, just as a martini or alcoholic beverage does for the drinker. It also gives one something to do with one's mouth. These nonverbal uses may be valuable in social settings for an anxious person, because they provide a chance to pause during conversations to puff on a cigarette or take a sip from one's cocktail, perhaps to think of some witty or clever thing to say.

The active pharmacological agent nicotine serves to produce activation at the physiological level, although the smoker tends to experience sedative effects. Jarvik (1970) indicated that the exact mechanism of these effects is not clear. Nicotine might act directly on organs to increase activation or indirectly through the release of other agents such as neurotransmitters known as *catecholamines*. Because these substances have been hypothesized (Kety and Schildkraut, 1967) to be responsible for general feelings of well-being and positive moods, it is plausible to conclude also that the relaxed and pleasurable effects of nicotine on smokers could stem from the release of catecholamines. This reinforcement mechanism involving nicotine must be potent in view of the difficulty experienced by smokers trying to quit.

As in the case of alcohol, then, we have a situation in which the use of a substance is initially unpleasant in taste but one that is a desired ingredient capable of eventually producing pleasurable effects, despite health hazards, moral disapproval, legal and age restrictions, etc. As with alcohol, once the habit is formed, tolerance develops and one must increase the amount of smoking in order to achieve the same effect previously created with a smaller amount. Both habits are exceedingly difficult to eliminate once they reach a certain stage, especially because discontinuation initially leads to such pronounced negative affects as craving and withdrawal symptoms such as tension and anxiety. Smoking, like drinking, seems to be a problem for only a small percentage of users fortunately. Exactly why others escape these ill effects is not clearly understood.

SMOKING AND PERSONALITY

Just as studies have shown the existence of personality differences among individuals who vary in their use of alcohol, it appears likely that differences should also distinguish smokers and nonsmokers, differences that might be similar to those found between heavy and light drinkers.

Matarazzo and Saslow (1960) compared smokers and nonsmokers on a number of variables. Their results, presented in Table 15–3, showed no differences in intelligence or socioeconomic status distinguishing smokers and nonsmokers. This finding occurred in three different populations: psychiatric patients, hospital nurses, and undergraduates. Some evidence suggested that, in some groups, smokers were more anxious, had more psychosomatic

TABLE 15–3.   Means and Ranges of Smokers and Nonsmokers

Variable	Psychiatric Patients (N = 40)		Student Nurses (N = 114)		University Undergraduates (N = 140)			
	Non-smokers (N = 9)	Smokers (N = 31)	Females		Females		Males	
			Non-smokers	Smokers	Non-smokers	Smokers	Non-smokers	Smokers
Socioeconomic Index:								
Mean	60.2	57.9	48.6	46.2	43.6	42.1	49.8	45.4
Range	44–73	14–77	11–73	11–77	11–71	11–73	11–77	11–73
IQ:								
Mean	93.6	98.8	117.6	118.4	110.9	109.2	107.9	109.2
Range	77–109	79–129	103–130	103–129	87–129	92–122	84–130	89–131
Anxiety level:								
Mean	28.9	25.9	12.3	14.8[a]	12.0	15.3	11.0	14.7[a]
Range	13–39	6–45	3–26	3–34	5–28	6–45	2–30	1–33
Psychosomatic Symptoms:								
Mean	12.1	13.9	6.3	8.2[a]	3.7	6.1	3.3	3.9
Range	2–23	1–44	0–22	0–18	0–14	0–18	0–12	0–19
Cups of Coffee:								
Mean	2.8	4.2	0.9	2.6[b]	1.5	2.7	1.0	3.5[b]
Range	0–8	0–15	0–6	0–10	0–10	0–6	0–6	0–12
Liquor Score:								
Mean	1.22	2.06	1.0	1.2[a]	1.3	1.5	1.5	2.2[b]
Range	1–2	1–6	1–2	1–2	1–2	1–2	1–5	1–6

[a] Mean differences significant at the .05 level.
[b] Mean differences significant at the .001 level.

Source. From "Psychological and Related Characteristics of Smokers and Nonsmokers" by J.D. Matarazzo and G. Saslow, *Psychological Bulletin*, 1960, *57*, 493-513. Copyright 1960 by the American Psychological Association. Reprinted by permission.

symptoms, and consumed greater quantities of coffee and liquor than non-smokers.

Eysenck (1965), among others, has found that smokers are more extraverted. This finding led him to question the idea that smoking per se is the major cause of the greater incidence of cancer found among smokers. He suggested that smokers, as a whole, have a lifestyle that involves more outgoing tendencies and greater risk taking, which may expose them to a variety of factors that increase the risk of cancer. Whether or not this latter conjecture is warranted, most studies of smokers dealing with the personality dimension of extraversion-introversion do agree in finding that smokers are more extraverted (Smith, 1970). Smith's review of the research also suggested that smokers may be more antisocial as well as more likely to believe in chance or fate.

A large-scale study by Coan (1973) involved the administration of a six-hour battery of tests to male and female college students. In general, smokers were found to be more extraverted, more distress prone, more liberal, more open to experience, and more inclined to favor spontaneity.

Coan (1973, p. 96) suggested that, "The smoker suffers more, but he is more likely to lead a full, rich life. He participates in a more varied way in all the acts that appear on the human stage. The nonsmoker settles for a more restricted pattern of living and thereby achieves more order and serenity. He is more certain of who he is and less aware of what he might be."

In addition, Coan argued that two distinct types of smokers may exist and that it may be misleading merely to contrast smokers as a whole category against nonsmokers. One type of smoker identified by Coan seems to be motivated by negative factors such as tension, whereas a second but smaller group of smokers appears to be oriented toward positive reasons such as relaxation.

The correlation between smoking and personality traits does not permit unequivocal interpretations regarding causality, because it is possible that the personality differences between smokers and nonsmokers are the consequences of differences in smoking behavior rather than causes of it. A longitudinal study by Stewart and Livson (1966) is valuable, because it obtained measures of personality and behavioral differences that existed prior to the onset of smoking. Using the data from the Oakland Growth Study (Jones, 1968), they established that children who eventually became smokers were already more rebellious even in elementary school and junior high school. These results fit in with Eysenck's (1965) view that smokers may be greater stress seekers and risk takers than nonsmokers.

SMOKING AND AFFECT

An interesting paradox about the phenomenology of smokers has been reported by Nesbitt (1972) in that they appear to "feel" less emotional, judging from their self-reports, whereas observers tend to judge them to be more emotional. In one experiment (Nesbitt, 1973), subjects were tested for pain tolerance to electric shocks under several conditions: no cigarette, low nicotine cigarette, and high nicotine cigarette. No differences between treatments were found with nonsmokers but for smokers, the more nicotine present, the more pain tolerance. Nesbitt suggests that one explanation is that smokers are less emotional and tolerate more pain when smoking because they may misattribute the feelings created by the shock to their cigarettes. Another possibility raised by Nesbitt is that smoking may increase arousal so that further increases from the shocks are relatively small increases and less painful.

Exactly why smokers can tolerate more pain is not answered but the phenomenon is intriguing. It fits in with the fact that many smokers claim that smoking calms them when they are under stress. Even though psycho-physiological evidence is to the contrary, the subjective feelings of stress reduction experienced while smoking are the primary determinants, leading to the continuation of smoking in the face of stress.

A similar emphasis on affective correlates of smoking guided a study by Ikard and Tomkins (1973) who observed situational determinants of smoking in an experimental setting. Two movies were shown, one positive and one negative in affective mood, in counterbalanced order to different subgroups of smokers. Observers watched the smoking behavior of subjects during the showing of the movies and classified smokers in three categories: smoked during positive affect movie only, smoked during negative affect movie only, smoked during both movies. In addition, self-reports of mood were obtained for each movie to see if subjects felt the way the movie was intended to influence their feeling states.

The results showed that in female smokers smoking occurred only during the negative mood movie, whereas in males most smoking also occurred during the negative movie but some also smoked during the positive mood movie. No subjects were observed who smoked only during the positive movie. Ikard and Tomkins suggested that different kinds of smokers exist, depending on the affective state that triggers smoking. However, it appears that for the most part, negative moods such as depression are more conducive to smoking than are positive moods.

In addition to smoking for affect, Ikard and Tomkins suggested that there are preaddictive and addictive smokers for whom smoking is such a strong habit that craving occurs when they have been deprived of cigarettes. Thus, they smoke not only for affective feeling but also to fulfill their cravings when deprived of cigarettes.

PARALLELS WITH SOME OTHER DRUGS

Despite the large gap in legal status, evidence on the nature of personality differences between smokers and nonsmokers of marijuana is surprisingly similar to those just described for cigarette smoking and alcohol drinking. Jessor, Jessor, and Finney (1973) extended their social-psychological analysis of the motives underlying alcohol use to the smoking of marijuana among junior high, senior high, and college students. Information about problem behavior, expectations for achievement, alienation, attitudes toward deviance, parent-peer influence, social support for drug use, and actual use of marijuana were among the items assessed.

At the time of the initial assessment, nonusers were identified who were reclassified a year later in a followup into two groups: those who began using marijuana and those who continued to abstain. The results were similar for junior and senior high school students, and although larger effects were found in males the general pattern was also noted with females. Marijuana users, compared to nonusers, valued achievement less but independence more, expressed greater alienation and social criticism, engaged less frequently in conventional activities such as attending church and were more prone to other types of problems such as those associated with alcohol or sex.

Because these differences were found to exist before the use of marijuana, they are more likely to be reflections of some general factors leading to deviant behavior rather than the effects of marijuana smoking per se. The interpretation of Jessor et al. involves both personality factors and social determinants and suggests that personal frustration, lack of perceived opportunity, social support and approval of deviance, etc. interact to increase the likelihood of marijuana use.

The fact that such correlates of marijuana use did not predict behavior of college students was attributed to the already high (70 per cent) usage of marijuana in the second year of the study among this group. Jessor et al. also suggested that college students may use marijuana more as an ideological symbol rather than as a means of coping with failure.

Finally, it should be noted that Blum (1969) found differences between users and nonusers of illicit drugs, which include hallucinogens, opiates, amphetamines, sedatives, and tranquilizers. This evidence provides another situation that parallels the preceding findings of differences among users and nonusers of alcohol, tobacco, and marijuana. The pattern may vary somewhat with the particular substance, the background of the individual, the age, sex, or education level of the person, but generally speaking the users tend to include the more adventuresome as well as the more desperate. Users appear to include experimenters and stimulation seekers as well as escapists from frustration and despair whereas nonusers tend to be more in control of themselves, for better or worse. In his study, Blum (1969) concluded that drug use can simultaneously serve ideological, social, and individualistic motives. Drug use can reflect dissatisfaction and pessimism as well as flexibility, openness to new experiences, and lesser commitment to institutional goals.

Blum also shed some interesting light on the motives of total abstainers, those few (4 per cent of his sample) college students who do not use tobacco, alcohol, marijuana or any drug for nonmedical purposes. Abstainers tend to be deeply religious, from conservative backgrounds, and generally satisfied and optimistic about life. When one considers the immense social pressures for the use of some of these substances in our society, it is not surprising that only 4 per cent of the students were total abstainers and that they differed from users in the ways they did. Our society attaches suspicion to abstainers, especially if they are male, because they seem too good to be true. As Ambrose Bierce defined an abstainer, he is "a weak person who yields to the temptation of denying himself a pleasure."

The contrast between the characteristics of abstainers and drug users again serves to suggest that a variety of motives ranging from boredom, curiosity, and risk taking to alienation, escapism, and frustration can motivate drug use, just as it seems to be the case in alcohol or marijuana use. Those few who are either satisfied or under such rigorous self-control that they can obey all the rules are the minority that abstains from using any of the substances discussed in this chapter. As in the case of alcohol drinking to excess, drug use may not cause the problems so often attributed to it so much as reflect the presence of some basic condition that leads not only to drug problems but other problems as well. As Nowlis (1969, p. 356) commented, "It is becoming increasingly evident that drug use does not cause but, rather, is caused by much of the behavior attributed to it and that drug use is only one manifestation of some fairly pervasive and basic problems. . . ." Such recognition may lead to society's giving more attention to such basic problems as poverty, lack of opportunity, boring schools, and other inequities. This emphasis may be more fruitful in the long run than attempting to outlaw all agents capable of altering states of consciousness such as drugs. For as Nowlis (1969, p. 357) noted, "If a student really wants to get high, there are more things with which he can accomplish this than we can possibly legislate against, even after we have identified them."

These latter observations concerning the use and control of illicit drugs are also directly relevant to the problems of alcohol, tobacco, and even marijuana with few differences. Attempts to get at the root causes of the negative conditions leading to the need for these substances are necessary if their abuse is to be reduced. Moral condemnation and legislative restriction have failed to reduce misuse and may have even contributed to greater use by increasing frustration, resentment, and anxiety.

In addition, some of the motives underlying the use of these controversial substances may be considered positive, provided excessive use or dependence on them does not occur. Although the use of tobacco and alcohol is generally accepted in our society, they also are seriously condemned in some quarters. Nevertheless, they produce some forms of pleasure and tension relief in many users and in their eyes this benefit seems to outweigh any negative consequences such as threats to health or social ostracism. As we noted in Chapter 10, humans are often motivated to seek arousal, varied stimulation, and altered states of consciousness. The use of alcohol, tobacco, marijuana, and other drugs is often motivated by the desire for these types of affective experiences.

Summary

The ingestion of substances such as tobacco, alcohol, marijuana, and other drugs is not necessary for biological survival, but throughout history humans have indulged in the use of some substances that produce marked changes in consciousness. Societies have ambivalent attitudes about such practices and usually have also tried to regulate, if not outlaw, the consumption of such substances.

The major focus of this chapter has been the drinking of alcoholic beverages with considerable attention also being given to the smoking of tobacco cigarettes. A few comparisons were also drawn between these behaviors and those related to the use of marijuana and drugs that entail more restrictive legal controls.

The discussion has been on the normative use of alcohol and tobacco, although the line between the use and abuse of these substances is often hazy especially in the mind of the user. Although the question of the motivation for abnormal or excessive use may be the more urgent social problem, the ultimate and more important question deals with the motives of the normal user. Why does anyone engage in the use of initially unpleasant tasting substances that are expensive and generally considered unhealthy? Furthermore their use is condemned by a large segment of society.

A brief description of the physiological effects of alcohol was followed by a discussion of some of the cultural and cognitive aspects of alcohol. The role of expectations and cultural attitudes can modify the behavioral reactions to alcohol despite the pharmacological effects of the substance. The need to consider the cultural context and meaning of drinking was illustrated by an example of drinking in rural Greece.

The social consequences of decisions to drink or not to drink as well as the altered states of consciousness created by alcohol are important factors to examine. Different drinkers imbibe to fulfill different motives. Personality comparisons of high versus low drinkers do not permit a clear determination of whether such differences are causes or effects of alcohol. Longitudinal studies, however, are able to identify differences that precede experiences with alcohol. They suggest that drinkers who differ in their consumption level were already different in personality earlier in life. These differences may not be specific to alcohol drinking but appear to be similar to the types of personality differences reported between smokers and nonsmokers as well as between users and nonusers of psychoactive drugs. There is also some suggestion that some of these differences are genetically determined.

Regardless of whether it is biological or environmental factors, or both, that produced the differences between users and nonusers of these substances, it appears important to consider the affective consequences of their use as motivating factors. Reduction of anxiety and tension, on the one hand, and escape from boredom, creation of "highs," and other good feelings, on the other, seem to be involved at various times in the use of these substances.

A consideration of all the negative consequences of the use of tobacco, alcohol, and the like might lead to the view that such behaviors are irrational or at least paradoxical. However, when the affective benefits are taken into account, these actions become both comprehensible and not unreasonable.

References

BACON, M. K., BARRY, H., and CHILD, I. L. A cross-cultural study of drinking: II. Relation to other features of culture. *Quarterly Journal of Studies on Alcohol,* 1965, *3,* 29–48.
BARRY, H., BUCHWALD, C., and CHILD, I. L., and BACON, M. K. A cross-cultural study of drinking: IV. Comparisons with Horton ratings. *Quarterly Journal of Studies on Alcohol,* 1965, 62–77. Supplement No. 3.
BECKER, H. On becoming a marihuana user. *American Journal of Sociology,* 1953, *59,* 235–242.
BLUM, R. H., and Associates. *Drugs II. Students and drugs.* San Francisco: Jossey Bass, 1969.
———, and BLUM, E. M. A cultural case study: Temperate Achilles. In R. H. Blum and Associates. *Society and drugs: Social and cultural observations.* San Francisco: Jossey Bass, 1969.
BORKENSTEIN, R. F., CROWTHER, C., SHUMATE, R. P., ZIEL, W. B., and ZYLMAN, R. *The role of the drinking driver in traffic accidents (the Grand Rapids Study).* Bloomington, Ind.: Department of Police Administration, Indiana University, 1964.
CAHALAN, D., CROSSLEY, I. H., and CISIN, H. M. *American drinking practices: A national survey of drinking behavior and attitudes.* Monograph No. 6, Rutgers Center of Alcohol Studies, New Brunswick, N.J.: Rutgers University, 1969.
COAN, R. W. Personality variables associated with cigarette smoking. *Journal of Personality and Social Psychology,* 1973, *26,* 86–104.
CONNER, R. G. The self-concepts of alcoholics. In D. J. Pittman and C. R. Snyder (Eds.), *Society, culture, and drinking patterns.* New York: Wiley, 1962.
EYSENCK, H. J. *Smoking, health, and personality.* London: Weidenfeld and Nicholson, 1965.
GOODWIN, D. W. Is alcoholism hereditary? A review and critique. *Archives of General Psychiatry,* 1971, *25,* 545–549.
———, SCHULSINGER, F., HERMANSEN, L., GUZE, S. B., and WINOKUR, G. Alcohol problems in adoptees raised apart from alcoholic biological parents. *Archives of General Psychiatry,* 1973, *28,* 238–243.
HORTON, D. The functions of alcohol in primitive societies: A cross-cultural study. *Quarterly Journal of Studies on Alcohol,* 1943, *4,* 199–320.
IKARD, F. F., and TOMKINS, S. S. The experience of affect as a determinant of smoking behavior: A series of validity studies. *Journal of Abnormal Psychology,* 1973, *81,* 172–181.
JARVIK, M. E. The role of nicotine in the smoking habit. In W. A. Hunt (Ed.), *Learning mechanisms in smoking.* Chicago: Aldine, 1970.
JESSOR, R., COLLINS, M. I., and JESSOR, S. L. On becoming a drinker: Social-psychological aspects of an adolescent transition. In F. E. Seixas (Ed.), *Nature and nurture in alcoholism.* New York: Annals of the New York Academy of Sciences, 1972.
———, JESSOR, S. L., and FINNEY, J. A social psychological analysis of marihuana use: Longitudinal studies of high school and college youth. *Journal of Personality and Social Psychology,* 1973, *26,* 1–15.
JONES, K. L., SMITH, D. W., STREISSGUTH, A. P., and MYRIANTHOPOULOS, N. C. Outcome in offspring of chronic alcoholic women. *Lancet,* June 1, 1974, No. 7866, 1076–1078.

Jones, M. C. Personality correlates and antecedents of drinking patterns in men. *Journal of Consulting and Clinical Psychology*, 1968, *32*, 2–12.

———. Personality antecedents and correlates of drinking patterns in women. *Journal of Consulting and Clinical Psychology*, 1971, *36*, 61–69.

Jung, J. Drinking motives and behavior in social drinkers. *Journal of Studies on Alcohol*, 1977, *38*, 944–952.

Kalin, R. Social drinking in different settings. In D. C. McClelland, W. N. Davis, R. Kalin, and E. Wanner (Eds.), *The drinking man: Alcohol and human motivation*. New York: Free Press, 1972.

Kaplan, J. *Marihuana—the new prohibition*. Cleveland, Ohio: World, 1970.

Kety, S. S., and Schildkraut, J. J. Biogenic amines and emotion. *Science*, 1967, *156*, 21–30.

Lolli, G., Serianni, E., Golder, G. M., and Luzzato-Fegiz, P. *Alcohol in Italian culture*. New York: Free Press, 1958.

McAndrew, C., and Edgerton, R. B. *Drunken comportment: A social explanation*. Chicago: Aldine, 1969.

McClelland, D. C., W. N. Davis, R. Kalin, and E. Wanner (Eds.), *The drinking man: Alcohol and human motivation*. New York: Free Press, 1972.

McCord, W., and McCord, J. *Origins of alcoholism*. Stanford, Calif.; Stanford University Press, 1960.

Matarazzo, J. D., and Saslow, G. Psychological and related characteristics of smokers and nonsmokers. *Psychological Bulletin*, 1960, *57*, 493–513.

Mello, N. K. Some aspects of the behavioral pharmacology of alcohol. In D. H. Efron et al. (Eds.), *Psychopharmacology: A review of progress*. Washington, D.C.: U.S. Government Printing Office, 1968.

Mulford, H. A., and Miller, D. E. Drinking in Iowa, Ill. A scale of definitions of alcohol related to drinking behavior. *Quarterly Journal of Studies on Alcohol*, 1960, *21*, 267–278.

Nesbitt, P. D. Chronic smoking and emotionality. *Journal of Applied Social Psychology*, 1972, *2*, 187–196.

———. Smoking, physiological arousal, and emotional response. *Journal of Personality and Social Psychology*, 1973, *25*, 137–144.

Neurhring, E., and Markle, G. E. Nicotine and norms: The re-emergence of a deviant behavior. *Social Problems*, 1974, *21*, 513–526.

Nowlis, H. Overview for administrators. In R. H. Blum (Ed.), *Drugs II. Students and drugs*. San Francisco: Jossey Bass, 1969.

Smith, G. Personality and smoking: A review of the empirical literature. In W. A. Hunt (Ed.), *Learning mechanisms in smoking*. Chicago: Aldine, 1970.

Snyder, C. R. *Alcohol and the Jews: A cultural study of drinking and sobriety*. Yale Center of Alcohol Studies Monograph 1, New York: Free Press, 1958.

Stewart, L., and Livson, N. Smoking and rebelliousness: A longitudinal study from childhood to maturity. *Journal of Consulting Psychology*, 1966, *30*, 225–229.

U.S. Public Health Service. *Smoking and health*. Report of the Advisory Committee to the Surgeon General of the Public Health Service. Washington, D.C.: U.S. Government Printing Office, 1962.

Williams, A. F. Self-concepts of college problem drinkers. *Quarterly Journal of Studies on Alcohol*, 1965, *26*, 586–594.

———. Self-concepts of college problem drinkers. 2. Heilbrun need scales. *Quarterly Journal of Studies on Alcohol*, 1967, *28*, 267–276.

Wilsnack, S. C. The effects of social drinking on women's fantasy. *Journal of Personality*, 1974, *42*, 43–61.

Wolff, P. Ethnic differences in alcohol sensitivity. *Science*, 1972, *175*, 449–456.

PART SIX

CHANGING MOTIVES and INDIVIDUAL DIFFERENCES

CHAPTER 16

You Can Lead a Horse to Water, but...

Many years ago, William Jones (1890) observed that "habit is the great flywheel of society." Most of our daily behavior reflects the influence of attitudes, beliefs, and values that we acquired in early childhood. Ingrained habits automatically determine much of our behavior without much awareness or reflection on our part. Most of the time this stability is economical of our efforts and compatible with situational demands. But when new situations or changing times are encountered, this same process may be quite unadaptive and rigid, preventing the individual from seeking or accepting novel and adaptive ways of responding to change.

We generally feel comfortable doing things in familiar ways, and sudden or drastic changes are often disruptive and anxiety producing. We are momentarily lost, for our old habits may be inadequate to deal with the new situation, and we must devise new solutions. Thus, we see that attempts to persuade people to change their attitudes and behaviors are usually met with resistance and hesitancy or the stance, "don't confuse me with facts, my mind's already made up." Even emotional appeals for change can be blocked by defensive responses such as the avoidance of views different from one's own. People do not go out of their way to learn facts or views contrary to their own. Thus, aside from a few hecklers, audiences attending political rallies are predominantly comprised of those who already support the candidate.

If most people are as rigidly set in their motives and behaviors as suggested here, one would expect little or no change in the overall society. Yet there is abundant evidence that enormous social changes have taken place in the past generation alone. Changing attitudes toward international relations, sexual freedom, civil rights, and educational philosophy, to name a few topics, have occurred even in the past decade. In view of the argument that individuals are highly resistant to change and the fact that society is a collection of individuals, how can we reconcile the obvious changes that have transpired?

Perhaps, on the other hand, these changes have not been as rapid as we might think at first. The fight for the rights of ethnic minorities and women, for example, did not begin recently but originated long in the past. Lincoln signed the Emancipation Proclamation over a century ago, and a score of years have passed since the Civil Rights Act was legislated. Similarly, the struggle for women's rights was prominent in the early part of this century only to become dormant until revived in its modern form. In other words, viewed against the long run, the changes we note today may have taken longer than it might appear. The faster changes seen in some areas of social revolution today are the result of earlier campaigns, which met substantial resistance and active opposition initially. Society was not ready to accept these changes at those earlier periods but those early crusaders laid the groundwork that, in combination with other complex historical and social factors, has made these changes more acceptable in today's society.

Methods of Changing Motives and Behavior

Society influences and controls our behavior in numerous ways, ranging from the subtle conventions we rarely notice such as driving on the right-hand side of the road to legal sanctions whereby certain behaviors are expressly forbidden under threat of punishment by fines, penalties, or imprisonment.

LEGAL MEANS

Compliance with laws is not always willing, but most citizens both respect and fear the law. Laws are accepted by many citizens as immutable commands to be obeyed without question. Even unapprehended transgressions create substantial guilt and anxiety that aid in the prevention of subsequent violations. Consequently, laws are generally effective external controls on the behavior of most persons.

Nonetheless, laws are far from ideal forms of control precisely because they are external rather than internal. Unless they are periodically enforced so that a reasonably high percentage of violators are punished, even good citizens will come to ignore the prohibition, such as in the case of jaywalking, which is generally not a violation that is enforced. Even if apprehended violators are punished, the reliance on external control means that authorities must search and patrol for violations. The cost is prohibitive for the apprehension of all violators, as is realized by all drivers who occasionally speed when they think no police are present.

Some laws, especially the ones we disagree with in philosophy, generate resentment. Whereas an apprehended speeding driver may accept fault because he or she can accept that he or she represented a danger to other drivers, legal attempts to control behavior in the areas of desegregation of schools or busing of students create substantial resistance among those who disagree with the ideological goals of the social change. Brehm (1966) used the term *reactance* to describe the tendency of people to balk at coercive or restrictive efforts by external forces to limit their own freedom of choice.

Legal means of control and change will be dealt with at greater length in Chapter 17, whereas this chapter will focus first on gentler methods of producing changes.

EMOTIONAL APPEALS

One of the most common tactics to influence behavior and motives is the use of fear and other emotional states. The campaign to change the smoking habits of millions of Americans that emphasizes the health hazards of smoking is a good example. Although factual information is also employed, the major focus of these efforts involves the elicitation of fear and anxiety about the threats to health created by cigarette smoking, as illustrated by the requirement by the Surgeon General's Office that all cigarette packages carry explicit warnings about health hazards.

This campaign, along with related efforts to control the televised advertising of cigarettes, temporarily reduced the sales of cigarettes, but it does not appear that permanent reductions occurred in already habitual smokers, if cigarette sales figures are a good index. As in other instances, fear campaigns have not been highly effective against smoking practices.

Griep (1970) has similarly questioned the effectiveness of the negative tone of highway safety campaigns that emphasize the hazards of unsafe driving, on the grounds that most drivers probably regard themselves as safe and responsible drivers. It is the other driver who is wild and reckless.

A more specific situation involving the use of scare tactics to change driving behavior is the threat to revoke driving privileges for traffic violations. In one of the few evaluative studies available, Kaestner, Warmoth, and Syring (1967) mailed one of three messages to different groups of traffic offenders that were from the category of under twenty-five-year-old males. One group received a Xerox threat of license suspension for future violations, a second group received a personalized letter that contained the same threat, and a third group received a soft-sell letter that attempted to persuade the violator of the safety aspects of good driving. A fourth group served as a control and received no communication. Followup records of the driving violations of these offenders found no benefits from the Xerox threat, slight improvement with the personalized threat, but the best results with the soft sell.

Why does fear fail to motivate change? The research of Irving Janis and his colleagues suggests that fear may lead to defensive avoidance such that high fear may lead the individual to think about other more pleasant topics or at least avoid facing the issue about which the fear-arousing communication is concerned. In a classic experiment, Janis and Feshbach (1953) presented three lectures differing in the extent of fear arousal to three different groups of high school students concerning the health benefits of toothbrushing.

Measures were taken before and one week after the lectures concerning the students' attitudes toward and habits in dental care. The results showed that there was an inverse relationship between improvement in toothbrushing and the level of fear aroused. This is not to argue that high fear never works, as subsequent studies have shown it can (Janis, 1967; McGuire, 1969), but this evidence does suggest how high fear can sometimes backfire. The kind of persuasive communication that an individual is apt to regard as threatening depends on numerous factors such as personality, the availability of counter resources such as knowledge that allows the subject to question the validity of an emotion-laden argument, and the alternative responses available. As a consequence, communications that the experimenter may assume are neutral or fear arousing may have a different impact on the recipient, sometimes making it difficult to draw firm conclusions about the effects of fear on motivation. About the best we can conclude at present is that high fear does not always serve to bring about changes in attitudes and behavior, as it has sometimes been assumed.

One factor that might determine whether or not fear would motivate change in behavior is the availability of some immediate activity relevant to the issue. Leventhal and Niles (1964) conducted a field study at a health exposition in which they created three different levels of fear among viewers of a film on smoking and cancer. Intentions to stop smoking were highest among the low fear or control group, once again showing that high fear may be ineffective.

However, noting that large individual differences existed within each group, Leventhal and Niles reanalyzed their data and found positive correlations between fear and intentions to stop smoking as well as with plans to take recommended x-rays. They argued that these latter findings show that fear can lead to desired changes in behavior for a short while such as in making plans to stop smoking or take x-rays. A check of records at the x-ray booth at the exposition later showed that high-fear subjects did tend to fulfill their intentions of taking x-rays more often than moderate- or low-fear subjects did. Whether or not high-fear subjects also stopped smoking, however, is another question and deals with a long-term outcome, where Leventhal and Niles agree that fear is probably ineffective.

EDUCATIONAL APPEALS

It is sometimes difficult to draw the line between emotional and educational persuasion for as we have seen both factors can be present in health campaigns. By educational appeals, we refer to those campaigns in which the emphasis is factual and little attempt is made to draw attention to fear-producing aspects or moral issues.

One of the great social problems today is the increased use of drugs, especially among youth. Attempts to reduce this tendency have often assumed that any intelligent person given adequate information about the potential dangers of the use of hard drugs would never begin or would soon stop using them.

The evidence, however, suggests that drug education programs have generally failed. In the first place, many adolescents already know much information about drugs so that education based campaigns to prevent their use may fail because they are redundant. In addition, users may have already decided the risks are worthwhile because of the greater psychological and physiological rewards they experience or anticipate. They may think that they can be exceptions to the rule in that they can consume drugs without becoming addicted or dependent.

Attempts to dissuade by education may also have an unintended effect of piquing the curiosity or resistance of those who previously were uninterested in drug use. If it is forbidden, maybe it is really worth trying. Youth is especially prone to be suspicious and distrustful of adult intentions when it appears their behavior is being regulated. All these factors contribute to the ineffectiveness of educational appeals to control behavior.

According to DeLone (1972) the U.S. Office of Education invested $13 million in 1972 to fund drug education in the schools. Other federal and state funds were also available, so that a conservative estimate of the total expenditure is around $100 million per year nationwide. Despite these efforts to inform the teenager about the dangers of drug abuse, DeLone suggested that there is little evidence that such programs are effective and went so far as to indicate that the opposite effect may occur whereby information promoted drug use.

Similar ineffectiveness has been reported by Haskins (1969) in programs aimed at reducing drinking and driving problems. Many of these programs may claim success, but they are difficult to evaluate because alternative explanations cannot always be excluded. Thus if accidents decline following a traffic safety campaign, it could stem from other simultaneously occurring events rather than the campaign per se. Campbell (1969), for example, cited the faulty conclusion that was reached in Connecticut after a period of more stringent law enforcement against speeding. Although statistics reported for the pre- and postcampaign periods showed a decline in accidents, it was also the case that adverse weather conditions prevailed at the time of the cam-

FIGURE 16–1. Feiffer's commentary on the ineffectiveness of education in producing change. [Reprinted by permission of author.]

paign and that they may have produced some or most of the improvement.

The same type of problem must be faced in assessing the assumed benefits of safety campaigns during holiday periods in reducing driving and drinking accidents. To rule out concomitant factors in evaluating the impact of a campaign, it is necessary to include a control group that is not exposed to the campaign.

Studies that do not include a control group are inconclusive, because we do not know the extent to which those persons who show changes are the type who would have changed even without the communication. Furthermore, if we find that people who are the most informed on an issue also show the most change we do not know if there is a causal effect, because a selective process may occur in which those who are most interested in a topic will voluntarily seek information, whereas those who are disinterested will avoid it.

Exactly why educational efforts frequently fail is not clear. The reason may vary with the type of situation or degree of prior commitment to a position. The extent to which a person will be embarrassed if he or she should change views may be important. If the person regards change as an admission of error, he or she is likely to resist persuasion. The persuasiveness of the ineffectiveness of educational attempts to induce change is aptly conveyed by Feiffer's cartoon.

MORAL PERSUASION

Social and religious reformers may try to modify or control behavior with sermons and lectures on morality. Violations of the social norms and expected behaviors are seen as undesirable and condemned. Lectures on the immorality of these behaviors are generally unsuccessful in promoting change because there is a strong tone of "repent or be punished" rather than gentle persuasion. In addition, making some behavior taboo and forbidden can also add attractiveness to it. Books or movies promoted as censored or restricted to adults only kindle the curiosity of most people.

Self-interest is often in conflict with the proper moral course of action. One may condemn prejudice in the name of humanity and justice but even relatively unbigoted individuals are apt to become more worried about their own property values than about social justice when some of "those people" move into their neighborhoods. Moralizing may arouse some pangs of guilt, but they are generally inadequate to offset the fears about one's own interests.

Perhaps one reason moral approaches fail is that they place too much emphasis on threats against noncompliance rather than actually deal with moral choices. The sense of social and moral conscience should, ideally, involve internal rather than external controls, so that a moral person should believe that his or her actions are voluntary actions in accord with his or her beliefs and values. It may be argued that in actuality moral behavior may be the consequence of guilt feelings or other negative consequences rather than moral convictions. Nonetheless, from the individual's perspective, unless behavior is perceived as voluntary, he or she will feel resentment, as would be the case if he or she felt coerced.

Some Reasons People Are Hard to Change

Some of the major reasons attempts to change the attitudes and behavior of others have failed in the past and will continue to fail will now be summarized, followed by a case history of the attempts to control population growth cited as an example involving some of these weaknesses. Our discussion is probably not exhaustive in identifying all the reasons and some of them overlap or occur together, but we hope our discussion will help focus on the problem.

First, and perhaps foremost, any attempt to change another person who realizes someone else is making his or her decisions is apt to create resistance or reactance. As DeCharms (1968) noted, no one wants to feel like a pawn but prefers being the origin of his or her own behavior. Even if the behavior is to be modified in ways that are good for the individual, acceptance will not automatically occur as any mother who has tried to feed her child nutritious food can attest. Somehow one must find an *ethically acceptable* manner of convincing the person that he or she made the decision to do what you think is best for him or her. Trickery, such as forbidding a child to do precisely what you wanted in the first place, will usually achieve the desired behavior but involves questionable ethics. Most of the time, however, the line can be quite thin between what might be viewed as helping a person make up his or her mind and forcing or steering him or her in a given direction.

Second, many attempts to change behavior do not first identify the motives underlying the existing attitudes and behavior. Are the current motives based on positive factors such as sincere belief or do they involve fear or inertia? Is the present undesired behavior due to tradition or inertia rather than to conviction? Is the lack of change due to anxiety about change per se rather than to dislike of the specific change?

Ernest Dichter, the head of a successful motivation research organization that applies psychology to marketing and consumer behavior, observed that, "Changing human behavior without understanding motivations is like trying to start a stalled car by kicking it" (Dichter, 1971, p. 79). In other words, our knowledge or our assumptions about the motives underlying a behavior to be changed can influence the choice of our method for bringing such change about. Yet, many campaigns and programs aimed at change seem to ignore this common-sensical observation and thereby reduce their chances of success. Thus, to expect fear appeals to induce sports-car drivers to wear seat belts may be unrealistic if the wearing of seat belts is perceived as conservative by people who like to appear daring and sporty. To curb smoking, we need to know why people like to smoke instead of focusing only on the health hazards that are apparently seen as a small price to pay by most smokers.

A third factor frequently present in change attempts that guarantees failure or, at best, compliance as long as one is being observed is the emphasis on punishment, moral condemnation, and social stigma. Rules and regulations are posted telling us what not to do and violations lead to guilt feelings, social censure, or some form of penalty or fine. Unsafe drivers may lose their licenses, but what recognition or reward can be given to safe drivers? The example set by insurance companies of providing lower premiums for safe drivers should be followed more frequently.

In short, a brief look at the reward structure in our society confirms the popular belief that monetary rewards and punishments are powerful determinants of human behavior. The profit motive and the law of least cost are not limited to business enterprises but extend to many other forms of human activities. If a given behavior provides financial advantages, it is unlikely that that behavior will be terminated voluntarily. Whether it be the operation of a respectable or disreputable endeavor, if it pays well it will continue. Conversely, most activities that lead to financial disincentives, fines, penalties, or losses will be modified or reduced.

Accumulation and preservation of financial assets is a central goal of most individuals, a value that has received surprisingly little psychological research. Money is important for a variety of reasons, and different persons may not share the same reasons. Because money is a medium of exchange, it affords the holder a wide range of choices in its use. It may be hoarded or accumulated as a form of security, status, and power. It may be invested in hopes that it will generate more of the same commodity. It can be spent to acquire material possessions, to influence others, or to receive services. In short, money is a form of power above and beyond mere physical survival.

Viewed in this light, it is understandable why some behaviors do not readily change if to do so is to incur costs. The polluter is not necessarily motivated from perversity or a desire to devastate the environment, the pornographer is not necessarily motivated to corrupt the sexual values of others, and the opponent of equal opportunity for jobs or fair housing is not necessarily a racist. All three want to maximize their gains, albeit at the expense of others. This situation pits one person against another, so that one person's profit is another's loss.

If desired behavior is not evident, society must find ways of providing positive rewards to encourage it. At the same time, undesirable behaviors that do exist will continue unless ways of reducing or eliminating the positive gains for such behaviors are devised.

Self-dissatisfaction and Change

If, as we noted above, coercion and external pressure for change is self-defeating because it generates a threat to one's sense of personal control, it would appear that somehow the individual must become dissatisfied with his or her present condition, if change is to occur readily. Persuasion and education may help engender this state of dissonance, but, in the final analysis, the individual must experience this cognitive imbalance before he or she will be motivated to attempt to change voluntarily.

Consider the numerous methods developed to change eating, smoking, and drinking habits that are threats to health. Few of them have worked very successfully, often because the person does not really want to change and is being cajoled and nagged by friends, family, or physician without anyone's trying to persuade the person himself or herself that he or she wants to change. In a discussion of smokers who successfully quit, apparently without undergoing therapy or professional treatment, Premack (1970) cites the importance of humiliation as a determinant of self-control. He is not referring to deliberate attempts of others to humiliate the smoker but to instances in which the smoker suddenly examines smoking and becomes humiliated or embarrassed by a new perception of his or her behavior. A man who smoked two packs daily for twenty years and then quit abruptly described his transformation in these vivid terms, "It is humiliating to be duped by those goddamn cigarette companies. They know their product causes cancer, but they do absolutely nothing to prevent it. Instead they spend millions on advertising, to keep all the old suckers smoking and to start as many new suckers as possible . . ." (Premack, 1970, p. 114).

Regardless of the accuracy of his perceptions, this individual suddenly felt manipulated and exploited by cigarette manufacturers and quit for this reason, not because of fear of health hazards, per se. Premack's example illustrates the central role of cognitive factors, showing that dissatisfaction with one's behavior can succeed in producing change, whereas techniques such as behavior modification, group psychotherapy, or psychoanalysis often fail. The same process may occur among successful dieters, abstainers, and others who are able to modify behavior usually highly resistant to change.

A similar emphasis on the importance of self-dissatisfaction as an antecedent of changed attitudes, values, and behavior is held by Rokeach (1973). His monograph detailed a large-scale experiment in which exposure to contrived norms about social values led to long-term changes in values of college students such as freedom and equality, improved attitudes toward blacks and other oppressed groups, and fostered support of a civil rights group.

A brief description of the complex study will be given to show the manner in which self-dissatisfaction was involved as a change agent. First, subjects rank-ordered a list of values according to the importance they attached to them. Values on the scale included items such as *a comfortable life, a world at peace, equality, freedom, pleasure, salvation,* and *wisdom.* Then they were shown a contrived set of norms (see Table 16–1) based on the views of other students, which showed *freedom* ranked first and *equality* ranked much lower. The experimenter moralized a bit and noted that these norms showed how selfish it is to rate one's own freedom above equality or the freedom of others.

TABLE 16–1. "Table 1" Shown to Experimental Subjects in Experiments 1, 2, and 3.

Experiment 1	Experiments 2 and 3
Table 1: Rank order of importance to 444 Michigan State Students	*Table 1:* Rank order of importance to 298 Michigan State Students
10 A comfortable life	13 A comfortable life
2 A meaningful life	12 An exciting life
3 A world at peace	6 A sense of accomplishment
6 Equality	10 A world at peace
1 Freedom	17 A world of beauty
8 Maturity	11 Equality
11 National security	9 Family security
9 Respect for others	1 Freedom
7 Respect from others	2 Happiness
12 Salvation	8 Inner harmony
4 True friendship	5 Mature love
5 Wisdom	16 National security
	18 Pleasure
	14 Salvation
	15 Social recognition
	4 Self-respect
	7 True friendship
	3 Wisdom

Source: From *The Nature of Human Values* by M. Rokeach, New York: Free Press, 1973. Copyright 1973 by Macmillan Publishing Co., Inc. Reprinted by permission.

After they had a chance to compare their own ratings with the norms, they were asked whether or not they had participated in civil rights activities. Then they were shown fake data again, as shown in Table 16–2, this time showing that, among other subjects, civil rights activists rated *equality* over *freedom* whereas the reverse was true for nonactivists. Another brief lecture was given by the experimenter about the selfishness of those who rate their own freedom above that of others, as reflected by those students also being against civil rights.

Control group subjects went through the same routine essentially except that they were never exposed to the value rankings or data showing the civil rights participation of the other students.

Measurements were assessed before the experiment on attitudes toward several topics, including equality of rights of blacks and toward all people in general. Post-tests were also taken at varying intervals after the experimental session, ranging from three weeks to about fifteen to seventeen months later, in the three different experiments conducted. In addition, in two studies the subjects received a letter from the National Association for the Advancement of Colored People (NAACP) about three to five months later asking them to join for a $1.00 membership. This contrived measure of behavior was not identified in any way with the experiment and was possible through the co-operation of the local NAACP branch.

The rationale underlying the study was that the exposure to social norms plus the lectures would induce self-dissatisfaction among the subjects in the experimental group. Compared to the control group, which would not encounter this dissatisfaction, more change in the direction of greater valuation of equality, positive attitudes towards blacks, and joining the NAACP should occur in the experimental group. These predictions were generally upheld

TABLE 16–2.   "Table 2" Shown to Experimental Subjects in Experiments 1, 2, and 3.

Table 2: Average Rankings of *Freedom* and *Equality* by Michigan State University Students for and against Civil Rights

		Yes, and Have Participated	Yes, but Have Not Participated	No, not Sympathetic to Civil Rights
Experiment 1	FREEDOM	1	1	2
	EQUALITY	3	6	11
	DIFFERENCE	2	5	9
Experiments 2 and 3	FREEDOM	6	1	2
	EQUALITY	5	11	17
	DIFFERENCE	+1	−10	−15

Source: From *The Nature of Human Values* by M. Rokeach, New York: Free Press, 1973. Copyright 1973 by Macmillan Publishing Co., Inc. Reprinted by permission.

even though only one session was used to induce the dissatisfaction and the effect lasted over several months.

Rokeach's paradigm for inducing change raises ethical questions. Is it proper to change the attitudes, values, and behavior of others through the use of deception? How does one decide which values or behaviors are the desirable ones? What happens if the technique is misused by the wrong people? Unlike naturalistic situations, such as in the example of the man who quit smoking after he felt humiliated by his perception of his behavior, Rokeach employed subtle means in modifying his subjects' views and his results suggest that the changes lasted over a year.

There are no simple answers to the ethical questions, but they must be faced. We cite this important study, because it illustrates the potential usefulness of self-dissatisfaction rather than external control of an explicit nature in promoting change. Rokeach's technique represents an external method of control, but one that is not seen as such by the recipient, thus enhancing its chances of success.

Relationships among Motives of Different Individuals and Groups

The behavior of one person does not exist in a vacuum but is highly interrelated to the behavior of others. Attempts to change a person have usually tried to modify his or her motives without examining these interactions. It may be essential, however, to examine these interrelated parts of the system if we are to understand how to change behavior. For example, punishing a child for aggression may not change this behavior, because he or she is receiving attention or social approval of peers, which is more rewarding. Professors lament students focusing on grades and exhort them to learn for learning's sake, ignoring the conflicting pressure on students to get high grades for graduate school admission, as shown in Figure 16–2. Students condemn faculty for poor teaching and advising, but this negative feedback does not bring about much improvement, because (as Fig. 16–2 also illustrates) faculty are often more attuned to research publications in order to obtain such reinforcements from their peers as recognition and promotion. Obligations to the administration also compete with research to weaken the faculty attention to the best interests of students. As in any system, change in the behavior of one element or part has implications for the other components. Resistance will develop in those parts that regard a contemplated change in another as having adverse consequences for themselves. Changes at the level of the individual are often difficult, because the other elements of the system are not personal agents but large-scale societal factors, impersonal institutional or organizational obstacles, or collective entities such as the public, community standards, or the taxpayers.

It is therefore quixotic to expect a significant change to occur in an indi-

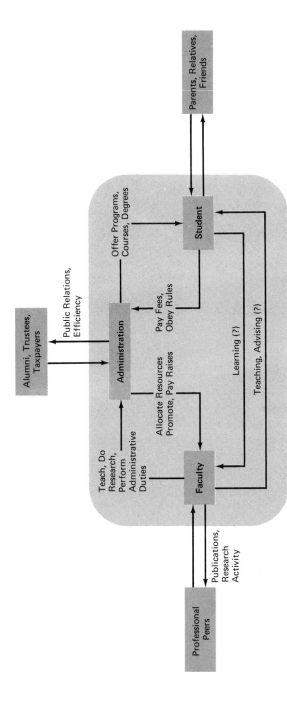

FIGURE 16–2. Schematic representation of the three major components of a university or college system and their responsibilities and obligations to each other. Note the question marks (?) next to the relationships between faculty and students, which suggest that these ideal functions are sometimes degraded into poor teaching and poor learning. Each component within the system is also affected by relationships with some external factors and these obligations compete and disrupt the fulfillment of the obligations of the internal components to each other. For example, students may become "grade grubbers" instead of creative and genuine learners because of pressure from parents, graduate school requirements, etc. Similarly, faculty teaching is sometimes weakened because of pressures to publish in scholarly journals in order to impress peers or earn promotions.

vidual if efforts are made only at that level. Etzioni (1972), a sociologist, has argued, ". . . to solve social problems by changing people is more expensive and usually less productive than approaches that accept people as they are and (we should) seek to mend not them but the circumstances around them" (p. 46). He cited the example of the failure of compensatory education to help disadvantaged groups as stemming basically from the fact that these children are locked into a system that includes poverty, discrimination, etc., and not only lack of educational skills. To change one aspect of the situation, it is necessary to modify the others as well.

DIFFICULTIES IN CHANGING PART
OF A SYSTEM

An example of institutional obstacles to change is provided by Repucci and Saunders (1974) who discussed the serious difficulties faced in implementing change programs in natural environments such as public schools, prisons, or mental hospitals. They wanted to employ token economies in a school for delinquent boys in which youngsters performing various chores would be awarded points or tokens, which could later be exchanged for rewards. This type of behavior modification program is based on the principles derived from laboratory studies of operant conditioning; although they should succeed in theory, the actual implementation of them is not easy.

Repucci and Saunders related the bureaucratic obstacles they encountered, hurdles inherent in large organizations and somewhat independent of the specific individual occupying key administrative positions. In their case, the highest administrator felt that the proposed research needed the approval of the state legislature. The head of the business office at the school did not think that his office should become involved in the exchange of tokens for money for the boys. Resistance from staff supervisors was encountered, as they worried that the program would impair their own effectiveness.

Regardless of the merits of the planned study then, the fact that the school for these boys was part of a larger system made it necessary to bring about changes in these other components before attempting to change the behavior of the boys.

Obstacles to change should not be viewed only in a negative perspective. Not all changes are desirable nor are the kinds of changes that one person might seek equally attractive to someone else. The obstacles to change that exist in the interrelationships among several elements of a system operate as a set of mutual checks and balances just as the legislative, judicial, and executive components of our government are supposed to act. If one element gains unchecked power to impose changes without the approval of the other parts, tyranny is the eventual outcome.

As Bandura (1974, p. 868) commented, "The most reliable source of opposition to manipulative control resides in the reciprocal consequences of human interactions. . . . Because of reciprocal consequences, no one is able to manipulate others at will, and everyone experiences some feeling of powerlessness in getting what they want. This is true at all levels of functioning, individual and collective."

The checks and balances of reciprocal influence can be shown to be valuable then. Bandura (1974, p. 869) does not see change as impossible and in fact considers social change even more likely because, "If anything, the recent years have witnessed a diffusion of power, creating increased opportunities for reciprocal influence. This has enabled people to challenge social inequities, to effect changes in institutional practices, to counteract infringements on their rights, and to extend grievance procedures and due process of law to activities in social contexts that hitherto operated under unilateral control."

According to this view, change was difficult in the past, because the power of the status quo was too formidable to challenge. As power has been more evenly distributed, each component of the system has more reciprocal influence on the other and more substantial changes are possible than in the past. Although this argument seems reasonable, it does not mean that change is easy in an absolute sense. Resistance to external influence, defense of vested interests, and anxiety over change will still exist to impede change.

CHANGING A SYSTEM BY OUTSIDE FORCES

Given these problems, it is not surprising that significant changes are rare or slow. How can change occur, especially when systems of interrelated parts are involved? Lon Hefferlin (1969) made a perceptive study of the factors that make colleges and universities the conservative institutions they are. For one matter, until recently they held a monopoly on one recognized avenue to success in life, the college diploma. Like any other organization free to regulate itself, the college tends to maintain the traditional status quo and resist change or innovation. As Lon Hefferlin (p. 146) noted, "Outsiders initiate: institutions react." Thus, feedback and reaction from factors external to an institution are more likely to foster change than ideas coming from within, assuming any would arise from internal sources. The benefactors who provide financial support to the institution can demand policies, whereas the students and faculty would be ineffective, for the most part, in calling for changes.

The closed system, then, is unlikely to change just as colleges did not until the past decade. As long as students were available in large supply, they could be ignored, but in the early 1970s enrollments began to drop for a variety of reasons, not the least of which was the changing belief that a college education was needed to get ahead in life. This changing situation has probably brought about more innovation and student-oriented change in higher learning institutions than even the student demonstrations of the late 1960s, because it has attacked the financial basis of their existence.

Lon Hefferlin is careful to emphasize that the opposite strategy of placing total control of colleges in external hands is not the solution either. What is needed is an open system in which there is responsiveness to all the components of the system as well as to outsiders connected with learning institutions such as alumni, trustees, and patrons. The role of the outsiders is regarded by Lon Hefferlin as avuncular or uncle-like rather than patriarchial. This awkward term is a useful conceptual distinction, however, for it defines the role of outsiders as like that of a relative "who provides experience but not discipline and who is available for aid without being omnipresent" (p. 178).

An avuncular influence may avoid the usual problem created by external change agents of resentment and resistance. At the same time the system is no longer closed but can receive and respond to the necessary external forces that can prevent it from falling into a state of inertia.

The factors that might promote change in academic institutions also can be seen in business and economic situations in which the failure to react to the needs of consumers and to changing economic conditions spell bankruptcy. But there are also situations in which voluntary change is not likely because self-interest may conflict with the interests of others, as in the case of racial prejudice. Recent American history provides vivid illustrations of the need to resort to external coercion in the form of legal means to produce social change in race relations. This type of situation will be discussed further in Chapter 17.

In concluding this chapter on the motivation of voluntary change, we will examine the specific issue of population control to see how the points we have been discussing are relevant to this social issue.

An Example: The Population Explosion

Although Rev. Thomas Malthus warned about the dangers of overpopulation back in 1798, his dire predictions have yet to come true. However, his prophecy has received renewed attention and concern in the past decade. Organizations ranging from voluntary groups such as Zero Population Growth (ZPG) to a federal commission on Population Growth and the American Future have called for a halt to population growth, because of the threat it poses to the quality of life and to future economic resources.

Although some skeptics disagree and doubt that the consequences will be as bad as forecast, let us assume for the moment that overpopulation is a problem of some magnitude. How does one persuade the public to change their attitudes and practices with respect to family size?

EDUCATIONAL EFFORTS

One means is the use of information campaigns to convey to citizens the costs of having a large family. Attempts to persuade people that a small family also provides benefits whereas a large family lowers one's quality of life can be made. A striking example is the lead headline in the *Los Angeles Times* of March 12, 1972, which asserted "Zero Growth held 'Choice' of Nation." A subhead went on to add, "Two-child family would ease ills of society, population panel says." The article (1972) was dealing with the report of the National Population Commission that emphasized the economic benefits of small families that would then contribute to the quality of the family's life as well as to other social benefits.

In addition to these tactics, specific information about contraceptive methods has been disseminated. Opportunities for voluntary sterilization, vasectomy, and even abortion have increased, although there is obviously much disagreement about the legal and ethical aspects of the latter solution.

These procedures are relatively mild attempts inasmuch as the individual presumably makes the final decision even though social pressure is directed at limiting family size. Garrett Hardin (1968) is not optimistic that enough people will cooperate in order to control population growth if left to their own decisions. The "tragedy of the commons," as this biologist likes to call it, involves situations in which individual interests are at odds with the best interests of the society, as when individual farmers allow their herds to overgraze a common pasture. Each individual may realize his or her behavior conflicts with long-range social goals but prefers to let the others restrain themselves; in the end, no one does and the tragedy happens.

ECONOMIC INCENTIVES

Hardin considers other tactics such as inculcating young children with the belief that childlessness is acceptable and not unnatural, but his ultimate solution involves some form of coercion. Although he recognized the ethical and practical problems of coercion such as tax incentives for smaller families, he implies that such solutions may be necessary. Similar material and social incentives were suggested as a means of population control by Lipe (1971).

How likely are such attempts ranging from education and persuasion, on the one hand, to mild coercion, on the other to succeed in restricting population? Current data showing some stabilization of population growth cannot be attributed entirely to these programs, because other social movements such as Women's Liberation and alternative styles of living may also reduce population growth. Therefore our discussion of specific attempts to change family size traditions will be somewhat speculative.

CONFLICTING VALUES

There is evidence that these attempts have created resentment as well as suspicion of ulterior motives, especially by minority groups such as Chicano and black populations. Buckhout (1972), for instance, collected responses to a questionnaire concerning family plans of college students and found that minority group members not only wanted more children than white students did but also expressed suspicion and resentment against population control. Fears that such programs were genocidal or that minorities need *more* population, rather than less, in order to achieve their rights were expressed.

Tax incentives for smaller families, although rewarding the socially desired behavior, has distinct disadvantages in promoting change in this aspect of behavior. Smith (1972) has questioned the ethical propriety of these financial incentives, because they put more pressure on the poor and therefore are more coercive for them. He does allow for the "planned manipulation of incentives" (Smith, 1972, p. 12) but it is not clear where he would draw the line between the ethical and the unethical.

In addition, to these shortcomings of present programs to limit population, there tends to be ignorance or disregard of the motives for people having children in the first place. This is not to say that population growth should not be reduced, but we cannot achieve this goal if we ignore the fact that for many people children are regarded as a sign of fertility, prestige, immortality, or personal enjoyment. Cultural traditions about family size have been followed for generations among some groups. These psychological reasons, even if unsound, cannot easily be undone in the name of ecology, quality of life, etc.

Even if some people can be persuaded that the logic for having fewer children is sound, as Hardin has suggested, unless everyone complies, there will be a tendency to do as one pleases while expecting the other couples to control their family sizes. This problem extends between as well as within societies. Even if the United States is able collectively to change its rate of growth, what guarantees are there that other nations, especially those that are small or underpopulated, will follow our lead? In short, although it may be likely that all humankind will suffer in the future from failure to curb population growth, it is psychologically difficult for one group or nation to take the initiative for fear that other nations will not follow suit. Although there are important differences, there is some parallel in the problem of arms races, where nations will not unilaterally disarm for fear their foes will gain an advantage over them. To produce change in one part of the system, it is necessary to bring about changes in the other parts as well.

Moralizing about the irresponsibility of large family size will not produce the desired effect either, because people are not motivated to have large families to be immoral. Education and contraception will lower family size among those who previously lacked the knowledge and means for birth control and were desirous of fewer children in the first place. But for those whose cultural and psychological needs are fulfilled by having children, these methods will be inadequate.

In analyzing the world population problem, DuBos (1965) has emphasized the inadequacy of approaches based on provision of contraceptive knowledge and materials as a means of curbing growth. It is precisely in some of the less economically advantaged countries that children are highly valued. Dubos (1965, p. 307) noted, "Under restricted conditions of existence, children usually constitute the only hope of reward. They provide labor on the farm and insurance against the solitude and trials of old age; they are the most reliable and often the only source of deep emotional satisfaction; finally and probably most important, they symbolize hope and eternity."

He admonished those who would criticize people of other nations for not controlling population growth that they might ". . . ponder on the unwillingness of Western people to change their own ways with regard to cigarette smoking, overeating, or lack of physical exercise, despite the wide publicity given to the relation between these practices and various forms of illness" (Dubos, 1965, pp. 306–307).

Dubos' observations illustrate the dangers of one group attempting to change the behavior of another by assuming that its own values are shared by others to the same extent. He suggested that the prerequisite for fostering population control in other countries must be the creation of a genuine desire to do so on their part, perhaps by showing them first that such a goal is beneficial to them, as well as to everyone else.

Summary

Once people form habitual patterns of responding, it is often difficult if not impossible to get them to change. Familiar ways are comfortable, whereas change involves uncertainty and anxiety. In addition, many attempts to change the attitudes and habits of others have employed some type of coercion such as direct force or the threat of punishment for noncompliance. These approaches seem to generate a stubbornness and rebelliousness against external control, as most people like to feel that their choices and decisions are voluntary and free. This psychological state, called reactance, decreases the likelihood of behavioral change even when it might be in the best interests of those who are resisting.

Several types of social control attempt to influence our behavior. At one extreme are laws that can lead to fines and imprisonment for behavior that violates them. Laws, even good ones, generate resentment even though compliance may generally occur. They are also expensive to enforce and many violators are not apprehended. It would seem preferable to use other methods of control, if possible.

Emotional appeals such as those based on fear, shame, or guilt are aimed at creating unpleasant internal feelings that will inhibit wrong doing and encourage moral behavior. Use of excessively high levels of emotion can backfire and even produce undesired negative side effects. Persuasion by highly fearful messages, for example, may lead to inattention or other defenses that discredit the message.

Educational approaches emphasize the dissemination of facts and assume that once a person knows the facts, he or she will act in a different manner consistent with his or her new knowledge. Health issues are a good example. In the case of drug abuse it is assumed that once the addict or abuser knows certain facts about the health hazards, he or she will immediately change behavior to reduce the health risk. Many of these attempts have failed badly, because they do not realize that drug abuse can still produce consequences desired by the user that outweigh the perceived possible dangers.

Moral approaches to bringing about change often employ emotional arousal as well, because the appeal is to one's sense of right or wrong. Presumably, guilt feelings will be activated if our behavior is regarded as wrong or immoral and we will act to change. However, because moral persuasion is still perceived as external control, it often fails to work and even where it does succeed, resentment may accompany any change.

Greater attention to the use of positive incentives such as offering rewards may be more effective in changing behavior than most of the procedures emphasizing negative consequences.

Change appears to be more likely if the individual reaches a state of self-dissatisfaction so that he or she will want to change voluntarily. Appeals to one's own sense of vanity, intelligence, and internal consistency might lead the individual to change if he or she perceived that the behavior was contrary to these positively valued attributes.

Important in the discussion of changing individual behavior are the facts that no one is free from the influence of other individuals as well as from social institutions and that these factors can often prevent desired changes from occurring. Change in one part of a system of interrelated elements implies changes for the other parts as well. If benefits are not involved for all components, it may be difficult to produce any change in some elements because the other parts are acting to prevent it. Change of a system, therefore, is usually activated from agents or forces outside rather than within that system.

An example illustrated the main points of this chapter using current concerns about overpopulation as a model.

References

BANDURA, A. Behavior theory and the models of man. *American Psychologist,* 1974, *29,* 859–869.

BREHM, J. W. *A theory of psychological reactance.* New York: Academic Press, 1966.

BUCKOUT, R. Toward a two-child norm; changing family planning attitudes. *American Psychologist,* 1972, *27,* 16–26.

CAMPBELL, D. T. Reforms as experiments. *American Psychologist,* 1969, *24,* 409–429.

DECHARMS, R. *Personal causation: The internal affective determinants of behavior.* New York: Academic, 1968.

DELONE, R. H. The ups and downs of drug-abuse education. *Saturday Review,* Nov. 11, 1972, 27–32.

DICHTER, E. *Motivating behavior.* New York: McGraw-Hill, 1971.

DUBOS, R. *Man adapting.* New Haven, Conn.: Yale University Press, 1965.

ETZIONI, A. Human beings are not so very easy to change after all. *Saturday Review,* June 3, 1972, 45–47.

GRIEP, D. J. Propaganda and alternative countermeasures for road safety. *Accident Analysis and Prevention,* 1970, *2,* 127–140.

HARDIN, G. The tragedy of the commons. *Science,* 1968, *162,* 1243–1248.

HASKINS, J. B. Effects of safety communication campaigns: A review of the research evidence. *Journal of Safety Research,* 1969, *1,* 58–66.

JAMES, W. *The principles of psychology.* (Vols. 1 and 2). New York: Holt, 1890.

JANIS, I. L., and FESHBACH, S. Effects of fear-arousing communications. *Journal of Abnormal and Social Psychology,* 1953, *48,* 78–92.

KAESTNER, N., WARMOTH, E. J., and SYRING, E. M. Oregon study of advisory letters: the effectiveness of warning letters in driving improvement. *Traffic Safety Research Review,* 1967, *11,* 67–72.

LEVENTHAL, H., and NILES, P. A field experiment on fear arousal with data on the validity of questionnaire measures. *Journal of Personality,* 1964, *32,* 459–479.

LEVENTHAL, H., SINGER, R. P., and JONES, S. H. The effects of fear and specificity of recommendation. *Journal of Personality and Social Psychology,* 1965, *2,* 20–29.

LIPE, D. Incentives, fertility control, and research. *American Psychologist,* 1971, *26,* 617–625.

LON HEFFERLIN, J. B. *The dynamics of academic reform.* San Francisco: Jossey-Bass, 1969.

BURKE, V. J. Zero growth held "choice" of nation. *Los Angeles Times,* March 12, 1972.

MCGUIRE, W. The nature of attitudes and attitude change. In G. Lindzey and E. Aronson (Eds.), *Handbook of Social Psychology.* (Vol. 3.) Reading, Mass.: Addison-Wesley, 1969.

PREMACK, D. Mechanisms of self-control. In W. A. Hunt (Ed.), *Learning mechanisms in smoking.* Chicago, Aldine, 1970.

REPPUCCI, N. D., and SAUNDERS, J. T. Social psychology of behavior modification: Problems of implementation in natural settings. *American Psychologist,* 1974, *29,* 649–660.

ROKEACH, M. *The nature of human values.* New York: Free Press, 1973.

SMITH, M. B. Ethical implications of population policies: A psychologist's view. *American Psychologist,* 1972, *27,* 11–15.

CHAPTER 17

The Legislation of Morality

Voluntary behavior may fail to comply with the social norms, values, and mores of a society even though social censure and ostracism may be directed toward the transgressors, because the selfish gains achieved exceed the possible adverse consequences. Within some limits, minor violations by a small percentage of citizens can be tolerated by a society, but in other cases some form of legal control has been necessary to regulate the behavior of citizens. Legal means involve external control and the threat of fines or imprisonment for failure to comply. Laws are evil in the sense that they restrain the freedom of individuals to do as they please; at the same time they are sometimes necessary to prevent one individual from usurping the freedoms of others by his or her free actions. If everyone would voluntarily respect the rights of others, one could argue that laws would not be needed, but because this utopian situation does not exist, laws are a vital aspect of societies.

Laws are expensive, not only in the economic sense of the costs incurred in their enforcement, but also in terms of the psychological reaction of individuals who feel coerced by them, even if the laws may be for their own welfare, as in the case of statutes regarding health matters. A letter to the editor of a national newsmagazine (*Time,* May 20, 1974) vividly pinpoints the matter:

Sir/ The most irritating aspect of compulsory seat-belting is not so much the bother of it all as the violation of basic principles of individual freedom. By "protecting" individuals from the hazards of cigarette smoking, by banning cigarette commercials on TV, by requiring that autos carry seat belts that must be fastened in order to start the car, or (heaven forbid!) fining people for not fastening belts in the privacy of their own vehicles, we violate longstanding tenets of liberty.

468

Independence and self-reliance are rather old American principles, after all, which should not be forgotten as we approach our bicentennial.

Albert L. Weeks
New York City

As this letter writer indicated, a fundamental value in our society is freedom, a value that can be seen as threatened by virtually any type of law by one citizen or another. Even if the law is one concerning the mandatory use of seat belts, such as in Australia where the imposition of $20 fines for noncompliance has reportedly reduced highway fatalities by 20 per cent (Lamb, 1973), citizens do not like their governments to tell them what they must do.

Laws as a Last Resort

Consequently, attempts are generally made to educate and persuade compliance to guidelines, but if behavior does not change, laws become necessary. The change in the speed limits on American highways during the critical energy shortage at the end of 1973 is a typical example. Appeals to citizens to conserve gas by driving slower were unsuccessful, and it became necessary to pass a legal restriction of highway speeds to fifty-five miles per hour. Similarly, public information pleas for preventing littering are ignored by a sizable portion of the public. Even though fines exist for litterers in many states, it is difficult to enforce them. A different legal approach, adopted in 1971 by Oregon, outlawed pull-tab cans and required that all beer and soft-drink containers carry refundable deposits. This controversial law has apparently reduced the amount of highway litter (Kilpatrick, 1973) by attacking the bottle manufacturers and the stores directly rather than by trying to control the consumers' behavior directly. By requiring deposits, the law may make consumers more likely to return their bottles than to litter. In addition, other individuals may voluntarily clean up littered bottles to collect the deposits. Despite the success of this bill, which wisely uses economic incentives, it is still a law that creates some resentment at the external restriction of individual freedom to litter, even though the aesthetic benefits are desirable.

Laws and Victimless Crimes

Laws vary widely in their acceptability to the public. Although there is deep moral disagreement about the execution of murderers, there is consensus that laws must exist to protect the public from such criminals by restricting their freedoms in some way. On the other hand, whether laws should exist against the use of marijuana is a controversial matter, as was the case concerning prohibition of alcohol earlier in the century. The widespread disobeyance of the Volstead Act outlawing alcohol use eventually led to its necessary repeal.

A key difference between these two examples is the distinction between crimes with and without victims. Generally speaking, the public supports the idea that some kinds of laws are necessary to protect citizens being victimized physically or economically by criminal behavior. Assault, homicide, rape, robbery, embezzlement, and forgery, for example, threaten the physical and financial well being of the victims. The public agrees that when criminals jeopardize the rights and freedoms of their victims, it is necessary to apprehend and restrict the freedoms of the culprits.

Not all behaviors that threaten to create victims are seen as crimes, however, as can be seen in cases of discrimination and prejudice against racial, ethnic, religious, or sex minorities. Here are situations in which the exercise of the freedom of those in social power to do as they please simultaneously restricts and impedes the access of minorities to their freedoms.

Reliance on good will and humanitarian ideals alone did not improve the lot of the oppressed minorities, and in the past two decades we have witnessed increasing legislation to remove the impediments to social justice. These laws, ranging from the desegregation of public schools to fair housing laws to equal opportunity for employment, have provoked the strongest outcries among those in more privileged positions about the legislation of *their* morality and the threats to *their* personal liberties and rights.

Onerous as legal means may sometimes appear, it is safe to argue that without the passage of laws in the area of civil rights considerably less progress would have occurred in the improvement of social conditions for minorities. The price of reactance and resentment is a high one, but it may have been the only alternative to achieve the ideological values of freedom and justice for all.

Some laws aimed at protecting one set of victims may at the same time create another set of victims. That is, in redressing the grievances of the victims, laws may require changes perceived by another group as creating a new wrong. The example of school busing to achieve integrated education is relevant here. Whereas many whites who are opposed to such busing do so because of discriminatory attitudes, there are also whites who espouse equality of rights as an end but question the *means* of busing. Busing is seen as an infringement of individual rights. It is also feared because the white children might be sent to inferior schools, inadequate facilities, and tougher social environments. Complaints are also made about the extra time and money spent in transporting children away from schools in their own neighborhoods.

Proponents of busing regard these reasons as excuses and subterfuges for maintaining racist conditions. Some evidence based on a national probability sample survey, however, indicates that even though busing might promote equality, those who are opposed to this means are not motivated by racist

THE LEGISLATION OF MORALITY 481

attitudes. Kelley (1974) obtained data from 1352 nonblack respondents over eighteen years of age. The vast majority, 83 per cent, opposed busing despite the fact that 84 per cent were in favor of blacks and whites going to the same schools.

The survey also included items that measured racial attitudes. Scores on these items did not show any strong relationship with attitudes toward busing as one might expect if anti-busing sentiment reflected discriminatory attitudes. However, for a small subsample of college-educated respondents there was some indication that more prejudiced persons were also more opposed to busing.

Busing laws have been and will continue to be controversial. In general, we think that laws are necessary against situations in which there are victims. Racial discrimination is such a case just as much as is homicide. However, all laws aimed against discrimination are not good, just as all laws against any other crime are not. The main reason, in our opinion, why busing laws are so strongly opposed is that in redressing one evil, they create another one. This substitution of evils may be inherent in this type of problem, because one group's gain is a loss for another group. The challenge is to find ways to maximize the former and at the same time minimize the latter.

There is less agreement about whether victimless crimes should be treated by legal means than whether crimes involving victims of physical and economic consequences should be. On the negative side is the fact that considerable resentment is generated at the legal restriction of behavior that presumably does not harm anyone or anyone else. It is also expensive to enforce such laws, because the offenders are usually numerous as well as secretive about their activities. How effective such laws are in deterring offenses is difficult to know, but it is now clear that the existence of laws against immoral behavior does not eliminate it but merely makes it harder to detect. In fact, it may contribute to other criminal activities such as robbery and theft in order for individuals to engage in victimless crimes that become inflated in costs by being made illegal. Herron (1968), a tax agent, has pointed out some of the adverse effects of raising cigarette taxes as a means of discouraging smoking. Underground crime, bootlegging, and tax evasion are some of the unintended byproducts of imposing financial disincentives in the moral crusade against the use of substances such as cigarettes and liquor.

It is hardly surprising then that a perennial issue is whether unenforceable or unenforced laws against victimless crimes should be abolished. Those in favor of keeping ineffective laws argue that without them immorality would be even greater and that the laws, feeble as they might appear, do have some restraining effect. The key issue, then, is one of whether it is morally right to restrict civil liberties and legislate against certain forms of behaviors that do not harm the participants but offend the mores of others.

On some issues such as homosexual behavior or marijuana smoking where more liberal attitudes have developed in recent years, there is still considerable disagreement about the desirability of eliminating laws against these activities.

But on issues such as birth control, there is wide agreement that such behavior is moral except in some religious denominations. Yet, archaic laws against the sale and distribution of contraceptives are still in existence despite their widespread use which in effect makes a large portion of our population criminals. As Smith and Pollack (1971) recognized, it is very difficult to repeal morals laws even where there is high consensus because many people feel that "by advocating repeal, the conduct that heretofore has been forbidden is being endorsed" (p. 28).

When issues such as drug abuse are concerned, enforcement is pursued with more zeal than for outdated laws that gradually die out for lack of enforcement. Blumberg (1973) noted that civil liberties such as rights of privacy and personal safety are ignored often by law enforcement agencies, which resort to wiretapping, "no-knock" laws, and other tactics of a similar nature. The justification for such drastic actions is usually based on the association between drug abuse and crimes such as robbery, theft, etc., which do involve victims.

Blumberg (1973) insists, however, that placing the focus on drug use as the major cause of street crimes is misleading and also serves to conceal the role of other factors such as inflation, chronic unemployment, and social and economic problems. Compared to the amounts of federal spending to improve social conditions, the expenditure on the criminal justice system to deal with drug problems is much greater. Blumberg maintains that these efforts will not succeed in reducing drug abuse and associated crime unless a shift is made in emphasis to deal with the basic underlying social problems which lead to much drug abuse.

Whether or not one agrees with Blumberg's view that the crusade of law and order theme directed against drug abuse is part of an ideological war, it does seem apparent that legislation against drug use is not highly successful in curbing such behavior. If anything, it forces the illegal behavior to become concealed and the availability and price of the drugs increases so that the likelihood of crimes against property goes up.

The Example of Pornography

What would happen if laws and penalties did not exist for some types of moral crimes? It is dangerous to generalize from one topic to another but let us examine the matter of obscenity and pornography. Laws against the sales and distribution of such materials exist in most communities, but the precise definitions vary from community to community, as does the enforcement of such laws. It is generally felt by those who find these laws desirable that without them, obscene and pornographic materials would engulf the community, leading to the corruption of moral standards and increased sexual crimes.

CORRELATIONAL STUDIES

One type of evidence relevant to this question is a comparison of known sexual deviants with "normals" with regard to their past and present exposure to pornography. This kind of data is not conclusive, because it is usually based on retrospective report that is difficult to verify and easy to distort. Furthermore, such correlations may not prove that there is a causal relationship between exposure to pornography, per se, and sexual offenses. With these caveats in mind, it can be noted that a large scale study of 1,500 institutionalized sex offenders and their experience with pornography was conducted by Gebhard, Gagnon, Pomeroy, and Christenson (1965). Their reported arousal to pornography was compared with that of other institutionalized nonsex offenders as well as with a sample of noninstitutionalized controls. Although close to a third of the sex offenders reported experiencing sexual arousal to pornography, this was also true of slightly more of the control subjects. It does not appear that pornography differentially affects sexual arousal of sex offenders and controls, but of course this observation does not deal with the question of whether such arousal leads to differences in actual sexual conduct.

Goldstein and Kant (1973) also interviewed institutionalized sex offenders about their exposure to pornography. They included male samples of homosexuals, transexuals, and pornography users as well as a control group of noninstitutionalized "normals." The results dealing with adolescent experiences, shown in Figure 17–1, indicated that the percentage of subjects with exposure to all types of pornographic material seemed to be highest in the normal controls. It should be added that Goldstein and Kant's attempt to obtain controls who were matched with the sex offenders in important demographic features was not highly successful. In particular, the education level was appreciably higher for the normals and this factor must be considered in drawing conclusions.

Goldstein and Kant suggested that less-than-average exposure to pornography during adolescence may be a symptom of a restrictive and punitive upbringing about sexual matters. Erotica may be an important source of fantasy, which stimulates adolescent sexual curiosity. It may also serve as a source of sexual information and education unobtainable at home or in school. When adulthood is attained, as the study of the normals suggests, the reliance on pornography drops as gratification is then available from sexual partners.

In contrast, the sexual offenders who had little exposure to pornography as adolescents seemed to respond to erotica with masturbation, both during adolescence and adulthood, rather than with heterosexual activities. Goldstein and Kant found that the home environments of rapists tended to be very repressive about sexual matters. Sex guilt was associated with exposure to pornography, which may be responsible for the lesser contact with these ma-

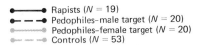

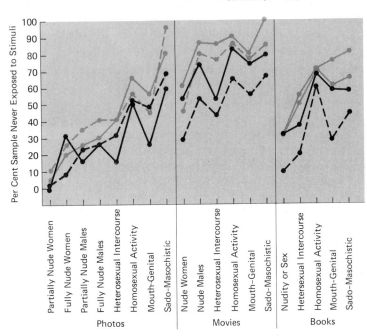

FIGURE 17–1. Adolescent reports of exposure to various erotic stimuli for institutionalized sex offenders versus Controls. [From *Pornography and Sexual Deviance,* by M. Goldstein and H. Kant, Berkeley: University of California Press, 1973. Copyright © 1973 by Michael Goldstein and Harold Sanford Kant; reprinted by permission of the University of California Press.]

terials by sex offenders. Therefore, Goldstein and Kant suggest that the sexual fantasies aroused by erotica in normals that serve positive functions in adolescent sexual development are minimized among sexual offenders. Exposure to pornography, they conclude, does not seem to be a factor leading to antisocial sexual behavior and, if anything, it can even serve a cathartic or tension-reducing function during adolescence.

In a somewhat similar way, it could be argued that the availability of pornography could reduce some forms of sexual offenses by providing a vicarious or substitute outlet. Kutchinsky (1973) noted that Denmark experienced a "porno wave" in the 1960s but that sex crimes tended to be inversely related to the availability of pornography. This effect could reflect an actual decrease in crimes, changes in attitudes of the public toward reporting offenses of certain types, or even changes in police enforcement and reporting of different offenses. Based on interviews with citizens and police, Kutchinsky concluded that some offenses such as exhibitionism were reported less often by the public, whereas the presence of pornography may have directly caused drops in offenses such as child molestation and peeping. The vicarious sexual arousal from pornographic materials may have satisfied the needs of these types of offenders.

The increased availability of pornography in countries such as Denmark with permissive laws may also have the effect of satiating consumers. Although other explanations can be offered, Cook (1972) suggested that the decreased profits of the pornography trade in Denmark might reflect such satiation.

EXPERIMENTAL STUDIES

A laboratory assessment of psychophysiological reactions in college-age males also indicated that overexposure, so to speak, to pornographic materials leads to habituation. Howard, Liptzin, and Reifler (1973) showed stag films to male subjects individually whose heart rate, temperature, pulse, and respiratory rates were measured. In addition, penile erection latency and turgidity was measured using a device known as a strain gauge, which the subjects wore around the penis while viewing the films.

Viewing one and one-half hours of these films everyday for a month took its toll and the men showed less sexual arousal as the study progressed. Other measures of mood, concentration, and sexual arousal outside the experiment during the month suggested that the viewing of these films had no adverse effects on the subjects. It must be kept in mind that these subjects were aware that they were being studied and similar effects might not occur if the films were viewed under real-life conditions.

The same limitation applies to another study assessing the effects of viewing several erotic and pornographic films over a month by married couples. Mann, Sidman, and Starr (1973) accepted only couples who had been married at least ten years and it is quite possible that the effects of pornography might be quite different on younger couples or on single individuals. Mann et al. had the couples complete eighty-four daily checklists regarding their behavior. They reported no adverse effects of the films but they did report more sexual activity on the nights following the film viewing, compared to reports from control groups. Whereas Mann et al. concluded that their findings showed no harmful effects of pornography on married couples, it is precisely this increased sexual activity that alarms those who would ban or censor pornography for fear that similar effects would occur in unmarried individuals, especially adolescents.

CONCLUSIONS

A report to Congress by the Commission on Obscenity and Pornography (1970), based on a review of the existing research, concluded that there was no evidence that exposure to pornography has a significant role in causing delinquency, crime, or sexual deviancy. It severely criticized present laws in this area, calling for their repeal. Not only were these laws regarded as in conflict with individual rights but the definitions of obscenity are generally vague and subjective, making it difficult to enforce them consistently.

As Wallace (1973) has demonstrated by a survey of over 1,000 adults in the Detroit area, there is no consensus as to what are "contemporary community standards" for defining pornography. The criterion also changes drastically over the years. As recently as the early 1960s, the publication of materials such as *Eros* magazine, tame by comparison with current materials, ended in a prison term for editor Ralph Ginsberg. In 1952, a popular movie called *The Moon is Blue* created mild controversy merely because the word *pregnant* was spoken in one scene.

The Commission was also influenced by the findings of a survey (Abelson, Cohen, Heaton, and Suder, 1970), which it authorized, that suggested that explicit sexual materials can have beneficial effects as well as harmful ones. Respondents indicated that these materials provided information about sex, constituted entertainment, and could improve sexual relations among some married couples.

In summary, although the conclusions of the Commission were controversial and not unanimously accepted, their call for the repeal of obscenity statutes suggests that legal means are unnecessary both because the harmful effects are not so demonstrable and because the rights of individuals who consent to receive these materials are denied. Furthermore such laws are highly ineffective in controlling pornography.

Alternatives to Legal Controls

The legislation of moral behavior is sometimes attractive because it may appear easy. If an undesirable behavior is not voluntarily terminated, it can be a tedious and difficult task to persuade and convince offenders to change, whereas a law is assumed to be a quicker and more effective remedy. Although this may sometimes be true, it may not be the best strategy in the long run.

Consider, for example, the new phenomenon of the 1970s known as *term-paper mills,* where students pay for someone else to provide term papers. Although this practice has occurred probably since the initiation of the term-paper assignment, it was usually done by a fellow student not a company. Academicians were horrified by the concept, as were many other members of the public. In California, a bill proposed in 1972 to outlaw such practices received the sponsorship of most higher institutions of learning in the state. However, the proposed law was defeated.

Instead of banning the practice by fiat, perhaps a more constructive approach would have been to examine the educational process to see if it had defects that encouraged such fraudulent activities. The pressure for grades, the competitive grading on the curve, or the lack of adequate interaction between professors and students in discussing term paper assignments—these, as well as a number of other factors might have contributed to the temptation to pay someone else to do the work.

Legal sanctions are negative approaches to changing or controlling the status quo. People are told what *not* to do and if they do not obey, punishments are meted out. In some types of situations, it may be possible to find positive approaches that reward moral behavior. At the very least, the removal of advantages and rewards for behaving in the immoral manner can also change behavior without the need for outright legal bans.

Consider laws against speeding. Although we might wish to continue fining offenders, what would happen if we randomly selected law-abiding drivers and gave them tickets worth $25 as rewards? Instead of fining car owners who fail to attach antipollution devices to their engines, why not give discounts on license fees for all owners who can prove that they have these devices? Instead of outlawing gambling, why not follow the leads of many states that run their own lotteries? Such laws do not really prevent gambling but only drive it underground. The urge to take risks can still be fulfilled but in a legal manner that also benefits the state coffers.

USE OF POSITIVE INCENTIVES

The costs of enforcing laws, apprehending offenders, and sometimes incarcerating them can be avoided where programs emphasizing positive incentives can be added or substituted for the negatively oriented laws proscribing certain behaviors. Where positive incentives are offered, the responsibility of claiming them is placed on the virtuous in contrast to the situation in which the burden of catching the wicked is placed on the state.

A concrete illustration of the usefulness of this alternative can be seen in studies showing the beneficial effects of positive reinforcement on litter reduction in settings as varied as movie theaters (Burgess, Clark, and Hendee, 1971), campground sites (Clark, Burgess and Hendee, 1972), and urban low income housing developments (Chapman and Risley, 1974). In these studies the general procedure has involved the payment of small cash or token rewards to children for collecting litter. Compared to other procedures such as verbal appeals or propaganda films urging clean environments, the use of positive incentives produced substantially greater return of litter by children as illustrated by the results of Burgess et al. (1971) in Figure 17–2.

It should be noted, however, that these studies do not say anything about the people who littered the landscape in the first place. These studies only

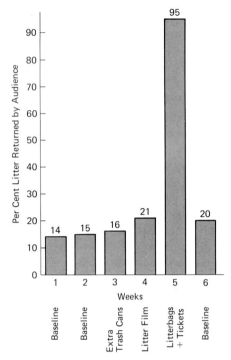

FIGURE 17–2. Per cent of total litter in Theater 2 returned by audience during successive experimental conditions. [From "An Experimental Analysis of Anti-litter Procedures," by R. L. Burgess, R. N. Clark, and J. Hendee, *Journal of Applied Behavior Analysis,* 1971, *4,* 71–76. Copyright 1971 by the Society for the Experimental Analysis of Behavior, Inc. Reprinted by permission.]

focus on finding ways of motivating people to pick up litter. Because we can not pay indefinitely for litter collection by citizens, the ultimate goal must be to find ways to encourage people not to litter in the first place.

There is another danger involved in payment for the collection of litter as a means for reducing it. Chapman and Risley (1974) paid some children on the basis of the volume of litter collected. Some enterprising children went beyond merely picking up litter and padded their litter bags with garbage-can contents as well.

These problems need not discourage attempts to improve the use of positive incentives as means of promoting socially desirable behaviors. The alternative use of negative incentives and legal controls often produces greater failures in changing behavior, except ironically in undesired directions due to the reactance and defiance induced by external threats of control.

Where crimes involving victims are concerned, laws and punishments are still necessary although positive incentives can sometimes be added in a supplementary way. But for victimless crimes and moral offenses, laws are ineffective and often counterproductive, sometimes increasing the tendency toward the commission of crimes involving victims by persons who are punished for victimless crimes. Legal means should be sought as a last, not as a first, resort in reducing the extent of victimless crime, because positive incentives may often be sufficient.

Summary

The use of legal means to control behavior is sometimes necessary even though it may create resentment and reactance. Appeals to voluntary actions aimed at the best interests of all often are inadequate and people behave in selfish ways. Although all laws arouse some resentment, there is generally agreement that laws are necessary, especially to prevent, minimize, or punish trangressions in which victims are involved. On the other hand, there is controversy over the desirability of legal sanctions against so-called victimless crimes, where there is no immediate or obvious victim.

Homosexual behavior among consenting adults, for example, can be viewed as a victimless crime that, because of social and legal attitudes, can create a myriad of problems for the participants. Critics of these kinds of laws see them as an infringement of civil liberties and a use of legal means to condemn the behavior of those whose values differ from those of the people in power. In short, there is an attempt to legislate moral behavior.

The line between victim and victimless crimes is not always clearcut. Laws against discriminatory behavior have been condemned as restricting individual rights by some groups, whereas others have regarded them as necessary to ensure that the rights of those discriminated against are not denied. Insofar as discrimination allows one group freedoms while simultaneously denying other groups those same as well as other freedoms, there is a victim and without legal controls it seems unlikely that changes that promote equal rights would occur.

Laws against immoral behavior such as victimless crimes are ineffective frequently because the behavior goes underground. If the behavior is widespread, such as the drinking of alcoholic beverages or gambling, laws succeed only in redefining more people as criminals. The behavior seems to occur despite the laws against such activities. In the instance of pornography, the suppression of these materials may even add to their attraction by making it more challenging to obtain them. Ironically, some evidence suggests that such laws are not necessary, because the pornographic materials may not have the corruptive influence commonly attributed to it. In fact, for some types of sexual crimes and deviance, it may even serve a therapeutic function. Under some conditions, reported exposure to pornography even reduces sexual arousal. A study with married couples, however, produced the opposite effects, so that it is obvious that a number of variables must be considered in making conclusions.

The heart of the matter for most laws against victimless crimes is the extent to which either the means or the ends are justified. Can one justify the restriction of individual freedoms to engage in activities the main elements of society find objectionable or unacceptable? Campaigns to legislate these forms of behavior do not accept the argument that there are no victims and usually try to prove that these behaviors lead to moral and spiritual decay as well as to serious crimes with victims such as robbery or theft.

References

ABELSON, H., COHEN, R., HEATON, E., and SUDER, C. *Public attitudes toward and experience with erotic materials.* Technical reports of the Commission on Obscenity and Pornography. (Vol. 6.) Washington, D.C.: U.S. Government Printing Office, 1970.

BLUMBERG, A. S. The politics of deviance: the case of drugs. *Journal of Drug Issues,* 1973, *3*, Spring, 105–114.

BURGESS, R. L., CLARK, R. N., and HENDEE, J. An experimental analysis of anti-litter procedures. *Journal of Applied Behavior Analysis,* 1971, *4*, 71–76.

CHAPMAN, C., and RISLEY, T. R. Anti-litter procedures in an urban high-density area. *Journal of Applied Behavior Analysis,* 1974, *7*, 377–383.

CLARK, R. N., BURGESS, R. L., and HENDEE, J. The development of anti-litter behavior in a forest campground. *Journal of Applied Behavior Analysis,* 1972, *5*, 1–6.

COOK, D. Danes grow weary of pornography scene. *Los Angeles Times,* Oct. 5, 1972.

GEBHARD, P. H., GAGNON, J. H., POMEROY, W. B., and CHRISTENSON, C. V. *Sex offenders.* New York: Harper, 1965.

GOLDSTEIN, M. J., and KANT, H. *Pornography and sexual deviance.* Berkeley: University of California Press, 1973.

HERRON, H. R. Socioeconomic effects of increasing state cigarette taxes. In E. F. Borgotta and R. R. Evans (Eds.), *Smoking, health, and behavior,* Chicago: Aldine, 1968.

HOWARD, J. L., LIPTZIN, M. B., and REIFLER, C. B. Is pornography a problem? *Journal of Social Issues,* 1973, *29*, 133–145.

KELLEY, J. The politics of school busing. *Public Opinion Quarterly,* 1974, *38*, 23–39.

KILPATRICK, J. J. Oregon "bottle bill" works, points the way for others. *Los Angeles Times,* July 13, 1973.

KUTCHINSKY, B. The effect of easy availability of pornography on the incidence of sex crimes: The Danish experience. *Journal of Social Issues,* 1973, *29*, 163–181.

LAMB, D. Seat belt law cuts Australia traffic deaths. *Los Angeles Times,* April 8, 1973.

MANN, J., SIDMAN, J., and STARR, S. Evaluating social consequences of erotic films: An experimental approach. *Journal of Social Issues,* 1973, *29*, 113–131.

SMITH, A. B., and POLLACK, H. Crimes without victims. *Saturday Review,* Dec. 4, 1971, 27–29.

The Report of the Commission on Obscenity and Pornography. New York: Bantam, 1970.

Time, Compulsory seat-belting. May 20, 1974.

WALLACE, D. H. Obscenity and contemporary community standards: A survey. *Journal of Social Issues,* 1973, *29,* 53–68.

CHAPTER 18

Insiders and Outsiders

An obvious fact to the most casual observer is the wide variation among individuals in behavior in a given situation. Many of the efforts described in the preceding two chapters dealing with motivating changes in behavior entail attempts to reduce such variation. We want people to conform to certain standards, and we are upset when people break traditions, customs, and formal laws.

Many of the variations in behavior are due to the fact that the cherished beliefs and values of one person may be rejected or of no consequence to another person. This conflict of values is hardly surprising, when one realizes the variety of different economic, political, religious, and ethnic backgrounds represented in our population.

Most textbooks on motivation ignore individual differences in motives, preferring to present a psychology of motivation for an *idealized average normal person,* whatever that may be. Throughout this book, we have pointed out the importance of the individual's perspective as a determinant of behavior. Due to this factor, it is important to examine individual differences rather than rely entirely on group averages. Because it is obviously not possible to examine all sources of individual differences in motivation, we will focus on individual differences in one major factor discussed at length in a different context in Chapter 5.

We are referring to the concept of personal power or the lack of it. Some individuals and groups within a society are those with power. They are the "haves" or the insiders, whereas those who are the "have nots" are the outsiders. This difference in personal power to affect what happens to one's life is not the only factor, but it is a major determinant of individual differences in motivation. As we shall see, those in power engage in certain behaviors that have the effect, if not the intent as well, of perserving the established social order by keeping the less powerful in their place. This subjugation need not be viewed as a malicious act, because it may stem from other factors such as fear of those whose lifestyles and values are incompatible with one's own. By rejecting or condemning the rival views of others, we defend and uphold the integrity of our own ways. We see ourselves as good, moral, and virtuous, while people whose behavior deviates from the norm are viewed as either misguided, wrong, or plain immoral. We tend to think in simple categories as we sort people into two distinct groups: the good guys like us and the bad guys like them.

People with different values will, of course, sort different people into the good and bad categories, which are not defined in any objective terms. The common feature of this process is for those persons and groups we define as part of "Us" to be seen as opposed by those with whom we differ. We tend to regard our side as normal and view the outsiders as deviant in some sense.

Is Deviancy Motivated?

How did "They" get to be the deviant weirdos that we see them as? Why do deviants violate the rules of normal conduct we normals have come to regard as sacred and inviolate? Are deviant tendencies inherited? Does environment, especially early upbringing, play an important role? Do deviants have character defects or lack a sense of conscience? Are they perhaps victims of mental illness?

These concerns are among the many motivational questions normals pose about deviant behavior. Since normals cannot comphrehend how anyone in his or her right mind would be deviant, the inference is often made that those people are crazy.

The question of conscious motivation invariably arises when the topic of deviant behavior is raised, especially if extreme forms of deviancy such as crimes are involved. It might appear to the normal and law-abiding citizen that deviant actions are freely chosen and preferred responses for the deviant. Thus, a robber can be seen as motivated by an easy access to money without having to work. Sexual deviance may be attributed to immorality or unbridled lust and evil. Drug addicts may be regarded as sensuous pleasure seekers. In short, deviant actions are seen as deliberate intentional actions that produce illegal or immoral rewards.

However, another possibility to consider is the lack of opportunity for deviants to choose behavior acceptable to those who have the power (in a given society) to define the terms of what is right or wrong, legal or illegal, moral or immoral. A person who cannot receive education or employment cannot earn money in the ways considered socially acceptable and may be forced to seek deviant or illegal means. Even the threat of imprisonment that would deter the law-abiding citizen is often inadequate to stop the desperate individual who perceives no other means.

Turning to moral issues such as in the case of sexual deviance and other forms of so-called victimless crimes, we see that it is quite likely that these behaviors are successfully labeled deviant because they offend the values of those in power. They may not be actions the moralistic or law-abiding citizen never wished to do himself or herself. The difference lies mainly in the fact that the latter has somehow managed to control his or her own desires whereas the deviant has not.

An interesting analysis of the situation in these terms was made by Becker (1963) who suggested that the proper question is not why are deviants motivated to transgress but rather why are normals unable or unwilling to follow some of their desires? Becker maintained that all of us have fantasies of engaging in the activities society labels as immoral or illegal but that those of us who own things are able to prevent these fantasies from becoming reality.

Becker pointed out that our reluctance to violate norms of social propriety stems from the fact that most of us have too much to lose if we are caught. In contrast, deviants are those people who have little or nothing to lose by their deviancy because they are already powerless, coming from the poor, the minorities, or the youth, for the most part. It is not that deviants so much prefer or choose deviancy but that in many cases they have no real alternatives.

Nor do deviants necessarily have a different sense of moral values or judgments than normals. According to Becker, normals may also be tempted to engage in some forms of immoral or illegal activities but fail to admit or recognize these tendencies. Instead, the normals define these illicit activities as forms of deviancy to be condemned and punished. It then becomes a puzzle to the normals as to why deviants behave in the reprehensible ways they do.

We normals are intrigued by these types of questions about the causes of the behavior of those who are radically different from ourselves. Our questions, however, rarely raise the possibility that we normals play any part in the creation of the deviant behavior of others. Instead, we imply that the fault lies within the deviant individual entirely and that the structure of society and the reactions of its normal members to deviant behaviors play no causal role in generating such behavior.

Methods of Maintaining Power

This chapter will examine the evidence that suggests that most behaviors generally considered deviant or abnormal are in fact highly influenced by the actions of normals. In the process of protecting itself from the threat of divergent values and life styles, the insider group seeks ways to enhance its own power. Self-enhancement through the creation of the impression of social power, exclusion of outsiders, and moral condemnation of deviants are examples of such activities by those in the mainstream of society that help keep the status quo intact.

CREATING THE IMPRESSION OF
SOCIAL POWER

What often counts in life is appearance rather than reality. Popular adages to the contrary, people do judge books by their covers. A casual glance at the sexually stimulating illustrations on the covers of paperback books on topics of almost every type certainly suggests that publishers believe people judge books by their covers.

A similar situation holds concerning impressions of social power. People assume that if you can convey to others that you have pull and connections, most of the battle is won. The age-old game of "keeping up with the Jones" is played with this philosophy in mind. For if one lags behind the Jones, the impression generated may be that you lack status, which is related to power.

Achieving and maintaining high social status is a primary goal for most of us. Buying name brand products, drinking twelve-year-old scotch, wearing the latest fashions, etc., seem necessary to impress others.

Thorstein Veblen, a famous economist of a generation ago, astutely recorded examples of what he termed, *conspicuous consumption,* a calculated form of economic wastefulness aimed at creating a type of status one-upmanship. In direct contrast to current concerns about ecology and conservation, the attitude of conspicuous consumption required extravagance, indulgence, and outright wastefulness. It served to call the attention of others to one's affluence, to prove one's value to others, as well as to oneself perhaps, by showing that one could afford waste. Whereas possessions were originally valued in themselves, they came eventually to represent evidence to others that the holder was powerful. Because esteem and respect was accorded to the wealthy, it was not surprising that conspicuous display of these resources occurred. Wastefulness, then, is one impressive means by which wealth and power can be demonstrated.

Regardless of whether our power is real or merely apparent, someone else must be in the position of having less power. That is, power being a relative matter, if some have power, others must be without it. Furthermore, those with it will strive to hold to it and prevent others from achieving it, because to have power is to be able to control one's own life, and, quite possibly, that of others as well.

Prejudice, especially of a racial variety, involves the restriction of opportunity for the minority groups by the more powerful majority group. The outsiders are assumed to hold different values and beliefs (Rokeach, Smith, and Evans, 1960; Rokeach and Mezei, 1966) and this perceived threat increases the efforts of the majority to control the lives of the minorities. Prejudice involves fear and hostility and is thus difficult to modify because it tends to prevent equal status contact or interaction between the minority and majority groups that might help reduce it.

Even when legal means are employed to give greater opportunity to minorities as in the case of school desegregation, the increased contact between blacks and whites have not produced consistent improvement in racial attitudes (Amir, 1969). The deep-rooted prejudices of the past, the fact that such contact is not based on genuine equal status, and the reactance to the feeling of coercion all serve to prevent significant or rapid improvement of relationships.

Moral crusades and campaigns against behavior considered to be immoral or evil also illustrate how perceived threats to the values of those in social power can arouse attacks on the deviants. Sinful activities in the areas of drinking alcohol, sexual deviancy, pornography, gambling, and the use of "hard" drugs have been especially capable of generating the indignation of the clean-living, law-abiding, and self-righteous citizens.

Gusfield (1963) has described the American temperance movement and shown how it developed as a means of preserving the established middle class American value system, which was perceived to be undermined by the alien working class use of alcohol. Their momentary success in establishing Prohibition represented a victory for the eroding moralistic middle class value system. Although alcohol still flowed, the moral crusade was able to cast stigma on it, because it was illegal and deviant behavior to drink alcohol.

Zurcher, Kirkpatrick, Cushing, and Bowman (1973) suggested that similar factors are involved in motivating the members of antipornography groups. They contacted two such organizations in different cities and interviewed their members. Rapid social change, especially in the sexual domain, was a threat to these individuals who held traditional values regarding not only sexual behavior but also religion, work, authority, and patriotism, among other topics. The moral decay they saw embodied in the increased amount of pornography became their target in their moral crusade. Members of these groups, compared with members of groups opposed to censorship, were middle-aged males from stable marriages. They came from smaller towns and were more religiously active and politically conservative. Scores on psychological tests showed that they were more intolerant of those with other views than their own.

Zurcher et al. draw several parallels between antipornography and temperance crusaders. Both seem to represent persons who believe in the traditional values but are worried by the trends toward new values. In retaliation, a campaign is waged to condemn the moral decay of the deviants. The antipornography campaign appears to be even less successful than the temperance movements were in eradicating its target but both crusades could still be regarded as symbolic efforts. Attacks upon the behavior of those with different values were waged as efforts in behalf of the virtuous and true against the evil and sinful.

EXCLUSION OF OTHERS

Those who share common values may develop a sense of closeness and togetherness augmented by a simultaneous opposition to those who hold conflicting values. The group with power is in a position to defend its values against those of less-powerful groups. Members of one's own group whose behavior is on the border between acceptability and deviancy may be excluded as well. Their presence may weaken the harmony within a group and jeopardize the likelihood of the group achieving its goals. To maintain its own effectiveness and power, a group may find it necessary to expel or ostracize members whose values create conflict.

An experimental analog of this situation can be found in a study by Schachter (1951) who invited students to participate in one of four different special interest club groups dealing with topics such as music, radio, journalism, and drama. After students first specified their preferences for the different groups, Schachter randomly assigned half of them to clubs with activities they preferred and half of them to clubs with activities in which they expressed little interest. It was assumed that the former clubs would consist of high cohesiveness groups, whereas the latter clubs would have low cohesiveness groups.

Each group contained seven members but three of them were confederates of the experimenter. At the first club meeting, each group received a description of Johnny Rocco, a delinquent, and was asked to discuss ways of dealing with him. During this forty-five minute group discussion one of the stooges adopted an extremely punitive attitude initially but then changed toward a moderate view, another stooge held a consistent moderate position, and the third stooge maintained a very punitive attitude throughout.

Then subjects had to rate group members. The stooge who held the deviant position advocating extreme punishment was rated lowest in likeability and most frequently nominated to serve on group committees involving unpleasant duties. These expressions of rejection of the deviant were stronger in the cohesive groups, which stood to suffer the most from group goals by the continued presence of the deviant member. Similar replications have been conducted in a number of European nations (Schachter, Nuttin, DeMonchaux, Maucorps, Osmer, Duijker, and Rommetveit, 1954) using groups of boys who were to build a model plane to enter in a competition for a prize. A stooge served as a deviant whose choice of the model for the group to build was clearly at odds with the choice of the other boys. As in the Schachter (1951) study, the deviant boy was generally rejected by his group in most of the replications.

A similar process occurs whenever insiders band together to exclude, censure, or criticize others whose views and behavior are unacceptable. By restricting the privilege of membership in our own group, we may also enhance the apparent value of our own membership. Even if a privilege is not intrinsically valuable, the very process of limiting access to it increases its value significantly. The outsider, who is denied this privilege, envies the insider. An illustration of this situation can be found in the case in which one person is keeping a secret from another. The secret itself may be trivial, but the knower and the outsider both regard it as valuable precisely because one person has access to it while the other does not. The possessor of the secret is regarded by both parties as in power and the outsider is seen as powerless by both parties, subject to the whims and dictates of the former.

When outsiders are excluded because of their deviant attitudes, values, and behaviors, the stigma of being considered an unworthy outcast along with the punitive treatment of society may generate more pronounced types and amounts of deviancy. A person who is denied a job because of unorthodox sexual practices cannot earn money by acceptable ways and may be forced to turn to socially unacceptable means of earning income. Deviants may band together and form their own subgroup that can tolerate, accept, and support its members. The belief that someone is deviant, then, becomes a self-fulfilling prophecy, because we treat that person in ways that restrict him or her from normal forms of behavior.

THE DEPRECIATION OF OTHERS

In order to justify its existence, the insider group may focus on why the outsiders should be regarded with contempt and disdain. If the actions of outsiders could be seen as evil, corrupt, or immoral, their exclusion would appear warranted to insiders. Furthermore, to preserve its own existence, the insider group might consider it necessary to imprison, regulate, or otherwise control the influence of the outsider's deviant ways.

All social groups create numerous rules, norms, and customs that specify the acceptable or proper behavior in various situations. These norms can serve as guides toward behavior that promotes the cohesiveness and integration of the social unit. Everyone commits deviant acts. We cannot conform to every social norm. Many of these transgressions, however, are invisible or can easily be remedied and do not lead to drastic consequences such as social rejection, fines, or imprisonment. On forms of deviance that violate strongly held morals, of course, the wrath of moral indignation and legal sanctions comes down quite severely. Sexual deviations, excessive use of select drugs, or radical religious or political beliefs, for example, have traditionally represented severe threats to those who have the power to retaliate against such deviance.

Although laws proscribe many of these forms of deviancy, many of them are rarely enforced directly and control is usually exerted in the form of harassment and ridicule. In contrast, direct threats to the person or property of others such as assault, robbery, or homicide are forms of deviancy that authorities make strong attempts to control by applying penalties and imprisonment to apprehended transgressors.

Becoming Deviant

The line between behavior that conforms to social conventions and that which is deviant can often be quite fine. Consider the example of swearing. Mild forms of swear expressions are generally tolerated by most persons, but some terms are frowned on as being too strong. Of course, the specific expletives that are offensive vary with time and place, and many swear words that were quite shocking a generation ago are considered rather mild nowadays. But every generation recognizes a set of words and expressions, often those having to do with sexual and eliminative functions, that are reserved for limited situations because of their emotional impact.

Most people swear to some extent but most of us keep within the bounds of social propriety. But a few individuals swear more vigorously and profanely and may suffer social reproach. Sometimes this reaction is precisely what is needed to encourage more swearing as in the case of a teenage boy who may enjoy shocking adults, especially if his peer group admires his earthy expressions.

What may happen in such a situation is that the person on the line between acceptable conformity and unacceptable deviancy may be gradually pushed beyond respectable bounds by the ostracism of those who are offended. At the same time, he or she may be pulled over the line, so to speak, by the social approval of those whose behavior is already deviant. With additional passage of time, the person is moved further from the edges of social acceptability and deeper into the category deemed deviant.

Darley and Darley (1973) similarly suggest that the process of becoming deviant begins when the justification for remaining within the confines of respectability is just barely insufficient. The person is able to refute successfully any arguments for conformity to norms in such a situation and in effect strengthens the rationale for engaging in deviant activities. Had a stronger argument for conformity been provided that the person could not have refuted, conformity would have been maintained.

INVOLUNTARY VS. VOLUNTARY DEVIANCE

The preceding analysis is not to say that all differences of behavior are due to involuntary exclusion. On the contrary, we may also distinguish a large number of voluntary departures from conventionality. Rival values and differences of belief systems may lead individuals or groups to reject the conventions and values of mainstream society. The beatniks of the 1950s and the hippies of the 1960s, for example, adopted lifestyles that did not conform to the usual norms of propriety and respectibility. These nonconformists or individualists voluntarily adopted customs, clothing, and verbal expressions that defied the prevailing standards as an expression either of indifference or protest against the traditional societal values.

The reaction of traditional society toward voluntary deviants may be stronger than that toward involuntary deviants. In either case, it is possible to regard both types of departures from conventionality as rival threats. To maintain the viability of the traditional ways, deviants could be both excluded and condemned as evil or corrupt. The alternative view that new values might have some validity or that the old ways were outmoded is not seriously considered because it would jeopardize one's own security and power.

Phenomenology of Deviance

What is it like to be a deviant? How does it feel to be rejected by others or at least expect such mistreatment because of one's atypical behavior or characteristics? How do these feelings influence other aspects of the deviant's behavior? One approach to finding answers to these kinds of questions is to become a member, albeit temporarily, of a deviant group and act as a participant observer. An extreme example is Griffin's (1961) well-known account, *Black Like Me,* based on his experiences disguised as a black man in the American south. He learned first hand what it is like to be a member of an oppressed minority.

PSYCHOLOGICAL EVIDENCE

An experimental approach to the problem by Freedman and Doob (1968) used Stanford University undergraduates, generally regarded as a rather elite group. They were tested in groups of five or six members on a series of personality type tests in which some ambiguity could exist as to which responses were normal. For example, tests similar to the Rorschach and the Thematic Apperception Test were used where presumably the subject projects his own personality through his responses to ambiguous stimuli. Other standardized multiple choice type personality tests were used as well. After each test was scored, subjects were shown the distribution of scores of group members before proceeding to the next test.

Two conditions were used, a deviant and a nondeviant, in order to examine how behavior is modified as a function of "feeling different." The deviant subject in the deviant group condition learned that his score was atypical from those of the rest of the group (see Figure 18–1); there was no value judgment rendered as to whether he was usually good or bad. All subjects in the nondeviant groups received scores that were closely bunched together (see Figure 18–2). Freedman and Doob felt that their paradigm would

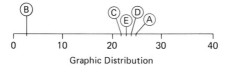

Graphic Distribution

FIGURE 18–1. Feedback for the deviant subject. [From *Deviancy: The Psychology of Being Different,* by J. L. Freedman and A. N. Doob, New York: Academic, 1968. Copyright 1968 by Academic Press. Reprinted by permission.]

enable them to identify some of the effects of being deviant, in general, rather than on a particular topic.

It was predicted that deviants would fear mistreatment from normals and that they would avoid them in preference to affiliating with other deviants. In one experiment subjects were shown the distribution of test scores for sixty-two different subjects. Later they were asked to serve in another study for which they had to choose three partners. The deviant subjects preferred choosing for partners other subjects whose scores were also deviant, even if the direction of their deviancy was not the same.

Another prediction about deviants made by Freedman and Doob was that they should try to conceal their deviancy by minimizing interaction with nondeviants. In an experiment subjects were asked to rate their preference for working on a task alone or with a group. Half of the deviants were led to think that their scores were public and known to other subjects, whereas the other half thought that their scores were not known by any other subjects. There was a tendency in the results for a greater preference for working alone by the deviants who thought their scores were private. Those deviants who knew that their scores were public knowledge were not so wary of group interaction, because they could no longer hide their scores.

Questions of ethical propriety may arise with respect to these experiments. Are we warranted in imposing feelings of deviancy on others for the purpose of measuring their effects? Freedman and Doob sidestep this issue, claiming that the deception was mild and produced no long lasting effects. Although this reassurance is comforting, the generalizability of such studies to the effects of being treated like real-life deviants is questionable. Stronger analogs of deviancy are needed if we wish to simulate the long-term rejection suffered by homosexuals, dope addicts, or the physically handicapped. We are by no means advocating such analogs if they become examples of unethical

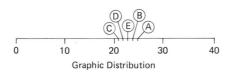

Graphic Distribution

FIGURE 18–2. Feedback for the nondeviant subject. [From *Deviancy: The Psychology of Being Different* by J. L. Freedman and A. N. Doob, New York: Academic, 1968. Copyright 1968 by Academic Press. Reprinted by permission.]

treatment of human subjects but wish to point out the limited value of permissible laboratory experiments in studying this type of issue. Perhaps sociological and anthropological field studies are better suited for the investigation of these questions.

SOCIOLOGICAL EVIDENCE

For example, the sociological studies of Erving Goffman (1963) on stigma deal directly with the experience of being deviant. In his analysis Goffman makes no clearcut division of people into deviant and nondeviant categories. Instead he suggests that everyone possesses some type of stigma at some time or another and that one can study the common features of the experience of bearing stigmas.

Mixed contacts between normals and the stigmatized are generally avoided, as mentioned by Freedman and Doob. Goffman suggests that one motive for the avoidance from the perspective of the normal person is the lack of knowledge about how to act toward the deviant. Inappropriate behavior could prove embarrassing or offensive. This discomfort can be avoided if encounters are prevented.

The stigmatized also face mixed encounters with dread, because they sometimes do not know whether they will be rejected or accepted. Or in cases such as ex-convicts, where the source of stigma is covert, there is the anxiety that someone will recognize him or that his past will somehow come out.

Consequently, deviants will prefer socializing with their own kind, even when it appears that normals might be willing to accept them or when it is unlikely that they will discover the stigma. Groups as diverse as Alcoholics Anonymous, Synanon, Weightwatchers, and Parents without Partners enable those who share the same source of societal rejection to enjoy each other's acceptance without undue anxiety.

Joining groups of one's own kind is not without some disadvantages, however. Although such association may enhance self-acceptance, the source of stigma might be promoted to the status of a virtue rather than a problem that needs to be solved. The relevance of this danger depends on the specific type of stigma.

Furthermore, inevitably one must leave the safety of one's own kind and deal with normals. What is the best strategy in such encounters? Should the stigmatized try to pass as a normal if the stigma is covert? Or should one be open about one's background and accept oneself as being as good as the next person? Thus, even if a normal might occasionally snub you, make fun of you, or even reject you, Goffman suggested that an open relationship in which you try to help normals understand and accept you might be effective, especially for those whose stigma cannot be hidden, as in cases of the physically handicapped.

Goffman assumes that normals reject deviants primarily out of fear and ignorance rather than out of malice. If the stigmatized person can accept himself or herself, Goffman feels that he or she can educate normals about the normalcy of the deviant in other areas and thereby accept him or her.

Although this approach may seem reasonable, it may be difficult for many bearers of stigma to accept because it means that deviants must accept themselves even if normals will not. Furthermore, deviants are asked to be forgiving and tolerant of normals for not understanding them. This "turn the other cheek" philosophy may occasionally work but for the most part it would appear to be unrealistic.

Normals often condemn, ridicule, and in some cases, aggress against deviants. Alcoholics, criminals, the mentally ill, and other social outcasts are looked on with self-righteous contempt. Better acceptance of the physically handicapped may exist, but only because they are regarded as objects of pity rather than of scorn since their differences are not of their own doing.

In contrast, deviant groups have little power to fight the prejudices, stereotypes, and rejection. Direct retaliation or confrontation may cost some groups the protection afforded by anonymity. Homosexuals, for instance, until recently have not dared to defend their rights because to do so was to leap from the frying pan into the fire by disclosing their identities.

The normals hold all the power and generally will not go out of their way to find ways of understanding and accepting those who are regarded as somewhat different in unfavorable ways. The so-called normals would face a conflict of interest since for many of them their own status depends on the existence of someone lower in power than themselves.

As Becker (1963) observed, "Those groups whose social position gives them weapons and power are best able to enforce their rules." This simple principle underlines such diverse situations as the fact that whites have traditionally defined the rules that imply that certain behavior of most blacks is deviant, men have specified the rules against which certain behavior of most women is deviant, and the middle class has determined the rules that define certain behavior of the lower class as deviant.

Relationship to Basic Themes of this Book

It is meaningless, then, to inquire about the nature of the underlying motives for many forms of behavior, especially those judged deviant by those with social power. Individual differences in behavior have generally been ignored by theorists interested in proposing general laws. Much of the research described in this book has been concerned with identifying such generalizations. As we noted in Chapter 1, this nomothetic approach is legitimate and useful but at the same time greater attention should be given to the idiographic aspect of psychology that deals more directly with the question of individual differences and their causes.

We have used the example of deviant behavior only as an illustration where attention to individual variation is more dramatic. We do *not* mean to imply that all types of individual differences are involuntary or imposed from external forces as in the types of deviant behavior described here. On the contrary, individual differences in motives do exist, as noted in the discussion of Chapter 4 on values and meaning. However, even when one freely chooses behavior it is likely that social forces will operate to restrict the degree of deviation from social norms.

Voluntary behavior that exceeds these limits will also be subject to the condemnation and ridicule of mainstream society. The behavior will be judged as deviant, according to the values of those holding social power.

Throughout this book we have pointed out the usefulness and necessity of evaluating the subjective and phenomenological interpretation an individual holds about himself or herself and the determinants of his or her behavior. The present discussion about deviancy is closely related to the ideas of powerlessness and learned helplessness discussed in Chapter 5. The cognitions that one is deviant, controlled by external forces, and is unable to be competent in dealing with the environment are similar in producing negative affective states such as depression and hopelessness. In turn, as we observed in Chapters 2 and 12, the lowered self-esteem of the individual stemming from such external attributions about the causes of one's behavior further undermines efforts to engage in socially acceptable and productive behavior.

Summary

Some forms of behavior are accepted as normal, whereas other types are regarded as abnormal or deviant. The specific behaviors assigned to these two broad categories are not identical for everyone but depend on the values of each individual. Those who behave in ways similar to ourselves are generally regarded as normal persons, whereas those who behave in ways that are unacceptable to us are regarded and treated as deviants.

Ostracism, exclusion, and condemnation are examples of reactions that deviants face from those who hold social power. The latter, by virtue of their power, define themselves as normal and, by contrast, equate deviants with abnormality. The effects of being labeled deviant can produce self-fulfilling predictions as the outcast reacts to the rejection. If one is denied employment opportunities, for example, because society considers an individual's sexual behavior to be unacceptable, such treatment is apt to create other forms of behavior that may also be regarded as deviant. Lowered self-esteem, alienation, and resentment may also develop as a consequence of being considered a deviant. Deviancy may also be self-chosen rather than involuntary as in the case of nonconformists who reject the values of mainstream society. Such deviancy, although self-imposed, is also likely to receive criticism by society.

The understanding of normal behavior is not possible without a consideration of deviant behavior. Since normals and deviants exist only in relation to each other, the behaviors of each type affect the other. Normals, having access to social power, exert more control over deviants than vice versa, although they rarely realize it and generally attribute the behavior of deviants to some irrational, perverse, or self-destructive motives.

References

AMIR, Y. Contact hypothesis in ethnic relations. *Psychological Bulletin,* 1969, *71,* 319–342.

BECKER, H. S. *Outsiders: Studies in the sociology of deviance.* New York: Free Press, 1963.

DARLEY, J. M., and DARLEY, S. A. *Conformity and deviation.* Morristown, N.J.: General Learning Press, 1973.

FREEDMAN, J. L., and DOOB, A. N. *Deviancy: The psychology of being different.* New York: Academic, 1968.

GOFFMAN, E. *Stigma: Notes on spoiled identity.* Englewood Cliffs, N.J.: Prentice-Hall, 1963.

GUSFIELD, J. R. *Symbolic crusade: Status politics and the American temperance movement.* Urbana: University of Illinois Press, 1966.

ROKEACH, M., and MEZEI, L. Race and shared belief as factors in social choice. *Science,* 1966, *151,* 167–172.

———, SMITH, P. W., and EVANS, R. I. Two kinds of prejudice or one? In M. Rokeach, *The open and closed mind.* New York: Basic Books, 1960.

SCHACHTER, S. Deviation, rejection, and communication. *Journal of Abnormal and Social Psychology,* 1951, *46,* 190–207.

———, NUTTIN, J., DEMONCHAUX, C., MAUCORPS, P. H., OSMER, D., DUIJ-KER, H., ROMMETREIT, R., and ISREAL, J. Cross-cultural experiments in threat and rejection. *Human Relations,* 1954, *7,* 403–439.

ZURCHER, L. A., JR., KIRKPATRICK, R. G., CUSHING, R. G., and BOWMAN, C. K. Ad hoc antipornography organizations and their active members: A research summary. *Journal of Social Issues,* 1973, *29,* 69–94.

Author Index

507

Subject Index

515